# The FIRESIDE Book of Baseball

## FOURTH EDITION

EDITED BY

## Charles Einstein

*With an Introduction by*
*Reggie Jackson*

A Fireside Book
Published by Simon & Schuster, Inc.
NEW YORK

Copyright © 1987 by Charles Einstein
All rights reserved including the right of reproduction in
whole or in part in any form.
A FIRESIDE BOOK
Published by Simon & Schuster, Inc.
Simon & Schuster Building
Rockefeller Center
1230 Avenue of the Americas
New York, NY 10020
FIRESIDE and colophon are registered trademarks of
Simon & Schuster, Inc.
Designed by Irving Perkins Associates
Manufactured in the United States of America

10  9  8  7  6  5  4  3  2  1

Library of Congress Cataloging in Publication Data

The Fireside book of baseball.

"A Fireside book."
Includes index.
1. Baseball—Miscellanea.     I. Einstein, Charles.
GV867.F49   1987        796.357       87-14943
ISBN 0-671-63812-2

# CONTENTS

## Contents

# Contents

# Contents

# Contents

I WAS TEN years old when the first *Fireside Book of Baseball* came out. Twelve years later, when the third *Fireside* book was published, I was in my first full season in the majors, with the Oakland A's. That was in 1968, and that was when I first got to meet Charlie Einstein, the editor of the *Fireside* series, who at the time was writing a baseball column for the *San Francisco Chronicle*.

Neither of us suspected that nineteen years later, I'd be back with the Oakland A's—and doing this introduction for the fourth *Fireside Book of Baseball*.

Things have a way of coming full circle. Here and there in these pages, among a thousand ballplayers and more—most of them real, some the figments of spectacular imagination—you may bump into one named Reggie Jackson. He is someone I knew in my baseball past and he is forever young.

But that is what the *Fireside* baseball books have meant, all the way back to the first volume of the series in 1956. There was a poem in that first book—"Polo Grounds," by Rolfe Humphries, saying:

> *The crowd and the players*
> *Are the same age always, but the man in the crowd*
> *Is older every season.*

And I think of A. Bartlett Giamatti, who this year went from being president of Yale University to being president of the National League. "It breaks your heart," he wrote a decade ago, in 1977. "It is designed to break your heart. The game begins in the spring, when everything else begins again, and it blossoms in the summer, filling the afternoons and evenings, and then as soon as the chill rains come, it stops and leaves you to face the fall alone."

Maybe not quite alone. Draw up a chair beside the fire. They don't call a book like this *Fireside* for nothing.

REGGIE JACKSON

IN THE remarkable afterglow of the 1986 baseball season, with this book by then less than a year away from publication, I found my thoughts being drawn increasingly to the words of two figures from the past.

One of them was Thomas Jefferson, who early in April of 1823, at the age of seventy-nine, sent a letter to a journalist friend, recommending against doing a biography until the subject had passed away. "It is impossible," Jefferson wrote, "that the writer's delicacy should permit him to speak as freely of the faults or errors of a living, as of a dead character."

*Ah there, Tom,* I found myself mumbling. Writer's delicacy, hey? Born 150 years too soon, you were. Never got to watch the Red Sox, or read Mike Royko after somebody attacked his beloved Cubs, or meet Gene Mauch. "There's not a hell of a lot to say," Mauch muttered after the improbable California Angels loss to Boston in the American League championship playoff of 1986 that left him still without a pennant after twenty-five years of managing. "I have an amazing ability to forget things. If only people would let me."

Let him? "The Red Sox did me a personal favor," proclaimed Newhouse News Service columnist John McLaughlin, a Phillies fan who had never forgotten the way his beloved team, under Mauch, blew the National League pennant in 1964. "I am not a hard man," he wrote now, twenty-two years later. "I do not hold grudges but there are some things that are unforgivable. . . . A pox on your pennant aspirations, Manager Mauch. The evil eye to you. May you never win a pennant, you who blighted my youth."

Be it as it may that the Red Sox did McLaughlin a favor; come the point in the World Series when, just like Mauch's Angels in the play-offs, the Sox found themselves only one pitch away from victory, somebody else became beneficiary of their largesse, and it was the Mets who wrote yet another chapter in a Doomsday book of Boston disappointment that by then dated back nearly seventy years. "One begins to see at last," Roger Angell wrote in *The New Yorker,* "that the true function of the Red Sox may be not to win but to provide New England authors with a theme, now that guilt and whaling have gone out of style."

Whether then the fixated McLaughlin, the fatalistic Angell, or (as we shall find later on in these pages) Mike Royko on an average day, we can only accept at face value a certain suspending of delicacy when it comes to writing about baseball and its living participants. It may even be one of the game's special charms. Woody Allen, interviewed by the French filmmaker and critic Robert Benayoun, compared Groucho Marx with baseball because of their shared qualities of cynicism and irreverence, and in truth the game holds little sacred. "Baseball teams do not carry chaplains, as do some football teams," former U.S. Senator Eugene McCarthy wrote in *The New Republic.* "They do not gather, kneeling or standing, in a group to pray or hold hands before the game, as basketball teams do, but proceed decently from locker room to dugout to playing field." Here and there, less temporal examples have surfaced, like the 1980 San Francisco Giants, whose more devout players tended to ascribe misfortune to the will of the Lord. Logically enough, they became known for a time as the "God Squad," but the public wasn't buying. "It is marvelous news that Jack Clark has found God," one fan wrote in a letter to the *San Francisco Chronicle.* "Perhaps one day soon he may also find the cutoff man."

All of this, you may say, could have left Thomas Jefferson a touch bewildered. Let us turn then to the words of the more contemporary statesman Casey Stengel, who late in February of 1965, at the age of seventy-five, commenced his final year as a baseball manager by issuing a directive to the rookies assembled before him for the start of spring training. "Line up in alphabetical order according to height," he told them.

Casey's command struck me as being peculiarly apropos for the way it could be used to describe the *Fireside* baseball experience, from the editor's standpoint, over the past thirty-one years. The preface to the first *Fireside Book of Baseball,* published in 1956, noted that neither of the customary methods of arranging the table of contents seemed to be right: "To arrange by category—such as fiction, spot reporting, autobiography, history, and so forth—would be artificial; many of the pieces fit more than one category, and many of the categories have been arbitrarily assigned. To arrange by chronology would be even harder—what year, or period of years, shall we assign to Connie Mack?" And so, because it made more sense than anything else, the contents were listed alphabetically by author, with category alongside, a textual format retained by the second *Fireside* volume in 1958, the third in 1968, and now this fourth book in 1987.

As for the height of the authors (or the length of their contributions), I suppose I can report pretty much the same success that Stengel got, which witnesses said didn't amount to all that much. The long and the short have a way of becoming commingled, along with everything else, so that the alphabetical imperative in the third *Fireside,* to take one example, produced consecutive entries by authors named Young—a piece by Dick, who was reporting a perfect game, directly in back of a piece by Cy, who pitched one. (Columnist Dick Young, who is honored by a plaque in the writers' wing of the Baseball Hall of Fame at Cooperstown, New York, has a history of following tough acts in the pages of the *Fireside*s. In the first book he was behind Rudy York's poignant and oft-reprinted ''A Letter to My Son''; in the second his article came directly after a box score printed entirely in Japanese; and here in this fourth volume he follows George Will's paean to the Louisville Slugger and the sound of bat on ball—''the sound the cosmos makes each spring when it clears its throat and says, 'We made it.' '' Ho boy.)

But the perils (and delights) of juxtaposition to one side, it was the greater purpose, again as set forth in the preface to the first *Fireside,* ''to try to spread-eagle the sport from Frank Merriwell to the kitchen sink''—a task whose happy hopelessness was symbolized perhaps by the fact that neither Merriwell nor the sink made it. Nor did they make it into the subsequent volumes of the series, though it wasn't for want of any respect for variety. This fourth book, for example, again may not go from Merriwell to the sink, but it does range from Heloise to ''Horseshoes''—from the homemaker's best friend, that is, to what may have been Ring Lardner's best story—not to mention the works of poets, journalists, novelists, historians, old-time ballplayers, a stand-up comic and the vice president of Nicaragua. The comfort of the familiar can, I hope, be found within these pages, but equally, in the informally established mode of the entire *Fireside* baseball series, the fun of the unfamiliar too.

One example of the latter would be the presence here of the motion filed in 1976 by attorneys for Bowie Kuhn, then the commissioner of baseball, to dismiss the lawsuit brought by Charles O. Finley, the owner of the Oakland A's, challenging Kuhn's refusal to let him sell off three of his star players in the middle of a pennant race. This was a typewritten document, the only public copy of which is on file in the U.S. District Court in Chicago, and so its use in these pages marks its first appearance anywhere in actual print. But its selection was hardly based on novelty alone; one of its fascinations indeed lies in the way it marks the approximate midpoint in the period between the third *Fireside* book and this one—a nineteen-year span more tightly gripped by ferment than any comparable time in baseball history.

The Kuhn motion to dismiss gives off the scent of those winds of change, as do a number of other pieces in these pages, but I found myself opposed to lacing the contents with an overabundance of socioeconomic detail. In rapid summary, what began in 1969 as an unsuccessful attempt by outfielder Curt Flood to litigate baseball's reserve clause, which bound players to their clubs even in the absence of a contract, would lead over the next dozen years to the longest player strike in sports history, a walkout lasting fifty days and wiping out the playing of 714 scheduled major league games at the heart of the 1981 season. Along the way, in 1973, an arbitrator had ruled that two pitchers, Andy Messersmith and Dave McNally, were free agents no longer bound to their respective clubs by the reserve clause; and the next year the same arbitrator, Peter M. Seitz, ruled the same way even though the pitcher in that case, Jim ''Catfish'' Hunter, actually had a contract with his club owner, the recurrent Finley. ''I am not an Abraham Lincoln signing the Emancipation Proclamation,'' Seitz said. ''Involuntary servitude has nothing to do with this case. The decision does not destroy baseball. But if the club owners think it will ruin baseball, they have it in their power to prevent the damage.''

The damage, as the owners professed to see it, was that the emergent free agents would all sell themselves instantly to the highest bidders, thus enabling the wealthiest teams to monopolize the talent and eliminating all meaningful pennant competition. As forebodings go, this one may have lost a little something in the translation. The six World Series held from the end of the player strike in 1981 through 1986 involved the maximum possible total of twelve different teams! Over the same period, no fewer than nine of the twelve National League and ten of the fourteen American League teams appeared in their respective League Championship play-offs. ''All other questions aside,'' editor Joe Reichler wrote in his preface to the sixth edition of *The Baseball Encyclopedia,* ''no one can deny that the years since the establishment of free agency have seen an extraordinary growth in the popularity of baseball.''

So Reichler wrote in 1985. In 1986, for the first time ever, each of the twenty-six teams in the majors drew more than a million home admissions, and the histrionics of the title play-offs in both leagues, followed—dare we say exceeded?—by those of the World Series, cast a luster that, judging by the visible effect of just one earlier encounter—the sixth game of the 1975 Series—must last for years to come. (Envisioning the contents of this book at long range, before the season began, I more or less routinely presupposed they would include no more than one game story, if even that, from 1986. Instead, there are five.)

The initial hard evidence of aftershock came in December of '86, with the baseball season by then six weeks into the past and the pro football, basketball and hockey campaigns in full cry. Despite the time of year, a survey conducted by *USA Today* found baseball ranked first not only as America's favorite game but in every subcategory in which fans were asked to choose between sports. Respondents picked the World Series as their favorite event and hitting a home run in the Series as their favorite fantasy. They even had advice for those recipients of college football's Heisman Trophy who, like Bo Jackson, the regnant Heisman winner, were all-around athletes. Asked "If your son had Bo Jackson's choice, would you want him to play baseball or football?" better than three out of four said baseball. (So did Bo.)

December saw publication too of *The World Almanac,* with its listing of the ten most dramatic sports events from November '85 through October '86. First place went actually not to a baseball game but to two baseball games: "The New York Mets, losing by two runs with two out and nobody on base in the bottom of the tenth inning, rallied to score three runs to win the sixth game of the World Series. In another come-from-behind effort, they defeated the Boston Red Sox in the seventh game to win the 1986 World Series." (In third and seventh places on this list were two other baseball games. No other sport in the top ten was mentioned more than once.)

But many observers believe there is a more lasting reason for such manifest extension of the game's hold on the public, and it has little to do with free agency or even the theatrical impact of recent postseason play, and just as little to do with any selected quotes from *USA Today* or *The Baseball Encyclopedia.*

Yet those two publications have more to do with it than any other single factor; and a clue to this seeming paradox can be found, it seems to me, in the very first selection in this book, "A Study in Suet," in which (speaking of lining up alphabetically according to height) the late Lee Allen dealt with the tendency of players to grow bigger over the years.

"Thanks to a rare book called simply *Baseball* and published in 1902 at San Francisco by S. R. Church, who was also the author, it is possible to get a fairly good line on how big players were in the old days," Allen writes. "Apparently Church intended to produce numerous volumes that would supply statistical data on all the players of major league history, a dream that has bemused numerous historians of the game."

That dream was still only that—a dream—when Allen published "A Study in Suet" in the mid-1950s, and his chart showing weight gain over the quarter century from 1929 through 1953 was the product of his own pencil-and-paper research and long division. I remember the feeling well, having worked for the old International News Service for a little over eight years in the immediate wake of World War II. The INS headquarters in New York in those days may have been the last of the great newsrooms. The staff included the only man who ever got a medical discharge from the French Foreign Legion, as well as a one-armed copy boy who, when harassed, would cry out, "For Christ's sake, I've only got two hands!" And dear to memory is the occasion when sports editor Lawton Carver phoned in from a Third Avenue tavern and told the switchboard operator, "Give me Einstein," meaning to dictate his next-day column to me. The operator was new and did not yet realize I worked there, but she did have a list of private telephone numbers for newsworthy celebrities. Accordingly she made the connection to a residence in Princeton, New Jersey, the occupant answered the phone, and Carver dictated his column about the Chicago Cubs to Prof. Albert Einstein. I found out about it the next day when Carver came in to the office. "You were drunk last night, you son of a bitch," he said to me.

Given that unusual introduction to the game, it is not recorded whether in his few remaining years the professor went on to become a serious fan. It was his kind of diversion, though, for baseball, with its endless numbers, has ever been the paradise of the cabalist. "And the next day in the paper:" wrote another naturalized American, the French-born Jacques Barzun, "learned comment, statistical summaries, and the verbal imagery of meta-euphoric experts. In the face of so much joy, one can only ask, Were you there when Dogface Joe parked the pellet beyond the pale?"

It was in those days at the old INS, in any event, that we kept a much-thumbed paperback, *Spalding's Ready Reckoner,* on the handiest shelf in the sports department. It carried page after page of precalculated won-and-lost percentages and batting averages, sparing us the dreary task of having to do the math ourselves. We were aware dimly, if at all, of a well-guarded operation at the Aberdeen Proving Ground in Maryland, where the newly established Department of Defense was beginning to test a first-generation computer, of the unwieldy size then in initial manufacture by IBM and Sperry-Rand. In due course a government scientist named Roger Baldwin and three of his associates at Aberdeen determined to put the machine to the ultimate test. Their findings, eventually published in September 1956 by the *Journal of the American Statistical Association,* showed that in the presence of correct player strategy, the casino's advantage in the game of blackjack was practically nonexistent.

To some people, like inmates of the Nevada penitentiary at Carson City, imprisoned in a jurisdiction where gambling was not only legal but viewed as a salutary form of convict recreation, this discovery did not exactly come as red-hot news. The breakthrough was to be found instead in the portent of how many different and previously unsuspected uses might be made of the new technology of data storage and retrieval. Barely a dozen years later, in 1969, the first edition of *The Baseball Encyclopedia* was published, its copyright shared, its data collected, even its pages set in type, by a computer.

For its wealth of statistical information on every player, manager, team and season dating back to the dawn of major league competition nearly a century before, this was Lee Allen's "historian's dream" come true, and how fitting to find his name accorded top billing among the credits listed for the *Encyclopedia*'s editorial staff. Well, next-to-top billing: *numero uno* was David S. Neft, director of research for Information Concepts Incorporated, the company that owned the computer.

Did you know that 1,142 major league players and managers were born in Pennsylvania, one in Alaska and one in China? That George McMullen, born in California, got one hit in twelve at-bats for New York of the American Association in 1887? That George McMillan, born in Evansville, Indiana, got five hits in thirty-five at-bats for New York of the National League in 1890 and was five-foot-eight, 175 pounds and nicknamed "Reddy"? That Fred McMullin, born Oct. 13, 1891, at Scammon, Kansas, batted and threw right-handed, was injured in 1916 while playing for the White Sox and ruled ineligible in 1920 for his participation in the Black Sox scandal, played a career total of 259 games at third base, 10 at second and 6 at short, and died Nov. 21, 1952, at Los Angeles? That Larry Pratt, born Lester John Pratt on Oct. 8, 1887, at Gibson City, Illinois, played for two teams in the Federal League in 1915, batting .184 in twenty games for Brooklyn and .500 in five games for Newark, while Frank Pratt, born Francis Bruce Pratt on Aug. 24, 1897, at Blocton, Alabama, and known as "Truckhorse," had a major league career consisting in its entirety of one time at bat?

I have already alluded to the inclusion in this *Fireside* volume of Ring Lardner's classic short story "Horseshoes." Page 2,334 of that first edition of *The Baseball Encyclopedia* tells us that in 1931 the rules of the game were rewritten to read, "A fair hit ball which bounces through or over a fence, or into the stands, is considered a ground rule double." Before then (as in 1914, when "Horseshoes" was first published), that kind of hit counted as a home run—a piece of information essential not just to the enjoyment but even to the basic comprehension of the Lardner story today. And similar acknowledgment is owed to data processing for its help in bringing into being a wide range of material to be found within the covers of this book, from the trivial pursuits of quizmaster Ted Misa to the dazzling extrapolations of "sabremetricians" Pete Palmer and John Thorn.

By now, indeed, acknowledgments in prefaces like this are as commonplace as the statistics themselves. "Recognition should be given to two books that are valuable sources for facts and ideas, and might be responsible in some measure for the booming interest in big-league baseball," goes one typical such salute, in *If at First . . .* , the diary of first baseman Keith Hernandez. "They are *The 1985 Elias Baseball Analyst,* by Seymour Siwoff, Steve Hirdt, and Peter Hirdt, and *The Bill James Baseball Abstract—1985.*" Swollen by constant updating, the baseball bookshelf, already by far the most crowded of any sport, sags with the glut of high technology.

But the numerical and other delicious minutiae of the era are hardly confined to books alone. The daily newsstand spews them out as well, thanks in the main to the satellite downlink that embodies the production of *USA Today,* a journal whose lust and capacity for statistical chic have spawned a rash of imitators. The Associated Press alone, utilizing material supplied by that longtime statistical repository, the Elias Sports Bureau, distributes 3,500 words per day of the new-style baseball numerology, and sports pages everywhere drip with the hard and soft data of the game, from This Day in Baseball History five and ten and twenty-five and fifty years ago to the official listing, in descending order, of Damaso Garcia's five favorite desserts. Even so mundane an element as the daily won-and-lost standing of the teams has become so reinforced with connective tissue as to radiate the gravity of the Dead Sea Scrolls.

No other sport ever came close to baseball in exerting this sort of grip on its followers, let alone the exponential effects of the computer—a point that even the nay-sayer concedes. "Statistics I detest," the veteran San Francisco sportswriter Abe Kemp, who favored horses over ballplayers, observed in the course of taping his thoughts for Jerry Holtzman's book *No Cheering in the Press Box.* "They're the scourge of the American sports page. The fifteenth time he wiped his ass, the sixteenth time he rubbed his nose. You're writing a story and you say he's six foot seven, he's four foot two, or his earned run average is _____. That's a lot of crap. You disturb the continuity of the story. But that's all you get today." And that was nearly twenty years ago—*before* the high-tech takeover—that Kemp was doing his complaining.

What has happened to the printed word has of course happened also to television, where new equipment and techniques have augmented the quality as well as the quantity of the coverage. The computer even plays a part in packaging the newest wrinkle of all: the "fantasy week," in the course of which the most spavined middle-aged fans foregather at a training site in Florida or Arizona, suit up and watch their lifelong dream as it struggles to take wing. "They come from all different walks of life and backgrounds," Mets telecaster Steve Zabriskie observed. "But once they put on that uniform—they're all bad!"

What sets fantasy week apart, however, is what sets baseball apart. When all is said and done, it's the only game in town. No fifty-two-year-old, 140-pound, five-foot-four accountant is going to plunk down $3,000 to spend a week somewhere one-on-one against Air Jordan or The Refrigerator. Know what baseball is, in the computer language of the eighties? User-friendly, that's what. That's a computerized tape, throwing those words up on the message board midway through the seventh inning. But what high-tech words do we read?

*For it's one, two, three strikes, you're out*
*At the old ball game!*

Truth is, it's still the old ball game, only more so. In the agonizing tension of those postseason moments in October of 1986, one realizes in retrospect, it didn't make any difference whether there was a designated hitter in anybody's lineup, or what time of day or night it might be, or that the stadium was outdoor or indoor, the surface of the field real or artificial, or who was getting what salary. No difference to the live spectators, the viewers at home and in the saloons, the vendors in the stands, the commissioner, the owners, the umpires, the players. Least of all the players. "Even if I field the ball," Bill Buckner was saying six months later, "Mookie still beats Stanley to the base." You want to know what this game is all about, *that's* what this game is all about. In the abiding words of Yogi Berra, it's déjà vu all over again.

Yet even here the numbers told their story. As fans were reminded repeatedly in print and over the air, in all of the 650-odd postseason games played before 1986, no

## MASCOTS . . .
Here are the two most popular mascots in all baseball—the San Diego Chicken and the Phillie Phanatic. The least popular mascot in all baseball—the San Francisco Crab—was going to be pictured here, too, but he declined permission to use his photo. (Photos © 1986 T.F.C., Inc., San Diego and © 1987 The Phillies)

team trailing by three or more runs when it came to bat in the ninth inning had ever rallied to win. In 1986, it happened three times in five days!*

And by now, I guess numbers may be used to describe the four *Fireside* baseball books, including as they do overall more than 400 text pieces totaling maybe 1,500,000 words, as well as some 400 illustrations.† Yet none of the four books, published though they were at intervals of two, then ten, now nineteen years, were creatures of their own time. Not even this fourth book, reflect though it may the coming of the computer and cold type, is in any way confined to any one period. The subject matter would never permit it. I can remember the spring of 1956 and a question from Peter Schwed, who is retired now but served first as editor, then as chairman of the editorial board, at Simon & Schuster and had supervision of the first three books in this series. I had just delivered the manuscript for the first *Fireside,* and he wanted to know whether it left out any truly important event in the annals of the game. "I wouldn't worry about it," I said, ever so modestly. "Not unless somebody pitches a perfect game in the World Series between now and publication day." I was right, of course. It was not before publication day but on it that Don Larsen pitched his perfect game in the '56 World Series.

So, like the three volumes before it, this one ranges over what by now is well over a century of baseball history; and the surface is barely scratched. The more baseball games you see, the more things you will be seeing for the very first time. My offhand guess is that every decade of baseball's existence is reflected in these pages; but, having said that, I call to mind the unforget-

table cry of the San Diego fans reacting to the visiting Detroits as they were introduced one by one before the start of the '84 World Series: *Who Cares?*

And as for the literature of the game, is there any other subject that can bring together a Robert Fitzgerald, a William Kennedy, a James Michener, a Chaim Potok, a Mordecai Richler, a Philip Roth, an Irwin Shaw and a John Updike, all within the pages of a single volume? Is there a gleam of quality in spot reporting that outshines the Moss Klein story in this book, or a chapter of history surpassing those here by Robert Creamer and Robert Smith? It's a long-established fact that baseball and good writing go together, and over all the *Fireside* years I've observed only one change in the writing: the people doing it these days seem to me, for some recondite reason, to be younger than they used to.

I am grateful to all of the contributors to this fourth volume in its series, and to a fond swarm of other writers, editors, baseball people and samaritans including Maury Allen, Neil Cohen, Stanley Cohen, John Creamer, Tony D'Antonio, David Einstein, Jim Fitzpatrick, Lee Hays, Bowie Kuhn, Matt Merola, Arthur Pincus, Harold Rosenthal, Tom Seeberg, Sharon Seeley, Al Silverman, Frank Slocum, and Eleanor Wood and the staff of her agency. And a special vote of thanks is owed to Tim McGinnis and the people of the Fireside division of Simon & Schuster, including in particular Joe Smith, Laura Yorke, Kalia Lulow, Bonni Leon, Robin Willig, Cathy Hemming, Herb Schaffner and Phil James.

Readers of the previous *Fireside* baseball books will recognize an old friend, cartoonist John Gallagher, whose works have prowled the pages of the series more often than those of any one other illustrator (and with good reason—take a look for yourself). How little indeed has changed in the thirty-one years of the *Fireside*s. As Hall-of-Famer Paul Waner puts it in his article toward the end of this book, "Somehow . . . I don't know . . . it seems like it all happened only yesterday."

It did. You could look it up.

CHARLES EINSTEIN
New York, 1987

---

* Like Roger Maris eclipsing Babe Ruth's one-season home run mark, this may be one of those records that needs an asterisk, so it gets one here. The Bobby Thomson "homer-heard-round-the-world" playoff finale in 1951, when the Giants entered the last of the ninth trailing the Dodgers 4–1 and wound up winning 5–4, was also a postseason game but strictly speaking doesn't count as one, since it predated the splitting of the leagues into divisions and its results went into the regular-season standings and averages.

† Whoever said one picture was worth a thousand words needed seven words to say it.

The work of the late Lee Allen, who served as historian at the Baseball Hall of Fame in Cooperstown, New York, is familiar to readers of the previous *Fireside* books. This piece was published in 1955.

# A Study in Suet

## LEE ALLEN

DURING THE nation's great depression when attendance dwindled and even major league teams faced an uncertain future, life was particularly burdensome for the two clubs in Philadelphia. Shibe Park, the home of the Athletics, and Baker Bowl, the shabby nesting place of the Phillies, were seldom filled to capacity. One dreary afternoon Dave Driscoll, business manager of the Dodgers, was walking in Philadelphia and chanced to pass Baker Bowl. The Phillies were on the road, but in spite of that a pathetic vendor of peanuts was hawking his wares before an imaginary crowd near the entrance to the bleachers.

"There won't be a crowd here today," Driscoll told him. "Why don't you go to Shibe Park?"

"I've been to Shibe Park," the vendor replied. "There's nobody there either."

It was this situation that helped explain a remark made at the time by Joe McCarthy, the great manager of the Yankees. McCarthy had a pitcher at New York by the name of Walter Brown, a mammoth righthander. Although possessed of a great number of physical assets, Brown was used sparingly. When he did work, it was usually in Philadelphia against the Athletics.

"Why is it you pitch Brown only in Philadelphia?" McCarthy was asked one day.

"It's the only way I know to fill Shibe Park," Joe quipped.

McCarthy's reasoning was impeccable, for Walter, at 265 pounds, was the heaviest player who had ever appeared on the major league scene. Strangely, he owed his start to one of the lightest men the game has ever known, Rabbit Maranville. During the season of 1925 Maranville managed the Cubs for about a month, and it was at that time that Brown, a sandlotter who had been pitching around Brockton, Massachusetts, reported to him. Walter was so heavy that he found traveling uncomfortable, but he was to do plenty of it during his career. The trail that began in Chicago led to Sarasota, New Orleans, Cleveland, Omaha, Oklahoma City, New York, Jersey City, Newark, Cincinnati and New York again before he wound up his career in 1941. He is now the proprietor of a sporting goods store at Freeport, Long Island.

The peculiar thing about Brown's weight was that he put on sixty-eight of his 265 pounds during a single winter. He belonged to Cleveland at the time and weighed only 197 at the close of the 1927 season. But after an operation for the removal of his tonsils, he shot up to 265, and despite working out five hours a day at the Y.M.C.A. gymnasium, he was never able to shed the excess suet.

But Brown was no clown. He pitched big league ball for twelve years and won more games than he lost. He was also a particular favorite at Newark, where he won twenty and lost six in 1934 and led the International League in earned run percentage. Hy Goldberg of the Newark *Evening News* was asked one day what sort of stuff Brown threw. "He throws a fast ball, curve and the biggest shadow in baseball." Goldberg sallied.

Players as fat as Brown usually delight the galleries. When a player can overcome the handicap of excess weight, it is usually because he has other assets that more than make up for his bulk. Cy Young, winner of more games than any pitcher in major league history, reached his greatest peak of popularity towards the end of his career, when a bulging paunch made it almost impossible for him to field bunts. Ernie Lombardi, who sometimes weighed close to 240, was the most popular performer that Cincinnati ever had.

Bob Fothergill was another of the game's famed fatties who attained a tremendous degree of popularity. A stroke cut him down at the age of thirty-nine in 1938, but he is still recalled with sweet nostalgia in Detroit, where the fans worshipped him and where he simply pulverized the ball from 1922 through 1929.

Waite Hoyt, one of the finest Yankee pitchers and now a Cincinnati broadcaster, still shudders whenever he thinks about pitching to Fothergill and his mates. "It was awful," Hoyt has frequently said. "The Yankees would go into Detroit for a series in August and find that the entire Tiger outfield would be hitting nearly .400. Ty Cobb and Harry Heilmann were bad enough, but in some ways Fothergill was the most frightening of all. He was murder!"

Fothergill weighed about 235 pounds when he was in shape, but he was surprisingly light on his feet. Once, thinking he had been thrown at by George Earnshaw of the Athletics, he smashed a majestic home run and then climaxed his tour of the bases with a somersault that saw him land on home plate with both feet.

His full name was Robert Roy Fothergill, and he carried a handsome suitcase around the American League that had his initials, R.R.F., in big letters. When asked what they stood for, he would always reply, "For Runs Responsible For."

Fothergill really belonged in a previous age. He was one of the last of those rare spirits who appeared to play for the fun of it, and he seemed able to extract the fullest amounts of pleasure from life. After the game you could find him with a thick porterhouse steak and a seidel of beer, and he would chuckle to himself and mumble out of the side of his mouth, "Imagine getting paid for a life like this!"

Finally Detroit sold him to the White Sox, but before leaving the team he made fifty-one separate bets with friends that he would get a safe hit the first time up in his new uniform. Several days later all fifty-one received identical telegrams: "Pay up. I singled to left."

Frank (Shanty) Hogan was a catcher whose dietary requirements startled John McGraw, led to frequent finings and were responsible for some of the game's most repeated stories. Hogan weighed about 240 when in his best form, and it is probable that at certain times he weighed almost as much as Walter Brown. This would be difficult to prove for, unlike Brown and Fothergill, Hogan was reluctant to get on the scales. Chief Bender, the veteran scout of the Athletics, recalls that when he was a coach for the Giants in 1931, Hogan bet four or five players five dollars each that he would weigh 230 or less when the season began, but that when the campaign did start, they could not induce him to settle the argument.

Hogan may have been fat, but he had plenty of courage. One day, after being hit on the jawbone by a fast ball from the hand of Guy Bush of the Cubs, he trotted to first base without even rubbing his chin.

Still another leading heavyweight was Garland Buckeye, a big bird from Heron Lake, Minnesota, who had trials with the Senators, Indians and Giants for a decade starting in 1918. Buckeye was a southpaw pitcher and his weight was officially listed at 238. He was also a good batter, but was far too portly to be used at any other position. His weight put him on the defensive, and he used to say, "I'm not fat really. Now just feel that leg. You can see I'm just big-boned." Buckeye did his last professional pitching at Milwaukee. One day he attempted to field a bunt, fell on his stomach and was helped to his feet by two infielders. That was enough to teach him it was time to quit the game.

Players in the major leagues today are getting heavier just as they are getting taller. The average major league recruit of 1953 weighed 184.6 pounds, and the average for the quarter century studied is 180.6. Here, year by year, is how they have grown:

| Year | New Players | Total Weight in Pounds | Average Weight in Pounds |
|------|-------------|------------------------|--------------------------|
| 1929 | 109 | 18,967 | 174.0 |
| 1930 | 98 | 17,377 | 177.3 |
| 1931 | 102 | 18,011 | 176.5 |
| 1932 | 93 | 16,409 | 176.4 |
| 1933 | 70 | 12,641 | 180.5 |
| 1934 | 113 | 20,322 | 179.8 |
| 1935 | 115 | 20,454 | 177.8 |
| 1936 | 100 | 18,025 | 180.2 |
| 1937 | 110 | 19,773 | 179.7 |
| 1938 | 109 | 19,439 | 178.3 |
| 1939 | 127 | 22,906 | 180.3 |
| 1940 | 104 | 18,970 | 182.4 |
| 1941 | 120 | 22,031 | 183.5 |
| 1942 | 110 | 20,086 | 182.6 |
| 1943 | 147 | 26,721 | 181.7 |
| 1944 | 153 | 27,603 | 180.4 |
| 1945 | 124 | 22,314 | 179.9 |
| 1946 | 107 | 19,608 | 183.2 |
| 1947 | 98 | 17,855 | 182.1 |
| 1948 | 114 | 20,920 | 183.5 |
| 1949 | 92 | 16,884 | 183.5 |
| 1950 | 105 | 19,080 | 183.4 |
| 1951 | 110 | 19,851 | 180.4 |
| 1952 | 114 | 20,980 | 184.0 |
| 1953 | 100 | 18,463 | 184.6 |
| | | | 180.6 |

Thus, about ten tons of ballplayers are annually deposited on the major league shores, and the 1953 crew was the heaviest in history.

Thanks to a rare book called simply *Baseball* and published in 1902 at San Francisco by S. R. Church, who was also the author, it is possible to get a fairly good line on how big players were in the old days. Apparently Church intended to produce numerous volumes that would supply statistical data on all the players of major league history, a dream that has bemused numerous historians of the game. Unfortunately, the only volume that Church published covered only the National Association of 1871 to 1875, the first major league. But of the 120 players who were in that circuit in

1871, Church has provided height and weight data on about half, and from other sources statistics have been obtained on some others. It can now be shown that the player of 1871, big league baseball's first season, averaged 68.54 inches in height and 156 pounds in weight. Ballplayers, then, have grown 3.4 inches and put on twenty-eight pounds in eighty-two years.

The game had a few big men in the old days. Pop Anson, first baseman and manager of the Chicago White Stockings, listed his weight at 227 pounds, and one of his leading pitchers, Jim McCormick, was only one pound lighter. Two early hitting stars, Dan Brouthers and Roger Connor, weighed in at 207 and 220 respectively.

Players with excess poundage became a subject of mirth very early in the game's development. In April, 1877, Louis Meacham, baseball editor of the Chicago *Tribune,* the first paper in that city to give adequate coverage to the game, printed this comment about a Cincinnati catcher, Nat Hicks:

> An Eastern paper prints the Cincinnati *Enquirer*'s description of the training undergone by the Red Stockings and gently scoffs at the idea of Hicks doing anything of the kind. By the way it is so rare that one gets a chance to describe a ballplayer right out of the Bible that such an opportunity must not be missed. The picture of Jeshurun fits Hicks so exactly it must be quoted: "But Jeshurun waxed fat and kicked; thou art waxen fat; thou art grown thick; thou art covered with fatness."—Deuteronomy XXXII–15.

The *Enquirer* wasted no time in replying to this friendly libel, as O. P. Caylor, the baseball editor, wrote: "Get thee to a nunnery, friend Meacham. You don't know what you're talking about. Hicks, though fat, is one of the most earnest, good-natured workers in the Cincinnati nine."

The first player to quit the game because of overweight was Ned Williamson of the Chicago White Stockings, considered the greatest third baseman who ever lived and a fine shortstop, as well, at the time of his death. Williamson was a member of a band of players that toured the world following the season of 1888, and in a game at Paris, France, he was injured in a strange manner, cutting his knee on a rock that lay on the field while sliding into third. The enforced idleness following his injury caused him to gain an enormous amount of weight and he was never able to regain his old form, abandoning the game after the season of 1890. He then became a victim of dropsy and died at Hot Springs, Arkansas, where he had gone for treatment, March 3, 1894.

When Babe Ruth started spraying home runs around American League lawns in 1919 and finished with twenty-nine for the season writers were hard put to discover whose record he had surpassed. At first it was believed that John (Buck) Freeman of Washington had set the mark at twenty-five in 1899, but then Ernest J. Lanigan, one of the game's foremost authorities, made it known that Williamson had hit twenty-seven for the White Stockings in 1884.

Actually, Williamson's home run record is somewhat tainted. Prior to 1884 all fair balls hit over the short fences at Chicago were ruled two-base hits. The rule was changed that winter, and the result was something of a joke. The 1884 National League schedule called for only fifty-six contests in each park, and the White Stockings connected for 131 home runs in their home games and their opponents sixty-one more. When Williamson socked three over the beckoning barrier in right in the second game on Decoration Day, he became the first major leaguer to account for that many in the same game. Of his twenty-seven homers only two were smashed out on the road, both at Buffalo.

Williamson and Ruth were alike in many ways. Ned was childless but, like Ruth, genuinely devoted to children. He always carried candy and pennies for them, and when his funeral was held at his home in Chicago, the house was jammed with hundreds of urchins who looked as if their hearts would break.

Players who have attracted attention because they were underweight have been much more rare than those who had to struggle to get the pounds off. One of the first was Frederick (Bones) Ely, a shortstop who lasted from 1884 to 1902. Ely's nickname is self-explanatory, and when he batted he presented such a delicate picture that fans were afraid a pitched ball might splinter him.

Most of the extremely light players attained prominence in the nineteenth century. William (Candy) Cummings, now immortalized at Cooperstown because he is believed to have discovered the curve ball, actually weighed only 120 in his prime. Dave Birdsall, with Boston of the old National Association, was the lightest catcher, at 126 pounds. Bobby Mitchell, who became the major leagues' first southpaw when he joined Cincinnati in 1877, weighed in at 135. Mitchell's catcher, George Miller, weighed only 150, and when they joined the Reds from a team at Springfield, Ohio, that year, they were known as the Pony Battery.

Bill Veeck's midget, Eddie Gaedel, of course, was the lightest player of all time. It seems unlikely that any professional of the future will weigh less than his sixty-five pounds.

There are other physical characteristics, aside from weight, that have made certain players stand out. Slowness of foot, small feet, bowleggedness, baldness and the wearing of glasses or moustache have often marked players for ridicule.

The smallest feet in major league history were the property of Art Herring, a pitcher who spent most of his career with the Tigers and Dodgers. He wore a size three shoe. Myril Hoag, an outfielder with the Yankees, also had a peculiar pair of feet, wearing a size four shoe on one tootsy and a four and one-half on the other.

Lave Cross, a catcher and third baseman who played in the majors for twenty-one years, mostly with the Philadelphia teams, was the most bowlegged player of all time, although, in this department Honus Wagner was not far behind.

Most players of today do not affect moustaches, and when they do, they wear trim, businesslike ones. The last moustache of the handlebar variety adorned the lip of Silent John Titus, outfielder of the Phillies from 1903 to 1912. After returning to his home at St. Clair, Pennsylvania, as a young man following the Spanish–American War, Titus grew his moustache, along with friends who were members of the St. Clair Athletic Club, as a group project. When he joined the Phillies, he retained it, and it made him recognizable on the field in the days when players were not numbered.

Titus also invariably draped a toothpick in his mouth, both at bat and in the field, claiming it kept chewing tobacco off his teeth. Rival pitchers always tried to knock it out of his mouth but none succeeded, although Albert (Lefty) Leifield of the Pirates came closest, knocking off his cap one day. Titus always kept the toothpick at the side of his mouth until he decided to take a swing at the ball, and then he moved it in towards the center. Pitchers eventually discovered this mannerism and forced him to hit at bad pitches whenever they saw the toothpick change position, and began to whittle down his batting average.

Full beards, of course, have disappeared from American faces, and except on the chins of eccentrics have not been seen for years. In his excellent book, *Lost Men of American History*, Stewart Holbrook has traced the history of beards and moustaches in the United States, pointing out that not a single signer of the Declaration of Independence wore one, but that they came into favor about 1860. In baseball there was an old belief that hair on the face was an aid to eyesight, and though players were ashamed to wear glasses, they raised moustaches instead. The last player in the majors to wear a full beard on the field was Jack Remsen, an outfielder with Brooklyn who last played in 1884. Clark Griffith, owner of the Washington Senators, signed a bearded pitcher, Allen Benson, in 1934, but that was mostly a stunt and Benson, a House of David alumnus, disappeared after working in only two games.

Bald players have long been grateful for the custom of wearing caps. Tony Rensa, a catcher with the Tigers and Phillies in 1930, was so sensitive about his bald pate that he fastened his cap to his head with great wads of chewing gum. Every time he threw off his mask to chase a high foul his cap remained on his head, and he was spared the indignity of titters from the crowd.

Jimmy Ring, who pitched for the Phillies when Art Fletcher managed the team, always refused to work in the opening game of the season, and Fletcher believed it was because he would have to bare his head when "The Star-Spangled Banner" was played. It seems that early in his career Ring was warming up to pitch an opener when the band began to blare, and there was nothing for him to do but expose his head of skin. Fletcher claimed that he found the remarks from the stands so embarrassing that he vowed never again to pitch an opening game. Fortunately for Jimmy he did his pitching in the days before World War II. Since that time the national anthem has been standard procedure at most parks, not only for the opener but every day.

After a two-year "trial," the American League voted in 1975 to adopt the designated hitter rule permanently.

# Designated Hitter (DH) Rule

## AMERICAN LEAGUE OF PROFESSIONAL BASEBALL CLUBS

A HITTER MAY be designated to bat for the starting pitcher and all subsequent pitchers in any game without otherwise affecting the status of the pitcher(s) in the game. A DH for the pitcher must be selected prior to the game and must be included in the lineup cards presented to the umpire-in-chief.

It is not mandatory that a club designate a hitter for the pitcher, but failure to do so prior to the game precludes the use of a DH for that game.

Pinch-hitters for a DH may be used. Any substitute for a DH himself becomes a DH. A replaced DH shall not re-enter the game in any capacity.

The DH may be used defensively, continuing to bat in the same position in the batting order, but the pitcher then must bat in the place of the substituted defensive player, unless more than one substitution is made, and the manager then must designate their spots in the batting order.

A runner may be substituted for the DH and the runner assumes the role of the DH.

A DH is "locked" into the batting order. No multiple substitutions may be made that will alter the batting rotation of the DH.

Once the game pitcher is switched from the mound to a defensive position this move shall terminate the DH role for the remainder of the game.

Once a pinch-hitter bats for any player in the batting order and then enters the game to pitch, this move shall terminate the DH role for the remainder of the game.

Once the game pitcher bats for the DH this move shall terminate the DH role for the remainder of the game. (The game pitcher may only pinch hit for the DH.)

Once a DH assumes a defensive position this move shall terminate the DH role for the remainder of the game.

A DH is eligible for all American League batting titles.

At one point during the 1977 season, Reggie Jackson was quoted as having made a remark that disparaged his Yankee teammate Thurman Munson. "Munson, naturally, was outraged," Dave Anderson of *The New York Times* would later recall. "Then the Jackson–Billy Martin feud was there on a Saturday-afternoon televised game for the nation to see. Martin benched Jackson in mid-inning for allegedly loafing on a looper that became a double. They almost had a fight in the dugout. Not long after that, Reggie suggested we have a drink after a game.

" 'I need somebody to talk to,' he said.

"We went out for a drink again a few weeks later. At the time, both conversations were off the record. But when I got home, I made notes on what Reggie had talked about. I've learned that, sooner or later, what is said off the record often becomes on the record. And if that happened in this situation, I wanted the quotes to be accurate. The night he emerged as the World Series hero, I asked him if, in order to put his accomplishment in perspective, I could now write what he told me when he was discouraged. He agreed."

What resulted was the following remarkable account, made even more poignant today by the death of Munson in the crash of his small plane in 1979.

# 1977: Reggie

## DAVE ANDERSON

NEARLY THREE HOURS after his three home runs had won the World Series for the Yankees and redemption for himself, Reggie Jackson, like almost everyone else, appeared in awe of what he had accomplished. "There's a part of me I don't know," he was saying softly at his locker. "There's the ballplayer in me who responds to all that pressure. I'm not sure I hit three home runs but the ballplayer in me did."

And above all his complex parts, Reggie Jackson is a ballplayer. When he took nearly $3 million from the Yankees, most people scoffed that he wasn't worth it. He even agreed he wasn't worth it. But he's worth it now. No matter what he does from now on is a bonus. What he did Tuesday night put Reggie Jackson up there with Muhammad Ali winning back the heavyweight title in Zaire, up there with Joe Namath and the Jets winning Super Bowl III, up there with Tom Seaver and the Mets winning the 1969 World Series, but to appreciate how the "part of me I don't know" put Reggie Jackson up there, it is necessary to remember how another part, his sensitive ego, put Reggie Jackson down so that he might ascend.

"I got to get dressed," he was saying now. "I told some people I'd meet them at Seventy-sixth and Third."

*In that same East Side area, at a sidewalk table at Arthur's Court in July, he was sipping white wine and saying, "I'm still the straw that stirs the drink. Not Munson, not nobody else on this club."*

All the other Yankees had dressed and departed Tuesday night except for Thurman Munson, who was on his way out now.

"Hey, coon," called the catcher, grinning. "Nice goin', coon."

Reggie Jackson laughed and hurried over and hugged the captain.

"I'm goin' down to that party here in the ballpark," Thurman Munson said, grinning again. "Just white people but they'll let you in. Come on down."

"I'll be there," Reggie Jackson said. "Wait for me."

*"I got to make myself go to the ballpark," he said in July. "I don't want to go."*

*"You'll change your mind," somebody told him.*

*"I don't want to change. I've closed my mind. Remember the thing in Boston," he said, referring to his*

*dugout confrontation with Billy Martin in Fenway Park,* "the next day we had a meeting in Gabe Paul's suite and Billy challenged me. He stood over me and said, 'I'll make you fight me, boy.' But there was no way I was going to fight him. I'm two hundred and fifteen pounds, he's almost fifty years old. I win the fight, but I lose."

In the manager's office half an hour earlier, Reggie Jackson and Billy Martin had finished a TV interview together when the slugger overheard the manager talking about punching somebody.

"Anybody fights, you, Skip," Reggie Jackson said, "he's got to fight both of us."

"And anybody who fights you," Billy Martin said, "got to fight the both of us."

*"We can't win this way,"* he said in July. "The Red Sox can hammer. We got nobody who can hammer except me. I should be batting third or clean-up, not sixth. I always hit third or clean-up."*

"How far did that last homer go?" the clean-up hitter asked.

"I figured it to be about four hundred and fifty feet," a sportswriter said.

"Make it four hundred and seventy-five, it sounds better," the clean-up hitter said, laughing. "I hit that one off a knuckler, the first two off fast balls. The general consensus on how to pitch to me is hard and in. On the first one, I knew [Burt] Hooton would pitch me there, but I had an inkling I'd hit one. As soon as they brought in [Elias] Sosa, I got on the phone to Stick [Gene Michael, the Yankee scout] upstairs and asked him about Sosa, because Sosa popped me up with a fast ball in spring training. Stick told me he throws hard stuff—fast ball, slider, good curve. I hit another fast ball. I hit the second one even better than I hit the third, the one off [Charley] Hough's knuckler. Brooks Robinson taught me how to hit a knuckler. Just time the ball."

"Hough said that knuckler didn't move much," somebody said.

"It didn't," Reggie Jackson said, "until I got hold of it."

*"I should've signed with the Padres,"* he said in July. "I'd be happy there. Or with the Dodgers."*

"Did you hear," Reggie Jackson was told, "what Steve Garvey said—that after your third homer, he applauded in his glove?"

"What a great player Steve Garvey is, what a great man," Reggie Jackson said. "He's the best all-around human being in baseball. My one regret about not playing with the Dodgers is not being around Steve Garvey, but I got a security blanket here, Fran Healy [the Yankees' bullpen catcher]. Before the game he told me I was swinging the bat good."

*"I don't need baseball,"* he said in July. "I'm a businessman. That means as much to me as baseball. I don't need cheers."*

"When you hit the third one," a visitor was saying now, "George Steinbrenner had tears in his eyes."

"Get my bat, Nick, please," Reggie Jackson told a clubhouse man. "I started using this bat Saturday after I broke one in Friday's game. Look at the wide grain. The older the tree, the wider the grain, the harder the wood. I think I'll give this bat to George, he'll appreciate it."

"George," somebody said, "ought to put a marker out there halfway up the bleachers where that third homer landed."

"That'd be something. Babe Ruth, Lou Gehrig, Joe DiMaggio, Mickey Mantle and Reggie Jackson. Somehow I don't fit."

*"You know what Bobby Vinton sings, 'Color Me Gone,' that's me,"* he said in July. "Color me gone. I want to hit .300, thirty homers, fifty doubles, drive in ninety runs, be the most valuable player in the World Series, get to win the World Series, and then go. Color me gone."*

Thurman Munson reappeared. "Hey, nigger, you're too slow, that party's over but I'll see you next year," the captain said, sticking out his hand. "I'll see you next year wherever I might be."

"You'll be back," Reggie Jackson said.

"Not me," said Thurman Munson, who has talked of demanding to be traded to the Cleveland Indians. "But you know who stuck up for you, nigger, you know who stuck up for you when you needed it."

"I know," Reggie Jackson said. "But you'll be here next year. We'll all be here."

The sixth game of the 1975 World Series. The masterful Roger Angell begins his account of that game by saying that even to describe it is to diminish it—and were it anyone but Angell at the typewriter, he'd have quite a point.

Maybe one thing that made this game so special is that no one can recall anything about it except its good parts: extraordinary work by the hitters, countered by brilliancy in the field: the perfect matching of offense and defense. This in contrast to, say, the equally memorable sixth game of the 1986 World Series, where the tying run scored on a wild pitch and the winner on a grotesque error.

Television deserves its due, too, particularly in the case of this game six of 1975. Not only did it deliver the contest to uncounted millions, it brought its viewers the shot of Carlton Fisk's body English the moment after he swung for the game-winning home run in the twelfth inning—something no one actually at Fenway Park was likely to have noticed.

Scores of longtime observers—I am among them—have called this the greatest game ever played.

# 1975:
# Boston Red Sox 7,
# Cincinnati Reds 6

## ROGER ANGELL

GAME SIX, Game Six . . . what can we say of it without seeming to diminish it by recapitulation or dull it with detail? Those of us who were there will remember it, surely, as long as we have any baseball memory, and those who wanted to be there and were not will be sorry always. Crispin Crispian: for Red Sox fans, this was Agincourt. The game also went out to sixty-two million television viewers, a good many millions of whom missed their bedtime. Three days of heavy rains had postponed things; the outfield grass was a lush, Amazon green, but there was a clear sky at last and a welcoming moon—a giant autumn squash that rose above the right-field Fenway bleachers during batting practice.

In silhouette, the game suggests a well-packed but dangerously overloaded canoe—with the high bulge of the Red Sox' three first-inning runs in the bow, then the much bulkier hump of six Cincinnati runs amidships, then the counterbalancing three Boston runs astern, and then, *way* aft, one more shape. But this picture needs colors: Fred Lynn clapping his hands once, quickly and happily, as his three-run opening shot flies over the Boston bullpen and into the bleachers . . . Luis Tiant fanning Perez with a curve and the Low-Flying Plane, then dispatching Foster with a Fall Off the Fence. Luis does not have his fastball, however. . . .

Pete Rose singles in the third. Perez singles in the fourth—his first real contact off Tiant in three games. Rose, up again in the fifth, with a man on base, fights off Tiant for seven pitches, then singles hard to center. Ken Griffey triples off the wall, exactly at the seam of the left-field and center-field angles; Fred Lynn, leaping up for the ball and missing it, falls backward into the wall and comes down heavily. He lies there, inert, in a terrible, awkwardly twisted position, and for an instant all of us think that he has been killed. He is up at last, though, and even stays in the lineup, but the noise and joy are gone out of the crowd, and the game is turned around. Tiant, tired and old and, in the end, bereft even of mannerisms, is rocked again and again—eight hits in three innings—and Johnson removes him, far too late, after Geronimo's first-pitch home run in the eighth has run the score to 6–3 for the visitors.

By now, I had begun to think sadly of distant friends of mine—faithful lifelong Red Sox fans all over New England, all over the East, whom I could almost see sitting silently at home and slowly shaking their heads as winter began to fall on them out of their sets. I scarcely noticed when Lynn led off the eighth with a single and Petrocelli walked. Sparky Anderson, flicking levers like a master back-hoe operator, now called in Eastwick, his sixth pitcher of the night, who fanned Evans and retired Burleson on a fly. Bernie Carbo, pinch-hitting, looked wholly overmatched against Eastwick, flailing at one inside fastball like someone fighting off a wasp with a croquet mallet. One more fastball arrived, high and over the middle of the plate, and Carbo smashed it in a gigantic, flattened parabola into the center-field bleachers, tying the game. Everyone out there—and everyone in the stands, too, I suppose—leaped to his feet and waved both arms exultantly, and the bleachers looked like the dark surface of a lake lashed with a sudden night squall.

The Sox, it will be recalled, nearly won it right away, when they loaded the bases in the ninth with none out, but an ill-advised dash home by Denny Doyle after a fly, and a cool, perfect peg to the plate by George Foster, snipped the chance. The balance of the game now swung back, as it so often does when opportunities are wasted. Drago pitched out of a jam in the tenth, but he flicked Pete Rose's uniform with a pitch to start the eleventh. Griffey bunted, and Fisk snatched up the ball and, risking all, fired to second for the force on Rose. Morgan was next, and I had very little hope left. He struck a drive on a quick, deadly rising line—you could still hear the loud *whock!* in the stands as the white blur went out over the infield—and for a moment I thought the ball would land ten or fifteen rows back in the right-field bleachers. But it wasn't hit quite that hard—it was traveling too fast, and there was no sail to it—and Dwight Evans, sprinting backward and watching the flight of it over his shoulder, made a last-second, half-staggering turn to his left, almost facing away from the plate at the end, and pulled the ball in over his head at the fence. The great catch made for two outs in the end, for Griffey had never stopped running and was easily doubled off first.

And so the swing of things was won back again. Carlton Fisk, leading off the bottom of the twelfth against Pat Darcy, the eighth Reds pitcher of the night—it was well into morning now, in fact—socked the second pitch up and out, farther and farther into the darkness above the lights, and when it came down at last, reilluminated, it struck the topmost, innermost edge of the screen inside the yellow left-field foul pole and glanced sharply down and bounced on the grass: a

fair ball, fair all the way. I was watching the ball, of course, so I missed what everyone on television saw—Fisk waving wildly, weaving and writhing and gyrating along the first-base line, as he wished the ball fair, *forced* it fair with his entire body. He circled the bases in triumph, in sudden company with several hundred fans, and jumped on home plate with both feet, and John Kiley, the Fenway Park organist, played Handel's "Hallelujah Chorus," *fortissimo,* and then followed with other appropriately exuberant classical selections, and for the second time that evening I suddenly remembered all my old absent and distant Sox-afflicted friends (and all the other Red Sox fans, all over New England), and I thought of them—in Brookline, Mass., and Brooklin, Maine; in Beverly Farms and Mashpee and Presque Isle and North Conway and Damariscotta; in Pomfret, Connecticut, and Pomfret, Vermont; in Wayland and Providence and Revere and Nashua, and in both the Concords and all five Manchesters; and in Raymond, New Hampshire (where Carlton Fisk lives), and Bellows Falls, Vermont (where Carlton Fisk was *born*), and I saw all of them dancing and shouting and kissing and leaping about like the fans at Fenway—jumping up and down in their bedrooms and kitchens and living rooms, and in bars and trailers, and even in some boats here and there, I suppose, and on back-country roads (a lone driver getting the news over the radio and blowing his horn over and over, and finally pulling up and getting out and leaping up and down on the cold macadam, yelling into the night), and all of them, for once at least, utterly joyful and believing in that joy—alight with it.

It should be added, of course, that very much the same sort of celebration probably took place the following night in the midlands towns and vicinities of the Reds' supporters—in Otterbein and Scioto; in Frankfort, Sardinia, and Summer Shade; in Zanesville and Louisville and Akron and French Lick and Loveland. I am not enough of a social geographer to know if the faith of the Red Sox fan is deeper or hardier than that of a Reds rooter (although I secretly believe that it may be, because of his longer and more bitter disappointments down the years). What I do know is that this belonging and caring is what our games are all about; this is what we come for. It is foolish and childish, on the face of it, to affiliate ourselves with anything so insignificant and patently contrived and commercially exploitative as a professional sports team, and the amused superiority and icy scorn that the non-fan directs at the sports nut (I know this look—I know it by heart) is understandable and almost unanswerable. Almost. What is left out of this calculation, it seems to me, is the business of caring—caring deeply and passionately, really *caring*—which is a capacity or an emotion that has almost gone out of our lives. And so it seems possible that we have come to a time when it no longer matters so much what the caring is about, how frail or foolish is the object of that concern, as long as the feeling itself can be saved.

Naïveté—the infantile and ignoble joy that sends a grown man or woman to dancing and shouting with joy in the middle of the night over the haphazardous flight of a distant ball—seems a small price to pay for such a gift.

# JAMES STEVENSON

*Drawing by Stevenson; © 1986 The New Yorker Magazine, Inc.*

*"I don't think that Bart Giamatti is actually going to play baseball, Miles. I believe he's going to more or less be on the management side."*

# Baseball's Longest-Running Trade

## MARTY APPEL

Into the clubhouse of Shibe Park in Philadelphia walked a six-foot-one 190-pounder, just 18 years old and quite a bit in awe of teammates like Jimmy Foxx, Lefty Grove, Mickey Cochrane and manager Connie Mack. His name was Frankie Hayes, and within a matter of months, Cochrane would be off to Detroit, and Hayes would become the new catcher of the Philadelphia Athletics. He'd hold onto the job for over seven years. It all began for him in 1933.

Out of the Yankee Stadium clubhouse strode six-foot-three 190-pounder Dave Righetti. The 1986 season was over, and it was a big one for Dave, who had set a new record for saves. A half-century had passed since Hayes had walked into the majors. And between Hayes and Righetti, two men who never heard of each other, wove baseball's longest-running trade. In the end, in a manner of speaking, it came down to whether George Steinbrenner had managed to pull a fast one on Connie Mack.

This baseball oddity makes the most sense by getting to the point. Through a series of fifteen trades, with the poetic license of dropping out of sequence on occasion, it is possible to determine that a single trade, sending Hayes back to the Athletics on February 17, 1944, is still alive. And when so many careers end with players getting optioned or released, that one could exist for so long is truly a baseball wonder.

Hayes, who had been dealt to the St. Louis Browns, was traded back to Philadelphia in that 1944 deal, with a pitcher named Sam Zoldak crossing over to the Browns. After five years there, Zoldak went to Cleveland in time for their pennant-winning season of 1948.

On April 30, 1951, he wound up back with the A's in a complicated three-way deal involving six players. One of the six was pitcher Lou Brissie, the World War II vet who had lost a leg in combat but was able to pitch just the same.

On that April day in 1951, as Brissie and Zoldak crossed paths, the three-way deal also made it possible for Brissie to cross paths with Minnie Minoso, who was moving from Cleveland to Chicago.

Minoso, then a 28-year-old rookie, went on to become a very popular White Sox outfielder and a "five-decade player" (appearing in games in the 1940s, 1950s, 1960s, 1970s and 1980s).

On December 4, 1957, Minoso was traded back to Cleveland, along with Fred Hatfield, for Al Smith and Early Wynn, two men who would help the White Sox to their 1959 pennant.

Wynn, who went on to win 300 games and enter the Hall of Fame, is our new torchbearer on this trade. But it's necessary to backtrack just a bit to establish the lineage.

On December 14, 1948, Wynn had been traded from Washington to Cleveland with Mickey Vernon, in exchange for Joe Haynes, Ed Klieman and Eddie Robinson.

Robinson, a first baseman, becomes an important link in the story. Not only is he now a player in the sequence of trades, but years later, as vice president of the Texas Rangers, he made one of the trades that kept the streak alive.

On December 5, 1956, Robinson and three other players were traded from Kansas City to Detroit in exchange for Ned Garver, Virgil Trucks and two minor leaguers. Garver became the new link on August 11, 1952, when he exchanged uniforms with, among others, the much-traveled Dick Littlefield. It was an eight-player deal between the Browns and the Tigers, and in Littlefield, we come to a man who played for a record ten teams—in an era of only sixteen!

Littlefield, the new link, was traded on April 16, 1957, by the New York Giants (their final season in New York, and the first time the National League got involved in this) to the Cincinnati Reds. The deal brought third baseman Ray Jablonski to New York.

Jablonski had accompanied pitcher Gerry Staley and a stack of cash from the Cardinals to the Reds on December 8, 1954, for a highly regarded pitcher named Frank Smith. And on June 10, 1961, just a year and a half after he had starred for the White Sox in their pennant season, Staley and three other players went to Kansas City for

"*Play me, or trade me!*"

Don Larsen, Andy Carey, Al Pilarcik and Ray Herbert.

Herbert, a pitcher, was traded to the Phillies on December 1, 1964, in a deal that brought rookie Danny Cater to the White Sox.

Cater worked his way through the American League, stopping in Chicago, Kansas City and Oakland before going to the Yankees in 1970. And on March 22, 1972, he was traded to Boston for relief ace Sparky Lyle.

Sparky spent six seasons with the Yankees, won the Cy Young Award in 1977, and set a record for most career appearances without making a start, 899.

By 1978, he had outlived his usefulness in New York, and the Yankees dealt him, along with rookies Larry McCall, Dave Rajsich, Mike Heath and Domingo Ramos, to the Texas Rangers, for Juan Beniquez, Greg Jemison, Paul Mirabella, Mike Griffin and Dave Righetti.

Eddie Robinson had kept the longest-running trade alive as the vice president of the Rangers, although he had no idea that he was doing it, nor that he himself had been one of the men in the link.

In brief:

| | |
|---|---|
| 1933 | Frankie Hayes debuts |
| 1944 | Hayes for Sam Zoldak |
| 1951 | Zoldak for Lou Brissie |
| 1951 | Brissie for Minnie Minoso |
| 1957 | Minoso for Early Wynn |
| 1948 | Wynn for Eddie Robinson |
| 1956 | Robinson for Ned Garver |
| 1952 | Garver for Dick Littlefield |
| 1957 | Littlefield for Ray Jablonski |
| 1954 | Jablonski for Frank Smith |
| 1954 | Smith for Gerry Staley |
| 1961 | Staley for Ray Herbert |
| 1964 | Herbert for Danny Cater |
| 1972 | Cater for Sparky Lyle |
| 1978 | Lyle for Dave Righetti |

As of 1986, with Righetti still active, the trade was still alive. Did Connie Mack outfox George Steinbrenner? Or did George steal one away from Connie? You call it.

# Pennant Races of the 1890s

## JIM BAKER

AMONG ITS many shortcomings, the twelve-team league produced very few good pennant races. From an inauspicious start in 1892 with the idea of a split season, which was reviled by everyone, the "big league" never produced a three-team race. Third-place teams never got closer than eight games off the mark. For the years 1893–99, the National League's third-place teams averaged ten games out of first.

And there were only a few decent two-team races. The 1895 race, though decided by only three games, was not especially climactic, since, in the last ten days of the season, Baltimore played seven games, and runner-up Cleveland played only two. Kind of slows down the scoreboard watching. . . . Baltimore went six and one while Cleveland split, so that the half game lead of September 21 edged up by the day, with Cleveland powerless to do anything about it.

There was a great two-team race in 1897. On August 21, the defending champion Baltimore Orioles trailed the Boston Beaneaters by three games. On the twenty-eighth, they had pulled ahead by percentage points, but were still a half game behind because they had played fewer games:

|  | Won | Lost | Pct. | GB |
|---|---|---|---|---|
| Baltimore | 69 | 32 | .683 | .5 |
| Boston | 72 | 34 | .679 | — |

And then, for twenty-eight days, the margin between the two teams never grew larger than one full game. Baltimore won eleven in a row from September 4 through September 16; Boston answered with eight out of nine. By the twenty-third, things hadn't changed much:

|  | Won | Lost | Pct. | GB |
|---|---|---|---|---|
| Baltimore | 87 | 36 | .707 | .5 |
| Boston | 89 | 37 | .706 | — |

Another problem with the twelve-team league, familiar to fans of the 1980s, is the dilution of the schedule; the two teams rarely met. But on this date, Boston began a three-game set in Baltimore; they would have only one series left when the series was over. A crowd of 12,900 turned out to see Boston move into first place with a 6–4 victory; the crowd included 135 "Rooters" down from Boston under the leadership of John Fitzgerald, wearing Red Badges and armed with tin horns. The Orioles had the tying runs on base when Willie Keeler ripped a liner that was speared by Herman Long, the great Boston shortstop, who doubled off second a runner "who had incautiously lit out for third when Keeler hit the ball."

On the twenty-fifth, Saturday, 18,750 people saw the Orioles come back, 6–3. The Orioles took a quick 3–0 lead, but the Beaneaters in the seventh had the tying run on third (Billy Hamilton) and another man on first (Bobby Lowe). When Lowe got caught in a rundown between first and second, Hamilton headed home, but Dirty Jack Doyle made a quick throw home and got him, with Wilbert Robinson landing hard on the tiny Hamilton, according to a newspaper report "almost crushing him with his two hundred and fifty pounds of solid flesh." The game was described as a "nerve destroyer," and it was said that the series so far had comprised two of the most exciting games in the history of baseball.

No Sunday ball. Game three was played on Monday, September 27, and was attended by 25,375 cranks, bringing the three-day total to a remarkable 57,000. It was a wide-open slugfest, common in 1897; Baltimore scored five early off the great Kid Nichols, but Boston exploded for nine runs in the seventh, and won it 19–10. Baltimore's three top pitchers all worked in the effort, but Boston was in first place with three to play.

The Baltimore crowd seemed to enjoy the barrage; the papers reported them laughing good-naturedly at the onslaught. Billy Hamilton was cheered lustily when, "after being trampled upon and severely stunned by Jennings at second, he made a grand run for home on Lowe's single, collided with Baltimore's fleshy backstop, and, falling heavily, pluckily crawled toward the base, almost fainting as he touched it." On-the-scene reports paint a pleasant picture, very different from the one we usually see of the period. When the game was over "ten thousand people congratulated the visitors with handshakes and cheers and told them what good fellows and fine players they were." Then again, the size of the crowd suggests that these were not so much the regular fans of the era as they were just some people who got caught up in passing excitement. The *Topeka Capital* lauded this demonstration of appreciation as "a fitting climax to the greatest spectacle Baltimore has ever seen."

In what was probably the greatest series in nineteenth-century baseball, Germany (Why-on-Earth-Aren't-You-in-the-Hall-of-Fame) Long had nine hits, three of them doubles, and scored four runs. Willie Keeler and Huey Jennings had seven hits apiece for Baltimore, Wilbert Robinson six. There were twenty-two doubles in the three games, four by Jennings.

Baltimore was one and a half back with one series remaining, and, since Boston won two of its three, out of the race.

Beginning with the 1976 season, certain established major leaguers could play out that year without signing a contract, then deal elsewhere for their services for the next year. It was a part of the revolution in free agency, and twenty-four players—five of them with the Oakland A's—opted for that course. Figuring that so long as he was going to lose them he might as well get something for them, A's owner Charles O. Finley traded two of them—Reggie Jackson and Ken Holtzman—to Baltimore just before the 1976 season started. Then in mid-June he sold three more stars—outfielder Joe Rudi and pitcher Rollie Fingers to the Boston Red Sox for $2 million and pitcher Vida Blue to the New York Yankees for $1.5 million.

That's what he thought. However, no player sale in baseball can be final until the commissioner says so. Commissioner Bowie Kuhn decided the Rudi/Fingers/Blue transactions would be bad for the game, and that was that.

That's what he thought. Finley sued him, claiming among other things that Kuhn had acted in restraint of trade. Legal sales had taken place between consenting parties, each of whom was to receive something of value, in the greatest tradition of this nation and the free enterprise system. By and large, the public, loudly led by the sporting press, agreed with Finley and forecast his victory in the trial that lay ahead.

That's what they thought. There was no trial—not on the main issues, anyway. Having read all the documents, including the one you are about to read, which was the crusher, Federal Judge Frank McGarr in Chicago simply threw the case out, concurring that among other things Finley was one of the club owners who specifically had hired Kuhn to do exactly what he did here in the exercise of his authority as commissioner.

Some months later, Judge McGarr did hold a trial, this one limited to seeing whether Kuhn had properly exercised the cosmetics of that authority—given all parties a chance to be heard, served due notice, that sort of thing. Kuhn, of course, won that one too.

As you read this, incidentally, you will get as good—and as enjoyable—an account of baseball's historical exemption from the antitrust laws as can be found anywhere. And you may find yourself shaking your head and wondering how anybody could have supposed Finley had a chance of winning.

# Motion to Dismiss

## — BAKER, McTURNAN, BLEAKLEY, NATHAN ET AL. —

IN THE UNITED STATES DISTRICT COURT FOR THE NORTHERN DISTRICT OF ILLINOIS, EASTERN DIVISION

---

CHARLES O. FINLEY &
CO. INC.,
an Illinois Corporation

     *Plaintiff,*

  v.          No. 76 C 2358

BOWIE K. KUHN, *et al.,*

     *Defendants.*

---

MEMORANDUM IN SUPPORT OF
MOTION OF DEFENDANT
BOWIE K. KUHN FOR SUMMARY JUDGMENT

By this lawsuit, plaintiff, owner of the Oakland A's major league baseball club, seeks to have this Court reverse the discretionary decision of the Commissioner of Baseball disapproving plaintiff's proposed transfer of three ball players in mid-season to competing teams. Notwithstanding a blunderbuss 38 page complaint—raising charges ranging from the Commissioner's alleged violations of the United States Constitution to a purported antitrust conspiracy against plaintiff involving the Commissioner and every other major league club—the critical material facts underlying this suit are undisputed and, we submit, entitle the Commissioner to summary judgment as a matter of law.

Plaintiff's complaint should be dismissed in its entirety with prejudice as a matter of law for the following reasons:

1. Plaintiff, as well as each of the other major league club owners, has entered into a lawful agreement "to be bound by the decisions of the Commissioner" as to all baseball disputes and controversies, including such matters as player transfers, and to "waive such rights of recourse to the courts as would otherwise have existed. . . ." Recognizing that the national pastime of baseball could not function if internal disputes and their resolution by the Commissioner were to become embroiled in protracted litigation—no more than if every ball and strike call by an umpire were appealable to higher authorities—the major league club owners have voluntarily, knowingly and with good reason agreed that the decisions of the Commissioner shall be final and unreviewable in a court of law, and have lawfully deprived themselves of recourse to this forum. Accordingly, this suit must be summarily dismissed for lack of subject matter jurisdiction.

2. Even if this Court were to assume jurisdiction, it would be required, based on the indisputable facts of record and the law of this jurisdiction for almost half a century,* to uphold the Commissioner's decision because:

    (a) The Commissioner's authority to approve or disapprove player transfers in accordance with the best interests of baseball is clearly delegated to him by the Major League Agreement and the Major League Rules promulgated thereunder;

    (b) The Commissioner acted after providing all interested parties with a fair and transcribed hearing, in which plaintiff participated without protest or objection; and

    (c) The Commissioner's written decision articulates the reasonable basis for his conclusion that the proposed $3.5 million sale of three mainstays of plaintiff's championship team in mid-season to plaintiff's wealthy competitors would not be in the best interests of baseball, thereby negating any possible claim that the decision is arbitrary or capricious.

3. Plaintiff's antitrust claim is untenable since the United States Supreme Court has ruled in an unbroken line of precedents—reaffirmed as recently as 1972—that professional baseball is not subject to the antitrust laws. *Flood* v. *Kuhn,* 407 U.S. 258 (1972); *Toolson* v. *New York Yankees, Inc.,* 346 U.S. 356 (1953); and *Federal Baseball Club of Baltimore* v. *National League,* 259 U.S. 200 (1922).

4. And finally, plaintiff's claim that the Commissioner

---

* *Milwaukee American Association* v. *Landis,* 49 F.2d 298 (N.D. Ill. 1931).

of Baseball, a private citizen responsible for overseeing the internal affairs of a private association, violated the due process and equal protection clauses of the Fifth and Fourteenth Amendments to the United States Constitution is patently without merit since the decision by the Commissioner to disapprove player transfers does not in any conceivable fashion constitute "state action."

In light of these fully dispositive legal grounds, the Commissioner of Baseball respectfully urges this Court to dismiss this action forthwith. Despite the multiple counts and theories in which plaintiff purports to cast its complaint, this case comes down to no more than a disagreement by one major league club owner with a judgmental decision rendered by the Commissioner in a matter expressly and exclusively delegated by plaintiff and all of the other major league club owners to the Commissioner's discretion. Put simply, the plaintiff disputes the "call" and improperly seeks to have this Court review and substitute its judgment for that of the Commissioner as to whether these proposed player transfers would be in the "best interests of baseball."

In addition to the standard reasons supporting the efficacy of summary judgment—including the conservation of judicial time and energy and the savings of substantial litigation costs by all parties—there is an overriding public interest in this case which justifies prompt dismissal. As plaintiff knew full well, both when it became a party to the Major League Agreement and agreed to be bound by the Commissioner's decisions, and when it participated without protest in the hearing before the Commissioner to determine whether to approve the player transfers in issue here, the public's continued confidence in the integrity of baseball requires that the decisions of the Commissioner be final and unreviewable by the courts.

The millions of baseball fans around the country must be assured that internal baseball disputes will be resolved expeditiously and authoritatively by the Commissioner, who is knowledgeable about and dedicated to protecting the best interests of the game, and not in complex, protracted judicial trials and appeals. In particular, the fans must be promptly assured that the three players in question here owe their full allegiance to plaintiff's team and have no reason to aid the teams to which plaintiff proposed to transfer them. The prolongation of this litigation—with protracted pretrial discovery, multiple evidentiary hearings and all of the attendant publicity—would totally frustrate these objectives and, in so doing, have a definite adverse impact on the public's confidence in and support for the national pastime.

In the following sections of this memorandum, defendant Commissioner Kuhn shall set forth in detail the undisputed material facts and governing legal precedents which, we submit, require the Court to dismiss the complaint with prejudice.

STATEMENT OF MATERIAL, UNCONTESTED FACTS*

The operative facts underlying this controversy can be simply stated: After conducting a full hearing,** the Commissioner of Baseball, acting under the Major League Agreement and the Major League Rules, issued a written decision disapproving plaintiff's proposed assignment in mid-season of the contracts of players Joe Rudi and Rollie Fingers to the Boston Red Sox for $2 million, and player Vida Blue to the New York Yankees for $1.5 million on the ground that the sales were not "consistent with baseball's best interests, the integrity of the game, and the maintenance of public confidence in it." (Kuhn Aff. ¶ 19.) The authority for and propriety of the Commissioner's action and its immunity from review in this forum are established by the following undisputed material facts.

*A. Organization of Baseball*

Defendant Bowie K. Kuhn is the Commissioner of Baseball. (Kuhn Aff. ¶ 1.) The office of the Commissioner was created by the Major League Agreement, which is a contract among the American and National Leagues and each of their 24 constituent ball clubs, including the Oakland A's Baseball Club, which is owned and operated by plaintiff. (Kuhn Aff. ¶ 5.) (A copy of the Agreement is attached as Exhibit A to the Kuhn Affidavit.) The Agreement, which establishes the organization and governmental structure of major league baseball, empowers the Commissioner, *inter alia:*

> "TO INVESTIGATE, either upon complaint or upon his own initiative, any act, transaction or practice charged, alleged or suspected to be not in the best interests of the national game of Baseball . . . [and]

* This statement of undisputed facts is drawn exclusively from the affidavit of Commissioner Bowie Kuhn attached hereto as Exhibit A, and the documents annexed thereto. While plaintiff can have no possible disagreement with the facts set forth in the affidavit or the contents of the documents, the complaint raises additional allegations, which defendant vigorously denies. However, defendant submits that for the reasons set forth below, the additional allegations, even if true, are legally irrelevant and immaterial and that the undisputed facts warrant dismissal.

** A copy of the transcript of the hearing is attached as Exhibit D to Commissioner Kuhn's Affidavit. Citations to the transcript are as follows, "Tr. p. —."

"TO DETERMINE, after investigation, what preventive, remedial or punitive action is appropriate in the premises, and to take such action either against Major Leagues, Major League Clubs or individuals, as the case may be." (Article I, Sections 2(a) and (b)) (Kuhn Aff. ¶ 8).

The most recently amended version of the Major League Agreement was adopted by all 24 major league club owners, including plaintiff, on January 1, 1975. (Kuhn Aff. ¶ 5.)

Articles II, IV and V of the Major League Agreement further provide for the promulgation of the Major League Rules. These rules are made "binding upon the Major Leagues and their constituent clubs." (Kuhn Aff. ¶ 9.) Rule 12(a) provides that no assignment of a player contract "shall be recognized as valid *unless* within fifteen (15) days after execution a counterpart original of the document shall be filed . . . *and approved by the Commissioner.*" (Kuhn Aff. ¶ 10) (emphasis added). (A copy of Rule 12 is attached as Exhibit B to the Kuhn Affidavit.)

The Major League Agreement expressly provides that each of the parties, including plaintiff, agreed to be bound by the decisions of the Commissioner and to waive any rights they might otherwise have to seek judicial review of the Commissioner's decisions. Thus, Article VII, Section 2, of the Agreement reads as follows:

"The Major Leagues and their constituent clubs, severally agree to be bound by the decisions of the Commissioner, and the discipline imposed by him under the provisions of this Agreement, *and severally waive such right of recourse to the courts as would otherwise have existed in their favor.*" (Emphasis added). (Kuhn Aff. ¶ 11.)

In explaining the reasons for the original incorporation of this provision in the Major League Agreement, the owners stated in a unanimous resolution attached to the Agreement:

"We, the undersigned, earnestly desirous of insuring to the public wholesome and high-class baseball, and believing that we ourselves should set for the players an example of sportsmanship which accepts the umpires' decisions without complaint, hereby pledge ourselves loyally to support the Commissioner in his important and difficult tasks; and we assure him that each of us will acquiesce in his decisions, even when we believe them mistaken, and that we will not discredit the sport by public criticism of him or of one another." (Kuhn Aff. ¶ 12.)

The language of Article VII was first incorporated in the Major League Agreement in 1921. In 1945, Article VII of the Major League Agreement was amended by deleting the clause in which the clubs explicitly waived their rights of recourse to the courts; the Agreement continued to provide that the clubs would be bound by the decisions and discipline imposed by the Commissioner. (Kuhn Aff. ¶ 13.) Effective January 1, 1965, Article VII of the Major League Agreement was amended, expressly restoring the provision that the clubs "severally waive such rights of recourse to the courts as otherwise would have existed in their favor." (Kuhn Aff. ¶ 13.) This language from the 1965 Agreement was readopted in the 1975 Agreement, which became effective approximately 18 months ago.

*B. Plaintiff's Proposed Transactions*

On June 15, 1976—the final day of the baseball season in which interclub player transactions are permitted under the Major League Rules—plaintiff negotiated tentative and unapproved agreements to assign the contracts of outfielder Joe Rudi and relief pitcher Rollie Fingers to the Boston Red Sox for a total of $2 million and the contract of starting pitcher Vida Blue to the New York Yankees for $1.5 million. (Complaint ¶ 11.) The A's, Red Sox and Yankees are all members of the American League and regularly compete against each other.

In the past five years, the Oakland A's baseball team has won five divisional titles, three American League pennants, and three world championships. (Tr. p. 10.) Throughout this period, the leading players for the A's have included Blue, Rudi, Fingers, as well as Reggie Jackson and Ken Holtzman. Earlier in the season, plaintiff traded Jackson and Holtzman to a competing team. (Tr. p. 10.)

Concerned about the large sums of cash involved, the impact on the competitive balance among teams in the American League, the absence of any players to be received by the A's in return for the sale of its stars and the substantial depletion of talent of a championship team, the Commissioner, pursuant to the authority vested in him by the Major League Agreement to initiate investigations into transactions which may not be in the best interests of baseball, invited all parties to a hearing on June 17, 1976, in his New York office. (Kuhn Aff. ¶ 15.) In a telegram sent to all of the parties, the Commissioner explained that the purpose of the hearing was "to provide a prompt means of establishing the full facts regarding these transactions and to afford all parties the opportunity to present their views and contentions as to their propriety." The telegram added, "All concerned are of course entitled to be represented by counsel if they desire.'' A copy of the telegram is attached as Exhibit C to Commissioner Kuhn's Affidavit.

## C. The Hearing Before the Commissioner

Appearing at the hearing before the Commissioner were Charles O. Finley, president of plaintiff, and his son, Paul Finley; the general partner, the president and counsel for the New York Yankees; the executive vice president and general manager, the treasurer and counsel for the Boston Red Sox; the president of the American League; and the executive director and counsel for the Major League Baseball Players Association. (Kuhn Aff. ¶ 17, Tr. p. 2.) A copy of the transcript of the hearing is attached as Exhibit D to the Kuhn Affidavit.

At the outset of the hearing, the Commissioner explained that the question presented was "whether these transactions are consistent with the best interests of baseball's integrity and maintenance of public confidence in the game." (Tr. p. 5.) The Commissioner invited the participants to set forth all "details or facts that you believe are relevant to the inquiry which I have described," reminding all of the participants that "it is at least possible that I might determine that the assignments here involved should not be approved." (Tr. pp. 5, 6.)

At no time before or during the hearing did plaintiff's representative challenge or even intimate any reservation about the authority of the Commissioner to approve or disapprove player transfers, nor did plaintiff's representative lodge any protest or objection to the procedures at the hearing. (Kuhn Aff. ¶ 18.) Instead, Mr. Charles Finley volunteered to begin the proceedings and made a vigorous presentation of all of the factors which, in his view, justified the Commissioner in approving the proposed transactions. (Tr. pp. 9–34.) Similarly, all of the other participants availed themselves of the opportunity to present the factors which they believed relevant to the Commissioner's decision to approve or disapprove the proposed player transfers. (Kuhn Aff. ¶ 18.)

## D. The Commissioner's Decision

On June 18, 1976, after considering the presentations made at the hearing, the Commissioner issued a written decision disapproving the proposed transfers of the player contracts in exchange for $3.5 million as "inconsistent with the best interests of Baseball, the integrity of the game and the maintenance of public confidence in it." (Kuhn Aff. ¶ 19.) A copy of the decision is attached as Exhibit E to the Kuhn Affidavit.

The decision does not contest the good faith of the club owners involved in negotiating the proposed player transfers. However, the decision reasons that, if the Commissioner approved the sales for enormous sums of cash of three stars of one team to wealthy competitors,

> "[T]he door would be opened wide to the buying of success by the more affluent clubs, public suspicion would be aroused, traditional and sound methods of player development and acquisition would be undermined and our efforts to preserve competitive balance would be greatly impaired."

In accordance with the responsibility expressly vested in him by the Major League Agreement to protect the best interests of baseball, the Commissioner's decision reflects his concern that both for the present season and for all future seasons baseball fans must be assured that each of the teams, not only those with large cash reserves, will be able "to compete effectively" in their respective pennant races.

In part, the decision was based on the Commissioner's concern that the Oakland A's "shorn of much of its finest talent in exchange for cash" would not be able to play competitively this season against the other teams in its league, thereby depriving the A's' fans of the team and caliber of play which they have supported in the past. More importantly, for the long run, the decision states the Commissioner's concern that baseball fans may not support a sport where all of the best talent is purchased by one or two of the wealthiest clubs and when all the remaining teams, consisting of inferior players, will not be able to mount serious competition to the wealthy few.

Finding that "public confidence in the integrity of club operations and in baseball would be gravely undermined should such assignments not be restrained," the Commissioner disapproved the proposed transfers and directed the three players to remain on the active roster of the Oakland A's and to be available to play in their games.

## E. The Complaint

Without seeking reconsideration by the Commissioner, plaintiff filed this suit on June 25, 1976, in the Northern District of Illinois. The suit seeks, in addition to monetary damages and other relief, an injunction from this Court "ordering defendant Kuhn to approve the assignments" of Rudi, Fingers and Blue and "ordering defendant Kuhn to rescind, reverse, nullify and withdraw his order of June 18, 1976, disapproving said assignments." (Complaint, p. 35.)

Neither of the other major league baseball clubs involved in the proposed transfer joined the A's in filing the suit, and the Yankees and Red Sox have been named as defendants along with the Commissioner, the American and National Leagues and the Executive Council of major league baseball.*

While the complaint contains seven counts, each of them is premised upon the Commissioner's disapproval of the proposed transfers. Counts 1 and 5 charge that the Commissioner's disapproval of the proposed assignments constitutes a breach of his employment contract with the major league baseball clubs and an inducement to the Yankees and Red Sox to breach their contracts to purchase the players. Count 2 alleges that the Commissioner's disapproval was part of a conspiracy in restraint of trade in violation of the Sherman Act, 15 U.S.C. § 1. Counts 3 and 4 charge that the Commissioner's disapproval constitutes a violation of the due process and equal protection clauses of the U.S. Constitution. Count 6 seeks a declaratory judgment that the Commissioner lacked the authority to disapprove the transfers, and Count 7 seeks to compel the Yankees and Red Sox to consummate the transfers, notwithstanding the Commissioner's disapproval.

### ARGUMENT

### • I. Plaintiff's lawful agreement to waive judicial review of the Commissioner's resolution of internal baseball disputes bars this action

Section 2 of Article VII of the Major League Agreement, the most recent version of which was adopted by plaintiff and every other major league club owner in 1975, provides:

> "The Major Leagues and their constituent clubs, severally agree to be bound by the decisions of the Commissioner, and the discipline imposed by him under the provisions of this Agreement, and *severally waive such right of recourse to the courts as would otherwise have existed in their favor.*" (Emphasis added).

The underscored portion of this fundamental provision was deliberately reinstated in the Major League Agree-

* The Executive Council, consisting of four major league club owners (two from each major league), the presidents of the two major leagues, and the Commissioner, was established by the owners in the Major League Agreement. Article II, Section 2(a) of the Agreement provides that it shall be the function of the Executive Council:

> "To COOPERATE, advise and confer with the Commissioner and other offices, agencies and individuals in an effort to perpetuate Baseball as the national game of America, and to surround it with such safeguards as may warrant absolute public confidence in its integrity, operations and methods." (Kuhn Aff. ¶ 4.)

ment in 1965 and reaffirmed by the major league owners in 1975 because they recognized that the Commissioner of Baseball would be unable to perform his "important and difficult tasks" unless all of the owners "assure him that each of us will acquiesce in his decisions" and that he will not be threatened by a lawsuit every time he makes a decision which displeases one of the 24 major league club owners. (Unanimous Resolution attached to original Major League Agreement.) (Kuhn Aff. ¶ 12.)

In order to preserve public confidence in the integrity of baseball—thereby insuring the public's continued patronage—the owners established, through the Major League Agreement, the Office of the Commissioner of Baseball, and granted him broad powers to prevent actions which might undermine public confidence in the integrity of the sport. The owners recognized that decisions made in the exercise of such powers by the Commissioner could be difficult and might displease one or more of the owners. For this reason, the owners adopted Article VII, Section 2 as a manifestation of their intent to shield the Commissioner from the risk that any of his decisions could subject him to protracted, expensive litigation (including, as in this case, a $10 million damage suit against him personally as well as in his capacity as Commissioner).

If the Commissioner of Baseball were forced to consider the cost of a possible lawsuit every time he made a decision which one or more club owners might consider adverse to their interests, he would not be able to perform the tasks assigned to him under the Major League Agreement. In certain cases, he might be discouraged from taking any appropriate action. In any event, the public would have reason to question whether the Commissioner's decisions were made "in the best interests of baseball" or in an effort to appease particular club owners and avoid litigation. Recognizing that public confidence in the integrity of baseball depends on the public's trust in the ability of the Commissioner to prevent conduct "not in the best interests of baseball," the club owners agreed that decisions made by the Commissioner were to be final and binding, and they agreed to waive such right of recourse to the courts as might otherwise have been available to them.

It has long been the rule that voluntary agreements to be bound by the decisions of nonjudicial tribunals and to waive judicial review are valid and binding. *See, e.g., Bower* v. *Eastern Airlines,* 214 F.2d 623 (3d Cir.), *cert. denied,* 348 U.S. 871 (1954); *Rossi* v. *TWA,* 350 F. Supp. 1263, 1269–70 (C.D. Cal. 1972), *aff'd,* 507 F.2d 404 (9th Cir. 1974); *Rood* v. *Railway Passenger & Freight Conductors' Mutual Benefit Ass'n,* 31 F. 62 (N.D. Ill. 1887); *Pacaud* v. *Waite,* 218 Ill. 138, 75 N.E. 779 (1905). Thus, in *Berlin* v. *Eureka Lodge,* 64 P. 254 (Cal., 1901), the court described as "settled law" that:

"[A] member of a lodge, by his subscribing to the by-laws, may waive his right to sue in the courts of law for the redress of his grievances; and, if such member brings an action in a court of law, it is a defense thereto if he has agreed within the order to look solely to its tribunals for the redress of those grievances, and those tribunals have decided against him upon the merits of his case." *Id.*

Similarly, the Illinois Supreme Court recognized in *Railway Passenger & Freight Conductors' Mutual Aid & Benefit Ass'n* v. *Robinson,* 147 Ill. 138, 35 N.E. 168, 176 (1893), that:

". . . [I]t is competent for members of societies of this character to so contract that their rights as members shall depend upon the determination of some tribunal of their own choice, and that such determination shall be conclusive, . . ."*

Particularly where, as here, the parties agree not only to be bound by the decision of a nonjudicial tribunal, but further expressly and unequivocally covenant to forego any recourse to the courts, complaints filed in breach of such agreements have been summarily dismissed. *See, e.g., Railway Passenger & Freight Conductors' Mutual Aid & Benefit Ass'n* v. *Robinson, supra; Supreme Lodge of Order of Select Friends* v. *Raymond,* 57 Kan. 647, 47 P. 533 (1897); *Wuerthner* v. *Workingmen's Benev. Soc.,* 121 Mich. 90, 79 N.W. 921 (1899).

Like agreements to compromise litigation prior to trial, agreements to waive judicial review are favored because they spare the caseload of overburdened courts and permit the parties to resolve their differences without the enormous cost and inconvenience of litigation. As one court emphasized in upholding the waiver of judicial review of an arbitrator's award:

"Such a policy of non-review is grounded in the desire to avoid litigation. In fact one must assume that the main reason the parties resorted to arbitration in the first place was to circumvent the identical protracted altercation Plaintiff now invites by coming into the Federal Courts. Both parties knew the arbitration process would be quick and cheap; moreover,

* The enforceability of agreements by private associations to forego resort to the courts is a corollary to the more general rule, recognized in this Circuit and in the Illinois state courts, that rules and bylaws of private associations governing the rights and obligations of their members shall be judicially enforced. *See, e.g., Talton* v. *Behncke,* 199 F.2d 471, 473 (7th Cir. 1952); *Parsons College* v. *North Central Association of Colleges and Secondary Schools,* 271 F. Supp. 65, 70 (N.D. Ill. 1967); *Engel* v. *Walsh,* 258 Ill. 98, 101 N.E. 222 (1913); *Bostedo* v. *Board of Trade,* 227 Ill. 90, 81 N.E. 42 (1907); *Werner* v. *International Association of Machinists,* 11 Ill. App. 2d 258, 137 N.E. 2d 100 (1956).

the differences would be resolved by people familiar with the practical intricacies of their particular occupation. We hesitate to cancel the advantages that both sides appreciated before and during their dispute." (citation omitted). *Rossi* v. *TWA,* 350 F. Supp. 1263, 1270 (C.D. Cal. 1972).

In short, plaintiff, like all of the other major league club owners, voluntarily, knowingly and with good reason agreed to be bound by the decisions of the Commissioner and expressly agreed to forego judicial review of the Commissioner's decisions. Because such voluntary, contractual arrangements are valid and enforceable, plaintiff is barred from maintaining this action. Accordingly, we request the Court to enter dismissal of the complaint in its entirety with prejudice.

## • II. The Commissioner's rational exercise of the authority vested in him by the Major League Agreement and Rules should be sustained

Even if this Court were to entertain jurisdiction in this suit, under well established precedents in this Circuit its review of the Commissioner's decision is limited to determining whether the Commissioner acted (1) within the scope of his authority; (2) with procedural fairness; and (3) upon a rational basis. *Milwaukee American Association* v. *Landis,* 49 F.2d 298 (N.D. Ill. 1931).*

In this case, the undisputed facts of record—more particularly, the Major League Agreement and Rules, the transcript of the hearing, and the Commissioner's written decision—establish that the Commissioner was authorized to disapprove the proposed player transfers and that his decision to disapprove them "in the best interests of baseball" was procedurally fair and reasonable.

### A. *The Commissioner Acted Within the Scope of the Authority Vested in Him by the Major League Agreement and Rules*

As set forth above, the Major League Agreement empowers the Commissioner to initiate investigations into any act or transaction "suspected not to be in the best interests of baseball," and to take such preventive or remedial actions as are appropriate under the circumstances. (Major League Agreement: Article I, Section 2). Without more, these broad powers would authorize the Commissioner to review proposed player assignments and disapprove them when he found that they were not in the best interests of baseball.

* This is the same standard applied in this Circuit to the review of decisions by all quasi-judicial tribunals of private associations. *See, e.g., Rosee* v. *Board of Trade of City of Chicago,* 311 F.2d 524, 527 (7th Cir.), *cert. denied,* 374 U.S. 806 (1963); *Parsons College* v. *North Central Association, supra,* 271 F. Supp. at 70.

But the Commissioner's authority to review proposed player transfers does not rest on these broad powers alone because Major League Rule 12(a) specifically provides that no assignment of a player contract "shall be recognized as valid unless within fifteen (15) days after execution a counterpart original of the document shall be filed . . . *and approved by the Commissioner.*" (Kuhn Aff. ¶ 10.) (Emphasis added.) In disapproving plaintiff's proposed player transfers, the Commissioner expressly relied on the authority vested in him by Rule 12(a) and the Major League Agreement.

In *Milwaukee American Association* v. *Landis,* 49 F.2d 298 (N.D. Ill. 1931), this Court described the broad authority vested in the Commissioner by the Major League Agreement:

"We have observed that, in addition to his jurisdiction over disputes certified to him, the commissioner is empowered to investigate upon his own initiative any act, transaction, or practice charged or alleged to be detrimental to the best interests of baseball, to determine what preventive, remedial or punitive action is appropriate in the premises and to take such action against leagues or clubs as the case may require. Certain acts are specified as detrimental to baseball, but it is expressly provided that nothing contained in the code should be construed as exclusively defining or otherwise limiting acts, practices or conduct detrimental to baseball. It is contended that this phrase should be so construed as to include only such conduct as is similar to that expressly mentioned. *However, the provisions are so unlimited in character that we can conclude only that the parties did not intend so to limit the meaning of conduct detrimental to baseball, but intended to vest in the Commissioner jurisdiction to prevent any conduct destructive of the aims of the code.* Apparently it was the intent of the parties to make the commissioner an arbiter, whose decisions made in good faith, upon evidence, upon all questions relating to the purpose of the organization and all conduct detrimental thereto, should be absolutely binding." (Emphasis added.) 49 F.2d at 302.*

---

\* Remarkably, the complaint avers that the Commissioner's power to remedy conduct deemed not to be in the best interests of baseball is limited to the five specific punishments listed in Article I, Section 3 of the Major League Agreement. (Complaint, ¶ 64.) This contention is patently erroneous and is inconsistent with the plain meaning of the Major League Agreement. Article I, Section 2(a) of the Agreement explicitly authorizes the Commissioner to determine *and take* whatever "preventive, remedial or punitive action is appropriate in the premises. . . ." This clearly encompasses disapproval of proposed transactions found not to be in the best interests of baseball. Moreover, Rule 12(a) specifically authorizes the Commissioner in his discretion to review and approve or disapprove transfers of player contracts.

Other courts which have considered the powers of the Commissioner of Baseball have agreed with this Court's analysis in *Landis* that the Commissioner possesses broad authority in determining what actions are not in the best interests of baseball. In *Livingston* v. *Shreveport-Texas League Baseball Corp.,* 128 F. Supp. 191 (W.D. La. 1955), *aff'd per curiam,* 228 F.2d 623 (5th Cir. 1956), the *Landis* holding was specifically approved:

"After careful consideration of the number and the technical nature of problems involved in the sport, we are convinced that this is as it should be. Surely the officials designated are best qualified by training, experience and practical judgment to pass upon such matters; and, if it were otherwise—if all the persons and organizations in baseball were required to litigate their many differences—endless delays and undue burdens upon the courts certainly would result. Not unlike a military organization, in baseball there must be a set of governing rules through which these officials speedily may pass upon and finally decide the multitude of disputes inherent in the game." 128 F. Supp. at 197–198.

In short, as plaintiff virtually conceded when it submitted without protest to the hearing before the Commissioner, there can be no question but that Article I of the Major League Agreement and Major League Rule 12(a) authorize the Commissioner to review and, in appropriate cases, disapprove proposed player transfers, such as plaintiff's cash sales of Rudi, Blue and Fingers.

B. *The Commissioner Scrupulously Followed Fair and Reasonable Procedures in Rendering His Decision*

At no time prior to the filing of the complaint did plaintiff or any other party suggest that the procedures followed by the Commissioner in rendering his decision were unfair or improper. A description of the procedures—including notice and a full opportunity to be heard—demonstrates that the Commissioner scrupulously adhered to procedures which were fair and reasonable to plaintiff.

The Commissioner learned of plaintiff's proposed player transfers on June 15, 1976. On June 16, he sent to all parties concerned a notice, advising them of his intention to hold a hearing, stating the time, place and issue to be considered at the hearing, permitting them an opportunity to present all relevant considerations and affording them the opportunity to be represented by counsel at the hearing.*

The hearing was conducted in accordance with the specific Rules of Procedure which the Commissioner had previously promulgated in accordance with Article I, Section 2(d) of the Major League Agreement. These Rules provide, in pertinent part, that:

"Proceedings before the Commissioner shall be conducted in general like judicial proceedings and with due regard for all of the principles of natural justice and fair play, but the Commissioner may proceed informally when he deems it desirable."

At the hearing, the Commissioner again advised the parties of the issue before him, and the possible options open to him, and asked each party to present all of the pertinent facts and considerations bearing on his decision. All of the parties, many of them represented by counsel, took full advantage of the opportunity to present what they deemed to be the material facts and considerations.

Following the hearing, the Commissioner issued a written decision, articulating his reasons for disapproving the proposed player transfers. Copies of this decision were sent by telegram to all parties on the date the decision was rendered.

In light of these indisputable facts, we submit that, in considering and reaching his decision, the Commissioner followed procedures that were impeccably fair and reasonable to plaintiff and all of the other parties.

### C. *The Commissioner's Exercise of Discretion Was Reasonable and Should Be Sustained by This Court*

As noted, it is well-established in this jurisdiction that the courts will refuse to hear *de novo* appeals from quasi-judicial tribunals of private associations and will limit their review to determining whether, based on the

* While the complaint alleges that these was inadequate time between the notice and the hearing, plaintiff raised no such objection at any time prior to or during the hearing. Nor does the complaint suggest any prejudice which plaintiff suffered from the alleged shortness, failing to enumerate any additional information which plaintiff might have adduced if there had been more time before the hearing. Further, since the American League championship season is in full progress, time was of the essence and, under these circumstances, the one-day notice was clearly reasonable. Moreover, as the Court stated in *Parsons College* v *North Central Association, supra,* "the nature of the hearing, if required by rudimentary due process, may properly be adjusted to the nature of the issue to be decided." 271 F. Supp. at 72.

record before him, the administrator's decision was arbitrary and capricious. *See, e.g., Parsons College* v. *North Central Association, supra; Robinson* v. *Illinois High School Association,* 45 Ill. App. 2d 277, 195 N.E.2d, 38 (1963).*

As one court explained, under this applicable standard of limited judicial review a court may not substitute its judgment for that of the Commissioner and "must guard against unduly interfering with the [Commissioner's] autonomy by substituting judicial judgment for that of the [Commissioner] in an area where the competence of the court does not equal that of the [Commissioner]." *Pinsker* v. *Pacific Coast Society of Orthodontists,* 526 P.2d 253, 266 (Cal., 1974). The court added that administrative actions would be set aside only when "contrary to established public policy or . . . 'so patently arbitrary and unreasonable' as to be 'beyond the pale of law'. . . ." *Ibid.*

In determining whether a decision is arbitrary and capricious, the Court must simply determine whether on the basis of the record before the administrator there is any reasonable basis for his decision. *See, e.g., Pauley* v. *United States,* 419 F.2d 1061, 1066 (7th Cir. 1969), in which the Seventh Circuit explained:

"*Administrative action may be regarded as arbitrary and capricious only where it is not supportable on any rational basis. . . .* The fact that on the same evidence a reviewing court could have reached a decision contrary to that reached by the agency will not support a determination that the administrative action was arbitrary and capricious." (citation omitted) (emphasis added).

Based on the materials of record in this proceeding— including the transcript of the hearing, the charter of the Commissioner set forth in the Major League Agreement, and the Commissioner's written decision—we submit that the Commissioner's exercise of the discretion vested in him was so clearly reasonable as to negate any

* The law in other jurisdictions is also that "courts will not interfere with the internal affairs of a private association so long as its affairs and proceedings are conducted fairly and honestly, and after due notice to anyone involved." *Sanders* v. *Louisiana High School Athletic Association,* 242 So. 2d 19, 26 (La. 1970); *see e.g., Pinsker* v. *Pacific Coast Society of Orthodontists,* 526 P.2d 253 (Cal., 1974); *Tennessee Secondary School Athletic Association* v. *Cox,* 221 Tenn. 164, 425 S.W.2d 597 (1968); *State ex rel. West Virginia Secondary School Activities Commission* v. *Oakley,* 152 W. Va. 533, 164 S.E.2d 775 (1968); *State ex rel. Ohio High School Athletic Association* v. *Judges of the Court of Common Pleas,* 173 Ohio 239, 181 N.E.2d 261 (1962); *Morrison* v. *Roberts,* 183 Okla. 359, 82 P.2d 1023 (1938).

possible claim that the decision was arbitrary or capricious.*

Relying on his expertise in this sport and fulfilling his obligation to act in accordance with his best judgment to protect the best interests of baseball, the Commissioner—after hearing testimony from representatives of the plaintiff, the other club owners involved and the players association—concluded that it would be detrimental to the best interests of the game if one team were to sell off in mid-season three of its most talented players for enormous sums of cash to two wealthy competitors. Under these circumstances, the Commissioner's written decision concluded that approval of plaintiff's proposed transactions would lead to, among other things, the loss of competitive balance in major league baseball.

The loss of competitive balance could be devastating to baseball which, as the Commissioner's decision notes, is engaged in a "highly competitive" contest for the public's support with many other sports and entertainments. The Commissioner was clearly reasonable in concluding that unless a number of teams are fairly evenly matched, resulting in close pennant races among a number of competitors, fan interest and support will wane. The Commissioner's decision explained that if a few wealthy clubs were free to buy all of the outstanding talent, the results of the pennant races would be foregone conclusions, competitive balance would be destroyed and the public's support of the game diminished.

Plaintiff challenges the reasonableness of the Commissioner's decision on the ground that it is allegedly "contrary to historical precedent." (Complaint, ¶ 14.) While Commissioner Kuhn denies this allegation, it is entirely irrelevant to this lawsuit whether the Commissioner's decision is or is not unprecedented. In his written decision, the Commissioner expressly determined that the cash sales negotiated by plaintiff were unique and completely distinguishable from "cash sales of player contracts in the past" because "there has been

no instance in my judgment which had the potential for harm to our game as do these assignments."

Specifically, the Commissioner determined that plaintiff's transactions were both unique and harmful to baseball because: (1) such transactions involved the simultaneous sale of three of the star players—the "finest talent"—of a championship club; (2) the transactions involved "enormous sums of cash," thereby assuring that the player contracts in question could be sold only to the wealthiest and most successful clubs; (3) the transactions would greatly impair the "competitive balance" among clubs which is essential to the maintenance of public interest in and support for professional baseball; and (4) the transactions were peculiarly harmful to baseball because they were made at a time when the "circumstances of baseball's reserve system" were "unsettled."*

While the Commissioner's decision was manifestly in the best interests of baseball, the correctness of his judgment is not the issue in this Court. The issue is not whether this Court would reach the same conclusion but, assuming *arguendo* the propriety of judicial review at all, the question for the Court is whether the Commissioner's decision was predicated upon a reasonable basis. As the court stated in *Livingston* v. *Shreveport-Texas League Baseball Club, supra,* 128 F. Supp. 197:

> "After careful consideration of the number and the technical nature of problems involved in the sport, we are convinced that this is as it should be. Surely the officials designated are best qualified by training, experience and practical judgment to pass upon such matters. . . ."†

In short, since the Commissioner's disapproval of the proposed player transfers was made in the exercise of his discretion, pursuant to the authority vested in him by the Major League Agreement and Rules, following fair and reasonable procedures and based upon eminently reason-

---

\* Apparently recognizing that no valid claim of arbitrariness can be sustained, plaintiff has salted its complaint with numerous derogatory epithets, impugning the good faith of the Commissioner in rendering his decision. While the Commissioner vigorously denies the allegations of "malice," "prejudice," and "bad faith," we submit that they are totally irrelevant because the Commissioner's written decision sets forth a fully rational and sustainable basis for his decision. That should be the end of this Court's inquiry. (*See, e.g., Parsons College* v *North Central Association, supra; Milwaukee American Association* v. *Landis, supra.*) If, upon a totally conclusionary, unparticularized and unsubstantiated cry of "malice," every decision of an administrator could be subjected to lengthy litigation—including extensive investigation into his state of mind—there would be no finality to an administrative decision and the well-established doctrine of limited judicial review of quasi-judicial decisions by private associations would be rendered meaningless.

\* Plaintiff's transactions took place during the brief hiatus between *Kansas City Royals Baseball Corp.* v. *Major League Baseball Players Ass'n,* 532 F.2d 615 (8th Cir. 1976), which upheld an arbitrator's decision restricting baseball's "reserve system" and the consensual establishment of a new "reserve system" via collective bargaining. On July 12, 1976, it was publicly announced that the Major League Baseball Players Association, representing the players, and the Player Relations Committee, representing the club owners, had reached an agreement on a new "reserve system"; the agreement requires ratification by both sides.

† This reasoning was applied by the court to uphold the discretionary judgment of National Football League Commissioner Rozelle in *Rentzel* v. *Rozelle,* No. C-63828 (Cal. Super. Ct. 1973). In that case, Commissioner Rozelle's suspension of player Lance Rentzel for "conduct detrimental to the NFL" was upheld on the basis that a court would not substitute its judgment for that of the Commissioner.

able considerations, we submit that the Commissioner's actions should be sustained by this Court.

### • III. The propriety of the Commissioner's actions under the Major League Agreement eliminates any possible claim of breach of contract or inducing breach of contract

The foregoing sections of this memorandum demonstrate that the Commissioner acted properly and reasonably within the scope of his authority under the Major League Agreement to determine whether the proposed player transfers were "in the best interests of baseball." This demonstration summarily disposes of plaintiff's claims for breach of contract and inducing breach of contract.

The complaint alleges that the Commissioner's disapproval of the proposed player transfers constituted (1) a breach of the Commissioner's employment contract with the major league clubs (Count 1) and (2) and inducement to the Yankees and Red Sox to breach their contracts to purchase the service of the three A's players (Count 5). In addition to damages, the complaint seeks a declaratory judgment that the disapprovals were improper (Count 6) and requests specific performance by the Yankees and Red Sox despite the Commissioner's disapproval (Count 7). None of these counts states a valid claim for relief in light of the clear propriety of the Commissioner's actions under the Major League Agreement and Rules.

### A. *The Commissioner Did Not Breach His Employment Contract*

As set forth in the Commissioner's Affidavit, as Commissioner of Baseball he is "obliged to faithfully perform and discharge to the best of [his] ability the duties of the Office of Commissioner of Baseball as provided in the Major League Agreement and the Major League Rules." (Kuhn Aff. ¶ 7.)

Thus, the Commissioner's contractual obligations to the owners are completely coterminous with his responsibilities under the Major League Agreement and the Major League Rules promulgated thereunder. Since we have established in the preceding section of this memorandum that the Commissioner properly exercised the discretionary authority vested in him by the Major League Agreement and Rules, it inexorably follows that he has not breached his employment contract. Accordingly, we submit that Count 1 must be summarily dismissed.

### B. *The Commissioner Did Not Induce a Breach of Contract by the Yankees and Red Sox*

Count 5 of the complaint alleges that the Commissioner's disapproval of plaintiff's proposed player contract trans-

fers induced the Yankees and Red Sox to breach their "contracts" with the plaintiff. The short and dispositive answer to this contention is that the Yankees and Red Sox have not breached their agreements; in the absence of the Commissioner's approval of the proposed transfers, these clubs had, and continue to have, no obligation to plaintiff.

The "contracts" which plaintiff negotiated with the Yankees and Red Sox were conditional agreements which, under the express terms of Major League Rule 12(a), were subject to the approval of the Commissioner. Rule 12(a) specifically provides that no transfer of player contracts "shall be recognized as valid unless" such transfer is "approved by the Commissioner." As the cases uniformly hold, in the absence of such approval, the contracts are neither valid nor binding and do not obligate the transferee club. *See, e.g., Los Angeles Rams Football Club* v. *Cannon,* 185 F. Supp. 717, 721 (S.D. Cal. 1960); *Detroit Football Co.* v. *Robinson,* 186 F. Supp. 933, 935 (E.D. La.), *aff'd,* 283 F.2d 657 (5th Cir. 1960). In *Los Angeles Rams Football Club* v. *Cannon, supra,* in interpreting a virtually identical clause in a National Football League contract, the court held that "approval by the [football] Commissioner is essential to the formation of a contract here . . . because the terms of the document make it so. . . . [T]he agreement shall only become valid and binding if, as and when approved by the Commissioner." 185 F. Supp. at 721, 722.

Since the Yankees and Red Sox were conditionally obligated to pay for the contracts of Rudi, Fingers and Blue only if, as and when the Commissioner of Baseball approved the proposed transfers, and since the Commissioner has not approved them, the Yankees and Red Sox have no obligation to plaintiff. In the absence of any such contractual obligation, it is clear that the Commissioner cannot be held liable for inducing a non-existent breach of contract. Accordingly, Count 5 should be summarily dismissed.

Count 6 (for declaratory relief) and Count 7 (for specific performance by the Yankees and Red Sox) are wholly dependant upon plaintiff's allegations that the Commissioner's disapproval was unauthorized by the Major League Agreement, and that the Commissioner breached his employment contract and induced a breach by the transferee clubs under their contracts with plaintiff. The foregoing discussion has demonstrated beyond question that the Commissioner acted properly within the scope of his authority under the Major League Agreement and Rules and, accordingly, did not constitute a breach of his employment contract and did not induce the Yankees and Red Sox to breach any agreement with plaintiff. Therefore, Counts 6 and 7 should similarly be dismissed.

• IV. Plaintiff's antitrust claim should be dismissed because professional baseball is exempt from the antitrust laws

Count 2 of the complaint charges that the Commissioner's disapproval of plaintiff's proposed player transfers was part of a conspiracy to restrain trade among all of the major league clubs, the two major leagues and baseball's executive council in alleged violation of the Sherman Antitrust Act, 15 U.S.C. § 1. Even if this were true—which the Commissioner vehemently denies—the allegation fails to state a valid claim for relief.

On three separate occasions—and as recently as 1972—the United States Supreme Court has definitively ruled that professional baseball is exempt from the antitrust laws. *Flood* v. *Kuhn*, 407 U.S. 258 (1972); *Toolson* v. *New York Yankees, Inc.*, 346 U.S. 356 (1953); *Federal Baseball Club of Baltimore* v. *National League*, 259 U.S. 200 (1922). Accordingly, the antitrust allegations contained in plaintiff's complaint fail to state any claim upon which relief may be granted and should be dismissed forthwith.

*Federal Baseball Club of Baltimore, supra,* was the first case in which the Court ruled that the antitrust laws do not apply to professional baseball. In that case, plaintiff baseball club sued the two major leagues, contending, among other things, that the refusal of the two leagues to permit plaintiff to play games against the leagues' teams constituted a boycott in violation of the Sherman Act which effectively forced plaintiff out of business. In an opinion by Justice Holmes, the Court rejected plaintiff's claims on the ground that professional baseball is not within the scope of the antitrust laws.

In *Toolson, supra,* the Supreme Court again ruled that the antitrust laws were inapplicable to professional baseball. *Toolson* was decided together with two companion cases, *Kowalski* v. *Chandler, Commissioner of Baseball* and *Corbett* v. *Chandler, Commissioner of Baseball.* In *Corbett,* plaintiff alleged that many aspects of professional baseball's structure violated the antitrust laws, including, *inter alia,* the Major League Agreement which, according to plaintiff, deprived the Pacific Coast League of Major League status, and unreasonably restricted the number and location of Major League franchises. After considering all three cases, the Court, in a *per curiam* opinion, explicitly reaffirmed the holding in *Federal Baseball Club of Baltimore* that professional baseball is not within the scope of the antitrust laws:

"In *Federal Baseball Club of Baltimore* v. *National League of Professional Baseball Clubs,* 259 U.S. 200 (1922), this Court held that the business of providing public baseball games for profit between clubs of professional baseball players was not within the scope

of the federal antitrust laws. Congress has had the ruling under consideration but has not seen fit to bring such business under these laws by legislation having prospective effect. The business has thus been left for thirty years to develop, on the understanding that it was not subject to existing antitrust legislation. The present cases ask us to overrule the prior decision and, with retrospective effect, hold the legislation applicable. We think that if there are evils in this field which now warrant application to it of the antitrust laws it should be by legislation. Without re-examination of the underlying issues, the judgments below are affirmed on the authority of *Federal Baseball Club of Baltimore* v. *National League of Professional Baseball Clubs, supra,* so far as that decision determines that Congress had no intention of including the business of baseball within the scope of the federal antitrust laws." 346 U.S. at 356–57.

In 1972, in *Flood, supra,* the Supreme Court reiterated for the third time, that professional baseball is exempt from the antitrust laws:

"We repeat for this case what was said in Toolson:

" 'Without re-examination of the underlying issues, the [judgment] below [is] affirmed on the authority of *Federal Baseball Club of Baltimore* v. *National League of Professional Baseball Clubs, supra,* so far as that decision determines that Congress had no intention of including the business of baseball within the scope of the federal antitrust laws.' 346 U.S. at 357.

"And what the Court said in Federal Baseball in 1922 and what it said in Toolson in 1953, we say again here in 1972: the remedy, if any is indicated, is for congressional, and not judicial, action." 407 U.S. at 285.

Despite the clear holdings in these cases that professional baseball as a whole is not subject to the antitrust laws, the complaint repeatedly suggests that only baseball's "reserve system" is exempt from the antitrust laws. This is not the first time that a plaintiff has attempted to effect a narrowing of baseball's antitrust immunity. In each previous case, however, the courts uniformly have sustained motions to dismiss antitrust claims brought against the Commissioner of Baseball, the two Major Leagues, or their member teams. For example, in *Portland Baseball Club, Inc.* v. *Kuhn,* 368 F. Supp. 1004 (D. Ore. 1971), *aff'd per curiam,* 491 F.2d 1101 (9th Cir. 1974), plaintiff, a member of the Pacific Coast League, brought suit against the Commissioner of Baseball, the two Major Leagues, and their member teams, alleging that the expansion of the Major Leagues into Seattle and San Diego (resulting in the displacement of Pacific Coast League franchises in those cities) violated the antitrust laws. Plaintiff there, as here, sought to distinguish *Flood, Toolson* and *Federal Baseball Club of Baltimore* by arguing that these decisions merely held that baseball's "reserve system" was exempt from the antitrust laws. The District Court, which granted defendant's motion to dismiss, specifically rejected this argument and held that, on the authority of the three Supreme Court decisions, professional baseball as a whole is exempt from the antitrust laws:

"On the basis of numerous cases which exempt professional baseball from the application of the federal anti-trust laws, I dismissed the claim of plaintiff based upon alleged violations of these laws by the professional baseball leagues." 368 F. Supp. at 1007.

This holding was explicitly affirmed by the Ninth Circuit. 491 F.2d 1101, 1103 (1974).

Even before the Supreme Court handed down the *Flood* decision, the federal courts, on the authority of *Toolson* and *Federal Baseball Club of Baltimore,* routinely dismissed antitrust claims brought against professional baseball. In *Salerno* v. *American League,* 429 F.2d 1003 (2d Cir. 1970), *cert. denied,* 400 U.S. 1001 (1971), the Second Circuit affirmed the dismissal of a claim brought against the American League and the Commissioner of Baseball by two discharged umpires who alleged that defendants unlawfully conspired to drive them out of baseball in violation of the Sherman and Clayton Antitrust Acts. The Court of Appeals explained that "professional baseball is not subject to the antitrust laws" because "the ground upon which *Toolson* rested was that Congress had no intention to bring baseball within the antitrust laws." 429 F.2d at 1005. Similarly, in *Portland Baseball Club, Inc.* v. *Baltimore Baseball Club, Inc.,* 282 F.2d 680 (9th Cir. 1960), the Ninth Circuit affirmed the dismissal of an antitrust claim against the Commissioner of Baseball, among others, on grounds that baseball is exempt from the antitrust laws.

In sum, based on the decisions of the Supreme Court in *Flood, Toolson* and *Federal Baseball Club of Baltimore,* the courts have ruled consistently that professional baseball, as a whole, is exempt from the antitrust laws. In light of this clear and unbroken chain of precedents, plaintiff's attempt to subject professional baseball to yet another antitrust challenge can only be regarded as frivolous. Accordingly, the antitrust claim set forth in Count 2 of plaintiff's complaint should be dismissed.

### • V. The due process and equal protection claims must be dismissed because the decision by the Commissioner of Baseball did not constitute "state action"

In Counts 3 and 4 of its complaint, plaintiff claims that it has been denied its Fourteenth Amendment rights to due process and equal protection by virtue of the Commissioner's decision not to approve the purported player transfers. However, the Fourteenth Amendment prohibits only those denials of due process or equal protection that result from "state action"; and, under well-established standards, the actions taken by the Commissioner of Baseball do not constitute "state action." Plaintiff's attempt to elevate its disagreement with the Commissioner to constitutional magnitude is therefore entirely unsupportable and must be dismissed.

It is indisputable that the Commissioner of Baseball is a private individual and that the Major League Executive Council, the National and American Leagues, and their 24 member teams are wholly private organizations. Moreover, the internal affairs of professional baseball—including the making, interpreting and enforcing of Major League Rules and the exercise of authority under the Major League Agreement by the Commissioner of Baseball—are carried on by these private entities free of any regulation by federal, state or local governments. Finally, it is indisputable that the specific action giving rise to this lawsuit—the Commissioner's decision to disapprove plaintiff's attempt to sell certain player contracts—was made without any involvement whatsoever by any organ of government.

Nevertheless, plaintiff alleges that the Commissioner's decision constituted "state action" because: (1) "Seventeen of the twenty-three major league clubs located in the United States make use of stadia owned by municipalities located within various states of these United States"; and (2) "Major League baseball enjoys a judicially created exemption for its reserve clause from the antitrust laws, and a legislatively-created exemption under 15 U.S.C. §§ 1291–1295 for agreements covering interstate telecasts of its contests." Clearly, the "connection" between professional baseball and the state set forth in plaintiff's complaint is so insignificant and, more important, so far removed from the activities which plaintiff has challenged in this lawsuit, that it falls far short of constituting the requisite "state action" necessary to invoke the Fourteenth Amendment.*

The courts have been unanimous in ruling that when an action by a private individual or organization is

---

* Even if there were "state action," the procedures followed by the Commissioner in reaching his decision were so clearly fair and his rationale so clearly reasonable as to rebut any contention that plaintiff was deprived of due process or equal protection of the laws. (See II(B), *supra.*)

challenged under the Fourteenth Amendment, the "state action" requirement is satisfied *only if there is a close nexus between the state and the particular action being challenged. Jackson* v. *Metropolitan Edison Co.*, 419 U.S. 345 (1974); *Cohen* v. *Illinois Institute of Technology*, 524 F.2d 818 (7th Cir. 1975); *Doe* v. *Bellin Memorial Hospital*, 479 F.2d 756 (7th Cir. 1973); *Gerrard* v. *Blackman*, 401 F. Supp. 1189 (N.D. Ill. 1975).

In *Jackson, supra*, a privately owned and operated utility (Metropolitan) held a license issued by the State of Pennsylvania and was otherwise subjected to extensive regulation by the state. Metropolitan, without holding a hearing, terminated service to petitioner, who claimed that the termination amounted to a denial of due process in contravention of the Fourteenth Amendment. In holding that the termination did not constitute "state action," the Supreme Court ruled that the action of a private business would be considered the action of the state *only when the particular action challenged* is the subject of extensive state regulation and involvement:

> "It may well be that acts of a heavily regulated utility with at least something of a governmentally protected monopoly will more readily be found to be 'state' acts than will the acts of an entity lacking these characteristics. But *the inquiry must be whether there is a sufficiently close nexus between the State and the challenged action of the regulated entity so that the action of the latter may be fairly treated as that of the State itself.*" (Emphasis added.) 419 U.S. at 350–351.

The rule that "state action" is present only when there is a close nexus between the state and the challenged activity has been applied consistently in the Seventh Circuit. *See, e.g., Cohen* v. *Illinois Institute of Technology*, 524 F.2d 818 (7th Cir. 1975) (per Judge, now Mr. Justice, Stevens); *Doe* v. *Bellin Memorial Hospital*, 479 F.2d 756 (7th Cir. 1973); *Gerrard* v. *Blackman*, 401 F. Supp. 1189 (N.D. Ill. 1975).

Plaintiff has not alleged that there is any nexus between any agency of government and the activity challenged in this lawsuit—that is, the decision by the Commissioner of Baseball, in the exercise of his authority under the Major League Agreement and the Major League Rules, to disapprove plaintiff's proposed transfers. Certainly the alleged leasing of municipally owned stadia to individual teams and the alleged judicial and legislative activity bearing on the status of baseball's reserve system and telecasting agreements under the antitrust laws have no relationship whatever to the activity challenged here. In these circumstances, it is clear that plaintiff has failed to make a sufficient allegation of "state action" to invoke the Fourteenth Amendment. Accordingly, plaintiff's constitutional claims must be dismissed.

### CONCLUSION

For the foregoing reasons, we respectfully urge that summary judgment be granted as to each and every count of the Complaint in favor of defendant Commissioner Bowie K. Kuhn.

Respectfully submitted,

James E. S. Baker
Lee B. McTurnan
One First National Plaza
Chicago, Illinois 60607
Telephone: 312-329-5400

Peter K. Bleakley
Irvin B. Nathan
1229 - 19th Street, N.W.
Washington, D.C. 20036
Telephone 202-872-6700

Attorneys for Defendant,
Bowie K. Kuhn

OF COUNSEL:

SIDLEY & AUSTIN
One First National Plaza
Chicago, Illinois 60607
Telephone: 312-329-5400

David R. Kentoff
Paul S. Reichler
Scott B. Schreiber
ARNOLD & PORTER
1229 - 19th Street, N.W.
Washington, D.C. 20036
Telephone: 202-872-6700

*Dated: July 19, 1976*

The place: Riverfront Stadium in Cincinnati. The date: September 11, 1985.

# 1985: 4,192

## IRA BERKOW

TEN MILES from the sandlots where he began playing baseball as a boy, Pete Rose, now 44 years old and in his 23d season in the major leagues, stepped to the plate tonight in the first inning at Riverfront Stadium. He came to bat on this warm, gentle evening with the chance to make baseball history.

The Reds' player-manager, the man who still plays with the joy of a boy, had a chance to break Ty Cobb's major-league career hit record, 4,191, which had stood since Cobb retired in 1928.

The sell-out crowd of 47,237 that packed the stadium hoping to see Rose do it now stood and cheered under a twilight blue sky beribboned with orange clouds.

Now he eased into his distinctive crouch from the left side of the plate, wrapping his white-gloved hands around the handle of his black bat. His red batting helmet gleamed in the lights. Everyone in the ball park was standing. The chant "Pete! Pete!" went higher and higher. Flashbulbs popped.

On the mound was the right-hander Eric Show of the San Diego Padres. Rose took the first pitch for a ball, fouled off the next pitch, took another ball. Show wound up and Rose swung and hit a line drive to left-center.

The ball dropped in and the ball park exploded. Fireworks being set off was one reason; the appreciative cries of the fans was another. Streamers and confetti floated onto the field.

Rose stood on first base and was quickly mobbed by everyone on the Reds' bench. The first base coach, Tommy Helms, one of Rose's oldest friends on the team, hugged him first. Tony Perez, Rose's longtime teammate, then lifted him.

Marge Schott, the owner of the Reds, came out and hugged Rose and kissed him on the cheek. A red Corvette was driven in from behind the outfield fence, a present from Mrs. Schott to her record-holder.

Meanwhile, the Padres, some of whom had come over to congratulate Rose, meandered here and there on the field, chatting with the umpires and among themselves, waiting for play to resume. Show took a seat on the rubber.

Rose had removed his batting helmet and waved with his gloves to the crowd. Then he stepped back on first, seemed to take a breath and turned to Helms, threw an arm around him and threw his head on his shoulder, crying.

The tough old ball player, his face as lined and rugged as a longshoreman's, was moved, perhaps even slightly embarrassed, by the tenderness shown him in the ball park.

Then from the dugout came a uniformed young man. This one was wearing the same number as Rose, 14, and had the same name on the back of his white jersey. Petey Rose, a 15-year-old redhead and sometime bat boy for as long as he can remember, fell into his pop's arms at first base, and the pair of Roses embraced. There were tears in their eyes.

Most people in the park were familiar with the Rose story. He had grown up, the son of a bank cashier, in the area in Cincinnati along the Ohio River known as Anderson Ferry. He had gone to Western Hills High School here for five years—repeating the 10th grade. "It gave me a chance to learn more baseball," he said, with a laugh.

He was only about 5-foot-10 and 150 pounds when he graduated, in 1960—he is now a burly 5-11 and 205— and the only scout who seemed to think he had talent enough to make the major leagues was his uncle, Buddy Bloebaum, who worked for the Reds.

Three years later he was starting at second base for the Reds, and got his first major league hit on April 13, 1963, a triple off Bob Friend of the Pittsburgh Pirates.

Rose was at first called, derisively, "Charlie Hustle." Soon, it became a badge of distinction. He made believers out of many who at first had deprecatory thoughts about this brash young rookie who ran to first on walks, who slid headfirst into bases, who sometimes taunted the opposition and barreled into them when they were in the way.

But never was there malicious intent, and he came to be loved and appreciated by teammates and opponents for his intense desire to, as he said, "play the game the way it's supposed to be played."

He began the season needing 95 hits to break Cobb's record, and as he drew closer and closer, the nation seemed to be watching and listening and wondering when "the big knock," as he called it, would come.

Tonight, he finished in a most typical and satisfying fashion. He got two hits—he tripled in the seventh inning—and walked once and flied to left in four times at bat. It wasn't just the personal considerations that he

holds dear. He cares about team accomplishments, he says his rings for World Series triumphs are his most cherished baseball possessions. And this night he scored the only two runs of the game, in the third and seventh innings, as the Reds won, 2–0.

After the game, in a celebration at home plate, Rose took a phone call from President Reagan that was relayed on the public address system.

The President congratulated him and said he had set "the most enduring record in sports history." He said Rose's record might be broken, but "your reputation and legacy will live for a long time."

"Thank you, Mr. President, for taking time from your busy schedule," said Rose. "And you missed a good ball game."

This piece appeared in *The Sporting News* in 1984, by which time two generations of sports fans had been reading stories by Furman Bisher, sports editor of *The Atlanta Journal*. Reading the stories and remembering them. Especially the way they ended.

# Dennis Dale McLain

## FURMAN BISHER

THE SIGN was still out front long after the proprietor had pulled stakes and the joint had gone dark. It hung under the marquee on the Ponce de Leon side of the Georgian Terrace Hotel, the neon tubing empty of color.

"Gaffer's" was the name Denny McLain put on his lounge, tavern, bistro, call it what you would. Another watering hole. It was located on the lower level of a once ornate hotel desperately trying to hold onto the last vestige of flossier times.

So in a sense was Denny McLain. His vestiges were threadbare even then, but you had to say this for the guy—he never saw a cloud in his sky. There was a pot of gold out there somewhere, if he could only find the rainbow.

Denny was the kind of guy who always figured he had the world by the tail, even when it was the other way around. He figured nothing could get at Big Denny. He was too smart. He had too much on the ball. He was Dennis Dale McLain, world's greatest baseball pitcher.

It didn't matter that his fast ball was gone, he was ingloriously out of condition, his earned-run average was about the size of his waistline, and that he was unemployed. Denny had the conviction that once a king, always a king. Once the greatest, always the greatest.

He didn't realize it then, but he had pitched and won his last major league game in Atlanta on August 8, 1972. He would never make it into another season. "Gaffer's" was his next act. He would become the world's next great nightclub operator. (His choice of a name for the place was out of character. A "gaffer" is an old man.)

Denny had developed another talent, playing the organ above hobby level. He would have made it in your average Holiday Inn cocktail lounge. So it was expected that he would play in his own parlor, offering himself as his star attraction. After all, he had produced one album.

During the World Series in 1968 he had played wildly into the night for kicks in the lounge of the St. Louis hotel where the Detroit Tigers put up.

No organ playing for him, he said to an interviewer. He would be the Toots Shor of the place, not the organ grinder.

I don't know when "Gaffer's" took the gas, but I drove past one day and it was shut tight. Denny was gone. He would have one more spring training, a halfhearted appearance. The Braves invited him, the courteous thing to do for the once greatest pitcher. It was an exercise in futility, considering his condition. Even in his myopic state that was one thing he could see clearly.

What he couldn't see was what a baseball derelict he was becoming. He'd been working at it since he was at his very peak. He bought jet planes he couldn't pay for. He had this brief vision of himself as an airline entrepreneur. He bought automobiles he couldn't pay for. He bought real estate he couldn't pay for. He tried to pay off his debts with his signature, which was worth something only on a baseball.

A classic pitching arm had come attached to a totally undisciplined character. Not since Lefty Grove had gone 31–4 in 1931 had there been such a season pitched in the major leagues as McLain's '68, when he was 31–6. Three seasons later he was 10–22.

In between, he had had one season of three won and five lost, but that was the season he did time in Bowie Kuhn's cooler. He'd run into trouble with the mob, he'd doused a reporter with a bucket of water, he'd been caught carrying a gat, but otherwise checked out as an exemplary citizen.

Atlanta was his last stop in uniform. Eddie Robinson gave up Orlando Cepeda to get him, and McLain paid for himself in one day. About 50,000 paid to watch him make his first start, which didn't last long. The three games he won for the Braves were strugglesome. He was through, washed up, and he wasn't 30 yet.

After life with "Gaffer's," McLain turned up in Memphis running a minor league team. The problem there involved missing funds, and he hit the road again. He managed to stay out of major print until the big storm broke over his head.

This time he was hit with the book, extortion, bookmaking, drug smuggling, and a few coattail charges. He was hauled in for indictment, which wasn't easy. In 1968, he weighed 186 pounds. In 1984, he has filled out, as they say, to 300 pounds. He could play the blimp at the county fair. He is tragic, pathetic, grotesque, all three. His is a textbook case of self-destruction.

His pitching companion in Detroit was Mickey Lolich, who picked up the Tigers and turned them around in the World Series of '68. He was of rather rotund construction even then, but kept his pitching condition long enough to win 217 games. When retirement time came, Lolich exited gracefully, went back to Detroit and opened a doughnut shop.

One morning last week, Mickey Lolich arose before dawn, as usual, and went to the shop to see that the doughnuts were properly prepared for the day. That same day in Tampa, Florida, the jury was picked to try Denny McLain. Seven women and five men.

This article appeared in *Sports Illustrated* in March of 1986, to mark the 100th anniversary of *The Sporting News*. Author Roy Blount, Jr., according to his editor's summary accompanying the article, visited the archives of the famed weekly in St. Louis and "passed through the looking glass into a wonderland of sacred relics and mythology."

# The Bible of Baseball

## ROY BLOUNT, JR.

I HAD BEEN into 1886 for no more than an hour, and lo!

"I've just found the first time the hidden-ball trick was played! In history!" I cried.

Mac Mac Farlane's eyes—as they were not reluctant to do, for all their venerability—twinkled. "Good going, Kid," he said.

Here it was on page 1 of the Sept. 13 issue of *The Sporting News*:

Foutz's sharp trick.
He Catches Pete Browning Napping at Second Base,
And Puts Him Out Without the Assist-
ance of Captain Comiskey

"It happened in a game between St. Louis and Louisville," I went on. "On September 8, 1886. 'In the presence of 6,000 persons, Foutz played the sharpest trick ever seen on the ball field.' Pete Browning was on first for Louisville, and took a big lead because Charley Comiskey was playing way off the base in rightfield. 'Pete had his back turned toward second base, and was keeping an eye on the movements of Comiskey, while he eagerly pranced back and forth to show the crowd that he was not afraid to steal off a bag. Foutz pretended not to watch Browning, but suddenly. . . .'

"Wait a minute," I said, my heart sinking. "What position did this guy Foutz play?"

Mac Farlane did not know, but moved to look it up in one of many volumes. This time, I was quicker. I advanced the microfilm to the box scores. They were old. They were faint. But there was the game in question, and there was Foutz.

"His name was Dave," said Mac Farlane. "He was . . ."

"He was pitching," I said. I had not found the first hidden-ball trick after all.

But I had found something pretty amazing. Something from the days when organized ball was as young as I was when I became a fan of it. The days when baseball was so young that almost anything could happen. I had found not only the first time but surely the last time that a pitcher picked a man with a .343 lifetime batting average off first base *without making a throw*.

. . . suddenly Bushong [the catcher] signaled; and Foutz dashed over toward first base with the ball in hand, touching Browning before the latter knew what had happened. Such a play was never before seen, and the spectators howled with delight. Pete was mighty mad, and, as he has a faculty for being caught napping, the play was

DOUBLY EMBARRASSING

"Pete Browning," mused Mac Farlane with relish. "An odd fellow. He didn't slide. Wouldn't slide. Another thing, he thought every bat had a certain number of hits in it, so when old Betsy got 19 hits he'd hang her up in his cellar. Had old Betsys hanging all over the place. He also thought it was smart when riding a train to open a window, stick his head out and catch soot from the smokestack. In his eyes. He thought that made his eyes water and cleaned out his sight."

"Wow," I observed. I had not observed "wow" in a number of years.

Pete Browning stories! Oh, I knew Browning was the guy who got Hillerich and Bradsby into the bat business when he brought them a wagon tongue or something and asked them to see what kind of old Betsy they could turn out on their lathe. It was the birth of the Louisville Slugger. But I had never heard any *other* Pete Browning stories.

"Neat," I observed, nearly aloud. "The last time I had

observed "neat" nearly aloud was when I took my son John to the Hall of Fame and he stood in Babe Ruth's actual locker and he observed "neat" aloud. It isn't easy to get young people to observe "neat" aloud about something that you think is just as neat as they do.

Now I am not in Babe Ruth's locker, but I am in a place just as wondrous. I am in the cubbyhole of Paul (Mac) Mac Farlane, 66, official historian of *The Sporting News*. I am unscrolling the Bible of Baseball. And as I do so, it is annotated by a high priest.

Mac Farlane used to pitch batting practice to Joe Cronin!

Mac Farlane had hung around with Hugh Duffy! One of the first things I remember learning in life, on my own, was that Hugh Duffy hit .438, the alltime major league standard, back before the modern era. Never in my wildest dreams—even when those dreams included being a baseball immortal myself—did I expect to hang around with anybody who had hung around with Hugh Duffy!

Mac Farlane has a stack of three-by-five cards, on which is recorded every time anybody hit for the cycle in the big leagues before 1977! Mac Farlane thinks all this is as neat as I think it is.

"Look at this," he says. He shows me a photograph taken around 1879, of the Providence Grays and the Boston Nationals lounging in shallow rightfield at the Messer Street baseball field in Providence. He points to one of the Grays.

"Paul Hines," he says. "Got hit by a pitch in the ear and turned deaf as a haddock. Invented the electrical acoustical cane. Sometimes, in the dark, deaf people have trouble getting their balance. Hines invented the electrical acoustical cane [Mac Farlane repeats this term with pleasure] so he could get a feeling of where he was. I don't know whether I ought to tell you how he died."

"Oh, come on."

"Got caught shoplifting. He was teched at the time and had the walk-arounds. He was as old as the hammers of Hades. He didn't know what he was doing. Shock of it killed him.

I'd never heard anybody say "old as the hammers of Hades" before. I am in a place where baseball is as old as the hammers of Hades, and as fresh.

I am in heaven.

March 17 is the 100th anniversary of *The Sporting News,* the weekly tabloid published in St. Louis that stood for decades as the Bible of Baseball, but in recent years has restructured itself into a condensation of the week's news in all major sports. For 91 years *The Sporting News* was owned by the Spink family, who devoted it to the idiosyncratic gratification of themselves and everyone else who was obsessed with baseball. In 1977 it was sold to the Times Mirror Company, which

has more than doubled the paper's circulation, to 711,000 by appealing (in the words of *Sporting News* chief executive officer Richard Waters) to "the yuppie group and on up." *The Sporting News* is still baseball's publication of record: Every major league box score since 1886 has been printed—with strict triple-checked accuracy—in its pages. There is talk now of dropping the box scores so that the eight pages they take up will be available for (in editor Tom Barnidge's words) "really dynamite feature stories."

But who wants to dwell for long upon contemporary publishing practices when we can contemplate mythological figures? Recently I spent a week in the offices of *The Sporting News* on Lindbergh Boulevard in St. Louis and I kept gravitating toward its historical storehouse, where Mac Farlane keeps the sacred relics, the temple jewels, the idols' eyes.

It doesn't look like a shrine. Things are lying around or stuffed away and Mac Farlane has to dig them out for you. But that is exactly what Mac Farlane loves to do, when the moment arises.

The Ty Cobb letters, for instance. I was deep into 1908. "Here's a great Cobb story," I said.

"Cobb, you know, was the Joe Namath of the American League," said Mac Farlane. "There was no denying it was a major league, with Cobb in it."

"I never thought of that," I said. I read aloud from the Cobb story, which appeared on Jan. 16, 1908.

WILL WATCH COBB.
OFTEN SNEAKED IN EXTRA BASE
LAST SEASON.
Tricks Can Not Be Turned if Members of
Fielding Side Are Always on the
Alert.

A safe bet is that when the several American League teams get down to training, each manager will take his first baseman aside and tell him in no uncertain tones that he must watch Ty Cobb more closely this year. The champion batsman of the league had a habit last season, when on first base, of going from that sack way around to third on a bunt or slow infield grounder. . . . Let an infielder or a pitcher fumble a bunt ever so little, and Ty was sure to attempt to take two bases. Let the first baseman be pulled off the bag a trifle in making the catch, and Ty was certain to go the limit. This year, however, all the first basemen will be watching out for just this play and Cobb will be lucky if he pulls it off as regularly as he did in 1907.

"Did I show you these?" Mac Farlane asked. He handed me a thick handful of handwritten letters. They were written to the late J.G. Taylor Spink, from 1914 to

1962 the publisher of *The Sporting News*. They were written by Cobb.

"Wow," I said. "Have Cobb's biographers read these?"

"Nah," said Mac Farlane.

I started reading them: "Anything I write you can be *assured* no one will know where it comes from . . . I will throw up a phoney story to hide real source."

This was dated 1955. Cobb was filling Spink in on Wahoo Sam Crawford, who had not yet been enshrined in the Hall of Fame. I knew Crawford hated Cobb during the years they played together. But I had never realized their non-speaking terms went as far as this. Crawford, Cobb wrote to Spink, "never helped in the outfield by calling, plenty of room, you take it, Etc." Not only that, but when Cobb tried to steal second to get into scoring position with Crawford at bat, Crawford would foul the ball off so Cobb would have to go back and the first baseman would have to hold him on, giving Crawford a bigger hole to hit through. According to Cobb, "I ran hundreds of miles in all and had to return to first."

However, Cobb urged Spink to support Crawford's Hall of Fame candidacy. Cobb said he had written on Crawford's behalf to Grantland Rice and other influential sportswriters. "Sam has had copies of my letters. I like the decent way, I like to return good for what I considered say evil. So I have been his booster and he knows it from me."

How Crawford must have hated that.

"Cobb was a bastard," said Mac Farlane. "But he was a factual bastard."

"And a fast bastard," I said.

"Mm," said Mac Farlane. "Did you see this?" He pointed to a handwritten quotation tacked to his wall:

"IF You Don't Live to get Old,
You Die Young!"
—Cool Papa Bell

"Ah, yes," I said. "Talking about fast." I had heard about Cool Papa Bell, the great star of the Negro leagues long before blacks were admitted to the teams that *The Sporting News* covered. Bell was said to be so fast he once hit a line drive up the middle and the ball hit his foot as he was sliding into second. "How fast was he really?" I asked Mac Farlane.

"Clocked in 12 seconds around the bases."

"*Really?*"

Mac Farlane's expression seemed to say, "What do you think I deal in here, but 'really'?"

"I mean . . ." I said, "I'd always heard Mantle had the fastest time, at 13.1 or something. Although I guess Vince Coleman and some of these later guys. . . . Twelve seconds?"

"Jamie will tell you himself," Mac said.

I tried to think who Jamie was. Must be somebody I ought to recognize. "I wish I could talk to Cool Papa himself," I said.

"Jamie," said Mac Farlane. "That's what I call him, but that's family. You should just call him Cool Papa at first." He picked up the phone, and the next thing I knew I had an appointment to visit Cool Papa Bell in his house on James "Cool Papa" Bell Avenue in St. Louis.

Cool Papa, who will be 83 on May 17, sat nonchalantly on his living room couch and told me how fast he was. In 1948, Satchel Paige talked him into playing against some barnstorming major league all-stars in Los Angeles. Bell didn't want to play because he was out of shape and hadn't felt quite himself since somebody practiced witchcraft on him and poisoned his food when he was in the Mexican League. But he agreed. Then he had to drag Paige out to the park and by the time they got there they had no time to loosen up. Bell hit a single off the all-stars' pitcher, Bob Lemon, and Paige laid down a sacrifice bunt. Bell had studied Lemon on television, so as soon as the pitcher looked over at him hard once and then turned back to the plate, Bell took off. Everybody converged on Paige's bunt except the shortstop, who covered second. By the time catcher Roy Partee started to throw to second, Bell was rounding it. And nobody was covering third. So Partee ran toward third. By the time Partee got to third, Bell was rounding it. And nobody was covering home. As Bell scored, Partee was running down the line hollering "Time! Time!" But you can't call time when the ball is in play, even against Cool Papa Bell.

"I got that on paper," Cool Papa said. "All on paper's not true, but that's true. I was sick, I was 45 years old when I did that. I did that a gang of times. They clocked me going around the bases in 12 seconds, but then another time I went from home plate to third in eight seconds. They wanted me to break my 12-second record but then it rained. And the league broke up."

What if *The Sporting News* had covered Cool Papa the way it covered the Georgia Peach? Bell doesn't let it bother him. "We never had no reading lessons in school, in Mississippi," he said. "Sitting on a hill, that's the only way it was a high school. I had to learn myself. I'd read *The Sporting News,* about Babe Ruth, Bill Terry, Chuck Klein. Seemed like everything it was, Chuck Klein was leading in it. I just liked a ballplayer."

I returned to Mac Farlane. "Cool Papa says he ran from home to third in eight seconds," I said. "That's . . ."

"Jamie," said Mac, "is factual."

Mac Farlane can be a factual bastard himself, at least from official baseball's viewpoint. Five years ago he uncovered evidence that in 1910 somebody altered the batting records of Cobb and Napoleon Lajoie. His research established that Lajoie, not Cobb, had won the batting championship that year and that Cobb's lifetime batting average was .366 instead of .367, and his career hit total was 4,190 instead of 4,191. But .367 and 4,191 are sacred numbers. Bowie Kuhn, then baseball's commissioner, refused to allow the new figures to be etched in stone. Mac Farlane can't get over this. "Baseball could never live with facts!" he says.

Mac Farlane can. There are no books of baseball statistics, except the ones painstakingly produced by *The Sporting News,* that Mac Farlane can't find mistakes in. He pulls out a copy of the *Official American League Batting Averages for 1973,* corrected by him in ink. Sal Bando hit .287, not .286; Brooks Robinson hit .257, not .256; it was George Brett, not Ken, who hit .125; Larry, not Fred, Haney hit .500 (1 for 2), not .000 (0 for 1), and so on. I must say I found this unsettling. What if I had been Haney? I would have turned to Mac Farlane.

In the May 24, 1886 issue, I read the following story filed by a Cincinnati correspondent but headlined in St. Louis:

AKIN TO REAL DEMONS.
That is What They say of the Saint
Louis Browns.
All Cincinnati Jealous of the Club that
Beat the Coming Champions

If it is any satisfaction for a player to maim or cripple a brother player, then let him continue in his good (?) work. If not then cry a halt before disastrous results ensue. The game that was lost to us [the Reds] Friday was due to Comiskey's throwing himself

FULL TILT

against McPhee, causing Bid to throw wild to first. . . .
The Browns personally are a clever set of men, but on the field they are akin to demons.
Oh, my! Oh, my oh!

"I thought these old guys were tough," I said. "Here's Charley Comiskey being called a 'demon' for going into the second baseman hard enough to break up a double play."

"Who's the second baseman?" asked Mac Farlane with asperity.

"Bid McPhee," I said. "I think I've heard of him."

Mac Farlane looked at me with an expression he was not reluctant to use when I fell short of his expectations. "Bid McPhee should be in the Hall of Fame," he said. "Wouldn't *you* let into the Hall of Fame a man who was voted by his peers the greatest second baseman up to 1900?"

"Oh, *I* would," I said hastily. "I guess I . . . don't go any further back, in second basemen, than Lajoie."

There was a pause. I had pronounced it—just as I have been pronouncing it in my mind since I was nine years old—La-*jo*-ey.

"He pronounced it *La*-jho-ay," said Mac Farlane, who then began speaking in French! Something about . . . *lanceurs.* . . . I couldn't follow it—oh, my, oh. Maybe I had no business in this sanctum after all. *French.* Was I being tested? I turned, meekly, from the microfilm machine. Mac Farlane was reading a letter aloud. A request for information.

"When letters come from France," explained Mac Farlane, "I translate."

"How did you learn such good French?" I asked.

He smiled like an owl in pleasant recollection. "Mm," he said. He looked over his glasses. "I'd rather not repeat it."

Mac Farlane will repeat many other things, however, such as what Hugh Duffy once said about what it takes to hit .400. Only I can't repeat that. I know an unprintable story about Hugh Duffy!

I also know, on Mac Farlane's authority, that Babe Ruth once described Lou Gehrig as "built like a four-car garage with five buses in it." I hadn't realized that Ruth ever said anything about anybody except himself. "You know, Ruth's favorite dessert was eels and ice cream," said Mac Farlane.

"It was?" I answered.

"Yes," said Mac Farlane.

But there is plenty of Ruth lore in circulation. Mac Farlane has Hugh Duffy lore. Duffy, a Hall of Famer whose career ended in 1906, was a scout for the Red Sox in the 1940s. Mac Farlane's father was a minority stockholder in the Sox, and Mac grew up around the team—talking to Harry Hooper while Hooper shagged flies, and getting to know Duffy "very well. You know he worked Jackie Robinson out before the Dodgers did. Thought Robinson was a little old to be a rookie and the Red Sox . . ."

"The *Red Sox?*"

". . . and Duffy thought he was excessively ding-toed at the time."

"You mean pigeon-toed?"

There was a pause such as might follow were an eminent jazz historian to describe Count Basie as cool and you were to say, "You mean groovy?"

"Ding-toed," said Mac Farlane.

The true story of baseball's color line has never been told, according to Mac Farlane, and it involves actual exclusionary legislation that has never come to light. He has been trying to get people to listen to the whole story, but they won't. Now he hopes to develop a TV documentary on the subject. "Branch Rickey was interested in Robinson as a gate attraction," he says. "My description of Rickey is a Bible-quoting thief."

Once, when Mac Farlane was a semi-pro player at Arlington, Mass. in 1937, he batted against Satchel Paige. "The ball looked like a ribbon," he says. "I struck out on three pitches."

Mac Farlane never batted against Walter Johnson, but he knew plenty of people who did. "From the tip of his finger to his wrist was 14 inches. People say he came over the top, but he threw sidearm. And he'd whip those long fingers around. . . . Three guys gave up and left the plate against him with only two strikes."

I don't remember how Johnson came up, but we got into Rube Waddell when I was reading "Gossip of the Players" from 1908. During the off-season in those days *The Sporting News* had four great tidbits columns: "Gossip of the Players," "Scribbled by Scribes," "Tips by the Managers," and "Said by the Magnates." I find it interesting that the money men have always had an important place in *Sporting News* coverage. This headline appeared on Nov. 24, 1910:

O, YOU MAGNATES!
CONTINUE TO OCCUPY LIMELIGHT
WITH THEIR TROUBLES.

But "Gossip of the Players" was by far my favorite. I was reading some 1908 quotes from Waddell, whom I always loved as a kid because his legend had to do with his chasing a fire engine or playing catch with kids or wrestling alligators when he was supposed to be pitching. As recorded by some period scribe, this is what Waddell was saying in 1908:

I have had good luck fishing, so far, and ought to be satisfied, but since I have been associated with that advanced financier, Jack O'Connor, I have developed a hankering for lucre. Jack has drilled it into me that I owe it to myself to go get the money. He may be right, but it is not clear to me how a fellow can owe himself anything in any way.

Ah, Rube. Here he was a few weeks earlier.

I want to call attention to the fact that few freak or fool stories were printed about me [during the preceding season] in the papers. Why up to this year I never knew when I got out of bed what I would read about myself. . . . I am not conservative or discreet, but I am not 'bughouse,' but if I have done all that has been said or written about me, I ought not to be at large.

Did Rube really talk like that? Well, did Samson or Delilah really talk the way *they* do in the Bible? All we can say is this: that legendary sports flakes have been saying that last thing (if they had really done all that has been said or written . . .) at least since Rube Waddell. After that winter Waddell pitched only two more years in the big leagues, and six years later, at 37, he was dead of tuberculosis. Cocaine was not a problem among players in those days, but liquor was. I read Waddell's quotes to Mac Farlane.

"One time," said Mac Farlane, "a detective brought Waddell into the hotel lobby and told Connie Mack he was arresting him. Said Rube had been making fresh remarks to ladies and disturbing the peace. Mack asked if there was any way to keep Waddell out of jail. The detective said, well, he supposed if Mack paid the $10 fine. . . . So Mack did. A little later Mack walked past a saloon down the street and through the window he saw Rube and the 'detective'—he was no detective, he was a friend of Rube's—drinking up Mack's $10."

*The Sporting News* was founded by Al Spink as a local magazine of all sports. In 1886, there was an item about W.C. Manning, THE CHAMPION ONE-LEGGED WRESTLER OF THE WORLD, which declared, "Manning has never been thrown, though he has met several two-legged men."

But when Al's brother Charles took over *The Sporting News* in 1887, he concentrated solely on baseball, and made it national. When Charles's son, Taylor, became publisher in 1914, baseball became the publication's holy cause. Taylor Spink was as obsessed with being the driving force behind the Bible of Baseball as Cobb was with being a better player than anybody else. "To Spink," says Mac Farlane, "the word 'vacation' was absolute blasphemy." The staff labored six or seven days a week, and Spink would call them up in the middle of the night to make sure they were thinking about *The Sporting News* in their sleep. "Pappy Spink drilled into us, Get everything right even if you have to call God Almighty. And if anything was wrong he raised *hell*."

Most of the writing was contributed by "beat guys," the newspaper reporters who followed the baseball teams everywhere and kept the nation's devotees up to date with weekly reports from the field. These days *The Sporting News* takes as its purview the whole sporting scene and, in order to make room for what is most topical across that broad scene each week, a beefed-up editorial staff boils down the beat guys' copy. "People today want a five-to-10-minute quick read—so they can go to a cocktail party and sound knowledgeable," says C.E.O. Waters. Editor Barnidge points out that "readers today are not as willing to work at reading." But in the old days, when scribes were paid by the inch and the Bible of Baseball was scripture. . . .

Do you have a few minutes?

Oct. 7, 1893. Harry Leach reporting from Chicago (again with one of those St. Louis headlines):

RESULTS OF OVER-EXERTION
How It Effects Some of Chicago's
Nervous Scribes

There are times when sobriety of temper is an essential precaution. Too much excitement is detrimental to the gearing of the nervous system. However thrilling an event may be, it is best to be calm. It is a medical fact that over exertion of the aexota, where the nerve center is situated, will, without fail, lead to cataclasm of the semi-colon and watery consummation of the lower lobe of the apocalypse. These facts were secured at the Pan-American congress of physicians after a large outlay of time and money. They are particularly pertinent at this time, because about 1000 cranks who witnessed that game of ball between Baltimore and Chicago last Friday are wandering around in the great throbbing world this morning with their semi-colons terribly cataclasted.

For eight innings neither side made a run.

There follows—well, here is some of what follows:

Never More Decker, eager to shatter anything he could, came up. There was a reverberating roar and the ball whistled away through the air in an opposite direction. McGraw and the ball met and stuck together like two lone girls when a tramp is trying to break in through the back door. That retired the side. . . .

And here is some more:

The air thumped like a volcano with the crater plugged up. Many a horny tongued son of toil on the bleacheries buried his teeth in the soft pine boards and pulled out knots in sheer anguish. . . .

And more:

Reitz seized himself passionately and bore down on the plate. Irwin shot the ball in with a scream of triumph and Reitz died. . . .

And then, finally, at the end of the 12th long paragraph, comes the end of the story, which is also the first mention of the final score:

That was the run of the game. It was too exciting to tell about.

And I believe it.

Have you ever wondered how ballplayers joshed in the early days of the 20th century? Here is how the Baltimore Orioles joshed in 1908, according to J.M.

Cummings in the May 28 *The Sporting News,* under this headline:

ORIOLES' OFF DAYS.
PASSED PLEASANTLY IN LOBBY OF HOTEL

"Waiter, remove these peas," he [manager Jack Dunn] demanded. "They won't stay on me knife. Bring me some split in half, that will. . . . Boys," he began. "I am seriously thinking about organizing the Baltimore Club into a minstrel troupe at the end of the season. Prithee, what thinkest thou? . . . Dessau and Pearson could figure as the P.-C.-M. kids in a knockabout comedy I have in mind to be called 'The higher up we go the better we like it, because it's so different, yet it ain't.' "

Hearne rose at this thrilling juncture, threw up his hands and in a stage whisper remarked: "I'm getting foolish."

"Not 'getting,' " replied the manager, and "Hughie" fell under the table.

"How do you feel, Pfyl?" inquired the manager. "Do you feel as though you could feel your way through some minor f-e-e-l-ing-in part? Just some little piece eloquent in -er-er-er its silence, for instance. Methinks thou wouldst fairly shine in some thinking part."

"Aw, quit your joshing, you distract my attention from my victuals," was all that could be got from the ambassador from the New York Giants.

In those days, Baltimore was in the minors. *The Sporting News* covered the minor leagues almost as thoroughly as it did the majors, hence headlines such as this one, from Wilkes-Barre:

BARONS STRONGER.
LEZOTTE HAS WEEDED OUT DUMB
ELEMENT.

And nine long paragraphs from Keokuk headlines UNJUST TO OSKALOOSA, all about the inequities of the Central Association schedule. Such coverage made *The Sporting News* not only the Bible but the *Variety* of baseball, and what is left of that coverage is still a big reason why players can be seen reading *The Sporting News* in clubhouses—checking up on their friends in the bushes.

An operation called *Baseball America* provides the most comprehensive coverage of the minor leagues, and *USA Today* prints a wealth of big-league statistics five days a week. By the time box scores come out in *The Sporting News* they are as much as 10 or 11 days old. It's a great thing for baseball writers to know they can always lay their hands on the season's box scores if they save *The Sporting News*. "But I don't know how many of our 700,000 readers are baseball writers,'' says Barnidge.

*The Sporting News*'s advertising revenues have doubled since 1981. It's a considerably more accessible and professional-looking product now than it was as holy writ under Taylor Spink. Old hands on the staff, who remember Pappy Spink the way old soldiers remember General Patton, say that the paper got better when Taylor died in 1962 and his mild-mannered son, C.C. Johnson Spink, started making some of the changes that the present owners have accelerated.

But there are several up-to-date sports publications. Only *The Sporting News* has 100 years of baseball fever behind it. Only *The Sporting News* can show you in its pages an endorsement of Coca-Cola by Hughie (Ee-yah) Jennings, in which he maintained that ''the hardest thing a ball player has to contend with is thirst, because if you try to satisfy it with water, you either get loggy or lose your 'Ginger' or it makes you sick, while alcoholic beverages are fatal to good ball.''

The newsstands are loaded with analyses of how baseball has been affected by artificial turf and free agency. Only *The Sporting News* can take you back to the days when scribes speculated that base stealing was on the decline because catchers were wearing ''the fat glove of the modern type. . . . When the catchers took the force of the fiercely projected ball on the thin glove of years ago their fingers gave way, forming a sort of spring box to receive the shock. So heavy was the impact that the hand naturally unconsciously recoiled, and the ball was delayed a fraction of a second before the catcher would gather it up and shoot it down to second. . . . It's different with the big glove, the ball whangs into the great fast cushion and its shock is killed instanter.'' (To counteract this development, a beat guy proposed in 1899 that second base be moved eight feet closer to first when a runner was on first; then if he reached second, second would be moved eight feet closer to third.)

*The Sporting News* has another unique resource. ''The FBI uses this,'' says Mac Farlane. It's a huge card catalog containing the transactional careers of everybody who *ever* signed a professional baseball contract, major or minor. ''Everybody? Are you *sure*?'' I asked Mac Farlane. His expression, while kindly, suggested that if there was anything he was unsure of, it was whether I knew what ''sure'' meant.

So I looked up the best player *I* ever threw batting practice to, the only kid from my high school team who signed a contract, Bobby DeFoor. And there he was: William Robert DeFoor, who kicked around a couple of years and then was put on injured reserve. (After that, I knew, came the Baptist ministry, but that was for a higher card catalog.)

You might think it struck me with a certain finality that I myself was not in that card catalog, what with my being 44 now and not gaining any steps. But it didn't. I was too busy turning over in my mind the possibility that Johnny Evers and I might have a lot in common.

I had been reading ''Gossip of the Players'' for Nov. 12, 1908. Johnny Evers had been giving a lot of thought to this whole problem of what to do when the other team has men on first and third. This is a problem that may seem primitive to fans of big-time baseball today. But it is a problem never resolved, very firmly, at any level of ball that I myself attained. As Evers put it:

If the catcher threw to second, the man on third would race home and the throw was too long from second to get him. Then the trick of the second baseman running in behind the pitcher on such occasions and stopping the throw and shooting it back to the plate was started. This worked for a while, but then the runner on third got to sticking to the bag, and as a result the man going from first to second would be safe at second.

Exactly. What was Evers's solution?

With much practice, I was able to run in on such plays, thus holding the runner at third, and with a good throw from the catcher I could take the ball and with the same movement pass it between my knees back to second base in time to nab the other runner. The catcher, of course, must make a good throw for the play to be a success.

Here we have Johnny Evers. The Evers of Tinker-to-Evers-to-Chance. The Evers who stole a pennant from the Giants in 1908 by calling for the ball when Merkle failed to touch second base. Here we have Johnny Evers with his thinking cap on, figuring out a way to avoid either going all to pieces or sitting there sullenly when the other team has men on first and third.

Exactly the kind of thing I worried about when I played ball. And if I had ever been able to do more than one thing—or even one whole thing—in the same movement, *I think that I might have come up with this same between-the-knees trick!*

I have problems identifying with contemporary baseball stars. They are so much richer than I am, and their gloves are so much better. They play in and on sleek synthetic fibers. They have got the other-team-with-the-guys-on-first-and-third problem licked. And if they're so great, where were they when I was a kid?

I know where Johnny Evers was. He was in my head, in undying verse (''pricking our [the Giants'] gonfalon bubble''), in a glove as scruffy and a uniform as baggy as mine.

A baseball fan, no matter how old, is always a kid, right? If only we could get back to baseball that kids and old guys—as opposed to yuppies and on up—can identify with.

Then again, in the bright lexicon of baseball, why should there be any "if only"? What happened when I told Mac Farlane I wished I could meet Cool Papa Bell? And what did Cool Papa himself reply, when I asked him the obligatory question: Did he regret having been excluded from the white majors? With a calm assurance not unlike Mac Farlane's, Bell replied: "People say, 'Isn't it a shame you couldn't play in the major leagues?'

Unh-uh. I *could* play. Like they used to say, 'You can't eat in this place.' And I would say, 'I *can*. Maybe you're not going to let me in there. But I can *eat* anywhere.' And I could play."

I thought of that as I peered at faint but enduring microfilm. Mac Farlane was saying, "Johnny Evers. A very *brainy* player. There haven't been many brainy players. Lots of *smart* players, but. . . ."

You know what I was reminded of? One of those movies where there's a kid and there's this old guy who knows karate mysteries or can train your foal to be Seabiscuit or has a time machine.

As chief sports columnist for The Associated Press, Hal Bock has a
by-line familiar to fans everywhere. Familiar, too, in the 1960s and
1970s was the name Richie Allen, until its owner forbade it: "I am Dick,
not Richie."

# The Vagabond

## HAL BOCK

DICK ALLEN IS one beautiful cat.
      He is the dictionary definition of a nonconform-
ist in a game chained by conformity. Everybody connected with baseball knows that it takes about six weeks
of spring training for a player to shake out the winter
cobwebs and ready himself for the long season ahead.
And everybody knows that for a hitter to stay sharp
during the season, he must take batting practice every
day.

Well, Dick Allen knows better.

Last February, when Florida and Arizona were being
inundated by migrating athletes, Dick Allen decided to
prolong his winter. This was a very unpopular and
puzzling decision in the training camp of the Chicago
White Sox.

The Sox had acquired Allen in a winter trade with Los
Angeles. The price was relatively light—utility infielder
Steve Huntz and Tommy John, a left-hander with a
losing record. Why would Allen, an acknowledged
slugger, come that cheaply? Well, the reason was
simple. The word was out on Allen. Baseball's establishment had tagged him as a disruptive force on a ball
club—a bad actor.

Manager Chuck Tanner of the White Sox wasn't
interested in Allen's dramatic talents. All Tanner knew
was this guy could hit a baseball great distances—an
ability missing in most of his other employees. He also
knew Allen's family because he lived in New Castle,
Pennsylvania, next door to Wampum, where the Allens
lived. If anybody could handle Dick Allen, Tanner
decided, he could do it.

So the Sox entered a bid on Allen, and the Dodgers
accepted the offer, shipping the muscled slugger to his
fourth team in as many years. Allen had worked—
sometimes—in Philadelphia in 1969, in St. Louis in
1970, in Los Angeles in 1971 and now he was moving

on to Chicago for 1972. He was fast becoming a baseball
vagabond.

Negotiations began between the slugger and the Sox,
and Allen demanded large numbers on his contract, something like $125,000, for his autograph. The Sox said
"sure," and then, inexplicably, Allen refused to sign.

Squeezing every last day out of winter, Allen stayed
home while the White Sox were soaking up the Sarasota,
Florida, sun and getting themselves in shape. There was
nothing wrong with the contract terms—just the time.
The baseball season wasn't supposed to start until April,
and Dick Allen wasn't going to start his season in
February.

Tanner stayed cool. Another manager might have
popped off at a player who insisted on a reporting date
all his own. Tanner knew better. He played the waiting
game. Finally, 23 days late, Allen showed up in camp.
He stayed—for one night—and then, like Duane
Thomas, he took off again.

Above everything else, you must understand that Dick
Allen marches to his own drummer. He is an independent cat who does his own thing. Chuck Tanner understood.

Spring training and its 25-some exhibition games had
run its course and the season was about to begin. Then
came a roadblock. A player strike. On Saturday, April
1, every player in major league baseball walked out.
One by one training camps shut down. And in Sarasota,
Florida, with every other major leaguer in America out
of work, Dick Allen decided to report to the Chicago
White Sox.

Beautiful.

"How long will it take you to get in condition,"
asked Tanner.

"About as long as it takes a pitcher to warm up,"
answered Allen.

With the White Sox camp shut down by the strike, Allen went to a nearby high school and took his first 1972 swings against a Chicago coach. He hit the fourth pitch through the window of a house some 450 feet away. So much for spring training.

Beautiful.

On Opening Day, Dick Allen hit a home run. It was the first of 37 homers that he slugged for the White Sox last season. He drove in 113 runs and batted .308. He won two-thirds of the Triple Crown, leading the league in homers and RBIs. He finished third in the batting average race, 10 points behind the leader, Minnesota's Rod Carew.

When they opened the Most Valuable Player ballots last November, his name was No. 1 on 21 of the 24 votes cast by the baseball writers' committee. Where the other three voters spent their summer remains undisclosed.

"He's Babe Ruth, Rogers Hornsby and Ty Cobb all put together," Manager Tanner decided one day last August, after watching Allen power a baseball some 470 feet and out of sight to win another ball game for the Sox. "The guy gives me chills," Tanner continued. "I'm surprised they even pitch to him at all. The guy's just super."

The Sox made a run at Oakland for the West Division title, and Allen was the man who kept Chicago's hopes alive. Day after incredible day, he would turn ball games around with his big bat. And the man who was booed out of Philadelphia and shunted aside by St. Louis and Los Angeles, took Chicago by storm. Fans packed Sox Park to watch his prodigious shots. And more often than not, he sent them home contented and determined to return another day to watch him hit another one.

Allen became the town's No. 1 hero. Fans cheered themselves hoarse when he hit one. And Allen, never the victim of overaffection in any of the other towns in which he had played baseball, basked in the attention.

"Did you hear the standing ovation I got?" he asked a visiting writer after he had beaten the Yankees with a huge home run that may still be traveling. "That was something else," exulted Allen. "So cool. I can't ever remember fans doing that for me. This has got to be the greatest place ever to play ball."

Tanner watched the love affair develop day by day. "He's taken this town by storm," the manager said. "He's the greatest thing in this town since Ernie Banks. He can own it if he wants."

He might be able to buy it after the Sox finish paying off for last year's exploits. Asked how much of a raise he wanted for 1973 after winning the MVP crown, he just grinned. "I don't know," he said, "how much do you have?"

Whatever the numbers, it will be hard for them to match what Allen meant to the White Sox in 1972, not only on the field but in the cashbox as well. This was a dying franchise. The team had lost 106 games in 1970, and with their crosstown rivals, the Cubs, competing for the National League pennant, the Sox were all but forgotten in Chicago.

The White Sox drew less than 500,000 customers that sorry season while the Cubs were attracting 1.6 million. Chicago clearly belonged to the National League club. Allen, not coincidentally, also belonged to a National League club at the time. Then came the winter 1971 trade to Chicago and last summer's excitement. The turnstiles clicked off 1,186,018 admissions, almost three times the 1970 total. The Sox were saved, thanks mainly to the slugger with the muttonchop sideburns.

But Allen's excitement didn't only bring money in through the gate and ensuing concession sales. There was the matter of the White Sox' TV-radio contract. The team was working on the final season of a five-year $1 million contract when Dick arrived. There was some skepticism over how much the rights would be worth when the Sox sat down to renegotiate them. General Manager Stu Holcomb was clearly concerned.

"If we don't get at least $600,000 for our media rights next year," said Holcomb during the spring, "I'm not sure what we'll do."

By the time October rolled around and Allen's super season was history, the Sox quietly signed a new broadcast pact. No figures were announced but it is the understanding of the industry that the ball club has returned to the $1 million class.

Thank you, Dick Allen. Beautiful.

Tanner sometimes sat in complete awe of Allen's feats. The slugger not only won games with his bat, but sometimes with his legs as well. He stole 19 bases. He became only the third man in history to hit two—count 'em, two—inside-the-park home runs in a single game.

"He is the best ballplayer I have ever seen in the major leagues," Tanner said simply, "and I played with some good ones—Hank Aaron, Eddie Mathews, Ernie Banks, Rocky Colavito, Minnie Minoso. Allen beats them all . . . fielding, running, hitting in the clutch, for average and power."

Allen has his own philosophy of hitting. He is concerned only with producing runs for his ball club.

"I never play for individual totals," he said. "It might be easier for me if I did. Guys like Joe Rudi or Rod Carew can bunt and help their batting average. I can bunt, but it doesn't make the Sox move.

"If I bunted, I might hit .330 or .340, but I might not be doing the other guys a favor. If I were playing for the batting title," he continued, "I'd bunt."

Did Allen's huge success with the White Sox embarrass the Dodgers, who had surrendered him so readily the previous winter?

"When you trade a fellow like Allen," said Al Campanis, the Dodger vice president who had engineered the trade, "you are leaving yourself wide open. He's a fine ballplayer. You know if he does something at his next stop, you are going to take a beating.

"We gave it a lot of thought," Campanis continued. "Long range, we thought we could do more winning with those who conform to the rules."

Rules, like going to spring training in February, not April, for example. Rules, like taking batting practice before every game even if you're the most productive hitter in the league. Rules, like being on the team bus when it is ready to leave.

There was one night during the season when Allen was detained in the dressing room after a game. The team bus was loaded with all of the club personnel including Manager Tanner. Five minutes passed, then 10. Finally, 15 minutes after the scheduled departure of the bus, Allen still was not aboard.

From the rear of the bus came a complaint. "The hell with him," snapped another player. "Let's get going. He can catch a cab. He makes enough money."

Tanner whirled.

"You can take the cab," snapped the manager, "I'm waiting for Dick Allen."

Beautiful.

The 1970s produced a new wave of excellence in baseball writing, much of it the work of "beat men" in their late twenties or early thirties, working for daily newspapers. A partial list would include Moss Klein in Newark, Mike Lupica, Ira Berkow and Murray Chass in New York, Glenn Schwartz in San Francisco—and most certainly Peter Gammons of *The Boston Globe* and Thomas Boswell of *The Washington Post*. The last two, like some of the others, reached the point early on where they wrote *only* baseball. The following piece, the title chapter from a book by Boswell, suggests why.

# From *Why Time Begins on Opening Day*

## THOMAS BOSWELL

WHY BASEBALL?

Millions of us have wondered. How can baseball maintain such a resolute grasp upon us? My own affection for the game has held steady for decades, maybe even grown with age. After twenty-five years of attachment, I have no sense of wanting to be weaned from this habit. What seems most strange is the way so many of us reserve a protected portion of our lives for a game which often seems like an interloper among our first-rate passions. What is *baseball* doing here, tucked on the same high shelf with our most entrenched emotions?

If asked where baseball stood amid such notions as country, family, love, honor, art and religion, we might say derisively, "Just a game." But, under oath, I'd abandon some of these Big Six before I'd give up baseball. Clearly, a game which becomes one of our basic fidelities is something more than "sport." Perhaps the proper analogy is to our other joyous, inexplicable addictions.

A thread runs through all these idle loves. Each, like baseball, brings us into a small and manageable world chocked with intriguing and unambiguous details; we are beckoned into tiny universes where the areas of certainty are large, where the regions of doubt are pleasantly small. The cook must wrestle with tarragon and basil, the gardener agonizes over his pruning. The baseball fan knows every batting average, down to the *thousandth* of a point. What steady ground on which to stand, if only in one corner of our lives! Each pastime has its own unstated set of values. That part of us which is a fly fisher or a curer of hams or an habitué of the bleachers shares fragments of a common viewpoint with others of the same tastes.

When we meet a bona fide fan—and baseball fanciers can be as snobbish as wine sippers or prize rose gardeners—we start from an assumption of kinship. Implicit is the sense that you endorse a whole range of civilized modern tastes; if you'd lived in the sixteenth century, you would probably have liked Montaigne. By and large, baseball fans tend to prefer pastoral, slyly anecdotal, proven-if-slightly-dated things over those which are urban or pretentious or trendy. We choose the gentle grandstand conversations, beer in hand, on a soft spring night over the raucous forty-yard-line scream, whiskey-in-fist, on a brisk autumn afternoon. Our presumption of comradeship is considerable. Anyone who shares our range of wise opinion must do dastardly deeds to lose our good will.

In sum, what baseball provides is fact. Fact in a butter sauce of tone. Fact as in the sense of detail and concreteness. Tone as in style and spirit.

In contrast to the unwieldy world which we hold in common, baseball offers a kingdom built to human scale. Its problems and questions are exactly our size. Here we may come when we feel a need for a rooted point of reference. In much the same way, we take a long hike or look for hard work when we suspect what's bothering us is either too foolish or too serious to permit a solution.

Baseball isn't necessarily an escape from reality, though it can be; it's merely one of our many refuges *within* the real where we try to create a sense of order on our own terms. Born to an age where horror has become commonplace, where tragedy has, by its monotonous repetition, become a parody of sorrow, we need to fence off a few parks where humans try to be fair, where skill has some hope of reward, where absurdity has a harder time than usual getting a ticket.

In those moments when we have had our bellyful of abstractions, it is detail, the richness of the particular, which restores us to ourselves. There are oceans of consolation, seas of restored appetite, in as humble a thing as a baseball season. This great therapeutic wash of fact and anecdote draws us back to ourselves when we catch ourselves, like Ishmael, water-gazing too long.

In part, our attachment to the game stems from a persistent feeling that major-leaguers tend to give the best of themselves to their game, even at peril to other parts of their lives. One big-leaguer, known for his drinking as well as his fear that the bottle might be mastering him, once told me, defiantly and proudly, that in his whole career he had "never had one drink from the time I woke up until the game was over." Of course, sometimes this future Hall of Famer didn't wake up until the afternoon.

His point, ambiguous as it may have been, was that, as long as he could function, the game would get his best. Not because he owed it to the sport, but because he assumed that the baseball part of him was the best part, the piece he'd fight longest to hold. Many creative people see their talent in this light; whatever else must be pruned or neglected, their painting or writing or composing will be given a full chance to prosper. Part of the power of baseball is this sense that ballplayers tend to be obsessed with their work. It is this that gives them added stature as well as an intimation of tragedy. An air of danger and courage surrounds anyone who devotes himself to the long shot of art, who has burned the bridges back to a conventional life. In their uncompromising confidence, in their sometimes stunningly inaccurate appraisals of themselves, ballplayers are linked—though they might never recognize it—to others of their generation who are living on the edge.

The notion that such internally driven people can become slipshod overnight just because they're stupefyingly overpaid, is bogus. By the time a man is established in the majors, his personality has been in place for a long time. For every player who counts his money and "retires" while still playing, there are more who are doubly motivated by the promise of greater wealth or by fear of public embarrassment or simply by a feeling of responsibility to live up to those fleeting gifts which distinguish them from other men.

The career athlete who is perceived to have fulfilled his potential is, within the jock community, given a sort of lifetime pass, a character reference that can never be revoked by misfortune. And the athlete whose peers believe that he wasted his talent is, in a way, never forgiven, no matter how hale a fellow he may pass for to the rest of us.

In baseball today, the twin internal dynamics of competition and artistry are still much stronger than the degenerative effects of riches. Consequently, we can still truly enjoy baseball. If we feel that the performers care deeply, genuinely judge themselves by their acts, then the game is worth watching. Craft is the surest proof of sincerity.

Once, I sat next to Gaylord Perry, three-hundred-game winner and curmudgeon, at a winter banquet. Initially he despised me, as I assumed he would, since I was one of those slimy reporters who nag him about his spitball, his feuds with teammates, his undermining of managers and his love of a dollar. But the only thing Perry really loves to talk about, besides his tobacco crop, is baseball, and that link soon erased our differences.

"During games, I'll sit alone down at one end of the dugout and talk baseball," said Perry, then forty-four and an ancient Seattle Mariner. "Pretty soon, the young players would kinda gather around me. If anybody brings up any other subject, I just say, 'We're talkin' baseball down here. These are working hours. You wanna talk about something else, go the hell down to the other end.'

"It was amazing what those kids don't know, and I enjoyed watchin' their eyes get big. I can tell a hitter's weaknesses the first time I ever see him, just by watching him take his stance. Like, if a hitter carries the bat high and wraps it back around his neck [giving a casual demonstration of the cocked wrists], well, then you know he can't hit the fastball in on his hands. It takes him too long to get the bat started and clear his hips out of the way.

"And if the hitter holds the bat low or lays it out away from him, then he can't hit the outside pitch with authority, especially the breaking ball. You can get him to pull the trigger too soon.

"Also, you gotta watch their feet. The good hitters, like Rod Carew or Eddie Murray, they've got a half-dozen different stances and they'll change 'em between pitches. That's how you tell what they're guessing."

"What if they change stances," I asked, "as you're winding up?"

Perry raised one eyebrow.

"Oh," I muttered, "you drill him."

"I hope so," said Perry.

If one quality distinguishes baseball as seen from a distance, from the game as it is at point-blank range, it's just this sort of ambiance which mixes constant technical analysis with an equal amount of prickly agitating. My favorite clubhouse was that of the '77–'78 New York Yankees. Those world champs were perhaps the most acid-tongued, thick-skinned, insult-you-to-your-face team that ever spit tobacco juice on a teammate's new Gucci loafers. A perfect Yankee day came late in '77 when Steinbrenner decided the item he needed to complete his circus was reclusive Dave Kingman. "We already have Captain Moody [Thurman Munson], Lieutenant Moody [Mickey Rivers], Sergeant Moody [Ken Holtzman] and Private Moody [Willie Randolph]," said third baseman Graig Nettles. "Now Dave can be Commander Moody."

The heirs to that tradition were the '82 Brewers, led by Cy Young winner Pete Vuckovich. When it's time to form a new musical-chairs group called Down with People, or if you want a cover photo for a new book called "I'm Not O.K. and Neither Are You," start with Vuke.

Catching sight of Gorman Thomas' great mane of shaggy hair, his unfriendly mustache, his chaw of 'baccy, his third-world teeth and his dirty uniform, the glowering Vuckovich accosted his roommate, saying, "You are the ugliest."

"No, *you* are the ugliest," said Thomas, running his eye over Vuckovich's pockmarked skin, his mass-murderer hair, his beer belly, his whole cultivated mien of mayhem. "In fact, you are the absolute worst in every way."

Most people might take offense at such perspicacity. Not Vuke.

"Well," he said proudly, "somebody's got to be."

Men with personalities as flinty, minds as sharp and tongues as tart as Perry, Nettles, Vuckovich and Thomas are the sort who define what we might call the big-league point of view. When I covered my first major-league game, in 1972, I assumed I had a respectable knowledge of the subject. Now, after a thousand and one nights in the ballpark, I may know half as much as I thought I knew then. I stepped into the dugouts of the major leagues with an outsider's approach to the sport. With the years, I've gradually altered that angle of vision until, while still half outsider, I'm also half insider.

What *is* this big-league point of view?

In many ways, the pros watch a game, a season, just as we do; when a flyball is heading for the fence, they root exactly like the folks in the bleachers. However, more often than not, the ballplayer sees things much differently from the rest of us. If we truly want to taste the facts of the game, get the flavors right, then we must add this insider's perspective to our own. Let's have a preliminary Ten Commandments of the Dugout:

• Judge slowly.

No, even more slowly than that.

Never judge a player over a unit of time shorter than a month. A game or even a week is nothing; you must see a player hot, cold and in between before you can put

## JOHN GALLAGHER

*"He was a great painter until his arm went."*

the whole package together. Sometimes, in the case of a proven player, a whole season is not enough time to judge, especially if there are extenuating circumstances. In '81, Fred Lynn, traded from Boston to the Angels, batted .219 with five homers; the quick judgment was that Lynn was a Fenway Park hitter who would never be an All-Star away from it. In '82, Lynn was healthy, made his technical adjustments at the plate and saw his stats go back close to their .300-with-power, Fenway levels.

The rush to judge is the most certain sign of a baseball outsider. When, in '82, George Steinbrenner tried to *run* his Yankees, as well as own them, he made all the sort of shoot-from-the-hip judgments of a guy in the cheap seats who's had one beer too many; the results were a disaster. Steinbrenner, with his football and business backgrounds, didn't have the patience to come to sound, fully digested decisions; why, the man made judgments of players based on just one game—absolute proof of not having baseball sense. The baseball person is usually the last to work his way to a firm opinion, and also the last to abandon it. Steinbrenner is always the first on the boat and the first off.

- Assume everybody is trying reasonably hard.

Of all the factors at work in baseball, effort is the last to consider. In the majors, you seldom try your hardest; giving 110 percent, as a general mode of operation, would be counterproductive for most players. The issue in baseball is finding the proper balance between effort and relaxation. Usually, something on the order of 80 percent effort is about right. Few players have trouble revving that high. Many can't get down that low. Physical sluggishness, called "jaking," is relatively rare, except among heavy drug users whose heads are temporarily on call to another star system.

- Physical errors, even the most grotesque, should be forgiven.

On good teams, the physical limitations of players are nearly ignored. The short hop that eats an infielder alive, the ball in the dirt that goes to the screen, the hitter who is hopelessly overpowered by a pitcher—all these hideous phenomena are treated as though they never happened. "Forget it," players say to each other, reflexively. It's assumed that every player is physically capable of performing every duty asked of him. If he can't, it's never his fault. His mistake is simply regarded as part of a professional's natural human margin of error.

Even if a player consistently makes physical blunders, it's *still* not his fault and he's never blamed. It's the front office's fault for not coming up with a better player; the assumption is that while stars are rare, there is always an abundance of competent professionals. Or it's the manager's fault for putting a player in a situation beyond his talents. You don't ask Roy Howell to hit Ron Guidry. And if you do, his strikeout is your fault, not his.

- Conversely, mental errors are judged as harshly as physical errors are ignored. The distinction as to whether a mistake has been made "from the neck up or the neck down" is always made.

Mental errors, however, can cover a wide range. Failure in any fundamental—laying down a sacrifice bunt, hitting the cutoff man, covering or backing up bases, receiving or relaying a sign, even catching a windblown pop-up—is considered a sort of quasi-mental error. Why? Because, with the proper mental discipline, you could have learned to master those basic skills.

As an extreme example, a pitcher who walks home the winning run is guilty of a grievous mental error, because a major-league pitcher is assumed to be able to throw a strike whenever he absolutely must. If he can't, the problem usually has more to do with poise or preparation or proper thinking on the mound, than with the physical act of throwing the ball.

- Pay more attention to the mundane than the spectacular.

Baseball is a game of huge samplings. The necessity for consistency usually outweighs the need for the inspired. In judging any player, never measure him by his greatest catch, his longest home run, his best-pitched game. That is the exception; baseball is the game of the rule.

- Pay more attention to the theory of the game than to the outcome of the game. Don't let your evaluations be swayed too greatly by the final score.

The most common error of novice reporters is their tendency to watch what happens, rather than study the principles under the action. You don't ask, "Did that pinch hitter get a hit?" In a sense, that's a matter of chance. The worst hitter will succeed one time in five, while the best hitter will fail two times in three. Instead ask, "Given all the factors in play at that moment, was he the correct man to use in that situation?"

Only then will you begin to sense the game as a team does. If a team loses a game but has used its resources properly—relieved its starting pitcher at a sensible juncture, used the proper strategy during its rallies, minimized its mental and fundamental mistakes, had the proper pinch hitters at the plate with the game on the line in the late innings—then that team is often able to ignore defeat utterly. Players say, "We did everything right but win."

If you do everything right every day, you'll still lose 40 percent of your games—but you'll also end up in the World Series. Nowhere is defeat so meaningless as in baseball. And nowhere are the theories and broad tactics that run under the game so important.

• Players always know best how they're playing.

At the technical level, they seldom fool themselves—the stakes are too high. Self-criticism is ingrained. If a player on a ten-game hitting streak says he's in a slump, then he is; if a player who's one for fifteen says that he's "on" every pitch, but that he's hitting a lot of "atom" balls ("right at-'em"), then assume he's about to go on a tear.

There are exceptions: Jim Palmer always thought his arm was about to fall off and once alternately begged and cursed his manager in hopes of being taken out of the last three innings of a game in which he ended up pitching a one-hit shutout. Al Oliver, owner of the game's best superiority complex, believed the only reason he never had a hundred-RBI year until his twelfth season was that "I always seem to hit in bad luck."

• Stay *ahead* of the action, not behind it or even neck and neck with it.

Remember, the immediate past is almost always prelude. Ask hurlers how they go about selecting their pitches and they invariably say, "By watching the previous pitch." The thrower plans his game in advance; the pitcher creates it as he goes. A veteran pitcher usually doesn't know what he'll throw on his second pitch until he sees what happens to the first. "Don't judge your fastball by those darn radar guns," says Perry. "Judge by how the hitters act."

Was that batter taking or swinging? Was he ahead of the curveball or behind the fastball? Was he trying to pull, to go to the opposite field, or simply "go with the pitch"? Was he trying for power or contact? And just as important, how has he reacted to these factors in the past? Does he tend to adjust from pitch to pitch (which is unusual)? From at-bat to at-bat (which is more common)? Or is he so stubborn that he has a plan for the whole game and will "sit on the fastball" or "wait for that change-up all night" in hopes of seeing one pitch that he can poleax?

That's how baseball has been watched in every respectable dugout for as long as the oldest hands can remember. And the closer you come to that sort of reflective, sifting, tendency-spotting habit of viewers, the more enjoyable and open the game will seem. Of all our major sports, baseball comes closest to rewarding the spectator in direct proportion to his effort.

Pay particular attention to the first inning. Study the starting pitcher and study him hard. Both he and his foes are trying to figure out what he's got that night; his first dozen pitches will often set the tone for the first half of the game. Don't ask, "Does he have his control?" Instead, go through this checklist: Can he get his fastball over for strikes? Can he throw his fastball to *spots* within the strike zone? Is he throwing his breaking ball for strikes, or just showcasing it? Does he trust his off-speed pitch enough to throw it when he's behind in the count? Is he tempting batters into getting themselves out on borderline pitches or balls?

What does he tend to throw on each of the sport's most important counts: 0–0, 2–2 and the cripples (2–0 and 3–1)?

In other words:

What does he rely upon to *start* hitters—i.e., 0–0?

What "out pitch" does he use to *finish* hitters—that's the moment-of-truth, 2–2 pitch. Players call the 2–2 pitch "the end of the line," because pitchers hate to go from 2–2 to 3–2. *Never* take a nap on a 2–2 pitch. That's when you're most likely to find out the pitcher's true opinion of both his strength and the batter's weakness.

Finally, what does the pitcher select when he's nibbled himself into a corner: the 2–0 and the 3–1 "cripple" pitches? What is his tight-spot pitch?

As an almost clinical example, the '82 Cy Young winner, Vuckovich of Milwaukee, was often two different pitchers in the same game.

He'd go through the lineup the first time, when he was still fresh, like an utterly conventional "power" pitcher. He'd "pitch the counts," as it's called.

That means on neutral counts—like 0–0, 1–1 and 2–2—he'd use his bread-and-butter—the fastball or hard slider—trying to stay ahead of the count and "challenge the hitters."

On all the "hitter's counts"—like 1–0, 2–1 and 3–2—he'd also bravely confront the hitters with hard stuff, often on a corner or the fists.

On all the "pitcher's counts"—like 0–1, 1–2 and 2–2—he'd throw tormenting breaking balls at the corners. On cripples, he'd go macho, throwing hard strikes; on waste pitches, he'd also play fair, bouncing curves in the other batter's box or coming up and in.

Then, sometimes in the middle innings, Vuckovich—having established that he could succeed with old-fashioned, no-imagination power pitching—would begin to "contradict the counts."

That's upsetting to hitters, because they're taught to believe pitchers won't change tactics until they're forced. Vuckovich would occasionally mix in breaking balls on neutral counts or even on hitters' counts. When he was ahead, and presumably didn't need to challenge hitters, that's when he'd show the fastball, though just off the plate. Suddenly the cripples would be change-ups, and the waste pitches would be smoke on the black.

Finally, by the late innings, Vuckovich would be "reversing the counts."

Neutral counts and even cripples would, almost invariably, be nasty off-speed pitches, always nibbling; often, with men on base, Vuckovich would, almost deliberately it seemed, fall behind in a count, then "reverse the count" and get an inning-ending double play.

When he got ahead of the count, Vuke would do anything, including throw his best remaining fastball for a high strike in hopes of a fly out.

Milwaukee general manager Harry Dalton was like a kid with candy watching Vuckovich at work constantly playing mind games with hitters. "A lot of pitchers, like Nolan Ryan, can perform," said Dalton one night. "Give me Vuckovich. He competes."

Vuckovich could be several contradictory pitchers all wrapped in one for two unique reasons: First, though he weighed two hundred fifty pounds and played the role of mound thug, he was actually more a curveball control pitcher than a fastballer. Second, for some reason, Vuke felt comfortable pitching behind in counts or with tons of men on base. The more a hitter thought he had Vuckovich backed into a corner where he would have to throw either a fastball, a strike or both, the more likely Vuckovich was to throw a breaking ball just off the corner—and get the hitter out with it.

Vuckovich was a student of expectation. That is, a student of baseball.

Baseball offers us pleasure and insight at so many levels and in so many forms that, when we try to grasp the whole sport in our two hands, we end up with nothing. The game, because it is no one thing but, rather, dozens of things, has slipped through our fingers again.

As each season begins, we always feel the desire to capsulize and define the source of the sharp anticipation that we feel as opening day approaches. We know that something fine, almost wonderful, is about to begin, but we can't quite say why baseball seems so valuable, almost indispensable, to us. The game, which remains one of our broadest sources of metaphor, changes with our angle of vision, our mood; there seems to be no end to our succession of lucky discoveries.

When opening day arrives, think how many baseball worlds begin revolving for seven months.

As history, baseball has given us an annual chapter each year since 1869. Each team will add a page to its franchise's epic. Countless questions that attach themselves to the baseball continuum will be answered. Will Pete Rose find a way to break Ty Cobb's record for hits? Will Reggie Jackson get his five hundredth home run? Will Terry Felton—oh-for-sixteen in his career and back in the minors again—ever win a game? Yes, we walk with giants.

As living theater and physical poetry, the game will be available in twenty-six ballparks on more than two thousand occasions. Baseball is always there when we want it—seven days a week, seven months a year. All the tactile pleasures of the park are ready when the proper mood strikes us: evening twilights, sundowns, hot summer Sunday afternoons, the cool of the dark late innings of night games, quiet drives home as we decompress and digest.

Then, just when we think the game is essentially mellow and reflective, we find ourselves looped in the twists and coils of a 5–4 barn burner between two contenders. When the centerfielder jumps above the fence in the bottom of the ninth and comes down with the ball and the game in his hand, we realize that two to three hours is just the proper amount of time to tighten the mainspring of tension before letting us explode in one, final cheer. We leave with a glowing tiredness, delighted by the memories of this impromptu and virile ballet, all choreographed by the capricious flight of a ball.

Despite all this, baseball may give us more pleasure, more gentle, unobtrusive sustenance, away from the park than it does inside it.

With breakfast, we have our ten minutes of box scores—enough to travel to thirteen cities, see thirteen games in our mind's eye, note at a glance what five hundred players did or failed to do. Dave Righetti, five walks in four innings, still can't get his delivery in synch. Tony Armas, three for four, out of his latest slump, will probably go right into a streak and hit five homers by next Friday.

On Sunday, the breakfast process takes an extra ten minutes, since The Averages must be consumed. We imagine the state of mind of dozens of players and their teammates. (Who ever thought Seaver had another good season in him? Kingman's down to .196; bet that bum's a prince to be around.)

Then, in odd parts of the day, the game drifts into the mind. Who's pitching tonight? Is it on TV? At worst, the home team is on the radio; catch the last few innings. "Double-play grounder to Ozzie Smith deep in the hole, Billy Russell's chugging toward first, Steve Sax trying to take out Tommy Herr."

Why, it doesn't even have to happen to be real.

The ways that baseball insinuates itself into the empty corners, cheering up the odd hour, are almost too ingrained to notice. Tape at eleven, the scores before bed, the Monday and Saturday games of the week. Into how many conversations does George Steinbrenner's name creep, so that we may gauge the judgments of our friends, catch a glimpse of their values on the sly? The amateur statistician and the armchair strategist in us is aroused. What fan doesn't have a new system for grading relief pitchers, or a theory on why the Expos never win?

Sure, opening day is baseball's bandwagon. Pundits and politicians and every prose poet on the continent jumps on board for a few days. But they're gone soon, off in search of some other windy event worthy of their attention. Then, once more, all those long, slow months of baseball are left to us. And our time can begin again.

Published in 1970, *Ball Four* was an instantaneous and overwhelming hit, to the point where many people today remember it as the first of the diary-type sports books. It wasn't that, of course. In football, Jerry Kramer's *Instant Replay* was published during the 1960s; and in baseball, even earlier, Jim Brosnan's *The Long Season*.

But for all the diaries before or since, *Ball Four* retains a quality—call it irreverence, if you will—somehow all its own. In this chapter, author Jim Bouton details his salary history with the New York Yankees—a history that suggests why, come 1969, he found himself pitching for the Seattle Pilots.

# From *Ball Four*

## JIM BOUTON *edited by* LEONARD SHECTER

I SIGNED my contract today to play for the Seattle Pilots at a salary of $22,000 and it was a letdown because I didn't have to bargain. There was no struggle, none of the give and take that I look forward to every year. Most players don't like to haggle. They just want to get it over with. Not me. With me signing a contract has been a yearly adventure.

The reason for no adventure this year is the way I pitched last year. It ranged from awful to terrible to pretty good. When it was terrible, and I had a record of 0 and 7, or 2 and 7 maybe, I had to do some serious thinking about whether it was all over for me. I was pitching for the Seattle Angels of the Pacific Coast League. The next year, 1969, under expansion, the club would become the Seattle Pilots of the American League. The New York Yankees had sold me to Seattle for $20,000 and were so eager to get rid of me they paid $8,000 of my $22,000 salary. This means I was actually sold for $12,000, less than half the waiver price. Makes a man think.

In the middle of August I went to see Marvin Milkes, the general manager of the Seattle Angels. I told him that I wanted some kind of guarantee from him about next year. There were some businesses with long-range potential I could go into over the winter and I would if I was certain I wasn't going to be playing ball.

"What I would like," I told him, "is an understanding that no matter what kind of contract you give me, major league or minor league, that it will be for a certain minimum amount. Now, I realize you don't know how

much value I will be for you since you haven't gone through the expansion draft and don't know the kind of players you'll have. So I'm not asking for a major-league contract, but just a certain minimum amount of money."

"How much money are you talking about?" Milkes said shrewdly.

"I talked it over with my wife and we arrived at a figure of $15 or $16,000. That's the minimum I could afford to play for, majors or minors. Otherwise I got to go to work."

To this Milkes said simply, "No."

I couldn't say I blamed him.

It was right about then, though, that the knuckleball I'd been experimenting with for a couple of months began to do things. I won two games in five days, going all the way, giving up only two or three hits. I was really doing a good job and everyone was kind of shocked. As the season drew to a close I did better and better. The last five days of the season I finished with a flurry, and my earned-run average throwing the knuckleball was 1.90, which is very good.

The last day of the season I was in the clubhouse and Milkes said he wanted to see me for a minute. I went up to his office and he said, "We're going to give you the same contract for next year. We'll guarantee you $22,000." This means if I didn't get released I'd be getting it even if I was sent down to the minors. I felt like kissing him on both cheeks. I also felt like I had a new lease on life. A knuckleball had to be pretty impressive to impress a general manager $7,000 worth. Don't ever think $7,000 isn't a lot of money in baseball. I've had huge arguments over a lot less.

When I started out in 1959 I was ready to love the baseball establishment. In fact I thought big business had all the answers to any question I could ask. As far as I was concerned clubowners were benevolent old men who wanted to hang around the locker room and were willing to pay a price for it, so there would never be any problem about getting paid decently. I suppose I got that way reading Arthur Daley in *The New York Times*. And reading about those big salaries. I read that Ted Williams was making $125,000 and figured that Billy Goodman made $60,000. That was, of course, a mistake.

I signed my first major-league contract at Yankee Stadium fifteen minutes before they played "The Star-Spangled Banner" on opening day, 1962. That's because my making the team was a surprise. But I'd had a hell of a spring. Just before the game was about to start Roy Hamey, the general manager, came into the clubhouse and shoved a contract under my nose. "Here's your contract," he said. "Sign it. Everybody gets $7,000 their first year."

Hamey had a voice like B. S. Pully's, only louder. I signed. It wasn't a bad contract. I'd gotten $3,000 for playing all summer in Amarillo, Texas, the year before.

I finished the season with a 7–7 record and we won the pennant and the World Series, so I collected another $10,000, which was nice. I was much better toward the end of the season than at the beginning. Like I was 4–7 early but then won three in a row, and Ralph Houk, the manager, listed me as one of his six pitchers for the stretch pennant race and the Series.

All winter I thought about what I should ask for and finally decided to demand $12,000 and settle for $11,000. This seemed to me an eminently reasonable figure. When I reported to spring training in Ft. Lauderdale—a bit late because I'd spent six months in the army—Dan Topping, Jr., son of the owner, and the guy who was supposed to sign all the lower-echelon players like me, handed me a contract and said, "Just sign here, on the bottom line."

I unfolded the contract and it was for $9,000—if I made the team. I'd get $7,000 if I didn't.

*If I made the team?*

"Don't forget you get a World Series share," Topping said. He had a boarding-school accent that always made me feel like my fly was open or something. "You can always count on that."

"Fine," I said. "I'll sign a contract that guarantees me $10,000 more at the end of the season if we don't win the pennant."

He was shocked. "Oh, we can't do that."

"Then what advantage is it to me to take less money?"

"That's what we're offering."

"I can't sign it."

"Then you'll have to go home."

"All right, I'll go home."

"Well, give me a call in the morning, before you leave."

I called him the next morning and he said to come over and see him. "I'll tell you what we're going to do," he said. "We don't usually do this, but we'll make a big concession. I talked with my dad, with Hamey, and we've decided to eliminate the contingency clause—you get $9,000 whether you make the club or not."

"Wow!" I said. Then I said no.

"That's our final offer, take it or leave it. You know, people don't usually do this. You're the first holdout we've had in I don't know how many years."

I said I was sorry. I hated to mess up Yankee tradition, but I wasn't going to sign for a $2,000 raise. And I got up to go.

"Before you go, let me call Hamey," Topping said. He told Hamey I was going home and Hamey said he wanted to talk to me. I held the phone four inches from my ear. If you were within a mile of him, Hamey really didn't need a telephone. "Lookit, son," he yelled. "You better sign that contract, that's all there's gonna be. That's it. You don't sign that contract you're making the biggest mistake of your life."

I was twenty-four years old. And scared. Also stubborn. I said I wouldn't sign and hung up.

"All right," Topping said, "how much do you want?"

"I was thinking about $12,000," I said, but not with much conviction.

"Out of the question," Topping said. "Tell you what. We'll give you $10,000."

My heart jumped. "Make it ten-five," I said.

"All right," he said. "Ten-five."

The bastards really fight you.

For my ten-five that year I won 21 games and lost only 7. I had a 2.53 earned-run average. I couldn't wait to see my next contract.

By contract time Yogi Berra was the manager and Houk had been promoted to general manager. I decided to let Houk off easy. I'd ask for $25,000 and settle for $20,000, and I'd be worth every nickel of it. Houk offered me $15,500. Houk can look as sincere as hell with those big blue eyes of his and when he calls you "podner" it's hard to argue with him. He said the reason he was willing to give me such a big raise right off was that he didn't want to haggle, he just wanted to give me a top salary, more than any second-year pitcher had ever made with the Yankees, and forget about it.

"How many guys have you had who won 21 games in their second year?" I asked him.

He said he didn't know. And, despite all the "pod-ners," I didn't sign.

This was around January 15. I didn't hear from Houk again until two weeks before spring training, when he came up another thousand, to $16,500. This was definitely final. He'd talked to Topping, called him on his boat, ship to shore. Very definitely final.

I said it wasn't final for me, I wanted $20,000.

"Well, you can't make twenty," Houk said. "We never double contracts. It's a rule."

It's a rule he made up right there, I'd bet. And a silly one anyway, because it wouldn't mean anything to a guy making $40,000, only to somebody like me, who was making very little to start with.

The day before spring training began he went up another two thousand to $18,500. After all-night consultations with Topping, of course. "Ralph," I said, real friendly, "under ordinary circumstances I might have signed this contract. If you had come with it sooner, and if I hadn't had the problem I had last year trying to get $3,000 out of Dan Topping, Jr. But I can't, because it's become a matter of principle."

He has his rules, I have my principles.

Now I'm a holdout again. Two weeks into spring training and I was enjoying every minute of it. The phone never stopped ringing and I was having a good time. Of course, the Yankees weren't too happy. One reason is that they knew they were being unfair and they didn't want anybody to know it. But I was giving out straight figures, telling everybody exactly what I'd made and what they were offering and the trouble I'd had with Dan Topping, Jr.

One time Houk called and said, "Why are you telling everybody what you're making?"

"If I don't tell them, Ralph," I said, "maybe they'll think I'm asking for ridiculous figures. They might even think I asked for $15,000 last year and that I'm asking for thirty now. I just want them to know I'm being reasonable."

And Houk said something that sounded like: "*Row-orrowrowrr.*" You ever hear a lion grumble?

You know, players are always told that they're not to discuss salaries with each other. They want to keep us dumb. Because if Joe Pepitone knows what Tom Tresh is making and Tresh knows what Phil Linz is making, then we can all bargain better, based on what we all know. If one of us makes a breakthrough, then we can all take advantage of it. But they want to keep us ignorant, and it works. Most ballplayers in the big leagues do not know what their teammates are making.

And they think you're strange if you tell. (Tom Tresh, Joe Pepitone, Phil Linz and I agreed, as rookies, to always tell. After a while only Phil and I told.)

Anyway, on March 8, my birthday, Houk called me and said he was going to deduct $100 a day from his offer for every day I held out beyond March 10. It amounted to a fine for not signing, no matter what Houk said. What he said was, "Oh no, it's not a fine. I don't believe in fining people." And I'm sure it never occurred to him just how unfair a tactic this was. Baseball people are so used to having their own way and not getting any argument that they just don't think they *can* be unfair. When I called Joe Cronin, president of the league, to ask if Houk could, legally, fine me, he said, "Walk around the block, then go back in and talk some more."

After walking around the block and talking it over with my dad, I chickened out. Sorry about that. I called Houk and said, "Okay, you win. I'm on my way down." I salved my wounds with the thought that if I had any kind of a year this time I'd really sock it to him.

Still, if I knew then what I know now, I wouldn't have signed. I'd have called him back and said, "Okay, Ralph, I'm having a press conference of my own to announce that for every day you don't meet my demand of $25,000 it will cost you $500 a day. Think that one over."

Maybe I wouldn't have gotten $25,000, but I bet I would've gotten more than eighteen-five. I could tell from the negative reaction Ralph got in the press. And I got a lot of letters from distinguished citizens and season-ticket holders, all of them expressing outrage at Houk. That's when I realized I should have held out. It was also when Ralph Houk, I think, started to hate me.

The real kicker came the following year. I had won eighteen games and two in the World Series. Call from Houk:

"Well, what do you want?"

"Ordinarily, I'd say winning eighteen and two in the Series would be worth about an $8,000 raise."

"Good, I'll send you a contract calling for twenty-six-five."

"But in view of what's happened, last year and the year before that, it will have to be more."

"How much more?"

"At least thirty."

"We couldn't do that. It's out of the question."

A couple of days later he called again. "Does $28,000 sound fair to you?"

"Yes, it does, very fair. In fact there are a lot of fair figures. Twenty-eight, twenty-nine, thirty, thirty-two. I'd say thirty-three would be too high and twenty-seven on down would be unfair on your part."

"So you're prepared to sign now."

"Not yet. I haven't decided."

A week later he called again and said he'd sent me the contract I wanted—$28,000.

"Now, wait a minute. I didn't say I'd sign for that."

"But you said it was a fair figure."

"I said there were a lot of fair figures in there. I said thirty-two was fair too."

"You going back on your word? You trying to pull a fast one on me?"

"I'm not trying to pull anything on you. I just haven't decided what I'm going to sign for. I just know that twenty-eight isn't it."

By now he's shouting. "Goddammit, you're trying to renege on a deal."

So I shouted back. "Who the hell do you people think you are, trying to bully people around? You have a goddam one-way contract, and you won't let a guy negotiate. You bulldozed me into a contract my first year when I didn't know any better, you tried to fine me for not signing last year, and now you're trying to catch me in a lie. Why don't you just be decent about it? What's an extra thousand or two to the New York Yankees? You wonder why you get bad publicity. Well, here it is. As soon as the people find out the kind of numbers you're talking about they realize how mean and stupid you are."

"All right. Okay. Okay. No use getting all hot about it."

When the contract came it was like he said, $28,000. I called and told him I wouldn't sign it. I told him I wouldn't play unless I got thirty.

"No deal," he said, and hung up.

Moments later the phone rang. Houk: "Okay, you get your thirty. Under one condition. That you don't tell anybody you're getting it."

"Ralph, I can't do that. I've told everybody the numbers before. I can't stop now."

Softly. "Well, I wish you wouldn't."

Just as softly. "Well, maybe I won't."

When the newspaper guys got to me I felt like a jerk. I also felt I owed Ralph a little something. So when they said, "Did you get what you wanted?" I said, "Yeah." And when they said, "What did you want?" I said, "Thirty." But I said it very low.

Now, I think, Ralph really hated my guts. Not so much because I told about the thirty but because he thought I went back on my word.

Four years later Ralph Houk was still angry. By this time I had started up a little real-estate business in New Jersey. A few friends, relatives and I pooled our money, bought some older houses in good neighborhoods, fixed them up and rented them to executives who come to New York on temporary assignment. Houses like that are hard to find and Houk, who lives in Florida, needed

one for the '69 season. After a long search he found exactly what he wanted. Then he found out I owned it. He didn't take it. Too bad, it might have been kind of fun to be his landlord.

Of course, I may misunderstand the whole thing. It's easy to misunderstand things around a baseball club. Else how do you explain my friend Elston Howard? We both live in New Jersey and during my salary fights we'd work out a bit together. And he always told me, "Stick to your guns. Don't let them push you around." Then he'd go down to spring training and he'd say to the other guys, "That Bouton is really something. Who does he think he is holding out every year? How are we gonna win a pennant if the guys don't get in shape? He should be down here helping the club."

I didn't help the club much in 1965, which was the year the Yankees stopped winning pennants. I always had a big overhand motion and people said that it looked, on every pitch, as though my arm was going to fall off with my cap. I used to laugh, because I didn't know what they meant. In 1965 I figured it out. It was my first sore arm. It was my only sore arm. And it made me what I am today, an aging knuckleballer.

My record that year was 4–15, and we finished sixth. It wasn't all my fault. I needed lots of help and got it. Nevertheless my spirits were high waiting for my contract because of something Houk had said. He'd been painted into a corner with Roger Maris. There was a story around that after Maris hit the 61 home runs he got a five-year, no-cut contract. But he'd had a series of bad years and should have been cut. So to take himself off the hook with Maris, Houk said that anybody who had a poor year because of injuries would not be cut. Fabulous, man, I thought. That's me.

When I got my contract it called for $23,000, a $7,000 cut.

"But, Ralph, I was injured and you said . . ."

"You weren't injured."

"The hell I wasn't."

"Then how come you pitched 150 innings?"

"I was trying to do what I could, build my arm up, trying to help the team."

Somehow he remained unmoved. I guessed it was my turn to be humble. "Look, Ralph, I know that people think you lost the battle with me last year and I know some of the players are upset that I got $30,000. So I know there are reasons you have to cut me. Tell you what. Even though I could stand firm on the injury thing if I wanted to, I'll make a deal with you. Cut me $3,000 and we can both be happy." He said okay.

After that, it was all downhill. Which is how come I was happy to be making $22,000 with the Seattle Pilots.

This article appeared in *USA Weekend* in 1986.

# The Best in the Land

## ERIK BRADY

Do you know him?

Probably not. He doesn't even have an American Express card.

But maybe you should know *about* Craig Elliott: He's the best softball player in the land. And that's saying a lot, since about 22 million people in the USA play the game.

"I'm not sure I'm *the* best," Elliott says. "There are two or three other guys in the running."

Maybe so, but Elliott, 34, is softball's answer to Babe Ruth—from his prodigious home runs to his size 40 waist.

And his team, Steele's Sports Co. of Grafton, Ohio, is softball's answer to Ruth's Yankees: Next month, it will defend its slow-pitch super division title and Elliott his MVP award.

Still not convinced? In 1983 Elliott hit a record *390* homers.

Anything else? Well, yeah. But let Elliott tell it. "Once I came up and there were no outfielders. I didn't know what was going on, but then there they were, all four of 'em, standing *behind* the outfield fence, waving their gloves at me. That was a good one."

How else do you stop a 6-foot-4, 300-pound behemoth with the fluid swing of a big league batting champ? The answer: 7 times out of 10, you don't.

When Elliott strides into a pitch, arms extended, weight behind him, the result is often the same. *Thunk!* Home run. "I'm a tough guy to get out," he says.

Elliott is an affable Alabaman with a profitable paving business in Wadley, a town with fewer citizens—532—than his 708 runs batted in last season.

Wife Susan and children John, 6, and Jeni, 4, see a lot of softball. "We all love it," says Susan, "which is a lucky thing."

Elliott began Little League baseball at age 7 and softball at 15. Now, 19 years, 175 pounds and thousands of home runs later, he is softball's superstar.

Elliott rises at 4 or 5 on summer mornings so he can be off work in time for hitting clinics.

"If I had my way I would play softball from dawn to dusk," he says. "There is nothing in the world I would rather do."

And it doesn't matter at what position. Elliott can be pitcher, catcher or designated hitter.

But hitting is his specialty—.711 in last season's playoffs. His goal is a repeat next month, "only I want more homers."

Always does. When he hit 390, Elliott wished for 10 more. "Nothing like the sight of a softball dropping over the fence."

Especially when it means money in his pocket. Elliott is an amateur in name only. He has a personal services contract with Steele's to promote its products.

Steele's sells softball equipment, including a 35-ounce aluminum bat called "The Elliott" (price: $44). Its namesake could make as much as $100,000 over three seasons.

On weekends he flies to wherever Steele's plays. This weekend he's in Philadelphia and Trenton, N.J. Next weekend he'll be in Rochester, N.Y.

Elliott admits he swings for the fences 99 percent of the time. But he never points beyond the outfield in the manner of Babe Ruth calling a home run. "I'm cocky," Elliott says, "but not that cocky."

Just how cocksure is this guy? He says if you put baseball's best hitters on a softball diamond to play Steele's, it would be no contest. "We'd beat 'em bad," he says. "Shoot, yeah!"

The film version of this novel is rated (see Bert Sugar's entry later in this volume) as one of the ten best baseball movies ever made. A lot of people think the book was even more fun. This section takes up just after Bingo Long has decided to form his own team.

# From *The Bingo Long Traveling All-Stars and Motor Kings*

## WILLIAM BRASHLER

BINGO AND Leon were stooped under the hood of Bingo's Auburn when Louis drove up in front of Chessie Joy's place in his 1938 Lincoln V-12 convertible. Bingo was fingering his spark plug cables, making sure his man at the garage had put them in shape for the road. Louis left his Lincoln idling and hopped out with Mungo Redd, Splinter Tommy Washington, Isaac Nettles, and Fat Sam Popper. Bingo had talked each one of them into jumping the Aces for his All-Stars. The only Ace infielder to balk at the offer was Gerald Purvis, and he was into Sallie for a thousand because of a new La Salle. If Gerald took off and left the La Salle behind, Sallie would grab it and keep what Gerald had already paid him. Gerald was the only player Sallie had comfortably over the barrel. The others had grown wary of Sallie's financial setups long ago. When Bingo approached them with his offer and his sales pitch, they were easily persuaded. He had enough money up front to turn their heads.

Since second-line pitcher Turkey Travis had agreed to come along, Bingo needed only a center fielder and a first baseman to fill out his squad. He let Ezell Carter paint the team's name on the side of his Auburn with whitewash. Ezell messed up "Traveling" and "Motor Kings" pretty bad, but he got Bingo Long spelled right, so Bingo told him it was a good job. Louis had the initials "B.L.T.A.S.M.K. #2" painted on his Lincoln and he added a few five-point stars for class.

Louis was dressed in his custom blue pin-striped suit and vest. But the clothes couldn't begin to disguise that on all of Louis's five feet eleven inches hung only 140 pounds. His neck sprouted out of his collar into a wide, wet smile, giving him a look like he'd just finished his high school graduation. He cocked a skinny-visored touring cap on his head and, for the occasion, he sported a pair of snow white spats.

"Oh, there is a pretty partner!" Bingo howled when he laid eyes on him.

"Dressed up for the leaving," Louis said. He spun around and jerked his hips. "This town is seeing the last of this third baseman for a time."

"My, my, what a dandy," Leon said as he and the others looked Louis over. They were wearing suits as well; Bingo featured his usual carnation in the lapel.

"When you touring you got to do it in fashion," said Bingo. "The people got to know you in town."

Louis's Lincoln was long and spacious, and Bingo's Auburn could easily seat six, so the team had plenty of room for the small satchels they carried with them. Bingo put most of the equipment, the bats and balls he could scrape up, in his trunk. He and Leon drove together since most of the others preferred to go with Louis and sit in the open convertible.

Just before starting off, Isaac Nettles yelled at Bingo and walked over to talk with him. Isaac, who was thirty-eight and showing wisps of gray throughout his scalp, pinched the lines of his brow together as he talked. He was the darkest of all the Aces, with a dour, narrow face. His expression betrayed his age and the fact that he became more concerned about things than did most of the others.

"Hey, what you think about a suggestion I got to make the team complete?" Isaac said.

"Shoot," said Bingo. "I'm open for anything."

"Let's go to Raymond's and take him along. He could be manager or traveling secretary or something like that. Man, it would make it for him."

"Damn, I never thought about that. What you think, Leon?"

Leon looked up at the sky. "Foolish," he said.

"Why? Now just why?" objected Isaac.

"Money," said Leon. "Raymond's dead weight if he can't play. A traveling team can't afford no luxuries."

"Who says?" said Bingo.

Leon shook his head. "Damn, Bingo, common sense says it."

"Shit. Let's show Sallie how to take care of a top-rate ball player. Raymond can manage things like Isaac said, like counting up the take and all, until he gets his wheel back in shape."

"You a good man, Bingo," Isaac said. "Raymond will fly when we shows up."

Isaac ran back to Louis's car and the two autos started out. Leon hung his head off to the side of the seat. Bingo grinned at him. "You got to have understanding when you running a ball team, Leon. That's what it's about." He turned the car onto Raymond's street.

Bingo had not broken the final news of the team's formation to Sallie in person. He preferred instead to get his men together on that Friday morning and quietly leave for Pittsburgh. It was best not to get Sallie into another argument, for then Sallie would let loose with a bunch of threats in desperation just to keep his team. He would have to carry out the threats sooner or later or admit that he was licked. Lionel had told Bingo to break without that kind of fuss. It lacked style but the effect would be just as permanent. Sallie would have to cancel most of his league commitments unless he could assemble a ghost squad in time. Even then, he would lose his gate as soon as the people saw that Bingo, Leon, and most of the rest of the regulars were missing. The timing was also good, for Sallie was in hot water with the local politicians because of a craps operation he was running out of his restaurant. He wouldn't have a prayer in court if he tried to bring Bingo and the others in for breach of contract. He'd have to get back at Bingo on his own, and that gave Bingo the benefit of time. Bingo could have his team halfway across the country before Sallie could do anything to stop him, if he could stop him at all. The only thing Bingo knew for certain was that Sallie, sooner or later, would try.

Lionel Foster stood outside his Chop House eying the automobiles which had just parked in front of him. "So we have the Motor Kings, yes we do," he announced. A pair of his counter girls stepped out onto the sidewalk. They smiled at Bingo and Louis and rubbed the door of Louis's Lincoln as if it were too hot to touch.

"We is made for the open road," yelled Bingo.

"Lionel, you ever dream we'd be looking this good?"

Louis got out of his car and clicked his heels. The girls stroked their thighs and purred at him.

"Now we only wonders if you can play some ball," Lionel said and ushered Bingo into the restaurant.

He set the team up with beers and steaks and then sat down at a table with Bingo and Leon.

"Glad to see the old man with you," Lionel said, nodding at Leon. "I thought you was a slave to Sallie's plantation for good, Leon. I did."

Leon looked at Lionel out of the corner of his eye but said nothing.

"I talk faster than Sallie, that's all," Bingo said.

"Or you got to say something different," said Lionel. He shook the ice in his whiskey. "But I'm glad to see you, Leon, because you is another reason why this might turn out to be some good money spent. Just so things don't get away from my man Bingo here. How about it, Bingo? Sallie fight you before you got away?"

"I did it like you said to, Lionel. We played Wednesday some boys from Ranolia and yesterday when we had off I did my packing and this morning we was gone. Sallie couldn't done it better hisself."

"He going to fight you every way. But if you got the odds, you can keep him off you until you rich enough to come back and do anything you want. Them papers ain't worth much to Sallie if he ain't got the boys to go with them. He can't do nothing because them courts is glad to see colored stumble around after themselves. Judge told me I was too rich for any nigger so he wasn't going to help me get more. That's what they going to tell Sallie when he try to get you."

"Funny talk coming from you," Leon said.

"Ain't it though?" Lionel agreed. "Here I is pulling for you boys like you was runaway slaves on the river." Lionel laughed out loud.

"Who says we ain't," said Leon.

"Ain't no slave ever run away with the money you got in your pocket, Leon. Remember that when you feeling like a slave sometime." Lionel finished his drink.

Bingo sawed at his steak. "I just brought Leon along to keep things laughing, Lionel. You know he ain't worth a nickel."

Lionel smiled once again and refilled his glass from the bottle on the table. He had always liked Bingo. Bingo never made trouble, never raised a fuss. He leaned over to him.

"You know what you got to do to make this thing move. You been on the road before so you know. The big cities is easy because the people know you and there is a lot of colored to come out. But when you get to those one-lump towns you is going to have to *sell* the product, you know that, Bingo. They ain't going to be putting out just to see their boys beat by the darkies so you got to show them something they ain't seen before and take your chances. You know you got to show first and win second before you going to take their money.''

"Yeah, yeah, I know," said Bingo.

"Good. And watch out for the police because they can cut you when they wants to. There ain't no money sitting in the can."

"What our suits look like? You got them, Lionel?"

"The ladies is going on them. They some Elite suits with some fancy lettering. Don't worry about the out-fits," he said.

"Okay, I won't," said Bingo.

Lionel gave Bingo Donus Youngs, a good fielding first baseman, and a kid outfielder by the name of Joe Calloway. Calloway had been a bat boy until he was old enough to try out for the Elite Giants. He was only eighteen, but Lionel thought he might be good enough to travel with Bingo and learn what he could from the Stars. Bingo named him Esquire Joe and told him not to let anything get by him in right field. Joe was tall and bony and Lionel said he had an arm like a rifle.

The uniforms were Elite Giant green and white, with pin stripes and five green stars running across the chest. Bingo had wanted "Bingo's All-Stars" over the numbers in back but Lionel said he didn't have the time for that. Bingo had to admit, though, that the uniforms were top rate, as sharp as any around. In Chicago he would pick up a set of two-tone caps, green bills and white crowns, to complete the outfit.

When they trotted out onto the field for the second game of the Elite Giants doubleheader, the Pittsburgh crowd gave them a loud welcome. Bingo led the team on with his lumbering walk and a smile from ear to ear. When he got to the infield he stopped and bowed to the people. His Stars circled him like elephants in the circus. They had used this entrance on other trips and the crowd loved it. When they stopped running they took out four balls and shuttled them from man to man, crisscross within the circle. They called it hotball because the ball never stopped changing hands and never touched the ground. Louis Keystone finally ended it by grabbing all four balls and putting them in his back pocket. But that did not stop the motions, and for a minute or so the Stars wildly pantomimed hotball with nothing but fresh air changing hands. The fans laughed and whistled, the kids in the crowd tried to figure out what was going on.

Louis, Mungo Redd, and Splinter Tommy Washington went through their routines in infield practice. As they moved, the three of them in their baggy whites and script letters looked identical even though Louis was twice as skinny and taller than the others and Mungo

wore a pair of glasses that all but hid his eyes beneath the bill of his cap and Splinter, for all of his grace and casual nonchalance around the bag, sported a set of teeth so crooked they made him feel awkward and self-conscious off the field. But in the dust of the warm-up, Mungo and Tommy gobbled up double-play balls and skipped through the relay without a bobble. Tommy went across the bag and pivoted in the air with the toss to first. Louis at third took ground balls that skipped at him like stones on cement. After he gloved one, he flipped the ball backhand to a ball boy behind him and then waited for another. To finish up, the infield went through their routine without a ball, jumping and throwing and slapping their gloves in place of it. It was a smooth sight, even better than the hotball act, and the crowd applauded as if the Stars had just pulled one out in the ninth.

Yet there was nothing as sweet as watching Bingo take batting practice. He leaned into each pitch with his huge arms, whipping the bat around and cracking the ball. His usual blast was as high as it was far. At the peak of its ascent it hung in the sky like a dirigible about to burst, and then it lazily fell behind the fence. The kids in blue jeans and barebacks stood behind the backstop and winced each time Bingo smashed one. Some mim-icked him, swinging an imaginary bat as he swung his, and then gazed off into the sky following the ball. They could feel the power, the icy connection stinging through them just as if they had swatted the ball like a fat bug and then circled the bases and heard the cheers. Bingo grinned at them, flexed the muscle in his right arm, and then fouled one straight back into the screen about head-high on the kids. It jolted the wires and sent them ducking and yelling.

Over on the sidelines Leon Carter was warming up. He was to pitch four innings and Turkey Travis would follow up. Louis Keystone was standing next to Leon, priming the crowd for a pregame contest. Four or five men leaned on the fence and listened to Louis's propo-sition.

"A little money against Mr. Leon's arm here. Can I interest a gambling man? Anyone among you all who can take a dollar away from me?"

He waved his hands in front of the men, pointing at Leon's arm as the pitcher warmed up with Sam Popper. Then Louis took out a few one-dollar bills from his back pocket and held them up.

"Right here now. A little money on Mr. Leon's arm. Take no chances, just bet against the man's skill. You win, I'll double your money. Two you take against my one."

Leon threw nonchalantly.

"Popper just holds his glove on a chewing gum wrapper, that's all," Louis said. "He don't move it a half inch, no sir. And old Leon throws the fastball over the wrapper. If he does I take your dollar, if he don't you take two from me. Ain't no man perfect, and that's the game. C'mon, gentlemen, you be the judge. Just a friendly gamble among us.''

He flashed his bills up and fanned them. Three of the men held up a dollar. Fat Sam wadded up a wrapper and tossed it in front of him. Then he held his glove over it. Leon wound up and threw, and he missed the wrapper by a foot on the right.

''Oh, man, you is losing it and costing me money right off,'' Louis yelped.

He walked in front of the three men and peeled off two bucks for each. He then repeated the challenge. The same three and two more held up a buck. Leon wound and threw; Sam Popper never budged his mitt. The ball streaked into it like a beam of light. Louis hopped down the row of men and took their bills. All five put another in the air. Leon again reached back and threw and Fat Sam's mitt didn't move. Louis quickly grabbed his money. He held the bills up and called the bettors.

''Now it's a man's game, boys. You seen him do it and you seen him miss. Old Louis here is the fool because I plays every time and pays every time. Put your money against the man's arm. Show me what you got.''

The first three men flashed bills again. Leon uncorked another fastball over the wrapper. Only two men followed with bills. Leon threw another down the center. Louis took their money. Four in a row. Louis didn't advertise anymore, but stared at Popper's mitt. Five was a good number; four men put their money up. Leon split the wrapper again. Louis hustled to collect. Only one man put up his dollar after that. But Leon hit home once more. Each ball had been thrown the same, like a machine had done it, and Sam never moved his mitt enough to raise a question about it. The man flashed another dollar. He glared at Leon, daring him to throw another strike. Leon threw, Louis took the dollar. Once more, Leon threw a submarine fastball, and Louis snatched the bill.

The man fanned his face with his hat. ''You is worse than craps, Carter,'' he said. He waved Louis away. Louis stuffed the bills into his back pocket and trotted to the bench. Leon split the wrapper a few more times and put his warm-up jacket on. Then he walked to the bench to get his money from Louis.

The All-Stars met little resistance from the Elite Giants. It was the Giants' second game of the day, an ''appearance'' game as they called it, a game set up for the fans instead of the players. They played nonchalantly, kidding the All-Stars about the routines Bingo made them go through. Leon glided through the line-up with an assortment of experimental pitches, and Bingo's men jumped on three Elite pitchers for nine runs. Only

Esquire Joe Calloway showed badly with three swinging strike-outs, but he did bring in a long drive over his shoulder near the right-field fence. Bingo liked him, he liked how the kid galloped along the grass, he liked the kid's arm, and he liked Joe's big, level swing, even though it didn't hit anything that afternoon. Most of all, Bingo liked the way Esquire Joe seemed to enjoy himself while he played. He held a loose, close-mouthed grin on his face as he cradled long flies. There were few things Bingo liked better than watching an outfielder outrun a high blast and then bring it home like a soft peach off a tree.

''You boys doing good, real good,'' Lionel said to Bingo as they walked from the field after the game. ''You got class and you got talent like nobody I seen around. You play it right, Bingo, and you ain't going to be able to keep the people from giving you their money.''

Lionel had contacted some of the big promoters in the Midwest and set up a half dozen games in Cleveland, Toledo, and Chicago. These were all league towns, so the All-Stars had to work around schedules to get their games. After Chicago they could hit Milwaukee and then head west across Wisconsin and Iowa.

''You got to watch out for the other barnstormers like Max Helverton's Hooley Speedballers and them white teams from Michigan, them House of David boys with the beards,'' Lionel told Bingo. ''You can't follow them because you lose the edge on the towns. You can play them but when you is done you should go in the opposite direction. It ain't trouble; it's just good business. And remember too, Bingo, that you got to hit those towns when they ain't doing nothing big like harvesting or something because then you lose your crowd. Otherwise they going to welcome you like you was a circus.''

Bingo already knew most of what Lionel was telling him, but he listened anyway because Lionel had run almost every kind of traveling show around. Lionel helped him get up some paper for advertising and letters to send to town post offices announcing the All-Stars' arrival. The night before the team took off for Cleveland, Bingo sat down with Lionel and went over possible routines and antics to please the crowds. ''Remember,'' Lionel said, ''ain't nothing around pleases more than good ball playing. Better than folks has ever seen. They remember it because it *amazes* them. Yeah, it does.''

Bingo called a meeting that night after the players had come in from the Chop House.

''I been doing some talking and some planning and I'm ready to present you with what we going to be doing on this tour. Now you all know how to play and how to look good like we did yesterday with the Giants. And when we be playing the big teams like the Detroit

Cubans and the Velvets in Chicago and around in there
we won't have no trouble either because they is our own
people watching and we know what they likes. But some
of you ain't been past Chicago and you don't know what
happens out there. In them dog towns we got to play it
with our nose. We got to please the people who works
them farms. And if they want to see us clown then we
clown them until they dead. But if they want to see us
play straight then we do and take our chances against
what they got. We just can't be looking bad or noncha-
lant or no good. Because then they be calling us a bunch
of shuffles and they ain't going to be throwing their
quarters in our socks. So they ain't much we can do until
we see what the situation is but we got to be ready. We
got to be polite and cheerful all the time even when we
ain't feeling it. If we get trouble we just be leaving by
the back way and getting on down the road with our
hands in our pockets and whistling like we stole the
lady's pie. Now that is something I thought I should say
right off so you know where this team stands. Lionel say
if we play it right we going to take their money. I think
he's right because he been around. He takes some lumps
too, yes he does. But that's what I got to say."

He stopped and wiped his mouth. Nobody said
anything. Then he went on.

"We going to be playing a lot of white outfits too.
Some of you ain't played much against white so you got
to be prepared. They take what they can out of you if
you don't be on your guard. They going to slide into
your leg and step on your foot if you leave it out there in
plain sight. They going to be saying the same old things
to rattle you and get you to forget how to play right. But
they ain't nothing. They got to pitch to you when you up
to the plate. I hit everything a white pitch can throw and
they don't like it but they can't do much but run after it.
So that's how we play them. You keep your heads
turned behind your back all the time for something
sneaking up on you. That's the way you play white."

Bingo stopped again and waited for a reaction. He
could feel himself getting excited. The players sat and
looked at him, blinking their eyes. Louis Keystone
yawned.

"That was a nice speech, Bingo. Real nice," Leon
finally said.

"Yeah, thanks, Leon," Bingo said, and he sat down
and pulled out a Lucky.

A picture spread in *The Second Fireside Book of Baseball* showed the way political cartoonists love to make use of baseball. This piece by David Broder and the ones by Tom Wicker and George Will toward the end of this volume exhibit the same love on the part of political columnists. It may indeed be the one thing they all agree on.

# 22nd Amendment: A Pitch for Repeal

## DAVID S. BRODER

WASHINGTON—WALKING down to the White House the other day, I encountered a rally of right-wing youths calling for repeal of the 22nd Amendment. It took all of my professional self-discipline to keep from grabbing a placard and joining in the demonstration.

Adding a provision to the Constitution to deny a president the option of running for a third term was a crackpot idea from the beginning. It was retroactive revenge by the Republicans against the ghost of Franklin D. Roosevelt. Having failed to defeat him in his lifetime, the frustrated conservatives wrote themselves an amendment guaranteeing no one else would ever occupy the White House as long as FDR had.

The ninnies didn't even realize that their own action would serve to certify his unique place in history. But all that is forgotten, and now the new generation of right-wingers wishes to repeal the 22nd Amendment, in order to perpetuate the wonders of the Reagan administration.

More power to them, say I. I don't give a hoot what their real motives may be. Some of them see it as a little bouquet for the president, who has made it clear he is going to retire in 1989, no matter what. Others see it as a nice fund-raising and organizing device. Still others are using it to send a not-too-subtle message of no confidence in George Bush as Reagan's successor.

Whatever their real game, I wish them every success. The Constitution can only be improved by pruning such extraneous and unwise growths as the 22nd Amendment. As President Reagan has said, each generation should be free to decide for itself whether to keep someone in the Oval Office for another four years or boot him out. It's a subject on which the Constitution was eloquently silent for a century and three-quarters and once again should be rendered mute.

But there is a stronger reason than constitutional theory for eliminating the 22nd Amendment—a reason of which I was particularly conscious this past weekend. I see repeal of the 22nd Amendment as a means to the more important end of bringing back baseball to Washington.

It was no coincidence, ladies and gentlemen, that the 22nd Amendment became law in 1951 and exactly 20 years later, in 1971, the Washington Senators left town. It took just that long for the greedy and not-too-bright owners of the team to realize that locking the door to a third term gave them an opening to skip to putatively greener pastures.

The Senators decamped on Richard Nixon's watch. This was not the Watergate-weakened Nixon of 1974, but a president enjoying his full authority. In 1971, Nixon was strong enough to impose wage and price controls on the American economy. But on the much more vital matter of saving baseball for the capital, the 22nd Amendment had rendered him a premature lame duck. In my reading of history, conservative tampering with the Constitution clearly cost Washington its team. Repeal of the 22nd Amendment will bring back baseball.

We need it back to improve the quality of life and of the presidency. Every real patriot cherishes the National Game. Few would ever seek employment in a city where they are denied the basic American right to go to the ballpark and root for the home team.

Ronald Reagan was persuaded to give up watching the Dodgers for eight years, but they had to promise him Normandy Beach, the Olympics and the Statue of Liberty in return. The best of his possible successors flatly refuse to seek the White House because of the absence of baseball in Washington. I am thinking of such statesmen as Lee Iacocca and Charlton Heston, who understandably will not give up their Tigers or Dodgers tickets to take a job which requires them to spend their summers in a city without baseball.

If we get rid of the 22nd Amendment and a newly inaugurated president thought he might be here as long as FDR, I guarantee you he would get a baseball franchise for Washington. That would, of course, be a blessing for those like myself, who are trapped in boring, dead-end jobs in Washington with no way out. But it would also be in the clearest self-interest of the voters and taxpayers of America to get baseball back into Washington as soon as possible.

Deficits will decrease, the bureaucrats will work harder and even the Senate will find agreement easier when once again the magic words can be uttered, "As soon as we're done, we can go out and catch the game."

There is no way the Senate would stay in session, spending your tax dollars, as it did last Saturday, a perfect baseball afternoon, if there were a game on tap three miles away.

The best program for constitutional and political reform in Washington can be summed up in two lines:

Repeal the Twenty-Second.

And bring back the Nine.

The first time I read this piece, I wondered how anybody could justify classifying it as poetry. The fifth time, I wondered how you could call it anything else.

# Rules for a Softball Game/Office Picnic, 1984

## BOBBY BYRD

1. ONE LADY ON THE FIELD AT ALL TIMES.
2. EVERY PLAYER MUST PLAY AT LEAST TWO INNINGS (CONSECUTIVE).
3. STRAIGHT SLOW PITCH.
4. NO UMPIRES?
5. NO WALKS.
6. NO STEALS.
7. NO BUNTS.
8. ONE BASE ON THROWAWAYS.
9. ONE GUY OVER 50 AT ALL TIMES.

This is one of a number of pieces collected in a remarkable book by Richard Grossinger called *The Temple of Baseball* and published by North Atlantic Books in (why not?) Berkeley, California.

# Playing Possum

———————— • JAMES B. CAROTHERS • ————————

THIS WAS in Virginia. That first year I was just an assistant coach. "How come there aren't any black kids playing ball in this league?" I said.

"What are you trying to do," they said, "start some kind of a crusade?"

The next year I was a head coach. The league had city-wide tryouts. "When I draft a black ballplayer," I said, "which one of you is going to burn a cross on my lawn?"

"What do you think we are, anyway," they said.

I waited until the last round to see if anybody else would do it.

"Clarence Williams," I said. "I draft Clarence Williams." They didn't say anything for a short minute.

"He's *colored*," one of them said.

"He looked like a ballplayer to me," I said.

"You better hope to hell you know what you're doing," another said.

"He didn't look to me like the only black kid at those tryouts who could play ball in this league," I said.

"We don't want to get too many," they said.

His birth certificate had said Clarence, but everyone but his mother called him the Possum. After our first practice I drove him home and told him what I thought he might be up against. "We be okay," he said. I told him about Jackie Robinson. "Jackie Robinson voted for Nixon," he said. "Ball is ball."

The Possum was flat-footed and pigeon-toed, but he could hit. He talked to the ball after he hit it, taking a sharp left-handed cut and watching the ball as he labored toward first base. "Get down, you mother. Get down." That first year I played him in left field and he hit .415 and led the league in RBI's. We won the league by three games.

"That's Black Power," I said.

The next year there were eight more black ballplayers in the league. I moved the Possum in to first base so he wouldn't have to do so much running. He was reading Eldridge Cleaver and Malcolm X and he wanted to change his name to Clarence X, but everyone still called him Possum. He got himself an enormous cheap yellow first-baseman's mitt somewhere and he covered it with a ball-point rainbow of names and shades and shapes: Clarence X, Soulpossum, *Didelphis virginiana*, The Poss. There was a clenched fist, and an upside-down American flag. And on the back of the wide thumbpiece in electric purple: *Up Against the Wall, Outfielder*. "She my tattooed Lady," he said, pounding his fist into the soft pocket. "We be going to the circus."

Also on the team that year was a big white kid named Bobby Foster. He hit the ball a long way once at the tryouts, and I picked him for that, but he never hit one that far again. He was just big, kind of sullen, and not too bright. He kept his hands tight to his body with the bat low, so he had a bad hitch in his swing and he couldn't get the bat around quickly or with any power.

Early that year I gave the team a speech about how there were probably 1,500 boys of baseball age in that town, but the league had only 120 uniforms, so if they didn't want to come to practice or show up for games on time we could find somebody else who would. Bobby Foster showed up, but he didn't get to play much. I kept the Possum out of one game because he showed up late, and he didn't say anything. Then his friend Swamp told me that the Possum had been made to work late at the store where he carried groceries to the cars. I apologized. "You should have said something," I said.

"I coulda been here," the Possum said. "You got your rule."

Now in July that year we were playing a game on a hot afternoon, the kind of day when the hitting is good. The field was set in front of an ancient concrete amphitheater where the fans sat. It was Saturday, so there were about a hundred people watching, fathers in sport shirts, mothers in double-knit slacks, and the old men, the casuals who are always at ball games. It was real heat. You could see it shimmering beyond the brown diamond above the green outfield. We were losing, and the other team had runners on second and third with two out. The batter fell away from a high, inside pitch and hit a looping pop fly off the handle of the bat deep down the first-base line. The Possum ran out after it as hard as he could go, with the runners tearing around the bases and the fans and coaches and players yelling, and he dived for the ball and speared it just above the grass. It was a tough play to make, probably the toughest for a first baseman. The Possum bounced up and showed the umpire the ball. It was stuck in the top of the web, a scoop of vanilla ice cream above the rainbow leather.

The team came running in from the field, still yelling. The Possum rolled the ball toward the pitcher's mound and trotted past our bench to the bat rack. A few of the fans were still clapping. "Way to go, Possum," said Bobby Foster, jumping up from the bench. "Nice catch, boy."

Possum wheeled from the bat rack. He slammed the rainbow mitt into the dust and looked at Bobby Foster. "What you say to me?"

Bobby Foster grinned. The regulars rarely acknowledged him. "I said nice catch, boy." The Possum strode hotly toward the bigger boy and bumped him with his chest. Bobby Foster stumbled backwards in surprise. "Whassamatter, boy? I said NICE CATCH!" Our other players were crowding around. I could see the other team's shortstop take a practice throw and hold the ball,

watching. Behind us, from the concrete amphitheater above the diamond, there was a murmur.

Bobby Foster was sweating now. "Did I say something wrong?" He appealed to me. "You heard what I said, Coach. All I ever said was Way to Go and Nice Catch."

I was watching the Possum. He turned toward the bat rack and selected a bat. "Bobby Foster," he said slowly, "you is sooo dumb." Then he turned to me. I was watching the bat in his clenched fist. "Fifteen hundred kids in this town could be playin' ball," he said, shaking his head in disbelief, "and *you* go and pick Bobby Foster."

He walked away from the bench toward the on-deck circle, flexing the bat behind his shoulders. "Ain't it somethin'," he said to no one in particular. "Ain't it somethin' how the man that makes a great play in the field is always first man up in the next inning." He whipped the bat through the hot air. "Let's go get us some runs. We in this thing."

The Possum drifted away from the team toward the end of the season. We were out of the race early, and I began to play some of the younger kids. I made a few phone calls and drove around town looking for the Possum, but no one seemed to know where he was. The manager of the store where he worked said he'd just quit. "What kind of trouble's he in?" he asked me. "He told somebody here he was going to Pittsburgh."

During infield practice before a game I asked Swamp about this. Swamp considered the matter briefly, looking down and kicking at the dirt by the third base line with his spiked shoe. "Naw," he said decisively, "I don't know where he's at. But he didn't go to no Pittsburgh."

This one went 16 innings, a record for any postseason game, and the Mets, with their second consecutive extra-inning victory over the Houston Astros, won the 1986 National League playoff. "All I know," said Wally Backman, the New York second baseman, "is if my kid was playing, I would have had a heart attack and I might have had more than one." More than one sports reporter called it the best game in playoff history. (Three days earlier, as Dan Castellano's *Newark Star-Ledger* colleague Moss Klein reports at another place in this book, they were saying the same thing about the Red Sox and Angels in the American League playoff. Who was right? Everybody, that's who.)

# 1986:
# New York Mets 7,
# Houston Astros 6

## DAN CASTELLANO

THEY FELT the National League pennant would be theirs from the first day of the season. They were patient as they went through a season that produced a club-record 108 victories. They were patient after clinching their division early and sitting back to wait for the playoffs to begin.

But they were never more patient than yesterday, when they had to sit through 16 innings and endure four hours, 42 minutes of incredible baseball.

Finally, it was over. After scoring three runs in the top half of the 16th inning, the Mets suffered through one more Astros' rally that produced two runs and had an Astrodome crowd of 45,718 on its feet and a national television audience absolutely spellbound.

Then, Jesse Orosco struck out Kevin Bass with two men on and the Mets had themselves a 7–6 victory in Game Six of this incredibly exciting playoff series, giving them the series, four games to two, and a berth in the World Series for the third time in their 25-year history, the first since 1973. They'll open the Series Saturday night in New York against the Red Sox.

Ironically, it happened on Oct. 15, making it the 17th anniversary of their only World Series championship, when they defeated the Baltimore Orioles in five games, winning it on Oct. 15, 1969.

"Is that right?" asked Davey Johnson, the man who made the final out for the Orioles in '69 and who now has taken the Mets to the World Series in his third season as their manager.

"I'll tell you this, it wasn't easy," Johnson went on. "This game gave me a headache. But we never panicked and we managed to come back, the way we have all year.

"This was major league baseball at its finest. If you didn't enjoy this, you don't enjoy anything."

Astros' manager Hal Lanier had a different viewpoint. After taking the Astros to the N.L. West title in his rookie year as manager, Lanier fought the favored Mets in a six-game playoff that produced four one-run games and two extra-inning games.

"You have to hand it to the Astros' organization," said Mets' vice president Joe McIlvaine in the jubilant Mets' clubhouse as he wiped his head with a towel following a champagne bath. "Sitting in the stands and watching this game, I felt like I was on Iwo Jima."

What he sat and watched was his own ballclub, the best hitting team in the league this season, continue their offensive frustrations for the first eight innings against Bob Knepper, who took a two-hit shutout and a 3–0 lead into the ninth as the Astros looked like they were going to force a seventh game and another confrontation between the Mets' hitters and Mike Scott.

Scott, of course, had complete game victories in both the Astros' triumphs in the series, limiting the Mets to one run on eight hits in 18 innings, a performance that earned him the Most Valuable Player award for the series, despite the Astros losing.

The Mets didn't really have one hero, one MVP. They had many. But the one who was mentioned most by his teammates in the aftermath of victory yesterday was Lenny Dykstra, whose pinch-hit triple off Knepper in the ninth got the Mets started on a three-run rally that made Knepper's pitching a footnote to what many described as the greatest game they have ever witnessed.

Dykstra's triple to the wall in right-center, only the third hit off Knepper, was followed by Mookie Wilson's soft line drive off second baseman Bill Doran's glove that went into center field for an RBI single.

Kevin Mitchell grounded out, sending Wilson to second, and Keith Hernandez followed with a double to right-center that drove in Wilson and made it a 3-2 ballgame.

Lanier removed Knepper for his ace reliever, Dave Smith, at that point, but Smith, who saved 33 games for the Astros this season but blew Game Three of the playoffs when he gave up Dykstra's ninth inning, game-winning home run, blew another one for Knepper.

He walked Gary Carter and Darryl Strawberry to load the bases before Ray Knight came through with a sacrifice fly to right that scored Hernandez with the tying run.

So they played on, and on, until the 14th inning when Carter opened with a single to right off Aurelio Lopez, who followed that by walking Strawberry. Knight bunted into a force play at third, but Wally Backman, who had entered the game as a pinch-hitter in the ninth and remained in it at second base, lined a single to right to drive in Strawberry with the go-ahead run.

With the champagne in the clubhouse now getting ready to be opened, Jesse Orosco, who had pitched so well in the series, came on to try and save it for Roger McDowell, who pitched five scoreless innings, the longest outing of his career, allowing only one hit.

Orosco struck out Doran, then went to 2–2 on Billy Hatcher before breaking off a wicked slider that appeared to be strike three. Not so, according to plate umpire Fred Brocklander, who had an erratic day at best.

Orosco's next pitch was a hit a ton down the left field line, where it nicked the foul pole for a game-tying home run.

So they played some more. In the 16th, Strawberry got it started against Lopez with a short fly to center that fell in front of Hatcher for a double. Knight singled to right to drive in the go-ahead run. The Mets added two more in the inning when Jeff Calhoun came into the game for Houston and threw two wild pitches to force in one run, then gave up an RBI single to Dykstra.

And Orosco needed each of those runs when he went out to face the persistent Astros in the bottom of the inning. There was a one-out walk to Davey Lopes, a single by Doran, an RBI single by Hatcher and a force-out grounder by Denny Walling that left runners on first and third with two-out and the lead down to a precarious two runs.

Glenn Davis blooped a single to center to drive in Doran and that lead was now one as the Astrodome shook with the delirium of the masses.

But Orosco struck out Bass, throwing him nothing but sliders, and the Mets' celebration began.

"He wasn't gonna give me anything to hit," said Bass, "just nasty sliders down and in. It was kind of like I was up there swatting flies. I'm not stupid. I knew what was coming. I just couldn't hit it."

"This is the most satisfying point of my career," said Hernandez. "All the players in the National League wanted to see us get beat. I don't care how they feel now. But they have to respect us as a team.

"As for my feelings, I did not want to go to Game Seven. Let Mike Scott put his arm on the shelf until next spring."

"I don't drink," said Wilson. "I hate champagne. But I'm drinking it now. When that last out was made, I thought it was a dream. I've waited so long for this moment, playing with a lot of bad ballclubs here. But it's all worth it.

"And I don't think anything that happens in the World Series can match this."

"I agree," said Johnson. "We can't top this feeling. This is the ultimate for me."

*"If they make three outs, then we get up."*

This story is actually just one-third of the mind-boggling pine tar incident. The second part came a couple of days later, when Lee MacPhail, then president of the American League, reversed the umpires, and the third some time afterward when, taking up where they had left off in the ninth, the two teams, performing in an all-but-empty Yankee Stadium, played out the rest of the game, this time with Brett's homer counting and giving the Royals a 5–4 victory.

This first part of the story made page one of *The New York Times*. So did the second part. So did the third part.

# 1983:
# New York Yankees 4,
# Kansas City Royals 3 (or 5)

## MURRAY CHASS

BASEBALL GAMES often end with home runs, but until yesterday the team that hit the home run always won. At Yankee Stadium yesterday, the team that hit the home run lost.

If that unusual development produced a sticky situation, blame it on pine tar.

With two out in the ninth inning, George Brett of the Kansas City Royals hit a two-run home run against Rich Gossage that for several minutes gave the Royals a 5–4 lead over the Yankees. But Brett was called out by the umpires for using an illegal bat—one with an excessive amount of pine tar. The ruling, after a protest by Billy Martin, the Yankees' manager, enabled the Yankees to wind up with a 4–3 victory.

"I can sympathize with George," Gossage remarked after the game, "but not that much."

The outcome, which the Royals immediately protested, is certain to be talked about for years to come, because it was one of the more bizarre finishes any game has ever had.

"I couldn't believe it," Brett said, infinitely more calm than when he charged at the umpires after their controversial call.

"It knocks you to your knees," added Dick Howser, the Kansas City manager. "I'm sick about it. I don't like it. I don't like it at all. I don't expect my players to accept it."

What the Royals refused to believe or accept was that the umpires ruled the home run did not count because Brett's bat had too much pine tar on it.

Pine tar is a sticky brown substance batters apply to their bats to give them a better grip. Baseball rule 1.10 (b) says a bat may not be covered by such a substance more than 18 inches from the tip of the handle. Joe Brinkman, the chief of the crew that umpired the game, said Brett's bat had "heavy pine tar" 19 or 20 inches from the tip of the handle and lighter pine tar for another three or four inches.

The umpires did not use a ruler to measure the pine tar on Brett's 34½-inch bat; they didn't have one. So they placed it across home plate, which measures 17 inches across.

When they did, they saw that the pine tar exceeded the legal limit. The four umpires conferred again, and then Tim McClelland, the home plate umpire, thrust his right arm in the air, signaling that Brett was out. His call prompted two reactions:

Brett, enraged, raced out of the dugout and looked as if he would run over McClelland. Brinkman, however, intercepted him, grabbing him around the neck. "In that situation," Brinkman said later, "you know something's going to happen. It was quite traumatic. He was upset."

Gaylord Perry of the Royals, who has been long accused of doing things illegal with a baseball, tried to swipe the evidence, according to Brinkman.

"Gaylord got the bat and passed it back and tried to

get it to the clubhouse," Brinkman said. "The security people went after it, but I got in there and got it. Steve Renko, another Kansas City pitcher, had it. He was the last in line. He didn't have anyone to hand it to."

Why the stadium security men went after the bat was not clear.

"I didn't know what was going on," Howser said. "I saw guys in sport coats and ties trying to intercept the bat. It was like a Brink's robbery. Who's got the gold? Our players had it, the umpires had it. I don't know who has it—the C.I.A., a think tank at the Pentagon."

Brinkman, when asked about the stadium security's bat force, said, "Maybe if it had been reversed, the bat might be gone."

The umpires declined to show the bat, which they said was on its way to the American League office. Presumably, Lee MacPhail, the league president, will study the bat and measure the pine tar today, then rule on the Royals' protest.

Martin, who has had a few violent encounters with umpires himself, was as peaceful and as smug as he could be about the whole incident.

"We noticed the pine tar on his bat in Kansas City," he said, alluding to the team's visit there two weeks ago. "You don't call him on it if he makes an out. After he hit the home run, I went out and said he's using an illegal bat."

"It's a terrible rule, but if it had happened to me I would have accepted it," Martin said. "It turned out to be a lovely Sunday afternoon."

It was also a bizarre Sunday afternoon—so bizarre, in fact, that the Yankees' computer couldn't digest it. When the operator of the computer tried to expunge Brett's home run, which he had already fed into the computer, it balked and refused to spit out the box score of the game and updated Yankee statistics.

As Brett, by now in the dugout after his triumphant trot around the bases, watched the discussion on the field, he laughed. "They didn't have a case," the Royals' leading hitter said.

But the umpires obviously thought Martin did have a case, although Brinkman acknowledged that pine tar, unlike cork or nails, has no effect on the distance a ball will travel.

"I was aware of the rule," Brett said, "but I thought it couldn't go past the label. Some umpires, when they see the pine tar too high, will say, 'Hey, George, clean up your bat.' "

Why was the pine tar that high on Brett's bat?

"I don't wear batting gloves," Brett explained, showing his calloused hands. "I like the feel of raw skin on raw wood. But you also don't want to hold the bat where pine tar is, so you put it up higher on the bat, get some on your hands when you need it, and then go back to the bottom of the bat. Where I hit that ball, it was on the meat part of the bat, about five inches from the end. There's no pine tar 29 inches from the handle. That ball wasn't even close enough to the pine tar to smell it."

Brett said he especially liked the bat, not for the pine tar but for the kind of wood with which it was made. He called it a seven-grainer ("the fewer grains a bat has, the better it is") and said it is the best bat he has ever had.

"I want my bat back," he said.

What the Royals really want back is their 5–4 lead. But only MacPhail can give it to them. If the league president should uphold their protest, the game would be resumed from Brett's home run, with two out in the Kansas City ninth. If MacPhail denies the protest, the Yankees' 4–3 victory will stand.

"It's unfortunate for them, but it's fortunate for us, of course," said Gossage, who gave up a memorable home run to Brett that clinched the 1980 league championship series for the Royals. "That's what he gets for hitting it."

The Yankees scored their runs presumably with legal bats. Dave Winfield hit a home run about 450 feet into the monuments in left-center field in the second inning, then singled home the third run of the Yankees' three-run rally in the sixth inning that overcame a 3–1 Kansas City lead. Don Baylor, who scored on the single, had tripled home the first two runs.

The Bird, they called him, and for one brief shining season—1976, when he won 19 games for the Detroits—he was youth, he was joy. And after that, he was what the poet says:

# Mark Fidrych

## TOM CLARK

Nobody ever rode a higher wave or gave us more
                back of what it taught
Or thought less of it,
Shrugging off the fame it
             brought, calling it "no big deal"
And, once it was taken
           away, refusing bitterness with such
Amazing grace.
Absence of damage limits one's perception
               of existence.
Suffering, while not to be pursued,
Yields at least what Mark
             termed "trains of thoughts,"
Those late, sad milk runs to Evansville
             and Pawtucket
Which he viewed
         not simply as pilgrimages
Of loss, but as interesting trips
In themselves—tickets to ride
           that long dark tunnel through
Which everybody—even those less gifted—must sooner
Or later pass
Because, "hey, that's what you call life."

# A Love of the Game

## LOWELL COHN

Jim Lefebvre, batting coach for the San Francisco Giants, is not a man you'd accuse of being a poet. He played his entire major league career for the Dodgers, was rookie of the year in 1965, once hit 24 home runs in a season, was part of the Dodgers all-switch hitting infield, played five years in Japan, has a square jaw and rough-hewn good looks, and once decked Dodger manager Tom Lasorda.

You expect a lot of things from Lefebvre. You just don't expect him to resort to poetry. But that's exactly what he did last week in the deserted dugout at Phoenix Stadium. He was a John Keats in baseball togs.

Lefebvre was telling a writer about the function of spring training, the usual rededication stuff, when all of a sudden, he was *overcome*. That's the only word for it.

"When I think of a stadium, it's like a temple," Lefebvre said. "It's religious. Sometimes I'd go into Dodger Stadium just to be alone. The game might start at 8 and I'd get there at 1 and sit in the stands and look at the field. It was that beautiful. No one would be there—only the birds chirping. And I'd see the sky and the grass. What a feeling!

"After a while, things began to happen. The vendors would come in slowly. The place was beginning to come alive. It was like it had a heart and it was beating slowly, softly—*Boom, boom*. (As he said this, Lefebvre began to pump his right hand—open, shut, open, shut—like a man preparing to give blood.)

"The fans started to arrive. The lights went on. *Boom, boom*. (Open, shut, open, shut.) The visiting team arrived. You could see them in their dugout and you'd look at them. *Boom, boom*. And the game was getting closer. And the heart was beating faster. (Open, shut,

open, shut.) And the game started. BOOM, BOOM! It was loud now, crashing, beating wildly. (He was squeezing so fast the veins popped out in his arm.)

"And then it was over. Just like that. The vendors left. The visiting team was gone. The heart stopped.

"I think a baseball field must be the most beautiful thing in the world. It's so honest and precise. And we play on it. Every star gets humbled. Every mediocre player has a great moment.

"The field is beautiful in spring. I smell the grass again and remember how I loved the smell, the way it came into my nostrils and filled me up."

"Did artificial turf change that?" the writer asked.

"Artificial turf was a desecration." Lefebvre said. "It violated the temple."

"Which stadium is the most special?" the writer asked.

"Yankee Stadium," he said. "I was a Yankee fan until the day I signed with the Dodgers. I had always dreamed of playing there, but I was never in it until . . . (Lefebvre paused, did a quick calculation.) It was the World Series, just after Junior (Gilliam) died, 1978."

"What was it like when you were finally in Yankee Stadium?" the writer asked.

"I went in there and I almost cried," Lefebvre said. "It was very moving. My God, Ruth played there and Gehrig. They were heroes and they hit in the same box, ran the same bases. They left their spirits there. I know it."

Lefebvre paused, looked at the writer and blushed. He had been caught with his sensibility down.

"I hope I made myself clear," he said shyly. "I've never said those things before. I didn't know they were in me."

The second book in this *Fireside* series contained an instructional entry on how to simulate a baseball game with dice. At the time, the distinguished author Robert Coover was at work on his own version, and ten years later it was published as a novel starring a middle-aged accountant named J. Henry Waugh who had a pair of dice and, in Jerry Holtzman's phrasing, "a mythical league that comes alive nightly on his kitchen table."

# From *The Universal Baseball Association, Inc.*

## ROBERT COOVER

BOTTOM HALF of the seventh, Brock's boy had made it through another inning unscratched, one! two! three! Twenty-one down and just six outs to go! and Henry's heart was racing, he was sweating with relief and tension all at once, unable to sit, unable to think, *in* there, *with* them! Oh yes, boys, it was on! He was sure of it! More than just another ball game now: history! And Damon Rutherford was making it. Ho ho! too good to be true! And yes, the stands were charged with it, turned on, it was the old days all over again, and with one voice they rent the air as the Haymaker Star Hamilton Craft spun himself right off his feet in a futile cut at Damon's third strike—zing! whoosh! *zap! OUT!* Henry laughed, watched the hometown Pioneer fans cheer the boy, cry out his name, then stretch—not just stretch—*leap up* for luck. He saw beers bought and drunk, hot dogs eaten, timeless gestures passed. Yes, yes, they nodded, and crossed their fingers and knocked on wood and rubbed their palms and kissed their fingertips and clapped their hands, and laughed how they were all caught up in it, witnessing it, how he was all caught up in it, this great ball game, event of the first order, tremendous moment: *Rookie pitcher Damon Rutherford, son of the incomparable Brock Rutherford, was two innings—six outs—from a perfect game!* Henry, licking his lips, dry from excitement, squinted at the sun high over the Pioneer Park, then at his watch: nearly eleven, Diskin's closing hour. So he took the occasion of this seventh-inning hometown stretch to hurry downstairs to the delicatessen to get a couple sandwiches. Might be a long night: the Pioneers hadn't scored off old Swanee Law yet either.

A small warm bulb, unfrosted, its little sallow arc so remote from its fathering force as to seem more akin to the glowworm than lightning, gleamed outside his door and showed where the landing ended; the steps themselves were dark, but Henry, through long usage, knew them all by heart. Cold bluish streetlight lit the bottom, intruding damply, seeming to hover unrelated to the floor, but Henry hardly noticed: his eye was on the game, on the great new Rookie pitcher Damon Rutherford, seeking this afternoon his sixth straight win . . . and maybe more. Maybe: immortality. And now, as Henry skipped out onto the sidewalk, then turned into the front door of Diskin's Delicatessen, he saw the opposing pitcher, Ace Swanee Law of the hard-bitten Haymakers, taking the mound, tossing warm-up pitches, and he knew he had to hurry.

"Two pastrami, Benny," he said to the boy sweeping up, Mr. Diskin's son—third or fourth, though, not the second. "And a cold six-pack."

"Aw, I just put everything away, Mr. Waugh," the boy whined, but he went to get the pastrami anyway.

Now Swanee Law was tough, an ace, seven-year veteran, top rookie himself in his own day, one of the main reasons Rag Rooney's Rubes had finished no worse than third from Year L through Year LIV. Ninety-nine wins, sixty-one losses, fast ball that got faster every year, most consistent, most imperturbable, and most vociferous of the Haymaker moundsmen. Big man who just reared back and hummed her in. Phenomenal staying power, the kind old Brock used to have. But he didn't have Brock Rutherford's class, that sweet smooth delivery, that virile calm. Mean man to beat, just the same, and to be sure he still had a shutout going for him this afternoon, and after all, it was a big day for him, too, going for that milestone hundredth win. Of course, he had a Rookie catcher in there to throw to, young Bingham Hill, and who knows? maybe they weren't getting along too well; could be. Law was never an easy man to get along with, too pushy, too much steam, and Hill was said to be excitable. Maybe Rooney had better send in reliable old Maggie Everts, Law's favorite battery mate. What about it? Haymaker manager Rag (Pappy) Rooney stroked his lean grizzly jaw, gave the nod to Everts.

"How's that, Mr. Waugh?"

"Did you put the pickle?"

"We're all out, sold the last one about thirty minutes ago."

A lie. Henry sighed. He'd considered using the name Ben Diskin, solid name for an outfielder, there was a certain power in it, but Benny spoiled it. A good boy, but nothing there. "That's okay, Benny. I'll take two next time."

"Working hard tonight, Mr. Waugh?" Benny rang up the sale, gave change.

"As always."

"Better take it easy. You been looking a little run-down lately."

Henry winced impatiently, forced a smile. "Never felt better," he said, and exited.

It was true: the work, or what he called his work, though it was more than that, much more, was good for him. Thing was, nobody realized he was just four years shy of sixty. They were always shocked when he told them. It was his Association that kept him young.

Mounting the stairs, Henry heard the roar of the crowd, saw them take their seats. Bowlegged old Maggie Everts trundled out of the Haymaker dugout to replace Hill. That gave cause for a few more warm-up pitches, so Henry slowed, took the top steps one at a time. Law grinned, nodded at old Maggie, stuffed a chaw of gum into his cheek. In the kitchen, he tore open the six-pack of beer, punched a can, slid the others into the refrigerator, took a long greedy drink of what the boys used to call German tea. Then, while Law tossed to Everts, Henry chewed his pastrami and studied the line-ups. Grammercy Locke up for the Pioneers, followed by three Star batters. Locke had been rapping the ball well lately, but Pioneer manager Barney Bancroft pulled him out, playing percentages, called in pinch-hitter Tuck Wilson, a great Star in his prime, now nearing the end of his career. Wilson selected a couple bats, exercised them, chose one, tugged his hat, and stepped in.

Henry sat down, picked up the dice, approved Everts'

signal. "Wilson batting for Locke!" he announced over the loudspeaker, and they gave the old hero a big hometown hand. Henry rolled, bit into pastrami. Wilson swung at the first pitch, in across the knuckles, pulling it down the line. Haymaker third-sacker Hamilton Craft hopped to his right, fielded the ball, spun, threw to first—*wide!* Wilson: safe on first! Henry marked the error, flashed it on the scoreboard. Craft, one of the best, kicked the bag at third sullenly, scrubbed his nose, stared hard at Hatrack Hines, stepping now into the box. Bancroft sent speedster Hillyer Bryan in to run for Wilson.

"Awright! now come on, you guys! a little action!" Henry shouted, Bancroft shouted, clapping his hands, and the Pioneers kept the pepper up, they hollered in the stands.

"Got them Rubes rattled, boys! Let's bat around!"

"Lean into it, Hatrack, baby! Swanee's done for the day!"

"Send him down the river!"

"Dee-ee-eep water, Swanee boy!"

"Hey, Hatrack! Just slap it down to Craft there, he's all butter!"

The dice rattled in Henry's fist, tumbled out on the kitchen table: *crack!* hard grounder. Craft jumped on it this time, whipped the ball to second, one out—but young Bryan broke up the double play by flying in heels high! Still in there! Bancroft took a calculated risk: sent Hatrack scampering for second on Law's second pitch to Witness York—*safe!* Finishing his sandwich, Henry wondered: Would the Rookie Bingham Hill, pulled for inexperience, have nailed Hines at second? Maybe he would have. Pappy Rooney, the graybeard Haymaker boss, spat disdainfully. He knew what he was doing. Who knows? Hill might have thrown wild.

Anyway, it didn't matter. Pioneer Star center-fielder Witness York stepped back in, squeezed his bat for luck, swung, and whaled out his eleventh home run of the season, scoring Hines in front of him, and before Law had got his wind back, big Stan Patterson, Star right fielder, had followed with his ninth. Wham! bam! thank you, ma'am! And finally that was how the seventh inning ended: Pioneers 3, Haymakers 0. And now it was up to Damon Rutherford.

Henry stood, drank beer, joined in spirit with the Pioneer fans in their heated cries. Could the boy do it? All knew what, but none named it. The bullish roar of the crowd sounded like a single hoarse monosyllable, yet within it, Henry could pick out the ripple of Damon's famous surname, not so glorified in this stadium in over twenty years. Then it was for the boy's father, the all-time great Brock Rutherford, one of the game's most illustrious Aces back in what seemed now like the foundling days of the Universal Baseball Association, even-tempered fireballing no-pitches-wasted right-handed bellwether of the Pioneers who led them to nine pennants in a span of fourteen years. The Glorious XX's! Celebrated Era of the Pioneers! Barney Bancroft himself was there; he knew, he remembered! One of the fastest men the UBA had ever seen, out there guarding center. Barney the Old Philosopher, flanked by Willie O'Leary and Surrey Moss, and around the infield: Mose Stanford, Frosty Young, Jonathan Noon, and Gabe Burdette, timid Holly Tibbett behind the plate. Tooth-brush Terrigan pitched, and Birdie Deaton and Chad-bourne Collins . . . and Brock. Brock had come up as a Rookie in Year XX—no, XIX, that's right, it would have to be (Henry paused to look it up; yes, correct: XIX), just a kid off the farm, seemed happy-go-lucky and even lackadaisical, but he had powered his way to an Ace position that first year, winning six straight ball games at the end of the season, three of them shutouts, lifting the long-suffering Pioneers out of second division into second place. A great year! great teams! and next year the pennant! Brock the Great! maybe the greatest of them all! He had stayed up in the Association for seventeen years before giving way to age and a trouble-some shoulder. Still held the record to this day for total lifetime wins: 311. 311! Brock Rutherford . . . well, well, time gets on. Henry felt a tightness in his chest, shook it off. Foolish. He sighed, picked up the dice. Brock the Great. Hall of Fame, of course.

And now: now it was his boy who stood there on the mound. Tall, lithe, wirier build than his dad's, but just as fast, just as smooth. Smoother. More serious some-how. Yes, there was something more pensive about Damon, a meditative calm, a gentle brooding concern. The calm they shared, Rutherford gene, but where in Brock it had taken on the color of a kind of cocky, almost rustic power, in Damon it was self-assurance ennobled with a sense of . . . what? Responsibility maybe. Accountability. Brock was a public phenome-non, Damon a self-enclosed yet participating mystery. His own man, yet at home in the world, part of it, involved, every inch of him a participant, maybe that was all it was: his total involvement, his oneness with UBA. Henry mused, fingering the dice. The Pioneer infielders tossed the ball around. Catcher Royce Ingram talked quietly with Damon out on the mound.

Of course, Pappy Rooney cared little for the peculiar aesthetics of the moment. It was his job not only to break up the no-hitter, but to beat the kid. Anyway, old Pappy had no love for the Rutherfords. Already a Haymaker Star and veteran of two world championships, four times the all-star first baseman of the Association, when Dad Rutherford first laced on a pair of cleats for the Pioneers, Rag Rooney had suffered through season after season of

Haymaker failure to break the Pioneer grip on the UBA leadership, had gone down swinging futilely at Brock's fireball as often as the next man. So maybe that was why it was that, when the Haymaker right fielder, due to lead off in the top of the eighth, remarked that the Rutherford kid sure was tough today, Rooney snapped back: "Ya don't say. Well, mister, take your goddamn seat." And called in a pinch hitter.

Not that it did any good. Henry was convinced it was Damon's day, and nothing the uncanny Rooney came up with today could break the young Pioneer's spell. He laughed, and almost carelessly, with that easy abandon of old man Brock, pitched the dice, watched Damon Rutherford mow them down. One! Two! Three! And then nonchalantly, but not arrogantly, just casually, part of any working day, walk to the dugout. As though nothing were happening. *Nothing!* Henry found himself hopping up and down. One more inning! He drank beer, reared back, fired the empty can at the plastic garbage bucket near the sink. In there! *Zap!* "Go get 'em!" he cried.

First, of course, the Pioneers had their own eighth round at the plate, and there was no reason not to use it to stretch their lead, fatten averages a little, rub old Swanee's nose in it. Even if the Haymakers got lucky in the ninth and spoiled Damon's no-hitter, there was no reason to lose the ball game. After all, Damon was short some 300-and-some wins if he wanted to top his old man, which meant he needed every one he could get. Henry laughed irreverently.

Goodman James, young Pioneer first baseman making his second try for a permanent place in the line-up after a couple years back in the minors, picked out a bat, stepped lean-legged into the batter's box. Swanee fed him the old Law Special, a sizzling sinker in at the knees, and James bounced it down the line to first base: easy out. Damon Rutherford received a tremendous ovation when he came out—his dad would have ac-knowledged it with an open grin up at the stands; Damon knocked dirt from his cleats, seemed not to hear it. Wasn't pride. It was just that he understood it, accepted it, but was too modest, too *knowing,* to insist on any uniqueness of his own apart from it. He took a couple casual swings with his bat, moved up to the plate, waited Law out, but finally popped up: not much of a hitter. But to hear the crowd cheer as he trotted back to the dugout (one of the coaches met him halfway with a jacket), one would have thought he'd at least homered. Henry smiled. Lead-off man Toby Ramsey grounded out, short to first. Three up, three down. Those back-to-back homers had only made Law tougher than ever. "It's when Ah got baseballs flyin' round mah ears, that's when Ah'm really at mah meanest!"

Top of the ninth.

This was it.

Odds against him, of course. Had to remember that; be prepared for the lucky hit that really wouldn't be lucky at all, but merely in the course of things. Exceedingly rare, no-hitters; much more so, perfect games. How many in history? two, three. And a Rookie: no, it had never been done. In seventeen matchless years, his dad had pitched only two no-hitters, never had a perfect game. Henry paced the kitchen, drinking beer, trying to calm himself, to prepare himself, but he couldn't get it out of his head: *it was on!*

The afternoon sun waned, cast a golden glint off the mowed grass that haloed the infield. No sound in the stands now: breathless. Of course, no matter what happened, even if he lost the game, they'd cheer him, fabulous game regardless; yes, they'd love him, they'd let him know it . . . but still they wanted it. Oh yes, how they wanted it! Damon warmed up, throwing loosely to catcher Ingram. Henry watched him, felt the boy's inner excitement, shook his head in amazement at his outer serenity. "Nothing like this before." Yes, there was a soft murmur pulsing through the stands: nothing like it,

electrifying, new, a new thing, happening here and now! Henry paused to urinate.

Manager Barney Bancroft watched from the Pioneer dugout, leaning on a pillar, thinking about Damon's father, about the years they played together, the games fought, the races won, the celebrations and the sufferings, roommates when on the road several of those years. Brock was great and this kid was great, but he was no carbon copy. Brock had raised his two sons to be more than ballplayers, or maybe it wasn't Brock's work, maybe it was just the name that had ennobled them, for in a way, they were—Bancroft smiled at the idea, but it was largely true—they were, in a way, the Association's first real aristocrats. There were already some fourth-generation boys playing ball in the league—the Keystones' Kester Flint, for example, and Jock Casey and Paddy Sullivan—but there'd been none before like the Rutherford boys. Even Brock Jr., though failing as a ballplayer, had had this quality, this poise, a gently ironic grace on him that his dad had never had, for all his raw jubilant power. Ingram threw the ball to second-baseman Ramsey, who flipped it to shortstop Wilder,

## JOHN GALLAGHER

". . . *And it looks like that's going to be all for the kid today.*"

who underhanded it to third-baseman Hines, now half-way to the mound, who in turn tossed it to Damon. Here we go.

Bancroft watched Haymaker backstop Maggie Everts move toward the plate, wielding a thick stubby bat. Rookie Rodney Holt crouched in the on-deck circle, working a pair of bats menacingly between his legs. Everts tipped his hat out toward the mound, then stepped into the box: dangerous. Yes, he was. The old man could bring the kid down. Still able to come through with the clutch hit. Lovable guy, old Maggie, great heart, Bancroft was fond of him, but that counted for nothing in the ninth inning of a history-making ball game. Rooney, of course, would send a pinch hitter in for Law. Bancroft knew he should order a couple relief pitchers to the bull pen just in case, but something held him back. Bancroft thought it was on, too.

Rooney noticed the empty bullpen. Bancroft was overconfident, was ripe for a surprise, but what could he do about it? He had no goddamn hitters. Even Ham Craft was in a bad slump. Should pull him out, cool his ass on the bench awhile, but, hell, he had nobody else. Pappy was in his fifteenth year as Haymaker manager, the old man of the Association's coaching staffs, and he just wasn't too sure, way things were going, that he and his ulcer were going to see a sixteenth. Two pennants, six times the league runner-up, never out of first division until last year when they dropped to fifth . . . and that was where his Rubes were now, with things looking like they were apt to get worse before they got better. He watched Everts, with a count of two and two on him, stand flatfooted as a third strike shot by so fast he hardly even saw it. That young bastard out there on the rubber was good, all right, fast as lightning—but what was it? Rooney couldn't quite put his finger on it . . . a little too narrow in the shoulders maybe, slight in the chest, too much a thoroughbred, not enough of the old man's big-boned stamina. And then he thought: shit, I can still beat this kid! And turning his scowl on the Haymaker bench, he hollered at Abernathy to pinch-hit for Holt.

Henry realized he had another beer in his hand and didn't remember having opened it. Now he was saying it out loud: "It's on! Come on, boy!" For the first time in this long game, the odds were with Damon: roughly 4–to–3 that he'd get both Abernathy and—who? Horvath, Rooney was sending in Hard John Horvath to bat for Law. Get them both and rack it up: the perfect game!

Henry hadn't been so excited in weeks. Months. That was the way it was, some days seemed to pass almost without being seen, games lived through, decisions made, averages rising or dipping, and all of it happening in a kind of fog, until one day that astonishing event would occur that brought sudden life and immediacy to the Association, and everybody would suddenly wake up and wonder at the time that had got by them, go back to the box scores, try to find out what had happened. During those dull-minded stretches, even a home run was nothing more than an HR penned into the box score; sure, there was a fence and a ball sailing over it, but Henry didn't see them—oh, he heard the shouting of the faithful, yes, they stayed with it, they had to, but to him it was just a distant echo, static that let you know it was still going on. But then, contrarily, when someone like Damon Rutherford came along to flip the switch, turn things on, why, even a pop-up to the pitcher took on excitement, a certain dimension, color. *The magic of excellence.* Under its charm, he threw the dice: Abernathy struck out. Two down, *one to go!* It could happen, *it could happen!* Henry reeled around his chair a couple times, laughing out loud, went to urinate again.

Royce Ingram walked out to the mound. Ten-year veteran, generally acknowledged the best catcher in the UBA. He didn't go out to calm the kid down, but just because it was what everybody expected him to do at such a moment. Besides, Damon was the only sonuva-bitch on the whole field not about to crap his pants from excitement. Even the Haymakers, screaming for the spoiler, were out of their seats, and to the man, hanging on his every pitch. The kid really had it, okay. Not just control either, but stuff, too. Ingram had never caught anybody so good, and he'd caught some pretty good ones. Just twenty years old, what's more: plenty of time to get even better. If it's possible. Royce tipped up his mask, grinned. "Ever hear the one about the farmer who stuck corks in his pigs' assholes to make them grow?" he asked.

"Yes, I heard that one, Royce," Damon said and grinned back. "What made you think of that one—you having cramps?"

Ingram laughed. "How'd you guess?"

"Me too," the kid confessed, and toed a pebble off the rubber. Ingram felt an inexplicable relief flood through him, and he took a deep breath. We're gonna make it, he thought. They listened to the loudspeaker announcing Horvath batting for Law. "Where does he like it?"

"Keep it in tight and tit-high, and the old man won't even see it," Ingram said. He found he couldn't even grin, so he pulled his mask down. "Plenty of stuff," he added meaninglessly. Damon nodded. Ingram expected him to reach for the rosin bag or wipe his hands on his shirt or tug at his cap or something, but he didn't: he just stood there waiting. Ingram wheeled around, hustled back behind the plate, asked Horvath what he was sweating about, underwear too tight on him or some-thing? which made Hard John give an uneasy tug at his balls, and when, in his squat behind the plate, he looked back out at Rutherford, he saw that the kid still hadn't moved, still poised there on the rise, coolly waiting, ball resting solidly in one hand, both hands at his sides, head tilted slightly to the right, face expressionless but eyes alert. Ingram laughed. "You're dead, man," he told Horvath. Henry zipped up.

Of course, it was just the occasion for the storybook spoiler. Yes, too obvious. Perfect game, two down in the ninth, and a pinch hitter scratches out a history-shriveling single. How many times it had already happened! The epochal event reduced to a commonplace by something or someone even less than commonplace, a mediocrity, a blooper worth forgetting, a utility ball-player never worth much and out of the league a year later. All the No-Hit Nealys that Sandy sang about . . .

> *No-Hit Nealy, somethin' in his eye,*
> *When they pitched low, he swung high,*
> *Hadn't had a hit in ninety-nine years,*
> *And then they sent him out agin*
> *the Pi-yo-neers!*

Henry turned water on to wash, then hesitated. Not that he felt superstitious about it exactly, but he saw Damon Rutherford standing there on the mound, hands not on the rosin bag, not in the armpits, not squeezing the ball, just at his side—dry, strong, patient—and he felt as though washing his hands might somehow spoil Damon's pitch. From the bathroom door, he could see the kitchen table. His Association lay there in ordered stacks of paper. The dice sat there, three ivory cubes, heedless of history yet makers of it, still proclaiming Abernathy's strike-out. Damon Rutherford waited there. Henry held his breath, walked straight to the table, picked up the dice, and tossed them down.

Hard John Horvath took a cut at Rutherford's second pitch, a letter-high inside curve, pulled it down the third-base line: Hatrack Hines took it backhanded, paused one mighty spellbinding moment—then fired across the diamond to Goodman James, and Horvath was out.

The game was over.

Giddily, Henry returned to the bathroom and washed his hands. He stared down at his wet hands, thinking: he did it! And then, at the top of his voice, "WA-*HOO!*" he bellowed, and went leaping back into the kitchen, feeling like he could damn well take off and soar if he had anyplace to go. *"HOO-HAH!"*

And the fans blew the roof off. They leaped the wall, slid down the dugout roofs, overran the cops, flooded in from the outfield bleachers, threw hats and scorecards into the air. Rooney hustled his Haymakers to the showers, but couldn't stop the Pioneer fans from lifting poor Horvath to their shoulders. There was a fight and

Hard John bloodied a couple noses, but nobody even bothered to swing back at him. And old lady blew him kisses. Partly to keep Rutherford from getting mobbed and partly just because they couldn't stop themselves, his Pioneer teammates got to him first, had him on their own shoulders before the frenzied hometown rooters could close in and tear him apart out of sheer love. From above, it looked like a great roiling whirlpool with Damon afloat in the vortex—but then York popped up like a cork, and then Patterson and Hines, and finally the manager Barney Bancroft, lifted up by fans too delirious even to know for sure anymore what it was they were celebrating, and the whirlpool uncoiled and surged toward the Pioneer locker rooms.

"Ah!" said Henry, and: *"Ah!"*

And even bobbingly afloat there on those rocky shoulders, there in that knock-and-tumble flood of fans, in a wild world that had literally, for the moment, blown its top, Damon Rutherford preserved his incredible equanimity, hands at his knees except for an occasional wave, face lit with pleasure at what he'd done, but in no way distorted with the excitement of it all: tall, right, and true. People screamed for the ball. Royce Ingram, whose shoulder was one of those he rode on, handed it up to him. Women shrieked, arms supplicating. He smiled at them, but tossed the ball out to a small boy standing at the crowd's edge.

Henry opened the refrigerator, reached for the last can of beer, then glanced at his watch: almost midnight—changed his mind. He peered out at the space between his kitchen window and the street lamp: lot of moisture in the air still, but hard to tell if it was falling or rising. He'd brooded over it, coming home from work: that piled-up mid-autumn feeling, pregnant with the vague threat of confusion and emptiness—but this boy had cut clean through it, let light and health in, and you don't go to bed on an event like this! Henry reknotted his tie, put on hat and raincoat, hooked his umbrella over one arm, and went out to get a drink. He glanced back at the kitchen table once more before pulling the door to, saw the dice there, grinned at them, for once adjuncts to grandeur, then hustled down the stairs like a happy Pioneer headed for the showers. He stepped quickly through the disembodied street lamp glow at the bottom, and whirling his umbrella like a drum major's baton, marched springily up the street to Pete's, the neighborhood bar.

> *N-o-O-O-o Hit Nealy!*
> *Won his fame*
> *Spoilin' Birdie Deaton's*
> *Per-her-fect game!*

Here is a chapter from *Babe,* which has been called the best baseball biography ever done. There have been other pieces about Babe Ruth in the previous *Fireside* volumes, of course, but none that zeroed in on what a punster might call his flip side. The title to this chapter says it all.

# The Left-handed Genius: Best Pitcher in Baseball

## ROBERT W. CREAMER

THE FEDERAL League died at the end of 1915, and with its death the major league owners reverted to type and began to slash player salaries. During the two-year war, salaries had soared, particularly for star players. Now, with no place to jump to, or threaten to jump to, the players lost their only effective weapon and were more or less helpless. The demise of the Federal League meant there was a horde of ballplayers scrambling for places on the rosters of the legitimate big league teams. It was a buyer's market, and the owners wasted no time in letting the players understand that. The hitherto generous Lannin was no exception.

Ruth was not affected, because he still had a year to go on the three-season contract he signed in the summer of 1914, but Joe Wood, whose 34 victories in 1912 moved him well up in the salary scale even before the Federal League came into being, was cut so drastically that he refused to report to the Hot Springs training camp in 1916. His friend Speaker agreed to report and work out, but he too refused to sign the contract Lannin offered him. In 1914, when the Federals were throwing money like rose petals at the feet of major league stars, Lannin paid Speaker a $5000 bonus to stick with the Red Sox and gave him a two-year contract at $15,000 a year, which was very close to being the highest salary in the majors. Now, in 1916, Speaker accepted the reality that he would have to take a salary cut, which was remarkably understanding when you consider that he was the star of the World Champions, the only .300 hitter in the Boston lineup in both 1914 and 1915 and by all standards the best fielding outfielder in baseball. When he found out what the Red Sox were planning to pay him, Speaker stopped being so understanding. Lannin was offering $9000, a 60 per cent cut. Speaker said he might accept $12,000, but that was the lowest figure he

could even consider. All through spring training he and the Red Sox owner sparred. Lannin, adamant, said $9000 was his top price; if Speaker wanted to play with the Red Sox, that is what he would have to sign for. Speaker continued to train but would not sign.

Despite the salary disputes the Red Sox looked very strong that spring. Even though Wood was not there and Ray Collins had gone the way of all failing ballplayers, Carrigan had a wealth of superior starting pitchers. Ruth, the erstwhile erratic rookie, was still clowning around off the field, and his gargantuan appetite had ballooned his weight to 212 pounds, but on the mound he showed every sign of maturity. Mays too looked impressive. And in Shore, Foster and Leonard he had three of the best pitchers in baseball. The rest of the lineup was solid and set. The Lewis-Speaker-Hooper outfield had been playing as a unit since 1910, and all three were in their prime. Hoblitzell at first base and Gardner at third were fixtures. Scott, a rookie at shortstop in 1914, was good enough in 1915 to make the nonpareil Barry shift to second, and behind that pair was the graceful Janvrin. Thomas and Cady were fine catchers. It was a very solid team, a little weak at bat, of course, but nonetheless the class of the league. It was a big favorite to retain the pennant.

The Speaker thing was still unsettled as the Red Sox made their way toward Boston for the opening of the season, but the players—notably Ruth—were bubbling with enthusiasm and optimism. A week before the season began they played Jack Dunn's Orioles in Baltimore, and Ruth appeared before the home folks for the first time as a major leaguer. The next day Lannin announced, almost incidentally, that he had bought an outfielder named Clarence (Tilly) Walker from the Philadelphia Athletics. That was not startling news, since hardly a day went by without someone buying a player from Connie Mack. Walker, who hit the ball hard, had been around the league for five years with Washington and St. Louis and had ended up with Mack that winter as an offshoot of the Federal League settlement. A couple of Federal League owners had been allowed to buy legitimate big league franchises. One of these was Phil Ball of St. Louis, who bought the Browns. Among his Federal League stars was Eddie Plank, who jumped from the Athletics after the 1914 season. It was agreed that Ball could keep Plank with him in St. Louis, but in return he had to give Walker to Philadelphia. Mack, who needed money, decided to sell him. Lannin's decision to buy Walker made sense, everyone agreed, because Duffy Lewis had been slightly injured that spring and it never hurt to have a little insurance. No one thought about the new outfielder as a possible replacement for Speaker—except Lannin, who had been doing some maneuvering behind the scenes.

The day after Walker's purchase the Red Sox lost to Brooklyn, 3–2, in an exhibition game; Speaker, still unsigned but in top form, got Boston its two runs with a pair of homers. Opening day was only five days away, but Bostonians were sure the disagreement between Lannin and his star outfielder would be settled by then. They were right. On the Saturday before the season opened, Lannin stunned players, fans, sportswriters and half the country by announcing he had sold Speaker to the second-division Cleveland Indians. The price was $50,000, the largest amount ever paid for one player up to that time. Two unimportant young Cleveland players also came to Boston in the deal. One of them, Sam Jones, eventually became one of the best pitchers in the American League, but no one knew anything about that in April 1916. It was Speaker for cash, and it was almost unbelievable. It was impossible for Boston to accept the news at first. The Red Sox sell Speaker! He was the big man, the hero of the team. More practically, he was the only really good hitter on a weak offensive club. The Red Sox players walked around shaking their heads. Ruth said he felt as though a rug had been pulled out from under him. What did this do to their pennant chances? Speaker was gone. Wood was gone. (Joe, who held out all season, ultimately was sent to Cleveland, where he rejoined Speaker, gave up pitching and became an outfielder; he hit .366 one season as a part-time player). Downcast, the players muttered and grumbled.

Carrigan, as hurt as any of them by the deal, which was completely Lannin's idea, reacted the way a leader should. He gathered his team together and chewed them out in his tough no-nonsense way. "All right," he said. "We've lost Speaker. That means we're not going to score as many runs. But we're still a good team. We

have the pitching. We have the fielding. And we'll hit well enough. We'll win the pennant again if you guys will just stop your goddamned moaning and get down to business." Fired up, the Red Sox opened the season by winning their first four games and six of their first eight. Ruth, now a major factor in Carrigan's strategy, pitched the opening game and won it, 2–1. In his second start he was sent against Walter Johnson, the best pitcher in American League history. Babe had pitched against Johnson once in 1915 and beat him, 4–3; now he defeated the great Walter again, 5–1.

Babe won his first four starts, the club was in first place and everything seemed to be going swimmingly. But it was not so, not really. The team was not hitting at all. It was shut out in New York and shut out again in Washington; in its first 15 games it was able to score as many as three runs only six times. Inevitably, the defeats began to come. The team slid out of the league lead as April ended, Ruth lost his first game on the first of May and the club began to stumble badly. Carrigan was most disturbed by his unsettled outfield, hitherto the team's pride. Walker was late in reporting and Carrigan put Lewis, who had recovered from his injury, in center and Chick Shorten, a rookie, in left. When Walker was ready, Carrigan put him in left. But Lewis was uncomfortable in center, so Carrigan shifted him back to left and put Shorten, a weak hitter but a capable fielder, in center. Finally he stuck Walker in center and left him there, even though the newcomer was a hitter more than he was a fielder.

For almost two months, through May and most of June, the Red Sox played sluggish .500 ball in a league that had turned upside down because of the infusion of Federal League players. The big teams—the Red Sox, Tigers and White Sox—were far behind, while the perennially weak Yankees, Indians and Senators were taking turns in first place. Speaker, playing like a man possessed, was leading the league in hitting and had lifted drab Cleveland into contention. In May, when the Indians played in Boston for the first time, a delegation of Boston fans gave Speaker a silver loving cup, partly as a gesture to their departed hero, partly as a slap at owner Lannin. The next afternoon, with Tris starring, the Indians walloped Ruth, and the Red Sox fans didn't know whether to cheer or cry. It was an unhappy spring for Boston.

The hitting picked up a little with Walker in the lineup, but then the pitching began to go bad. Something was wrong with Shore. Foster was not right. Mays pitched very little. There were fits and starts of brightness. Leonard's first three starts were shutouts, and Ruth was generally superb. Late in May he pitched a shutout against Detroit. On June 1 he beat Walter Johnson again, this time 1–0. Four days later he pitched another shutout, stopping Cleveland after the Indians had beaten Boston two days running by big scores. Speaker went 0 for 4 against him this time, which made the victory that much more satisfying, and the Babe, who was beginning to hit after a slow start, had two singles and scored a run.

He lost to Detroit a few days later, after holding a 4–1 lead in the eighth inning, but he had a perfect day at bat and even hit a home run, his first since the previous July. Three days later, in St. Louis, Carrigan had him pinch-hit with two men on base and the Red Sox behind 3–0. Ruth hit a three-run homer over the bleachers in right field to tie the score. He pitched against the Browns the next afternoon, won 5–3, had another perfect day at bat and hit another home run, his third in three games, which created a sensation. (Oddly, these three were the only home runs he hit all season.) His batting average jumped to .300, and people were remembering all over again what a powerful batter he was. The Red Sox scored fewer runs than any team in the league except the last-place Athletics, and Carrigan, talking about Ruth's home runs, wondered out loud if he ought not put the Babe in the outfield to fill some of the hitting void that Speaker had left. Carrigan was only speculating. He was essentially conservative when it came to baseball. He always put Ruth in the ninth spot in the batting order, the traditional place for a pitcher, despite Babe's obvious hitting ability, and he was not going to gamble with the man who was now his best pitcher. Indeed, Ruth was not only Boston's best, he was the best pitcher in the league that year, including Walter Johnson.

He was beginning to be something of a character too. Everyone was aware of his amazing appetite and his love of night life (though he really was not much of a drinker yet, except for beer). Now his trait of not remembering names was becoming part of the growing legend. One evening in Philadelphia he was in the hotel lobby after defeating the Athletics that afternoon, when Stuffy McInnis, the Philadelphia first baseman, came in. McInnis was from Massachusetts and he had stopped by to visit some of his old Boston friends. When he saw Ruth he walked over and said, "Babe, that was a hell of a fine game you pitched this afternoon." It was a significant compliment. McInnis had been in the league since 1909, had played on four pennant-winning teams, was, like Barry, a widely publicized member of the famous $100,000 infield and had played against Ruth frequently since Babe's debut against the Athletics in North Carolina in the spring of 1914. Ruth looked at him blandly and said, "Thanks, keed, that's very nice of you. Glad you were able to come out and watch us play." McInnis nodded dumbly and more or less staggered away. "He didn't know me," he would say in awe to people to whom he would tell the story. "He didn't even know I was a ballplayer."

Late in June things began to swing Boston's way. Foster pitched a no-hitter, Ruth and Shore followed with shutouts and Mays and Leonard won a doubleheader to make it five straight. The beautiful pitching staff was in top form again, and with improved hitting the Red Sox began to move steadily upward. The last three months of the season were much more fun than the first three. There was a lovely fight in Washington one day after a Mays pitch hit George McBride, the Senators' veteran shortstop. McBride threw his bat, à la Cobb, and Sam Agnew, a third-string catcher Boston recently acquired, raged at McBride. Carrigan came off his bench, Clark Griffith, the Washington manager, came off his, Agnew punched Griffith, the police arrested Agnew (he had to pay $50 bail at a police station) and Ban Johnson suspended Carrigan for five days.

Cleveland and the Yankees were still wrestling for first place, but the Red Sox were coming on, winning two games for every one they lost, getting closer and closer to the top. By late July Boston was only half a game off the lead, and after they won three straight in Detroit, including a 6–0 shutout by Ruth, they moved into first place. They fell back again when they lost three games in St. Louis, but in Chicago they took three of four and regained the lead. They were a strong road club, and after this trip they had a commanding lead.

Ruth's pitching sloughed off briefly, but by mid-August he was riding high again. He beat Washington, 2–1, came back three days later to beat Johnson, 1–0, in thirteen innings, beat Cleveland, 2–1, four days after that and shut out Detroit, 3–0, in his next start. The Red Sox lead widened to six and a half games and it seemed as though they would win the pennant easily. But as September began they slumped, and Detroit and Chicago closed in for the long anticipated pennant battle among the three best teams in the league. On September 9 Ruth beat Johnson, 2–1, for his fifth in a row over the Washington star, but Detroit was only one game behind and Chicago two. On September 12 Carrigan sent Ruth against Johnson again, and Walter finally won one, 4–3, in ten innings, although Ruth, who was taken out in the ninth after losing a 2–0 lead, was not charged with the defeat.

That same day, just as the club was about to leave on its last western trip of the season, Lannin revealed that Carrigan was planning to retire at the end of the season. Whether this news upset the players is conjectural, but they lost two of their first three games in the west and fell from first to third place. Then, in that curious way baseball has, the next two days abruptly settled the pennant race. On Sunday, September 17, the Red Sox met the White Sox before more than 40,000 people, the largest crowd in the history of Chicago baseball to that time. Ruth won the game, 6–2, for his 20th victory of the season and lifted the Red Sox past Chicago into second place behind Detroit. The next day Shore defeated the White Sox again and Boston found itself back in the lead, because that afternoon the Tigers suffered an astonishing 2–0 defeat at the hands of the Athletics. To appreciate the impact of Detroit's defeat you must know that the Tigers had won 35 of their previous 50 games, a vigorous .700 pace, and had charged up from the second division into first place. The Athletics, on the other hand, were at the absolute nadir of the worst season any team has had in the modern history of major league baseball. The Mets in their abysmal 1962 season won 40 games and lost 120 for a .250 winning percentage. The 1916 Athletics won 38 games and lost 117 for a .238 percentage, which was bad enough, but on that Monday in September when they beat the Tigers their record was 30 won and 108 lost, a percentage of .217. When the Mets finished last in 1962, they were 18 games behind the next worst team, a staggering margin when you consider that a team is said to have run away with a pennant when it wins by 12 games. But the Athletics—stand back, now—finished 40½ games behind the team next above them in the standings. They had one pitcher who lost 23 games, another who lost 22, a third with a record of one and 19 and a fourth who was one and 16. And yet in the midst of a pennant race this majestically inept team beat Ty Cobb and the Tigers, the hardest-hitting team in baseball, shut them out and knocked them out of first place.

The next day the Red Sox arrived in Detroit for a three-game series, swept all three (Ruth won the final game, 10–2), and that was the end of the season, practically speaking. Boston finished its triumphant road trip by beating Speaker and the Indians three out of four. Ruth shut out Cleveland in the last game there and four days later in Boston blanked the Yankees for his ninth shutout of the season, which a half century later was still the American League record for a lefthanded pitcher. It was also his 23rd and final victory of the season.

It was a year of singular achievement for Ruth—23 wins, nine shutouts, league-leading earned-run average, the three home runs in three games, the 20th victory before the huge crowd in Chicago that started Boston on its final drive to the pennant, the thirteen-inning 1–0 defeat of Walter Johnson—but his biggest moment of the season was still to come.

The 1916 World Series matched the Red Sox with the Brooklyn Dodgers, and Ruth pitched the second game. Carrigan had passed over him for the opener, had used Ernie Shore instead and had won. That first game was played on a Saturday in Boston, and Ruth's game was to be the following Monday, since Sunday was always an off-day in staid Boston. Hugh Fullerton, the old sportswriter, wrote that the players "spent a Boston sabbath, which is considerable sabbath," and things were indeed quiet everywhere in the city except at the Brunswick Hotel, which was World Series headquarters. There, Joe Lannin saw Charlie Ebbets, the Dodgers' owner, and asked him casually if he had arranged for tickets at Ebbets Field for Boston's Royal Rooters, a considerable segment of whom were planning to travel to Brooklyn for the third and fourth games. Ebbets looked at Lannin angrily and said, "No, but I'll do it right now." He picked up a telephone and put in a long distance call to Brooklyn. When he was connected with his Ebbets Field ticket office he said loudly, "I want you to hold out some of the best reserved seats for Tuesday's game. And while you're at it, save 250 of the worst seats in the grandstand for the Boston Rooters." He hung up the phone and glared at Lannin, who stared back in stunned silence for a moment before turning and walking out of the hotel. Ebbets, who was ill (he was suffering from dizzy spells and had disobeyed doctors' orders in order to come to Boston for the Series), was obviously upset. Asked for an explanation of his behavior, he said, "We received very bad treatment in the first game here. The seats the Brooklyn Boosters got were the worst in the ballpark. I am only retaliating." Ah, the good old days.

Boston's Royal Rooters were much in evidence the next afternoon, sitting in a group, complete with red-coated band, near the Red Sox dugout. Over and over the band played and the Rooters sang a tune called "Tessie," which for some inane reason had become their fight song. "Tessie," they sang, "you make me feel so bahadly. Why don't you turn around? Tessie, you know I love you sadly, babe. My heart weighs about a pound." Tessie might have been popular with the Royal Rooters, but followers of rival teams found her an agonizing bore. "That measly, monotonous melody," one newspaperman called it, but the Rooters, from politicians like James Michael Curley and Honey Fitzgerald down, sang it gleefully, soulfully and repeatedly.

When Ruth took the mound to start what was to become one of the most memorable of all World Series games, dark clouds were hanging low over Boston and rain was threatening. Ruth got rid of the first two Brooklyn batters with dispatch but the third man, Hy Myers, a stocky righthanded-hitting outfielder, hit Babe's second pitch on a line to right center field. Speaker might have caught the ball if he had still been playing center for the Red Sox, but Walker tripped as he started after it and fell. Hooper, coming over from right field, also stumbled, and the ball bounded through for extra bases. Hooper retrieved the ball near the fence and threw it in. The relay was bobbled and Myers, who never stopped running, beat the throw easily with a colorful but totally unnecessary head-first slide into home plate. It was an inside-the-park home run, and it put Brooklyn ahead, 1–0. It was also the only run the Dodgers were to score in the game, which lasted fourteen innings, although they came very close a couple of times.

In the third inning Ruth's rival pitcher, the lefthanded Sherry Smith, hit a clean double down the right field line but was out at third when he tried to stretch it into a triple; if he had stopped at second he most likely would have scored a moment later, because the next batter singled. The Dodgers went out without scoring, but the Red Sox picked up a run in their half of the inning when Ruth grounded out with a man on third. The base runner scored and Babe was credited with batting in a run.

The score was now tied, and it remained tied for eleven more innings, through a succession of melodramatic events. In the fifth, Thomas of the Red Sox hit a double and was tripped by Ivy Olson, the Dodger shortstop, as he tried for third. He was awarded the extra base by the umpires, who then had to break up a fight that erupted between Olson and Heinie Wagner, the Boston third base coach. After all that, Ruth struck out to end the inning.

The Red Sox might have scored in the sixth, except for a diving, rolling catch of a line drive by Myers in center field. In the seventh a Dodger rally was aborted and a furious argument begun when Myers—who seemed to be in the middle of everything—was called out at first base on an obviously bad decision by the umpire. In the eighth the Dodgers should have scored. Mike Mowrey, the third baseman, singled and was sacrificed to second. Otto Miller, the catcher, followed with a clean single to left, but the cautious Mowrey stopped at third. The throw from the outfield to the plate was wide, and Mowrey would have scored easily had he tried. The next batter hit a grounder to Scott at shortstop, and on this one Mowrey started for the plate. Scott threw home. Mowrey stopped halfway, backtracked and was immediately caught in a rundown: catcher to the third baseman to Ruth, who made the tag on the baseline.

When the Red Sox came to bat in the last of the ninth, it was becoming dark, the gloom of the heavy overcast aggravated by the early October dusk. Janvrin opened the inning with a line-drive double off Zach Wheat's glove in left field. Walker tried to sacrifice but hit a little foul ball off to one side of the plate. Carrigan, who wanted the runner moved over to third base, immediately took Walker out of the game and sent a substitute outfielder named Jimmy Walsh to bat in his place. Walsh bunted directly to the pitcher, and Smith pounced

on it and threw to Mowrey at third in time to catch Janvrin. The umpire had lifted his arm to call Janvrin out when the ball trickled from Mowrey's glove. The decision was reversed, and there were the Red Sox with men on first and third and no one out in the last half of the ninth inning of a tie ball game. Hoblitzell, the dependable, was up, and sure enough he lifted a fly ball into center field. Janvrin tagged up at third and the crowd began moving toward the exits. But Myers—who else?—took the fly ball on the run, threw perfectly to the plate and Janvrin was out by a foot.

The game went into extra innings. Boston almost scored in the eleventh when Scott singled and went to second on a sacrifice. After Ruth struck out, Hooper hit a ground ball off Mowrey's glove and Scott, moving as the ball was hit, went safely into third. The third baseman chased the ball to his left, picked it up and started to throw to first in an apparently hopeless attempt to get Hooper. It was a fake, but Scott fell for it. He took a couple of strides toward home plate and was tagged out when Mowrey turned and threw to Olson, the shortstop, who had come up behind the base.

Smith was in trouble each inning now, but Ruth, who had difficulty earlier, looked stronger than ever. He had given up six hits and three walks in the first seven innings, but from the eighth inning on he allowed no hits at all and only one walk. Boston was oozing confidence. When the popular Lewis came to bat in the eleventh with a man on first and two out, the Royal Rooters came to life. "Tessie!" they sang, and the band blared its accompaniment. Wilbert Robinson, the rotund Brooklyn manager, came red-faced and fuming off the Dodger bench and complained bitterly to the umpires, who dutifully ordered the Royal Rooters to knock it off. Nothing happened in the twelfth except that Ruth with two outs tried to bunt for a base hit and was thrown out. In the thirteenth Mowrey reached second for the Dodgers on an error and a sacrifice. Smith, a good hitting pitcher, poked a blooper into left field for what seemed a certain hit and an almost certain run. But Lewis came sprinting in and caught the ball off his shoe tops for the third out. You should have heard the Rooters sing "Tessie" then.

In the last of the fourteenth Smith, very tired, opened the inning by walking Hoblitzell for the fourth time. Lewis sacrificed him to second. It was so dark now that it was hard to see the ball. Carrigan therefore put Del Gainor, a righthander, in to bat for the usually dependable Gardner, who hit lefthanded, against the lefthanded Smith. Carrigan felt a righthanded batter would be better able to follow Smith's pitches in the murky light. And using all his weapons, he sent slim young Mike McNally in to run for the heavy-footed Hoblitzell. The wheels of baseball strategy turned even then, but Carrigan's maneuvers paid off. Gainor took a ball and a strike and then hit a liner over the third baseman's head. Most of the spectators could not tell where the ball went, but they could see Wheat, the left fielder, running desperately toward the foul line. McNally was around third and on his way to the plate before Wheat picked up the ball, and he scored easily with the winning run. Pandemonium. More "Tessie." And Babe Ruth, in his World Series debut, unless you count that pinch-hitting effort against Alexander the year before, had a 2–1, fourteen-inning victory in the longest and one of the most exciting World Series games ever played.

Ruth was roaring and shouting and jumping around the clubhouse afterwards like a high school kid. He grabbed Carrigan and yelled at him, "I told you a year ago I could take care of those National League bums, and you never gave me a chance." Carrigan, easing out of the Ruthian bear hug, laughed and said, "Forget it, Babe. You made monkeys out of them today."

It was Ruth's only appearance in the Series, which the Red Sox won, four games to one. Mays was the only Boston pitcher to lose, dropping the third game to the veteran Jack Coombs, who had previously been a star with the Philadelphia Athletics during their pennant-winning years. Ruth, in his ingenuously boorish way, tried to comfort the bad-tempered Mays by saying, "Well, if we had to lose one I'm glad it was to an old American Leaguer." Mays's reply was not recorded.

Comedian Billy Crystal, as here revealed in brief extracts from the pages of his autobiography, had a secret desire to be a baseball player. Come to think of it, who didn't?

# From *Absolutely Mahvelous*

## BILLY CRYSTAL *with* DICK SCHAAP

JOEL CAME up with a terrific idea, too. He invented the baseball game we played in our backyard when we weren't lip-synching Spike Jones records. We used a Little League bat and a badminton shuttlecock, and we laid out a baseball field, in miniature, to the exact proportions of Yankee Stadium—very short right field, very deep center. Joel, who became an art teacher, made a cutout of a catcher, and that was our backstop. If the pitcher threw the shuttlecock and hit the backstop, it was a strike. We called the game "Bird," even before Mark Fidrych.

We played an eighty-game season, with day games and night games. For night games, we took all my mother's lamps out of the living room and put them on extension cords, spreading them around the field with no shades on so they'd give off a good ballpark glow. We had a whole league with standings, batting and pitching averages, an official newsletter and even feuds among players. Little Al Jackson used to throw at Tom Tresh all the time. We had a postgame interview show in the garage—*Crystal's Corner.* On Oldtimers' Day we played a two-inning game as old people. We marked our foul lines with fertilizer. It stunk, and we loved it.

I really wanted to be a professional baseball player, but I had a problem. I know it's hard to believe, but I was short as a child. Very short. My brothers were both taller. Much taller.

*Don't get me started.*

The saddest words I ever heard were, "Maybe five-foot-nine." That's what the doctor said when my mother took me in to be examined for shortness two months before my bar mitzvah. "Maybe five-foot-nine."

Mom was afraid she had a midget wrestler on her hands. The doctor gave me appetite pills. I gained thirty pounds in two months, but I didn't grow an inch. At my bar mitzvah, I stood on a soda box two feet high. I was bursting out of my bar mitzvah suit.

*I hate when that happens.*

I played baseball anyway. I was shortstop and captain of the high school team. Tony Kornheiser, who's a sports columnist for the Washington *Post,* grew up in Long Beach around the same time I did, and Tony tells people I was a good player. For my size. He says I could've made Triple-A if I'd only been taller. I coulda been a contender.

I went to Marshall University in Huntington, West Virginia, to play second base. I had never been away from home before, not even to camp. The night I arrived, I went to a diner, and the man behind the counter pointed to a sign saying, WE RESERVE THE RIGHT TO REFUSE SERVICE TO ANYONE, then pointed to the mezuzah on my chest and said, "I won't serve you." Welcome to the USA.

Then I found out Marshall had eliminated its baseball program. Not because I was Jewish. They had no money. They also had no dorms. I lived in a hotel for a year. My roommate was twenty-six years old and rebelling against an Amish upbringing. It was a weird year.

I had a radio show on the campus station. It was a call-in show. I used to call in to myself. I'd put my questions on tape and then I'd do the answers live. I'd ask questions like: Should there be an IQ test for basketball players?

When I went home for the summer, I met Janice. We had our first date on July 30, 1966. We went to see the New York Mets play at Shea Stadium and celebrate Casey Stengel's seventy-sixth birthday. He rode in from center field in a chariot.

*He looked mahvelous.*

• • • • • • • • •

I worshiped Mickey Mantle. The first game I went to at Yankee Stadium, in 1956, I sat in Louis Armstrong's seats, and Mickey signed my scorecard and hit a home run, and from then on, whenever I went to the Stadium, I thought Mickey knew I was there and was telling himself, "Billy's here. I better have a good day. I better try to hit one for him."

More than a quarter of a century later, Mickey and I worked together on a baseball special preceding the All-Star Game, and at the end of the show—I had written the script—we stood on a field in Cooperstown, where the game was invented, and we tossed a ball back and forth. "Nice catch, kid," Mickey said, and then,

when I threw a ball wildly beyond his reach, he yelled, "Hey, don't make me run. If I could run, I'd still be playing." And I grinned, with tears in my eyes.

• • • • • • • • •

I was playing shortstop in a celebrity game at Dodger Stadium in front of 50,000 people, and on a ground ball up the middle, I raced over, fought off a bad hop, cut off the ball, spun and threw to Kareem Abdul-Jabbar at first base for the out. "Hey, that was a major-league play," said Reggie Smith of the Dodgers. Later, I hit a triple to

## ROBERT MANKOFF

*Drawing by Mankoff; © 1986 The New Yorker Magazine, Inc.*

*"Ken bats left-handed, enjoys cultural as well as outdoor activities, and seeks a sensitive, non-smoking woman for a lasting partnership that includes long walks, good music, and fielding practice."*

the opposite field, and after the game one of the Dodger officials asked me how old I was. "Early thirties," I said, and he looked disappointed. "Good game, anyway," he said. I got the feeling that if I had said eighteen, I might have had a shot at Albuquerque next year.

. . . . . . . . .

I never saw Joe DiMaggio play, but my father pointed him out to me at an oldtimers' game and told me he was the greatest. Years later, the night of the Ali-Holmes fight, I went out to dinner in Las Vegas with a group of people, and DiMaggio happened to be in the group. He spoke only once during dinner, to the maître d'. "Too much cheese in the antipasto," Joe D. said. He left the dining room with his strong, special stride, a John Wayne walk, and I heard someone say, "Look, there goes Mr. Coffee."

A movie was made from this novel, starring Ray Milland as the mild-mannered college professor Vernon Simpson who discovers a miracle "hair tonic" that repels anything made of wood, like a baseball bat. Under the name of King Kelly, he becomes a professional ballplayer, applies the tonic to the baseball, and pitches the St. Louis team into the World Series.

And then . . .

# From *It Happens Every Spring*

## VALENTINE DAVIES

WORLD SERIES fever hit St. Louis in a big way. Hotels were crowded and theatres were jammed. Mt. Stone could have sold every seat in his ball park many times over. A pair of bleacher seats and a brand-new Cadillac were considered about an even exchange. All normal activities came to a standstill during the afternoon of the game. Nor was the campus immune to all this excitement. There were few faculty members who had not smuggled radios into their offices to listen to the Series broadcast, play by play. The fall semester had just begun, and students crowded every radio, public and private—in cars; in drugstores; in fraternity houses—everywhere—tense, silent groups of undergraduates clustered about a loud-speaker or a television screen.

The lucky ones, who were able to wangle seats— professors, instructors and students alike—shamelessly cut classes to attend the game. Mixed in with the typical crowd of baseball fans, who jammed the stadium, were a surprising number of staid professors who had not witnessed a baseball game since the turn of the century. And many an elderly dean was astonished to find himself rooting and shouting with the best of them in a most undignified manner.

For King Kelly was the hero of the Series, and by this time there were few people connected with the University who did not know that he was Teaching Fellow Vernon Simpson.

Having enjoyed a four-day rest, Vernon pitched the opening game and won it handily. But New York came back the next day with a vengeance and blasted poor Hooper for six runs in one explosive inning. St. Louis was clearly out of the running for the rest of the afternoon.

With the score tied at one game each, the Series moved to New York. Debbie and her mother spent anxious hours each afternoon huddled over the radio in the living room, hanging on every word.

Before a record crowd, in the vast New York stadium, Vernon stifled the big-city sluggers and won the third game, giving St. Louis a 2 to 1 lead. But next day the New Yorkers staged another seventh-inning uprising, this time at the expense of Erickson, and pulled up even again at two games all. With only one day off, Kelly was forced to pitch the fifth game. The strain was beginning to show, and he wasn't having an easy time of it. In fact, he came up to the last half of the ninth with a very shaky one-run lead. Vernon walked the first man up and allowed the second to fly out to Bevan in deep right field. Bearing down now, he struck out the next batter, but not before a wild pitch had put the tying run on third. With two out, Vernon worked the count on Rudnik to three and two.

Listening to the broadcast, Debbie and Mrs. Greenleaf sat petrified, holding their breath.

"Here comes the pitch!" The sportscaster's voice was hoarse with tension. "It's got to be good this time! . . . It is! Rudnik swings—and he misses! . . . And that's the game, folks, Kelly's done it again!"

Debbie jumped up cheering and hugging her mother in wild excitement. Then suddenly she stopped and switched off the radio as her father entered the room. But Mrs. Greenleaf was too excited to think.

"Hurray!" she shouted, happily, "Vernon won again!"

Debbie's gasp was followed by a deathly silence. Mrs. Greenleaf's hand went up to her mouth; she looked at Debbie, horrified. Debbie turned to her father.

"Yes, it's true, Dad," she said calmly. "You may not believe it but—Vernon is King Kelly."

Dr. Greenleaf looked from one to the other in surprise. "Have you just found that out?" he said.

"No, Dad," said Debbie, lamely, "but we didn't think you knew . . ."

"Why didn't you say something, Alfred?" his wife demanded indignantly.

"Because there didn't appear to be anything to say. If Debbie wants to marry a baseball player, that's her affair . . ."

"But he's not just a baseball player, Dad," said Debbie. "He's Vernon . . . !"

Her father shook his head slowly. "He's just a baseball player now," he said.

St. Louis returned home with a 3 to 2 lead in games. All they needed was one more victory to win the Series. But now Jimmy Dolan had to do some fateful masterminding. The obvious move was to put Kelly in to pitch the next game and end the Series then and there. But King Kelly had pitched three out of the five long, hard-fought games, and he had been none too steady in the last one. If he should pitch the next game and drop it, Jimmy would lose his ace-in-the-hole, and the Series would be as good as over. On the other hand, if he sent Hooper in, the worst that could happen, if he lost, was that the Series would be tied again and he would have Kelly, refreshed and ready after a two-day rest, to pitch the final and deciding game. After many long powwows with Mr. Stone and others, Dolan decided to take a chance on Hooper and save Kelly for the final game.

And Hooper almost made it, too. Rising to unprecedented heights, he held the explosive gang from Gotham in check for eight tight, tingling innings. But then in the ninth, with two men on, he made the fatal error of trying to slip a slow ball past blockbuster Billy Marx. There was a sharp resounding crack, a roar from the crowd, a scuffle in the right-field bleachers, and three New York runners went trotting merrily around the diamond.

Sitting in the dugout, Monk and Vernon looked at each other glumly.

"There goes the old ball game," Monk said.

He slapped Vernon gently on the knee. "You better get a good night's rest, kid," he told him, "you're gonna have a busy day tomorrow."

Vernon slept long and peacefully, and awoke next morning, refreshed and eager. The fact that he was to pitch the deciding game of the World Series did not disturb him unduly. It would no doubt be a somewhat strenuous and exciting afternoon, but Vernon felt that he had plenty of justification for his calm, unruffled confidence. Monk was still snoring gently in the next bed, as Vernon tiptoed into the bathroom to take a shower, and

was still blissfully sleeping when Vernon had finished dressing. Taking advantage of the privacy, Vernon took his little sponge in its pliofilm bag into the bathroom to fill it for the last time. He opened the medicine cabinet and took out the bottle which contained his precious "hair tonic." To his surprise, the bottle was almost empty. He was quite certain that it had been more than half full the day before. It didn't matter, of course; he still had one full bottle left in his suitcase. Nevertheless, it seemed odd. He couldn't understand it.

He emptied what little liquid there was onto the sponge and returned to the bedroom to get the other bottle. As he did so, he glanced at his watch. It was high time Monk was up, too.

He crossed to Monk's bed and reached out his hand to shake him. But instead, he stopped and stared incredulously. Monk had rolled over in his sleep so that the shiny bald center of his cranium was less than half an inch from the wooden headboard of the bed. The wiry wreath of hair surrounding his bald spot was shiny with grease. With each breath, his head moved closer to the wood, and as it did so, his stiff crown of hair flattened and rose again in gently rhythmic waves. Vernon watched the strange undulations with a mixture of anxiety and amusement. That explained what had happened to the rest of the "hair tonic" in the bottle.

Vernon went to his suitcase to get the other bottle. He couldn't find it. He searched through the suitcase feverishly, scrambling its contents and scattering them all over the floor. He had seen the bottle there when he had packed to leave the train. But now it was gone!

He turned and grabbed Monk's shoulder and shook him violently.

"Monk . . . ! Monk . . . !" he said.

Lanigan rolled over and opened one eye.

"Monk, did you take a bottle out of my suitcase?"

"Huh?" said Monk. "Bottle? Bottle of what?"

"Hair tonic," said Vernon, tensely. "Did you take the bottle out of my suitcase?"

"Oh . . . the hair tonic . . . yeah," said Monk sitting up sleepily. "I meant to tell you. I seen it in there yesterday. I didn't think you'd mind."

He yawned and stretched elaborately.

"But it's my last bottle," said Vernon. "What did you do with it?"

"Why I gave it to Jimmy. He's gettin' pretty thin on top, too." He rubbed his bald spot. "It done me a lot of good, kid—look, I'm growin' a whole new . . ."

But Vernon had gone, slamming the door behind him. Monk looked after him, shaking his head.

"Jumpin' Jupiter," he said, "what a character!"

Vernon tore down the hall to Dolan's room at a dead run. He knocked at the door. There was no answer. He knocked again—louder. Still no answer. He tried the door; it was unlocked. He opened it cautiously and entered the room. Through the open bathroom door he saw Jimmy at the washstand. The water was running full force and Jimmy was splashing generous handfuls onto his face. Vernon crossed the room and stood in the doorway.

"Jimmy," he said, "I'm sorry to bother you . . ."

Dolan went on splashing away.

"Jimmy . . . !" Vernon shouted.

But the roar of the faucet drowned him out. He entered the bathroom and awkwardly tapped Dolan on the shoulder. Jimmy turned with a start and squinted at Vernon, his hands and face dripping with water.

"Oh," he said, "it's you, Kelly . . ."

"Er—I wanted to talk to you," said Vernon.

"What did you say?" said Dolan.

"I want to talk to you!" Vernon shouted.

"Okay," said Jimmy, "what's on your mind?"

"It's about the hair tonic," said Vernon, loudly.

"About what?"

"The hair tonic!" Vernon bellowed. "Monk said he gave you a bottle of my hair tonic."

"Oh, yeah," said Jimmy, returning to his ablutions. "Monk said it'll grow hair on a billiard ball. Kind of an insult."

"It's a very rare solution. It can't be duplicated."

"Okay," said Dolan. "I'm willing to pay for it. How much do you . . . ?"

"No, no!" Vernon shouted anxiously. "It's not that. It's my last bottle, Jimmy—I need it!"

Dolan turned and looked at Vernon.

"*You* need it? What for? You want to play for the House of David?"

Vernon could think of no plausible explanation. He cursed his own stupidity. Why had he ever said it was hair tonic? He could have told Monk it was any one of a dozen other things—a special medicine, for instance—anything but hair tonic.

"It's just a peculiarity—a superstition," he said. "And especially today."

Dolan shook his head. "I've heard of rabbits' feet and elks' teeth—but lucky hair tonic—that's a new one!"

"Please," said Vernon desperately. "Have you got it, Jimmy?"

"Yeah, yeah," said Jimmy. "If that's going to make you happy."

He opened the medicine cabinet with his wet hands and looked inside, blinking.

"Where did I put it?" he said. "Oh, yeah, there it is."

He reached up and grabbed the bottle. A larger one started to topple off the crowded shelf and he juggled the two bottles with his slippery wet hands. Vernon watched in agonized horror, involuntarily reaching out. But it

was too late. The little bottle slipped from Dolan's hand and fell into the basin with a crash. Vernon stood there, dumb and helpless, watching the World Series running down the drain.

The eyes and ears of the nation were on Vernon as he walked out to the mound to start the game. Newsreel and television cameras were focused on him. Sportscasters described every move to a nation-wide network. The stands were packed to overflowing with a tense, excited crowd. Monk had been faithful to the last, and Debbie sat between her mother and Mr. Forsythe in a safe location in the upper stand.

Vernon's calm, almost leisurely appearance gave no indication of what was going on inside him. The sponge in his pocket held less than half the amount of the magic solution he needed for a full nine-inning game. Vernon was facing almost certain disaster and he knew it. But he was not entirely without resources. He had worked out a plan of campaign. He knew that by now he had a tremendous psychological advantage over the batters, and he planned to make the utmost use of it. He would start by anointing the ball for at least the first two innings before hazarding any pitching on his own. From then on he would use the liquid as sparingly as possible, rubbing the ball into his glove only in the pinches, and he would hope and pray for the breaks.

The first three innings went surprisingly well. Even after he had stopped using the solution, he was able to hold the New York batters scoreless while St. Louis built up a two-run lead.

It wasn't until the middle of the fourth that Hammond stunned the crowd by connecting for a solid two-base hit off Kelly. Such a thing was practically unheard of and it shook Vernon quite as badly as it did the fans. In fact, he was so disturbed that he hit the next man, Sterling, on the sleeve, with an inside pitch, and walked Brown, the New York catcher after that. With the bases full and one out, he used a little of the fluid to strike the next man out. He decided to take his chances against Creston, the New York pitcher who came up next, but Creston rapped out an unexpected single which brought in one run, and now he faced Arizola, the head of the New York list. Vernon took no more chances. He pounded the ball into his glove and Arizola went down swinging.

Neither team got anywhere in the fifth, but in the first half of the sixth Vernon was in serious trouble again. His sponge was almost dry now, and what little liquid he had left he could use only in dire emergency. The bitter lesson of the two hits in the fourth had made him very leery of putting any straight clean pitches over the plate, and in trying to cut the corners he had walked three men. The bases were full, and now he was facing Lefty Hiller, one of the most consistent sluggers in either league. To put it straight over was an obvious form of suicide, and to walk him meant a run. Mustering all the control he had, Vernon managed to work the count to three and two. Lefty took a determined stand and swung his big bat ominously. Vernon threw one for the inside corner.

"Bawl Four!" roared Brannick, the umpire behind the plate.

Lanigan was beside himself as Hiller and the other New York runners happily trotted ahead a base. He tore off his mask and started bellowing at the umpire. The stands were in an uproar as the tying run came in.

The calm and jovial Mr. Forsythe jumped to his feet.

"Kill the ump!" he roared.

Debbie frantically pulled at his sleeve. "Sit down, sit down before Vernon sees you!"

Still fuming and grumbling, Forsythe sat.

At the plate, Monk was stamping and raging and waving his arms, describing Brannick's optical deficiencies in no uncertain terms. Nor was Brannick suffering this abuse in silence. He was shouting and threatening and waving his finger under Lanigan's nose as Vernon walked calmly in from the mound.

"Take it easy, Monk," he said. "I'm sorry, but Brannick's right. I missed the corner by six inches."

Monk was too flabbergasted to reply. He stood there with his mouth open, staring incredulously at Vernon. But to Brannick, such calm agreement was unheard of. He turned on Vernon suspiciously.

"Say, what's the matter with you?" he said.

Some good luck, good fielding and a double play pulled Vernon through the first half of the seventh. And in the last half, St. Louis went on a hitting spree which knocked Creston and Jacobs out of the box and gave them a two-run lead. With two men on and none out, it looked as if the game would be sewed up right there. But Harry Bevan hit into a double play and Manning, the next St. Louis batter, had been hitting badly all afternoon.

Sitting in the dugout next to Vernon, Monk looked very unhappy. "Judas, that's tough," he said. "I thought we was gonna put it on ice right now."

He took off his cap and scratched his head. Vernon looked over at Monk's circle of greasy hair. His face lit up. He reached out his right hand and rubbed his fingers through the thick grease. Lanigan turned and looked at Vernon, startled.

"Hey, Kelly, what's eatin' you?"

Vernon looked at his hand. His fingers were shining. Perhaps he could get enough for one or two pitches.

"I just did it for luck, Monk," he said, and rubbed Lanigan's head again.

Monk gave him a worried look and quickly put on his cap.

Manning had popped out, and Vernon followed Monk

from the dugout carefully guarding his right hand as he walked across to the mound. He refused any warm-up pitches and beckoned Granite, the first New York batter, into the box. Before he wound up, he rubbed his greasy fingers on the ball.

It worked. Granite swung at two beauties and missed them clean. But Vernon made the mistake of trying to stretch it for a third, and Granite connected for a two-base Texas Leaguer.

The next man up was Hammond. The same Hammond who had caused Vernon all the trouble in the fourth. Whatever else happened, he was not going to let him have two long hits in a row. He used the last bit of his solution and struck Hammond out.

It was then that the mayhem really began. Sterling got a double, and Brown and Wheeler a single each. The score was tied again.

Debbie turned and looked at Mr. Forsythe, bewildered. "I don't understand it," she said. "They've never done this to Vernon before."

"Nonsense," said Forsythe, indignantly. "They've used three pitchers against him, and Vernon's holding his own against all three of them."

He heard a sharp crack and turned his head to see the ball sailing over the shortstop's head as another runner crossed the plate.

Mrs. Greenleaf glanced at the scoreboard. New York had five runs; St. Louis—four.

"I'm afraid he's not holding his own any more," she said.

Monk rubbed up a new ball and walked slowly out toward the mound and handed it to Kelly.

"Where's that old hop, kid?" he said.

Vernon shook his head grimly. "I haven't got it any more . . . It's gone," he said.

"Okay, kid, just relax. Let 'em connect. You got seven men behind you. They'll handle 'em. They're a great ball team." He turned and walked back to the plate.

They'd better be, thought Vernon, as he returned to the mound. There was nothing he could do to help them any more. He looked over toward the bull pen, hopefully. But Dolan hadn't even sent another pitcher out to warm up. After all these months, not even Dolan could believe what was happening to Kelly.

Vernon steeled himself, and pitched. The batter swung sharply, and the ball came bounding across the infield toward third. With lightning precision, Whitey Davis came in on it, scooped up the ball and whipped it across to Baker at second. Baker shot it on to first for a dazzling double play.

As Vernon slowly crossed the infield toward the dugout, he was lost in thought. The beautiful precision of that double play had made him realize the truth of what Lanigan had said. They *were* a great ball team—all of them. They were real ball players. He felt a wave of gratitude and affection for his teammates, and an added sense of responsibility. He put on his jacket and sat unhappily in a corner of the dugout.

"What did I tell you, Kelly?" said Monk, gleefully, as he sat down next to Vernon. "Quit worryin' out there. This game ain't over yet!"

"I wish it were," said Vernon.

"You gotta keep your chin up, kid. You gotta go out there lookin' cocky. You gotta keep bluffin', see?"

"I'm afraid they've called my bluff," said Vernon.

But Monk didn't hear him. He was on his feet cheering. Whitey Davis had rapped out a whistling single.

Dolan was pacing back and forth in front of the dugout, changing his strategy to meet each new development of the game. Now he sent Rogers in to pinch-hit for Bailey, and he sent Hooper and Erickson out to the bull pen to warm up. Rogers completed his mission perfectly, laying down a delicate sacrifice bunt which sent Whitey to second. And then Bronco Turner rocked the ball park with a home run high into the left-field stands. The next two batters went out in rapid succession, but nobody cared. St. Louis was ahead again, 6 to 5, and if they could only manage to hold the fighting, slugging invaders scoreless for just this one more inning, the game, the Series and the world would all be theirs.

As his teammates leapt out of the dugout and scattered to their positions, Vernon rose and looked at Dolan uncertainly. Jimmy nodded and gave him a slap on the back.

"I'm leaving you in there, Kelly," he said. "It's your game to win or lose."

Vernon stood there. He started to say something and then he stopped. He slipped off his jacket and Dolan took it from him. Vernon turned and walked grimly toward the mound. He would have to face New York's heaviest hitters, one right after the other. He knew what was going to happen. He knew it was hopeless. But all his emotions were frozen inside him now; he was beyond despair or terror. He was numb and dazed. He couldn't feel—he could only think in a strange, detached and logical sort of way.

Winters, the first man up, hit the first ball Vernon pitched for a ringing single which he nearly stretched into a two-bagger. This was the beginning, thought Vernon. And it was going to end in a debacle. It was merely a question of how long Dolan would leave him in.

Vernon braced himself and went on pitching with grim, automaton-like persistence. While Winters danced tormentingly back and forth off first, Vernon laboriously worked out his string on Pike to three and two. Monk called for an inside pitch and Vernon tried his best. But Brannick called a ball and sent Pike trotting happily down to first.

Vernon caught Monk's return and stood poised in the pitcher's box. His face was a white mask. The winning run was on first—one good long hit and the Series would be over. The next three batters were Hiller, Granite and Hammond. All three of them had been socking him unmercifully. What was the use? He might just as well quit right now.

But something within him refused to accept this verdict; some crazy, illogical spark insisted that he keep on trying.

He gave a quick glance toward first and pitched. Hiller took a swift cut at the ball and sent it shooting straight up into the sky. When it came down, Monk was under it and there was one out.

Well, that was an unexpected piece of luck, thought Vernon, but it didn't alter the situation. There was still Granite and Hammond. And Granite was already in the batter's box, brandishing his war club menacingly and grinning at Kelly confidently.

Vernon took a deep breath and pitched. He saw Granite swing and connect and he saw the ball go sailing in a high rising arc. He turned in the box and followed it with his eyes. This was it. This was the end. Far away in right field he saw Bevan leap high into the air, his glove flat against the concrete wall. He saw him miraculously spear the ball and come tumbling to the ground with a jarring, bruising thud, and then he saw him jump up, still clinging to the ball.

As the crowd roared its appreciation, Vernon felt another sharp wave of gratitude. Once more he had been saved by the skill of his teammates.

And now he faced Hammond, the power-house. In each of his last two trips to the plate he had smashed out a two-bagger.

Mr. Forsythe turned to Debbie.

"Two out and Hammond up," he said. "This is the game right here."

There was a deathly silence in the stands as Vernon pitched. The ball was high and wide and Hammond let it go. How long could this ordeal last? It seemed to Vernon that he had been out there on that pitcher's box for hours. He wiped the cold sweat from his forehead and set himself to pitch again. He tried to keep it low and close, but the ball came across the plate just the way Hammond liked it. He hit it squarely on the nose. With a sinking, hopeless feeling of disaster, Vernon saw the ball coming straight toward him, high above his head. Reaching up, he made a blind, desperate leap into the air. Then he felt a sharp, stinging blow that sent him reeling backward off his feet. He landed sprawling on his back with a violent jolt that knocked his wind out. He lay there for an instant, stunned. Then he looked up. His hand felt numb and dead, but the ball remained stuck in his glove.

Still lying there, he frowned as he tried to collect himself. He was aware of a mighty roar, and the air seemed to be filled with flying cushions and paper and score cards. He craned his neck and looked about. His teammates were rushing towards him from all sides. He slowly began to pick himself up, and it was only then that it dawned on him that his ordeal was over; that the reason for all the roaring and the excitement was that he had won the game.

For wind and wildness, no major league All-Star Game ever has come close to the one played in 1961 at San Francisco's Candlestick Park. If seven errors, a hit batsman, a passed ball, and a pitcher being charged with a balk when he was blown off the mound don't grab you, consider that no fewer than *fifteen* of the players in this game went on to be voted into the Hall of Fame: Yogi Berra, Stan Musial, Mickey Mantle, Al Kaline, Hoyt Wilhelm, Brooks Robinson, Whitey Ford, Harmon Killebrew, Eddie Mathews, Sandy Koufax, Hank Aaron, Frank Robinson, and Warren Spahn—plus Willie Mays and Roberto Clemente, who drove in the tying and winning runs, respectively, in the bottom of the 10th. (A sixteenth player in that game, Nellie Fox, may yet make it into the Hall.)

# 1961:
# National League 5,
# American League 4

## JOHN DREBINGER

IN AS loosely played a game as baseball's midsummer classic ever has known, the National League today defeated the American League in the first of 1961's two all-star games before a roaring crowd of 44,115 fans.

Seven errors were committed, five by the Nationals and two by the Americans. The total broke the all-star record of six set at Ebbets Field in 1949.

The National Leaguers won it in the last of the tenth, 5 to 4. A two-bagger by the Giants' redoubtable Willie Mays drove in the first tally and a single by Bob Clemente sent Willie across the plate with the winning run.

But minutes before this, Danny Murtagh's Nationals all but had the victory blown out of their grasp as their players were caught in the swirling winds of San Francisco's Candlestick Park. They made four errors in the last two innings while the Americans tied the score with two runs in the ninth and then moved one ahead in the top of the tenth.

For eight innings, in the stillness of an unusually hot and almost windless afternoon, brilliant National League pitching, starting with Warren Spahn, had held the vaunted American League power to just one hit while the senior loop piled up a 3–1 lead.

That one hit had been a homer by Harmon Killebrew as he entered in the sixth inning as a pinch-hitter. It was smacked off Mike McCormick of the Giants.

But by then the Nationals already had scored a run off Paul Richards' starter, Whitey Ford. Clemente of the Pirates drove this one home in the second with a triple. In the fourth the Nationals picked up their second tally with the help of an American League misplay. And in the eighth, George Altman, a Cub outfielder, stroked a homer over the right-field barrier.

That had the Nationals two in front as the encounter moved into the ninth. With a spanking breeze already stirring up a lot of dust, local fans, knowing full well what was coming, were heading for the exits before being blown into the bay.

But within minutes, more than wind was swirling in the arena. Mickey Mantle, hitless in three tries at bat, was no longer in the American League lineup as the wind and everything else hit the stunned National Leaguers from all sides.

With one out and Elroy Face, the Pirates' star reliever, all set to lock up the victory, Norm Cash started the Americans' ninth-inning drive with a two-bagger.

It was the second hit for the harried Richards forces. The third one followed immediately as Al Kaline,

Mantle's replacement, singled to score the Detroit first baseman.

Now Manager Murtagh began reaching desperately into his bullpen. Out popped Sandy Koufax, a Dodger left-hander, only to be slapped for a single by Roger Maris. It scored Nellie Fox, who had gone in to run for Cash. That was all for Sandy, and the Giants' Stu Miller took over.

It was now blowing in lively fashion and, if what followed seems an incredible performance for men considered the highest craftsmen in their profession, it nevertheless was excusable.

Miller, a diminutive right-hander, immediately committed a balk that advanced Kaline and Maris to third and second respectively. Rocky Colavito followed with a grounder that Ken Boyer, crack third baseman of the Cardinals, stumbled all over for an error.

Kaline scored the tying run while Maris held up at second. The scoring for the inning ended here, but not the errors, which continued to give Candlestick's record crowd a violent case of jitters.

The catcher, Smoky Burgess, dropped a foul near the plate on Tony Kubek, who then struck out. Yogi Berra, appearing as a pinch-hitter, grounded to the second baseman, Don Zimmer, whose wide throw to first pulled Bill White off the bag. However, that merely filled the bases, and the gathering, which had tossed $250,230.81 into the players' pension pool, was still breathing, but with difficulty.

When Dick Howser followed with the third out, leaving the score tied, the sigh of relief from the fans almost matched the ever-increasing gale.

But the folks were still uneasy when Hoyt Wilhelm, the sixth and last of the American League hurlers Richards trotted out, held the Nationals scoreless in the last of the ninth.

In the tenth they nearly died. With one out, Miller walked Fox, who had remained in the game as the Americans' second baseman. Then Boyer followed with his second error, the most ghastly of the afternoon. The Cards' third baseman, scooping up Kaline's grounder, fired the ball into right field and Fox scored all the way from first.

That had the Americans in front for the first time, but the lead was brief. Hank Aaron, the noted Braves' slugger, pinch-hitting for Miller, opened the Nationals' tenth with a single to center.

Berra, who had remained as a catcher in the ninth, only to give way immediately to Elston Howard because of Wilhelm's exclusive knuckleball, now was to see his Yankee team-mate have his troubles. Howard let one of Wilhelm's flutter balls get away for a passed ball while Hoyt was pitching to Mays.

That put Aaron on second. When Willie the Wonder followed with his two-bagger, Aaron galloped home to tie the score again.

The wind was now even raising havoc with Wilhelm's knuckler. The Orioles' brilliant reliever hit Frank Robinson with a stray pitch.

A moment later, Clemente, who had driven in the Nationals' second tally of the afternoon with a sacrifice fly in the fourth, ended it all with a sharp single to right. Almost casually Mays jogged in from second and that was it.

With this victory the onrushing Nationals have now whittled the American League lead in all-star competition to a 16–14 margin. It was the Nationals' fourth triumph in the last five games and tenth in the last fourteen.

The Americans, for all the flurry they made at the end, connected for only four hits. The National League pitchers fanned a total of twelve batters, which tied an all-star record.

Out-of-towners, who had been hearing tales of the frosty gales that in the twinkling of an eye convert Candlestick Park into an icy wind tunnel, were more than a mite mystified as they entered the picturesque, sun-drenched arena nestled under the lee of Morvey's Hill.

In no time at all, they were in their shirtsleeves and perspiring as profusely as if they were sitting under the lee of Coogan's Bluff watching a July 4 double-header between the Giants and the Dodgers in the old Polo Grounds.

There was scarcely a breath of air stirring and the thermometer read 85 degrees. It could have been Kansas City or a place they rarely mention in these parts. On a map it's called Los Angeles. The wind was still to come.

It was, however, a gay and festive gathering, and there were lusty cheers for all the stars as they were formally introduced in the pre-game ceremonies. But the noisiest ovation of all was saved for the National League's "grand old man," the 40-year-old Stan Musial, who was appearing in his twentieth all-star game.

And there were still some pre-game cheers left when Casey Stengel, as guest of Commissioner Ford C. Frick, reared back to toss out the first ball. It was a well-delivered, left-handed pitch by the one-time left-handed dental student who ranked as one of baseball's greatest managers.

As the game got on the way, it was even more difficult to grasp the idea that baseball is a young man's game. For no sooner had the opening salute to Musial died down than the fans began cheering another 40-year-old, Spahn of the Braves.

Last April 28, the Milwaukee southpaw hurled a no-hitter. He might well have repeated that performance today were it not for all-star rules that bar a pitcher from working more than three innings. Spahn's three innings were letter perfect. He faced nine batters and they went down like tenpins, three of them on strikes.

Meanwhile, Ford, the American League's sixteen-game winner, was still having trouble shedding his all-star jinx of long standing, although Whitey acquitted himself better than in most of his previous midsummer appearances.

With one out in the second, Clemente drove a liner to the wire railing in right center. As Mantle and Maris converged on the ball, Maris reached it first. For a moment it looked as if the Yankee right-fielder had made a backhand catch of the ball. But he couldn't hold it and before Mantle could recover the ball and get it to the infield, Clemente was on third with a triple. He scored on Bill White's sacrifice fly by Mantle in center.

Although stung for a two-bagger by a pinch-hitter, Dick Stuart, in the third, Ford finished his three-inning stint without further trouble.

But with the fourth, fresh annoyances cropped up for the American Leaguers. As Frank Lary, the Tigers' ace right-hander, stepped to the mound, Kubek, the Yanks' crack shortstop, made a two-base boot of Mays' sharp grounder on the first play.

At the same time Lary had to leave the game. The Detroit star, who had pitched a nine-inning, three-hit shutout against the Angels on Sunday, complained of an ailing right shoulder and the Senators' Dick Donovan was hastily called in from the bullpen. Later it was learned that Lary was suffering from an inflamed tendon in his right shoulder.

Donovan couldn't prevent Mays from scoring. Willie advanced to third on Orlando Cepeda's infield out and galloped home, with cap flying off, on Clemente's sacrifice fly to Maris in right.

Incidentally, that tally enabled Mays to set an all-star record of most runs scored, with a total of twelve. He had been tied with Musial at eleven.

In the fifth Musial made his official bow and exit, as a pinch-hitter. With two on, he flied to left. Though Mays then singled, filling the bases, Donovan got out of this jam.

While this was going on, the Nationals continued to get two more innings of flawless pitching from the Reds' Bob Purkey, who had replaced Spahn after the third.

Even the fact that Cepeda opened the fourth by making a two-base muff of Johnny Temple's fly in left did not seem to disturb the Cincinnati right-hander. He snuffed out the next three batters to end the fourth and repeated the performance in the fifth.

With the sixth, however, the American League's power finally asserted itself long enough to crack the Nationals' two-run lead in half. With one out and the Giants' McCormick on the mound, Killebrew belted a towering fly toward left. It cleared the barrier just beyond Cepeda's reach.

According to local authorities, it was one of the highest flies ever to clear that sector of the park, where the prevailing wind blows from left to right. It had not started to blow yet. However, with the eighth, there was a spanking breeze blowing as Altman, a Cub outfielder, belted one over the 375-foot marker in right center and into the bleachers just beyond.

Mike Fornieles of the Red Sox, who had just replaced Jim Bunning in this inning, was the victim of that shot. It was made on Mike's first pitch. When Frank Robinson followed with a single, along with a stolen base, Richards brought in his own ace reliever, Wilhelm.

The latter made quick work of the next two batters and that is the way matters stood as the struggle moved into its windblown finale, the Nationals leading by two, but not for long.

# 1974: 715

## JOSEPH DURSO

ATLANTA, APRIL 8—Henry Aaron ended the great chase tonight and passed Babe Ruth as the leading home-run hitter in baseball history when he hit No. 715 before a national television audience and 53,775 persons in Atlanta Stadium.

The 40-year-old outfielder for the Atlanta Braves broke the record on his second time at bat, but on his first swing of a clamorous evening. It was a soaring drive in the fourth inning off Al Downing of the Los Angeles Dodgers, and it cleared the fence in left-center field, 385 feet from home plate.

Skyrockets arched over the jammed stadium in the rain as the man from Mobile trotted around the bases for the 715th time in a career that began a quarter of a century ago with the Indianapolis Clowns in the old Negro leagues.

It was 9:07 o'clock, 39 years after Ruth had hit his 714th and four days after Aaron had hit his 714th on his first swing of the bat in the opening game of the season.

The history-making home run carried into the Atlanta bull pen, where a relief pitcher named Tom House made a dazzling one-handed catch against the auxiliary scoreboard. He clutched it against the boards, far below the grandstand seats, where the customers in "Home-Run Alley" were massed, waiting to retrieve a cowhide ball that in recent days had been valued as high as $25,000 on the auction market.

So Aaron not only ended the great home-run derby, but also ended the controversy that had surrounded it. His employers had wanted him to hit No. 715 in Atlanta, and had even benched him on alien soil in Cincinnati.

The commissioner of baseball, Bowie Kuhn, ordered the Braves to start their star yesterday or face "serious penalties." And tonight the dispute and the marathon finally came home to Atlanta in a razzle-dazzle setting.

The stadium was packed with its largest crowd since the Braves left Milwaukee and brought major league baseball to the Deep South nine years ago. Pearl Bailey sang the national anthem; the Jonesboro High School band marched; balloons and fireworks filled the overcast sky before the game; Aaron's life was dramatized on a huge color map of the United States painted across the outfield grass, and Bad Henry was serenaded by the Atlanta Boy Choir, which now includes girls.

The commissioner was missing, pleading that a "previous commitment" required his presence tomorrow in Cleveland, and his emissary was roundly booed when he mentioned Kuhn's name. But Gov. Jimmy Carter was there, along with Mayor Maynard Jackson, Sammy Davis Jr. and broadcasters and writers from as far away as Japan, South America and Britain.

To many Atlantans, it was like the city's festive premiere of "Gone With the Wind" during the 1930's when Babe Ruth was still the hero of the New York Yankees and the titan of professional sports. All that was needed to complete the evening was home run No. 715, and Aaron supplied that.

The first time he batted, leading off the second inning, Aaron never got the bat off his shoulder. Downing, a onetime pitcher for the Yankees, wearing No. 44, threw a ball and a called strike and then three more balls. Aaron, wearing his own No. 44, watched them all and then took first base while the crowd hooted and booed because their home town hero had been walked.

A few moments later, Henry scored on a double by Dusty Baker and an error in left field, and even made a little history doing that.

It was the 2,063d time he had crossed home plate in his 21-year career in the majors, breaking the National League record held by Willie Mays and placing Aaron behind Ty Cobb and Ruth, both American Leaguers.

Then came the fourth inning, with the Dodgers leading by 3–1 and the rain falling, with colored umbrellas raised in the stands and the crowd roaring every time Aaron appeared. Darrell Evans led off for Atlanta with a grounder behind second base that the shortstop, Bill Russell, juggled long enough for an error. And up came Henry for the eighth time this season and the second this evening.

Downing pitched ball one inside, and Aaron watched impassively. Then came the second pitch, and this time Henry took his first cut of the night. The ball rose high toward left-center as the crowd came to its feet shouting, and as it dropped over the inside fence separating the outfield from the bull pen area, the skyrockets were fired and the scoreboard lights flashed in six-foot numerals: "715."

Aaron, head slightly bowed and elbows turned out, slowly circled the bases as the uproar grew. At second base he received a handshake from Dave Lopes of the Dodgers, and between second and third from Russell.

By now two young men from the seats had joined Aaron, but did not interfere with his 360-foot trip around the bases into the record books.

As he neared home plate, the rest of the Atlanta team had already massed beyond it as a welcoming delegation. But Aaron's 65-year-old father, Herbert Aaron Sr., had jumped out of the family's special field-level box and outraced everybody to the man who had broken Babe Ruth's record.

By then the entire Atlanta bull pen corps had started to race in to join the fun, with House leading them, the ball gripped tightly in his hand. He delivered it to Aaron, who was besieged on the grass about 20 feet in front of the field boxes near the Braves' dugout.

Besides the ball, Henry received a plaque from the owner of the team, Bill Bartholomay; congratulations from Monte Irvin, the emissary from Commissioner Kuhn, and a howling, standing ovation from the crowd.

The game was interrupted for 11 minutes during all the commotion, after which the Braves got back to work and went on to win their second straight, this time by 7–4. The Dodgers, apparently shaken by history, made six errors and lost their first game after three straight victories.

"It was a fastball, right down the middle of the upper part of the plate," Downing said later. "I was trying to get it down to him, but I didn't and he hit it good—as he would."

"When he first hit it, I didn't think it might be going. But like a great hitter, when he picks his pitch, chances are he's going to hit it pretty good."

Afterward the Braves locked their clubhouse for a time so that they could toast Aaron in champagne. Then the new home-run king reflected on his feat and on some intimations that he had not been "trying" to break the record in Cincinnati.

"I have never gone out on a ball field and given less than my level best," he said. "When I hit it tonight, all I thought about was that I wanted to touch all the bases."

In 1966, a survey of major league managers, carried by *Sport* magazine, named Willie Mays as the most feared hitter in baseball when the chips were down. The following extract from my memoir *Willie's Time*, which was published just before Mays entered the Hall of Fame in 1979, includes a summary of three clutch situations in 1962—his last time at bat in the regular season, the playoff, and the World Series, with the game on the line each time. The result? Home run, single, double.

# From *Willie's Time*

## CHARLES EINSTEIN

WILLIE MAYS led the National League in runs scored in 1961. Most of that season, as for most of his career, he batted third in the lineup, as did so many other champion-class hitters, like Ruth and Williams. (No other spot in the batting order so maximizes the combined potential for runners to drive in and hitters to drive you in.) It is fascinating how near-equal will be the great hitters' totals for runs scored and batted in. For Mays over his major league career, he would score 2,062, bat in 1,903. For Stan Musial, who like Mays played 22 seasons, the totals were 1,949 and 1,951! Babe Ruth, also in 22 seasons, drove in just 42 runs more than he scored, Ted Williams 41. With numbers so equal as those, is it fantasizing to point out that among these four all-time batting greats Mays was the only one who scored more runs than he batted in? Possibly not, for in Willie's case there was the extra dimension in run-scoring: he stole 113 more bases than Ruth, Musial, and Williams combined! . . . *Statistics:* I can hear Abe Kemp snarling the word, yet the fact obtains that among the game's top sluggers, Willie's 1:2 ratio of stolen bases:home runs is unique.

Having earned $85,000 in 1961, Mays went to $90,000 in 1962 and in 1963 became the highest-salaried player in history at $105,000. (Shortly after he signed at that figure, Mickey Mantle signed with the Yankees for $100,000, and columnist Jimmy Cannon wrote that Mantle actually had signed first for his $100,000 and Horace Stoneham gave Mays $105,000 only to top the Yankees and keep Mantle from being known as the game's first $100,000 player. Cannon's timetable was wrong, but that would be moot, because his history was wrong too. Fifteen years earlier, in 1948,

Joe DiMaggio had signed for $100,000. And from the standpoint of greatest purchasing power and least taxation, none of the above came close to Babe Ruth's $80,000 in the depths of the Depression. Told this would pay him more than President Hoover was earning, Ruth got off his deathless line: "I had a better year than he did.")

What can be said is that the Mays and Mantle raises in 1963 had to be honestly come by, since both had keyed their clubs into the World Series of 1962. Willie's work was especially vivid: he led his league in home runs with 49 and had career-high totals of 130 runs scored and 141 batted in. In winning, the Giants provided the National League with its fifth different league champion in as many years, and it was to be the Giants' only pennant in the fourteen seasons Mays was with them on the Coast. (The league broke into two divisions in 1969, and the Giants won their division in 1971, but then lost to Pittsburgh in the pennant playoff.) Mantle with the Yankees, on the other hand, was with a team that won 12 pennants during his career. Was a Mantle more important to his team's success than a Mays to his team's success? In his book *A Thinking Man's Guide to Baseball,* Leonard Koppett took up the question:

> Only a handful of players, in all baseball history, have been as important to winning teams, and have been able to contribute as much to eventual victory, rather than statistics, as Mickey Mantle.
>
> Willie, on the other hand, I can sum up very simply: he's the best baseball player I ever saw.

"The Great Debate," Koppett labeled that chapter in his book. Interestingly, it had by then replaced the earlier Great Debate, involving Mantle's predecessor Joe DiMaggio vs. Mays. A part of this shift could be attributed to the passage of the years: 1962 was the Giants' fifth season in San Francisco, and inevitably passions for Lefty O'Doul and the old Seals would begin to spend themselves and recede into history. Another fact was that after five years of seeing what Mays could do, a number of locals began to agree that the center fielder from New York rather did know how to play this game. And another fact joined the testimonials. One such came from Tommy Henrich, who'd played right field alongside DiMaggio with the Yankees and who later became a Giant coach and saw Willie make one of his fabled catches off Roberto Clemente in a game at Pittsburgh. Inevitably, Henrich was asked if DiMaggio could have made the same play. His answer was a study. "I think," he said slowly, "that DiMag *might* have covered that same distance in the same amount of time, and *might* have got a glove on the ball." He took a deep breath. "But he couldn't have caught it." And in 1962, another of DiMaggio's ex-teammates—Joe Gordon, a longtime favorite among Coast fans—spoke at a banquet and found himself being asked The Question: DiMaggio or Mays, who was the greatest he ever saw? "You're not going to like this," Gordon said flat-out, "but the greatest player I ever saw is Willie Mays."

(Not to be overlooked here is that San Francisco's memories of DiMaggio were memories of the great Yankee dynasty of the late thirties, and that was a Yankee team that had other San Franciscans in its lineup as well, like the sterling second base–shortstop combination of Tony Lazzeri and Frankie Crosetti. Another front-line Yankee of those days, pitcher Lefty Gomez was from the town of Rodeo, just across the Bay. Understandably, San Franciscans viewed those Yankees not just as DiMaggio's team but as their team. On occasion, the view got house support, such as the time Gomez was pitching in a bases-loaded situation and suddenly wheeled and threw the ball to Lazzeri, who was at his customary fielding post in between first and second. Puzzled, Lazzeri brought the ball back to the mound. "Why'd you do that?" he asked. Gomez shrugged. "I read a piece in the paper yesterday about how smart you were, so I wanted to see what *you'd* do."

(Now Gomez pitched out the inning successfully, and when he reached the bench Yankee manager Joe Mc-Carthy asked him the same question Lazzeri had asked. This time Gomez had a different answer. "We've got so many San Francisco Italians on this team I got confused," he said. McCarthy stared at him. "You've got one in center field," he said. "Why didn't you throw it to him?")

If the Giants could not have won the pennant in 1962 without Mays, neither could they have won it without Billy Pierce, a lefthanded pitcher acquired from the White Sox in a midwinter trade, who had a won-and-lost record of 13-and-0 at Candlestick in 1962. The prevailing winds at Candlestick make it a good park for lefthanded pitchers, and Pierce got added help from the Giants' chief groundskeeper, Matty Schwab. Any time they played the Dodgers, Schwab would ostentatiously wet down the dirt area around first base—so much so that on more than one occasion the umpires ordered him to put sand on the man-made swamp—presumably to keep Dodger base stealer Maury Wills from getting a jump on the pitch. It made for headlines and controversy. What made for neither was Schwab's far more private exercise in wetting down the grass on the left side of the infield hours before game time on days when Pierce was scheduled to pitch. This had the effect of slowing down ground balls that righthanded batsmen would get off lefthanded pitching, reducing the number of hits that would go through to the outfield.

All told, Pierce had 16 victories in 1962—Jack Sanford had 24, Billy O'Dell 19, and Juan Marichal 18. One thanked God for a Matty Schwab, for five other teams in the league had better pitching, gauged by earned-run average. Lowest ERA on the Giants belonged to Marichal, but his 3.36 was grievously above his career figure. The Giant starting lineup had an infield of Cepeda, Hiller, Pagan, and Davenport, an outfield of Felipe Alou, Mays, and Kuenn, and the catching shared by Tom Haller and Ed Bailey. Chief pinch hitters and part-time outfielders were McCovey and Matty Alou. The leading relief pitcher was Stu Miller, known as the killer moth, who threw change-ups (slow balls) and nothing else. Miller was an interesting man. Owner of a slew of master points, he was easily the best bridge player in the in-flight game whose other participants were Dark, Kuenn, and me, and he had other intellectual feats to his credit. Once he threw a spitball to strike out Frank Bolling of the Braves. The rules said anyone detected throwing a spitter would be ejected from the contest. But Miller's pitch to Bolling was the last pitch of the game. How do you eject a man from a game that's already over?

The spectacle of the slight-built Miller pitching to the Dodgers' 6-foot-7, 250-pound behemoth Frank Howard was worth the price of admission all by itself. Time and again, Howard would miss connections, flailing at Miller's change-up like a housewife attacking a hovering bumblebee with a broomstick. On one memorable occasion, the confrontation took place with neither man in the game. In a tight Dodger-Giant game, pinch hitter Howard stood up in the Dodger dugout. Instantly, relief pitcher Miller stood up in the Giant bullpen. Noting this, Howard sat down again. Noting that, so did Miller. One time, he mentioned idly to Mays that he had been a catcher in high school. Mays was interested. "What'd you throw to second?" he asked. "The change?"

The 1962 Giants were noteworthy also for their complement of Spanish-speaking players: Marichal, Cepeda, Pagan, the two Alous. They were wont to jabber to one another in the native tongue, and this occasionally upset the enemy. One Cincinnati pitcher stepped off the mound, glared at Cepeda as the latter led off second base, and said, "Don't you know how to talk English?" "Kiss my ass, you cocksucker," Cepeda replied. "Is that English enough for you?"

The actual pennant race that year was theater-of-the-absurd. The Giants trailed the Dodgers by four games with seven left to play, lost two of those seven, and still wound up in a tie for first place. One of the games they lost featured a Willie Mays who wandered off third base, thinking three were out when it was only two, and got tagged. This points to the mythology that grows around any great ballplayer, to the extent that in memories, not just of the fans, but even his own ex-teammates, no one can ever recall his ever making a mistake. One point of interest here is the way the less two players got along, the more one would praise the other on his departure. Men who disliked Babe Ruth the most were the first to say they never saw him make a bad play. Casey Stengel, who managed Joe DiMaggio in the latter's final years, heaped the same praise on DiMag. Yet as Phil Rizzuto recalled for Maury Allen:

I think the real trouble with DiMaggio and Stengel happened when DiMaggio was hurting and playing this game. He was in center field and all of a sudden here comes Cliff Mapes. Stengel had decided to make a change and he didn't wait until DiMaggio was on the bench. He was going to take him right off the field. You can't do that to a great star like DiMaggio. He has too much pride. Mapes got to center field and DiMaggio waved him back to the dugout. "I'll tell Casey when I want you to come out." DiMaggio came to the bench when the inning was over and went right to the clubhouse without a word. I don't they they ever talked again.

One reads today that DiMaggio never had a hitting slump. I saw him in the course of one: he was something like 0-for-August, and finally beat out a hit to the shortstop. As he then took his lead off first, you could see his shoulders sag in relief. He took a deep breath, put his hands on his knees, and relaxed in the knowledge that the hitless streak was over. He was still standing that way when the pitcher threw over to first and picked him off.

Ruth had his times, too. He came to bat with two out in the last of the ninth in the seventh and final game of the 1926 World Series. The Yankees trailed the Cardinals 3–2. Bases were empty. Ruth walked. Now coming to bat in order were the other two .300 hitters in the Yankee lineup that year, Bob Meusel and Lou Gehrig. Meusel, from the batter's box, and Gehrig, from the on-deck circle, looked on transfixed as Ruth got it into his head to steal second base. He was out from here to breakfast and the Series was over.

As in the case of pitchers throwing record-setting home runs to hitters, baseball has an engaging way of making celebrities out of sinners. It goes back to Casey at the Bat, and includes the Merkles who forgot to touch second, the Snodgrasses who dropped the ball, the Peskys who held the ball instead of throwing it; the case of Babe Herman, who is supposed to have doubled into a triple play (in real life he tripled into a double play), and the well-remembered Smead Jolley, who once made three errors on the same play: playing left field at the old League Park in Cleveland, he let a hit go through his legs for an error; turning to play it off the wall, he saw the ball go through his legs again coming back; retrieving it finally, he threw it into the dugout. There was Gee Walker of the Tigers, who got picked off first so often he finally was ordered to take no lead at all, but simply to tap his foot repeatedly on the base as evidence of contact. Promptly the pitcher picked him off. "He got me between taps," Walker explained. One of my favorites involves a Mets outfielder named Don Hahn, who passed teammate Rusty Staub on the bases. Realizing his mistake, he doubled back and passed Staub again, this time going the other way. Momentarily crazed, the nearest umpire called him out twice. And there was the case of Ping Bodie, another San Francisco product whose true name was Francesco Stephano Pezzolo. Like Ruth in the 1926 Series, Bodie sometimes got it into his head to steal against the odds. "He had larceny in his heart," Bugs Baer wrote. "But his feet were honest."

It was not for any mistake he had made, however, that the San Francisco fans booed Willie Mays when he came to bat for the first time on the final day of the 1962 season. To force a playoff for the National League pennant that day, the Giants not only had to win over Houston; the Dodgers had to lose to St. Louis. The parlay was not a particularly bright one for San Franciscans, and they held Mays primarily responsible for it— not for the way he played, but the way he didn't.

(When he became Giant manager in 1961, Alvin Dark was told the San Francisco team had never won a game in which Mays did not play. Since the number of such occasions could be counted on the fingers of one hand, Dark professed not to take it seriously. "We'll be resting him from time to time," he said. "Willie comes on just that much stronger after he's had a day off."

(But as it turned out, Dark rested Mays only one game in all of 1961. "The point wasn't that Mays shouldn't be given a rest," *Examiner* sports editor Curley Grieve wrote after that game. "It just wasn't the right time or place." Actually it was mid-June, and Willie's arm was hurting. Doc Bowman diagnosed it as a cold that had settled in his shoulder. It happened in Milwaukee the night after the Giants had played an exhibition game against their farm team at Tacoma, and manager Dark had another theory: "I don't think there *is* anything wrong with his arm," he told Bob Stevens and me. "I could be wrong. What happened last night in Tacoma was that we had to play the regulars, because it's the one chance those people get to come out and see the big-league stars in the Giant organization. Anyway, Cepeda came out of the game before Willie did, and I think Willie noticed it. *He* had to stay in. He sees other players getting time off, and he isn't getting any."

(I said, "I don't think he'd quit.")

("It's not a question of his quitting," Dark said. "He told me he'd play tonight if I wanted him to."

("But," Stevens said, "you said you didn't think there was anything wrong with his arm."

("It can hurt," Dark said, "without there being anything wrong with it."

(Such theorizing to one side, the record was kept intact: Mays didn't play that one game in Milwaukee in 1961, and the Giants didn't win.)

Again, in 1962, Dark renewed his pledge to rest Willie. By September 12, with the Giants at that point trailing the Dodgers by half a game in the standings, Mays had appeared in every game. That night, in the second inning of a game at Cincinnati, he collapsed in the dugout. He regained consciousness almost immediately, but an ambulance rushed him to the hospital. He was kept there for three days, under diagnosis of tension and exhaustion (the doctors found nothing clinically wrong). All three of those days, once again to keep the record intact, the Giants lost. Mays rejoined the team in Pittsburgh, and a wire service photo showed a miserable ballplayer hunched in a jacket. ACHING TO PLAY, the caption said. This was true, though it was a photo of the wrong man, a reserve outfielder named Carl Boles who bore considerable facial resemblance to Mays and who *was* aching to play.

Mays celebrated his return to the lineup the following day with a game-tying three-run homer, and the team was to come out of its spin. But it had lost precious ground to the Dodgers, and once again manager Dark may have had a private reservation or two about the non-playing Mays. Asked when Willie would re-enter the lineup, he said cryptically, "When he says he's ready." And far less private were the rumors printed in the San Francisco papers. One said Mays had had a heart attack, another an epileptic seizure, another that he was an alcoholic, another—cited by the city's leading columnist, Herb Caen of the *Chronicle*—that he had been punched by a teammate.

So the large Candlestick crowd for the season's last day, September 30, 1962—a crowd grown all the larger for the fact that it was Fan Appreciation Day and the Giants were giving away five automobiles and other prizes—vented the baseball portion of its interest by booing Willie when he came to bat in the first inning. In his first at-bat on opening day that year, Mays had hit Warren Spahn's first pitch, as of yore, for a home run. As he had done with his first pitch of the regular season, so today would he do with his last, slamming a long drive into the left-field seats off Turk Farrell in the eighth inning to break a 1–1 tie and bring his team a 2–1 victory.

The boos changed to cheers, mingled with new injections of hope supplied by the bulletins from Los Angeles, where the Dodgers and Cardinals were locked in a scoreless battle. Los Angeles was considered a good liberty town, and we heard that the Cards, on their final road swing with nothing at stake for themselves, were taking complete advantage of its attractions. One story said they were so drunk the catchers were calling audibles.

But at least they were loose, while the Dodgers—no reproduction of the Boys of Summer, that club found it difficult to remember the last time they'd even scored a run. Pitching was their forte in any event, and their offense was geared to the stolen base and the odd run it might produce. Maury Wills stole 104 bases that year, and the league's runner-up in that category, with 32, was his own teammate, Willie Davis; the rest of the Dodgers stole more bases than did any of four other entire *teams* in the league. There was some good hitting from Tommy Davis, the league batting champion, but he was the only Dodger over .300, and the demands on the club's pitching staff remained severe. On one occasion, Don Drysdale, having pitched and won the evening before, was enjoying a night off away from the ball park when a phone call reached him with the news that teammate Sandy Koufax had just pitched a no-hitter. "Did he win?" Drysdale asked.

The famine in runs was to cost the Dodgers a 1–0 loss to the Cardinals on the last day of the season and force a best-of-three Giant-Dodger playoff beginning in San Francisco the following day. In this one, with Mays homering twice, Billy Pierce pitched the Giants to an 8–0 triumph. And in the second game next day, held at Los Angeles, the Giants held a 5–0 lead going into the last of the sixth. At that point, the Dodgers, having now gone 35 innings without scoring, broke through for a 7-run inning and held on to win, 8–7. And so, eleven years to the day of the third playoff game between the two teams in New York in 1951, they met again in California to settle a near-identical playoff. Again, as before, the Giants had won the first game, the Dodgers the second. Again as before, the Giants would come up in the ninth inning trailing in the score, and it was almost the same score as before: 4–2 this time, as opposed to the 4–1 in 1951.

One difference was that this time the Giants were the visiting team, but all that meant was a difference in crowd noise—which in this case was no noise at all. The Giants, who had broken through for four runs in the ninth in 1951, would break through for four runs in the ninth again in 1962. But they managed it this time on only two hits, an inning-opening single by Matty Alou and a key single, ripped off the glove of pitcher Ed Roebuck, by Willie Mays.

Alou had been forced at second by Kuenn after his hit, but Willie McCovey walked, and so did Felipe Alou, loading the bases. Now came a moment that did distinguish 1962 from 1951. The same Willie Mays who as a rookie was sick with fear he might have to come to bat now stood in the batter's box with bases loaded, coolly and characteristically tamping down the dirt with his right foot so he could dig in. So subdued were the Los Angeles fans that the nationwide television audience could hear the encouraging shouts of the Giants as they called Willie's name—a mini-babel in itself, since to his friends he had several names, used interchangeably. They called him Willie, and Will, and 24 (for his uniform number), and Buck (for Buckduck, his boyhood nickname, itself a transfiguration of "Duck-butt" . . . "He always had a high behind," his Aunt Ernestine explained). Now Roebuck threw and Buck-24-Willie-Will rifled a base hit up the middle for one run, leaving the Dodgers ahead 4–3, bases still loaded, still one out.

Los Angeles manager Walter Alston brought Stan Williams in to replace Roebuck and pitch to Orlando Cepeda, who flied to right field, scoring pinch runner Ernie Bowman from third after the catch to tie the score at 4–4. A wild pitch now put runners at second and third and dictated an intentional walk to Ed Bailey. And then, quite unintentionally, Williams walked Jim Davenport, forcing in Felipe Alou with the go-ahead run. Ron Perranoski replaced Williams, and a moment later Dodger second baseman Larry Burright kicked a ground ball and Mays scored to make it 6–4.

Billy Pierce came on to pitch the last of the ninth for the Giants, and got Maury Wills on a grounder and Jim Gilliam on a fly. Then pinch hitter Lee Walls hit a 1-and-1 pitch on a line into right center. The crowd yelped in sudden hope, but the Giant center fielder, moving to his left, struck the pocket of his glove with the

fist of his right hand as he ran. With Mays that was a reflex signal meaning only one thing: no problem. "Minute I saw Buck pound that pood, I knew we were home," catcher Bailey said. Mays was waiting for the ball when it got there. He caught it chest high for the final out and then, in an unusual gesture of personal celebration, threw it into the right-field grandstand. (Throughout his career, Mays would eschew the hand slaps, hugs, and dancing that came more and more to characterize the joyous athletic moment. Not for him was it to spike the ball or boogie in somebody's end zone. His reserve was honestly come by, for even as early as 1962, at the age of thirty-one, he represented baseball's older generation. After just five seasons in San Francisco, he was the only Giant left from the team that had come west from New York, and to the rookies on the club, few if any of them old enough to remember *not* seeing his name in a big-league box score or the headlines trumpeting his accomplishments, he was known in simple logic as the old man.)

In the clubhouse following the pennant clincher, someone asked Mays why he had not used his basket catch on Walls's game-ending ball. Willie's high laugh was tinged with amazement at the question. "You crazy?" he responded. "That was $15,000 a man!" Now the Giants dressed and flew home to San Francisco, where a crowd of 75,000 overran the taxiways to make a shambles of airport traffic control. Delayed in landing, the Giants' plane finally got down and was shunted to a remote area where a couple of taxicabs and a bus awaited. Two or three in the traveling party, Mays included, made their getaway by cab, but the crowd caught up with the others and surrounded the bus. "We want Willie!" the people roared. "We want Willie!" Inside the bus, another reserve Giant outfielder, Bob Nieman, looked around uncomfortably. "For God's sake," he husked, "throw 'em Boles and let's get out of here!"

Downtown San Francisco was just as much a mess, wall to wall with celebrants, automobiles, church bells, horns, and firecrackers; and—precisely as had happened eleven years before—the ensuing World Series with the Yankees would prove to be an anticlimax. Again as in 1951, the chief emotional binge, and the most lasting memory, would be provided not by the Series but by the outcome of the playoff. Maybe Bobby Thomson's home run had the theatrical edge over four walks, a couple of singles, an error, and a sacrifice fly (*maybe?*), but both times the Giants had turned defeat into victory with a four-run ninth in the final inning of the final playoff game, and when the Series began the following day it was difficult to care. The '62 Series was subject too to record prolongation. To two days of travel, add four of rain, and the thing lasted thirteen days. That includes the fact that it went the full seven-game distance and came down to the ninth inning of the final game, when with two out, the tying run on third, and the winning run on second, Willie McCovey smote a savage low liner only to see it picked off by the perfectly positioned Yankee second baseman, Bobby Richardson.

It was the rain that saved Alvin Dark from a second guess that would have been both virulent and rather unfair. The instant in point came in the fifth inning of the fourth game of the Series, at New York. Giant pitcher Juan Marichal was tooling along with a 2–0 lead at the time, having among other things struck out Mickey Mantle swinging twice in a row, and now was at bat with one out, teammates on first and third, and a count of two strikes. At this juncture, Dark signaled for a squeeze bunt—though if Marichal bunted foul, it would go as a strikeout. Marichal did bunt foul. Worse than that, the pitch struck the index finger of his pitching hand. But the Giants went on to win that game, and after that the rains did come, resting the other Giant pitchers so there was no call on the injured Marichal. The second guess never materialized.

Dark was a curio with Marichal and the other Latin players on the team. At one point he called Marichal the best pitcher he ever saw at protecting a lead in the late innings. At another, Marichal was motoring along with a 6–3 lead over the Dodgers. It was the top of the eighth inning. He had struck out pinch hitter Duke Snider on three straight pitches to end the Dodger seventh, and now started off the Dodger eighth by striking out Willie Davis. By this point in the game, he had struck out twelve men. Now Tommy Davis dribbled a ball to the left side and beat it out. Instantly Dark emerged from the dugout, waved to the bullpen for a relief pitcher, and strode to the mound.

Marichal could not believe it. "You taking me out?"

"Yes."

"Why?"

"Just to be safe. You may be tired."

"I strike out Snider and Davis. Is that being tired?"

"I want to make sure I win this one," Dark said. "You get credit for the win even if I take you out. And ain't no way you can be the losing pitcher. So don't complain."

(The Giants lost the game 8–7. Later the same season Dark staged an innovation, again with Marichal pitching. This time there was *no one* occupying the bullpen. "I just got tired of seeing my starting pitchers standing out there and looking for help," Dark explained.)

The baserunner setup for McCovey's Series-ending liner had been established by the previous hitter, who was Mays and who had doubled to right field with Matty Alou on first base. This completed a Mays trilogy that went as follows:

- Last game of regular season, 8th inning, Giants tied, none on, none out: Mays homered.
- Last game of playoff, 9th inning, Giants trailing 4–2, three on, one out: Mays singled.
- Last game of World Series, 9th inning, Giants trailing 1–0, one on, two out: Mays doubled.

(Extra-base hits tend to speak for themselves, but most vivid in my memory is the ninth-inning single off the pitcher's glove in the playoff at Los Angeles. I am not alone in this reminiscence. More than sixteen years afterward, veteran St. Louis sportswriter Bob Broeg, recollecting Willie's career, said that 1962 single was hit "as hard as I ever saw.")

Yet Mays had been booed when he first came to bat for the last game of the regular '62 season. A principal reason for that has already been reviewed here. A secondary reason was that he'd gone hitless the day before, while the Giants were splitting a doubleheader. And all the time, Alvin Dark was keeping a private "book" on his hitters. Mays, he announced after the season was over, was his best clutch hitter. But Cepeda was awful. He could not deliver in the clutch. *Look* magazine did a story on it, and Cepeda sued. The suit was unsuccessful. Yet in the ninth inning of the final playoff game at Los Angeles, Cepeda was the Giant who hit the ball the farthest—the long sacrifice fly that tied the game. I asked Mays privately what he thought of Dark's estimate of Cepeda. "Shit," Willie said, "a man hits .300 and bats in 100 runs, how you gonna say he can't hit?"

Mays himself conformed to no pattern. "I always start good," he explained to one reporter who sought an explanation of one hot early season. "I always start bad," he explained to another who sought an explanation of a cold one. One such cold one was 1963. Willie was swinging late, bailing out, popping up, striking out. I wandered into Dark's clubhouse office one noontime and found the manager in consultation with club vice-president Chub Feeney.

"Listen," Dark said to me. "When Willie had his physical this winter, did they check his eyes?"

"How do I know?" I said.

"It could be his eyesight," Feeney said.

"Why don't you ask him?"

"No," Feeney said. "You know how he is when he's not hitting. You can't get near him."

"We were thinking," Dark said helpfully, "that you and he being as close as you are . . ."

"Oh, fine," I said. "You want me to bell the cat."

"You could just mention it to him," Feeney said. "You know, just in passing."

"Kind of like an idle question," Dark said. "It's like that if it comes from you, it's not official. It's like that he won't know you've been talking to us."

"Sure he won't," I said, and went out through the tunnel to the field where the Giants were taking batting practice. I fell in alongside Mays at the cage. "Say, Buck," I said to him, "you notice how many players are wearing glasses this year?"

"Like who?" he said.

"Well," I said, "Howard—Frank Howard. He's got glasses."

"He ain't hittin' either," Mays said.

Here is an umpire spending the winter in the knowledge that (a) he blew
a call and (b) half the country thinks it cost their team the World Series.

# In the Eye of the Storm

## RON FIMRITE

DON DENKINGER (the name sound familiar?) is, by any accounting, a pillar of Waterloo, Iowa—a native of adjacent Cedar Falls where he was a star athlete in the '50s, a lifelong resident of the area, a popular restaurateur in town and a member of the Shrine, Rotary, Elks Club and Zion Lutheran Church. His wife of 23 years, Gayle, taught at the local high school, was an active Junior Leaguer and worked in the local Red Cross chapter. The Denkingers have three bright and attractive daughters, Darcy, 20, Denise, 18, and Dana, 17, and a perky little schnauzer named Schatzie as well. They live in a fine house. They're a very sociable family, and Don, with his roots so deeply embedded in the community, is a soft touch for any civic endeavor. The Denkingers are well-known, well-liked and definitely respected. But you would never know any of this from the letters and phone calls they've been receiving lately.

The phone calls, though always unnerving, are relatively easy to deal with. After the first burst of profanity, one simply hangs up. Don't even consider collect calls. The mail is a little trickier. One letter, addressed to Gayle, begins, flatteringly enough, "I have always had the greatest respect for your advice and I was wondering if you could help me with this problem." What follows is a recounting of the letter writer's family history, a history so repellent as to make the Snopeses seem wholesome by comparison. And then the kicker: Should the correspondent inform his fiancée, herself a convicted felon, "that my brother is an American League umpire?" This one, though steeped in vulgarity, at least represents some conscious effort at composition. Most of the 200 or more letters the Denkingers have received over the past two months are simple explosions of bile. Most suggest that Denkinger, if not legally blind, should at least seek treatment for advanced myopia. One communication proposes that Don use makeup in all future television appearances because, "You're an ugly

bleep." (Not true.) Another, after a full page of billingsgate, closes chummily with, "Give my best to your wife and kids."

There is irony: "Congratulations on changing history." Pathos: "I just wish you could see my tears." Venom: "I wish you the worst." And malapropism: "The mistake you made will go down in the *annuals* of baseball." They are variously signed. "A. Fan," "Louie St. Louis," "Fellow Admirer," "Whitey and Joaquin." Some of the most vicious are, predictably, unsigned. You get the point: Opening the mail has not become a highlight of the Denkingers' day. Even when his equipment bag arrived by air freight from Kansas City, Denkinger found taped to it the unsigned message: YOU BLEW THE CALL.

Denkinger—wearing spectacles, his antagonists will be pleased to learn—reads this scabrous prose in the cozy den of his house in Waterloo with the weary resignation of one long accustomed to abusive language. "I think I've always realized there were those kinds of people out there," he says sadly. Denkinger is, after all, an umpire. More specifically, he is *the* umpire who, in the irrational view of St. Louis baseball fans everywhere (and their number is obviously legion), cost the Cardinals the 1985 World Series. Denkinger's call is, if not yet actually in the "annuals," quickly becoming part of Series lore. As you may remember:

It is the last half of the ninth inning of the sixth game, and the Cardinals, needing only one more win to take the championship, are leading 1–0. The leadoff batter for Kansas City is Jorge Orta, a left-handed hitter. He is facing Todd Worrell, a six-foot-five right-handed reliever. Worrell gets two strikes on Orta right off. His fourth pitch is nubbed softly to the first-base side of the mound. First baseman Jack Clark charges over to field it, and Worrell, who thought about going for it himself, runs to cover first. Clark lobs the ball to him high but on target as Orta rushes down the line. Denkinger is in position to make the call. He is in foul territory about eight feet from the bag. Runner and ball arrive almost, but not quite, at the same time. Denkinger calls the runner safe. Cardinal manager Whitey Herzog explodes from the dugout. There is an argument, but the decision holds. "We can't seem to draw a break," Herzog angrily tells the umpire. He's right. Video replays clearly show that Orta was out. All hell breaks loose after this call: a misjudged pop-up, a hit, a passed ball, a walk and, finally, a bases-loaded single by pinch hitter Dane Iorg that wins the game for the Royals 2–1. The Series is tied. Herzog is fit to be tied. "We're going to win the World Series and that bleeper [Denkinger] blows the call," he says. "Now we've got the bleeper behind the plate tomorrow. We've got about as much chance as the man in the moon." He's right again.

The Cardinals lose the seventh game 11–0 and the Series and their senses. In the fifth inning, with the score 10–0, St. Louis pitcher Joaquin Andujar complains to Denkinger, the plate umpire, about a ball three call on Jim Sundberg. Herzog rushes out, allegedly to calm his pitcher but really to berate Denkinger again for the Orta call. Denkinger ejects him. When Denkinger calls Andujar's next pitch a ball, the pitcher storms off the mound in a terrible rage. Denkinger ejects him. It is the first time in 50 years both a manager and a player have been kicked out of a World Series game. The Cardinals behave afterward like petulant schoolboys. Their fans are inflamed.

Gayle is in Kansas City for the game while Denkinger's daughters and his mother-in-law, Margaret Price, watch this ugly spectacle on TV in the family home back in Waterloo. Seeing their father assaulted from all sides is such an unsettling experience for the girls that they begin to cry. Denkinger's fellow American League umpires Dave Phillips and Rich Garcia, themselves disturbed by the Game 7 tumult, call the house to offer counsel to the family. Friends in Waterloo and elsewhere call. It's only a game, after all, the girls are told. It will soon be forgotten. And then the other calls start. "A St. Louis disc jockey gave out my address and phone number on the radio," says Denkinger. The girls, still upset by the nasty scene on television, are now exposed to a succession of obscene calls that lasts through the night. And the next night. And the next. Their father's life is threatened. Price calls a friend, who then telephones the local police to ask for protection. The Waterloo police call their counterparts in St. Louis, asking that the inflammatory deejay be ordered to desist.

Denkinger and Gayle drove home from Kansas City on Monday. He had a "sinking feeling" that there might be further trouble. "I could sense there was some

**KELLER**

*"He throws things at the umpire."*

frustration.'' But he thought any trouble resulting from the Series would quickly dissipate. In 26 years as an umpire, 17 in the American League, nine as a crew chief, he had been exposed to any number of cruel stunts. The air had been let out of his car tires. Somebody had put Limburger cheese in the manifold. Young toughs had tailgated him out of town in the minor leagues. Penny-ante stuff. But when he got home to Waterloo, he found his house under the watchful eye of the police and his daughters in a troubled state. "And then," he says, "two or three days later the mail started coming in," so much of it, in fact, that the post office didn't even bother to deliver it at all. "Sometimes," he says, "you can't really know what you're dealing with out there."

Denkinger, who is 49, had never planned to be an umpire. He had been a track man, a wrestler (137 to 157 pounds) and a football player at Cedar Falls High and at Wartburg College in Waverly, Iowa. He was drafted into the Army after 2½ years of college and sent, finally, to a missile base in New Mexico. It was his first prolonged stay away from home. He had planned to return to college after his discharge, but an Army buddy, Master Sergeant Bob Henrion, persuaded him to join him at the Al Somers School for Umpires in Daytona Beach, Fla. Denkinger went on a lark—"I couldn't even fathom what it was an umpire was supposed to do"—but he finished as most likely to succeed among 85 students. He was hooked. "I'm in a unique profession," he says, "one that people don't know a lot about. Oh, yes, I know we have this hateful image, but it's totally untrue that we lead a miserable, lonely life. Why, I've got friends in every city we go to."

Denkinger didn't see the tapes of his historic mistake in the sixth game until the Tuesday following the Series. He had purposely avoided reading the papers, watching television or listening to the radio between games, so as to preserve his objectivity. If he heard actual replays of Herzog's angry denunciations of him, he had feared, his judgment might be colored in some subtle way. Denkinger had already worked two World Series, in 1974 and '80, but the thrill of calling an important game meant fully as much to him as playing in one did to the ballplayers. But with it all over and the dust cleared, he felt it was time to reflect. He was sitting alone in his family room composing his report on the seventh-game mess to commissioner Peter Ueberroth when, to his ultimate dismay, he saw out of the corner of his eye the Orta play being rerun on his television set. He paused in his writing to watch.

"They were calling it the biggest bonehead play of the year," Denkinger recalls. "They must've shown it six times, from every angle. Well, it soon became obvious to me that, let's say, there was a very great possibility the ball beat the runner to the bag. In fact, I was astute enough to recognize that the man was clearly out. The call was wrong. I was in good position, but Worrell is a tall man, the throw was high and I couldn't watch both his glove and his feet at the same time. There was so much crowd noise I couldn't hear the ball hit the glove. Besides, it was a soft throw. My first responsibility is to make sure the ball is caught. Had I been maybe 15 feet back, instead of eight, I might have made the right call.

"I didn't like what I saw. No one wants to be embarrassed like that. My job is predicated on being right all the time, and I like to be right all the time. But [melancholy laughter] we're only human, and now it's history. I can't change anything. Even admitting I was wrong doesn't change anything. But I do know that I didn't cost the Cardinals the World Series, not with all that happened afterward. There were too many 'what ifs' in the game. I think what worries all umpires is the violent reaction to things now. In Yankee Stadium, God save us, there was even a shooting. Please tell me what a man is doing with a gun in the ball park? We have to be concerned about these things, because it's obvious the situation is getting worse. I love baseball and I'm not all that disillusioned by what's happened to me. I'll continue to do what I've always done, which is to take every game very seriously and do my best."

The calls and the letters keep coming in, but there has been no violence to his person, his family or his home. Denkinger is a man with a keenly honed sense of irony, and that has helped him ride over the rough spots. He observes, laughing, that his newfound notoriety has at least given him a certain cachet on the banquet circuit. And he takes special pleasure in one of the neon signs that flash behind the bar of his Silver Fox restaurant in downtown Waterloo. It's the first thing he'll show visitors to the place. "Gussie Busch's company [the *Braumeister* also owns the Cardinals] gave one of these to all the umpires," he says, standing beneath the glittering prize. The sign reads: THIS BUD'S FOR YOU.

The late Robert Fitzgerald was Professor of Rhetoric and Oratory at Harvard University and a Chancellor of the Academy of American Poets. His works include translations of *The Iliad, The Odyssey,* and, most recently, *The Aeneid. Cobb Would Have Caught It* was first published in 1943.

# Cobb Would Have Caught It

## — ROBERT FITZGERALD —

In sunburnt parks where Sundays lie,
Or the wide wastes beyond the cities,
Teams in grey deploy through sunlight.

Talk it up, boys, a little practice,
Coming in stubby and fast, the baseman
Gathers a grounder in fat green grass.
Picks it up stinging and clipped as wit
Into the leather: a swinging step
Wings it deadeye down to first.
Smack. Oh, atta boy, atta old boy.

Catcher reverses his cap, pulls down
Sweaty casque, and squats in the dust;
Pitcher rubs new ball on his pants,
Chewing, puts a jet behind him;
Nods past batter, taking his time.

Batter settles, tugs at his cap:
A spinning ball: step and swing to it,
Caught like a cheek before it ducks
By shivery hickory: socko, baby:
Cleats dig into dust. Outfielder,
On his own way, looking over shoulder,
Makes it a triple; A long peg home.

Innings and afternoons. Fly lost in sunset.
Throwing arm gone bad. There's your ball game.
Cool reek of the field. Reek of companions.

# The Base Stealer

## ROBERT FRANCIS

Poised between going on and back, pulled
Both ways taut like a tightrope-walker,
Fingertips pointing the opposites,
Now bouncing tiptoe like a dropped ball
Or a kid skipping rope, come on, come on,
Running a scattering of steps sidewise,
How he teeters, skitters, tingles, teases,
Taunts them, hovers like an ecstatic bird,
He's only flirting, crowd him, crowd him,
Delicate, delicate, delicate, delicate—now!

This may have been a more curious story in 1954, when it was first
published, than it is today. Today all the umpires dress that way.

# The Umpire's Revolt

## PAUL GALLICO

SURELY THERE will be none to whom our national
pastime is meat and drink who will have forgotten
Cassaday's Revolt, that near catastrophe that took place
some years ago. It came close not only to costing the
beloved Brooklyns the pennant and star pitcher Rafe
Lustig his coveted $7500 bonus, but rocked organized
baseball to its foundation.

The principal who gave his name and deed to the
insurrection, Mr. Rowan (Concrete) Cassaday, uncor-
ruptible, unbudgeable chief umpire of umpires of the
National League, was supposed to have started it all.
Actually, he didn't.

It is a fact that newspapers which focus the pitiless
spotlight of publicity upon practically everyone connected with baseball, from magnate to bat boy, have a
curiously blind side when it comes to umpires. They
rarely seem to bother about what the sterling arbiters are
up to, once the game is over.

Thus, at the beginning of this lamentable affair, no
one had the slightest inkling that actually something had
been invented capable of moving the immovable Concrete Cassaday, before whose glare the toughest player
quailed and from whose infallible dictum there was no
reprieve. That something was a woman, Miss Molly
McGuire, queen of the lovely Canarsie section of
Brooklyn, hard by fragrant Jamaica Bay.

The truth was, when umpire Cassaday went acourting
Molly McGuire of a warm September night and sat with
her on the stoop of the old brownstone house where she
lived with her father, the retired boulevard besomer, Old
Man McGuire, he was no longer concrete, but sludge.
When the solid man looked up into the beautifully kept
garden of Molly's face with its forget-me-not eyes,
slipperflower nose, anemone mouth, and hair the gloss
and color of the midnight pansy, you could have ladled
him up with a spoon.

Old Man McGuire, ex-street-cleaning department,
once he had ascertained that Cassaday could not further

his yearning to become the possessor of a lifetime pass to
Ebbets Field, such as are owned by politicians or bigwigs,
left them to their wooing. However, he took his grief for
assuaging—since he considered it something of a disgrace
that his daughter should have taken up with that enemy of
all mankind, and in particular the Brooklyns, an umpire—
to the Old Heidelberg Tavern, presided over by handsome
and capable Widow Katina Schultz.

This was in a sense patriotic as well as neighborly and
practical, since everyone knew that blond widow Schultz
was engaged to be married to Rafe Lustig, sensational
Brooklyn right-hander. Rafe had been promised a bonus
of $7500 if he won twenty-two games that season, which
money he was intending to invest in Old Heidelberg to
rescue it and his ladylove from the hands of the
mortgage holders.

There was some division of opinion as to the manner
in which Rowan Cassaday had acquired the nickname
"Concrete." Ballplayers indicated that it referred un-
questionably to the composition of his skull, but others
said it was because of his square jaw, square shoulders,
huge square head and square buttocks. Clad in his lumpy
blue serge suit, pockets bulging with baseballs, masked
and chest-protected, he resembled nothing so much as,
in the words of a famous sports columnist, a concrete—
ah—shelter.

Whatever, he was unbudgeable in his decisions,
which were rarely wrong, for he had a photographic eye
imprinting an infallible record on his brain, which made
him invaluable.

You would think it would have been sufficient for
Molly, one hundred and three pounds of Irish enchant-
ress, to have so solid and august a being helplessly in
love with her. But it was also a fact that Molly was a
woman, a creature who, even when most attractive and
sure of herself, sometimes has to have a little tamper
with fate or inaugurate a kind of test just to make certain.
Molly's tamper, let it be said, was a beaut.

It was a sultry evening in mid-September, with the Dodgers a game or two away from grabbing the banner, and the Giants, Cards and Bucs all breathing down their necks. Molly perched on the top step of the stoop, with Concrete adoring her from three below. Old Man McGuire still sat in the window of the front parlor, collarless, with his feet on the open window ledge, reading *The Sporting News*.

Miss McGuire, who had attended the game that afternoon, looked down at her burly admirer and remarked casually, "Rowan, dear, do you know what? I've been thinking about the old blue serge suit you always wear on the ball field. It's most unbecoming to you."

"Eh?" Cassaday exclaimed, startled, for he had never given it so much as a thought. For years, the blue serge suit, belted at the back, with oversize patch pockets and the stiff-visored blue cap, had been as much a part of him as his skin.

"Uh-huh! It makes you look pounds heavier and yards broader, like the old car barns back of Ebbets Field. My girl friend who was with me at the game was saying what a pity, on account of you were such a fine figure of a man. Can't you wear something else for a change, Rowan, darling?"

A bewildered expression came into Cassaday's eyes and he stammered, "Wear s-something else? Molly, baby, you know there's nothing I wouldn't do for you, but the blue serge suit is the uniform and mark of me trade!"

"Oh, is it?" she asked, and stared down at him in a manner to cause icicles to form about his heart. "So you don't care about my being humiliated, sitting up there in the stands with my girl friend on Ladies' Day? And anyway, who said you had to wear it? Is there any rule about it?"

"Sure," replied Cassaday. "There must be—I mean there ought to—that is, I'd have to look it up." For he was suddenly assailed with the strangest doubt. If there was any man who was wholly conversant with the rules and regulations of baseball, it was he, and he could not recall at that moment ever having seen one that applied to his dress. "What did you have in mind, darling?"

"Why, just that it's a free country and you're entitled to wear something a little more suitable to your personality, a man with a fine build like yours."

"Do you really think so, then?"

"Of course I do. When you bend over to dust off the plate at the start of the game, every eye in the park is on you, and I won't have my friends passing remarks about your shape. Next Monday when the Jints come to Ebbets Field, I'll expect to see you dressed a little more classy."

Cassaday fluttered feebly once more, "It would be against all precedent, Molly. You wouldn't want—"

"What I don't want is to see you in that awful suit again, either on or off the field," Molly concluded finally for him. "And I don't think I wish to talk about it any longer. But remember. I'll be at the game next Monday."

Concrete Cassaday, the terror of the National League, looked up at Molly McGuire and cooed, "Give us a kiss, Molly. I'm crazy about you."

"I don't know that I shall, naughty boy."

"Molly, baby, there's nothing I wouldn't do for you."

"I guess I'm crazy about you, too, honey."

With a pained expression on his wizened jockey's face, Old Man McGuire arose, descended the stoop and headed for Old Heidelberg, never dreaming at the moment the importance of what he had overheard.

I will refresh your memory as to some of the events of that awful Monday, when the Brooks trotted onto the cleanly outlined Ebbets Field diamond against the hated Giants. Big Rafe Lustig, who had won twenty-one games, and had warmed up beautifully, took the mound to win his twenty-second game. This would clinch the $7500 bonus destined for the support of the tottering Old Heidelberg and just about put Brooklyn out of reach in the scamper for the rag down the homestretch.

Umpires Syme and Tarbolt had already taken up their stations at first and third. The head of the Giant batting order was aggressively swinging three war clubs. The batteries had been announced. Pregame tension was electric. Into this, marching stolidly from the dugout onto the field, looking neither right nor left, walked the apparition that was Concrete Cassaday.

He wore gray checked trousers, a horrid mustard-colored tweed coat with a plaid check overlay in red and green. His shirt was a gray-and-brown awning stripe worn with an orange necktie. From his pocket peered a dreadful Paisley handkerchief of red and yellow. On his head he wore a broad flat steamer cap of Kelly green with a white button in the center. Concrete Cassaday, at the behest of his ladylove, and, no doubt, some long-dormant inner urge to express himself, had let himself go.

This sartorial catastrophe stalked to the plate, turned the ghastly cap around backward like a turn-of-the-century automobilist, and against a gasping roar that shook the girders of the field dedicated to Charlie Ebbets, called, "Play ball! Anybody makes any cracks is out of the game!"

Unfortunately, the storm of cheers and catcalls arising from the stands at the spectacle drowned out this fair warning, and Pat Coe, the manager, advancing on Cassaday with, "What the hell is this, Cassaday—

Weber and Fields?'' found himself thumbed from the premises before the words were out of his mouth.

Rafe Lustig, who had the misfortune to possess a sense of humor, fared even worse. With a whoop, he threw the ball over the top of the grandstand and, clutching at his eyes, ran around shouting, ''I'm blind! I'm blind!'' evoking roars of laughter until he fetched smack up against the object of his derision, who said, ''Blind, are you, Rafe? Then ye can't pitch. And what's more, as long as I'm wearing this suit, you'll not pitch! Now beat it!''

Too late, Rafe sobered. ''Aw, now, Concrete, have a—''

''Git!''

Wardrobe or no wardrobe, when Cassaday said, ''Git!'' they got.

Slidey Simpson, the big, good-natured Negro first baseman, said, ''Who-ee-ee, Mr. Cassaday! You sure enough dressed up like Harlem on Sunday night.''

''March!'' said Concrete.

Slidey marched with an expression of genuine grievance on his face, for he had really meant to be complimentary. Butts Barry, the heavy-hitting catcher, merely whinnied like a horse and found himself heading for his street clothes; Harry Stutz, the second baseman, was nailed making a rude gesture, and banished; Pads Franklin, the third baseman, went off the field for a look on his face; Allie Munson was caught by telepathy, apparently doing something derogatory all the way out in left field, and was waved off.

Sheltered by the dugout, the Giants somehow avoided the disaster that was engulfing the Brooklyn team. By the time Pat Coe managed to send word from the dressing room to lay off Cassaday and play ball, the Brooks fielded a heterogeneous mob of substitutes, utility infielders and bench-warmers including a deaf-and-dumb pitcher newly arrived from Hartford, whom the joyous and half-hysterical Giants proceeded to take apart.

Heinz Zimmer, the president of the club, had been thrown off the field by Cassaday for protesting, and was on the telephone to the office of the league president, who, advised of potential sabotage and riot at Ebbets Field, and the enormity of Cassaday's breach of everything sacred to the national sport, was frantically buzzing the office of the high commissioner of baseball.

Down on the diamond, the Giants were spattering hits against all walls and scoring runs in clusters; the fickle fans were hooting the hapless Dodger remnants. The press box was in an uproar. Photographers shot Cassaday from every angle, and even in color. All in all, it was an afternoon of the sheerest horror.

There was just one person in the park who was wholly and thoroughly pleased. This was Miss Molly McGuire.

You well remember the drama of the subsequent days, when the example set by Umpire Cassaday spread to other cities in both leagues, indicating that the revolt had struck a sympathetic chord in many umpirical hearts.

Indeed, there did not appear to be an arbiter in either circuit but seemed to be sick unto death of the blue serge suit. Ossa piled upon Pelion as reports came in from Detroit that Slats Owney had turned up in Navin Field in golf knickers and a plaid hunting cap; that in Cleveland, Iron Spine McGoorty had discarded his blue serge for fawn-colored slacks and a Harry Truman shirt, and that Mike O'Halloran had caused a near riot in the bleachers at St. Louis by appearing in white cricket flannels and shirt and an Old School tie.

As the climax to all this came the long-awaited ruling from the office of the high commissioner, a bureau noted from the days of Kenesaw Mountain Landis for incorruptible honesty. It was a bombshell to the effect that, after delving into files, clippings and yellowing documents dating back to the days of Abner Doubleday, there was no written rule of any kind with regard to the garb that shall be worn by a baseball umpire.

As far as regulations or possible penalties for infractions were concerned, an umpire might take the field in his pajamas, or wearing a ballet tutu, a pair of jodhpurs, a sarong or a set of hunting pinks complete with silk topper, and no one could penalize him or fine him a penny for it.

While the fans roared with laughter, the press fulminated and Rafe Lustig continued not to occupy the mound for Brooklyn; Concrete Cassaday, still hideously garbed, went on to render his impeccable decisions as the shattered Dodgers staggered under defeat after defeat, and no one knew just what to do.

A rule would undoubtedly have to be made up and incorporated, but the high commissioner was one who did not care to write rules while under fire. To force the maverick Cassaday back into his blue serge retroactively was not consonant with his ideas of good discipline and the best for the game. It was, as you recall, touch-and-go for a while. The revolt might burn itself out. And, on the other hand, it could, as it seemed to be doing, spread to the point where, by creating ridicule, it would do the grand old game an irreparable mischief.

That much you know because you remember the hoohaw. But you weren't around a joint in Canarsie known as The Old Heidelberg when a stricken old ex–asphalt polisher moaned audibly into his lager over the evil case to which his beloved Brooklyns had been brought because his wicked and headstrong daughter had seduced the chief of all the umpires into masquerading as a racehorse tout or the opening act at Loew's Flatbush Avenue Theater. And the sharp ears of a certain widow Katina Schultz, whose business was going out the window on the wings of Rafe Lustig's apparent permanent banishment from the chance to twirl bonus-winning No. 22, picked it up.

Miss Plevin, the secretary, entered the commissioner's office and said, "There's a Mrs. Schultz and a Mr. McGuire to see you, sir. They've been waiting all morning. Something to do with the Cassaday affair," she said.

"What?" cried the commissioner, now ready to grasp at any straw. "Why didn't you say so before? Send them in."

Mrs. Katina Schultz was a handsome blond woman in her thirties, with undoubted strength of character, not to mention of grip, for that was what she had on the arm of a small, unhappy-looking Irishman.

Holding firmly to him, Mrs. Schultz said, "Go on. Tell him what you told me down in the tavern last night."

With a surprising show of stubbornness, Old Man McGuire said, "I'll not! Oh, the shame of it will bring me to an early grave!"

"Oh, you are the most exasperating old man!" wailed Katina, and looked as though she were about to shake him. She turned to the commissioner and said, "My Rafe is losing his bonus, the Dodgers are blowing the pennant and he knows why Umpire Cassaday stopped wearing his blue suit. He says he wants a gold pass or something."

"Hah!" cried the commissioner. "If he knows any way to get Cassaday back into his blue serge suit, he can have a platinum pass studded with—"

Old Man McGuire managed to look as cunning as a monkey, but in a way also as pathetic. "Just plain gold, ye honor," he said. "A lifetime pass to Ebbets Field. I'm an old man and not long for this world."

"O.K. It's yours. Now what's the story?"

"It's me daughter, Molly, as good as betrothed to Rowan Cassaday, the Evil One fly away with all umpires. She put him up to it." And he told of what he had overheard that evening on the stoop.

"Good grief!" the commissioner exploded. "A woman behind it. I didn't know that umpires ever—I beg your pardon. See here, Mr. McGuire. Do you think that if your daughter persuaded Umpire Cassaday into the revolting—ah—unusual outfit, she might likewise persuade him out of it and back into—"

"With a nod of her head, he's that soft about her," Old Man McGuire replied. "But she won't."

"Why not?"

"She's a stubborn lass. Everybody in Canarsie is talking about her as the power behind Cassaday's Revolt. We've been at her, but she says Cassaday's within his rights and nobody but her can stop him. She's

jealous over her influence with him, and it's gone to her head."

"H'm'm," mused the commissioner, "I see. And what is your interest in this affair, Mrs. Schultz?"

Katina explained the insoluble dilemma of the mortgage on Old Heidelberg, the $7500 bonus, the fading season and Cassaday's ultimatum to Rafe Lustig.

The commissioner nodded. "Cassaday is a valuable umpire, perhaps the most valuable we have, even though a little headstrong. I should not like to lose him. Still, if we can't make a rule now to order him back into his uniform, perhaps we—" And here he paused as one suddenly riven with an idea.

Then he smiled quietly and said, "Go home, old man. Maybe you've earned your lifetime pass."

When they had left, he searched his drawer and gave Miss Plevin a telephone number to call. Electrical impulses surged through a copper wire, causing a bell to ring in a small office on Broadway in the Fifties with the legend SIME HOLTZMAN, PUBLICITY lettered on the grimy glass door.

"Sime, this is your old pal," said the commissioner, and told him what was on his mind.

At his end, Sime doodled a moment on a pad, chewing on a cigar, and then said, "Boy, you're in luck. I got just what you want. She's a real phony from Czechoslovakia and hasn't paid me for six months. Can she lay it on thick! She oozes that foreign charm that will drive any self-respecting American girl off her chump. You leave it to me, kid."

Thus it was that after the game the following afternoon, which the Bucs won from Brooklyn by the score thirteen runs to one, a flashy redhead, her age artfully concealed beneath six layers of make-up, sat in an even flashier sports roadster at the players' entrance to Ebbets Field, nursing a large bundle of roses, accompanied by Sime Holtzman and a considerable number of photographers.

When Umpire Cassaday, still in his rebel's outfit, mustard-colored coat, green cap and all, emerged, Sime blocked his path for the cameramen.

"Mr. Cassaday," Holtzman said, "allow me to present Miss Anya Bouquette of Prague, in Czechoslovakia. Miss Bouquette represents the Free Czechoslovakian Film Colony in the United States. They have chosen you the best-dressed umpire and she wishes to make the presentation—"

At this point, Umpire Cassaday found himself with a bunch of roses in his arms and Miss Bouquette, a fragrant and not exactly repulsive bundle of femininity, draped about his neck, cooing in a thick Slavic accent, "Oooo! I am so hoppy because you are so beautifuls! I geev you wan kees, two kees, three kees—

"I congratulates you, Mr. Cassaday!" she declaimed,

accenting the second syllable. "In Czechoslovakia, thees costume would be the mos' best and would cotch all the girls for to marry. I am Czech. I love the United States and Freedom, and therefore I am loving you too. I geev you wan kees, two kees, three kees—"

Thereafter, wherever Umpire Cassaday was, Mademoiselle Bouquette and the photographers were never far away. Holtzman worked out a regular schedule, duly noted in the press: Morning in the Brooklyn Museum, where she taught him European culture; lunch at Sardi's; dinner at 21 with the attaché of the Free Czechs, where Miss Bouquette announced that all men ought to dress like Mr. Cassaday; and so on.

In the meantime, word leaked from the commissioner's office that while no rule forcing umpires to wear blue serge was contemplated at the moment, so high was the esteem and regard in which Umpire Cassaday was held that consideration was being given to the idea of making his startling outfit the official uniform for all umpires.

The climax came the next afternoon at Ebbets Field, where the Pirates were playing their last game before the Giants returned for a short series, the last of the season, and the one that would decide the pennant.

In a box back of home plate, resplendent in a set of white fox furs purchased on credit restored by the new-found publicity and covered with orchids, sat Mademoiselle Anya Bouquette. This time she had a horseshoe of carnations and a huge parchment scroll, gold-embossed and dangling a red seal.

Umpire Cassaday had just emerged from the dugout, headed for home plate, when Sime Holtzman had a finger in his buttonhole and was hauling him toward the field box. Concrete had time only for one bewildered protest, "What, again?" smothered by Holtzman's "It's the Yugoslavs this time. They're crazy about your outfit. They've asked Miss Bouquette to present you with a scroll."

But upon this occasion the fans were ready. As Umpire Cassaday, with ears slightly reddened, stood with the floral horseshoe about his neck and Mademoiselle Bouquette arose with the parchment scroll unfurled, the united fanry of Flatbush, Jamaica Bay, Canarsie, Gowanus and other famous localities began to chant in unison, with a mighty handclap punctuating each digit.

"I geev you wan kees, two kees, three kees—"

They had reached "eight kees," when a very small contretemps took place which was hardly noticed by anyone.

Four boxes away there sat a most exquisite-looking young lady, in a dark Irish way. Between the count of eight and nine kees, Miss Molly McGuire arose from her seat and marched from the premises. As I said, very few noticed this. One of those who did, out of the corner of his eye, was Umpire Rowan (Concrete) Cassaday.

This was the game, as I remember, in which Umpire Cassaday made one of the few palpable miscalls of his career. Pads Franklin, the Brooklyn lead-off hitter, looked at a ball that was so far over his head that the Buc catcher had to call for a ladder to pull it down. Concrete called him out on a third strike.

It was again a sultry September night. On the top of the stoop of the brownstone house in Canarsie sat Molly McGuire, fanning herself vigorously. Below her—many, many steps below her, almost at the bottom, in fact—crouched Rowan Concrete Cassaday, an unhappy and bewildered man, for he was up against the unsolvable.

"But, Molly, darling," he was protesting. "I only wanted to make you and your girl friend proud of me. Gosh, wasn't I voted the best-dressed umpire by the Free Czechoslovakian Film Players and awarded a certificate by Miss Anya Bouquette herself to prove—"

Miss Molly McGuire's sniff echoed four blocks to the very edge of Jamaica Bay. "Rowan Cassaday! If you ever mention that woman's name in my presence again, our engagement is off!"

The square bulk of Umpire Cassaday edged upward one step. "But, Molly, baby, believe me. She doesn't mean a thing to me. I was only trying to please you, in the first place, by wearing something snappy. Why, the commissioner is even thinking of making it the regular—"

Molly gave a little shudder at the prospect of Mademoiselle Bouquette forever buzzing around her too generous wildflower. "If you want to please me, Rowan Cassaday, you'll climb right back into your blue serge suit and cap again, and start looking like the chief of all the umpires ought to look!"

"But, Molly, baby, that's what I was doing in the first place, when you—"

"Then do it for me, darling! Tomorrow!"

A glazed look came into the eyes of Rowan Cassaday, as it does into the eyes of all men when confronted by the awful, unanswerable, moonstruck logic of women. Nevertheless, he gained six steps without protest, and was able thus to arrive back where he had started from a hideous ten days ago—at the hem of her dainty skirt. And thus peace descended once more upon Flatbush.

Remember that wonderful day—a Thursday, I believe it was—when out from the dugout at game time marched that massive concrete figure once more impregnably armored, cap-a-pie, in shiny blue serge, the belted back spread to the load of league baseballs stuffed in the capacious pockets.

What a cheer greeted his appearance, and then what a roar went up as Rafe Lustig emerged from the dugout, swinging his glove and sweater. The historic exchange between the two will never be forgotten.

Rafe said, "Hi, Rowan."

Concrete replied, "Hi, Rafe."

What a day that was. How the long-silent bats of the Brooks pummeled the unhappy Jints. How the long-rested arm of Rafe Lustig, twirling out the $7500-bonus game and the everlasting rescue of Old Heidelberg, tamed the interlopers from Manhattan, disposing of them with no more than a single scratch hit. How the word spread like wildfire through the cities of the league that Cassaday's Revolt was over and blue serge once again was the order of the day.

Witness to all this was a happy Molly McGuire in a box back of home plate. Absent from the festivities was Mademoiselle Anya Bouquette, who, it seems, could not abide blue serge, for it reminded her of gloomy Sunday and an unhappy childhood in Prague, with people jumping off bridges.

And yet, if you looked closely, there was one difference to be observed, which, in a sense, gave notice who would wear the pants in the Cassaday household, came that day. For while indeed Concrete was poured back into the lumpy anonymity of the traditional garments—serge cap, coat, tie, breeches—yet from the breast pocket fluttered the tip of that awful red-and-yellow Paisley kerchief.

This was all that was left of Cassaday's Revolt. He had tasted individuality. He would never quite be the same again. But the object in his breast pocket remained unnoticed and unmentioned, except for the quiet smile of triumph reflected from the well-kept garden of the countenance of Miss Molly McGuire.

On July 17 of the 1978 American League season, the Red Sox led the Yankees by 14 games. Then something happened. The something happened in two parts. The first part is told here by Peter Gammons. The second part is told a bit farther on in these pages by Sparky Lyle. Hint: The second part don't change the title none.

# 1978: The Boston Massacre

## PETER GAMMONS

THE MAN had on a gray Brooks Brothers suit, which made him look for all the world as if he were Harvard '44, and he was leaning over the railing of the box next to the Red Sox dugout. "Zimmer!" he screamed, but Don Zimmer just stared dead ahead. The score at that point in last Friday night's game was 13–0 in favor of the Yankees and except to change pitchers a few times the Red Sox manager hadn't moved in three hours. He had stared as Mickey Rivers stood on third just two pitches into the game. He had stared as, for the second straight night, a Yankee batter got his third hit before Boston's ninth hitter, Butch Hobson, even got to the plate. He had stared as the Red Sox made seven errors. And now he stared as the man kept screaming his name.

"I've been a Red Sox fan for twenty years," the man hollered. "A diehard Red Sox fan. I've put up with a lot of heartaches. But this time you've really done it. This time my heart's been broken for good." Finally Zimmer looked up, just as security guards hauled the man away.

From Eastport to Block Island, New Englanders were screaming mad. Only a couple of weeks before, the Red Sox had been baseball's one sure thing, but now Fenway Park was like St. Petersburg in the last days of Czar Nicholas. Back in July, when Billy Martin still sat in the Yankee manager's office and New York was in the process of falling fourteen games behind the Sox, Reggie Jackson had said, "Not even Affirmed can catch them." But by late last Sunday afternoon, when the 1978 version of the Boston Massacre concluded with New York's fourth win in a row over the Red Sox, the Yankees had caught them. And the Yanks had gained a tie for first in the American League East in such awesome fashion—winning sixteen of their last eighteen, including the lopsided victories that comprised the

Massacre—that Saturday night a New Yorker named Dick Waterman walked into a Cambridge bar, announced, "For the first time a first-place team has been mathematically eliminated," and held up a sign that read: NY 35–49–4, BOS 5–16–11. Those figures were the combined line score of last weekend's first three games. The disparity between those sets of numbers, as much as the losses themselves, was what so deeply depressed Red Sox fans. "It's 1929 all over again," mourned Robert Crane, treasurer of the Commonwealth of Massachusetts.

The Red Sox and Yankees began their two-city, seven-game, eleven-day showdown in Boston last Thursday—it will continue with three games this weekend in New York—and it quickly became apparent that this confrontation would be quite different from their six-game shoot-out in late June and early July. On that occasion the Red Sox had beaten the Yanks four times and opened up a lead that appeared insurmountable. Back then the Yankees had so few healthy bodies that Catcher Thurman Munson was trying to become a right fielder, and one day a minor league pitcher named Paul Semall drove from West Haven, Connecticut, to Boston to throw batting practice. Had the New York brass liked the way he threw, Semall would have stayed with the Yankees and become a starter. By midnight, Semall was driving back to West Haven, and soon thereafter injuries became so rife among New York pitchers that reserve first baseman Jim Spencer was warming up in the bullpen.

Rivers, the center fielder and key to the Yankee offense, had a broken wrist. Both members of the double-play combination, Willie Randolph and Bucky Dent, were injured and out of the lineup. To complete the up-the-middle collapse, Munson was playing—

sometimes behind the plate and sometimes in right—with a bad leg, and the pitching staff had been reduced to *Gong Show* contestants. Paul Semall got gonged. Dave Rajsich got gonged. Larry McCall got gonged. Catfish Hunter, Ed Figueroa, Dick Tidrow, Ken Clay, Andy Messersmith, and Don Gullett were all hurt or soon to be injured. Only the brilliant Ron Guidry stayed healthy. Almost singlehandedly he kept the bottom from falling out during July and early August.

Then, as the regulars gradually began getting back into the lineup, the blow-up between owner George Steinbrenner and Martin occurred. Martin resigned on July 24, and the next day Bob Lemon, who had recently been canned by the White Sox, took over. "The season starts today," Lemon told the Yankees. "Go have some fun." Considering the disarray in New York during the preceding year and a half, that seemed a bit much to ask. So was catching Boston. No American League team had ever changed managers in midseason and won a championship. "Under Lemon we became a completely different team," says Spencer. "If Martin were still here, we wouldn't be," snaps one player. "We'd have quit. Rivers and Jackson couldn't play for him. But Lemon gave us a fresh spirit. We kept playing. We looked up, and Boston was right in front of us." The fact that a suddenly revived Hunter had won six straight, that Figueroa had regained health and happiness, that Tidrow had again become hale and that rookie right hander Jim Beattie had returned from the minors with his self-confidence restored didn't hurt.

And while the Yankees arrived in Boston 30–13 under Lemon and 35–14 since July 17—the night they fell fourteen games behind—the Red Sox had been stumbling. They were 25–24 since July 17. Their thirty-nine-year-old leader, Carl Yastrzemski, had suffered back and shoulder ailments in mid-July, and then he pulled ligaments in his right wrist that left him taped up and in and out of the lineup. He had hit three homers in two months. Second baseman Jerry Remy fractured a bone in his left wrist on August 25 and had not appeared in the lineup thereafter.

Catcher Carlton Fisk had been playing with a cracked rib, which he said made him feel as if "someone is sticking a sword in my side" every time he threw. Third baseman Butch Hobson has cartilage and ligament damage in both knees and bone chips in his right elbow. The chips are so painful that one night he had to run off the field during infield practice; his elbow had locked up on him. When New York came to town, he had a major-league–leading thirty-eight errors, most of them the result of bad throws made with his bad arm. Right fielder Dwight Evans had been beaned on August 29 and was experiencing dizziness whenever he ran. Reliever Bill Campbell, who had thirty-one saves and thirteen

wins in 1977, had suffered from elbow and shoulder soreness all season.

The injuries tended to dampen Boston's already erratic, one-dimensional offense, which relies too heavily on power hitting even when everyone is healthy. They also ruined the Sox defense, which had been the facet of play most responsible for giving the Red Sox a ten-game lead over their nearest challenger, Milwaukee, on July 8. No wonder the pitching went sour, with Mike Torrez going 4–4 since the All-Star Game, Luis Tiant 3–7 since June 24, and Bill Lee 0–7 since July 15. And as Boston awaited its confrontation with the Yankees, it lost three out of five to Toronto and Oakland and two of three in Baltimore. The Sox' only lift came in Wednesday's 2–0 win over the Orioles. Tiant pitched a two-hitter that night, and Yaz, his wrist looking like a mummy's, hit a two-run homer. It was one of only two hits the Sox got off Dennis Martinez.

As play began Thursday night at Fenway Park, the Red Sox lead had dwindled to four games with twenty-four to play. "We'll be happy with a split," Lemon said. By 9:05 P.M. Friday—during the third inning of Game 2—Lemon turned to pitching coach–scout Clyde King and said, "Now I'll only be happy with three out of four." Right about then *The Washington Post*'s Tom Boswell was writing his lead: "*Ibid,* for details, see yesterday's paper." The details were downright embarrassing to the Red Sox.

The embarrassments had begun with a Hobson error in the first inning Thursday. Then a Munson single. And a Jackson single. Zap, the Yankees had two unearned runs. After giving up four straight singles to start the second inning, Torrez went to the showers. Munson had three hits—and the Yankees seven runs—before Hobson got his first at bat in the bottom of the third. After the seventh inning, someone in the press box looked up at the New York line on the scoreboard—2–3–2–5–0–1–0—and dialed the number. It was disconnected. When the game ended, the Yankees had twenty-one hits and a 15–3 victory.

New York's joy was tempered by two injuries. Hunter left the game with a pulled groin muscle in the fourth, too soon to get the victory, though the Yanks were leading 12–0. "The bullpen phone rang and six of us fought to answer it," said Clay, who won the phone call and the game. Hunter, it turned out, would probably miss only one start. In the sixth inning, Munson was beaned by Dick Drago. Though dizzy, Munson said he would be behind the plate Friday. "He smells blood," Jackson said.

The next night, the Yankees not only drained Boston's blood but also its dignity. Rivers hit rookie right hander Jim Wright's first pitch past first baseman George Scott into right field. On the second pitch, he stole second and cruised on into third as Fisk's throw bounced away from shortstop Rick Burleson. Wright had thrown two pitches, and Rivers was peering at him from third base. Wright went on to get four outs, one more than Torrez had; he was relieved after allowing four runs. His replacement, Tom Burgmeier, immediately gave up a single and walk before surrendering a mighty home run by Jackson.

Beattie, who in his Fenway appearance in June had been knocked out in the third inning and optioned to

---

# GEORGE PRICE

*Drawing by Geo. Price;* © *1986 The New Yorker Magazine, Inc.*

*"Why anyone should look forward to a subway series is beyond me."*

Tacoma in the sixth, retired eighteen in a row in one stretch, while the Red Sox self-destructed in the field. Evans, who had not dropped a fly in his first five and three-quarters years in the majors, dropped his second one of the week and had to leave the game. "I can't look up or down without getting dizzy," he said. Fisk had two throws bounce away for errors. Rivers hit a routine ground ball to Scott in the third and beat Scott to the bag, making him three-for-three before Hobson ever got up. The game ended with a 13–2 score and the seven Red Sox errors.

"I can't believe what I've been seeing," said King, who has watched about forty Red Sox games this season. "I could understand if an expansion team fell apart like that, but Boston's got the best record in baseball. It can't go on." On Saturday afternoon, Guidry took his 20–2 record to the mound. It went on.

This was to be the showdown of the aces. Dennis Eckersley, 16–6, was 9–0 in Fenway and had not been knocked out before the fifth inning all season. He had beaten the Yankees three times in a twelve-day stretch earlier in the year. When he blew a third strike past Jackson to end the bottom of the first, he had done what Torrez and Wright had not been able to do—shut the Yankees out in the first inning.

"It looked like it was going to be a 1–0 game, what with the wind whipping in and Eckersley looking like he'd put us back together," said Zimmer. After Burleson led off Boston's first with a single, Fred Lynn bunted. Guidry, who could have cut down Burleson at second, hesitated and ended up throwing to first. Then Dent bobbled Jim Rice's grounder in the hole for an infield single. Two on. But Guidry busted fastballs in on the hands of Yastrzemski and Fisk, getting them out on a weak grounder and called third strike, respectively. Despite leadoff walks in the next two Boston at bats, the Sox hitters were finished for the day. Rice's grounder would be their second and last hit of the afternoon.

Yastrzemski seemed to lift his catatonic team in the fourth with a twisting, leaping catch on the dead run that he turned into a double play. But three batters later, with two on and two out, all that Yaz and Eckersley had done to heighten Boston's morale unraveled when Lou Piniella sliced a pop fly into the gale in right center.

"It must have blown a hundred feet across, like a Frisbee coming back," says Eckersley. Lynn came in a few steps but he had no chance. Burleson made chase from shortstop, Scott took off from first. The ball was out of reach of both. Rice, who was playing near the warning track in right, could not get there. Frank Duffy, the second baseman, did, but when he turned and looked up into the sun he lost sight of the ball. It landed in front of him. It was 1–0. After an intentional walk to Graig Nettles, Dent dunked a two-strike pitch into left for two more runs. "That broke my back," said Eckersley. By the time the inning had ended, Eckersley was gone. There had been another walk, an error, a wild pitch, and a passed ball. Seven runs had scored. "This is the first time I've seen a first-place team chasing a second-place team," said NBC's Tony Kubek.

Guidry had not only become the second left hander to pitch a complete game against the Red Sox in Fenway all season, but also was the first lefty to shut them out at home since 1974. "Pitchers are afraid to pitch inside here," he said. "But that's where you've got to."

The victory brought Guidry's record to 21–2, his earned-run average to 1.77, and his strikeouts to 220; it also brought the New York staff's ERA to 2.07 over the last twenty-six games. "They must be cheating," said Lynn. "Those aren't the same Yankees we saw before. I think George Steinbrenner used his clone money. I think those were Yankee clones out there from teams of the past."

"These guys are—I hope you understand how I use the word—nasty," said Jackson. "This is a pro's game, and this team is loaded with professionals. Tough guys. Nasty."

"This is two years in a row we've finished like this, so it must say something about the team's character," Tidrow said. Before Lemon took over, the only times the word "character" was used in the Yankee clubhouse it was invariably followed by the word "assassination."

With the 7–0 loss figured in, the Red Sox had lost eight out of ten. In those games they had committed twenty-four errors good for twenty unearned runs. Twice pop-ups to shallow right had dropped, leading to two losses and ten earned runs.

Tiant had been the only starting pitcher to win. Evans, Scott, Hobson, and Jack Brohamer, who most of the time were the bottom four in the batting order, were twelve for 123—or .098. "How can a team get thirty-something games over .500 in July and then in September see its pitching, hitting, and fielding all fall apart at the same time?" wondered Fisk.

After being bombarded in the first three games, all that the Red Sox could come up with in their effort to prevent the Yankees from gaining a first-place tie on Sunday was rookie left hander Bobby Sprowl. In June, while the Sox were beating the Yankees, Sprowl was pitching for the Bristol Red Sox against the West Haven Yankees.

Clearly he was not ready for their New York namesakes. He began by walking Rivers and Willie Randolph, lasted only two-thirds of an inning, and was charged with three runs. The most damaging blow came after Sprowl gave way to reliever Bob Stanley, who promptly yielded a single to Nettles that drove in two runners whom Sprowl had allowed to reach base. The

Yankees would build a 6–0 bulge before coasting to an eighteen-hit, 7–4 victory. Suddenly, New York not only had a psychological edge on the Red Sox, but it also had pulled even with them in the standings.

"It's never easy to win a pennant," said Yastrzemski. "We've got three weeks to play. We've got three games in Yankee Stadium next weekend. Anything can happen." He stared into his locker. Anything already had.

This piece appeared in *Advertising Age* just before the start of the baseball season. Which season? Who cares?

# Baseball's Walk of Life

## BOB GARFIELD

THE FLAGS are flapping heavily over Waveland Avenue. That is a given. The ivy is rooting itself still more firmly in the outfield brick. Obviously. But consider this: On the north side of Chicago, in the broad shadow of Wrigley Field, long-suffering homeowners are commencing to be ticked off. A new season begins, and with it cars and clogged streets and drunks tramping happily across strange lawns.

Baseball is back. Also beer cans in the shrubbery.

To San Francisco comes another season of winter sport. Candlestick Park is the frigid home of 24 lackluster players, who will rattle chilled metacarpals with every batted ball through 729 innings of inferior play. The players, their mid-season replacements and 900,000 shivering fans will hate it and love it.

Baseball is back, in varying degrees.

In Cleveland, the Easter promise of rebirth once again is a cruel tease. Decades of sporting futility cannot harden an Indians partisan; desperate people cling to desperate hope and speak with pathetic expectation of a young righthander called Candiotti. April is a giddy month. Even the Tribe isn't yet mathematically eliminated.

Baseball is back, and none too soon. Now that the weather's nice, we need this game to remind us how miserable we are.

Everybody has an idea of what makes the national game so enduring a phenomenon. People talk about baseball's strategy, culture, statistical tidiness. Some like its color, its folklore, its excruciating tension.

All true, I suppose. But the big thing is misery—misery in the quest for redemption—which, curiously enough, is the story of life. And therein lies the lure of the game: Baseball is a metaphor for our existence on Earth.

Oh, you think that's overstated? Here is a sport evolved from a lower form, enhanced through natural selection and half populated by losers. Journeymen are many, heroes are few and every error is recorded in perpetuity. And look here: Baseball is savored for its excitement and surprises, but isn't it more typically routine and discouraging? Is one season materially different from another? No. The names change, but the events are predictable as can be. And if you doubt me on that point, here's an assortment of things that will happen this year.

A bad team will burst from the starting gate, win its first nine games, and make an entire city suspend its rational understanding that the club, ultimately, is going nowhere.

A hulking cleanup hitter will take a fastball square in the shoulder and will jog to first base without so much as rubbing the welt.

The following night, in the ninth inning, his team down by a run, the same man will be batting with a runner on second and nobody out. His only job will be to put the ball in play, on the ground or in the air, on the right side of the diamond. He will strike out.

In the clubhouse after the game, the manager will rehash the ninth in a tense peculiar to baseball: the present hypothetical. "Tom gets his bat on the ball, Mike goes to third and Julio's fly ball scores the run and we tie the game." Woulda, coulda, shoulda. The press will leave the room and the manager will get dressed in red slacks, white shoes and a red-and-white houndstooth sportcoat, each of which houndsteeth is the size of a silver dollar. (Before season's end, he will be fired and be made a superscout with the Kansas City organization. People whom he forgot he knew will phone him for free Royals tickets.)

Somewhere in America, a fan will scale five levels of ramp and 61 concrete steps, shuffle sideways to the middle of a row, crane his neck to see past the foul pole 465 feet from home plate, turn to his buddy and say in absolute sincerity: "Hey, great seats!"

In the row beneath him, a man will eyeball the popcorn vender four sections away and wave him over. The vender will trip over four rows of feet, scale 60 concrete steps and hear the fan say, "Send the beer man around." The fan will elbow the guy next to him and laugh. The vender will descend down 60 concrete steps

thinking terrible thoughts.

Baseball *is* life—so thank heaven it's back, as precious as can be.

### TESTIMONIALS . . .

Walter Johnson. Left: the back page of *The Sporting News* for Ronald Reagan. (Walter Johnson ad reprinted by permission of the Coca-Cola Company; Chesterfield ad reprinted by permission of *The Sporting News*)

In this same column giving the origins of *bullpen, southpaw, bunt* and *rookie,* the author also furnished "a word to add to your vocabulary: *xanthodontous.*" It means "having yellow teeth." I couldn't think of a baseball connection there, but the more I think about it now—a coach I knew in the Coast League that time . . .

# Words

## MICHAEL GARTNER

IN THE good old days, the days before million-dollar contracts and arbitration and tv rights, there were at many ballparks outdoor boards advertising Bull Durham tobacco. This was in the days before night baseball, and pitchers warming up for relief duty often chose to limber up in the shade of those big signs. The signs since have given way to exploding scoreboards and the like, but the bull lives on in baseball language: It's because of him that today we call the pitchers' warmup area the *bull pen.*

In those days, most ballparks were built so batters standing at home plate faced east as they looked at the pitcher. The parks were built that way so batters wouldn't be looking into the afternoon sun. Right-handed pitchers thus threw from the north side, and left-handers threw from the south. That's why someone in the 1880s started calling left-handed pitchers *southpaws,* and that's why today left-handers, be they pitchers or tuba players, are called southpaws.

In 1872, a fellow named Pearce of the Brooklyn Atlantics decided that instead of taking a full swing at a pitch, he'd just butt it with his bat, much like a goat butts an intruder. The strategy apparently worked, and the butt became a part of baseball. It quickly became known as a *bunt,* probably because someone misheard the word in Brooklyn.

In baseball, as in anything else, a new player is a *recruit* (a word that comes from a Latin word that means, roughly, "new growth"). Baseball players started slurring that word, and by 1892 they had turned it into *rookie,* which still today means an untrained recruit, especially in sports.

# The Aerodynamics of an Irishman

## BARRY GIFFORD

THERE WAS a man on our block named Rooney Sullavan who'd often come walking down the street while the kids would be playing ball in front of my house or Johnny McLaughlin's house. He would always stop and ask if he'd ever shown us how he used to throw the knuckleball when he pitched for Kankakee in 1930.

"Plenty of times, Rooney," Billy Cunningham would say. "No knuckles about it, right?" Tommy Ryan would say. "No knuckles about it, right!" Rooney Sullavan would say. "Give it here and I'll show you." One of us would reluctantly toss Rooney the ball and we'd step up so he could demonstrate for the fortieth or fiftieth time how he held the ball by his fingertips only, no knuckles about it.

"Don't know how it ever got the name knuckler," Rooney'd say. "I call mine The Rooneyball." Then he'd tell one of us, usually Billy because he had the catcher's glove, the old fat-heeled kind that didn't bend unless somebody stepped on it, a big black mitt that Billy's dad had handed down to him from *his* days at Kankakee or Rock Island or someplace, to get sixty feet away so Rooney could see if he could "still make it wrinkle."

Billy would pace off twelve squares of sidewalk, each square being approximately five feet long, the length of one nine year old boy's body stretched head to toe lying flat, squat down and stick his big black glove out in front of his face. With his right hand he'd cover his crotch in case the pitch got away and short-hopped off the cement where he couldn't block it with the mitt. The knuckleball was unpredictable, not even Rooney could tell what would happen to it once he let it go.

"It's the air makes it hop," Rooney claimed. His leather jacket creaked as he bent, wound up, rotated his right arm like nobody'd done since Chief Bender, crossed his runny grey eyes and released the ball from the tips of his fingers. We watched as it sailed straight up at first then sort of floated on an invisible wave before plunging the last ten feet like a balloon that had been pierced by a dart.

Billy always went down on his knees, the back of his right hand stiffened over his crotch, and stuck out his gloved hand at the slowly whirling Rooneyball. Just before it got to Billy's mitt the ball would give out entirely and sink rapidly, inducing Billy to lean forward in order to catch it, only he couldn't because at the last instant it would make a final, sneaky hop before bouncing surprisingly hard off Billy's unprotected chest.

"*Just* like I told you," Rooney Sullavan would exclaim. "All it takes is plain old air."

Billy would come up with the ball in his upturned glove, his right hand rubbing the place on his chest where the pitch had hit. "You all right, son?" Rooney would ask, and Billy would nod. "Tough kid," Rooney'd say. "I'd like to stay out with you fellas all day, but I got responsibilities." Rooney would muss up Billy's hair with the hand that held the secret to The Rooneyball and walk away whistling "When Irish Eyes Are Smiling" or "My Wild Irish Rose." Rooney was about forty-five or fifty years old and lived with his mother in a bungalow at the corner. He worked nights for Wanzer Dairy, washing out returned milk bottles.

Tommy Ryan would grab the ball out of Billy's mitt and hold it by the tips of his fingers like Rooney Sullavan did, and Billy would go sit on the stoop in front of the closest house and rub his chest. "No way," Tommy would say, considering the prospect of his ever duplicating Rooney's feat. "There must be something he's not telling us."

This is the opening chapter in the book *Gifford on Courage*.

# Herb Score

## ——— FRANK GIFFORD *with* CHARLES MANGEL ———

IT WAS Bob Feller all over again. A kid who could move from the dirt ballfield and splintered stands behind the high school gym right into the major leagues and take on Williams and Mantle and the rest on even terms. He had a fast ball that Yogi Berra called "unfair," a curve that broke almost at a right angle, and if he could only get his control into shape, why he was sure to win 20 games his first year and, lord, maybe into infinity.

He set people dreaming. Even hard-nosed pros, who watched pretenders come up and go down every year, saw visions: Hal Newhouser, Prince Hal, the strongman of the Detroit pitching staff finishing his career with Cleveland, said, "I wish I had his future rather than my past." Tris Speaker, the old centerfielder against whom all centerfielders are measured, said, "He'll be the greatest." Flat out. No qualification. Men who played with Feller said the kid's fast ball was faster than Feller's and if Feller disagreed he kept it to himself.

His first trip—age 18—to meet the Cleveland brass might have been the wish of a Little Leaguer. "Just warm up, son, and we'll see what you have." The first few pitches crack into the catcher's mitt and a coach roars out of the dugout screaming, "I told you to take it easy; don't bear down until you're warm." And the apologetic response: "I'm not bearing down, sir." The catcher surreptitiously slips a sponge rubber pad into his glove.

We revel in new heroes, a fresh name to take its place beside Grove, Alexander, Johnson, Spahn in the pantheon of our memories. Young, skinny Herb Score seemed destined. Three fantastic years in succession, one in the highest rung of the minors, two in the majors. He wins 36 and loses 19 those two years with Cleveland. He strikes out 245 the first year and 263 the second. Both records. (Feller didn't strike out 240 until his third year; Grove, whom many call the best lefthander ever, until his sixth.) He wins Rookie of the Year in the minors and repeats the next year with Cleveland.

Then he's through. He doesn't have another winning season. In the baseball vernacular, he loses his arm.

Herb Score. Mention his name even to a marginal baseball fan and you'll hear, "Oh, yeah, he was the guy who was hit in the eye by McDougald's line drive. Shame. Great promise. Knocked him right out of baseball."

Did it? How *does* an arm go bad? When a spur begins to grow? When strain distorts a tendon? When the chill of a spring night game subtly alters musculature? When a baseball traveling 130 miles an hour smashes into an eye? So much the magic of medicine can't tell us; along with the diseases that ravage man, why does a pitcher suddenly lose his arm?

Herbert Score, 41 and totally gray, sportscaster for the Indians, is doing some missionary work before a room jammed with members of the Napoleon, Ohio, Kiwanis Club (they even permitted a few eager wives in this night; but *after* dinner). Score speaks well, with a fine self-directed wit.

"During my first season with Cleveland, we made an early visit to New York where I was born. I was hoping to pitch against the Yankees. I figured I'd walk onto that field and every kid I'd gone to school with would be there and I'd show them what I'd become. But Al Lopez was a bright manager. He wasn't going to use me. It would be Early Wynn Friday night, Mike Garcia Saturday and Bob Lemon Sunday. Saturday afternoon, Lemon is running in the outfield and pulls a muscle in his leg. After the game Saturday, Lopez tells me, 'We don't know if Lemon's leg will be all right tomorrow. If he can't pitch, you're going to start against the Yankees. Get to bed early tonight.'

"Next morning it's Sunday and I decide to go to St. Patrick's Cathedral. I'm in there kneeling, praying. And as I'm meditating and praying, I said, 'Lord, Bob Lemon hurt his leg yesterday. They don't know how serious it is and he's been awfully nice to me, taken me to dinner. He's a great pitcher, won 20 games six or seven times and he's just an outstanding person. But if you could see your way clear he couldn't walk today, I'd appreciate it.'

"I get to the ballpark and they're still not sure if Lemon's going to be able to play, so they tell us both to warm up. If Lemon's leg doesn't hurt, he'll pitch. About 10 minutes go by and they decide he's okay and tell me to sit down. It's about time for the game to start and rather than run across the field to the bullpen, I decide to walk underneath the stadium concourse.

"I start out and I'm passing the concessions. You know, nothing smells as good as hot dogs at a ballpark. Absolutely nothing. I'm walking and I'm smelling. If I only had some money, I'd buy some hot dogs. In those days, I was always hungry. I strike up a conversation with a couple of fellows. Pretty soon I have two hot dogs. I keep walking and I hear the game start. At the head of the ramp going down to the bullpen, there's another concession stand. I thought, the hot dogs were good. A little ice cream to wash it down wouldn't be bad. Sure enough, another conversation; I end up with a box of ice cream.

"Sit down on the bench and by now the Yankees are at bat. I open my shirt, take off my cap, close my eyes and I'm ready to take a little sun. All of a sudden, I feel a tug at my sleeve and I open my eyes and there's Mel Harder, our pitching coach. He's pointing toward the mound. I see Lopez standing there waving his left hand. Harder says, 'I think he wants you.' And I say, 'That's what I'm afraid of.'

"I climb over the railing and start across the outfield toward the mound. Yankee Stadium, 60,000 people, something I've dreamed of since I was a kid and here I am gurgling with every step.

"Finally get to the mound, Lopez tells me Lemon's leg is hurting, the umpires realize this and I can take all the time I need to warm up. I figured it might take three days. But we get under way and it gets into the fifth or sixth inning and somehow the Yankees load the bases and there are no outs. I look up and here's Mickey Mantle at the plate. We all know there's a lot of criticism of baseball for being a long game, being too slow, and usually they blame the pitcher and they say how come he holds the ball so long. As long as I'm holding it, he can't hit it.

"I know I have to do something and then I hear someone call time out. Al Rosen's playing third base, sort of the unofficial team captain. He's called time and he's going to walk over and I know I'm going to get this wonderful piece of advice.

"Rosen calls the shortstop and they have a little meeting. Now Rosen comes to the mound. He and the shortstop have worked it all out. 'Hey, kid,' he says, 'you're really in trouble.'

"The mind is a wonderful thing and frequently we're able to forget unhappy events. I don't remember the details from that point, except learning why Mantle is paid all that salary, but I'm young and I'll have lots of chances at the Yankees and we continue to Boston.

"I had heard a lot about Ted Williams and I'm looking forward to pitching against him. So the first time we play the Red Sox, I'm geared up to face Williams. But he's not in the line-up. Has the flu. Two weeks later, we have another series with Boston. And again, I'm ready for Williams. Again, he's not in the line-up. A suspicion grows. Possibly Williams doesn't want to face Score. It's understandable. He's getting on—34, 35 years old—and his reflexes are shot and he possibly couldn't get around on a fast ball any more. I'd been having a good spring. Won a couple of games. I could understand his reluctance.

"It gets to be June and the Red Sox are in Cleveland. Finally, Williams is going to meet Score. I know this because they have it in the newspaper and they're never wrong. I could hardly wait to warm up. It's the first inning and here comes Williams, batting third. I'm not the kind of pitcher, incidentally, who looks back to see where his fielders are playing each batter. I didn't know where I was going to throw it, so I sure didn't know where they were going to hit it.

"But I notice suddenly that the team is shifting way over to the right, the Boudreau shift. The shortstop is on the right side of second base, the second baseman almost in right field, Rosen all alone on the left side of the infield. I was thinking, if I say anything to them, they'll think I'm a fresh rookie and I shouldn't talk, all those veteran ballplayers. There's no way Williams can pull me, not *my* fast ball, but I figure they'll find out for themselves. Count gets to be three balls and a strike and Williams hits a little fly ball into left centerfield.

"The Cleveland stadium sits out there on the lake and very unusual wind currents blow off the water. Somehow this ball gets up into one of those unusual currents and that lazy fly ball hits the fence 385 feet away. Williams has a double. I'm undaunted. He didn't *pull* the ball. When he comes up next time, I'll reach back, give it a little extra push and zip right on by him. He comes up two innings later, I reach back for a little extra, he hits it into the upper deck in right field. In his first 16 times at bat, Williams hits four home runs, a double, and a single off me.

"So, next trip to Boston, Williams is in the line-up again. He's obviously regained his confidence as far as Score is concerned. Now I've rarely been able to get ahead of Williams. It's always two balls and no strikes, three balls and maybe one strike. I have two pitches, a fast ball and a curve, and the curve I usually don't get over. So if you want to guess what's coming, you have a pretty good percentage. I'd have Williams 3–0 and he'd say to himself, he's going to throw me a fast ball and I'm going to hit it 100 miles. And I'd say to myself, I'm going to throw him a fast ball and he's going to hit it 100 miles.

"But, now, I do get ahead of him. I get two strikes, no balls. I've got him. I've pitched a whole year and I know how to do this. I'm going to bounce the curve in front of home plate. Then I'm going to stomp around on the mound and kick some dirt and fume and Williams is going to say, ahah, he still can't get that curve over. Then I'm going to throw a fast ball right up under his chin. He's going to jump back and he's going to say, ahah, now he'll have to come in with a fast ball and then I'm going to throw the curve over the outside corner; he'll be so surprised he won't even swing, strike three. All figured out.

"I bounce the curve in front of the plate, stomp around, put on a pretty good show. Now I'm ready. Someone once told me it takes two-fifths of a second from the time a pitcher releases until the batter swings. You'd be amazed what goes through your mind in two-fifths of a second. I throw the ball. I see him start to swing. I notice he has a lovely swing. I see the ball over my head, and I think, boy, he sure didn't pull my pitch. I look back and all I can see is the centerfielder's number. I'm thinking, it carried pretty good, Larry Doby's going to have to hurry to catch it. Then I realize he's not going to catch it. He's going to play it off the wall in centerfield. Then I realize it's not going to hit the wall."

His audience warm, Score talked about prospects for the current Indians and then asked for questions. Two routine queries, and a hand goes up hesitantly: "Herb, what happened with McDougald?" Nineteen years later and they still ask. A pitcher with extraordinary skills loses them and people still wonder.

Six no-hitters and three perfect games in three years of high school ball, a total of eight hits allowed his entire junior year, brought scouts from 14 of the then-16 major league teams to his family's home. Ten offered bonuses up to $80,000 if he would sign with them; four said simply, "Tell us your best offer and we'll top it."

Herb and his mother had very little money but passed up the dollar hunt and chose a friend instead. Cy Slapnicka, the man who had signed Feller as a 17-year-old in Iowa, wintered in Score's hometown of Lake Worth, Florida. Told by a city cop one day about a freshman at Lake Worth High, Slapnicka went to watch—and kept his seat behind home plate for three seasons. Major league rules prevented him from talking contract until the youngster turned 19; but he could talk about other things, couldn't he? He could take Herb, his

mother and two sisters out to dinner now and then. And, if the talk got around to baseball, he might mention a few of the nice things about the people he worked for. There's no law against that, is there?

So Slap and the family became genuinely great friends. And by the start of Herb's junior year, when the other scouts began to show in packs, it really was too late. (Even though Herb coincidentally had been dating the pretty daughter of one of them.) Slap offered $60,000. Herb took it, bought his mother a house and himself a record player.

Baseball was more than a game to Score, however talented he was; it was—well, it was communication. He was—still is—shy and modest. But intense, too, if that doesn't seem contradictory. "The reason I played so hard at baseball," he says, "was because that was the one thing *I could do,* the only thing that would lift me out of the crowd. We had no money. People knew my father drank a lot and someone would come by and say your father's down there somewhere drunk. My parents separated. We moved to Florida and sports was the only way I could 'say' something."

Some intangible within Score forced him to make his "statement" clear and sharp. "Players, great players, come to the majors all the time with extraordinary talent," says Rocky Colavito, Score's friend, teammate, and later, a coach, "but often they try to get by with just their God-given skills. I never saw any pitcher come up with the natural equipment Herb had, but that wasn't enough for him. He made perfect seem like second-rate. He had a burning desire to excel. In warm-ups he didn't jog, he ran. In playing catch along the sidelines, he didn't lob. He threw. Even after he won a game, he talked to me for hours about how *he* might have played better. He wouldn't accept an average performance."

No one could ever suggest that Score was not giving his best. In Indianapolis, manager Kerby Farrell walked out to the mound to remove Score after he had walked three successive batters. "Herb," he said, "you're not trying to relax." Score didn't hear the last two words and snapped, "Get away from me before I push your nose through your face." Score left the game and put the runway to the locker room into temporary eclipse by breaking every light bulb en route. Then he tore the locker room apart. Suddenly, Herb realized what he had done. From that point he kept his furies to himself. "If I don't pitch well, why should I take it out on other people?" he told me. "Why should people have to walk carefully around me?" No one, in the ballpark or at home, ever saw him angry again. When he was displeased with the way he pitched, he would wait until he got into his car after the game, roll up the windows and scream at the top of his voice.

In demand from his first year in Cleveland as a

speaker at sports affairs, Score was politic and always said what the audience wanted to hear. But there was one exception. At a high school dinner, the baseball coach preceded Score and said that while the team had not done too well, "We all had fun." Score, always slow to criticize, had to disagree. "I don't understand how you could have fun while you were losing. I'll tell you honestly, it kills me."

Every batter was Herb's personal antagonist. "Every hit against me was a slap in my face," he says. "I hated that batter." Score can't remember those he got out, but he will give you—30 years later—clinical details of everyone who hit him going back to high school. He didn't walk too many in those days because high school kids scare. They see a wild fastballer, take three strikes and sit down, relieved they're still whole.

At that, perhaps they weren't too different from major leaguers. Frank Frisch, manager and second baseman of the Cardinals, watched a fast, wild Feller warm up before pitching against the Cards in an exhibition game in 1936. After one of Feller's errant pitches splintered a section of the backstop, Frisch called rookie Lynn King.

"Young man," he asked, "have you ever played second base?"

"No sir," King replied.

"Well, you're playing there today."

Feller struck out eight men in the first three innings of that game. One of them was shortstop Leo Durocher. Durocher looked at the first two strikes and, as legend has it, turned and walked away.

"Wait a minute," the umpire said. "You have another strike coming."

"Thanks," said Durocher. "I don't want it."

Score could have come directly to the Indians when he signed his contract in June 1952, but there were Wynn, Lemon and Garcia, each winning 20 games a year or more, and Feller, fading but good for 10 or 15 wins a season. Lopez wanted Score to pitch regularly and get over his wildness. In the closing months of the '52 season, Score went to Indianapolis, the Indians' top farm club, and walked 62 in 62 innings. He was demoted to Reading. There the next year, he walked 126 in 98 innings (and during warmup one day badly dented a new car waiting alongside the first baseline to be given away).

The Indians brought Score back to Indianapolis for spring training in 1954 and turned the matter over to Ted Wilks, the old Cardinal reliever who was then the Indianapolis pitching coach. Wilks' style was unusual. He swore a lot. From the dugout in full earshot of two city blocks: "Keep your damn head level. Watch the goddamn plate. Look where you're throwing if you want the ball to get there."

A pitcher's motion is a many-faceted and fragile thing. Every part of the motion—kick, step, release, follow-through—must be synchronized if the ball is to get where the pitcher wants it, to a piece of a strike zone 17 inches wide. Before Wilks, Herb just leaned back as far as he could behind a high leg kick to get as much "body" into each throw as possible. But the kick pulled his head back so he lost sight of catcher, plate and batter. His head bobbed as he came forward. After Score released the ball, his hard delivery carried him so far forward that his left elbow slammed into his right knee. In self-defense, he had long before strapped a rubber pad to his knee.

Wilks lowered Score's leg kick considerably. He taught Score to pivot, to get his power by swiveling his hips rather than by tilting backward as much as he had. And to keep his eyes on the target until he released the ball. The follow-through wasn't changed much, however; Score frequently finished a pitch with his back turned to the plate. Score often had been hit by batted balls he never saw.

Herb remained with Wilks in 1954 and pitched Indianapolis to a pennant. He reduced his walks to 140 in 252 innings, acceptable by any measurement, struck out 330, won 22 games and lost only 5. He was hit hard in only one game all season, a 6–5 loss to Louisville. His other four losses: 2–1 twice, 1–0, 4–3. He was elected Most Valuable Player in the league as well as Rookie of the Year. *The Sporting News,* the sports bible, chose him the number-one player in the minor leagues.

Herb was extremely popular, too. He became an instant kid brother to many athletes whose careers had ended and were hanging on perhaps for another year or two. During Herb's first visit to Indianapolis, a former major league pitcher named Johnny Hutchings was a coach. Herb, extremely thin, always had trouble with his uniforms, especially the pants.

Because of his fierce windup, his socks and the bottom of each pant leg would fall down continually. Herb would spend much of each ball game pulling up his trousers and socks. One afternoon, Hutchings called time out, picked up a roll of tape, and walked out to the mound. A huge man, weighing well over 300 pounds, Hutchings bent over laboriously, pulled up one of Herb's pant legs, then pulled up the sock, taped the sock to the pant leg just above the calf, adjusted the pant leg, did the same with the other leg, pulled the trouser leg and sock up, taped it, adjusted it. All in slow motion. When he finished, he stepped back a pace or two to survey his work, then walked up to Herb, took off Herb's cap and kissed him on the cheek. (When Hutchings died 10 years later, his will asked that Herb be a pallbearer.)

Gossip in spring training is almost as much a part of that annual ritual as baseball itself. Two hundred and seventy-two minor leaguers were in camps in 1955—Elston Howard, Most Valuable Player in the International League the year before, and Ken Boyer among them—trying to win a spot in the majors. But it seemed most of the sportswriters were looking at the quiet left hander from Indianapolis who was not yet old enough to vote.

In the hierarchy of baseball players, the fastballer stands first—higher than the Ruths, Aarons and Gehrigs. Brains can create a crafty pitcher, even a junk ball hurler who wins by virtue of experience and guile and, maybe, an occasional spitter. But a fireballer is nature's gift. And baseball men stand in awe. Dazzy Vance, an excellent speed baller in his own right, was warming up one day near the end of his career to pitch an exhibition against Feller, just 17. A photographer came up to Vance and asked if he would mind posing with the young kid. "Ask him," said Vance, "if he would mind posing with me." Hierarchies within hierarchies. Herb Score fit. He, with the classic overhand fireball delivered almost javelin-like with the full stretch of his six-foot-two body.

A natural pitching motion or a batter's natural swing can exceed for pure beauty most things created by man. John McGraw ordered 16-year-old Mel Ott not to take any hitting advice even though Ott swung with his forward foot up in the air. Lopez told Score he'd fine him if he ever saw Herb comparing pitching styles with the other men on the team. When Herb experimented one day with a change-up ball, a new pitch, Lopez threatened to send him back to Indianapolis.

At the Indians' camp in Tucson that spring in 1955, Score pitched as if he feared he would be cut. His reputation as a perfectionist had preceded him. Coaches watched to see that he didn't drive himself too hard. Score admitted to one writer that he "didn't know how to throw easy. Every batter is tough for me. I even bear down on the pitcher."

Herb had one goal—formed back in Rosedale, N.Y., when he was in eighth grade—and he didn't want to lose it now. He didn't have to worry. Cleveland couldn't keep him in the minors any longer. The club had won 111 games and the pennant in 1954 with Wynn, Lemon and Garcia winning 55 games among them and Feller contributing 13. Could Score crack that starting rotation? He could and Lemon soon was moved to coin a couplet of sorts: "There's no big four any more/Score's got to stay in the store."

The lefthander became the Indians' most effective pitcher that season. He struck out 245 batters in 227 innings—an average 9.70 for nine innings—breaking a 44-year-old record for rookies set by Grover Cleveland Alexander. No previous pitcher, not even Feller, had ever been able to strike out batters at that pace for a full

season. Feller's best was 7.3, Walter Johnson's, 6.9. Score allowed only 2.85 earned runs per game, won 16 games and lost 10. Once again, he was voted Rookie of the Year. He pitched a one-hitter, a two-hitter, three three-hitters and struck out 16 batters in one game, only two less than the record of the time, 18, held by Feller. During one game in 1955, Detroit somehow successfully intercepted all of Herb's pitching signals, yet still lost, 3–1.

The following year was even better. Score won 20 and lost 9. He struck out 263—setting an unofficial freshman-sophomore record of 547—and brought his walks down to an average five per nine-inning game. He battled New York's Whitey Ford to the final days of the season for the earned-run title. Ford won with 2.47, .06 better than Score's. The Indian pitching staff slumped in 1956. Garcia was 11–12 and Feller was 0–4. "During the last half of the season," someone cracked, "Cleveland's big three were Score, Don Mossi and Ray Narleski." Mossi and Narleski were the Indians' relief pitchers. Even though the Indians lost the pennant to the Yankees by nine games, attention focused on Score during the last half of the season as he won 10 games and lost only one. Few pros had ever seen anyone who could pitch almost as hard and effectively at the end of a game as at the beginning.

Wilks, at Indianapolis, continued to monitor Score, in person when he could, other times on television. When the Indians came to Indianapolis for periodic exhibition games, Wilks would always meet Score at the airport, bellowing for all to hear, "You're not keeping your goddamn eyes on the batter."

At spring training in 1957, Mickey Mantle—who was to bat .365 that season—called Score the toughest pitcher he had ever hit against; the Boston Red Sox offered Cleveland $1 million cash for Score, the largest bid ever made for a ballplayer (the worth of the entire Cleveland franchise was estimated at $3 million); and *The Sporting News* asked, "Will Score become the greatest lefthander in the history of baseball?"

Four weeks later, Score's career effectively ended. It was his fourth start of the season, May 7, and he was in the first inning against the Yankees. He retired Hank Bauer and then came Gil McDougald, Yankee shortstop. With the count 2 and 2, McDougald had to swing at the fast ball belt high on the outside. He lined it back at the pitcher's mound. Score, as usual, had turned his eyes away in his follow-through. He looked up in time to see a flash of white before the ball hit him squarely in the right eye.

He crumbled, but never lost consciousness. He had remarkable presence of mind. He poked around in his mouth to see if he had swallowed his bridgework. Then he felt his ears to determine if he was bleeding from them. He knew he was bleeding badly; he could taste the blood in his mouth and from his nose. Colavito raced in from right field and then stood there, helpless. He finally put his glove under Score's head so Herb's face wouldn't have to be on the dirt.

The public address system announcer asked if there were any doctors in the stands; within minutes, six were at the pitcher's mound. Score was carried into the clubhouse and placed on the trainer's table. Pain, the real pain, hadn't started yet. By this time, the team's doctor, driving nearby, had heard of the accident on the radio and reached the ballpark. He got there in time to hear Herb crack, "Now I know how Fullmer felt last week." (Ray Robinson only days earlier had punched Gene Fullmer silly in a middleweight title bout.) At the end of the inning, Colavito raced to the clubhouse to find out how Score was doing and was greeted by mock anger: "What are you doing here? Get back to work." An ambulance brought Score to a hospital where an ophthalmologist was waiting.

Herb asked only one question. "Am I blind?" The physician, Dr. Charles I. Thomas, said, "I don't know. I can't tell the condition of your eye because it's swollen and hemorrhaging so badly." Drugs were administered to help stop the bleeding. Herb asked for a radio so he could listen to the rest of the game. (Cleveland won.)

Dr. Thomas made Herb lie still. He didn't want any pupil movement. He bandaged the left eye so Score wouldn't move that pupil which of course would cause the pupil in the right eye to move as well. Then the pain began, from the pressure in the right eye and from the fracture in his nose and a displaced right cheekbone.

Herb lay still for eight days. By then, the swelling around the eye had receded sufficiently so Dr. Thomas was able to have a clear field. The retina had been torn, but not completely. The physician hoped that surgery to repair the rip would not be necessary. Score would not be blind in that eye but might have a blind spot.

Three weeks later, he was discharged. His vision from the damaged eye was blurred for almost a year. No one knew if he would pitch again. Herb had been placed on large doses of cortisone and it took five months to wean him from that drug. He was finished with baseball for the balance of the season.

No one suggested to Score that he might not be able to come back from the injury, but there was concern. Herb had little depth perception; he couldn't tell if a ball thrown to him was three or 30 feet away. Exercises during the winter returned his depth perception to normal. Score asked Colavito to report early to spring training with him so he could pitch to Rocky with the usual waist-high batting-practice shield removed. Colavito was hesitant, but Herb, in his customary straight-out manner, said, "Rocky, I've got to know if I'm gun shy

and now is as good a time as any." Colavito sprayed line drives and grounders throughout the infield and pitching area; Score didn't let up.

Herb lost his first game of the season but seemed to dispel all doubts in his second start, against the Chicago White Sox. He gave up two hits, struck out 14 and won, 3–0. "That convinced me," he said, "that I have everything I had before the accident."

He still hadn't regained his old pitching rhythm, but he wasn't worried. Spring that year was cold and rainy, not ideal conditions for a pitcher, especially one who had laid off for a year. Rain washed out what would have been Score's next two starts. Nine days later, he opened against the Senators on a damp, cold night. He was winning in the fourth inning when he attempted a curve and felt a strain in his forearm just below the elbow. In the seventh inning, a fast ball failed to reach the batter. Actually bounced in front of the plate. Incredulously, Herb tried again; same result. Now his arm began to hurt. He called manager Bobby Bragan to the mound and told him what happened. Score left the game. Next morning, his arm was swollen so badly he could hardly get it through the sleeve of his coat.

He was examined by the Washington team's physician who told him to rest the arm for a few days. Five days later, Herb tried to throw again. The pain was unbearable. Score consulted the Indians' doctor. He advised him not to pitch for 10 days. After 10 days, the arm continued to hurt, but Score thought he could work the pain out by throwing.

Finally, Herb went to Johns Hopkins, one of the outstanding hospitals in the country. There, he was told that he had torn a tendon back in April against Washington. Again, Herb was told to rest the arm, this time for 30 days. He obeyed, then began to throw again, in warmups, in batting practice, trying to get his arm back into condition. He threw hard a couple of times and felt no pain. Bragan asked him if he thought he could finish the last three innings of a game in Washington. Score got nine consecutive batters out, six by strike-outs. On the last pitch of the game, Score felt a sharp stabbing pain in his arm again, this time accompanied by a popping sound in his elbow.

Again the arm blew up. Score rested several weeks, then began to throw. He could still break off his curve as effectively as ever but his arm hurt every time he attempted a fast ball. Anxious about the amount of time he had missed, he began to press. He modified his throwing motion slightly to end the pain from the fast ball and told Bragan he was ready to go.

Several days later, he was called in from the bullpen in the fourth inning against the Yankees. (Ironically, the first batter was McDougald, the first time they had faced each other since the accident.) Herb had nothing on the ball except a curve and a slow change of pace—the same pitch Lopez had banned angrily two years earlier. Score struck out McDougald and finished the game without giving up any runs. But he knew he couldn't throw well.

The agony lasted the remainder of that season—he finished with 2 wins and 3 losses. "I had spent practically two full seasons without pitching," Herb said. "All that time, I was developing bad habits. When I tried to work, I favored my elbow. If I threw low in a certain way, I wouldn't strain my arm, but I lost my fluid motion and my rhythm and I never recovered it." At midyear in 1959, Score had won nine games and lost four, mainly by careful use of his curve and the change-up. He no longer had the looseness he had before. He was throwing as hard, but the ball was nowhere near as fast as it had been.

Yet, 9–4 at the All-Star midyear break; he wasn't doing too badly. Joe Gordon, the new manager, suggested cutting down Herb's full motion drastically. Herb put unfamiliar stresses on his arm. He became a sore-arm pitcher. As his confidence began to ebb, so did his remaining effectiveness. He didn't win another game that season and lost seven more.

Gordon and general manager Frank Lane gave up on Score. Indian management would not let Herb be traded to anyone but Lopez, his first-year manager who was then handling the White Sox. Lopez had been watching his former pitcher closely and had seen what he believed were flashes of the 1955 Score. Shortly before the 1960 season began, Score, age 27, went to the Sox.

"Of course, there was an element of selfishness to it," Lopez says. "I hoped to profit by having Herb make good with the White Sox. But I also had another motive. In all my years in baseball, I never met a finer man. I felt I might be able to help him."

Lopez, some said, brought the guesswork of handling a pitcher to an art form. Perhaps it was his training as a catcher. He had the uncanny ability, for example, to pull a pitcher out of a game before maximum damage was done. He seemed to *know* before a pitcher stayed a bit too long, before a fast ball failed to jump, before a curve started to roll, even before a man's spirit failed. He never asked a pitcher. And for some reason understood by none, he was usually right.

But Lopez had no magic for Herb. The ordeal was not to end. Score started 22 games that year, finished only five. In six of those early games, he made it past the fourth inning only once. He twice put 12 runners on base in less than four innings. "I was throwing the ball well and the pain was gone. But I just couldn't hit a groove, get the ball over. When I did get it over, there wasn't that much on it." There were brief moments, even games, when "all of a sudden, it looked like it was coming back. Then—nothing." He began "aiming" the ball, placing too much emphasis on his arm in an attempt to get the ball where it should go; in the process, whatever "stuff" he had on the ball would disappear.

The next season was worse; Herb started five games, finished one. About midseason, Score opened a night game in Baltimore, pitched to five batters and allowed four runs before Lopez sent in another pitcher.

Neither Lopez nor Score had an easy answer. And, of course, there was none. Herb felt well, the best in years, he told Chicago writers. Why was he pitching so "lousy," as he put it?

Lopez suggested Herb go down to San Diego, then a minor league team, for several weeks. There he could work regularly, pitch every four days in rotation, something not possible with Chicago. Herb, after talking it over with Nancy, a classmate from Lake Worth High whom he had married in 1957, agreed.

So Score went to San Diego. "In my own mind, I knew that I would never be what I once was," he said afterward. "But I was hoping that I could still pitch reasonably well, still win." His delivery became a parody of what it had been. He kept getting extreme periods of wildness, worse than when he had been a rookie. His arm would come to a kind of halt at the end of the windup and he seemed to be pushing the ball.

The old natural motion when he just reared back and threw now was replaced with constant planning. He explained it to writer Jack Olsen: "If I throw the ball and I haven't followed through or I land wrong, this would tell me that I'm not throwing right and I would say to myself, 'Let me pivot a little slower, let me bring my arm up higher,' and these are things you don't normally have to think about. You should get the sign from the catcher; then the only thing you should think about is I'm gonna throw this fast ball low and across the inside and concentrate only on that. But I would wind up and tell myself, 'Now make sure you pivot right, don't lean back too far, hold your head level,' and you can't do all that. And then I get behind a batter, maybe two balls and no strikes, and I begin to aim. I'd be better off if I just slung the ball and it wound up in the grandstand."

One holiday in San Diego, Score started the first game of a doubleheader against Seattle. He faced 11 batters in two innings, gave up two home runs, a double, two singles and walked three. He was brought in to relieve in the fourth inning of the second game. Seattle reached him for two singles, two doubles, two triples and six runs. In four innings, the pitcher who was to surpass Grove had given up 13 runs. In 133⅔ innings at San Diego, he walked 136, made 15 wild pitches, allowed 103 hits.

He went to the minors twice more after San Diego. In 1962 and again in 1963, he attempted a comeback with Indianapolis where he had started. He would not quit until he was sure he had given himself the time he needed. "I didn't want to think 15 years later that I could have pitched if I had tried a little longer. I went out and proved I couldn't pitch." *Then* it was time to stop.

"I'm grateful to have played in the major leagues and to have had some degree of success," he told reporters then. "I'm retiring sooner than I wanted to. That's nothing to be sad about."

As a measure of the respect men throughout baseball had for him, he was immediately asked to come back to Cleveland to broadcast its games. And that seemed fine to him. Because he loved baseball and now could stay with it.

Many skilled athletes have legends created about them: Williams, full of self-generated demons but, often, as gentle as a child; Cobb, noisy, hostile and cruel; Koufax, shy and private but extraordinarily principled. Score, too, created a legend quite apart from his ballplaying: a good man with the potential for athletic greatness who didn't complain when the vision died young. Lopez, his first—and last—major league manager, may have said it best: "Herb, if my son was to be a baseball player, you're the one I'd want him to model himself after."

Courage is an ill-defined term. Certainly, it is not the exclusive property of athletes who come back from problems to their former renown. It belongs, too, to those like Score who labor with little success for six years in the hope they may find some part of their former brilliance. Score found none and who is to blame it on the eye injury or the torn tendon? Who even cares? He could have quit many times and none would have raised a voice against him. I know many athletes, in a variety of sports, who have quit for less—and demanded public sympathy as well.

What must it be like to realize that an eighth-grade dream—a reality well into manhood—is perishing? Within the context of sports, Herb's story is one of the saddest I know. Talent so great should wither gracefully so the rest of us can prepare for the end of something bestowed on few. One talks now to Herb and Nancy and expects to find—what? Disappointment—certainly. Bitterness—possibly. After all he was "sure" to make the Hall of Fame. He began pitching when salaries were just beginning to rival those of movie starlets. Not small losses. Yet he laughs when I suggest fate played a poor trick on him and turns the topic to something else.

Long after Herb went into decline, he was pitching the second game of a doubleheader against the Red Sox. It was late in the season, the temperature was about 94° and neither team was going anywhere in the pennant race. Score had absolutely nothing on the ball. Pitching just by instinct, he kept the Sox scoreless. His team managed a run to go ahead, 1–0, entering the ninth inning. Score got the first two batters out.

Ted Williams no longer played the second game of doubleheaders, but now he came in to pinch-hit. Score was perspiring, sick about the season he was having and struggling with every pitch. He got two strikes on Williams. Always an overhand pitcher, Score experimented with a side arm curve and, because of his fatigue or maybe his sweaty fingers slipping, the ball took a couple of unexpected dips. Williams stared at it—the pitch was a long time getting to the plate—and he finally swung as if he had an axe in his hand, almost straight down, and he missed.

Score didn't know it, but that was the last shutout he would pitch in the majors. His arm was dead and hurting and he knew it was a matter of time before he would have to stop playing. But on that hot Sunday in Boston with absolutely nothing at stake he had to win.

Pete Reiser, the old Dodger outfielder, would understand that. Reiser crashed into so many outfield walls trying to catch long drives that he shortened his career considerably. One July afternoon in 1942, Brooklyn was leading the league by 13½ games and the Cardinals were in town. It was the second game of a doubleheader, there was no score and it was in extra innings. Enos Slaughter belted a ball deep to centerfield. Racing for it, Reiser thought, "If I don't get it, it's a triple and there could go the game."

He slammed into the wall at full speed, dropped the ball and knocked himself out. In the hospital, he learned he had a fractured skull. "Was I being foolhardy in going after that ball the way I did?" Reiser asked years later.* "After all, we had a 13½ game lead. . . . You can slow up in those circumstances, can't you? No, you can't. You slow up a half step and it's the beginning of your last ball game. You can't turn it on and off any time you want to. Not if you take pride in yourself."

On the morning that Herb's and Nancy's second child was delivered—mongoloid—Herb had been scheduled to speak before a father and son Communion breakfast at their church. He didn't want to go, but Nancy insisted. Those who were there said Herb spoke without notes, without mentioning what had happened that morning— no one there knew until later. He spoke longer than he usually did. Quietly, he spoke of family, of love, of doing one's best at whatever one does and of accepting what life offers without complaint. He could have been thinking of the damaged daughter who the next day would be christened Susan Jane; he could also have been thinking of an arm that mysteriously died. Those who were there said no talk of Herb's ever moved them more.

*In *Baseball When the Grass Was Green* by Donald Honig.

This is a chapter from the book *Spartan Seasons*—subtitled, "How Baseball Survived the Second World War."

# Spring Training in the Snow

## RICHARD GOLDSTEIN

PIRATE PITCHER Rip Sewell relaxed under the palms, enjoying a breeze created by manager Frankie Frisch, who stood over him waving a towel converted into a fan. True, baseball was beginning to feel a manpower pinch. But it was not every day the boss provided such personal services for his charges.

Sewell and Frisch were merely teaming up for a gag photo—posing beside a potted palm inside the lobby of the Hotel Roberts in Muncie, Indiana, to display their longing for the warm weather of springtimes past. It was March 1943 and spring training, wartime style, had arrived.

With the railroads jammed by soldiers reporting to camps or embarkation points and civilians journeying to war plant jobs near the big cities, federal authorities looked for ways to cut nonessential travel. Their eyes turned to baseball. The game, they pointed out, could make a contribution to travel conservation by shifting spring training to northern sites, thereby eliminating the traditional barn-storming trips home from Florida and California.

Although the movement of sixteen ball clubs could hardly have a major impact on scarce rail facilities, baseball would, of course, do its patriotic duty. And so, beginning in the spring of 1943 and continuing for the following two exhibition seasons, ballplayers would battle frigid temperatures, rain, and an occasional snowstorm at a string of training camps near their home parks.

Big league teams had been training in the South since well before the turn of the century. As far back as 1886, the Chicago White Stockings worked out in Hot Springs, Arkansas—a favorite sobering up spot for grog shop devotees—and the Phillies went to Charleston, South Carolina. The 1888 Washington club, whose roster included a catcher named Connie Mack, may have been the first ball club to train in Florida, going to Jacksonville. Prior to World War I, most of the major league camps were in Texas or Georgia. But by the spring of

1942, twelve teams were training in Florida and the other four in California.

Baseball was advised to begin looking elsewhere via a letter from Joseph Eastman, director of the Office of Defense Transportation, one of the numerous federal agencies created to oversee the war effort. Writing to Landis, Frick, and Harridge on November 30, 1942, Eastman asked that the major league meetings scheduled for the first week in December "give careful consideration to the problem of how your basic travel requirements can be met without a waste in space or mileage."

The official had a few thoughts of his own, suggesting "the elimination or drastic curtailment of preseason exhibition schedules requiring travel."

An obvious way to accomplish this, Eastman pointed out, would be "the selection of a training site as near as possible to the permanent headquarters of the team."

The club owners announced at their December session that they would cut rail mileage during the regular season by scheduling only three intersectional trips instead of the normal four, but they took no immediate action on shifting the spring camps.

There were faint hopes that the government might permit training along the South Atlantic Coast. The Senators envisioned a move from Orlando to their minor league park in Charlotte and the Giants, who had trained in Miami, received an invitation from Statesville, North Carolina. The Browns and Pirates, who had been spending their springs in California, looked, meanwhile, into the possibility of resurrecting Hot Springs as a training camp. A more realistic Branch Rickey conferred during December with Yale University officials on use of their field house, but was advised it might be needed for servicemen's physical training programs. Ed Barrow had a simple solution: the clubs could train in their own ballparks, waiting until early April to get under way, with the start of the regular season to be pushed back by two weeks.

As December moved along, Landis sent a letter to the ball clubs advising that they abandon Florida and California, then followed up with a note telling them to forget about relocating anywhere in the Southeast. Just before the end of the year, the commissioner went to Washington to thrash out the 1943 spring training boundaries with Eastman.

"Nobody needs to enter any orders on us," Landis told reporters covering the meeting, asserting the majors would be "happy to cooperate" with transportation authorities as "a very small contribution to the war effort on our part."

Eastman publicly confined himself to the hope that baseball "would serve as a guide for others" in cutting back on unnecessary travel, saying he had no specific proposals beyond those in his letter.

But definite ground rules there would be. Landis called an emergency session of the club owners for Chicago's Palmer House, where on January 5, 1943, what would be known as the Eastman–Landis line was drawn up. With the exception of the two St. Louis teams, who of course could hold their camps in Missouri, training would be confined to an area east of the Mississippi River and north of the Ohio and Potomac rivers. Eastman was pleased, commenting, "The example which such an important national industry as this has set will have, I am sure, a most beneficial influence throughout the nation. I hope and believe there will be many who will follow this fine example."

The Red Sox were the first team to settle on a northern camp, announcing even a week before the Chicago meeting that they would go to Tufts College in Medford, Massachusetts, and use an indoor batting cage. The following day the White Sox and Cubs reported they would both train at French Lick, Indiana, 278 miles south of Chicago. Soon the other clubs moved into line, creating a 1943 spring training map showing camps in Connecticut, New York, New Jersey, Pennsylvania, Delaware, Maryland, Illinois, and Missouri, as well as Massachusetts and Indiana.

The players coped, having no other choice, but it wasn't easy.

Though there would be some stretches of mild weather, long underwear quickly became a part of the training camp attire. The Athletics would ride sleighs to an indoor workout at their Frederick, Maryland, training site, and the Dodgers would try out skis at their Bear Mountain, New York, camp—a snowstorm blanketing the East Coast in March '44. The French Lick ballfields and the Cardinals' training field in Cairo, Illinois, would be hit by floods.

Some clubs were fortunate to have good indoor facilities for days when the weather was too frosty to practice outside. The Dodgers were allowed to use the spacious batting cage at the U.S. Military Academy, down the road from Bear Mountain. But the Yankees at one point had to make do with an abandoned Navy aircraft hangar, and the Cubs and White Sox limbered up in what had once been a stable.

Could the ballplayers get into a semblance of reasonably decent shape? This depended to a large degree on the individual. A youngster would require less conditioning than an old-timer and anyone who had done some exercising through the winter was that much better off.

Pitchers could always find a place to warm up. One day, the White Sox hurlers threw inside their hotel ballroom. But with travel curbs and poor weather cutting the spring training schedule, the batters—especially those on clubs unable to obtain an indoor cage—were hard pressed to get their timing down.

There were some baseball people who felt workouts in a field house or gymnasium, where there could be no sunlight or wind, would never be of much value.

"The sport is essentially an outdoor one and indoor training is of little help," Joe McCarthy told reporters at the Yankees' 1943 camp in Asbury Park, New Jersey. The manager was, however, quick to add, "We are willing to do all in our power to cooperate with the war effort, and do not let this be analyzed in the slightest as any sort of beef. It is just a technical diagnosis of training."

A few clubs tried to gain an edge by stepping up physical conditioning programs.

The Reds hired a $100-a-day muscle relaxation specialist named Bill Miller for their spring camp at Indiana University. Miller had helped train the Tulsa University football team that went undefeated in 1942 before losing to Tennessee in the Sugar Bowl and taught body control to Army aviation cadets so that they would not freeze up in an emergency.

"We called him Yogi Miller, he was what I'd call the relaxer, he tried to teach you how to relax," remembers Frank McCormick, an outstanding first baseman for the Reds from 1934 through the end of the war.

Seated at his desk in Yankee Stadium, where he directs group ticket sales, McCormick picked up a paper cup and let it fall to the floor.

"Miller would tell you, if you dropped this, don't grab for it, pick it up slowly," he explained, reaching down easily to retrieve the cup.

"We went through exercises sort of limp, with no tension," McCormick added, slowly flapping his arms.

Besides the repertoire of slow motion exercises, Miller had the players do an occasional rhumba in the Indiana field house to loosen up. On one occasion the team put on a production number of sorts for the benefit of newsreels. The chief choreographer was Tommy de la

Cruz, a Cuban pitcher whose brother sang with Xavier Cugat's band. Nancy Uland, a local high school student, provided accompaniment on an accordion. As the players shook their hips, soldiers passing by en route to physical training programs in the field house couldn't resist a snicker or two.

As for whether all this helped round the players into shape, McCormick says, "The field house was acceptable, but of course we preferred sunny Florida. I didn't feel like I was getting in condition inside, I just didn't feel it."

The Bloomington, Indiana, camps did produce one major dividend, McCormick recalls. "We got Ted Kluszewski because of training there. The college groundskeeper recommended him so we took a look."

The muscular first baseman, an Indiana student at the time, would make his debut with the Reds in 1947.

Ill-fated Phillie owner Bill Cox brought Harold Bruce, his prep school track coach and later a trainer of Olympic runners, to the club's 1943 spring camp in Hershey, Pennsylvania.

"He was a good man, our ball club was well conditioned," says Danny Litwhiler. "We were probably in as good a shape as any team as far as conditioning is concerned. The main thing was run, run, run."

Remembering the abbreviated exhibition schedule, Litwhiler adds, chuckling, "We didn't get a chance to play ball, but we sure ran a lot."

Bruce also had some definite ideas about the training table menu. Litwhiler recalls, "He liked fruits, he thought that was one of the good things in a diet."

It was this penchant that gave Bucky Harris the pretext for firing the trainer, a move which angered Cox and led to the ousting of the manager himself. Harris, a member of the old school who didn't have much use for conditioning programs, finally decided to get rid of Cox's mentor when, it was said, Bruce fell asleep on the bench amid a mess of sliced orange quarters.

Another traditionalist was Cub manager Jimmy Wilson, who told reporters at his 1944 training camp, "Calisthenics stink as a baseball conditioner. A player goes through all of those monotonous drills and when he gets through he's sore all over. He has exercised muscles he never knew he had, muscles that won't help him one bit when he's out there in a game."

Whatever alternative the manager had in mind for getting his players ready for the season didn't work out too well, however. The Cubs went on to lose nine of their first ten games, at which point Wilson was fired.

A few older ballplayers who lived in the South were excused from the first weeks of camp on the theory they could better limber up their bones working out near home.

Bobo Newsom, who joined the Athletics in 1944 at age thirty-six after making the rounds of the Dodgers, Browns, and Senators the previous season—he would be traded sixteen times in a twenty-year career—was permitted by Connie Mack to remain at his Hartsville, South Carolina, home while the rest of the team drilled in Frederick, Maryland.

Among the ballplayers in the Frederick camp was a twenty-one-year-old rookie who would win the third baseman's job and go on to play fifteen seasons in the American League. Now behind the microphone for the Tigers, George Kell chatted about Bobo Newsom one afternoon over a cup of coffee before telecasting a game at Yankee Stadium that featured a latter-day pitching flake—Mark Fidrych.

"Bobo would not report," Kell recalled. "He told Mr. Mack he could get in better shape at home. Everybody was horrified that Mr. Mack agreed to it. But when Bobo finally got there, he did pitch.

"He was some kind of character," Kell added with a smile. "I don't remember anybody talking back to Mr. Mack—except Bobo Newsom."

Newsom stayed home during the first few weeks of both the 1944 and 1945 A's camps. One Wednesday afternoon well into the last wartime spring, the pitcher telephoned Mack long distance and was reported to have told his patient manager, "I read in the papers that your men haven't been doing so good so far. I guess I'd better come up and help you out. I'll be in Baltimore to pitch Sunday and I'll win twenty games for you this year. I've been running over the hills and pitching to the high school kids."

On Sunday, a big car carrying Newsom, his wife, and their three dogs pulled into the parking lot outside the Baltimore Orioles' ballpark. The late arrival pitched three innings against the International League club, giving up two runs. Newsom did attain a twenty-game milestone that year, but not the way he had envisioned: he won eight games and *lost* twenty.

Perhaps Bobo would have fared even worse had he reported in chilly March. The Dodgers' thirty-five-year-old Whitlow Wyatt, coming off a 19–7 record, sought permission to work out near his Buchanan, Georgia, home during the spring of 1943, but was turned down by Branch Rickey. So Wyatt went to Bear Mountain, and promptly developed a sore arm. The veteran right-hander wasn't back in the groove until July, when he began a ten-game winning streak, finishing out the year 14–5. The following training season, Rickey allowed Wyatt to stay at home and permitted Paul Waner and Johnny Cooney, his forty-year-old-plus outfielders, to try getting into shape in the Sarasota area.

With federal authorities frowning on side trips between major league training camps, one way to get an exhibition game was to visit an Army or Navy installation, since the military was happy to provide bus or plane transportation. Bizarre as training generally was in the North, there was a special aura of absurdity in the military posts when it came to baseball.

An April '43 game at Camp Kilmer, New Jersey, between the Giants and their Jersey City farm team was declared off limits to reporters. Because the installation was a point of embarkation, the Army feared some tidbits on troop movements might be divulged inadvertently in the sportswriters' stories. A post public relations officer transmitted a play-by-play summary for the press, providing such gems as: "Poland, batting for Mancuso, cleared the bases when his single into left went by Brack for a homer." The *New York Herald Tribune* headlined its secondhand story, "Giants Belabor Jersey City 17–7 in Secret Game."

Fortunately, reporters were not barred from an exhibition between the same teams a few days later at the Lakehurst Naval Air Station in New Jersey, else they would have missed perhaps the longest home run in baseball history. A ball hit by the Giants' Babe Barna over the head of Jersey City outfielder Howie Moss came to a stop out of sight—the field was a vast, dirt landing terrain without fences. Barna could have circled the bases several times, since the ball landed 450 feet from home plate and then rolled another 200 feet before Moss caught up with it. The game was delayed while a jeep retrieved the out-of-breath fielder.

Lakehurst provided a variety of challenges. On a windy, cold day in April '44, the Navy dropped baseballs from a blimp four hundred feet in the air to Giant players poised on the landing terrain. First baseman Phil Weintraub and Danny Gardella, an eccentric outfielder who had trouble with routine flies, were the only ones to make a catch.

While northern spring training games often would be curtailed by bad weather, an exhibition the Pirates played at Fort Benjamin Harrison, Indiana, was halted after the seventh inning for a different reason—the crowd of two thousand GIs had been summoned to mess call.

The Fort Meade, Maryland, Army base was the site of particularly strange doings.

The Washington Senators and Philadelphia Athletics, arriving there for a game in April '43, were treated by the post mess to a delightful ration-free spread: a main course of steak along with hard-to-get trimmings such as genuine coffee, sugar, and butter. But a vital ingredient was missing so far as the ballfield was concerned.

George Case recalls, "We were gonna cancel out because of bad weather, but they were expecting a huge crowd. The commander called Mr. Griffith and said, 'If you could bring the ball club down, it would mean a lot to the boys.' So we got there and the field was rimmed

with soldiers. But there were no bases. They couldn't find the bases. So they put down towels. Well, we didn't slide anyway because it was too wet."

The game stands out in Case's memory for another reason. While it was an occasion where the spectators—ten thousand GIs—should have been properly appreciative, "There were some soldiers in the crowd who yelled 'get a gun' and all that. The MPs got them away or shut them up."

"You know," Case continues, "that was the only time we had trouble at a camp. There was very little resentment otherwise."

When the Senators played the Baltimore Orioles at Fort Meade, the ball clubs weren't the only source of entertainment. A band composed of Italian prisoners of war tooted away on the sidelines.

Two Wacs helped warm the Athletics' bench during a Fort Meade game with the International League's Buffalo Bisons and a male lieutenant served as home plate umpire. Italian POWs were on hand again, this time in a different role. Four of them were used as groundskeepers, raking the infield.

"We were told they were POWs, but I didn't know from where," says George Kell. "They didn't look like soldiers, but you knew they weren't civilians. They wore what looked like denim prison garb so you figured what they told you was true."

An umpire became a prisoner of sorts during an April '43 exhibition game in the Midwest. American League ump Art Passarella, having almost been beaned the previous spring by that irate fan throwing back a foul, found himself in another unhappy situation while calling balls and strikes at Vincennes, Indiana, in a game between the White Sox and the host Camp George air base team.

The shortstop for the service team got into a heated argument with Passarella in the bottom of the eighth and naturally lost. But his mates obtained their revenge. A group of MPs pulled up at home plate in a jeep, bundled the umpire inside, and drove him off to the guardhouse. By the time Passarella was given his liberty, the game was over.

When the White Sox later visited Camp Grant, Illinois, Passarella was behind the plate again, but this time his sympathies lay with the Army team—he had been drafted and was stationed at the post, umpiring in his spare time. Now he could turn the MPs loose for his own purposes, getting even with Jimmy Dykes for past tirades. The Sox manager later recounted his ordeal:

"My personal Gestapo agents tip me off that Passarella is all set to have me thrown into the clink if I open my trap even once so I keep nice and quiet. I won't even talk to him. But by the ninth inning I begin to get curious. So I tell Mike Tresh, my catcher, to object to a decision. As soon as he does, I rush over to the plate and raise Cain, kick dirt all over Art and everything. Before I know what's happening, the MPs whisk me out of there and bring me before a major.''

'' 'What's the charge?' he asks. Then he adds, 'Oh, never mind, leave the charge open. Into the guardhouse with him.' I'm in there awhile and Passarella comes to see me. 'Get me out of here,' I tell him. 'Sorry Jimmy,' he says, 'I'm just a private in this man's Army. I haven't any influence.'

''They left me in there at least half an hour before releasing me. I sweated so much I was wringing wet. It taught me that the Four Freedoms are not enough. There should be a fifth one—guaranteeing that Dykes will be kept out in the open air.''

The individual major league camps had their own share of oddities. In the East, the ball clubs were housed, among other places, at a New England prep school, a ski lodge, and a mansion once owned by John D. Rockefeller.

The Braves settled in at the exclusive Choate School in Wallingford, Connecticut. Since students were away for spring recess, the team bedded down in vacant dormitory rooms and a wing of the infirmary. Casey Stengel, who wasn't the ''Ol' Professor'' for nothing, made the photographers happy by lecturing to his players in an academic cap and gown. While the atmosphere was pleasant, the weather wasn't. After two springs at Choate, the club switched to Georgetown University in Washington, D.C., for the final wartime camp. Medical students attending classes in a building along the campus ballfield's left field foul line would wander over to take in workouts when tired of their cadavers.

The Red Sox stayed close to home the first two wartime springs, drilling in the batting cage at Tufts College, which was a six-mile trolley ride from the Hotel Kenmore in downtown Boston, where the players were housed. The team headed south—relatively speaking—for the 1945 camp, going to Atlantic City. The ballplayers were put up at the popular Claridge Hotel, doing their outdoor drills on a high school field in the nearby town of Pleasantville. The Army Air Corps was kind enough to let the club hold an occasional calisthenics session or pepper game inside the Atlantic City Convention Hall, which had been taken over to house servicemen awaiting reassignment.

One warm, sunny day in March '43, a middle-aged lady carrying the cowbell that had become her trademark arrived at the ferry slip off Manhattan's West Forty-Second Street. Hilda Chester, most zealous of all Dodger rooters, the personification of Ebbets Field fanaticism, was seeing her heroes off for their first wartime spring training camp. She tinkled her bell good-bye to an advance party of eight players who boarded the ferry ''Catskill'' for a brief trip across the Hudson River and then transferred to the West Shore Rail Road for a forty-five mile ride northward. The contingent would have been wise to soak up the sun that afternoon. It wouldn't be shining very often over the next three springs at Bear Mountain.

The Dodgers arrived at the resort complex to find a caretaker hard at work on their ballfield, which happened to be laid out near the foot of a ski jump and toboggan slide. The groundskeeper was building a fire over first base, trying to take the frost out of the ground.

There would not be too many days when the diamond could be used, but Branch Rickey had planned well, obtaining one of the best indoor facilities of any training camp—the spacious, steam-heated West Point field house, complete with batting cage and dirt floor. The club practiced at the well-lit field house—a five-mile bus ride from Bear Mountain—for the first nine days of the 1943 camp and could count on it whenever the weather was frosty. The workouts had to be scheduled, however, around cadet activities. During the 1944 camp, the Dodgers drilled in the field house from noon to 1:00 P.M., then returned at 5:45 P.M. (A surveying class occupied the facility during the afternoons.) Leo Durocher returned the hospitality by serving as adviser to the military academy baseball team.

Home was a rustic lodge called the Bear Mountain Inn, whose proprietors were anxious to keep the players as happy as possible, providing game rooms with pool tables and roaring log fires. At dinnertime, the dessert menu featured Jelly Roll a la Higbe, Stewed Mixed Fruits Fitzsimmons, and Ice Cream Puff Medwick.

The Dodgers weren't the only distinguished visitors. The day the 1943 camp opened, Mme. Chiang Kai-shek and party arrived for lunch at Stone Cottage, next door to Hessian Lodge, the section of the inn where the players were housed. The public relations man for the Palisades Interstate Park Commission, which ran the Bear Mountain facilities, tried to get Mme. Chiang to pose with the team, but she declined the honor.

The Giants found spring training headquarters with an elegant past: the grounds of the old John D. Rockefeller estate in Lakewood, New Jersey. The Meadow Brook Country Club in Westbury, Long Island, and the Westchester Country Club in Rye, New York, also wanted the team, but a nine-hole golf course where the oil baron played daily while in residence at an adjoining forty-seven-room mansion would be the Giants' springtime ballfield.

The complex, which had become public parkland after Rockefeller's death in 1937, was not chosen for any residual snob appeal. Although Lakewood was only sixty-five miles south of New York City, temperatures were said to be, on the average, ten degrees warmer than in the city. The golf course diamond drained well and sections surrounded by thick pines provided some shelter from brisk March winds. It was also a homecoming after almost five decades, the Giants having trained at Lakewood in 1895 and 1896 when they were owned by Andrew Freedman. An active member of Tammany Hall, Freedman had chosen the Jersey resort town because the Democratic bigwigs held their annual spring meetings there—he could attend to politics and baseball at the same time.

Lakewood was thrilled to have the ball club back. The two dozen Giants arriving as advance guard for the first camp were met at the railroad station by a crowd of 1,200, headed by Mayor William Curtis, and given a ride to their hotel in horse-drawn victorias, a mode of transportation revived in the war era to symbolize gasoline conservation efforts. When the Rockefellers and the Goulds (Georgian Court, the former estate of financier George Gould, was also in town) played an intrasquad game, some twenty-five hundred school children were given a half-day off to watch.

What the town fathers couldn't produce was a decent facility for indoor workouts. The Giants had to settle for a YMCA gym so small that no more than ten players could toss a ball around at the same time. The 1944 team, able to play a total of 8 exhibition games in a snow-plagued spring training season, was described by Mel Ott as "the worst conditioned club in Giant history."

During their first two springs at Lakewood, the Giants stayed in hotels, but no space was available for 1945. Declaring "anything the Giants want in Lakewood they can have," Ocean County Freeholder Alfred Brown solved the problem by helping to arrange for the team to take over the county-owned Rockefeller mansion. The three-story estate, containing seventeen baths to go with the forty-seven rooms, had been kept much as the Rockefeller family left it. Rich oriental rugs and plush chairs abounded. There were bedrooms done up in yellow, and if that wasn't his favorite color, a ballplayer could select buff or lavender quarters. Meals were taken on glassed-in porches. They may not have rounded into shape, but the Giants sure were comfortable.

The Yankees held their first camp 17 miles from Lakewood, choosing the New Jersey shore community of Asbury Park, which boasted a summer population of 100,000. Only 14,000 people, however, found the community attractive enough to live in on days like those of the chilly early spring. The winds were blowing and the mercury was flirting with the forty-degree mark when the Yanks held their first workout on the local high school field. Five hundred hardy souls looked on. The *New York Times* reported, "The athletes were red and

purple and blue by turns, but all thawed out in the clubhouse, where scout Paul Krichell's pot-bellied, wood-burning stove did overtime duty."

The ballplayers might have done well to sleep in their stove-heated clubhouse. A fuel shortage made for nippy nights in their rooms at the Hotel Albion. As for indoor drilling, there was but a high school gym best suited for calisthenics and basketball.

Though the locals were anxious to please—a candy firm supplied the players with saltwater taffy—the Yankees decided, not surprisingly, that one spring in Asbury Park was enough. The team shoved on to Atlantic City, sixty miles farther south, for its last two wartime camps.

Some twelve thousand cubic yards of rich, imported sod were transplanted from the $500,000 beachfront mansion of the late Mrs. Isabelle Fishblatt to the Yankees' Atlantic City practice diamond, a municipal field formerly used for football. A few thousand portable seats were added. They weren't put to much use in the spring of 1944, however, since the weather permitted only six days of outdoor work.

The indoor facility, something of an improvement over the Asbury Park gym, was the larger 112th Field Artillery Armory, whose floor was covered with a layer of soil taken from Convention Hall, where football had been played prior to the Air Corps' arrival. But the team was still without an indoor batting cage, and confined its activity at the armory to pepper games, except for the day Joe McCarthy broke up the monotony with a potato race. In the last wartime spring, the armory was requisitioned by the military to house wounded servicemen. The Yanks would hold their final indoor drills on the concrete floor of an abandoned Navy aircraft hangar behind the left-field fence of the Atlantic City ballpark.

Club headquarters was the modern, 300-room Senator Hotel, whose management was every bit as generous as the folks in Asbury Park—here, too, the players were stuffed with saltwater taffy.

The Athletics pitched their initial wartime camp at Wilmington, Delaware, limbering up with a snowball fight the first day of training. Wilmington produced what must have been the smallest turnout in history for a game involving a big league team—the A's defeated the University of Delaware, 2–0, one day in a contest that attracted six spectators.

Anticipating better weather and perhaps even larger turnouts, Connie Mack took his men to Frederick, Maryland, in the Blue Ridge Mountains for the following two spring camps. The right-field fence at McCurdy Field, the local ballpark, was 506 feet from home plate, and the only indoor facilities were an armory and a YMCA. But at least the players could pick up an education. If nothing else, Frederick was historic.

The 200-room hotel housing the team was named the

Francis Scott Key. The man responsible for the lyrics being sung before every game had been born on the outskirts of Frederick, practiced law there, and was buried in the community's Mount Olivet Cemetery.

Another headstone was that of the old lady whose supposed courage had inspired John Greenleaf Whittier's poem ''Barbara Frietchie.''

According to legend, as Stonewall Jackson was passing through Frederick with his troops in 1862, he noticed a Union flag flying from the second-story window of Mrs. Frietchie's home and ordered that it be fired upon. Moments later, the ninety-six-year-old woman seized the riddled banner and waved it defiantly. Rather than seek retribution, Jackson, touched by the old woman's spirit, decreed death to any Confederate soldier who might harm her.

The tale made an impression on the Athletics, who lined up for intrasquad games as the Stonewall Jacksons versus the Barbara Frietchies. It was, however, apparently apocryphal. Jackson's staff and Mrs. Frietchie's family subsequently reported that the two had never laid eyes on each other. She is conceded to have feebly waved a small American flag at Union soldiers passing through Frederick six days after Jackson left town.

At any rate, a reconstructed version of the Frietchie home at 156 West Patrick Street in downtown Frederick was a tourist attraction.

''My wife, who was a schoolteacher, was very much interested, she took me to all these places,'' recalls George Kell. ''She had a ball, it was a very historic town.''

Less attractive was the weather. But Connie Mack, who by now had presumably seen everything, was undeterred. During a 1944 snowstorm, he ordered sleighs to transport the players to an indoor workout. When the weather was good enough for drills at McCurdy Field, Mack dispensed with the horses.

''Mr. Mack would lead us out of the hotel,'' Kell remembers. ''He'd say, 'Hey, we're gonna walk.' It was about a mile to the ballpark. There were no buses and we had no cars, so we walked. He led the way.''

At times there wasn't much competition around, even by the lowly Athletics' standards. The A's beat the Martin Bombers, a semipro aircraft plant team, 20–0, in a game halted by cold after seven innings. On another occasion, they took on the Frederick Hustlers, an outfit described by the *Philadelphia Inquirer* as ''made up of the grocery clerk, baggage man, a salesman, two schoolboys, a serviceman on furlough, and four young, married men.'' That made ten players, but the Athletics triumphed nonetheless, 7–1.

The Phillies tried Hershey, Pennsylvania, for their first northern camp, playing on a field not too much larger than latter-day Little League parks. Any ball well

hit to left field would land in Cocoa Creek. When the team visited Yale, owner Bill Cox was behind the plate while the university's athletic director, Ogden Miller, switched allegiance to start on the mound. The pair didn't fare badly. Cox drew a base on balls in his one time at bat while Miller pitched a scoreless inning. The battery-mates were then relieved by catcher Tom Padden and hurler Al Gerheauser.

With the Wilmington-based Carpenter family taking over before the 1944 season, the Phillies spent the last two wartime springs in the Delaware city, abandoned by the Athletics in favor of Barbara Frietchieland.

The 1944 camp didn't begin very auspiciously. Snow fell as the ballplayers, bundled up in overcoats, scarves, and hats, left Philadelphia's Thirtieth Street Station for a twenty-eight-mile rail trip south. The first four days at Wilmington were spent inside a state armory, where manager Freddie Fitzsimmons kept the boys puffing by having them run up twenty-five steps of a corner staircase, then hustle along a fifty-yard balcony, and scamper down another twenty-five steps at the opposite end. One such session lasted for three-quarters of an hour. Not called Fat Freddie for nothing, the skipper just supervised. The players finally got outdoors on the fifth day but their ballfield was still too damp for full-scale workouts, so they contented themselves with bunting practice on the cinder surface of a parking lot.

When the weather relented sufficiently to allow for some baseball, the attendance was up sharply from the turnout of a half-dozen at the A's–University of Delaware game in Wilmington during the spring of 1943. A crowd of ninety-seven showed up to watch the Phils battle the Martin Bombers.

The Senators stayed at the University of Maryland in College Park, ten miles outside the District of Columbia. '' 'Curley' Byrd, the president of the university, was an avid baseball fan and he offered the facilities,'' says George Case. ''We'd take over a whole dorm, there weren't too many students during the war. We ate in the guest house. Mr. Griffith hired his own cook and he managed to get pretty good steaks for us occasionally.''

Case continues, ''The first year the weather was nice, but the second year it was miserable. We were playing in bad weather all that spring.''

Latin ballplayers (most of them Cubans), whom the Senators had made a specialty of signing, particularly suffered during the frigid spring of 1944.

Among more than a dozen recruits experiencing wintry weather for the first time was a twenty-year-old shortstop who would have a brief playing career in the big leagues but would return to the majors many years after the war to manage and coach.

Reached at his Santa Monica home one day during the Dodgers' dismal 1979 season, Preston Gomez—then the

Los Angeles third base coach and later to be named manager of the Cubs—thought back to hard times of a different sort thirty-five years before. He remembered how it was when he arrived at College Park fresh from amateur ball in Havana.

"We got a little snow in March and it was very cold. I liked to keep inside. When I had to go outside, I would suffer," Gomez recalled. "I'll never forget, I tried to go out one day to take ground balls and hit wearing my big jacket, and the manager, Ossie Bluege, called me over and said, 'you cannot do things like that.' I didn't know how to explain to him I was too cold. Finally, Gil Torres [a Cuban infielder with experience in organized ball] came over and explained that if I trained this way, I wouldn't be able to move. And he was right. That's the problem we had most, getting used to the climate."

While half the clubs trained along the eastern seaboard, the other eight teams were in the Midwest. The Cardinals chose the town of Cairo, Illinois, on the east bank of the Mississippi River; their Sportsman's Park colleagues, the Browns, went to Cape Girardeau, Missouri, forty miles upstream on the west bank. The Reds, Indians, Pirates, Tigers, Cubs, and White Sox were spread out over Indiana.

In the months before the Cardinals arrived at Cairo, what passed for the local ballpark, a place called Cotter Field, had become pretty much a municipal dump, strewn with tin cans and broken glass. But the townspeople cleaned things up, put down fresh sod, and transferred seven hundred portable seats from the high school gym. They hardly need have bothered. Isolated from the other major league camps—at least by the standards of wartime travel—the Cards could do little more than stage intrasquad contests. During their entire time at Cairo, they played only two real games, both against the Army's Fourth Ferrying Group from Memphis.

Although the team was able to drill outdoors most days during the first two springs, the weather was far from accommodating. Danny Litwhiler, traded from the Phils to the Cards during the 1943 season, has chilly memories of the 1944 camp.

"An awful lot of us got sick there," he recalls. "Colds, you know, real bad colds. Everybody, the ballplayers, the wives, the kids. You'd call it flu today, but we called it colds. It was just so damp and so cold there."

When the ballplayers arrived for their 1945 camp, they found Cotter Field under four feet of water, the runoff from a rain-swollen Ohio River, which meets the Mississippi at Cairo. A fire department pump was pressed into service, but the waters kept rising as fast as they could be channeled into sewers and drainage ditches. Photographers got a rookie named Red Schoen-

dienst to pose with two teammates on swings. The caption read, "It's about the only baseball training, even in name, the Cards have been able to do."

After five days of futile efforts to dry out the field, the Cardinals packed up and went to St. Louis, working out for the rest of the spring at Sportsman's Park.

The only indoor facility at Cairo had been a high school gym. The locals tried hard, installing four extra showers—making a grand total of eight—and building a large wooden locker for drying uniforms, but it hardly would do. Billy Southworth commented after watching his players run relay races one day, "We're making the best of it, but a wooden gymnasium floor is no place to prepare to play baseball. I admit I'm relieved each time we get out of a crowded gym with all the players intact."

Up at Cape Girardeau, the Browns played on a municipal ballfield and also set up mounds for pitching drills in a wind-sheltered natural amphitheater belonging to Southeast Missouri State Teachers College. Providing competition for exhibition games were the Toledo Mud Hens, the Brownies' American Association farm team that shared the complex.

Indoor workouts were held at the Arena, a building on the edge of town built for horse shows and livestock exhibits. The facility had a six-inch soil base and was large enough to hold a batting cage.

Here, too, the townspeople were eager to help out, furnishing Browns officials with unrationed gasoline from fire department pumps when club affairs required a 240-mile round trip to St. Louis.

The Cards and Browns had each other for a brief period at the end of each spring, playing a city series in Sportsman's Park for their only big league training season competition.

Of the six ball clubs training in Indiana, the Indians and Reds were best off, enjoying the use of Big Ten field houses during bad weather.

The Cleveland club originally eyed Marietta College in Ohio, where a field house had been built with funds donated by alumnus Ban Johnson. The college expressed reluctance, however, to pack the floor with soil, so the Indians went, instead, to the West Lafayette, Indiana, campus of Purdue University, which had a 300 × 160–foot field house already covered with dirt.

The facility boasted a cage to accommodate batting and pitching drills, but hurler Vern Kennedy was particularly interested in the equipment belonging to the Purdue track and field team. Finding its pole vault unattended one day, Kennedy lifted himself over the bar at the nine-foot mark and came up smiling. Asked if he recalls the feat, Kennedy's old manager, Lou Boudreau, says, "If he did that, he did it without my noticing it."

The Reds quickly realized how lucky they were to

have the dirt-surfaced Indiana University field house—five inches of rain hit Bloomington the first week of the 1943 camp. Track team equipment was a lure there, too, with unhappy consequences for pitcher Bucky Walters. On the first day of training, Walters tried to leap over a hurdle, caught a spike, and sprained his left ankle. He didn't get into form until mid-season. In an authorized exercise, the players studied batting stance flaws by gazing into a large mirror used by the Indiana track team to examine starting-block form.

The team dressed in locker rooms underneath the football stadium and held outdoor workouts at Jordan Field, the university's baseball diamond. There were those who displayed something less than the hospitality afforded big league clubs elsewhere. Three of the Reds' windbreakers were stolen one day while the club drilled on the ballfield.

Both the Indians and Reds stayed in downtown hotels not far from their respective campuses.

The Pirates did without a field house at their Muncie, Indiana, camp—a small gym was the only available indoor facility—but the local officialdom certainly was nice. Honus Wagner, brought back by the team as a coach, was given a silver badge by Mayor John Hampton designating the Hall of Famer an honorary policeman. In return, Hizzoner got to umpire at home plate in an intrasquad game. Housed in town at the Hotel Roberts, the club worked out on the Ball State Teachers College field when the weather permitted. Manager Frankie Frisch ordered long hikes when it didn't.

The Tigers, training in a minor league park at Evansville, Indiana, at one point faced the prospect of having their entire 1945 exhibition schedule wiped out by toughened travel curbs. It appeared that no games could be played without running afoul of the ban on side trips instituted by the Office of Defense Transportation. But general manager Jack Zeller had an idea. The players could get in a series by walking to the White Sox camp at Terre Haute—it was only 112 miles away.

"Have them carry their uniforms, bats, and toilet articles on their backs," Zeller told manager Steve O'Neill. "The players are supposed to be athletes in good condition. There are a few million boys who aren't athletes and are walking from ten to twenty miles a day in training camps in this country and they're carrying something heavier than uniforms and bats. They're carrying packs of from forty-five to sixty pounds on their backs. You could take five or six days to get there, stopping along the way."

O'Neill responded, "If they walk, they'll have to go without the manager. I can't foot it that far."

Dizzy Trout, once an Indiana farm boy, volunteered, "All I got to do is speak to some of my farm friends around here. They'll drive us over in hayracks paced by

a hillbilly band. We'll each take a basket of lunch."

A compromise was suggested by second baseman Eddie Mayo: "Why should we do all the walking, why can't we meet the Sox halfway and play them on the most convenient hayfield?"

The idea for the stroll was dropped, but the Tigers did get to Terre Haute. They took a train to the White Sox camp and instead of returning to Evansville after the series, stayed around for a few practice sessions, then continued on to St. Louis when time came for the season's opener.

The White Sox had repaired to Terre Haute after two unhappy exhibition seasons elsewhere. The Sox and Cubs had trained together during the springs of 1943 and 1944 in the resort community of French Lick, Indiana, but they were not, it developed, very neighborly. For the better part of the two springs, the clubs argued over use of a golf course that turned out to be the only available playing field in sight.

Both teams were housed in the seven-hundred-room French Lick Springs Hotel, centerpiece of a resort area known for its natural springs and baths. The Cubs laid out their diamond on a golf course outside the hotel while the White Sox made arrangements to use a semipro park down the road at West Baden. But they were thrown together in both '43 and '44 by heavy spring rains swelling the Lost River, its overflow flooding both ballfields. The Cubs' turf drained well and would be playable only a few days after being inundated. The White Sox field, however, became a muddy mess. And so, with nowhere else to go, Jimmy Dykes moved in on his rivals. The squabbling over practice time on the golf greens made for lively newspaper copy. Cub general manager Jimmy Gallagher put up an arch proclaiming the golf course his club's exclusive territory. Jimmy Dykes in turn called the Cubs a "bush league outfit." And one day in April '44, the GIs became involved. The White Sox scheduled a 2:30 P.M. game on the golf course with the 820th Tank Destroyer Batallion from Camp Breckenridge, Kentucky. But the Cubs, having previously planned a workout for 2:00 P.M., invoked a veto. A saddened Jimmy Dykes told reporters, "I have been forced to cancel the game with the soldier boys."

Indoor training put a premium on improvisation, there being nary a YMCA in town. The White Sox pitchers, working out in the ballroom of their hotel, propped mattresses against the walls as backstops. In the spring of 1945, the Cub players did their calisthenics in the ballroom to a piano accompaniment by manager Charlie Grimm, Jimmy Wilson's successor. Also available to provide some shelter from the elements was an abandoned stable.

One ballplayer may have had a premonition that

French Lick was a place to stay away from. Cub pitcher Vallie Eaves went out to California in the spring of 1943 to report as usual for training on Catalina Island. Traveling secretary Bob Lewis sent him word there was a war on and provided a bus ticket to Indiana.

Len Merullo, the Cubs' shortstop through the war years and now a talent hunter for the Major League Scouting Bureau—a consortium of seventeen clubs—has some rather fond memories of French Lick. He reminisced one day upon returning to his Reading, Massachusetts, home after a busy '79 spring preparing reports for the free agent draft.

"The French Lick Springs Hotel had the finest of everything; the wealthy people, businessmen, used to go there. The leading bands were still coming in, fellows like Glen Gray," he recalls. "Of course, it was a health spa, with the natural springs. It's famous for steam baths, hot baths and all that bit. The players were allowed to go through this procedure and it was great; it was something we had never experienced before. The big fellas, especially, went down there to lose weight."

"You know what I remember most about French Lick?" Merullo continues. "These old-timers that would come down there. It was the home of Pluto water, very famous for cleaning your body out. They would have this path through the woods and it was just beautiful, but every so many yards there would be these little outhouses. The old-timers got up before breakfast and they'd give them the Pluto water. Then they would hand them a cane and they'd take a walk through the woods. Well, when they got the urge, they'd just put their cane on the outhouse door, that meant it was occupied. Then they would come back and have their breakfast. This was the first step, in other words, back to good health."

At times, however, there was just too much water around.

"The river would come up every spring and the golf course would be just flooded over," Merullo remembers. "Don Johnson and myself and Phil Cavarretta and Peanuts Lowrey posed for a group photo supposedly fishing in our baseball uniforms."

In the spring of 1945, not only did the Lost River overflow for the third time in three years, but the train to French Lick was taken out of service by the government. Coach Red Smith had to drive eighteen miles to Orleans, Indiana, which had become the end of the line, to pick up arriving ballplayers.

The White Sox by then were off to Terre Haute, where they found themselves more than welcome for a change. When Jimmy Dykes complained about having to walk twenty-six blocks every day from his hotel to the training field, Mayor Vern McMillan had the police pick him up in a Model T paddy wagon. (Despite all good intentions, the thing broke down en route to the ballpark.)

Did the bizarre conditions provoke grumbling? Ballplayers looking back on the wartime camps say they were resigned to the situation and, give or take a field house or two, knew everyone was experiencing the same hardships.

Virgil Trucks, talking about the Tiger base at Evansville, Indiana, says, "It was quite cool, it was always wet, it wasn't anywhere near like Florida weather, but you could train, you could do running. It wasn't an ideal area for spring training, but since the circumstances called for that, nobody complained about it, we all went about our jobs."

Then, turning his thoughts to the modern-day ballplayer, Trucks adds with a chuckle, "I don't know what they would do if they had to go through that today. Probably all rebel, pay their own way and go to Florida."

As this article suggests, and the one later in this book by Mordecai Richler confirms, Montreal fans are—well, *different*.

# Quattrocento Baseball

## ADAM GOPNIK

I AM BY vocation a student of fifteenth-century Italian art and a fan of the Montreal Expos. It is a mixture of callings that provokes more indulgent smiles than raised eyebrows, as though my penchant for wearing my Expos cap, peak backward, to seminars at the Institute of Fine Arts were a kind of sophisticated joke, a put-on—as though I were simply one more pop ironist "thoroughly bemused by the myths of popular culture," as Hilton Kramer puts it, "but differentiated from the mass audience by virtue of [a] consciousness of [his] own taste." This kind of well-meaning misunderstanding has led me to brood a great deal on the relationship of the one passion to the other, and, more generally, on what I suppose I have to call the aesthetics of sport, and of baseball in particular. I have tried to imagine a pasture on the slopes of Parnassus where Bill Lee plays pepper with Giorgione, and Fra Filippo Lippi calls off Warren Cromartie.

To be sure, it has been submitted by a few nearsighted observers that I admire the Expos precisely because they are *not* like Carpaccio or Sassetta, because they "provide an outlet" for my need to be attached to something that is neither Catholic nor half a millennium away. It has occurred to others—for example, to my wife, whom I met in a Verrocchio seminar—that I am attracted to the Expos because participation in their cult provides a very close modern equivalent of the kind of communal involvement with spectacle which was so crucial a part of the original experience of fifteenth-century Italian art. My passion for the Expos, she argues, is at heart a way of re-creating an essential piece of the Quattrocento aesthetic—fellowship achieved through a formal object—which the passage of time has replaced with one or another kind of detached and devitalized "appreciation." It is a nice theory, and may go a long way toward explaining my nearly equal passion for the Montreal Canadiens, but I don't think it has much to say about the Expos. In 1981, the Expos won their division and

participated in the Championship Series for the first time, and surely, if my wife's theory is correct, this should have been sheer epiphany for me; I should have felt as the people of Siena felt when they marched through the streets with Duccio's "Maestà." Yet, while I found that series by turns elating and heartbreaking, I was struck most by how *different,* how disagreeably different, it was from my everyday, high-summer experience of watching the Expos play. By the sixth inning of the final match, my "involvement" with the destiny of the Expos had become so intense that I no longer took any pleasure in the game. I wanted only a climax, a *result*—my triumph or my doom. It was, in short, sport deprived of anything like a detached aesthetic experience—or anything like the pleasurably removed delight I take in a Carpaccio or a Giorgione—and I sensed, suddenly, that it is precisely the kinship of my normal experience of baseball with my normal experience of Italian painting that has held me, and this suggested, in turn, that there must be some substratum of pure aesthetic experience, divorced from symbolism or civic feeling, that can account for the curious twinning of my obsessions.

There's no shortage of literature on the supposed aesthetic appeal of various sports; most of it involves assimilating the activities of one or another sport to the practice of one or another of the performing arts. This is the kind of comparison that is accomplished with a few pious references to the athleticism of Villella or the balletic grace of Lynn Swann, say, or with a few lyrical descriptions of acrobatic catches. There's nothing wrong with one kind of creative endeavor imitating the forms and strategies of another—every student of fifteenth-century Italian painting knows that it discovered itself only when it began to aspire to the condition of poetry— but I think it's obvious that playing baseball has nothing to do with dancing. Most of the actions central to the game and expressive of its essence—waiting out a fly ball, making sure of a grounder—are only minimally "dramatic" or fluid of movement. It is possible to achieve real distinction as a baseball player while attaining grace perhaps only in the most religious sense: one thinks of the earthbound Woody Fryman, and of Rusty Staub, who hit like a god but ran like a mortal. In football, of course, the spectacular catch is much more to the point. It is also really quite rare, and football fans do indeed seem like fans of the older performing arts in their willingness to put up with hours of deadening boredom and repetition in exchange for one or two epiphanic moments (although even in this they seem to me more like lovers of the opera than like lovers of the dance). That is why the N.F.L. is so well served by its highlight films: "N.F.L. Week in Review" can include in a half hour everything that was heart-stopping in the previous week's games without altering their essential meaning. The response of organized baseball, the syndicated program called "This Week in Baseball," is inevitably dull and unrealized; the only equivalents the producers can find for the self-contained moments of football lie in the weekly montage of mistakes and curiosities—flubbed catches, rhubarbs with umpires—that can be wrenched from their context without losing whatever meaning it is they have. That is the kind of "highlight" that Joe Garagiola now takes onto the "Tonight Show," too, to everyone's apparent delight, and it suggests the depressing thought that television is now aggressively trying to reduce baseball to the aesthetic of pro football.

"In its special mode of handling its given material, each art may be observed to pass into the condition of some other art," writes Pater in the most famous passage on aesthetic transferal. Baseball, I believe, aspires to the condition of painting. The blank, affectless description of any particular moment in the game has in common with great painting a certain puzzling first-glance banality. A child sits on the lap of a woman who sits on a rock. A very old man is seen against a neutral background in dim light. A fuzzy black square rests on a fuzzy maroon rectangle against a blood-red background. Now baseball: A man stands, stares, rocks, and throws a ball—almost too quickly to be seen—at a second man. The second actor, frozen in place, lunges at the near-invisible object with a club. Two other men, one dressed in formal clothes, squat and watch them. We see this action repeated, unchanged, again and again. Surely this sounds more like what goes on in a performance space in SoHo on an off night, or like a passage from one of the lesser works of Robert Wilson, than like a public spectacle that could become the national obsession of a restless and impatient people. Baseball can't be grasped by a formalist aesthetic; the appeal of the game can't be understood by an analysis of its moments. As in painting, the expressive effect, the spell, of baseball depends on our understanding of context, of the way what is being made now collects its meaning from what has gone before and what may come next. E. H. Gombrich has championed this view of how the meanings of pictures must be understood—not as a series of acts but as a series of choices within a context, an organized medium. The weight of Giotto becomes apparent only against the weightlessness of Duccio; the humidity of Giorgione becomes apparent only against the clarity of Mantegna. And just as Masaccio comes to alter irrevocably our understanding of Giotto, so each inning alters irrevocably the meaning of every inning that has preceded it: Henry Aaron's first at-bat in 1974, as he approaches Babe Ruth's record, suddenly lends an entirely new meaning, an unlooked-for centrality, to some nearly forgotten Aaron home run back in 1959. The significance of every action in the game depends entirely on its place within a history, on our recognition of it as one possibility, one choice, within a series of alternatives. The batter swings freely, the way the painter paints, but the swing itself is bound about by the ghosts of every other swing.

Just as painting, then, seems able to be better grasped by a historical than by a purely critical imagination, so baseball's most inspired observers are essentially historians, and do their best work at a distance. Baseball inspires reminiscence not because of the sentiment of its devotees but, rather, because the meaning of its forms—of a crucial lapse, a fabled stat—can only be clarified by time. Statistics, like the best kind of art history, are not basically an attendant or peripheral activity. They are the means by which the act becomes articulate. And in baseball, as in painting, the presence of history—of the weight of tradition—is both bequest and burden. Each game, each season must recapitulate all the cycles of the larger history, from nascent opportunity to exhaustion. Spring is the time of Giotto, where there is an April freshness and the rebirth of miraculous possibility. July is the Quattrocento, where history begins to give shape to that possibility, to set problems without precluding any outcome. August is baroque: the weight of history, of the season's corrosive and insistent patterns, demands an inflation of effects and complicated new forms—shuffled rotations, patched lineups, gimmicky plays. September is wholly modern: the presence of tradition becomes oppressive and begins to generate anxiety; we turn self-conscious, pray that nerve and daring, the bravura gesture, alone may see us through.

October, my memory and my father remind me, was once both climax and renewal. The World Series celebrated our escape from history, and held out the promise of another spring, as though we could applaud Frank

Stella and then begin all over again with the Arena Chapel. Now we escape from the context of the season only to enter the horrible context of prime-time entertainment, as if, just as in much contemporary art, there were nothing left for us at the end but an extended mockery of the same values that our calling once upheld. There was a time, just a few years ago, when the World Series was dominated by the Dodgers and the Yankees. No accident, it seems to me, for these two teams have precisely the kind of smug, sneering hardiness that I associate with much postmodern art and architecture. The Dodgers seem like a Robert Venturi version of a Monticello house: a familiar vernacular form like team spirit, which was once touching in its innocence and good cheer, is transformed by the Dodgers into an effect to be cultivated and exploited. The tastes of the fan, of the gallerygoer, are jeered at and gratified at the same time. The Yankees, too, seem to me to operate by taking an archetypal bit of folklore—the interfering owner meets the prima-donna player—and turning it into something rigged and artificial, mechanical in its self-consciousness. (Think of how natural and funny this trope seemed just a few years ago in Oakland!) Steinbrenner's exploitation of the Yankees' tradition is exactly like Michael Graves' exploitation of classical architectural form: not an imaginative extension but a cynical appropriation. October these days seems to share the central, miserable feature of postmodernism—the displacement of the vernacular into a mode of irony.

Am I so bitter about October because of the continuing failures—once last-minute, now apparently sealed by the third week of the season—of my Expos over the past few years? Perhaps—although the Expos, with their prolific, uncynical energy, did seem to promise precisely the kind of natural, eager, unforced voice that art and baseball alike demand at the moment. Of course, a few turncoat Expos fans have now placed their aesthetic bets on the increasingly successful Toronto Blue Jays. I don't know; the Blue Jays seem to me suspiciously skilled at embodying the virtues of their city: dogged adherence to a goal and the subordination of the individual to a team ethic. I feel about the Torontonians' methodical approach to the pennant more or less the way that the Sienese painters' guild must have felt about the Florentine discovery of linear perspective—that this is precisely the kind of depressing gimmick you would expect from a town like that. The difference between the Expos' André Dawson, who many people came to think was the best player in baseball simply because he *looked* like the best player in baseball (he never really was), and, say, the Blue Jays' Jesse Barfield, is precisely the difference between a Sassetta saint and a Masaccio saint. Their guys are probably a lot closer to the real thing, but ours look more holy.

If I can find any consolation in recent Octobers, it is this: While meaning in baseball depends on context, perhaps only part of that context is provided by public history, by the official chronicle of box scores and All-Star ballots. For each game belongs to a private chronicle, too. Perhaps there is somewhere a fan who sees the Yankees or the Dodgers not in the context of the history of the game but in the context of his own history, whose real unhappiness ennobles their squabbling, and whose rituals (the cap worn just so, the radio placed just so), unknown to them, guarantee their victories. If he exists, then there is hope for rebirth in April after all.

# Couplet

## DONALD HALL

*Old-Timers' Day,*
*Fenway Park, 1 May 1982*

When the tall puffy
figure wearing number
nine starts
late for the fly ball,
laboring forward
like a lame truckhorse
startled by a gartersnake,
—this old fellow
whose body we remember
as sleek and nervous
as a filly's—

and barely catches it
in his glove's
tip, we rise
and applaud weeping:
On a green field
we observe the ruin
of even the bravest
body, as Odysseus
wept to glimpse
among shades the shadow
of Achilles.

This is true history, in that it corrects a lasting false impression. Few are the fans who at one point or another have not seen what they assume is the TV kinescope of Bobby Thomson's pennant-winning "home run heard round the world" in 1951, with the voice of broadcaster Russ Hodges suddenly gone insane as he screamed, "The Giants win the pennant! . . . The Giants win the pennant!" over and over.

But what televiewers saw that day was not what has been replayed ever since. There was no video taping in those days, and kinescoping of any quality could be done only on prepared stage-sets. So what has been preserved is the silent newsreel footage of the Thomson homer. And Hodges' voice was grafted against it, thanks to a fan in Brooklyn who had made a tape from the Hodges *radio* (not television) account, and later sent Russ a recording of it.

To this day, hardly anyone knows that the actual telecast is never shown in the replays, and the voice of that telecast was that of Ernie Harwell, whose permanent baseball home turned out to be Detroit, where he has been describing the Tiger games for nearly thirty years now.

And he and the late Russ Hodges are both enshrined in baseball's Hall of Fame.

# From *Tuned to Baseball*

## ——— ERNIE HARWELL ———

THE GIANTS' victory over Boston had come earlier that Sunday afternoon. So, we had to wait on the Dodger-Philly result. I remember listening to the radio in the Giant clubhouse. When we left for the train station the Phils were leading. We finally got the word in Providence. Chub Feeney, the Giants' VP then, re-boarded the train.

"Dodgers won," he said. "Robinson hit a homer in the fourteenth to win it, 9–8. Show up at Ebbets Field tomorrow for the first playoff game."

This was the first sport series ever telecast coast-to-coast. Before then, any telecast in New York was seen two days later on the West Coast. Now, because of the co-axial cable, the Dodger-Giant series would be viewed as it happened. CBS-TV picked up the Dodger broadcast of that first game and sent it across the nation.

Jim Hearn pitched the biggest game of his career and the Giants won the first game, 3–1. Bobby Thomson's two-run homer was the vital blow.

The two teams moved to the Polo Grounds. It was the Giants' broadcasters' turn to go coast-to-coast. NBC-TV picked up our telecast. Russ Hodges worked the first and last three innings and I telecast the middle three. We had a rain delay of about 50 minutes during my portion of the telecast. I remember filling all the time myself. Our booth was so cramped it was impossible to get anybody else to the mike for an interview.

We had a great shot of Yankee Stadium, across the river. The Yanks had won the American League pennant and would host the winner of the National League playoffs in the first World Series game.

"So near and yet so far, for these two teams here today at the Polo Grounds," I said. "But one of them will be there."

The Dodgers won that second game, 10–0, behind Clem Labine, a young right-hander who had spent most of the season in the bullpen. That set the stage for the big one.

These two teams had played 156 games each and they were still tied. One more and it would all be over.

I had a feeling at the time that both teams were weary and that everybody was pushing to get through that final meeting.

As I drove to the Polo Grounds from my Larchmont

home, I told myself how lucky I was to be in on this one. I would be on NBC-TV coast-to-coast on the biggest game in baseball history. Hodges, my partner, would have to settle for radio. I would be the only TV announcer, but there were at least four other radio broadcasts: the Dodger network, Liberty, Mutual, and KMOX of St. Louis.

When Russ and I were eating lunch, he said: "Ernie, I think it's my time today on TV."

"No," I said. "Remember, you were on yesterday. I did the middle three of that game on TV. I've got the first and last three on TV today."

"Oh," he said. "I guess you're right."

So, I was on NBC-TV coast-to-coast when Bob Thomson hit his famous home run in the ninth to win the game for the Giants, 5–4.

Over the years people have asked me: "Ernie, what did you say when Thomson hit his home run?"

"It's gone," I tell them. As soon as Bobby hit the ball I said, "It's gone." Then I let the picture tell the story. Right after I had said those two words I had quick misgivings. Andy Pafko had backed up against the left-field wall and was waiting. "Oh," I told myself, "suppose Andy catches it!" But the ball sailed into the seats and history was made.

When the old New York *Sun* folded in 1949, there were many sad and appropriate comments on the passing of such a venerable newspaper. And one of the most appropriate may have been the way *The New Yorker* noted the event: not by any comment, but by printing a solved crossword puzzle.

In any event, W. C. Heinz was writing sports for the *Sun* at the time. He then turned to free-lancing, some of it in the now-all-but-vanished mode of the "short-short" story. Here's one of his best-remembered examples.

# One Throw

## W. C. HEINZ

I CHECKED INTO a hotel called the Olympia, which is right on the main street and the only hotel in the town. After lunch I was hanging around the lobby, and I got to talking to the guy at the desk. I asked him if this wasn't the town where that kid named Maneri played ball.

"That's right," the guy said. "He's a pretty good ballplayer."

"He should be," I said. "I read that he was the new Phil Rizzuto."

"That's what they said," the guy said.

"What's the matter with him?" I said. "I mean if he's such a good ballplayer what's he doing in this league?"

"I don't know," the guy said. "I guess the Yankees know what they're doing."

"What kind of a kid is he?"

"He's a nice kid," the guy said. "He plays good ball, but I feel sorry for him. He thought he'd be playing for the Yankees soon, and here he is in this town. You can see it's got him down."

"He lives here in this hotel?"

"That's right," the guy said. "Most of the older ballplayers stay in rooming houses, but Pete and a couple other kids live here."

He was leaning on the desk, talking to me and looking across the hotel lobby. He nodded his head. "This is a funny thing," he said. "Here he comes now."

The kid had come through the door from the street. He had on a light gray sport shirt and a pair of gray flannel slacks.

I could see why, when he showed up with the Yankees in spring training, he made them all think of Rizzuto. He isn't any bigger than Rizzuto, and he looks just like him.

"Hello, Nick," he said to the guy at the desk.

"Hello, Pete," the guy at the desk said. "How goes it today?"

"All right," the kid said but you could see he was exaggerating.

"I'm sorry, Pete," the guy at the desk said, "but no mail today."

"That's all right, Nick," the kid said. "I'm used to it."

"Excuse me," I said, "but you're Pete Maneri?"

"That's right," the kid said, turning and looking at me.

"Excuse me," the guy at the desk said, introducing us. "Pete, this is Mr. Franklin."

"Harry Franklin," I said.

"I'm glad to know you," the kid said, shaking my hand.

"I recognize you from your pictures," I said.

"Pete's a good ballplayer," the guy at the desk said.

"Not very," the kid said.

"Don't take his word for it, Mr. Franklin," the guy said.

"I'm a great ball fan," I said to the kid. "Do you people play tonight?"

"We play two games," the kid said.

"The first game's at six o'clock," the guy at the desk said. "They play pretty good ball."

"I'll be there," I said. "I used to play a little ball myself."

"You did?" the kid said.

"With Columbus," I said. "That's twenty years ago."

"Is that right?" the kid said. . . .

That's the way I got to talking with the kid. They had one of those pine-paneled taprooms in the basement of the hotel, and we went down there. I had a couple and the kid had a Coke, and I told him a few stories and he turned out to be a real good listener.

"But what do you do now, Mr. Franklin?" he said after a while.

"I sell hardware," I said. "I can think of some things I'd like better, but I was going to ask you how you like playing in this league."

"Well," the kid said, "I suppose it's all right. I guess I've got no kick coming."

"Oh, I don't know," I said. "I understand you're too good for this league. What are they trying to do to you?"

"I don't know," the kid said. "I can't understand it."

"What's the trouble?"

"Well," the kid said, "I don't get along very well here. I mean there's nothing wrong with my playing. I'm hitting .365 right now. I lead the league in stolen bases. There's nobody can field with me, but who cares?"

"Who manages this ball club?"

"Al Dall," the kid said. "You remember, he played in the outfield for the Yankees for about four years."

"I remember."

"Maybe he is all right," the kid said, "but I don't get along with him. He's on my neck all the time."

"Well," I said, "that's the way they are in the minors sometimes. You have to remember the guy is looking out for himself and his ball club first. He's not worried about you."

"I know that," the kid said. "If I get the big hit or make the play he never says anything. The other night I tried to take second on a loose ball and I got caught in the run-down. He bawls me out in front of everybody. There's nothing I can do."

"Oh, I don't know," I said. "This is probably a guy who knows he's got a good thing in you, and he's looking to keep you around. You people lead the league, and that makes him look good. He doesn't want to lose you to Kansas City or the Yankees."

"That's what I mean," the kid said. "When the Yankees sent me down here they said, 'Don't worry. We'll keep an eye on you.' So Dall never sends a good report on me. Nobody ever comes down to look me over. What chance is there for a guy like Eddie Brown or somebody like that coming down to see me in this town?"

"You have to remember that Eddie Brown's the big shot," I said, "the great Yankee scout."

"Sure," the kid said. "I never even saw him, and I'll never see him in this place. I have an idea that if they ever ask Dall about me he keeps knocking me down."

"Why don't you go after Dall?" I said. "I had trouble like that once myself, but I figured out a way to get attention."

"You did?" the kid said.

"I threw a couple of balls over the first baseman's head," I said. "I threw a couple of games away, and that really got the manager sore. I was lousing up his ball club and his record. So what does he do? He blows the whistle on me, and what happens? That gets the brass curious, and they send down to see what's wrong."

"Is that so?" the kid said. "What happened?"

"Two weeks later," I said, "I was up with Columbus."

"Is that right?" the kid said.

"Sure," I said, egging him on. "What have you got to lose?"

"Nothing," the kid said. "I haven't got anything to lose."

"I'd try it," I said.

"I might try it," the kid said. "I might try it tonight if the spot comes up."

I could see from the way he said it that he was madder than he'd said. Maybe you think this is mean to steam a kid up like this, but I do some strange things.

"Take over," I said. "Don't let this guy ruin your career."

"I'll try it," the kid said. "Are you coming out to the park tonight?"

"I wouldn't miss it," I said. "This will be better than making out route sheets and sales orders."

It's not much ball park in this town—old wooden bleachers and an old wooden fence and about four hundred people in the stands. The first game wasn't much either, with the home club winning something like 8 to 1.

The kid didn't have any hard chances, but I could see he was a ballplayer, with a double and a couple of walks and a lot of speed.

The second game was different, though. The other club got a couple of runs and then the home club picked up three runs in one, and they were in the top of the ninth with a 3–2 lead and two outs when the pitching began to fall apart and they loaded the bases.

I was trying to wish the ball down to the kid, just to see what he'd do with it, when the batter drives one on one big bounce to the kid's right.

The kid was off for it when the ball started. He made a backhand stab and grabbed it. He was deep now, and he turned in the air and fired. If it goes over the first baseman's head, it's two runs in and a panic—but it's the prettiest throw you'd want to see. It's right on a line, and the runner is out by a step, and it's the ball game.

I walked back to the hotel, thinking about the kid. I sat around the lobby until I saw him come in, and then I walked toward the elevator like I was going to my room, but so I'd meet him. And I could see he didn't want to talk.

"How about a Coke?" I said.

"No," he said. "Thanks, but I'm going to bed."

"Look," I said. "Forget it. You did the right thing. Have a Coke."

We were sitting in the taproom again. The kid wasn't saying anything.

"Why didn't you throw that ball away?" I said.

"I don't know," the kid said. "I had it in my mind before he hit it, but I couldn't."

"Why?"

"I don't know why."

"I know why," I said.

The kid didn't say anything. He just sat looking down.

"Do you know why you couldn't throw that ball away?" I said.

"No," the kid said.

"You couldn't throw that ball away," I said, "because you're going to be a major-league ballplayer someday."

The kid just looked at me. He had that same sore expression.

"Do you know why you're going to be a major-league ballplayer?" I said.

The kid was just looking down again, shaking his head. I never got more of a kick out of anything in my life.

"You're going to be a major-league ballplayer," I said, "because you couldn't throw that ball away, and because I'm not a hardware salesman and my name's not Harry Franklin."

"What do you mean?" the kid said.

"I mean," I explained to him, "that I tried to needle you into throwing that ball away because I'm Eddie Brown."

*Hints from Heloise* may be the most widely syndicated newspaper feature of all. This particular one may be the most valuable piece in this book.

# Hint from Heloise

## HELOISE

DEAR HELOISE:

I have a lot of baseball caps with different company insignias on them. They seem to get dirty and then I have to throw them away.

Do you have any suggestions on cleaning them? I wear them all the time so I hate to throw them out.

—J.C. Major

Most baseball type caps can be washed in the washing machine with other clothes. You should wash them in cold water on the gentle cycle and hang them outside to dry. If the bill needs stiffening, you can use spray starch and then let it dry.

Another method you can try is washing them in the sink in a mild detergent. Use a soft brush to scrub the cap but don't scrub too hard as it could remove the lettering. Then rinse the cap well and let it dry by placing it on an upside-down two-quart saucepan. Shape the bill and the top of the cap and leave it to dry.

Put the pan and cap on a surface so that when it is drying the water won't harm anything. It usually takes overnight for it to dry.

—Heloise

A Chicago baseball writer for more than forty years, Jerry Holtzman has served also as perhaps the foremost steward for all baseball writers. His books have included *No Cheering in the Press Box,* which did for old-time writers what *The Glory of Their Times* did for old-time players, and *Fielder's Choice,* with little doubt the best concentrated collection of baseball fiction ever put together.

Moe Berg, the subject of this Holtzman obituary, broke in as an infielder but spent the last twelve of his fifteen seasons—this was in the 1920s and 1930s—as a catcher. As Holtzman points out, he spoke ten languages, studied at the Sorbonne, took one degree from Princeton and another (in the law) from Columbia, and . . . well, this article is not about any of those things.

# A Great Companion

## JEROME HOLTZMAN

M OE BERG is dead and now I can tell the story. He would like that.

Many times, in recent years, I'd say to him, "Moe, you old son of a gun, when you die, I'm going to write your story, what you're really like."

Moe would laugh. He always was laughing, always enjoying himself. "Wonderful," he would shout, "marvelous." To him, so many things were wonderful and marvelous. They were his favorite words. Then he'd say, "Do it, do it, tell everything."

So I'll do it.

Moe was my roommate for the last 10 or 12 years. Whenever I'd come into New York, either with the Cubs or the White Sox, he would room with me. He knew the schedules and could estimate the arrival time. I would know, within minutes after checking in, if Moe was in town. He would call from the lobby and I'd say, "Moe, c'mon up," and we would spend the next three or four days together.

Life can be lonesome on the road and I always looked forward to seeing him. Sometimes he would join me in Baltimore, or in Boston, or in Philadelphia or in Washington. The Eastern Seaboard was his province.

We spent little time together during the day. We would lie awake, after night games, talking about everything, including the game, and then he would ask, "What time do you want to get up?" He was an early riser, up and out by 7.

I never saw him when he awoke in the mornings, but I knew his routine. He would buy the newspapers, then go to a cafeteria for what he always called "a coffee." At 9 or 9:30, or whatever the specified time, he would call the room and announce: "Time to get up."

He would surface again at the dinner hour, when it was time to start for the ball park. Usually we would take the subway, either to Yankee Stadium or to Shea Stadium. He always lightened my load and carried my briefcase. Most of the time, but not always, he would sit next to me during the game.

After the game, while I was writing my story, he would wait in the press room. Then we would return to Manhattan. Usually we would stop for something to eat, mostly at the Stage Delicatessen. If I ordered a salami omelette, Moe ordered a salami omelette. Food didn't interest him but, like a camel, he would stoke up.

Clothes didn't interest him, either. He always wore the same suit, a wash-and-wear charcoal gray, with a shirt and thin black tie. But he was meticulous about his person and each night would wash his clothes and hang them to dry. Many times, when he would see me packing, he would chide me and say, "What do you need all those clothes for?" One suit, he was convinced, was enough for any man.

Most former ballplayers wouldn't walk across the street to see a ball game. But not Moe. He loved baseball. He would attend as many as 50 to 60 games each season, maybe more. He often said the ball park was his theater—and it was. He watched every pitch and every move of the catcher. He had been a catcher and he often criticized the catchers, not so much for what they did, but more for what they didn't do.

I can still recall the night last year when Baltimore beat Vida Blue in the first American League playoff game. Moe was impressed with Blue. The critical moment of the game came in the seventh inning when Blue was pitching to Paul Blair. Blue got two strikes on Blair and then fired four or five fast balls in succession, each pitch coming in with the same lightning speed.

With each succeeding pitch, Blair improved his timing, getting a little slice of the ball at first, then a bigger piece, then, his timing down perfect, Blair pulled a game-winning double to left field.

In the room that night, Moe repeatedly said, in anger, "Why didn't he give him the hook? Why didn't he throw the hook?" Moe knew that if Blue had changed speeds and thrown a curve, Blair, most likely, would have struck out, lunging. Typically, Moe didn't blame Blue. The Oakland catcher was at fault. It was the catcher's responsibility to call for the curve.

Moe didn't like to meet the modern players, but it wasn't because he thought the moderns weren't as good as the ancients. Not at all. He often said Johnny Bench of Cincinnati was the best catcher he ever saw. But many times, when we were together, there would be ballplayers nearby and I would ask Moe if he wanted to be introduced. He didn't. Later, I understood why.

He didn't want a player, or players, asking who he was, when he played and who he played with, etc. He considered such identification demeaning.

"They think it all started with them," Moe would say. "Don't they know there were many of us here before they got here?" The modern players' lack of baseball history and their indifference to the past nettled Moe. So he did the gentlemanly thing. He avoided them.

Moe was the happiest, I think, at World Series time. He would see the games, return to the room for a nap and take a long and leisurely bath. He was always taking baths. He would then set out for the press hospitality room where he would have dinner and remain until closing time. Wherever Moe sat became the head of the table.

In the main, his dinner companions usually were the genuine aristocrats of sportswriting, men such as the late Frank Graham, Red Smith, Arthur Daley, Leonard Koppett and Jimmy Cannon of New York, Fred Russell of Nashville, Allen Lewis of Philadelphia and Harold Kaese of Boston. Moe often said if he had to miss a game and was limited to only one account of the game, he would want Kaese's story. Kaese, he was confident, would come closest to telling him everything he wanted to know.

When Moe saw a good newspaper story, he would tear it out and show it around. He enjoyed Dick Young's stuff. More than 10 years ago, Young did a piece that had to do with the members of the proposed Continental League (which died aborning but forced expansion) meeting with the executives from the established major leagues. Young wrote that the Continentals likely would be advised to try another sport, "like flying a kite." Moe carried that story with him for months. "Isn't that a wonderful description?" he would say.

Generally, Moe was impressed with the current generation of baseball writers. He regarded the game stories of the 1971 World Series by Joe Durso of the New York Times as beautifully done. "Durso makes a narrative out of the game," Moe said.

But Moe had a vehement dislike of the so-called "chipmunks" and the new tendency to rush to the clubhouse and fill an entire story with locker-room quotes. "Just give me the facts, that's all I want," he would say.

He also said John McGraw couldn't manage today because of the demands of the press. He couldn't imagine McGraw defending or explaining his strategy to writers.

Moe had a working knowledge of about 10 languages and, of course, was highly educated. He had degrees from Princeton University and the University of Columbia Law School and he studied at the Sorbonne in Paris. Of his scholarly attainments, the only one I ever heard him express any pride about was that he was a founding member of America's most prestigious linguistic society.

Moe employed his knowledge of languages mostly when he was meeting people for the first time—and he was constantly making new acquaintances. If he met a waitress and her name was Standish or Stanislawski, he would spend 10 minutes dissecting her name, telling how and where the name originated, etc. Once I accused him of using his languages only to meet women. He laughed and indicated his father had told him the same thing.

Only once did I see him with a book. It was a dictionary of Sanskrit which needed bindery repair. It occurred to me at that time that Moe certainly wasn't any intellectual in the usual sense. I never heard him engage in philosophical discussion or expound on great ideas or great books. He even refused to open Jim Bouton's "Ball Four," which was warmly received by the intellectual establishment. Moe regarded it as gossip.

Moe didn't read magazines and had no interest in television, but he devoured newspapers. He repeatedly insisted that anybody could get a good education simply by reading the New York Times every day, which he did. He also bought the Washington Post and the Boston Globe.

My guess is that he turned to the sports sections first and I'm certain he would prefer to spend an afternoon with former teammates such as Heinie Manush and Joe Cronin, who, incidentally, was Moe's life-long friend, than with a Shakespearean scholar or a scientist.

The New York baseball writers saw Moe several times a week, always at the ball parks or in the press room. Many times they referred to him as "Mysterious Moe." In reply, Moe invariably would put an index finger to his lips, confirming and sealing the mysteriousness of it all. It was a takeoff on the old World War II posters: "A slip of the lip can sink a ship."

Moe, of course, was pressed into service as a secret agent in World War II, working out of the Office of Strategic Services. He seldom spoke about his role as a spy.

I certainly don't want to diminish Moe's cloak-and-dagger contributions to the victory or to our acquisition of atomic secrets. I can only say that Moe was considerably more delighted to tell of the women he had known—a veritable chorus line of the countesses and duchesses stretching from Italy and Denmark to the Baltic Sea. Though a bachelor, Moe had a fundamental appreciation of the feminine form.

But Moe did have a secret. He didn't have a regular job. He must have been rooming with me four or five years before this occurred to me. When I confronted him with my discovery, he would offer faint denials. Often he would mention he was involved in a shipment of aircraft to a foreign power or that he had a connection with the Arthur Little Co. in Boston.

Above all, he was a free man, uncluttered and unencumbered. I can see him now striding down the avenue, newspapers folded under his arm and observing the world as it passed before him in review and saying, "Isn't that wonderful?" or "marvelous, marvelous."

One trivia question—and a trick trivia question at that—seeks the names of two brothers who won 372 games between them while pitching for the same team. The answer is Christy and Henry Mathewson. The former won 372 games for the New York Giants, the latter none.

The prolific baseball historian Donald Honig has, fittingly enough, nothing to say about Henry, but a good deal to say about his brother.

# From *Baseball America*

## DONALD HONIG

THE PUBLIC's dubious regard of professional baseball players—"You're all right, but please don't try and join the family"—continued for the better part of the century's first two decades. It revealed a curious ambivalence in the country's attitude toward its favorite game. The game was an entity unto itself, part of the American ethos, exemplifying cherished national virtues and qualities, but paradoxically divorced from its most gifted practitioners who were to be cheered, applauded, admired, and fussed over, but not invited to dinner. It pointed up the sharply differing areas of fantasy and reality that, in other contexts, the game still occupies in the minds of its devotees.

The man who more than any other began to force a modification of the public's opinion of its favorite athletes was Christy Mathewson. In his youthful photographs, with his pressed suit, tie, white shirt with batwing collar, his frank, open face with its full lips and wide, intelligent eyes, and parted hair lying neatly. Christy Mathewson looks like a medical student or a budding young attorney destined for the United States Senate; looks anything, in fact, but what he became—a superbly gifted righthanded pitcher who would dominate with class and style a realm of social pariahs.

Mathewson was born on August 12, 1880, in Factoryville, a small town in northeastern Pennsylvania that lay in the heart of the state's anthracite coal region. Unlike many of his friends, young Christopher did not head for the mines as soon as he was of age. Son of a gentleman farmer and a mother described as monied, Mathewson, oldest of five children, attended Keystone Academy, a junior college founded by his grandmother. Here the studious young man was lacquered with poise and purpose and sent on to Bucknell University. At Buck-

nell, Mathewson made the invention of Frank Merriwell superfluous. His good looks were at once sturdy, distinguished, and boyish. He excelled at baseball and football; indeed, he was called "the greatest drop-kicker in America" by Walter Camp, the most celebrated football coach of the era.

In contrast to some latter-day college athletes, Mathewson found diversions other than athletics available on campus and took advantage of them: things like opening books, taking exams, and thinking. But of course that was to be expected back then. Today, college sports are an industry and the public image of a star athlete is that of someone being led around the campus on a chain. Mathewson, however, was a born overachiever. In addition to being a star athlete, he was also class president, a member of the glee club (the only time, apparently, he was known to raise his voice), active in several literary societies, a member of the Phi Gamma Delta fraternity, and a champion checker player. A nice boy to have around. Overlooking nothing, he even found himself a campus sweetheart, whom he married a few years later. Naturally, the marriage was a happy one. This was America's first golden boy and for a long time nothing was going to go wrong; it simply would not be allowed, because America needed Christy Mathewson, baseball needed him, New York needed him, and John McGraw needed him—four natural forces that in conjunction could roll back tidal waves and paralyze tornadoes.

Today, however, it would all be stored and dust-laden in some ancestral attic if not for the young man's uncanny way with a baseball. There is no record of what Matty's family said when their young prince announced he was opting for a career as a professional baseball player (apparently his mother had been hoping he would take up a career in the ministry, but the closest he came to this was a promise that he would never play ball on Sunday, a promise he seems never to have broken). The family was probably so mesmerized by him that they assumed anything Christopher did was all right. Or they may have tried to stop him, but history tells us there is no use trying to stop a legend-to-be from hacking out its niche with those golden hammers and chisels. So, almost like a missionary from the gardens of the true and the good, he set forth, converting by deed and not word.

If Mathewson had pursued a different career and become, say, a United States senator or the most successful physician in Scranton, Pennsylvania, he might well have been marked down as a snob. Part of the Mathewson legend is the very fact that Christy was bred differently from the vast majority of his ballplaying colleagues; like another American objet d'art whose appeal approached canonization, Joe DiMaggio, he could be aloof and reserved. His teammates, as Emerson said of Thoreau, would as soon have taken the limb of a tree as the arm of their mighty star. He once refused to greet the friends of a teammate who had traveled a long distance to see him pitch. When the train carrying the Giants pulled into a small-town depot he was known to lower the window shade where he was sitting so as to conceal himself from the view of those on the platform. To the sportswriters, those instant historians whose fervent bouquets of prose helped create and perpetuate much of the Mathewson legend, the great pitcher was only as cordial as he had to be. These are the behavioral patterns of royalty, and the citizens of Matty's democratic land loved him for it. They had enthroned him because of his reserve and his dignity, and any deviation from the image on his part would have been viewed as an act of *lèse majesté*.

The image was so without blemish that some sportswriters felt compelled to point out that Matty, while indeed perfect, was also human. He took a sip now and then—in moderation of course—and did occasionally smoke a pipe or cigarette, and when properly aroused could and did let fly with some language not found in McGuffey's readers. He loved to gamble at cards and now and then at dice. Once when McGraw caught Matty rattling the bones with some teammates, the irate skipper fined the mere mortals ten dollars each, while Matty was drenched with a hundred-dollar fine, because, as McGraw explained, "With your intelligence you should be setting a good example for those guys." The responsibilities of a legend were onerous, and the price could be high. When Mathewson's image began growing dangerously marmoreal, Mrs. Mathewson felt impelled to say that while Christy was a good man, "he was not a goody-goody."

The Mathewson legend began modestly. He started pitching when he was eleven years old, diagraming his future on the playing fields of Factoryville. When he was a teenager he was getting a buck a game to silence the bats of older boys, doing it with his healthy fastball and a roundhouse curve, of which he was very proud. In the summer of 1896, when John McGraw was giving the hip to opposing baserunners, the man who was going to make him famous was sixteen years old and pitching semipro ball in Scranton, a few miles down the road from Factoryville. While at Bucknell, Matty continued pitching semipro for a couple of hundred a month—in those days college athletes were allowed to earn money without jeopardizing their amateur status. (They still are today, except that it's more fashionable to pretend otherwise.)

Mathewson started his professional career in 1899 in Taunton, Massachusetts, a small industrial city in the New England League, about thirty miles south of Boston. It was here, laboring for ninety dollars a month, that he began perfecting the pitch that was to make him famous. Already gifted with a smoking fastball and a good curve, and with masterly control of each, the addition of the new pitch was another case of the rich getting richer and the poor not being able to buy a base hit.

As with many momentous discoveries, there remains a residue of uncertainty as to just when Mathewson stumbled upon his famous "fadeaway" pitch. Whenever or wherever, he was definitely throwing it at Taunton in 1899. The fadeaway, so called because it broke suddenly and sharply and was no longer there for the batter to whale at, was today's screwball. Basically, the pitch is a reverse curve, thrown by twisting the thumb toward the body. Since the ball curves in the direction in which it is spinning, this pitch, when thrown by a righthander, drops and breaks in on a righthanded batter and away from a left. Today the pitch is thrown by a number of pitchers; back in the age of innocence it was considered exotic. Also, very few pitchers could control it. Mathewson's mastery of this "freak delivery" made him preeminent among pitchers. And it added to his mystique, for he alone had full command of it; but because its delivery put so taut a strain on his arm, he seldom threw it more than ten or twelve times a game.

A year later, in 1900, Christy Mathewson served notice. He was a formidable figure now, with his prepossessing manner that exuded a mature strength, dignity, and self-confidence. He was full grown now, six feet one-and-one-half inches tall and 190 muscular, well-proportioned pounds. He was considered tall for his time—six-footers were thought to have snow on their heads in those days. He was working the mounds of the Virginia League that year, pitching for Norfolk and having the time of his life. The perfect man was the nearly perfect pitcher in that summer that broke the seal on the new century. By the end of July his record was 20–2. They were coming from all over the Norfolk area to see the young man pitch, coming on horseback and by wagon and one-horse shay, because they knew a pitcher this good wasn't going to be theirs for long. They knew there were big leagues, big cities, and big money beckoning, and that their gifted athletes, like their gifted young in any activity or profession, were sworn to a dream and were marking time and listening for the train whistle and their journey to glory and success.

Twenty wins and two losses by the end of July was as good a ticket out of town as an affair with the police chief's daughter, and for Matty the ticket was punched for New York, that bustling, hustling, cavernous jaw of opportunity and temptation that another small-town boy, O. Henry, would soon label Baghdad-on-the-Subway. Mathewson's contract was bought by the New York Giants. The purchase price was around $2,000.

John McGraw was picking up ground balls in St. Louis that summer, and managing the Giants was one George Davis, also the club's shortstop. On a warm afternoon in late July, Davis's new recruit showed up at the Polo Grounds. Built in 1889, the field lay in uptown Manhattan, at 155th Street and Eighth Avenue, in the shadow of Coogan's Bluff, a broad, steep-faced cliff. Davis asked the new man to throw batting practice, with the skipper taking first cuts. Davis approved of Matty's fastball, told him to forget the roundhouse curve that had been wowing 'em since Keystone Academy days, and like the overhand curve (called a drop back then). When asked if he had anything else, Matty shyly conceded he had ''a sort of freak ball.'' Ordered to throw it, he did. Davis, a perennial .300 hitter, had trouble putting wood on the pitch. Supposedly it was Davis who named the pitch by saying, ''It sort of fades out of sight. A fadeaway.'' This is as forthcoming as mute old history is about the christening of baseball's most famous delivery.

Nevertheless, the young man was not quite ready for the big push. Used sparingly during the final two months of the season, Mathewson logged an 0–3 record and did not pitch impressively. By season's end the Giants were disenchanted and returned him to Norfolk. But this is how it should be, how any good scenarist with an eye on the coming cheers and trumpets would have it—''Too bad, kid, but I guess New York ain't Norfolk,'' and the legend-to-be, with the first bitter taste of failure on his palate, packs his straw suitcase and heads dejectedly toward a lonely train ride, shaking a figurative fist at the big city and vowing to return and make good. Return and conquer he did, of course, but how Christy Mathewson returned to New York is in itself a story of the ethics then prevailing in America's favorite game.

The Cincinnati Reds drafted Mathewson from the Norfolk club for $100 and almost immediately traded him to the Giants for right-handed pitcher Amos Rusie, something of a flaming legend himself. Rusie was one of those pitchers who threw so hard people wondered his arm didn't come flying in after the ball. His quickie earned the Indiana-born Amos the nickname Hoosier Thunderbolt. Pitching for New York, Rusie helped make the nineties gay in the big city, winning over thirty games three times and leading in strikeouts six straight years. He also led in bases on balls five times, which meant that, like most thunderbolts, his rarely struck twice in the same place. Connie Mack, a most reliable witness who seemed to have entered the game at about the same time as the round ball, described Rusie as fearsome. And fearsome the big fellow must have been, for he forced a rules change for which all hitters are to this day grateful, even though most of them never heard of Amos Rusie. Up until 1892 the pitching mound was a neighborly fifty feet away from home plate, giving a wallbreaker like Rusie what was finally deemed an unfair advantage. Accordingly, in 1893 the mound was hauled back to its present sixty feet six inches. The National League's collective batting average promptly jumped from .245 in 1892 to .280 in 1893 and then to .309 a year later, when a good time was had by all except the pitchers. (To this day psychological studies of pitchers come up with persecution disorders, dating back to 1893.) Today, the thought of a Nolan Ryan or a Goose Gossage pitching from fifty feet would be enough to make big-league batters perspire unto dehydration.

In those days pitchers were little more than dray horses, harnessed to the mound. What they started they were expected to finish. Rusie had for five straight years burned it in for over 400 innings, three times over 500. By 1898 the toll was beginning to show on the twenty-seven-year-old pitcher's powerful right arm. Following that season, when he posted a 20–10 record (fancy doings by today's standards, but fourteen National League pitchers won more than Amos that season), the Giants decided to cut his salary from $3,000 to $2,000. This action struck Rusie in the pocketbook and in his pride, and the twice-wounded pitcher went home to Indiana where he sat out the next two seasons.

In 1901 the Cincinnati Reds decided the inactive, one-time Thunderbolt was just the man for them. Or so it seemed. The truth of the matter is less savory. Running the Reds was the devious John T. Brush, who already knew he was going to New York to assume ownership of the Giants. In order to get the brooding Rusie off of New York's hands (and thus, soon, his own), he agreed to swap them Christopher Mathewson of Factoryville, Pennsylvania, Bucknell University, and future resident of Mount Olympus.

So Mathewson returned to New York in 1901 and this

time made it stick. (Rusie pitched three games for Cincinnati, was 0–1 and took a hike back to Indiana, his thunderbolts turned to cabbage. Mathewson went on to win 372 games for the Giants. So when out-of-towners voice their suspicions of the machinations of big-city folk, pay heed.)

If a legend may be said to be a thing woven, then Matty went right to the loom his first full year in New York. For a seventh-place club he won 20 games and lost 17, completing 36 of 38 starts. That complete-game statistic is impressive today, but back then it was the norm. While America may have had lots of unfinished business in 1901, that state of affairs had nothing to do with the pitching mound, although it should be stated that only two pitchers in the league, Cincinnati's Noodles Hahn and Matty's teammate Dummy Taylor completed more games than the imminent legend. Note, if you will, those nicknames—Noodles and Dummy. This was a more homespun, less refined society that these boys sprouted up from. Nicknames could be brutally literal—Luther (Dummy) Taylor, for instance, was a deaf-mute. Another of Matty's teammates was Charley (Piano Legs) Hickman, which gives us a fairly graphic mental snapshot of Charley, at least from the waist down. Looking around the National League during that 1901 season we find Bones Ely, Ginger Beaumont, Jiggs Donohue, Klondike Douglass, Cozy Dolan, Snags Heidrick, Daff Gammons, Cupid Childs, Topsy Hartsel, Brickyard Kennedy, Snake Wiltse, Wild Bill Donovan, as well as a number of Kids and Docs. The American League had its own crowd of colorful handles, like Nixey Callahan, Zaza Harvey, Socks Seybold, Farmer Steelman, Boileryard Clarke, Crazy Schmit, and Pink Hawley. The Detroit Tigers were the champs in the identity-crisis sweepstakes, their starting lineup including two Docs, two Kids, one Pop, and one Ducky. Nicknames have, of course, always been a colorful adjunct to the game, as latter-day saints rechristened Dizzy, Yogi, Harry the Cat, and Mark the Bird can attest, but nothing like the plethora and apparent literalness that obtained back then. Special players, if not tagged with some pedestrian nickname like Lefty, were later accorded an approximation of knighthood with alliterative titles like Larrupin' Lou (Gehrig), Joltin' Joe (DiMaggio), The Splendid Splinter (Ted Williams), Rapid Robert (Feller), Hammerin' Hank (Greenberg or Aaron), or Pistol Pete (Reiser).

They called Mathewson Big Six, and the origin of the name is somewhat in question. Some say it was in tribute to his imposing height, others that it was after a famed New York City fire wagon of the day that was noted for its efficiency in speeding to the scene of the fire and dousing the flames. In any event, the nickname was unique and had dignity. No Boileryards or Klondikes would do for Christopher Mathewson of the New York Giants.

Mathewson must have been a perfect, unoffending mix of aristocrat and regular guy. His cultured, slightly stand-offish ways gave affront to no one. To the opposition he was an Olympian who scaled heights loftier than a mound and was to be respected. His teammates worshiped him. Pitcher Rube Marquard: "What a grand guy he was!" Catcher Chief Meyers: "How we loved to play for him! We'd break our necks for that guy. If you made an error behind him or anything of that sort, he'd never get mad or sulk. He'd come over and pat you on the back. He had the sweetest, most gentle nature." Outfielder Fred Snodgrass: "He was a wonderful, wonderful man, too, a reserved sort of fellow, a little hard to get close to. But once you got to know him, he was a truly good friend." To all who played with or against him during the first decade of the century, he was, without reservation, the greatest pitcher they ever saw. Reminiscing about Mathewson, Marquard, a year or two before he died in 1980, said, "Sitting on the bench watching him pitch, I often forgot I was a ballplayer, a pitcher myself. I became a fan. That's how good he was. I've seen every pitcher you can name for the last twenty years, but Matty was the only one who ever made me feel like a fan."

By 1903 Mathewson was a 30-game winner (30–13). A year later he was 33–12. In 1905 he was 31–9. It was that October that he applied the seal of flawlessness to his achievements, crowning them with an autumnal splendor to match America's color-drenched landscape. As a great athlete must, he did it in the glare of his sport's most conspicuous event, the World Series. In 1905, the Series was being played for only the second time, but it had already laid its grip upon the national imagination and become, as it still is, the most momentous athletic clash of the year, sports' most supple springboard for fame and notoriety. Most of baseball's great pitchers have worked in a World Series; none have come close to Mathewson's performance against the Philadelphia Athletics in 1905.

The Series opened on October 9, in Philadelphia. Mathewson shut out the A's on four hits, 3–0. On October 12, celebrating Columbus Day in his own fashion, he again allowed just four hits in shutting down the A's, 9–0. Taking one day of rest, he came back on October 14 at New York's Polo Grounds and, allowing six hits, completed his lamination of the Athletics by a 2–0 score, locking up the title for the Giants. (In fact, every game of that Series ended in a shutout, Joe McGinnity winning the Giants' other game 2–0, while Chief Bender won the A's lone game by a 3–0 score. In that Series, score first and the game was yours.) In the space of six days Mathewson had—in a World Series—pitched twenty-seven innings of shutout ball, allowing just fourteen hits and one base on balls. With that kind of performance, you become an empyrean one-man fraternity, and everybody wants to join you.

*The New York Times*'s account of the day's events began:

> Two neatly dressed, ruddy faced athletic looking young men, grinning broadly; one a giant in contrast to the squattiness of the other, walked along the veranda of the clubhouse at the Polo Grounds about 5 o'clock yesterday afternoon. Below them was a sea of 10,000 faces, wildly emitting a thunderous eruption of enthusiasm. The two young men looked down upon the reverberating ocean of humanity for a moment, and then walked to a point directly in front of the plaza, where they were in view of all. The ten thousand throats bellowed forth a tribute that would have almost drowned a broadside of twelve-inch guns.

> The two smiling athletes stopped, one of them drew forth a long sheet of yellow paper rolled under his arm. As the crowd pushed and fought and cheered he unwrapped an impromptu banner and let it flutter on the breeze. The multitude pressed forward like a wave to read this inscription:

THE GIANTS, WORLD'S CHAMPIONS, 1905

> Geological records show that Vesuvius disturbs the earth and that seismic demonstrations are felt by the greater number. But if that doctrine had been promulgated in the vicinity of the Polo Grounds yesterday, as Christie Mathewson and Roger Bresnahan of the New York Baseball Club unfurled their victorious banner, it would have been minimized. For, as volcanoes assert themselves upon the earth's surface surely must that deafening, reverberating roar have lifted Manhattan's soil from its base.

The story went on to proclaim "Christie Mathewson, the giant slabman, who made the world's championship possible for New York, may be legitimately designated as the premier pitching wonder of all baseball records." At the conclusion of this tumultuous ceremony, the *Times* went on, Mathewson responded with "a half-suppressed smile and bow." Nobility's acknowledgement of the crowd.

This was Mathewson's sublime moment. At twenty-five he had it all, as only a revered athlete can have it all. Monarch of the mound, he was as royal as a democratic people can allow, a hero to his peers, a model for American youth, an example cited from the pulpits of the land. But it was dangerous to sit so loftily, to be so enviably perfect, for the gods, they say, are jealous, and the panegyric from the Polo Grounds that day must have rattled the shutters of other realms, for little more than a decade later the vipers would begin to gather around his feet and a miasma drift toward him.

But that would come later. The glories had to mount before the tragedy could match the man, before the pure gold became as fragile as crystal. In 1905 he seemed as mighty, as invincible, and as abundantly blessed as a man could hope to be. Not even the irascible, bullying John McGraw could disturb this obelisk of splendor. The fact of the matter is, the two men regarded each other warmly and affectionately.

The relationship between John McGraw and Christy Mathewson fascinates. Antagonism between the two seemed inevitable. But the flinty soul of John McGraw melted before the radiance of his ace. McGraw demanded his players be tough and combative and disciplined, and Mathewson surely delivered these qualities, but with a distinction that made him as unique a person, in his element, as his right arm made him a pitcher. Mathewson exemplified a credo of sportsmanship and fair play his skipper disdained; yet McGraw never tried to roughen the edges of his great pitcher. Of course there was no need to, for Mathewson won, consistently and effectively, in his own way. Mathewson was too vast, complex, and mysterious a machine for even McGraw to try to tinker with. It was a case of both sides of the tracks conjoining to produce the desired result, for if McGraw never tried to influence Mathewson, neither did the pitcher object to his manager's sarcasm, vulgarities, and uncompromising demand for discipline, for those relentlessly drilled, hard-driven, tongue-lashed teams were scoring the runs and making the plays that Mathewson needed. Mathewson had the highest regard for McGraw, whose baseball acumen impressed him immensely. In a book he authored in 1912, *Pitching in a Pinch*, Matty wrote: "Around McGraw revolves the game of the Giants. He plans every move, most of the hitters going to the plate with definite instructions from him as to what to try to do." Mathewson was an extremely competitive man, very passionate about baseball, proud of his ability, and himself a sharp student of the game and its players. But McGraw knew even more and was willing to take chances based on the cutting edge of his intellect, and this fascinated and intrigued his great pitcher. Matty was in awe of his manager's constantly clicking and evaluating and devising mind. McGraw's concentration during a game was so intense, Matty wrote, that it induced his players to speak in whispers around him, if they spoke at all. "He was the game," said Mathewson.

For the McGraws and the Mathewsons, husbands and wives both, it was a lifelong friendship, warm and affectionate. The two couples even shared a New York apartment one summer, a unique arrangement, since many players find it difficult to share even the dugout with their boss for a few hours each day. For the childless McGraw, Matty was the son he never had.

*The Third Fireside Book of Baseball* reprinted several entries from Lawrence Ritter's book *The Glory of Their Times,* and so will this fourth one. So did *The Saturday Evening Post,* when the book was published in 1966. Ritter and his tape recorder captured the memories of one old-time baseball great after another, and the result was that rarity of publishing rarities: the instant classic.

People are always talking about the greatest all-time outfield. If by that they mean the three best oufielders on the same team at the same time, then quite possibly they mean the 1912 Red Sox, with its outfield of Tris Speaker in center, Duffy Lewis in left, and the author of this piece, Harry Hooper, in right. John McGraw thought Speaker, Hooper and Ty Cobb would be the greatest outfield of the entire American League. He didn't live to see DiMaggio or Williams or Reggie. He saw Ruth but didn't include him. What a wondrous world this is!

# "This Hooper Appears to Be a Good Prospect"

## HARRY HOOPER

Sure, I still follow baseball. *Of course* I do. What a question to ask! Those darn Giants . . . sometimes I can't sleep for worrying over them. It didn't used to be so bad. But now that they're only about 75 miles away and I can hear all the games the situation has gotten impossible.

That Willie Mays, he's one of the greatest center fielders who ever lived. You can go back as far as you want and name all the great ones—Tris Speaker, Eddie Roush, Max Carey, Earle Combs, Joe DiMaggio. I don't care *who* you name, Mays is just as good, maybe better. He's a throwback to the old days. A guy who can do everything, and plays like he loves it. And that Koufax. You name a better left-hander in the history of baseball and I'll eat my hat.

I played my first professional baseball right here, in the California State League, in 1907. Actually, I never had any intention of taking up baseball as a career. I expected to be an engineer. Went to St. Mary's College and got my degree in Civil Engineering in 1907. After graduation, I played with the Sacramento club, mainly because they promised to get me a surveying job.

And they did. When I wasn't playing ball I worked as a surveyor for the Western Pacific Railroad. I got $85 a month for playing ball, and $75 a month as a surveyor. I guess you might say that was my bonus, a surveying job.

Actually, my "bonus" was $12.50. Before I graduated I played a few games in that same league, the California State League, with Alameda. That was right near school. This fellow who owned the Alameda club—Mr. McMinnamen—asked me if I'd play on the team the last few months of my senior year, and I agreed, with the understanding that he'd give me my release as soon as I got out of college.

Well, just about the time college was letting out we played a game at Sacramento, and I did pretty well. Charlie Graham was managing Sacramento at the time and he went to Mr. McMinnamen and wanted to buy me, not knowing, of course, that I was due to get my release any day.

So Mr. McMinnamen came to me and said, "Look, I've got a chance to sell you to Sacramento. If you don't say anything about this agreement we have to release you, I'll give you half of whatever we can get."

"OK," I said, "but you better warn them that I'm going to stop playing as soon as I get the right kind of an engineering job. I'll probably quit at the end of the summer."

"All right," he said, "I'll do that. But don't you mention anything about your release."

Later, Charlie Graham told me how the conversation went. First of all, the Alameda owner did tell him about my being an engineer.

"OK," Charlie said, "I understand that. I think we can get him an engineering job he can work at and play ball both. How much do you want for him?"

"Oh, about $200."

"How about $10," Charlie countered.

"Make it $50."

"I'll make it $20."

And they settled on $25. I was sold for $25 lousy dollars. Talk about deflating a guy's ego! So my "bonus" was half of the sale price, namely $12.50.

Later, Charlie told me he smelled a rat the minute the guy asked for $200 when he should have asked for $500. "So I went as low as I could," he said, "just to test the situation out a little more, and it worked."

I had two pretty good years with Sacramento, surveying all the while, when one day near the end of the 1908 season Charlie Graham came to me in the hotel lobby.

"Well," he says, "how would you like to take a look at the Big Indian?"

"Huh?" I didn't know what he was talking about.

"The Big Indian! Boston! How would you like to play with the Boston Red Sox?" he says. "John I. Taylor, the owner of the Red Sox, is coming to town next week and I think he's interested in you."

"Well, I don't know," I said. "I'm not a ballplayer. I'm an engineer. I'm doing real well at the Western Pacific Railroad and I like my job."

You see, *he* figured I was a ballplayer who did "this other stuff" on the side. But *I* figured I was an engineer who played ball on the side.

"Why not give it a whirl?" he said. "What have you got to lose? You're only twenty-one, and even if you played ball another two years you could still take up 'this other stuff' at the age of twenty-three."

"Well, it would be a nice trip, Boston and all. Get to see some of the country," I thought. "OK, I'll do it. I'll talk to the guy. How much salary do you think I ought to ask for?"

"How much do you think you should get?"

"I have no idea," I said. "Would $2,500 be about right?"

"I think it would," Charlie said. "But that means you should ask for $3,000. Then maybe he'll give you the $2,500."

The California State League, see, was an outlaw league, not in organized baseball. So the Red Sox couldn't just buy my contract. They had to negotiate with me as though I was a free agent. (That didn't hold for the deal where I was sold by Alameda to Sacramento, because they respected each other's contracts within the league. As an outlaw league, they didn't steal players from each other, just from everybody else!)

So one warm August day in 1908 I met Mr. John I.

Taylor, owner of the Boston Red Sox, at the corner of 8th and J Streets in Sacramento. We went into a bar and had a glass of beer.

"I hear you're an engineer," he says.

"Yes, I am," I said.

"Well, that's very interesting," he says. "It so happens that we are thinking of building a new ball park in the not too distant future, and we may be looking for someone just like you. Your experience with the Western Pacific will no doubt prove invaluable. By the way, I also hear you are a baseball player."

"Yes, I am," I said.

"I was just wondering," he said, "given your qualifications in both lines of endeavor, how would you like to migrate to Boston."

"I wouldn't mind," I said.

"Well, we'd like to have you," he said. "At the moment, however, we are not in immediate need of engineering assistance. Considering that for the time being at least we would only require your services as a ballplayer, I was also wondering how much money you might want."

"How about $3,000?"

"I'll tell you," he said, "fact is, I was thinking of something in the neighborhood of $2,500. What do you say we compromise at $2,800."

"That seems very equitable to me," I said.

So I finished out the season with Sacramento, said good-bye to Charlie Graham—and told him that from then on he was my unofficial business advisor—resigned my job with the Western Pacific, and started on what I figured would be just a couple of years of playing baseball. And that was the last job I ever had that was connected with engineering.

Fenway Park was built in Boston, and Shibe Park in Philadelphia, and Yankee Stadium in New York, and all the while I was nowhere near a drafting board. I was out there in right field the whole time, drawing a line on a baseball instead of a chart. And, in case you're wondering, I have no regrets.

I joined the Red Sox for spring training in 1909, at Hot Springs, Arkansas. After a week or so I started to get a pretty good idea of my competition. Tris Speaker was there—he'd come up at the end of the previous season—and it looked like he had a stranglehold on the center-field job. There were three other outfielders there also, besides myself, and it looked to me like I belonged on that team: I thought I was as good or better than any of them. But everybody didn't seem to see things my way, because after about three weeks they decided who would be the regulars, and I wasn't among them.

We'd get the Boston papers and I read that ". . . this Hooper appears to be a good prospect, but he needs several years seasoning in the minors before he'll be ready.'' That made my blood boil. I *knew* I was good enough to make that team.

However, once they'd picked the regulars, us youngsters didn't get much chance to show what we could do. We never really got a proper opportunity during all of spring training. The old-timers kind of had the thing by the horns, you know. Wouldn't even let us have batting practice. A few of us wound up taking our bats into the outfield and having our own batting practice. Spring *training*. Training for what?

Well, we opened up in Philadelphia on April 12, 1909. Played three games there, in brand-new Shibe Park, and I sat on the bench the whole series. I didn't even have a road uniform, and I heard rumors that they were getting ready to ship me to the minors, to St. Paul in the American Association. I was getting hot under the collar, because I knew if they gave me a chance I could do the job.

From Philadelphia we went to Washington. I climbed up to the top of the Washington Monument the first morning there (had to get *some* exercise), and then went out to the ball park, expecting to sit on the bench through another game. But I'd hardly gotten into the clubhouse before the manager—Fred Lake—comes over to me. "Here's a uniform," he says. "You're going to play today."

A lucky combination of circumstances. One of the outfielders was hurt, and another had to go in and play first base because the first baseman was sick. They *had* to play me because they didn't have anybody else. Well, if I'd been ballyhooed as a wonder or something, I'd probably have been a little shaky. But the way it was, nobody expected anything of me, and I went out there determined to show them.

The first time it was my turn at bat we had a chance to score a run. Man on second and two out. On the bench I could hear everyone saying, "Who's up? Who's up?"

And then, "Oh, it's Hooper—well, too bad."

But I went up there and drove in that run. I got another hit that day, and would have had a third if the pitcher hadn't stabbed a liner headed right for his forehead. One of those instinctive grabs, you know. And in the field I handled myself OK. In other words, everything went just fine. Before the day was over, John I. Taylor was going around shaking everyone's hand, saying, "That's the boy I signed up in California."

And that's how come I never went to St. Paul. I had a good start and a little bit of luck when I needed it. You have to have a little luck, you know. That year and the next we started to form the nucleus of what was to become a great, great Red Sox ball club. We won the American League pennant in 1912, '15, '16, and '18, and in between we finished second twice. From 1912 to 1918 we won four pennants *and* four World Series.

They never did beat us in a World Series. Never. We played four different National League teams in four different World Series and only one of them even came close. That was the Giants, in 1912. We beat them four games to three. We beat Grover Cleveland Alexander and the Phillies four games to one in 1915, the Dodgers four games to one in 1916, and the Cubs four to two in 1918. The best team in all of baseball for close to a decade!

There really were *two* teams, the 1912 team and the 1915 one. The outfield was the same on both—Tris Speaker, Duffy Lewis, and myself—I think acknowledged by most as easily the greatest defensive outfield ever. Larry Gardner was at third base on both teams, and Bill Carrigan and Forrest Cady caught that whole time. But at first base it was first Jake Stahl and then Doc Hoblitzel; at second Steve Yerkes was eventually replaced by Jack Barry; and at short it was first Heinie Wagner and then Everett Scott. And, of course, the whole pitching staff turned over—from Smoky Joe Wood, Hugh Bedient, Charlie Hall, and Buck O'Brien in 1912, it became Ernie Shore, Dutch Leonard, Carl Mays, George Foster, Joe Bush, Sam Jones, and Babe Ruth in 1915 or so.

Babe Ruth joined us in the middle of 1914, a nineteen-year-old kid. He was a left-handed pitcher then, and a good one. He had never been anywhere, didn't know anything about manners or how to behave among people—just a big overgrown green pea. You probably remember him with that big belly he got later on. But that wasn't there in 1914. George was six foot two and weighed 198 pounds, all of it muscle. He had a slim waist, huge biceps, no self-discipline, and not much education—not so very different from a lot of other nineteen-year-old would-be ballplayers. Except for two things: he could eat more than anyone else, and he could hit a baseball further.

Lord, he ate too much. He'd stop along the road when we were traveling and order a half a dozen hot dogs and as many bottles of soda pop, stuff them in, one after the other, give a few big belches, and then roar, "OK, boys, let's go." That would hold Babe for a couple of hours, and then he'd be at it again. A nineteen-year-old youngster, mind you!

He was such a rube that he got more than his share of teasing, some of it not too pleasant. "The Big Baboon" some of them used to call him behind his back, and then a few got up enough nerve to ridicule him to his face. This started to get under his skin, and when they didn't let up he finally challenged the whole ball club. Nobody was so dumb as to take him up on it, so that put an end to that.

You know, I saw it all happen, from beginning to end. But sometimes I still can't believe what I saw: this nineteen-year-old kid, crude, poorly educated, only lightly brushed by the social veneer we call civilization, gradually transformed into the idol of American youth and the symbol of baseball the world over—a man loved by more people and with an intensity of feeling that perhaps has never been equaled before or since. I saw a man transformed from a human being into something pretty close to a god. If somebody had predicted that back on the Boston Red Sox in 1914, he would have been thrown into a lunatic asylum.

I still remember when the Babe was switched from pitching to become an outfielder. I finally convined Ed Barrow to play him out there to get his bat in the lineup every day. That was in 1919, and I was the team captain by then. Barrow technically was the manager, but I ran the team on the field, and I finally talked Ed into converting Ruth from a pitcher into an outfielder. Well, Ruth might have been a natural as a pitcher and as a hitter, but he sure wasn't a born outfielder.

I was playing center field myself, so I put the Babe in right field. On the other side of me was a fellow named Braggo Roth, another wild man. Sakes alive, I'd be playing out there in the middle between those two fellows, and I began to fear for my life. Both of them were galloping around that outfield without regard for life or limb, hollering all the time, running like maniacs after every ball! A week of that was enough for me. I shifted the Babe to center and I moved to right, so I could keep clear of those two.

Sheer self-preservation on my part, pure and simple. I'm still amazed that playing side by side those two never plowed into each other with the impact of two runaway freight trains. If they had, the crash would have shaken the Boston Commons.

Of all the pennants and World Series we won, I guess 1912 was the most exciting. That was the first year the Lewis-Speaker-Hooper outfield really became famous, that was the year Smoky Joe Wood won 16 straight games, the year Snodgrass muffed that fly ball in the last game of the Series—well, all in all, so many things happened that season that it's hard to find another that can compare with it.

I think the thing I remember best about 1912, though, is the pitching of Smoky Joe Wood. Was he ever something! I've seen a lot of great pitching in my lifetime, but never anything to compare with him in 1912. In 1917, for instance, I was in right field for the Red Sox when Ernie Shore pitched his perfect game (against the Senators, I think it was). And in 1922 I was in right field for the White Sox when Charlie Robertson pitched *his* perfect game (against Detroit). I guess there haven't been more than about half a dozen *perfect* games pitched in the history of baseball, and I was the right fielder in two of them. On two different teams, too.

So you might say I've seen some pretty good pitching. But I've never seen anything like Smoky Joe Wood in 1912. He won 34 games that year, 10 of them shutouts, and 16 of those wins were in a row. It so happened that that was the same year Walter Johnson *also* won 16 in a row. (That's *still* the record in the American league, by the way.) And the fact that both of those fellows were so unbeatable that year gave rise to one of the greatest games in the history of baseball.

You see, Walter Johnson set his record first. Walter finally lost a game in August, ending his streak at 16. But Walter hardly had time to accept congratulations, before up loomed Joe Wood, who looked as though he'd take the record right away from Walter before that very season had come to an end.

When Walter's streak ended at 16 in August, Joe Wood had won about 9 or 10 in a row. But then Joe kept adding to it . . . 11 straight . . . 12 straight . . . 13 straight. In early September we were scheduled to play Washington, and the public started to clamor for Walter Johnson himself to be allowed to pitch for Washington when Joe Wood went for us.

"Let Walter defend his record!" That was the cry.

Well, the owners were no fools. So when the Senators came to Boston for this series it was arranged that Walter Johnson and Joe Wood would oppose each other in one of the games. The crowd that jammed Fenway Park that day poured out onto the field, and the team benches were moved out along the foul lines so the fans could be packed in behind them. People were also standing all around on the outfield grass, held back by ropes.

By then Joe had won 13 straight, and Walter really *was* defending his new record. Well, to make a long story short, Joe Wood beat Walter Johnson that day, and the score was exactly what you'd expect—one to nothing. In the sixth inning Tris Speaker hit one into the crowd standing in left field for a ground-rule double, he scored on a double by Duffy Lewis, and that was the whole story. Not another runner crossed home plate all day. That was probably the most exciting game I ever played in or saw.

After that, Joe won two more games to tie Johnson's record at 16, and then he lost the next time out on an error that let a couple of unearned runs score in the eight or ninth inning. So now they both hold the record. Funny thing, that's also the same year Marquard won 19 straight in the National League.

The tension on Joe was just terrific all that season. First the 16 straight, and then the World Series. I still remember talking to him before one of the Series games and suddenly realizing that he couldn't speak. Couldn't say a word. The strain had started to get too much for him. Well, what can you expect? I think he was only about twenty-two when all this was happening. Mighty young to be under such pressure for so many months.

But he still won three games in that 1912 World Series. The last inning of the last game of that Series was quite a doozy. That's one they'll never forget. The Giants took a 2–1 lead in the top of the tenth, and the first man up for us in the bottom of the tenth was Clyde Engle, pinch-hitting for Joe Wood. He hit the fly ball that Fred Snodgrass dropped. The famous Snodgrass muff. It could happen to anybody.

I was up next and I tried to bunt, but I fouled it off. On the next pitch I hit a line drive into left center that looked like a sure triple. Ninety-nine times out of a hundred no outfielder could possibly have come close to that ball. But in some way, I don't know how, Snodgrass ran like the wind, and dang if he didn't catch it. I think he *outran* the ball. Robbed me of a sure triple.

I saw Snodgrass a couple of years ago at a function in Los Angeles, and I reminded him of that catch.

"Well, thank you," he said, "nobody ever mentions that catch to me. All they talk about is the muff."

I don't know about anybody else. But *I* remember that catch all right. I'm the one guy who'll never forget it.

After that, Steve Yerkes got a base on balls, and that brought up Tris Speaker. We're still behind, 2–1, and there's one out. Well, Spoke hit a little pop foul over near first base, and old Chief Meyers took off after it. He didn't have a chance, but Matty kept calling for him to take it. If he'd called for Merkle, it would have been an easy out. Or Matty could have taken it himself. But he kept hollering for the Chief to take it, and poor Chief— he never was too fast to begin with—he lumbered down that line after it as fast as his big legs would carry him, stuck out his big catcher's mitt—and just missed it.

Spoke went back to the batter's box and yelled to Mathewson. "Well, you just called for the wrong man. It's gonna cost you this ball game."

And on the next pitch, he hit a clean single that tied the game, and a couple of minutes later Larry Gardner drove in Yerkes with the run that won it.

After that wonderful season, Joe Wood never pitched successfully again. He hurt his arm and never was able to really throw that hummer any more, the way he did in 1912. Joe kept trying to come back as a pitcher, but never could do it. He had a lot of guts, though. He couldn't pitch any more, so he turned himself into an outfielder and became a good one. He could always hit. He played with Cleveland in the 1920 World Series as an outfielder. I think he's the only man besides Babe Ruth who was in one World Series as a pitcher and another as an outfielder.

Harry Frazee became the owner of the Red Sox in 1917, and before long he sold off all our best players and ruined the team. Sold them all to the Yankees—Ernie Shore, Duffy Lewis, Dutch Leonard, Carl Mays, Babe Ruth. Then Wally Schang and Herb Pennock and Joe Dugan and Sam Jones. I was disgusted. The Yankee dynasty of the twenties was three-quarters the Red Sox of a few years before. All Frazee wanted was the money. He was short of cash and he sold the whole team down the river to keep his dirty nose above water. What a way to end a wonderful ball club!

I got sick to my stomach at the whole business. After the 1920 season I held out for $15,000, and Frazee did me a favor by selling me to the Chicago White Sox. I was glad to get away from that graveyard.

At Chicago they gave me a blank three-year contract and told me to fill in the figure.

"Well," I thought, "I'll be doing business with Mr. Comiskey for some years, and I don't want to start off on the wrong foot."

So instead of filling in $15,000—which was what I'd been holding out for with the Red Sox—I put down $13,250. Well, I have five darn-good years with the White Sox, best hitting years I ever had. Hit .328 one year, and .327 another. But in 1926 I got a contract in the mail calling for $7,000. That's right—$7,000!

So I wrote to Comiskey and reminded him that when I'd signed with him in 1921 I'd been more than reasonable in filling in a blank contract. I said I thought perhaps that should sort of be taken into account now. Ha! He wrote back that he never heard of anyone getting a guarantee of anything in this business, and sent me my release along with the letter. And they really needed me that year; they had nobody to play right field.

Well, that was early in 1926, and I was thirty-eight years old. So I went into the real-estate business for a while, coached baseball at Princeton for a couple of years, and then during the depression I took a fill-in job here at Capitola as postmaster—and didn't leave it until 25 years later. Supposed to be a *temporary* job.

I enjoyed the couple of years I coached at Princeton very much. Still go back there every once in a while. Beautiful spot, Princeton. Speaking about that, today they make such a big deal about all the college men in baseball, and about how baseball today has such a "better class" of people in it than the "rowdies" of the old days. But that's not true at all. With respect to college men, let me give you an idea of what it was *really* like.

I joined the Boston Red Sox in 1909, and when I got there Bill Carrigan was the regular catcher. He'd gone to Holy Cross. At first base was Jake Stahl, from the University of Illinois, and at third was Larry Gardner, from the University of Vermont. In the outfield, I had gone to St. Mary's, and so had Duffy Lewis. On the pitching staff was Marty McHale of the University of Maine (another civil engineering graduate), Chris Mahoney from Fordham, and Ray Collins from Vermont.

That was just the Red Sox. In general, I'd say that back in my day maybe as many as about one out of every five or six Big Leaguers had gone to college. I don't know how many of them graduated, but that isn't the point. The point is that they came from colleges into professional baseball.

Of course, it's ridiculous to think that only college men are gentlemen, or are intelligent. That isn't even worth discussing. But it should certainly be clear that the impression that we were an uneducated bunch of "rowdies" is a lot of nonsense.

Most people know that Mathewson went to Bucknell, but they don't realize that Frank Chance went to Washington University, Hal Chase to Santa Clara, Buck Herzog to the University of Maryland, Orvie Overall to the University of California, Eddie Plank to Gettysburg College, Chief Bender to Dickinson College, Art Devlin to Georgetown, and so on.

And there were more. Ginger Beaumont went to Beloit College, Andy Coakley and Jack Barry to Holy Cross, Eddie Collins to Columbia, Eddie Grant to Harvard, Fred Tenney to Brown, Bob Bescher and Ed Reulbach to Notre Dame, Jack Coombs to Colby, Harry Davis to Girard College, Chief Meyers to Dartmouth, Davy Jones to Dixon College, et cetera, et cetera.

Why, Miller Huggins and Hugh Jennings were both lawyers—Huggins was a graduate of Cincinnati Law School and Jennings went to Cornell. Both of them went to law school *after* they were in the major leagues. Even John J. McGraw went to St. Bonaventure for a while, also after he was in the majors. And do you realize that every one of these fellows I've named was in the majors in 1910 or earlier, and most of them were there *before 1905*.

If you take into account the proportion of the total population that went to college back in those days, I think it's pretty clear that we had *more* than our share of college men in baseball. And it's also pretty clear that the usual picture you get of the old-time ballplayer as an illiterate rowdy contains an awful lot more fiction than it does fact.

# Brushback or Beanball

## JERRY IZENBERG

A RECENT WIRE service piece lamented the fact that the brushback pitch has gone the way of daytime baseball and the crewcut. There are places where you can see both but they are few and far between. The reasons for this can be interpreted in two ways:

A) Baseball players have become much more intelligent and both thrower and hitter understand that a 90 mile-an-hour fastball is not something you can bounce off a guy's skull and then simply say, "Ooops."

B) Everyone is making so much money that the pitchers take it far less personally when somebody hits one out on them.

In any event, attitudes have changed and there is far less of the kind of philosophy that used to be a set of daily Beatitudes to fellows like Early Wynn. The way one man best remembers Mr. Wynn, who pitched a long time and won a lot of games, is with his spikes off, his feet propped up on a stool in front of his locker out at the White Sox ball park, a bottle of beer in his hand and a great deal to say.

He was telling a man about why he spent so much time throwing so close to so many hitters. "The batter's box basically belongs to the guy with the bat," he grudgingly conceded, "but there's these six inches more that he always wants to take. Those six inches are part of my office and I do not recall ever inviting anyone else inside.

"All I'm doing is enforcing my 'no trespassing' sign."

For the record, Mr. Wynn had more than his share of on-field litigation in such matters and a great many clenched fists were waved in his direction.

It was the brushback or beanball (depending on whether you spoke to the pitcher or the hitter) which caused and still causes virtually all baseball fights. With fewer such pitches thrown, you obviously have fewer fights.

Essentially, baseball fights (most of which are greatly enjoyed by fans of Marcel Marceau and others who enjoy pantomime) begin in one of two ways.

The most common starts with a pitcher whose feelings are hurt (as Wynn's were) because he believes the batter is "taking liberties" with him. "Taking liberties" may run the gamut from leaning too far over the plate to hitting the ball out of the park. In such cases, the hitter glares at the pitcher a great deal. Sometimes he throws his bat. This second option does not happen very often, which is a great break for the third baseman, who generally gets hit with it by mistake.

Then there is the over-enthusiastic slide on the base-path. This dates back to that era when old base-runners filed their spikes and infielders threw dirt in their faces in self defense. Those days are definitely gone, but every once in a while some ballplayer picks up Ty Cobb's biography and all hell breaks loose for the next three games.

For the most part, the ensuing fights are only slightly less violent than the morning Herbie stole Melvin's peanut butter sandwich during recess at the Happy Hour Nursery School.

History shows that the real fights take place in the minors where both the meal money and the stadium lights leave something to be desired and a blend of rookies in a hurry and veterans trying to stop the clock can become seriously volatile.

What may have been the best baseball fight anywhere took place 30 years ago this summer in the American Association when Ralph Houk was managing Denver and the late Johnny Keane had the Cardinals' farm at Omaha.

A man named Frank Barnes, pitching for Omaha, was having great fun knocking down the Denver hitters. Consequently, when the Denver third base coach (who later became known for other things), a man named Tom Lasorda, fielded a foul grounder, he casually took aim and threw it as hard as he could at Barnes' head.

Barnes (no fool) ducked and the ball sailed into the Omaha dugout where an infielder named Ed Jok picked it up. Mr. Jok might have been a minor league infielder but he led all of baseball in major league logic. With the calm of a Biblical patriarch in search of an eye for an eye, he fired it across the field into the Denver dugout.

What followed was one of the classic baseball riots of all time. Even today, Ralph Houk would tell you that he doesn't think he hit anybody—but he still won't swear to it.

Such things happen a great deal in the minors and it is admittedly a surprise when major leaguers tear themselves away from their stock portfolios long enough to get angry at anybody.

Of course, the big leagues will have to go some to compete with a pair of former major leaguers who, assigned to the same minor league roster, had what is probably the strangest fight in the history of all of baseball. In happier days, each had played for major league pennant winners.

Now they were flying through the night aboard an airplane from Phoenix to another Pacific Coast League city when they suddenly raced down the aisle screaming and began pounding the hell out of each other.

At first, everyone was amazed to see two baseball players work themselves into such a physical fury.

Later, reliable witnesses explained they were fighting over the ownership of a bottle of whiskey.

## JOHN GALLAGHER

*"A relief pitcher is on the way."*

Bill James has been described (by Dan Okrent) as an eminent baseball analyst ''able to squeeze brilliant and fluid theories from rock-hard columns of statistics.'' That is true. But he is also the proprietor of *The Bill James Historical Baseball Abstract,* which another Bill—Billy Crystal—has called ''absolutely mahvelous.'' Crystal is right too. This story, from that book, is the flip side of Bill James: statistics, yes—but what have statistics got to do with the guy who'd like to put down ten grand on Thibodaux to beat New Iberia next Saturday?

# Life Begins at Houma

## BILL JAMES

BILL THOMAS won 383 games in the minor leagues, and never threw a pitch at the major league level. His won/lost records for most of his career aren't very good—a seemingly endless series of 15–18 and 20–17 seasons—but he was one of those guys who had a talent for picking losers. He went 16–17 with Charleroi in the Middle Atlantic League in 1927, but you have to understand that the rest of the pitchers on the Charleroi team were 26–58, so he was almost 200 points better-than-team. It took him several years to reach the good minor leagues (he took the 1930 season off, for some reason) and when he did it was with Indianapolis, a middle-of-the-pack American Association team, and later he pitched for several years with Portland and Hollywood, then the weak sisters of the Pacific Coast League. His records in what would now be called Triple A baseball total up to a little below .500. He was 17–9 for Mobile in the Southern League in 1944, and the team still finished eleven games under .500.

In 1946 he was forty-one years old, and he was pitching for Houma, which emerged as the powerhouse of the Evangeline League. Houma played 131 games that year. Thomas won 35 games and lost 7. Now granted, that wasn't much of a league, but 35 wins are a bunch. No other pitcher, anywhere in organized baseball, at any age, has won 35 games in any other season since 1922.

What happened then I have never been exactly able to figure out. The 1947 *Baseball Guide* contains a one-paragraph note ''Five Banned in Gambling Probe,'' and says that on January 25, 1947, five players were placed on Organized Baseball's Ineligible List after an investi-gation of allegations involving thrown games and asso-ciation with known gamblers. Thomas was one of the five. He was suspended for ''conduct detrimental to baseball''—something which, apparently, extended be-yond winning thirty-five games at the age of forty-one.

An article by George Hilton in the 1982 *Baseball Research Journal* discusses the Evangeline League scan-dal, which was the only one of its kind to hit organized baseball since 1919. It began when the owner of the Abbeville franchise, Mr. I. N. Goldberg, alleged that the players of Houma and Alexandria had conspired to fix the outcomes of three playoff games (the league had one of those consarned multitiered playoff systems, which beg to be abused). The allegation against Thomas was that he had been in contact with gamblers who had asked him to throw games; he testified that he had, indeed, been approached by one such gambler, but had categorically refused any such involvement, and had not gone even so far as to learn the man's name. Unfortu-nately for Thomas, Judge Landis had established the principle of expulsion for guilty knowledge.

As Jim Baker points out, this raises some fascinating questions, such as ''Where do you go to place a bet on the Evangeline League?'' I mean, do you just walk into a Las Vegas casino one afternoon and say, ''I'd like to put down ten grand on Thibodaux to beat New Iberia next Saturday''? How many bets do you think you can win like this before they find you hanging from the nearest cactus? Apparently, illegal gambling was then flourishing in Louisiana, and the primary beneficiary of these dark deeds was an Alexandria bookmaker.

Clearly, some seedy things were going on down there;

charges extended as far as money being handed into the dugout from the stands during and after games. It is not clear whether or not any games were successfully thrown; a Houma player, years later, said that all of the games that were supposed to be thrown were won by mistake, as the would-be Rothsteins were carrying insufficient protection, and one player accidently hit a double while attempting to strike out.

Anyway, for associating with these ne'er-do-wells, Thomas was banned from baseball. It is clear that Bill Thomas had not thrown any games; for one thing, he was 5–0 during the playoffs. He was angry and defiant about the banishment. Out of baseball, he worked as a roustabout in Texaco's refinery at Houma, and alternately threatened to sue and petitioned for reinstatement, which eventually was granted. Almost three years later. The next time he broke camp he was forty-five.

In 1950 Thomas went 23–8 for two teams in the Evangeline League. Then he moved on to the Rio Grande Valley League, where he pitched nine more games and pushed his season's record to 26–12. After that season, though, he was to win only twenty-three more games in the minor leagues.

Thomas was basically a control pitcher, and control pitchers (a) don't win with bad ball clubs, and (b) are always the last ones to catch a break. In almost 6,000 innings of minor league baseball, he walked less than two men per nine innings. Thomas would now be about eighty, and he may still be alive; it is not known where he lives or where he was buried. He was probably not a major league pitcher or at the least not very much of a major league pitcher, but at any level it doesn't seem right to let the memory of such a remarkable career drop entirely from sight. How many games he might have won with good minor league teams, and if he had had the four missing seasons of his career, it is impossible to imagine. It was a great service of Ray Nemec, Robert Hoie and the other SABR members who compiled the book, *Minor League Baseball Stars,* which traces the statistical outline of Thomas' career, and allows us to envision a memory of him.

Meet Davy Jones (also David Jefferson ''Kangaroo'' Jones), born June 30, 1880, at Cambria, Wisconsin, and witness to the day Germany Schaefer stole first base! Witness also to a side of Ty Cobb not everybody saw.

# ''Hurray, Schaefer!''

## DAVY JONES

Two or three years ago Base Ball critics in the East and West began to agitate the question of signaling by the umpires to announce their decisions.

At first the judges of play did not want to signal. They thought it detracted from their dignity to go through a dumb show resembling the waving of the arms of a semaphore.

That did not deter the Base Ball critics from their stand. With good-natured persistence they urged upon the umpires the necessity of the new idea, and by and by the officials of the league took up the subject and suggested that it would be worth a trial.

It was finally experimented with and has been one of the very best moves in Base Ball as a medium of rendering decisions intelligible, and now there is not an umpire but uses his arms to signal. If he did not, two-thirds of the spectators at the immense crowds, which have been patronizing Base Ball for the last two years, would be wholly at sea as to what was transpiring on the field, except as they might guess successfully.

Even the older umpires, who were more loath to give their consent to the new system on the field, are now frank enough to admit that it has been of invaluable assistance to them in making their decisions understood when the size of the crowd is such that it is impossible to make the human voice carry distinctly to all parts of the field.

—*Spaulding's Base Ball Guide,* 1909

OH, THE game was very different in my day from what it's like today. I don't mean just that the fences were further back and the ball was deader and things like that. I mean it was more *fun* to play ball then. The players were more colorful, you know, drawn from every walk of life, and the whole thing was sort of chaotic most of the time, not highly organized in every detail like it is nowadays.

I was playing in the Big Leagues in 1901, when Mr. William McKinley was President, and baseball attracted all sorts of people in those days. We had stupid guys, smart guys, tough guys, mild guys, crazy guys, college men, slickers from the city, and hicks from the country. And back then a country kid was likely to *really* be a country kid. We'd call them hayseeds or rubes. Nowadays I don't think there's much difference between city kids and country kids. Anyway, nothing like there used to be.

Back at the turn of the century, you know, we didn't have the mass communication and mass transportation that exist nowadays. We didn't have as much schooling, either. As a result, people were more unique then, more unusual, more different from each other. Now people are all more or less alike, company men, security minded, conformity—that sort of stuff. In everything, not just baseball.

Talk about colorful guys, take Rube Waddell or Germany Schaefer. I doubt if fellows like that could exist in baseball today. Too rambunctious, you know. They'd upset the applecart.

I played with Germany Schaefer on the Chicago Cubs in 1902, and again on the Detroit Tigers later on. What a man! What stunts he could pull! I used to laugh at that guy till I cried. Far and away the funniest man I ever saw. He beat Charlie Chaplin any day in the week.

One day when I was on the Tigers—I think it was 1906, my first year with Detroit—we were in Chicago, playing the White Sox. Red Donahue was pitching for us and Doc White, that great little left-hander, was pitching for the White Sox. We were behind, 2–1, going into the ninth inning. Then in the ninth we got a man on first base with two out, and the next man up was Donahue, who was easily one of the worst hitters in the league. So Bill Armour, who was managing Detroit then, looked up and down the bench and spotted Germany Schaefer sitting there—talking, as usual, to whoever would listen.

"How would you like to go up there and pinch-hit?" Bill asked him.

"Sure," he says, "I'd love to. I always could hit Doc White."

Meanwhile, Red Donahue is already getting all set in the batter's box. Red was an awful hitter, but there was nothing in the whole world he loved more than digging in at that plate and taking his cuts.

"Hey, Red," yells Schaefer, "the manager wants me to hit for you."

"What?" Red roars. "Who the hell are you to hit for me?" And he slams his bat down and comes back and sits way down at the end of the bench, with his arms folded across his chest. Madder than a wet hen.

Well, Schaefer walked out there and just as he was about to step into the batter's box he stopped, took off his cap, and faced the grandstand.

"Ladies and gentlemen," he announced, "you are now looking at Herman Schaefer, better known as Herman the Great, acknowledged by one and all to be the greatest pinch hitter in the world. I am now going to hit the ball into the left field bleachers. Thank you."

Then he turned around and stepped into the batter's box. Of course, everybody's giving him the old raspberry, because he never hit over two or three home runs in his life. But by golly, on the second ball Doc White pitched he did just exactly what he said he would: he hit it right smack into the left-field bleachers.

Boy oh boy, you should have seen him. He stood at that plate until the ball cleared the fence, and then he jumped straight up in the air, tore down to first base as fast as his legs would carry him, and proceeded to slide headfirst into the bag. After that he jumped up, yelled "Schaefer leads at the Quarter!" and started for second.

He slid into second—yelled "Schaefer leads at the Half!"—and continued the same way into third and then

home. After he slid into home he stood up and announced: "Schaefer wins by a nose!" Then he brushed himself off, took off his cap, and walked over to the grandstand again.

"Ladies and gentlemen," he said, "I thank you for your kind attention."

Back on the bench everybody was laughing so hard they were falling all over themselves. Everybody except Red Donahue. He's still sitting there at the end of the bench with his arms folded, like a stone image, without the slightest expression of any kind on his face.

The next day we went back to Detroit to play against Cleveland, and Bill Armour promptly put Germany right into the lineup, at second base. And, of course, everybody at the game had read about what Schaefer had done the day before. So in the first inning, when Schaefer comes up to bat for the first time, the crowd naturally gives him a terrific ovation. "Hurray, Schaefer!" And the stands are buzz, buzz, buzzing about what he'd done the day before.

Unfortunately, the Cleveland pitcher that day was Addie Joss, who Schaefer couldn't hit with a paddle. A corking good pitcher. Three swings, and Schaefer strikes out. Never came close to the ball.

The second time at bat it's still "Hurray, Schaefer!" but not quite as loud as the first time. Well, he strikes out again, just as badly as before. Third time up, no commotion at all. Silence. This time he popped up.

The fourth time it's Schaefer's turn to bat it's the ninth inning, I'm on first, and we're two runs behind. And as he approaches the plate for the last time that day the crowd starts to make just as much noise as they did the first time. Only this time they're all yelling, "Take him out. Take the bum out!"

Ha! That's baseball. A hero one day and a bum the next. But always lots of laughs. I saw all the great ones, you know, in *both* leagues. I was in the American League in 1901 and again from 1906 through 1913, and in the National League from 1902 through 1904. Actually, I played in *three* major leagues, because I jumped to the Federal League in 1914 and spent two years there. And, of course, I was in three World Series with the Detroit Tigers—1907, '08, and '09. So, all in all, there weren't very many topflight players between 1900 and 1915 who I didn't play either with or against at one time or another.

Funny thing, I never expected to be a ballplayer in the first place. I wanted to be a lawyer. Well, as a matter of fact I *became* a lawyer. I went to law school at Dixon College in Illinois and graduated in 1901, but I got to playing ball and never did go back to the law.

I received an athletic scholarship at Dixon, one that included both baseball and track. Actually, track was my real specialty back then. I was always very fast, fast enough to beat Archie Hahn several times before he won the Olympics in 1904. You probably don't remember Archie Hahn, but he was the fastest man in the world at the turn of the century. Won the 60-meter dash, the 100-meter dash, *and* the 200-meter dash in the 1904 Olympics. Ranks right up there with Jim Thorpe and Jesse Owens as one of the greatest runners who ever lived. Odd, isn't it, that Jim Thorpe and Jesse Owens are still very familiar names, but hardly anybody seems to remember Archie Hahn any more.

I also played baseball at Dixon College, and that led, accidentally, to my becoming a professional. In 1901, in my senior year, the Dixon team went up to Rockford, Illinois, to play an exhibition game with the Rockford Club in the Three-I League. I had a great day both at bat and in the field, and they offered me a contract: $85 a month. Well, I was a very poor boy, and the prospect of $85 a month right away, compared to years as a law clerk before I could start my own practice, made it hard to turn down. So I signed up and joined the Rockford Club right after graduation.

You realize, of course, that baseball wasn't a very respectable occupation back then. I figured I'd stay in it just a few years, and then go back to the law once I got on my feet financially. To give you an idea about its respectability, I was going with a girl at the time and after I became a professional ballplayer her parents refused to let her see me any more. Wouldn't let her have anything more to do with me. In those days a lot of people looked upon ballplayers as bums, too lazy to work for a living. So Margaret—that was her name— and I had to break up.

Later on I met another girl, a rare and lovely woman, and we got married. Married for 52 years before she passed away. I heard that Margaret married a doctor, a man who later became a famous heart specialist at the Mayo Clinic, and that they lived in Rochester, Minnesota.

Well, a few years ago, believe it or not, I ran into Margaret once again, for the first time in nearly 50 years. Turned out that both of us had been very happily married, but were now both widowed. To make a long story short, we found out we still enjoyed each other's company and decided to get married, over half a century since we'd been high-school sweethearts. That was she who opened the door for you when you first got here.

Anyway, I played six weeks in the summer of 1901 with Rockford in the Three-I League, hit .384, fielded like a blue streak, and before the season was over I was sold to the Chicago Cubs. However, the Milwaukee Brewers in the brand-new American League made me a good offer, so instead of reporting to Chicago I jumped to Milwaukee. See, the American League was an outlaw league in 1901, and Milwaukee was one of the eight teams in the league that very first year.

The next year, 1902, the Milwaukee franchise was transferred to St. Louis and we became the original St. Louis Browns. So not only did I play in the American League the very first year of its existence, but I'm also a charter member of *two* of the teams in that league. Neither one of which exists any longer, a fact for which I assure you I can in no way be held responsible.

I'd been with the St. Louis club about two or three weeks in the 1902 season when we went to Chicago to play the White Sox. It was a rainy Saturday, and as we sat on the bench waiting for the game to begin somebody pointed out Mr. Comiskey, the owner of the White Sox. He was out there in the infield, with his pants rolled up, soaking up water with a couple of sponges and wringing them into a pail, trying to get the diamond in shape to play. That was my first sight of Charles A. Comiskey.

After the game that day I got a phone call from James A. Hart, the owner of the Chicago Cubs. He'd been pretty sore ever since I'd jumped from the Cubs to the American League the previous August. Mr. Hart said he'd like me to come over and talk with him at his office the next morning. Well, why not?

"I see you're going pretty good," he said to me, after I got there.

"Yes, that's right," I said. "We've got a good club."

"You know," he said, "I've lost a lot of good ballplayers to the American League, men like Clark Griffith and Jimmy Callahan, not to mention yourself. I'd like to try to get some of you fellows to move the other way. What would you think about jumping back to the Chicago Cubs?"

"Well," I said, "what have you got to offer?"

So he thought a minute, got up, walked into the next room, and sent the clerk for some cash. I guess he thought I'd find green cash more tempting than a check. (He was right.)

Finally he came back. "How about a two-year contract for $3,600 a year, the highest salary on the club, plus a $500 bonus that you can have right now. Here's the $500!"

Well, what could I do? I was playing for $2,400, and here was a 50 percent raise plus $500 in cold cash stacked up right in front of me. And, after all, I wasn't even twenty-two years old yet. Besides, everybody was jumping all over the lot in those days: Sam Crawford, Larry Lajoie, Clark Griffith, Willie Keeler, Cy Young, Jack Chesbro, Ed Delahanty. You name him, he was jumping from one league to the other.

So I signed.

Mr. Hart immediately called up the ball park and got the manager of the Cubs, Frank Selee, on the phone. "I've just signed a new outfielder," he said. "I won't tell you who he is, but take it from me he's OK. Put him in center field this afternoon."

So Selee went out on the field and one of the players told me later he looked sort of bewildered.

"Mr. Hart just called me," he said. "He says we've got a new outfielder and I should play him today, but he won't tell me who he is. Things are getting funnier and funnier around this place."

For my part, I left Mr. Hart and went for a long walk. I didn't want to go back to my hotel while the Browns were still there, because I wasn't especially anxious to see any of my teammates. My *former* teammates, that is. After I was pretty sure they'd all gone out to the White Sox park, I went up to the room, packed my grip and bat bag—in those days, you know, we carried our own bats in a little bag—and took off for the Cubs' West Side Grounds at Lincoln and Polk Streets.

And that's the last time I jumped a ball club. Well, almost. The last time until 1914, anyway, when I jumped from the White Sox to the Pittsburgh club in the Federal League. But I was about all through by then, so it hardly counts.

I played three years in the Chicago Cubs' outfield, but in 1904 I got hurt and it looked as though I was finished. The next year I found myself back in the minors, with Minneapolis in the American Association. I came back strong, though, hit .346 that year, and at the end of the season I went back up to the Big Leagues with Detroit.

Which was a real break for me, of course, because, as you well know, we won the pennant in 1907, '08, and '09, and for seven years I got to play in the same outfield with two of the greatest ballplayers who ever lived, Ty Cobb and Sam Crawford. Of course, playing by the side of two fellows like that was a good deal like being a member of the chorus in a grand opera where there are two prima donnas.

I always got along with Sam just wonderfully. In a lot of ways we were very much alike. He's still one of my very best friends. Cobb, though—he was a very complex person—never did have many friends. Trouble was he had such a rotten disposition that it was damn hard to be his friend. I was probably the best friend he had on the club. I used to stick up for him, sit and talk with him on the long train trips, try to understand the man. He antagonized so many people that hardly anyone would speak to him, even among his own teammates.

Ty didn't have a sense of humor, see. Especially, he could never laugh at himself. Consequently, he took a lot of things the wrong way. What would usually be an innocent-enough wisecrack would become cause for a fist fight if Ty was involved. It was too bad. He was one of the greatest players who ever lived, and yet he had so few friends. I always felt sorry for him.

In many ways he was resented by a lot of people because he was so doggone good, and that plus being ignored because he had such a nasty disposition meant that the man was very lonely. Of course, he brought a lot of it on himself, no doubt about that. A lot of times it seemed as though he was just asking for trouble.

Like one time in Detroit, when Cobb was in a batting slump. When Cobb got in a slump you just couldn't talk to him. He'd get meaner than the devil himself. Well, we were playing Boston this day, and Ray Collins was pitching against us. Cobb never did hit Collins too well, so the idea of being in a slump and batting against Collins too didn't go down very well with Ty. He'd just as soon sit this one out.

In about the third or fourth inning of this game I got on base and Ty came up to bat. I watched him for the hit-and-run sign, like I always did, but he didn't flash any. Then suddenly, after the first pitch, he stepped out of the box and hollered down at me, "Don't you know what a hit-and-run sign is?" Yelled it right out at me.

Jake Stahl was the Boston first baseman and he said to me, "Boy, any guy would holler down here like that is nothing but a rotten skunk."

But I knew Cobb, so I just ignored him. Those were his ways, that's all. Well, the second pitch came in and curved over for strike two. And was Cobb ever mad then! He went over and sat down on the bench and yelled, "Anybody can't see a hit-and-run sign, by God, I'm not going to play with him." Meaning me.

He just sat there and wouldn't play. They had to put in another batter. All he wanted, of course, was to get out of the game because he couldn't hit that pitcher. That's all it was, and I was the fall guy. He put the blame on me.

Well, the next day he was still sulking. Wouldn't play, he said. Finally Mr. Navin, the president of the club, called him up to the front office and asked him what was going on.

"I won't play with Jones," Cobb said. "That bonehead can't even see the hit-and-run sign."

"Oh," Mr. Navin said, "suppose he did miss the sign, which the other players tell me he didn't. So what? That's no reason for you not to play. You're just making an excuse because you're not hitting."

"Who told you that?" says Cobb. "Just tell me, *who told you that?*"

"Never mind," Navin said, "that's none of your business. Now you're going to play today, and that's all there is to it. Otherwise you'll be suspended without pay. And it's out of the question to take Jones out of the game, so forget it."

Mr. Navin told me all that afterwards. Well, that shows what kind of a person Cobb could be. Picking on me, of all people! Practically his only friend on the club. But with all that, he was really *some* ballplayer. Corking!

I played in the outfield with Cobb and Crawford for seven years, 1906 through 1912, the greatest years in

Detroit's baseball history. Three pennants. What a team! I was generally the lead-off man in the batting order, because of my speed. Usually it was Jones leading off, then Germany Schaefer or Donie Bush, Sam Crawford batting third, Cobb fourth, Claude Rossman next, the first baseman, and then George Moriarty, the third baseman. Jimmy Delahanty was in there somewhere, and Charlie Schmidt, the big catcher.

Being the lead-off man, by the way, resulted in my holding the unique distinction of being the first man to ever face Walter Johnson in a major-league game. He broke in late in 1907, in a game against us, and since I led off, naturally I was the first man to face him. And that was the beginning of Walter's long and amazing career. The *very* beginning. Boy, could that guy ever fire that ball! He had those long arms, absolutely the longest arms I ever saw. They were like whips, that's what they were. He'd just *whip* that ball in there.

It was during those years, I think about 1908, that I saw Germany Schaefer steal first base. Yes, *first* base. They say it can't be done, but I saw him do it. In fact, I was standing right on third base, with my eyes popping out, when he did it.

We were playing Cleveland and the score was tied in a late inning. I was on third base, Schaefer on first, and Crawford was at bat. Before the pitcher wound up, Schaefer flashed me the sign for the double steal—meaning he'd take off for second on the next pitch, and when the catcher threw the ball to second I'd take off for home. Well, the pitcher wound up and pitched, and sure enough Schaefer stole second. But I had to stay right where I was, on third, because Nig Clarke, the Cleveland catcher, just held on to the ball. He refused to throw to second, knowing I'd probably make it home if he did.

So now we had men on second and third. Well, on the next pitch Schaefer yelled, "Let's try it again!" And with a blood-curdling shout he took off like a wild Indian *back to first base,* and dove in headfirst in a cloud of dust. He figured the catcher might throw to first—since he evidently wouldn't throw to second—and then I could come home same as before.

But nothing happened. Nothing at all. Everybody just stood there and watched Schaefer, with their mouths open, not knowing what the devil was going on. Me, too. Even if the catcher *had* thrown to first, I was too stunned to move, I'll tell you that. But the catcher didn't throw. He just stared! In fact, George Stovall, the Cleveland first baseman, was playing way back and didn't even come in to cover the bag. He just watched this madman running the wrong way on the base path and didn't know *what* to do.

The umpires were just as confused as everybody else. However, it turned out that at that time there wasn't any rule against a guy going from second back to first, if

that's the way he wanted to play baseball, so they had to let it stand.

So there we were, back where we started, with Schaefer on first and me on third. And on the next pitch darned if he didn't let out another war whoop and take off *again* for second base. By this time the Cleveland catcher evidently had enough, because he finally threw to second to get Schaefer, and when he did I took off for home and *both* of us were safe.

These are fond memories, you know. I haven't thought about these things in years. Yes, those were wonderful days. Of course, one sad thing, a lot of the boys didn't realize how short their baseball life would be, and they didn't prepare themselves for when their playing days would be over. I was very lucky, compared to most, having gone to college and all.

However, I never did return to the law. What happened was that I had a brother who worked in a drugstore back home in Cambria, Wisconsin, and on my baseball money I helped put him through a course in pharmacy at the University of Michigan. After he was through and had his license, we went into partnership and opened up Davy Jones' Drug Store in downtown Detroit. That was in 1910, while I was playing for Detroit, see.

Well, the thing was a huge success. After a home game I'd join him at the drugstore and jerk sodas and talk about the game. The fans loved it. Business was so terrific that after awhile we had *five* stores. I got so I was spending all my free time in the stores, and when we went on the road I took pharmacy textbooks along to study.

After I was through with baseball—that was in 1915, when I was thirty-five—I sublet my home in Detroit and went out to California for a vacation. I bummed around for a month or two, but soon I started to get restless. So I wound up taking a two-year course in pharmacy at the University of Southern California. I got my degree, came back and took my state board exam from the Michigan Board of Pharmacy, and stayed in the drug business until I retired, thirty-five years later.

But getting back to baseball, that story of Germany Schaefer running from second to first reminds me of another incident that happened when I was with the Chicago Cubs in 1902. We had a young pitcher on that club named Jimmy St. Vrain. He was a left-handed pitcher and a right-handed batter. But an absolutely terrible hitter—never even got a loud foul off anybody.

Well, one day we were playing the Pittsburgh Pirates and Jimmy was pitching for us. The first two times he went up to bat that day he looked simply awful. So when he came back after striking out the second time Frank Selee, our manager, said, "Jimmy, you're a left-handed pitcher, why don't you turn around and bat from the left side, too? Why not try it?"

Actually, Frank was half kidding, but Jimmy took him seriously. So the next time he went up he batted left-handed. Turned around and stood on the opposite side of the plate from where he was used to, you know. And darned if he didn't actually hit the ball. He tapped a slow roller down to Honus Wagner at shortstop and took off as fast as he could go . . . but instead of running to first base, he headed for *third!*

Oh, my God! What bedlam! Everybody yelling and screaming at poor Jimmy as he raced to third base, head down, spikes flying, determined to get there ahead of the throw. Later on, Honus told us that as a matter of fact he almost *did* throw the ball to third.

"I'm standing there with the ball in my hand," Honus said, "looking at this guy running from home to third, and for an instant there I swear I didn't know *where* to throw the damn ball. And when I finally did throw to first, I wasn't at all sure it was the right thing to do!"

## JOHN GALLAGHER

*"They're putting in a pinch-hitter for Whiffle."*

This article appeared in *Life* during the 1986 season.

# Delayed on Account of Rain

## PAT JORDAN

HARRY PLATT, 52, a squat, disheveled little man, glares out the window of the ticket booth—a wood structure about the size of a port-o-john. It's nine A.M. He is hemmed in on three sides by dozens of cardboard boxes rising almost to the ceiling. He hitches up his pants, and his elbow knocks a box to the floor, spilling its contents of baseball caps. Harry stares at the spilled caps, curses and then opens the window.

"Awright!" he says in a raspy voice. "Who's first?"

A boy of about 10 steps up to the window. A long line of similar boys stretches far out behind him, all the way to the gravel parking lot of Moana Stadium, home of the Reno Padres of the Class A California League.

Today is Hat Day, and the first 100 boys who purchase tickets for tonight's doubleheader against San Jose will receive a free souvenir hat that vaguely resembles the yellow and brown caps worn by the Padres. As business manager of the Padres, Harry Platt himself wears many hats. Among other things, he is paymaster, ticket seller and groundkeeper. His mood has already been soured by a torrential downpour that has left huge puddles all over the infield.

"I wanna small," says the first boy as he hands Harry some crumpled bills for a bleacher seat ticket. Harry fumbles through one of the boxes and thrusts a hat at the boy. The boy looks at it and checks inside. "This is a medium," he says, "I wanna small."

"We only got one size," says Harry. "Next!" The boy does not budge. He hands the hat back to Harry. Harry pulls his hands back as if refusing a summons. "I said, 'That's all we got!' " says Harry, hitching up his pants. "Don't worry, it'll fit. Next!" The boy tries the cap on. It falls below his ears and eyes. "See? Fits beautiful," says Harry. "Now, beat it!"

The team manager's office is located underneath the home plate bleachers. Its highest point is only six feet, so that the manager, who is exactly six feet tall, must move around his dark, musty office crouched over like an old stone-age savage in his lair. There is an open black medicine bag, spilling tape, in a corner; a wire shopping cart filled with broken bats and scuffed balls; a metal desk jammed up against the wall. It is noon. A portable fan stirs the air. The manager sits at the desk, illuminated by a bare, overhanging light bulb, making out his lineup for today's game. His name is Jack Maloof.

For 10 years, he played semi-pro and professional baseball in such places as Boulder, Colo.; Fairbanks, Alaska; Auburn, N.Y.; Orlando, Fla,; Tacoma; Honolulu; and Tokyo. This is his sixth season in management. He is 37 years old and balding. He has sad, green eyes, a droopy mustache and a chipped front tooth.

Maloof batted .402 in his first professional season as an outfielder, compiled a lifetime minor league average of .302 and yet never made it to the major leagues. He earned more than $15,000 only once in his career, when he played for the Seibu Lions in the Japanese major leagues in 1979. The Lions gave him a $50,000 signing bonus and a $50,000 salary. He responded by batting .290—good enough to make him the 17th top hitter in the league. But the following year the Lions failed to sign him to a new contract. "I was an American spray-hitter," Maloof explains. "You know, singles, doubles. They had plenty of Japanese singles hitters. They wanted a home run slugger."

No longer a player, Maloof insists that he has no regrets. "I played enough," he says. "Now my goal is to do the best job I can as a manager. Reno was a good place to begin." Maloof pauses a moment, spits into a coffee can and then looks up, those green eyes sad, and says, "I don't know if I'll ever make it to the bigs."

At six P.M. there's another heavy rain. Then at seven, a rainbow appears over Moana Stadium. Harry Platt, seated behind the desk in his tiny office, is screaming into the telephone. "For Christ's sake," he says, "I got 500 people in this ballpark for a doubleheader and the whole field is one goddamn puddle! All I'm asking is one helicopter—who'll miss it?''

Harry wipes his brow. The Nevada National Guard colonel on the other end of the receiver tries to explain to Harry that it is not the Guards' function to land helicopters behind second base of a minor league ballpark just so its whirling blades can dry off a drenched field and save the team's business manager the night's paid gate.

"Well, then, what the hell *do* I pay taxes for?" says Harry and slams down the receiver.

He puts his head in his hands and begins to moan softly. Suddenly he jumps up, leaves his office and scurries over to the concession stand behind the home plate bleachers, where a bearded man is selling popcorn, hot dogs, bowls of chili with onion, wine coolers and 48-ounce cups of Olympia beer to a long line of fans. The bearded man, who is wearing a white dress shirt buttoned at the throat and the wrists, bears a striking resemblance to Commander Whitehead of the old Schweppes tonic commercial. He seems flustered by all these people who are after his wares. A gold prospector, he does not like to leave his desert solitude except for a few weeks each year, when he comes down into town for a new grubstake. He waves Harry toward him.

"When the hell is the game gonna start?" he says. "I'm going nuts!"

"Soon!" says Harry. "Soon!"

"Jeez," says the man, "it better. Some kid just stole a bag of peanuts when I wasn't looking—then he had the nerve to bring 'em back and demand a refund."

Harry waves a hand as if he can't be bothered with such trivialities, then rushes off again with that duck-waddling, stomach-thrusting walk of his.

He reaches the open area between the home plate stands to his right and the third base bleachers to his left. The sun still has not set, and the rainbow is still up there, curving over Moana Stadium.

Harry counts the house. "A good crowd," he mumbles to himself and turns to check the playing field. The Reno players mill around their dugout talking to the boys and girls who have wandered onto the field. One of the players holds a baby in his arms; another pets a boy's mongrel dog; a third flirts with a teenage girl in a silver lamé blouse.

Across the field, the San Jose players sprawl across the exposed first base bleachers looking bored. Behind them is their bus.

At home plate three young umpires in blue, their hands clasped behind their backs, shake their heads ominously. The infield dirt is littered with puddles. The batter's box and the pitcher's mound are swamps. The umpires have spent too many nights in California towns like Bakersfield, Visalia, Fresno and Salinas and would

like nothing better than to call off tonight's doubleheader so they can go into Reno. But they have no jurisdiction over the game until it has officially begun. And deciding when to begin the game is Harry Platt's province.

"Grrr . . ." he mutters to himself. Harry hitches up his pants and waddles onto the playing field toward the umpires. The fans behind the Reno dugout applaud. Someone shouts, "Atta boy, Harry! It's about time!"

Harry confers with the umpires. The fans are strangely quiet, as if transfixed by the muffled confrontation. A farmer in bib overalls. A gas station attendant in a soiled chino shirt and pants. A woman in a nondescript cloth coat. A slatternly high school girl. A small boy with a dirty face and his new Reno baseball cap. A lone Oriental man in a navy windbreaker. A Mexican farm worker with Aztec cheekbones and a Zapata mustache. An old couple sitting on cushions to protect their bony behinds. Their son, a handsome, childlike man of about 30, sits beside them, his hands folded in his lap and his knees pressed together. He stares straight ahead with wide, unblinking, birdlike eyes.

The Padre loyalists are an army of the dispossessed. They are here because they have no place else to go tonight. They know all the players' names. They follow their progress, their wives, their children, as if the players were characters in a soap opera. The players, like the fans, are outsiders too. They are paid as little as $600 a month, and they live in cheap apartment complexes on the outskirts of town, sometimes six to a room. Their quarters have a few sticks of Danish modern furniture, a *Sporting News,* crumpled beer cans and an unfinished hand of solitaire on the scarred coffee table. An apartment has only four beds, so two of the players must take turns sleeping on the floor of the living room. When one of the players leaves his bed in the morning, another of the players on the floor rises groggily and wanders into the bedroom to take over.

Unlike the fans, however, the players will be here only a year, two at most, and then, if they are talented enough, they will move on to bigger towns, Las Vegas or Beaumont, Tex., maybe even San Diego, or be traded to Los Angeles or New York. The fans remain behind, sitting all summer at Moana Stadium watching a new batch of young athletes compete and dream.

It is dark now. The lights go on, and Harry Platt is brightly illuminated as he trots around the infield, pouring kerosene from a 10-gallon drum on top of all the puddles. The fans, players and umpires are dumbfounded. When Harry reaches home plate, he surveys his work, then withdraws a matchbook from his pants pocket. A fan gasps. Bullfight music explodes over the loudspeaker. Harry sets fire to the kerosene at home plate and steps back onto the infield grass.

Flames spring up, ripple down the first base line,

round the bag and head for second. The fans, momentarily stunned, begin to applaud and cheer as the flames cross second, head for third, round the bag and break for home. The bullfight music builds to a crescendo as the flames reach home plate. The entire dirt infield is enveloped in flames. Harry Platt, smiling, stands on the pitcher's mound with his hands on his hips. He is surrounded by flames, a sacrificial offering, then black smoke, and finally he disappears from sight. A fan cries out, "Harry'll burn himself up!" Another says, "Naw, Harry's awright."

When the fire dies down, Harry reappears, like a phoenix, out of the clouds of smoke. The puddles are gone now, and only a little of the infield grass has been singed black. Harry grabs a rake, and with the help of Maloof and three teenage assistants, he scrapes away at the infield dirt. Finally the doubleheader begins, two hours late.

Alone in the darkness beside the home plate stands, Harry Platt watches the first Reno batter step up to the plate. "If the fire got outta hand," says Harry, "so what? I always wanted a new stadium. Besides, the fans would be brokenhearted if I called the game. I remember one night—we made it Free Beer Night—when the opposing team's bus broke down in Modesto. I got all these people drinking forty-eight-ounce cups of beer and no ball game. Hell, they just sat there getting stoned and cheering batting practice for three hours." Harry shakes his head and chuckles.

"I had the National Guard here with tanks in the outfield one night," he says. "Every time a player hit a home run they fired a cannon. Shoot, we had fourteen home runs that night, and somebody called the cops. This cop tried to arrest the tank commander. 'You can't arrest me,' he said. 'I'm federal property.'

"Basically, this is a one-man operation. I work out of my office all winter long. It gets cold out here in the winter. I burn bats to keep warm. I got a bottle of Scotch for company, too. . . . Oh, yeah, and about a thousand ducks. They sit in the outfield. . . . What do you mean, what kind? A duck's a duck! Quack, quack. What the hell do I know from ducks? I'm a New Yorker. I took a Fifth Avenue bus to Central Park one day and ended up in Reno. How do I know where I went wrong in life? Listen, for years I told everyone I was Russian, and then my father passes away, and the newspaper obituary says he was born in Poland. I said to myself, 'This is terrible.' Well, it seems my father was born in a part of Poland occupied by the Russians in 1903, so he told everyone he was Russian all these years. Now I can't tell any more Polish jokes."

Suddenly, a small boy comes running up to Harry. He tells him that the bearded concession man is threatening to quit. Harry shakes his head, mutters and waddles off. The small boy trots alongside him. Harry hitches up his pants.

Bill Joyce was a third baseman and player-manager in the 1890s. Bill James came across the following quotation from Joyce in the 1916 *Spalding Base Ball Guide*.

# Not Like the Old Days

## BILL JOYCE

"BASE BALL today is not what it should be. The players do not try to learn all the fine points of the game as in the days of old, but simply try to get by. They content themselves if they get a couple of hits every day or play an errorless game. The first thing they do each morning is to get the papers and look at the hit and error columns. If they don't see them, some sportswriter gets terrific panning, of which he never hears.

"When I was playing ball, there was not a move made on the field that did not cause every one of the opposing team to mention something about it. All were trying to figure why it had been done and to watch and see what the result would be. That same move could never be pulled again without every one on our bench knowing just what was going to happen.

"I feel sure that the same conditions do not prevail today. The boys go out to the plate, take a slam at the ball, pray that they'll get a hit, and let it go at that. They are not fighting as in the days of old. Who ever heard of a gang of ball players after losing going into the clubhouse singing at the top of their voices? That's what happens every day after the games at the present time.

"In my days, the players went into the clubhouse after a losing game with murder in their hearts. They would have thrown out any guy on his neck if they had even suspected him of intentions of singing. In my days the man who was responsible for having lost a game was told in a man's way by a lot of men what a rotten ball player he really was. It makes me weep to think of the men of the old days who played the game and the boys of today. It's positively a shame, and they are getting big money for it, too."

*This is a chapter from Roger Kahn's book* The Boys of Summer, *which was published in 1971 and instantly became a linchpin in where-are-they-now literature. The Boys were, of course, the Brooklyn Dodgers of twenty years earlier. Here is one of them.*

# The Bishop's Brother

## ROGER KAHN

*Pozehnaj nas pane a tento pokrym ktory budeme pozivat, aby sme sa zachovali v tvojej svatej sluzbe. Amen.*

Bless us, Lord, and this food we are about to take that we may keep ourselves in Your holy service.

SLOVAKIAN MEALTIME PRAYER

GEORGE THOMAS Shuba, the second ball player who ever pinch-hit a World Series home run, had been wholly different from Clem Labine. He was a blunt, stolid athlete, a physical man mixing warmth with suspicion, a bachelor living alone and apart from most of the other players. His abiding love was hitting. All the rest was work. But touching a bat, blunt George became "The Shotgun," spraying line drives with a swing so compact and so fluid that it appeared as natural as a smile.

"Not yet," he said early in 1952, when I suggested a Sunday feature on his batting.

"Why not?"

"I haven't got enough hits."

A month later he approached and said, "Now."

"Now what?"

"I've gotten enough hits. Write the feature." It sounded like an order, but after the story appeared George said thank you for several days.

Joining such disparate people as Labine and Shuba was baseball's persistent encouragement toward self-involvement. "What did *you* throw?" reporters asked. Or, "What did *you* hit?" "How is *your* arm, *your* knee?" And, "*You* pitched a nice game" or "*You* really stroked that double." Even the converse from fans— "*You're* a bum, Clem; hey, George, *you're* bush"— focused a man's thinking on himself. During the prime of Clement Walter Labine and the boyhood of Clement Walter Labine, Jr., baseball was always pulling the father away on road trips and involving the father with

his own right arm rather than with his son's cares. It is the nature of the baseball business, and Shuba, through an episodic eight-year career in the major leagues, had decided privately, with no hints at all, to wait for the end of his baseball life before marrying. Now he had written:

It will be a great pleasure to have you visit our home in Youngstown. The wife and children (3) are waiting to meet you. I'll make a reservation for you at Williams Motel. Leave the Ohio Turnpike at Exit Seven. I put the Postal Inspectors there. As you know, I work for the Post Office.

Went to the last two games of the 1967 World Series at Boston. Saw the 1969 All-Star game at Washington. Drive carefully. See you soon.

On a long day's journey from Manhattan to Youngstown, one follows the appalling new American way west. You escape New York through a reeking tunnel that leads to the New Jersey Turnpike, where refineries pipe stench and smoke into the yellow air above grassless flats. It is three hours to the hills along the Pennsylvania Pike and your first sense or hope that mankind will not choke to death in another fifteen years.

The country levels as Pennsylvania meets Ohio, and the first Midwestern flatlands open toward prairies. Youngstown, 170,000 people strong, produces pig iron, steel, lamps and rubber, in a dozen factories along the Mahoning River, which bisects it. The Williams Motel, on the southern outskirts, turned out to be a brick rectangle, open on one side and comfortable but not lavish. Unlike the nearby Voyager Inn, it offers neither sauna baths nor pool. "We have your reservation," a lady said behind the front desk, a strong-featured woman who wore glasses with colorless plastic rims. "Mr. Shuba made it for you. Are you with the Post Office?"

"No."

"I thought maybe you were with the Post Office. Mr. Shuba puts the postal inspectors here."

"I'm not a postal inspector."

"Twenty-six," she said, losing interest and handing me a key.

I telephoned the main Youngstown post office and George came on, the voice plain, pleasant and tinged with a heaviness from East Europe. I knew then that George's father had been an immigrant. One never thought much about such things when traveling with the team. Black and white, not Slovak or Italian, was the issue.

"Is your room all right?" Shuba said.

"Fine. What are you doing?"

"Just finishing up."

"I mean what do you do at the post office?"

"Clerk-typist," Shuba said. "I knew the room would be good. I put all the inspectors in the Williams Motel. I'll be by soon as I finish. We've got a dinner you'll like."

"I haven't eaten much Slovakian food."

"It's lasagna," George said, sounding very serious. "Didn't you know? I married an Italian girl."

Unpacking, I remembered George on the day he had joined a radio engineer and myself batting a softball in Forest Park, St. Louis, and how, taking turns pitching, we worried about upsetting George's timing. "Just throw," he said, "just throw." He pulled low liners one after another in the park and that night did the same against a Cardinal pitcher called Cloyd Boyer. And then a year later a certain quickness went from his bat, and he was not a fierce hitter, although still dangerous, and outside the Schenley Hotel I saw him carrying a lightweight portable typewriter.

"What's that for, George?"

"Oh," he said, and looked around, as though afraid to be overheard. He winked. He had a plan. "I'm not gonna be through at thirty-five, like some. Maybe I'll be a reporter. Some of those guys go on working till seventy. Look at Roscoe McGowen. So I'm teaching myself how to type."

"George," I wanted to say, "to write, you have to read and know the language and how to organize and, damnit, spell." Thinking that, I said, "Could be a pretty good idea."

At the door leading into Room 26 at the Williams Motel, Shotgun Shuba, now a 46-year-old male clerk-typist in the U.S. Post Office in Youngstown, Ohio, appeared heavier. The face, a study in angles, sloping

brow, pointed nose, sharp chin, looked full. The middle was thick. But the sense was of solidity, rather than fat. I hadn't remembered him as so powerful. "You could still go nine," I said.

"Ah."

"Or pinch-hit."

"I got no time for that stuff. Come on. Dinner's waiting. We'll have some red wine. You like red wine? I'll drive."

In the car Shuba mentioned an old book I had written and a recent article. "About student rebels with long hair," he said, "or something like that."

"About the SDS coming apart in Chicago."

"Yeah. That was it. Why do you waste time writing about *them?*" There was no harshness in his voice. He simply did not understand why anyone who was a writer, a craft he respected, would spend time, thought and typing on the New Left.

"I try to write about a lot of things. It keeps you fresh."

George considered and turned into a street called Bent Willow Lane. "Kind of like exercising your mind, isn't it?" he said finally. "Yeah. That must be it. Move around. Do different things. Sure. Keeps up your enthusiasm." We had entered a middle-income neighborhood, of tract homes and roads that twisted, so drivers could not speed, and hyperfertilized lawns of brilliant, competitive green.

"I though Youngstown had mills, George," I said.

"Over there," he said, indicating the northeast. "You won't see any mills around where *I* live." He pulled up to a gray split-level, saying "This is it," and parked in an attached garage. "I finished this garage myself. I'm a home guy now. Wait till you meet my wife. She's taking courses at Youngstown University."

As we walked into her kitchen, Katherine Shuba, nine years younger than George, said a warm hello and called Marlene, Mary Kay and Michael, nine to four, who greeted me solemnly over giggles. Mrs. Shuba turned off a large color television that dominated the living room and placed the children at a kitchen table. We sat promptly in the dinette. It was six o'clock. Old ball players pursue the pleasures of eating with lupine directness. Suddenly George bowed his head. Katherine clasped her hands. The children fell silent.

"Bless us, Lord," George said, beginning Grace. Then, in almost apologetic explanation he said, "My father said Grace in Slovakian every day of his life. He died when I was pretty young, but I've never forgotten it."

"Well, it's something to remember."

"Ah," George said and we proceeded with an excellent Italian dinner, lasagna and salad, lightened, as George had promised, with red wine.

"So you don't play any more or coach?"

"I watch the kids. Maybe umpire a little. I don't coach small kids. It doesn't make sense to. With small kids, up till about fifteen, let 'em have fun. You know what's damn dumb? A father getting on a small kid, telling him this or that, stuff he can't use much yet. All the father does is spoil the fun."

"Somebody must have coached you."

"It was a different time, and nobody coached me that much anyway. My father, from the old country, what could he teach me about baseball? What did he know?"

"Your swing was natural."

"I worked very hard at it," Shuba said.

Katherine guided the children back to the living room, which was carpeted and comfortably furnished, but showed no sign that Shuba had hit for pennant winners or even that he had played professionally. "Oh, I've got some equipment still," he said. "Maybe after we finish the wine, if you like, we can have a catch."

He fished a half dozen gloves from the trunk of a car and we walked to the back of the house. Shuba's home shares three acres of greensward with other houses, framing a common play area. "If my little guy wants," Shuba said, "he can do some hitting here."

The dusk light held as we started to throw. Shuba did not have an outstanding major league arm. Scouts described it as uncertain, or weak. Now he cocked that arm and fired easily. The ball shot at my Adam's apple and I knew, with a clutch of anxiety, that I was overmatched.

In *Gamesmanship*, Stephen Potter describes that clutch seizing you on a tennis court when an opponent's service turns out to be overwhelming and you return it forty feet beyond the base line. "Cry, 'Where was it?' " Potter recommends.

" 'Where was what?'

" 'My shot, of course.'

" 'Why, it was out. It went over the fence back there.'

" 'Very well. In the future please indicate clearly whether my shots are in or out.' "

The Shubas of Youngstown live removed from English drollery and there was nothing clever or sensible to call at George. Weak or strong, he had a major league arm, and I knew what I would have to do, and hoped I could. Aim at face height and, while appearing to work easily, throw hard by snapping the forearm as I released the ball. That way there could be a rhythm to the catch, a kind of exchange. A good catch is made of sight, sensation, sound, all balancing from one side to the other. The ball is in white flight. Red stitches turning, it whacks a glove; it is back in flight and whacks the other mitt. You can tell quickly from the sound and the speed of the throws and even from the spin what is going on, who has the better arm.

George took my throw and returned it, again hard. My glove felt small. You try to catch a ball in the pocket, so that it strikes the leather at a point slightly lower than the webbing between the thumb and forefinger of the hand within the glove. There is control there without pain. Catch a baseball farther down and it stings. Catch it farther up and you lose control. When you catch a ball in the webbing, you may not realize that you have made a catch. Each point of impact creates a different sound: thin at the webbing, dull toward the heel, resonant and profoundly right in the pocket. Sound tells when you are playing catch, how the other man is grabbing them.

Shuba delivers a heavy ball; it smarts unless caught exactly right. Mostly he throws waist high, moving the ball from one side to the other. I caught mindlessly, ignoring slight stinging to concentrate on my throws. They sailed true, but after ten minutes a twinge raked the inside of my right elbow. We caught in silence, communicating, as it were, with ball and glove. George was studying me and I could feel his eyes and it was a warm evening and I was wondering about my arm and beginning to sweat.

"You've got good body control," Shuba called.

"Hey. You've made my day."

Ebullient, I relaxed. As soon as the next throw left my hand, I knew it was bad. The ball sailed low, but fairly hard to Shuba's backhand. Nimbly, angrily, he charged, scooped the ball on a short hop and fired at my face. The throw thwacked the small glove, low in the pocket, burning my hand.

"What are you trying to do," Shuba said, "make me look bad?"

"No, George," Then very slowly: "That's the way I *throw*."

"You're trying to make me look bad," Shuba said, pressing his lips and shaking his head.

"George, George. Believe me." All the years the other writers had made jokes—"Shuba fields with his bat"—had left scars. *They* should have played catch with him, I thought.

Half an hour of light remained. "Come on, George," I said. "Show me the old neighborhood."

"What for?"

"I want to see where you started playing ball."

"I don't know why you'd care about something like that," Shuba said, but led me back to the car.

Fernwood Street was where he lived when Bent Willow Road was part of a forgotten farmer's pasture. Wooden frame houses rise close to one another on Fernwood. Each one is painted white. "This neighborhood hasn't changed in forty years," Shuba said.

"Mostly Slovakians?"

"All Slovakians."

His father, John, or Jan, Shuba, left a farm in eastern

Czechoslovakia during 1912 and settled in Youngstown, where other Slovak Catholics had come, and took a job in a mill. George does not know why his father left Europe, but the reason was probably economic. Before 1930 Slovakian emigration was coincident with crop failure. Since then it has been political, to escape Hitler or Soviet Communism. Slovakians have contending symbols. The *drotar* is an itinerant tinker, never anxious to settle down, unable to make use of the resources of the soil. A cry rang through old Slovakia: "*Drotar* is here; have you something to repair?" Slovakians say that *drotari* were the first to emigrate to America. After the long journey, nomadic longings spent, *drotari* settled into jobs in mines and mills. The old itinerants then built fixed, unchanging neighborhoods. The other symbol is based on the historic figure Janosik, who fled a Slovakian seminary in the seventeenth century. Slovakia still was feudal and any lord had power of life and death, but Janosik became a bandit, along the lines of Robin Hood. Caught at length, he was hanged. Disciples of Janosik were called *zbojnici*. When *zbojnici* and their idolators found the relative freedom of the United States, they turned against the romance of roguery and, like Shotgun Shuba, stood strong for law, obedience and the Church.

"We like to keep things the way they were," Shuba said. He parked on Fernwood, in a dead-end block. All the houses rose two stories. "Here's where I first played," he said. "In this street. Day after day. Three on a side, when I was little. That's good baseball, three on a side. Each kid gets a chance." Tall maples made borders at the sidewalks. "We played so hard, when we were kids, you'd have thought we were playing for money.

"It was a big family. My brother John is a steel worker in a mill. Ed is a photographer for the Youngstown *Vindicator*. You know about my brother Joe. He's doing very good in the Church as a monsignor, in Toronto, Canada. I'm proud of him. Counting the ones born in Czechoslovakia there were eleven of us. I was the last. Some died over there. I had one brother died here. He got the flu. They didn't have fancy medicines. My mother gave him a lot of soup. Soup was good for the flu, but that brother died."

We were walking down Fernwood toward ball fields. "This is Borts Park," Shuba said. "Mrs. Borts gave it to the city. When I got older, instead of playing in the street, I played in Borts Park. I was a second baseman."

"Your father must have been proud of you."

We continued under the tall maples. "You don't understand the way it was. My father was forty-five years old when I was born. He never saw me play. Old country people. What did they care for baseball? He thought I should go and work in the mills like him and I didn't want to. I wanted to play."

The nearest diamond at Borts Field was bare; patches of grass had been worn off. "Boy, did I play here," Shuba said. "I had that quick bat. One year there was a Dodger tryout. It was 1943. I was seventeen, not in the mills. I was working in a grocery store. And at the cemetery on Sundays I'd pack black earth to fill around the graves. They could plant flowers in it. I'd get ten cents a box for the black dirt.

"The Dodgers didn't come to sign me. They wanted a pitcher. Alex Maceyko. They had me playing third. I had the quick bat, but Wid Matthews, who Rickey liked, was the scout and he signed somebody, Alex I guess, who never did much, and I went home, and forgot about it. Then it was February. I remember all the snow. Somebody come to the house on Fernwood and said, 'George, my name is Harold Roettger. I'm with the Brooklyn Dodgers. I want to see you about a contract.'

"I let him in and we sat down and he said he was going to offer me a bonus of $150 to sign. But I'd only collect if I was good enough to stay in baseball through July 1. I thought, hell, wouldn't it be better, a big outfit like the Dodgers to give $150, no strings or nothing? But that was the offer and I took it."

Night had come. Borts Field was quiet. "Well, George," I said, "your mother must have been proud."

"Ah," Shuba said. "You know what she told me. 'Get a job in the mills like Papa. There's lots of better ball players than you up there.' "

The night was warm and very still. "All right. I'll drive you to another part of the neighborhood," George said. It was so dark that all I could see were house lights and a bar with argon and neon signs advertising beer. George angled the car toward a corner grocery. "Dolak's," he said. "Where I worked. I loaded potatoes, fifty pounds to the bag, down in the basement, and carried them up. Years in the minors, they didn't pay me much. I was a ball player, but I still had to come back winters and load bags of potatoes for Dolak."

The signs in the store window were hand-lettered. "SPECIAL," one read, "HALUSKI."

"Like ravioli," Shuba said. "I delivered for Dolak, too, while I was in the bush leagues. Three miles from here is the cemetery where I packed the black dirt. I worked here and I walked to the other work and in the cold it was a long way. A long way a long time ago."

When we returned to the split-level on Bent Willow, Katherine was studying a text on the psychology of preschool children. She is a full-faced woman and she looked up with tired eyes, but cheerful to see people, and closed the book.

"We're going downstairs to talk," George said.

"Can I bring you anything?"

"Bring the V.O."

George loped downstairs. The large cellar was partly

finished. A table and two chairs stood in one corner. Files had been pressed against a wall nearby. Farther along the same wall old uniforms hung from a clothing rack. Across the room was a toilet, which George had not yet gotten around to enclosing. The floor was linoleum, patterned in green and white squares.

I walked to the rack; all the uniforms were Dodger blue and white. Across one shirt letters read "BEARS," for the Mobile farm team; across another "ROYALS," for Montreal. The old Brooklyn uniform bore a large blue Number 8 on the back.

"Let me show you some things." Shuba opened a file and took out scrapbooks. He turned the pages slowly without emotion.

"They started me at New Orleans, but I wasn't ready for that, and I came back to Olean and led the league in home runs that first year."

"So you kept the $150."

"Yeah, but they shoulda risked it."

Katherine came with the drinks. "Then to Mobile," George said, "and they moved me to the outfield. They were thinking of me for the major leagues and I didn't have, you know, that major league infielder's glove. But I knew about my bat and one day in Montreal a year or two later, the manager says to me in batting practice, where everyone was supposed to take four swings, 'Hey, Shuba, how come you're taking five?' I told him, 'Look, let somebody else shag flies. I'm a hitter.' "

I laughed, but George was serious. Nothing about hitting amused him. I told him Arthur Daley's story of a catcher chattering at Charlie Gehringer at bat. Finally Gehringer turned and said, "Shut up. I'm working."

"I'm in Mobile," Shuba said. "It's '47. I hit twenty-one homers. Knock in 110 runs. Next spring at Vero Rickey says, 'George, we're sending you back to Mobile. Fine power but not enough average. We can't promote you till you're a .300 hitter.' I shorten up. It's '48. I bat .389. The spring after that he sends me to Mobile *again*. 'Nice batting,' Rickey says, 'but your power fell off. We need someone who can hit them over that short right-field wall in Ebbets Field.' "

"What could I say? As long as he could option me, you know, send me down but keep me Dodger property, Rickey would do that so's he could keep some other guy whose option ran out. Property, that's what we were. But how many guys you know ever hit .389 and never got promoted?"

"There's no justice in the baseball business, George," I said.

The high-cheeked, Slavonic face turned hard. "The Saints want justice," he said. "The rest of us want mercy."

"I thought you had some fun," I said.

"It wasn't fun. I was struggling so much I couldn't enjoy it. Snider, Pafko, Furillo, they weren't humpties. I was fighting to stay alive. To play with guys that good was humbling. And I was kidded a lot about my fielding. In 1953 I went out to left field in Yankee Stadium for the second game of the Series. They're bad shadows out there in the fall. You remember I took you out and walked you around to show you the shadows and the haze from cigarette smoke.

"I went out and in the first inning someone hit a line drive and I didn't see it good and kind of grabbed. The ball rolled up my arms, but I held on to it. With two out, somebody else hit a long one into left center and maybe I started a little late, but I just got a glove on it and held it. When I came back to the dugout, Bobby Morgan said, very loud, 'Hey, I think they're going for our weak spot.' "

I laughed again. "Hey," Shuba said. "That's not funny. What he should have said was 'Nice catch.' "

"Now something *funny*, that came from an usher. I wasn't going good, and by this time all the bosses, O'Malley, Bavasi and Thompson, are Catholics, and my brother gets promoted to monsignor and word gets around. It's real early and I'm not hitting at all. Some usher hollers down, 'Hey, George. It's a good thing your brother's a bishop.' "

George smiled and sipped.

"When did it really end?" I said.

"All the time Rickey's keeping me in the minors doesn't do me any good and one year in Montreal I rip up my knee ligaments. That's where it started to end. When I made the club to stay in '52 that knee was gone already. It just kept getting worse and worse. Around 1955, I was only thirty-one, but the knee was so bad I couldn't do much. So I quit. That's all there was.

"I tried the sporting goods business. Up and down. So I went to work for the Post Office, steady and safe."

"Does all the excitement and the rest seem real to you now?"

"Oh, yeah. It's real." George was drumming his fingers on the wooden table.

"What do you think of it?"

"Doesn't mean much. When somebody would come up and ask for an autograph, I'd say, 'Is this for a kid?' And if it was, I'd give it to him. But if he said no, if it was for a man, I'd say, 'Ah. Don't be foolish. What does a grown man want something like that for?' I had my laughs. One day against the Cubs, Hank Sauer was on first and Ralph Kiner was on third and neither one could run. I hollered, 'Look for the double steal.' But what does it mean? Ruth died. Gehrig died."

The glasses were empty. He called and Katherine came downstairs and looked hopefully at George, wanting to be invited into the conversation, but Shuba has a

European sense of a woman's place. "Why don't you come upstairs and sit with me?" she said.

"Because we're talking," Shuba said. "Men's talk."

"There was this time," he said after fresh drinks had come, "in the World Series when I pinch-hit the home run."

"Sure—1953. Off Allie Reynolds."

"That's not what I'm talking about," Shuba said. "It was the first game of that Series and Reynolds was fast and the fellers were having trouble seeing the ball and he's got a shutout. I come up in the fifth and he throws that first pitch. I never saw it. It was a strike. If it had been inside, it would have killed me. Reynolds was in sun and I was in shadow. I never saw the ball. The next pitch he curved me. I only saw a little better. I was swinging, but I went down on one knee." Shuba was a formful batter, always in control; slipping to a knee was as humiliating as falling flat. "Now the next pitch. I still wasn't seeing the ball good, but I took my swing. My good swing. I hit it and it went to right field and I knew it would be long but maybe the right fielder could jump and as I trotted to first base I was saying, 'Hail Mary, get it up higher. Hail Mary.'

"Only the second time in history anybody pinch-hit a home run in the World Series," Shuba said, his face aglow. "But it wasn't me. There was something else guiding the bat. I couldn't see the ball, and you can think what you want, but another hand was guiding my bat."

"I don't know, George. Birdie Tebbetts was catching once when a batter crossed himself. Birdie called time, and crossed *himself*. And he told the hitter, 'Now it's all even with God. Let's see who's the better man.' "

"I don't care what Tebbetts did. Another hand was guiding my bat."

"Do you remember Ebbets Field, George? Now, if you close your eyes, can you see it?"

"Ah. That don't mean nothing."

"What means something?"

"The Church."

"I mean in this life."

He sprang up, reaching into a top drawer in the nearest file. "Marks in school," he said. "Look at Marlene's." He put one of the girl's report cards in front of me, then opened a notebook in which he had recorded her marks from term to term. "She had some trouble with arithmetic here in the second grade, but my wife talked to the Sister and worked with Marlene at home. Then Mary Kay . . ." He talked for another ten minutes about the way his children fared in school and how he, and his wife, kept notebook entries of their progress. He was still talking about the children when Katherine came downstairs again and without being asked refilled our glasses. "All that baseball was a preparation," Shuba

said. "You have certain phases in your life. Baseball prepared me for this. Raising my family."

"Which is more important?"

"This is the real part of my life."

"So all the rest was nothing?"

"Not nothing. Just not important. You do something important. Write. But playing ball." He jerked his head and looked at the beams in the cellar ceiling, "What the hell is that?"

"You might not understand this, or believe me, but I would have given anything to have had your natural swing."

"You could have," George said.

"What?" I said. "What do you mean I could have?" And I saw, again, George standing in to hit as I first saw him, in 1948, when I was twenty and a copyboy and he was twenty-four and trying to become a major leaguer. It was a very clear, bright picture in my mind, and I could not see the pitcher or the crowd or even whether it was day or night. But I still saw Shuba. It was late in the year, when they bring up the good youngsters for a few games. He balanced on the balls of the feet as he waited for the pitch, holding the bat far back, and there was confidence and, more than that, a beauty to his stance. My father said, "What's this Shuba's first name? Franz?" But I was trying to understand how one could stand that beautifully against a pitcher and I did not answer and Shuba hit a long drive to right center field on a rising line. At a point 390 feet from home plate the ball struck the wire screen above the fence. It was still moving fast, thirty feet up. "Pretty good shot for Franz," I said, but now my father, impressed, had fallen serious.

In the basement, Shuba said, "What did you swing?"

"Thirty-one, thirty-two ounces. Depends on the speed and the shape I was in."

"Here's what you do," Shuba said. "Bore a hole in the top of the bat. Pour lead in it. Ten ounces. Now you got a bat forty-one or forty-two ounces. That's what you want, to practice swinging. Builds up your shoulders and your chest and upper arms."

"I couldn't swing a bat that heavy." I sipped the V.O. The cellar had become uncomfortably hot.

George was standing. "You take a ball of string and you make knots in it," he said. "You make a lot of knots and it hangs in a clump." He walked from the table and reached up toward a beam. A string coiled down and suspended, the base multiknotted into a clump. It was waist-high. "That's the ball," George said. His eyes were shining.

A large-thewed arm reached toward a beam. "I got some bats up here." He chose two signed "George 'Shotgun' Shuba." Both had been drilled and filled with lead. He set his feet, balancing as he had when my father joked about Franz Shuba, and he looked at the clumped string and I rose and drew closer, and he swung the bat. It was the old swing yet, right before me in a cellar. He was heavier, to be sure, but still the swing was beautiful, and grunting softly he whipped the bat into the clumped string. Level and swift, the bat parted the air and made a whining sound. Again Shuba swung and again, controlled and terribly hard. It was the hardest swing I ever saw that close.

Sweat burst upon his neck. "Now you," he said, and handed me the bat.

"I've been drinking."

"Come on. Let me see you swing," he said. Cords stood out in Shuba's throat.

I set my feet on green and white linoleum. My palms were wet. "Okay, but I've been drinking. I'm telling you."

"Just swing," Shuba ordered.

I knew as I began. The bat felt odd. It slipped in my hands. My swing was stiff.

"Wrist," George commanded. "Wrist."

I swung again.

"You broke your wrists here." He indicated a point two-thirds through the arc of the swing. "Break 'em here." He held his hand at the center. I swung again. "Better," he said. "Now here." I swung, snapping my wrists almost at the start of the swing. "All right," he said, moving his hand still farther. "Snap 'em here. Snap 'em first thing you do. Think fast ball. Snap those wrists. The fast ball's by you. Come on, snap. That's it. Wrists. Swing flat. You're catching on."

"It's hot as hell, George."

"You're doing all right," he said.

"But you're a natural."

"Ah," Shuba said. "You talk like a sportswriter." He went to the file and pulled out a chart, marked with Xs. "In the winters," he said, "for fifteen years after loading potatoes or anything else, even when I was in the majors, I'd swing at the clump six hundred times. Every night, and after sixty I'd make an X. Ten Xs and I had my six hundred swings. Then I could go to bed.

"You call that natural? I swung a 44-ounce bat 600 times a night, 4,200 times a week, 47,200 swings every winter. Wrists. The fast ball's by you. You gotta wrist it out. Forty-seven thousand two hundred times."

"I wish I'd known this years ago," I said. George's face looked very open. "It would have helped my own hitting."

"Aah," Shuba said, in the stuffy cellar. "Don't let yourself think like that. The fast ball is by the both of us. Leave it to the younger guys."

I guess this is fiction, especially if you define fiction as fact that hasn't happened yet. Either way, its author, Garrison (Lake Wobegon) Keillor, writes funny stuff. This one first appeared in *The New Yorker*.

# What Did We Do Wrong?

## GARRISON KEILLOR

THE FIRST woman to reach the big leagues said she wanted to be treated like any other rookie, but she didn't have to worry about that. The Sparrows nicknamed her Chesty and then Big Numbers the first week of spring training, and loaded her bed at the Ramada with butterscotch pudding. Only the writers made a big thing about her being the First Woman. The Sparrows treated her like dirt.

Annie Szemanski arrived in camp fresh from the Federales League of Bolivia, the fourth second baseman on the Sparrows roster, and when Drayton stepped in a hole and broke his ankle Hemmie put her in the lineup, hoping she would break hers. "This was the front office's bright idea," he told the writers. "Off the record, I think it stinks." But when she got in she looked so good that by the third week of March she was a foregone conclusion. Even Hemmie had to admit it. A .346 average tells no lies. He disliked her purely because she was a woman—there was nothing personal about it. Because she was a woman, she was given the manager's dressing room, and Hemmie had to dress with the team. He was sixty-one, a heavyweight, and he had a possum tattooed on his belly alongside the name "Georgene," so he was shy about taking his shirt off in front of people. He hated her for making it necessary. Other than that, he thought she was a tremendous addition to the team.

Asked how she felt being the first woman to make a major-league team, she said, "Like a pig in mud," or words to that effect, and then turned and released a squirt of tobacco juice from the wad of rum-soaked plug in her right cheek. She chewed a rare brand of plug called Stuff It, which she learned to chew when she was playing Nicaraguan summer ball. She told the writers, "They were so mean to me down there you couldn't write it in your newspaper. I took a gun everywhere I went, even to bed. *Especially* to bed. Guys were after me like you

can't believe. That's when I started chewing tobacco—because no matter how bad anybody treats you, it's not as bad as this. This is the worst chew in the world. After this, everything else is peaches and cream." The writers elected Gentleman Jim, the Sparrows' P.R. guy, to bite off a chunk and tell them how it tasted, and as he sat and chewed it tears ran down his old sunburnt cheeks and he couldn't talk for a while. Then he whispered, "You've been chewing this for two years? God, I had no idea it was so hard to be a woman."

When thirty-two thousand fans came to Cold Spring Stadium on April 4th for Opening Day and saw the scrappy little freckle-faced woman with tousled black hair who they'd been reading about for almost two months, they were dizzy with devotion. They chanted her name and waved Annie flags and Annie caps ($8.95 and $4.95) and held up hand-painted bedsheets ("EVERY DAY IS LADIES' DAY," "A WOMAN'S PLACE—AT SECOND BASE," "E.R.A. & R.B.I." "THE GAME AIN'T OVER TILL THE BIG LADY BATS"), but when they saw No. 18 trot out to second with a load of chew as big as if she had the mumps it was a surprise. Then, bottom of the second, when she leaned over in the on-deck circle and dropped a stream of brown juice in the sod, the stadium experienced a moment of thoughtful silence.

One man in Section 31 said, "Hey, what's the beef? She can chew if she wants to. This is 1987. Grow up."

"I guess you're right," his next-seat neighbor said. "My first reaction was nausea, but I think you're right."

"Absolutely. She's a woman, but, more than that, she's a *person*."

Other folks said, "I'm with you on that. A woman can carry a quarter pound of chew in her cheek and spit in public, same as any man—why should there be any difference?"

*And yet.* Nobody wanted to say this, but the plain truth was that No. 18 was not handling her chew well at all. Juice ran down her chin and dripped onto her shirt. She's bit off more than she can chew, some people thought to themselves, but they didn't want to say that.

Arnie (the Old Gardener) Brixius mentioned it ever so gently in his "Hot Box" column the next day:

> It's only this scribe's opinion, but isn't it about time baseball cleaned up its act and left the tobacco in the locker? Surely big leaguers can go two hours without nicotine. Many a fan has turned away in disgust at the sight of grown men (and now a member of the fair sex) with a faceful, spitting gobs of the stuff in full view of paying customers. Would Frank Sinatra do this onstage? Or Anne Murray? Nuff said.

End of April, Annie was batting .278, with twelve R.B.I.s, which for the miserable Sparrows was stupendous, and at second base she was surprising a number of people, including base runners who thought she'd be a pushover on the double play. A runner heading for second quickly found out that Annie had knees like ball-peen hammers and if he tried to eliminate her from the play she might eliminate him from the rest of the week. One night, up at bat against the Orioles, she took a step toward the mound after an inside pitch and yelled some things, and when the dugouts emptied she was in the thick of it with men who had never been walloped by a woman before. The home-plate ump hauled her off a guy she was pounding the cookies out of, and a moment later he threw her out of the game for saying things to him, he said, that he had never heard in his nineteen years of umpiring. ("Like what, for example?" writers asked. "Just tell us one thing." But he couldn't; he was too upset.)

The next week, the United Baseball Office Workers local passed a resolution in support of Annie, as did the League of Women Voters and the Women's Softball Caucus, which stated, "Szemanski is a model for all women who are made to suffer guilt for their aggressiveness, and we declare our solidarity with her heads-up approach to the game. While we feel she is holding the bat too high and should bring her hips into her swing more, we're behind her one hundred per cent."

Then, May 4th, at home against Oakland—seventh inning, two outs, bases loaded—she dropped an easy pop-up and three runs came across home plate. The fans sent a few light boos her way to let her know they were paying attention, nothing serious or overtly political, just some folks grumbling, but she took a few steps toward the box seats and yelled something at them that sounded like—well, like something she shouldn't have said, and after the game she said some more things to the writers that Gentleman Jim pleaded with them not to print. One of them was Monica Lamarr, of the *Press*, who just laughed. She said, "Look. I spent two years in the Lifestyles section writing about motherhood vs. career and the biological clock. Sports is my way out of the gynecology ghetto, so don't ask me to eat this story. It's a hanging curve and I'm going for it. I'm never going to write about day care again." And she wrote it:

### SZEMANSKI RAPS FANS AS "SMALL PEOPLE" AFTER DUMB ERROR GIVES GAME TO A'S

#### First Woman Attributes Boos To Sexual Inadequacy in Stands

Jim made some phone calls and the story was yanked and only one truckload of papers went out with it, but word got around, and the next night, though Annie went three for four, the crowd was depressed, and even when she did great the rest of the home stand, and became the first woman to hit a major-league triple, the atmosphere at the ballpark was one of moodiness and deep hurt. Jim went to the men's room one night and found guys standing in line there, looking thoughtful and sad. One of them said, "She's a helluva ballplayer," and other guys murmured that yes, she was, and they wouldn't take anything away from her, she was great and it was wonderful that she had opened up baseball to women, and then they changed the subject to gardening, books, music, aesthetics, anything but baseball. They looked like men who had been stood up.

Gentleman Jim knocked on her door that night. She wore a blue chenille bathrobe flecked with brown tobacco-juice stains, and her black hair hung down in wet strands over her face. She spat into a Dixie cup she was carrying. "Hey! How the Fritos are you? I haven't seen your Big Mac for a while," she said, sort of. He told her she was a great person and a great ballplayer and that he loved her and wanted only the best for her, and he begged her to apologize to the fans.

"Make a gesture—*anything*. They *want* to like you. Give them a chance to like you."

She blew her nose into a towel. She said that she wasn't there to be liked, she was there to play ball.

It was a good road trip. The Sparrows won five out of ten, lifting their heads off the canvas, and Annie raised her average to .291 and hit the first major-league home run ever by a woman, up into the left-field screen at Fenway. Sox fans stood and cheered for fifteen minutes. They whistled, they stamped, they pleaded, the Sparrows pleaded, umpires pleaded, but she refused to come out and tip her hat until the public-address announcer said, "No. 18, please come out of the dugout and take a bow. No. 18, the applause is for you and is not intended as patronizing in any way,'' and then she stuck her head out for 1.5 seconds and did not tip but only touched the brim. Later, she told the writers that just because people had expectations didn't mean she had to fulfill them—she used other words to explain this, but her general drift was that she didn't care very much about living up to anyone else's image of her, and if anyone thought she should, they could go watch wrist wrestling.

The forty thousand who packed Cold Spring Stadium June 6th to see the Sparrows play the Yankees didn't come for a look at Ron Guidry banners hung from the second deck: "WHAT DID WE DO WRONG?" and "ANNIE COME HOME" and "WE LOVE YOU, WHY DO YOU TREAT US THIS WAY? and "IF YOU WOULD LIKE TO DISCUSS THIS IN A NON-CONFRONTATIONAL, MUTUALLY RESPECTFUL WAY, MEET US AFTER THE GAME AT GATE C." It was Snapshot Day, and all the Sparrows appeared on the field for photos with the fans except you know who. Hemmie begged her to go. "You owe it to them," he said.

"Owe?" she said. *"Owe?"*

"Sorry, wrong word," he said. "What if I put it this way: it's a sort of tradition."

*"Tradition?"* she said. "I'm supposed to worry about *tradition?"*

That day, she became the first woman to hit .300. A double in the fifth inning. The scoreboard flashed the message, and the crowd gave her a nice hand. A few people stood and cheered, but the fans around them told them to sit down. "She's not that kind of person," they said. "Cool it. Back off." The fans were trying to give her plenty of space. After the game, Guidry said, "I really have to respect her. She's got that small strike zone and she protects it well, so she makes you pitch to her." She said, "Guidry? Was that his name? I didn't know. Anyway, he didn't show me much. He throws funny, don't you think? He reminded me a little bit of a southpaw I saw down in Nicaragua, except she threw inside more."

All the writers were there, kneeling around her. One of them asked if Guidry had thrown her a lot of sliders.

She gave him a long, baleful look. "Jeez, you guys are out of shape," she said. "You're wheezing and panting and sucking air, and you just took the elevator *down* from the press box. You guys want to write about sports you ought to go into training. And then you ought to learn how to recognize a slider. Jeez, if you were writing about agriculture, would you have to ask someone if those were Holsteins?"

Tears came to the writer's eyes. "I'm trying to help," he said. "Can't you see that? Don't you know how much we care about you? Sometimes I think you put up this tough exterior to hide your own insecurity."

She laughed and brushed the wet hair back from her forehead. "It's no exterior," she said as she unbuttoned her jersey. "It's who I am." She peeled off her socks and stepped out of her cubicle a moment later, sweaty and stark naked. The towel hung from her hand. She walked slowly around them. "You guys learned all you know about women thirty years ago. That wasn't me back then, that was my mother." The writers bent over their notepads, writing down every word she said and punctuating carefully. Gentleman Jim took off his glasses. "My mother was a nice lady, but she couldn't hit the curve to save her Creamettes," she went on. "And now, gentlemen, if you'll excuse me. I'm going to take a shower." They pored over their notes until she was gone, and then they piled out into the hallway and hurried back to the press elevator.

Arnie stopped at the Shortstop for a load of Martinis before he went to the office to write the "Hot Box," which turned out to be about love:

> Baseball is a game but it's more than a game, baseball is people, dammit, and if you are around people you can't help but get involved in their lives and care about them and then you don't know how to talk to them or tell them how much you care and how come we know so much about pitching and we don't know squat about how to communicate? I guess that is the question.

The next afternoon, Arnie leaned against the batting cage before the game, hung over, and watched her hit line drives, fifteen straight, and each one made his head hurt. As she left the cage, he called over to her, "Later," she said. She also declined a pregame interview with Joe Garagiola, who had just told his NBC "Game of the Week" television audience, "This is a city in love with a little girl named Annie Szemanski," when he saw her in the dugout doing deep knee bends. "Annie! Annie!" he yelled over the air. "Let's see if we can't get her up here," he told the home audience. "Annie! Joe Garagiola!" She turned her back to him and went down into the dugout.

That afternoon, she became the first woman to steal two bases in one inning. She reached first on a base on balls, stole second, went to third on a sacrifice fly, and headed for home on the next pitch. The catcher came out to make the tag, she caught him with her elbow under the chin, and when the dust cleared she was grinning at the ump, the catcher was sprawled in the grass trying to inhale, and the ball was halfway to the backstop.

The TV camera zoomed in on her, head down, trotting toward the dugout steps, when suddenly she looked up. Some out-of-town fan had yelled at her from the box seats. ("A profanity which also refers to a female dog," the *News* said.) She smiled and, just before she stepped out of view beneath the dugout roof, millions observed her right hand uplifted in a familiar gesture. In bars around the country, men looked at each other and said, "Did she do what I think I saw her do? She didn't do that, did she?" In the booth, Joe Garagiola was observing that it was a clean play, that the runner has a right to the base path, but when her hand appeared on the screen he stopped. At home, it sounded as if he had been hit in the chest by a rock. The screen went blank, then went to a beer commercial. When the show resumed, it was the middle of the next inning.

On Monday, for "actions detrimental to the best interests of baseball," Annie was fined a thousand dollars by the Commissioner and suspended for two games. He deeply regretted the decision, etc. "I count myself among her most ardent fans. She is good for baseball, good for the cause of equal rights, good for America." He said he would be happy to suspend the suspension if she would make a public apology, which would make him the happiest man in America.

Gentleman Jim went to the bank Monday afternoon and got the money, a thousand dollars, in a cashier's check. All afternoon, he called Annie's number over and over, waiting thirty or forty rings, then trying again. He called from a pay phone at the Stop 'N' Shop, next door to the Cityview Apartments, where she lived, and between calls he sat in his car and watched the entrance, waiting for her to come out. Other men were parked there, too, in front, and some in back—men with Sparrows bumper stickers. After midnight, about eleven of them were left. "Care to share some onion chips and clam dip?" one guy said to another guy. Pretty soon all of them were standing around the trunk of the clam-dip guy's car, where he also had a case of beer.

"Here, let me pay you something for this beer," said a guy who had brought a giant box of pretzels.

"Hey, no. Really. It's just good to have other guys to talk to tonight," said the clam-dip owner.

"She changed a lot of very basic things about the whole way that I look at myself as a man," the pretzel guy said quietly.

"I'm in public relations," said Jim, "But even I don't understand all that she has meant to people."

"How can she do this to us?" said a potato-chip man. "All the love of the fans, how can she throw it away? Why can't she just play ball?"

Annie didn't look at it this way. "Pall Mall! I'm not going to crawl just because some Tootsie Roll says crawl, and if they don't like it, then Ritz, they can go Pepsi their Hostess Twinkies," she told the writers as she cleaned out her locker on Tuesday morning. They had never seen the inside of her locker before. It was stuffed with dirty socks, half unwrapped gifts from admiring fans, a set of ankle weights, and a small silver-plated pistol. "No way I'm going to pay a thousand dollars, and if they expect an apology—well, they better send out for lunch, because it's going to be a long wait. Gentlemen, goodbye and hang on to your valuable coupons." And she smiled her most winning smile and sprinted up the stairs to collect her paycheck. They waited for her outside the Sparrows office, twenty-six men, and then followed her down the ramp and out of Gate C. She broke into a run and disappeared into the lunchtime crowd on West Providence Avenue, and that was the last they saw of her—the woman of their dreams, the love of their lives, carrying a red gym bag, running easily away from them.

Winner of both the Pulitzer Prize and the National Book Award, William Kennedy's marvelous novel *Ironweed* has as its central character a haunted ex-ballplayer named Francis Phelan. The author's power is such (said *The Wall Street Journal*) "that the reader will follow him almost anywhere, to the edge of tragedy and back again to redemption."

# From *Ironweed*

## WILLIAM KENNEDY

ANNIE WAS setting the dining-room table with a white linen tablecloth, with the silver Iron Joe gave them for their wedding, and with china Francis did not recognize, when Daniel Quinn arrived home. The boy tossed his schoolbag in a corner of the dining room, then stopped in midmotion when he saw Francis standing in the doorway to the kitchen.

"Hulooo," Francis said to him.

"Danny, this is your grandfather," Annie said. "He just came to see us and he's staying for dinner." Daniel stared at Francis's face and slowly extended his right hand. Francis shook it.

"Pleased to meet you," Daniel said.

"The feeling's mutual, boy. You're a big lad for ten."

"I'll be eleven in January."

"You comin' from school, are ye?"

"From instructions, religion."

"Oh, religion. I guess I just seen you crossin' the street and didn't even know it. Learn anything, did you?"

"Learned about today. All Saints' Day."

"What about it?"

"It's a holy day. You have to go to church. It's the day we remember the martyrs who died for the faith and nobody knows their names."

"Oh yeah," Francis said. "I remember them fellas."

"What happened to your teeth?"

"Daniel."

"My teeth," Francis said. "Me and them parted company, most of 'em. I got a few left."

"Are you Grampa Phelan or Grampa Quinn?"

"Phelan," Annie said. "His name is Francis Aloysius Phelan."

"Francis Aloysius, right," said Francis with a chuckle. "Long time since I heard that."

"You're the ball player," Danny said. "The big-leaguer. You played with the Washington Senators."

"Used to. Don't play anymore."

"Billy says you taught him how to throw an inshoot."

"He remembers that, does he?"

"Will you teach me?"

"You a pitcher, are ye?"

"Sometimes. I can throw a knuckle ball."

"Change of pace. Hard to hit. You get a baseball, I'll show you how to hold it for an inshoot." And Daniel ran into the kitchen, then the pantry, and emerged with a ball and glove, which he handed to Francis. The glove was much too small for Francis's hand but he put a few fingers inside it and held the ball in his right hand, studied its seams. Then he gripped it with his thumb and one and a half fingers.

"What happened to your finger?" Daniel asked.

"Me and it parted company too. Sort of an accident."

"Does that make any difference throwing an inshoot?"

"Sure does, but not to me. I don't throw no more at all. Never was a pitcher, you know, but talked with plenty of 'em. Walter Johnson was my buddy. You know him? The Big Train?"

The boy shook his head.

"Don't matter. But he taught me how it was done and I ain't forgot. Put your first two fingers right on the seams, like this, and then you snap your wrist out, like this, and if you're a righty—are you a righty?"—and the boy nodded—"then the ball's gonna dance a little turnaround jig and head right inside at the batter's belly button, assumin', acourse, that he's a righty too. You followin' me?" And the boy nodded again. "Now the trick is, you got to throw the opposite of the outcurve, which is like this." And he snapped his wrist clockwise.

"You got to do it like this." And he snapped his wrist counterclockwise again. Then he had the boy try it both ways and patted him on the back.

"That's how it's done," he said. "You get so's you can do it, the batter's gonna think you got a little animal inside that ball, flyin' it like an airplane."

"Let's go outside and try it," Daniel said. "I'll get another glove."

"Glove," said Francis, and he turned to Annie. "By some fluke you still got my old glove stuck away somewhere in the house? That possible, Annie?"

"There's a whole trunk of your things in the attic," she said. "It might be there."

"It is," Daniel said. "I know it is. I saw it. I'll get it."

"You will not," Annie said. "That trunk is none of your affair."

"But I've already seen it. There's a pair of spikes too, and clothes and newspapers and old pictures."

"All that," Francis said to Annie. "You saved it."

"You had no business in that trunk," Annie said.

"Billy and I looked at the pictures and the clippings one day," Daniel said. "Billy looked just as much as I did. He's in lots of 'em." And he pointed at his grandfather.

"Maybe you'd want to have a look at what's there," Annie said to Francis.

"Could be. Might find me a new shoelace."

Annie led him up the stairs, Daniel already far ahead of them. They heard the boy saying: "Get up, Billy, Grandpa's here"; and when they reached the second floor Billy was standing in the doorway of his room, in his robe and white socks, disheveled and only half awake.

"Hey, Billy. How you gettin' on?" Francis said.

"Hey," said Billy. "You made it."

"Yep."

"I woulda bet against it happenin'."

"You'da lost. Brought a turkey too, like I said."

"A turkey, yeah?"

"We're having it for dinner," Annie said.

"I'm supposed to be downtown tonight," Billy said. "I just told Martin I'd meet him."

"Call him back," Annie said. "He'll understand."

"Red Tom Fitzsimmons and Martin both called to tell me things are all right again on Broadway. You know, I told you I had trouble with the McCalls," Billy said to his father.

"I 'member."

"I wouldn't do all they wanted and they marked me lousy. Couldn't gamble, couldn't even get a drink on Broadway."

"I read that story Martin wrote," Francis said. "He called you a magician."

"Martin's full of malarkey. I didn't do diddley. I just mentioned Newark to them and it turns out that's where they trapped some of the kidnap gang."

"You did somethin', then," Francis said. "Mentionin' Newark was somethin'. Who'd you mention it to?"

"Bindy. But I didn't know those guys were in Newark or I wouldn't of said anything. I could never rat on anybody."

"Then why'd you mention it?"

"I don't know."

"That's how come you're a magician."

"That's Martin's baloney. But he turned somebody's head around with it, 'cause I'm back in good odor with the pols, is how he put it on the phone. In other words, I don't stink to them no more."

Francis smelled himself and knew he had to wash as soon as possible. The junk wagon's stink and the bummy odor of his old suitcoat was unbearable now that he was among these people. Dirty butchers go out of business.

"You can't go out now, Billy," Annie said. "Not with your father home and staying for dinner. We're going up in the attic to look at his things."

"You like turkey?" Francis asked Billy.

"Who the hell don't like turkey, not to give you a short answer," Billy said. He looked at his father. "Listen, use my razor in the bathroom if you want to shave."

"Don't be telling people what to do," Annie said. "Get dressed and come downstairs."

And then Francis and Annie ascended the stairway to the attic.

When Francis opened the trunk lid the odor of lost time filled the attic air, a cloying reek of imprisoned flowers that unsettled the dust and fluttered the window shades. Francis felt drugged by the scent of the reconstituted past, and then stunned by his first look inside the trunk, for there, staring out from a photo, was his own face at age nineteen. The picture lay among rolled socks and a small American flag, a Washington Senators cap, a pile of newspaper clippings and other photos, all in a scatter on the trunk's tray. Francis stared up at himself from the bleachers in Chadwick Park on a day in 1899, his face unlined, his teeth all there, his collar open, his hair unruly in the afternoon's breeze. He lifted the picture for a closer look and saw himself among a group of men, tossing a baseball from bare right hand to gloved left hand. The flight of the ball had always made this photo mysterious to Francis, for the camera had caught the ball clutched in one hand and also in flight, arcing in a blur toward the glove. What the camera had caught was two instants in one: time separated and unified, the ball in two places at once, an eventuation as inexplicable as the Trinity itself. Francis now took the picture to be a Trinitarian talisman (a hand, a glove, a ball) for achieving the impossible: for he had always believed it impossible for him, ravaged man, failed human, to reenter history under this roof. Yet here he was in this aerie of reconstitutable time, touching untouchable artifacts of a self that did not yet know it was ruined, just as the ball, in its inanimate ignorance, did not know yet that it was going nowhere, was caught.

But the ball is really not yet caught, except by the camera, which has frozen only its situation in space.

And Francis is not yet ruined, except as an apparency in process.

The ball still flies.

Francis still lives to play another day.

Doesn't he?

The boy noticed the teeth. A man can get new teeth, store teeth. Annie got 'em.

Francis lifted the tray out of the trunk, revealing the spikes and the glove, which Daniel immediately grabbed, plus two suits of clothes, a pair of black oxfords and brown high-button shoes, maybe a dozen shirts and two dozen white collars, a stack of undershirts and shorts, a set of keys to long-forgotten locks, a razor strop and a hone, a shaving mug with an inch of soap in it, a shaving brush with bristles intact, seven straight razors in a case, each marked for a day of the week, socks, bow ties, suspenders, and a baseball, which Francis picked up and held out to Daniel.

"See that? See that name?"

The boy looked, shook his head. "I can't read it."

"Get it in the light, you'll read it. That's Ty Cobb. He signed that ball in 1911, the year he hit .420. A fella give it to me once and I always kept it. Mean guy, Cobb was, come in at me spikes up many a time. But you had to hand it to a man who played ball as good as he did. He was the best."

"Better than Babe Ruth?"

"Better and tougher and meaner and faster. Couldn't hit home runs like the Babe, but he did everything else better. You like to have that ball with his name on it?"

"Sure I would, sure! Yeah! Who wouldn't?"

"Then it's yours. But you better look him up, and Walter Johnson too. Find out for yourself how good they were. Still kickin', too, what I hear about Cobb. He ain't dead yet either."

"I remember that suit," Annie said, lifting the sleeve of a gray herringbone coat. "You wore it for dress-up."

"Wonder if it'd still fit me," Francis said, and stood up and held the pants to his waist and found out his legs had not grown any longer in the past twenty-two years.

"Take the suit downstairs," Annie said. "I'll sponge and press it."

"Press it?" Francis said, and he chuckled. "S'pose I could use a new outfit. Get rid of these rags."

He then singled out a full wardrobe, down to the handkerchief, and piled it all on the floor in front of the trunk.

"I'd like to look at these again," Annie said, lifting out the clippings and photos.

"Bring 'em down," Francis said, closing the lid.

"I'll carry the glove," Daniel said.

"And I'd like to borry the use of your bathroom," Francis said. "Take Billy up on that shave offer and try on some of these duds. I got me a shave last night but Billy thinks I oughta do it again."

"Don't pay any attention to Billy," Annie said. "You look fine."

She led him down the stairs and along a hallway where two rooms faced each other. She gestured at a bedroom where a single bed, a dresser, and a child's rolltop desk stood in quiet harmony.

"That's Danny's room," she said. "It's a nice big room and it gets the morning light." She took a towel down from a linen closet shelf and handed it to Francis. "Have a bath if you like."

Francis locked the bathroom door and tried on the trousers, which fit if he didn't button the top button. Wear the suspenders with 'em. The coat was twenty years out of style and offended Francis's residual sense of aptness. But he decided to wear it anyway, for its odor of time was infinitely superior to the stink of bumdom that infested the coat on his back. He stripped and let the bathwater run. He inspected the shirt he took from the trunk, but rejected it in favor of the white-on-white from the junk wagon. He tried the laceless black oxfords, all broken in, and found that even with calluses his feet had not grown in twenty-two years either.

He stepped into the bath and slid slowly beneath its vapors. He trembled with the heat, with astonishment that he was indeed here, as snug in this steaming tub as was the turkey in its roasting pan. He felt blessed. He stared at the bathroom sink, which now had an aura of sanctity about it, its faucets sacred, its drainpipe holy, and he wondered whether everything was blessed at some point in its existence, and he concluded yes. Sweat rolled down his forehead and dripped off his nose into the bath, a confluence of ancient and modern waters. And as it did, a great sunburst entered the darkening skies, a radiance so sudden that it seemed like a bolt of lightning; yet its brilliance remained, as if some angel of beatific lucidity were hovering outside the bathroom window. So enduring was the light, so intense beyond even sundown's final gloryburst, that

Francis raised himself up out of the tub and went to the window.

Below, in the yard, Aldo Campione, Fiddler Quain, Harold Allen, and Rowdy Dick Doolan were erecting a wooden structure that Francis was already able to recognize as bleachers.

He stepped back into the tub, soaped the long-handled brush, raised his left foot out of the water, scrubbed it clean, raised the right foot, scrubbed that.

Francis, that 1916 dude, came down the stairs in bow tie, white-on-white shirt, black laceless oxfords with a spit shine on them, the gray herringbone with lapels twenty-two years too narrow, with black silk socks and white silk boxer shorts, with his skin free of dirt everywhere, his hair washed twice, his fingernails cleaned, his leftover teeth brushed and the toothbrush washed with soap and dried and rehung, with no whiskers anymore, none, and his hair combed and rubbed with a dab of Vaseline so it'd stay in place, with a spring in his gait and a smile on his face; this Francis dude came down those stairs, yes, and stunned his family with his resurrectible good looks and stylish potential, and took their stares as applause.

And dance music rose in his brain.

"Holy Christ," said Billy.

"My oh my," said Annie.

"You look different," Daniel said.

"I kinda needed a sprucin'," Francis said. "Funny duds but I guess they'll do."

They all pulled back then, even Daniel, aware they should not dwell on the transformation, for it made Francis's previous condition so lowly, so awful.

"Gotta dump these rags," he said, and he lifted his bundle, tied with the arms of his old coat.

"Danny'll take them," Annie said. "Put them in the cellar," she told the boy.

Francis sat down on a bench in the breakfast nook, across the table from Billy. Annie had spread the clips and photos on the table and he and Billy looked them over. Among the clips Francis found a yellowed envelope postmarked June 2, 1910, and addressed to Mr. Francis Phelan, c/o Toronto Baseball Club, The Palmer House, Toronto, Ont. He opened it and read the letter inside, then pocketed it. Dinner advanced as Daniel and Annie peeled the potatoes at the sink. Billy, his hair combed slick, half a dude himself with open-collared starched white shirt, creased trousers, and pointy black shoes, was drinking from a quart bottle of Dobler beer and reading a clipping.

"I read these once," Billy said. "I never really knew how good you were. I heard stories and then one night downtown I heard a guy talking about you and he was ravin' that you were top-notch and I never knew just

how good. I knew this stuff was there. I seen it when we first moved here, so I went up and looked. You were really a hell of a ball player."

"Not bad," Francis said. "Coulda been worse."

"These sportswriters liked you."

"I did crazy things. I was good copy for them. And I had energy. Everybody likes energy."

Billy offered Francis a glass of beer but Francis declined and took, instead, from Billy's pack, a Camel cigarette; and then he perused the clips that told of him stealing the show with his fielding, or going four-for-four and driving in the winning run, or getting himself in trouble; such as the day he held the runner on third by the belt, an old John McGraw trick, and when a fly ball was hit, the runner got ready to tag and head home after the catch but found he could not move and turned and screamed at Francis in protest, at which point Francis let go of the belt and the runner ran, but the throw arrived first and he was out at home.

Nifty.

But Francis was thrown out of the game.

"Would you like to go out and look at the yard?" Annie said, suddenly beside Francis.

"Sure. See the dog."

"It's too bad the flowers are gone. We had so many flowers this year. Dahlias and snapdragons and pansies and asters. The asters lasted the longest."

"You still got them geraniums right here."

Annie nodded and put on her sweater and the two of them went out onto the back porch. The air was chilly and the light fading. She closed the door behind them and patted the dog, which barked twice at Francis and then accepted his presence. Annie went down the five steps to the yard, Francis and the dog following.

"Do you have a place to stay tonight, Fran?"

"Sure. Always got a place to stay."

"Do you want to come home permanent?" she asked, not looking at him, walking a few steps ahead toward the fence. "Is that why you've come to see us?"

"Nah, not much chance of that. I'd never fit in."

"I thought you might've had that in mind."

"I thought of it, I admit that. But I see it couldn't work, not after all these years."

"It'd take some doing, I know that."

"Take more than that."

"Stranger things have happened."

"Yeah? Name one."

"You going to the cemetery and talking to Gerald. I think maybe that's the strangest thing I ever heard in all my days."

"Wasn't strange. I just went and stood there and told him a bunch of stuff. It's nice where he is. It's pretty."

"That's the family plot."

"I know."

"There's a grave there for you, right at the stone, and one for me, and two for the children next to that if they need them. Peg'll have her own plot with George and the boy, I imagine."

"When did you do all that?" Francis asked.

"Oh years ago. I don't remember."

"You bought me a grave after I run off."

"I bought it for the family. You're part of the family."

"There was long times I didn't think so."

"Peg is very bitter about you staying away. I was too, for years and years, but that's all done with. I don't know why I'm not bitter anymore. I really don't. I called Peg and told her to get the cranberries and that you were here."

"Me and the cranberries. Easin' the shock some."

"I suppose."

"I'll move along, then. I don't want no fights, rile up the family."

"Nonsense. Stop it. You just talk to her. You've got to talk to her."

"I can't say nothin' that means anything. I couldn't say a straight word to you."

"I know what you said and what you didn't say. I know it's hard what you're doing."

"It's a bunch of nothin'. I don't know why I do anything in this goddamn life."

"You did something good coming home. It's something Danny'll always know about. And Billy. He was so glad to be able to help you, even though he'd never say it."

"He got a bum out of jail."

"You're so mean to yourself, Francis."

"Hell, I'm mean to everybody and everything."

The bleachers were all up, and men were filing silently into them and sitting down, right here in Annie's backyard, in front of God and the dog and all: Bill Corbin, who ran for sheriff in the nineties and got beat and turned Republican, and Perry Marsolais, who inherited a fortune from his mother and drank it up and ended up raking leaves for the city, and Iron Joe himself with his big mustache and big belly and big ruby stickpin, and Spiff Dwyer in his nifty pinched fedora, and young George Quinn and young Martin Daugherty, the bat-boys, and Martin's grandfather Emmett Daugherty, the wild Fenian who talked so fierce and splendid and put the radical light in Francis's eye with his stories of how moneymen used workers to get rich and treated the Irish like pigdog paddyniggers, and Patsy McCall, who grew up to run the city and was carrying his ball glove in his left hand, and some men Francis did not know even in 1899, for they were only hangers-on at the saloon, men who followed the doings of Iron Joe's Wheelbarrow Boys, and who came to the beer picnic this day to celebrate the Boys' winning the Albany-Troy League pennant.

They kept coming: forty-three men, four boys, and two mutts, ushered in by the Fiddler and his pals.

And there, between crazy Specky McManus in his derby and Jack Corbett in his vest and no collar, sat the runt, is it?

Is it now?

The runt with the piece out of his neck.

There's one in every crowd.

Francis closed his eyes to retch the vision out of his head, but when he opened them the bleachers still stood, the men seated as before. Only the light had changed, brighter now, and with it grew Francis's hatred of all fantasy, all insubstantiality. I am sick of you all, was his thought. I am sick of imagining what you became, what I might have become if I'd lived among you. I am sick of your melancholy histories, your sentimental pieties, your goddamned unchanging faces. I'd rather be dyin' in the weeds than standin' here lookin' at you pinin' away, like the dyin' Jesus pinin' for an end to it when he knew every stinkin' thing that was gonna happen not only to himself but to everybody around him, and to all those that wasn't even born yet. You ain't nothin' more than a photograph, you goddamn spooks. You ain't real and I ain't gonna be at your beck and call no more.

You're all dead, and if you ain't, you oughta be.

I'm the one is livin'. I'm the one puts you on the map.

You never knew no more about how things was than I did.

You'd never even be here in the damn yard if I didn't open that old trunk.

So get your ass gone!

"Hey Ma," Billy yelled out the window. "Peg's home."

"We'll be right in," Annie said. And when Billy closed the window she turned to Francis: "You want to tell me anything, ask me anything, before we get in front of the others?"

"Annie, I got five million things to ask you, and ten million things to tell. I'd like to eat all the dirt in this yard for you, eat the weeds, eat the dog bones too, if you asked me."

"I think you probably ate all that already," she said.

And then they went up the back stoop together.

When Francis first saw his daughter bent over the stove, already in her flowered apron and basting the turkey, he thought: She is too dressed up to be doing that. She wore a wristwatch on one arm, a bracelet on the other, and two rings on her wedding ring finger. She wore high heels, silk stockings with the seams inside out, and a lavender dress that was never intended as a kitchen costume. Her dark-brown hair, cut short, was waved in a soft marcel, and she wore lipstick and a bit of rouge, and her nails were long and painted dark red. She was a few, maybe even more than a few, pounds overweight, and she was beautiful, and Francis was immeasurably happy at having sired her.

"How ya doin', Margaret?" Francis asked when she straightened up and looked at him.

"I'm doing fine," she said, "no thanks to you."

"Yep," said Francis, and he turned away from her and sat across from Billy in the nook.

"Give him a break," Billy said. "He just got here, for chrissake."

"What break did he ever give me? Or you? Or any of us?"

"Aaahhh, blow it out your ear," Billy said.

"I'm saying what is," Peg said.

"Are you?" Annie asked. "Are you so sure of what is?"

"I surely am. I'm not going to be a hypocrite and welcome him back with open arms after what he did. You don't just pop up one day with a turkey and all is forgiven."

"I ain't expectin' to be forgiven," Francis said. "I'm way past that."

"Oh? And just where are you now?"

"Nowhere."

"Well that's no doubt very true. And if you're nowhere, why are you here? Why've you come back like a ghost we buried years ago to force a scrawny turkey on us? Is that your idea of restitution for letting us fend for ourselves for twenty-two years?"

"That's a twelve-and-a-half-pound turkey," Annie said.

"Why leave your nowhere and come here, is what I want to know. This is somewhere. This is a home you didn't build."

"I built you. Built Billy. Helped to."

"I wish you never did."

"Shut up, Peg," Billy yelled. "Rotten tongue of yours, shut it the hell UP!"

"He came to visit, that's all he did," Annie said softly. "I already asked him if he wanted to stay over and he said no. If he wanted to he surely could."

"Oh?" said Peg. "Then it's all decided?"

"Nothin' to decide," Francis said. "Like your mother says, I ain't stayin'. I'm movin' along." He touched the salt and pepper shaker on the table in front of him, pushed the sugar bowl against the wall.

"You're moving on," Peg said.

"Positively."

"Fine."

"That's it, that's enough!" Billy yelled, standing up from the bench. "You got the feelin's of a goddamn rattlesnake."

"Pardon me for having any feelings at all," Peg said, and she left the kitchen, slamming the swinging door, which had been standing open, slamming it so hard that it swung, and swung, and swung, until it stopped.

"Tough lady," Francis said.

"She's a creampuff," Billy said. "But she knows how to get her back up."

"She'll calm down," Annie said.

"I'm used to people screamin' at me," Francis said. "I got a hide like a hippo."

"You need it in this joint," Billy said.

"Where's the boy?" Francis asked. "He hear all that?"

"He's out playin' with the ball and glove you gave him," Billy said.

"I didn't give him the glove," Francis said. "I give him the ball with the Ty Cobb signature. That glove is yours. You wanna give it to him, it's okay by me. Ain't much of a glove compared to what they got these days. Danny's glove's twice the quality my glove ever was. But I always thought to myself: I'm givin' that old glove to Billy so's he'll have a touch of the big leagues somewhere in the house. That glove caught some mighty people. Line drive from Tris Speaker, taggin' out Cobb, runnin' Eddie Collins outa the baseline. Lotta that."

Billy nodded and turned away from Francis. "Okay," he said, and then he jumped up from the bench and left the kitchen so the old man could not see (though he saw) that he was choked up.

"Grew up nice, Billy did," Francis said. "Couple of tough bozos you raised, Annie."

"I wish they were tougher," Annie said.

The yard, now ablaze with new light against a black sky, caught Francis's attention. Men and boys, and even dogs, were holding lighted candles, the dogs holding them in their mouths sideways. Specky McManus, as usual bein' different, wore his candle on top of his derby. It was a garden of acolytes setting fire to the very air, and then, while Francis watched, the acolytes erupted in song, but a song without sense, a chant to which Francis listened carefully but could make out not a word. It was an antisyllabic lyric they sang, like the sibilance of the wren's softest whistle, or the tree frog's tonsillar wheeze. It was clear to Francis as he watched this performance (watched it with awe, for it was transcending what he expected from dream, from reverie, even from Sneaky Pete hallucinations) that it was happening in an arena of his existence over which he had less control than he first imagined when Aldo Campione boarded the bus. The signals from this time lock were ominous, the spooks utterly without humor. And then, when he saw the runt (who knew he was being watched, who knew he didn't belong in this picture) putting the lighted end of the candle into the hole in the back of his neck, and when Francis recognized the chant of the acolytes at last as the "Dies Irae," he grew fearful. He closed his eyes and buried his head in his hands and he tried to remember the name of his first dog.

It was a collie.

Billy came back, clear-eyed, sat across from Francis, and offered him another smoke, which he took. Billy topped his own beer and drank and then said, "George."

"Oh my God," Annie said. "We forgot all about George." And she went to the living room and called upstairs to Peg: "You should call George and tell him he can come home."

"Let her alone, I'll do it," Billy called to his mother.

"What about George?" Francis asked.

"The cops were here one night lookin' for him," Billy said. "It was Patsy McCall puttin' pressure on the family because of me. George writes numbers and they were probably gonna book him for gamblin' even though he had the okay. So he laid low up in Troy, and the poor bastard's been alone for days. But if I'm clear, then so is he."

"Some power the McCalls put together in this town."

"They got it all. They ever pay you the money they owed you for registerin' all those times?"

"Paid me the fifty I told you about, owe me another fifty-five. I'll never see it."

"You got it comin'."

"Once it got in the papers they wouldn't touch it. Mixin' themselves up with bums. You heard Martin tell me that. They'd also be suspicious that I'd set them up. I wouldn't set nobody up. Nobody."

"Then you got no cash."

"I got a little."

"How much?"

"I got some change. Cigarette money."

"You blew what you had on the turkey."

"That took a bit of it."

Billy handed him a ten, folded in half. "Put it in your pocket. You can't walk around broke."

Francis took it and snorted. "I been broke twenty-two years. But I thank ye, Billy, I'll make it up."

"You already made it up." And he went to the phone in the dining room to call George in Troy.

Annie came back to the kitchen and saw Francis looking at the Chadwick Park photo and looked over his shoulder. "That's a handsome picture of you," she said.

"Yeah," said Francis. "I was a good-lookin' devil."

"Some thought so, some didn't," Annie said. "I forgot about this picture."

"Oughta get it framed," Francis said. "Lot of North Enders in there. George and Martin as kids, and Patsy McCall too. And Iron Joe. Real good shot of Joe."

"It surely is," Annie said. "How fat and healthy he looks."

Billy came back and Annie put the photo on the table so that all three of them could look at it. They sat on the same bench with Francis in the middle and studied it, each singling out the men and boys they knew. Annie even knew one of the dogs.

"Oh that's a prize picture," she said, and stood up. "A prize picture."

"Well, it's yours, so get it framed."

"Mine? No, it's yours. It's baseball."

"Nah, nah, George'd like it too."

"Well I will frame it," Annie said. "I'll take it downtown and get it done up right."

"Sure," said Francis. "Here. Here's ten dollars toward the frame."

"Hey," Billy said.

"No," Francis said. "You let me do it, Billy."

Billy chuckled.

"I will not take any money," Annie said. "You put that back in your pocket."

Billy laughed and hit the table with the palm of his hand. "Now I know why you been broke twenty-two years. I know why we're all broke. It runs in the family."

"We're not all broke," Annie said. "We pay our way. Don't be telling people we're broke. You're broke because you made some crazy horse bet. But *we're* not broke. We've had bad times but we can still pay the rent. And we've never gone hungry."

"Peg's workin'," Francis said.

"A private secretary," Annie said. "To the owner of a tool company. She's very well liked."

"She's beautiful," Francis said. "Kinda nasty when she puts her mind to it, but beautiful."

"She shoulda been a model," Billy said.

"She should not," Annie said.

"Well she shoulda, goddamn it, she shoulda," said Billy. "They wanted her to model for Pepsodent toothpaste, but Mama wouldn't hear of it. Somebody over at church told her models were, you know, loose ladies. Get your picture taken, it turns you into a floozy."

"That had nothing to do with it," Annie said.

"Her teeth," Billy said. "She's got the most gorgeous teeth in North America. Better-lookin' teeth than Joan Crawford. What a smile! You ain't seen her smile yet, but that's a fantastic smile. Like Times Square is what it is. She coulda been on billboards coast to coast. We'd be hip-deep in toothpaste, and cash too. But no." And he jerked a thumb at his mother.

"She had a job," Annie said. "She didn't need that. I never liked that fellow that wanted to sign her up."

"He was all right," Billy said. "I checked him out. He was legitimate."

"How could you know what he was?"

"How could I know anything? I'm a goddamn genius."

"Clean up your mouth, genius. She would've had to go to New York for pictures."

"And she'd of never come back, right?"

"Maybe she would, maybe she wouldn't."

"Now you got it," Billy said to his father. "Mama likes to keep all the birds in the nest."

"Can't say as I blame her," Francis said.

"No," Billy said.

"I never liked that fellow," Annie said. "That's what it really was. I didn't trust him."

Nobody spoke.

"And she brought a paycheck home every week," Annie said. "Even when the tool company closed awhile, the owner put her to work as a cashier in a trading port he owned. Trading port and indoor golf. An enormous place. They almost brought Rudy Vallee there once. Peg got wonderful experience."

Nobody spoke.

"Cigarette?" Billy asked Francis.

"Sure," Francis said.

Annie stood up and went to the refrigerator in the pantry. She came back with the butter dish and put it on the dining-room table. Peg came through the swinging door, into the silence. She poked the potatoes with a fork, looked at the turkey, which was turning deep brown, and closed the oven door without basting it. She rummaged in the utensil drawer and found a can opener and punched it through a can of peas and put them in a pan to boil.

"Turkey smells real good," Francis said to her.

"Uh-huh, I bought a plum pudding," she said to all, showing them the can. She looked at her father. "Mama said you used to like it for dessert on holidays."

"I surely did. With that white sugar sauce. Mighty sweet."

"The sauce recipe's on the label," Annie said. "Give it here and I'll make it."

"I'll make it," Peg said.

"It's nice you remembered that," Francis said.

"It's no trouble," Peg said. "The pudding's already cooked. All you do is heat it up in the can."

Francis studied her and saw the venom was gone from her eyes. This lady goes up and down like a thermometer. When she saw him studying her she smiled slightly, not a billboard smile, not a smile to make anybody rich in toothpaste, but there it was. What the hell, she's got a right. Up and down, up and down. She come by it naturally.

"I got a letter maybe you'd all like to hear while that stuff's cookin' up," he said, and he took the yellowed envelope with a canceled two-cent stamp on it out of his inside coat pocket. On the back, written in his own hand, was: *First letter from Margaret.*

"I got this a few years back, quite a few," he said, and from the envelope he took out three small trifolded sheets of yellowed lined paper. "Come to me up in Canada in nineteen-ten, when I was with Toronto." He unfolded the sheets and moved them into the best possible light at longest possible arm's length, and then he read:

" 'Dear Poppy, I suppose you never think that you have a daughter that is waiting for a letter since you went away. I was so mad because you did not think of me that I was going to join the circus that was here last Friday. I am doing my lesson and there is an arithmetic example here that I cannot get. See if you can get it. I hope your leg is better and that you have good luck with the team. Do not run too much with your legs or you will have to be carried home. Mama and Billy are good. Mama has fourteen new little chickens out and she has two more hens sitting. There is a wild west circus coming the eighth. Won't you come home and see it? I am going to it. Billy is just going to bed and Mama is sitting on the bed watching me. Do not forget to answer this. I suppose you are having a lovely time. Do not let me find you with another girl or I will pull her hair. Yours truly, Peggy.' "

"Isn't that funny," Peg said, the fork still in her hand. "I don't remember writing that."

"Probably lots you don't remember about them days," Francis said. "You was only about eleven."

"Where did you ever find it?"

"Up in the trunk. Been saved all these years up there. Only letter I ever saved."

"Is that a fact?"

"It's a provable fact. All the papers I got in the world was in that trunk, except one other place I got a few more clips. But no letters noplace. It's a good old letter, I'd say."

"I'd say so too," Annie said. She and Billy were both staring at Peg.

"I remember Toronto in nineteen-ten," Francis said. "The game was full of crooks them days. Crooked umpire named Bates, one night it was deep dark but he wouldn't call the game. Folks was throwin' tomatoes and mudballs at him but he wouldn't call it 'cause we was winnin' and he was in with the other team. Pudge Howard was catchin' that night and he walks out and has a three-way confab on the mound with me and old Highpockets Wilson, who was pitchin'. Pudge comes back and squats behind the plate and Highpockets lets go a blazer and the ump calls it a ball, though nobody could see nothin' it was so dark. And Pudge turns to him and says: 'You call that pitch a ball?' 'I did,' says the ump. 'If that was a ball I'll eat it,' says Pudge. 'Then you better get eatin',' says the ump. And Pudge, he holds the ball up and takes a big bite out of it, 'cause it ain't no ball at all, it's a yellow apple I give Highpockets to throw. And of course that won us the game and the ump went down in history as Blindy Bates, who couldn't tell a baseball from a damn apple. Bates turned into a bookie after that. He was crooked at that too.''

"That's a great story," Billy said. "Funny stuff in them old days."

"Funny stuff happenin' all the time," Francis said.

Peg was suddenly tearful. She put the fork on the sink and went to her father, whose hands were folded on the table. She sat beside him and put her right hand on top of his.

After a while George Quinn came home from Troy, Annie served the turkey, and then the entire Phelan family sat down to dinner.

# Lights! Camera! Action!

## ARMEN KETEYIAN

THE FIRST assistant director checked the camera crew and eyed the extras in the stands. "All right, ladies and gentlemen," he boomed through a megaphone, *"this is a picture."*

We were filming *A Winner Never Quits—The Pete Gray Story,* an ABC made-for-TV docudrama, and for this scene we were in Long Beach, Calif., at Blair Field, which in a bit of creative casting was playing the part of Yankee Stadium. The plot, were it capsulized in snappy movie-speak, might read something like this: Son of a Pennsylvania coal miner struggles against adversity and prejudice to become the only one-armed ballplayer ever to reach the majors. *A Winner Never Quits* is also a true story, although many of the specifics in the film are fiction. Pete Gray really did play in the majors in 1945, with the St. Louis Browns, and his achievement was indeed a remarkable one—war years or no war years. Keith Carradine was cast as Gray, Dennis Weaver played his father, and Mare Winningham, hot off the set of *St. Elmo's Fire,* portrayed Gray's love interest.

But at this moment the stars weren't out. Scene No. 183, Take 1, was ready to roll. My scene. My catch. I had been cast as Phil Canzoni, a fictional leftfielder of the 1945 Browns. In the next few minutes (if I was lucky), Canzoni would make the greatest—and only—catch of his short-lived celluloid career, a diving, sprawling, four-star grab guaranteed to make the likes of Gene Siskel and Roger Ebert jump out of their reclining seats. The Catch would end a Yankee scoring threat and represent a fictional turning point in Gray's career. Canzoni, you see, would get hurt. Not hospital hurt, but whatever damage I could inflict after sprinting 15 yards and landing on my face would be just fine with the directors. Gray, naturally, would be called upon to finish the game. He would get a hit or two, make a great catch of his own and end our picture on a high note.

How did I get myself into this vintage gray wool Browns' uniform with the orange-and-brown piping? By breaking Vacation Rule No. 1: Thou shalt never answer a telephone before 8 A.M.

"How would you like to be an extra in a movie?" The

voice belonged to Frank Pace, coproducer on the Gray film and a good friend. He was short of ballplayers.

"Three days. Easy work. You get to meet Keith," said Pace.

I declined. I had never acted and had no desire to stand around for hours on end. Besides, I was a stone's throw from the beach in San Diego and not about to budge. "Sorry, Frank," I said. "Maybe some other time." That's when Pace played his trump card. "You get to make a great catch."

"What kind of catch?"

"I don't know, we haven't decided yet. Something spectacular. You'll get your own scene. It would be something to show your grandchildren." I was almost persuaded, but one thing worried me: I'm very near-sighted (20/200). I'm one of those people who has to remember where he puts his glasses at night in order to find them the next morning. I wore contacts while playing shortstop in college, but nowadays I wear horn-rimmed glasses during softball games in Central Park. I didn't remember anyone wearing Clark Kent–type glasses in the outfield in 1945.

"Frank," I said, "I can't see very well without my glasses."

"That's O.K.," said Pace. "You'll only have to run about 15 yards. Someone will throw you the ball. It shouldn't be too tough."

"Oh . . . O.K.," I said.

Pace caught my concern. "By the way," he said, "just how bad are your eyes?"

He found out the next day. I was standing in leftfield, worried. The only way I could focus on the batter was by blinking my eyes. After a while, I felt like a traffic light. The first ball hit to me—a hard grounder—bounced off my glove and rolled behind me.

"All right," said Pace, who was responsible for orchestrating the baseball scenes. "We're only live if the ball's hit to leftfield. We want to set up the Canzoni catch."

The hitter was Mike Paciorek, brother of Tom, the Texas Ranger utility man. Like his brother, Mike—who

**LEFT-HANDED ALL THE WAY . . .**
Pete Gray. Imported to the majors for morale purposes toward the end of World War II. (UPI/Bettmann Newsphotos)

played college ball at Michigan—is well built and hits with power. He ripped the next pitch, deep down the line. Instinctively, I turned, trying to focus on the blurry object, and sprinted to the wall—an imposing concrete slab 12 feet high. Miraculously—at this point I could have used a guide dog—I was able to make a beautiful running catch inches in front of the wall. Even my teammates let out a few congratulatory whoops.

"Nice grab," said Pace, as I ran off the field. "You didn't even turn and look at the wall. Good instincts. But don't get cocky. We'll need that tomorrow."

As I ran to the bench to rest, I noticed Carradine warming up. At 35, he has earned a reputation as an actor willing to take risks, to accept the offbeat. Gray's life story was no exception.

Gray was six years old when his right arm was crushed by a wheel of a milk truck and had to be amputated above the elbow. He worked endlessly at his game, earning a shot at the majors after winning the MVP award in the Class A Southern Association with Memphis in 1944. He hit .333 that year and tied the

league record with 68 stolen bases. His career was inspiring enough to warrant a movie, and, in fact, the notion of doing one had been talked about in Hollywood for almost 40 years. Among the obstacles that kept the cameras from rolling were the demands of the starring role. It required an actor to spend hours in a rigid shoulder harness that held the right arm snugly across the chest. Catching and throwing one-handed on the sidelines, Carradine wielded his black glove to snare the baseball, then slipped the mitt under his right armpit, pulled the ball out and threw. His throws were swift and accurate, remarkable because Carradine, a natural right-hander, was forced to learn to throw left-handed.

A gate attraction because of his handicap, Gray was hailed as an inspiration to wounded vets returning from World War II. His superb defensive skills won him the admiration of New York sportswriters, who dubbed him a "one-armed wonder." Gray did his best to downplay his disability. But as time wore on, the publicity surrounding the handicap began to bother him. He played 77 games with the Browns in 1945, hitting .218;

then the war ended and he returned to the minors. After leaving baseball in 1949, he had a bout with alcohol. He is described in stories written in the 1970s as a "frightened" and "bitter" man. Today a nondrinker, Gray, 68, guards his privacy. He lives in his hometown of Nanticoke, Pennsylvania, has no phone and resists all requests for interviews, "I don't want to be bothered, that's all," he says.

Bringing Gray's story to life, lacing fact with fiction (the Canzoni catch, Gray's climactic grab) was left to director Mel Damski, ex-Colgate catcher, Long Island sportswriter, full-time Mets fanatic. Up in the broadcast booth Phil Stone, an NBC football announcer and radio man for the San Francisco Giants, provided the play-by-play. It was Stone who would call the critical Canzoni catch, a day before we actually filmed it.

"How do you want to do this?" Stone asked Damski.

"I don't know," said the director. "Nothing's really set. Why don't you ad-lib it."

Ad-lib? Great. What if Stone, a friend, suddenly went Hollywood on me and turned my catch into a death-defying stunt?"

I need not have worried. Stone played his part perfectly: "We're in the bottom of the fifth, all tied at five, the Yanks have two on with two out and Oscar Grimes stepping in. Grimes, hitting .260, already has a double on the day. Here's the pitch. Grimes drills it hard to leftfield; it is hit a ton. Canzoni's on a dead run. He makes a diving catch. What a play by Phil Canzoni! Wait just a minute. Canzoni is down. He may have hurt himself on the play. The Browns' trainer is out checking on him. Oh my, it looks like that'll be all for him today. Well, folks, with the injury to Phil Canzoni, it looks like we're going to get a chance to see the man many people came to Yankee Stadium hoping to see: Pete Gray." When Stone finished, the actors and crew cheered as if he'd just hit a grand slam.

My catch was set for the following day. Between takes I'd done some scouting of my own: I needed a partner, someone to throw that perfect fly ball. It had to look as if it was coming off a bat and it had to fall into an area defined by Damski and his cameramen. I chose a strong-armed ex-minor league infielder named Jerry Lane and the newest, whitest ball around. Without my glasses I could leave nothing to chance.

As the cameras set up, I took some deep breaths, eyed my mark and mentally ran through the sequence I had worked out: sprint 15 yards, dive, *catch the ball*, pretend to pull a hamstring. About 100 extras—fans decked out in fedoras and zoot suits—filled a section of stands behind home plate. (In typical Hollywood fashion, home plate at Blair Field was leftfield at Yankee Stadium.)

I took a couple of practice runs. Lane, playing Dan Marino, threw two passes right on the button. I picked them both off, sprawling splendidly in the grass. "Great catches," said Pace as I warmed up again. "But save a couple, will ya?"

The director's slate snapped down. Two hundred people waited, watching my every move. For the only time in my life, I was an actor. People depended on me. Time and money were going to be wasted if I didn't make this catch.

"Ready, Camera A," someone said. "Ready, Camera B."

"O.K., action," said Damski.

Pounding my old, leatherless glove, which wasn't big enough to hold a dinner salad, I began my sprint, watching Lane, my eyes blinking once or twice.

The throw was perfect—looped, but with some mustard on it. It fell right into camera range. I dived, stretched and watched as the ball landed right in my mitt . . . and popped out.

"That's O.K.," said Damski. "Let's do it again." We should have been done after the second take. Another strike from Lane. Another perfect dive, the ball caught an inch off the grass as I slammed down. A nine on the Willie Mays Meter.

Suddenly directors and cameramen were huddled in conference. "Ah, crowd," said the assistant director, "you were a little weak on that one. Remember, this ends the inning. You're supposed to react to the catch. Get excited. O.K., let's do it again."

I flubbed the next throw, a perfect toss. "Damn," I muttered to myself, my pride beginning to hurt as much as my bloodied arms and aching knees. "You all right?" asked Damski. "You want some knee pads or something?"

I said, "No, fine, Mel. I just want to catch the damn ball."

I took another look at Lane. We both knew this couldn't go on all day. I started my sprint, Jerry firing, this time a tad too hard. Overthrow, I thought. I accelerated. The ball was dropping eight feet in front. It was a dive I had attempted dozens of times playing shortstop in high school and college. Do or die. Catch it or you don't. So I dived extending my left arm—a lifeguard reaching out to a floundering swimmer. Two inches off the turf, the baseball settled softly into the webbing of my glove. I bounced and remembered to stay down, to play out the scene. The crowd erupted.

I talked to Pace today. He says the Catch looks wonderful on film, the network likes the show, and to watch for Carradine and Canzoni on TV during the second week of the season. I'm busy planning the party, the big bash in honor of my alter ego, his catch and a movie even Pete Gray himself should enjoy.

For sheer drama, Game Five of the 1986 American League playoff was, as Moss Klein puts it here, "this decade's answer to game six of the 1975 World Series." The two games took place eleven years and a continent apart, but both of them went extra innings and both were won not only by the same team but by the same score (7–6 Red Sox)!

As for the Red Sox–Angels game reported here, comparisons could also be made with their game the day before, won by the Angels, 4–3. Both games went 11 innings; in each game, the team that eventually lost entered the ninth inning with a three-run lead and its ace on the mound; in each game, the star reliever was one strike away from escaping the ninth and saving a victory, but couldn't bring it off. "In fact," Klein was to write in a follow-up piece, "the two games could be viewed as one 22-inning, 7-hour, 44-minute marathon."

One difference: Had the Angels won Game Five, the playoff would have ended then and there. Instead, they had to return to Fenway, where the Red Sox blew them out 10–4 and 8–1 in the sixth and seventh games. So near and yet so far . . . the team with the haunted manager . . .

# 1986:
# Boston Red Sox 7,
# California Angels 6

## MOSS KLEIN

THE TEAMS are like two phantom ships, circling in the ocean, trying to elude all the old ghosts that have hounded them for so many years and break through, finally, to the sunlight of a championship.

The Boston Red Sox . . . the team that has endured so much heartbreak for so many seasons, the team that is never expected to win, the team that hasn't won a World Series since 1918 and whose only true believers are the occupants of the dugout.

The California Angels . . . the team that has never won a pennant in its 26 years of existence, with a haunted manager named Gene Mauch who has managed four different clubs during a 25-year period without winning a pennant.

The two ships collided at Anaheim Stadium yesterday and provided one of the most memorable games in playoff history, a game filled with more drama than is usually found in a week's worth of post-season affairs, this decade's answer to Game Six of the 1975 World Series between Boston and Cincinnati.

When it finally ended, when all the emotion had been wrung from the players and the managers and 64,223 fans, the Red Sox had won, 7–6, in 11 innings to force a sixth game in this best-of-seven American League playoff series.

Dave Henderson, a reserve outfielder who individually experienced the extremes of emotions more than anyone else in this roller-coaster come-to-life, appropriately brought home the winning run in the 11th with a sacrifice fly, driving in co-hero Don Baylor.

Henderson, who entered the game in the fifth inning after center fielder Tony Armas twisted an ankle, had literally created a two-run, go-ahead homer by Bobby Grich in the sixth when his almost-remarkable catch against the center field wall turned sour, with the ball dropping from his glove, over the wall for a 3–2 Angels' lead.

But then it was Henderson, batting with a runner on first and two out in the ninth, with the Red Sox season one strike from an end, who blasted a stunning, crowd-silencing, two-run homer off reliever Donnie Moore. That gave Boston a 6–5 lead, setting the stage for subsequent theatrics and, ultimately, for the game-winning sacrifice fly by Henderson, the man whose emotional gamut epitomized the game.

The Angels, who were one strike from winning their first pennant in the top of the ninth, who failed with the bases loaded and one out and the score tied in the bottom of the ninth, still lead, three-games-to-two, but must now return to Boston's Fenway Park for Game Six tomorrow night, Kirk McCaskill pitching against Boston's Oil Can Boyd.

This game goes far beyond normal description. As Phillies' reliever Tug McGraw once said of a roller-coaster 1980 playoff game against Houston. "It was like going through an art gallery on a skateboard. I know I saw all the pictures, but I can't remember them."

And there was so much worth remembering: The ninth inning alone included the two-run homers by Don Baylor and Henderson, the latest of Mauch's ill-fated pitching decisions, the Angels' rally with a tying hit by Rob Wilfong, the clutch relief of Steve Crawford, who retired old pros Doug DeCinces and Grich to escape the bases-loaded, game-on-the-line crisis.

The Angels, with ace Mike Witt pitching, had a 5–2 lead entering the ninth. Bob Boone's homer in the third and Grich's Henderson-aided homer in the sixth had overcome Rich Gedman's two-run homer in the second, and the Angels added two lucky-hop runs in the seventh.

But this was to be a reverse déjà-vu of Saturday night's game, when the Red Sox had a three-run lead with Roger Clemens pitching, and when relief ace Calvin Schiraldi was one strike from a victory, only to have the Red Sox lose in 11 innings.

This was the Red Sox' turn to rise, the Angels' turn to fail. Witt, pitching masterfully, gave up a leadoff single to Bill Buckner in the ninth, just beyond the diving reach of shortstop Dick Schofield. But Witt struck out Jim Rice on three pitches, and had a 2–2 count on Baylor when the powerful DH muscled a fastball over the wall in left-center. Now it was 5–4, but Witt retired Dwight Evans on a weak pop to third.

One out to go. One out from the first pennant for the 26-year-old team and the 25th-year manager. But Mauch, who has lived with pitching demons for 22 years, with the Jim Bunning–Chris Short overkill in the fold of the '64 Phillies, with a series of backfires in the '82 playoffs when the Angels won the first two and lost the next three to Milwaukee, played the percentages and called for lefty Gary Lucas to face lefty-hitting Gedman.

But Lucas, who had not hit a batter with a pitch in his 45⅔ innings this season, hit Gedman with his first pitch, putting the tying run on base.

Henderson was the batter, and the Red Sox couldn't have been encouraged. Henderson, acquired from Seattle on Aug. 17 for outfield protection, had batted .196,

with one homer and 15 strikeouts in 51 at-bats for Boston. He was hitless in his two playoff at-bats, and had struck out in the seventh inning.

Mauch sent for righty Moore, a dominant force last year who had been hindered by arm problems this season but still finished strong and managed 21 saves. The count went to 1–2, then 2–2. Henderson fouled a pitch, then another. And then, in the tradition of Bobby Thomson and Bill Mazeroski and Carlton Fisk and Chris Chambliss, Henderson lined a split-fingered fastball that carried over the left-field wall. Boston had the 6–5 lead . . . but this one was far from over.

Boone led off the Angels' ninth against Bob Stanley with a single and pinch-runner Ruppert Jones was sacrificed to second. Lefty Joe Sambito came in and Wilfong, whose chopped double had produced a run in the two-run seventh, lined a single to right. Right fielder Evans made a strong throw to the plate but catcher Gedman had to move up a step and Jones—with third-base coach Moose Stubing never hesitating to wave this time—slid around the sweeping tag.

The score was tied, Henderson's homer had been negated and the Angels still had a chance to end their 26-year hunt. Crawford replaced Sambito and gave up a single to Dick Schofield, a sharp grounder to the right of first baseman Dave Stapleton, who had been a pinch-runner for Buckner in the ninth. Buckner, who wears his glove on his right hand, might have grabbed the ball; Stapleton, with his glove on his left hand, couldn't.

Wilfong raced to third and Downing was given an intentional walk, loading the bases with one out. The pennant was there to be won and Crawford, who had been added to the playoff roster because of Tom Seaver's injury, who during the season had an 0–2 record and 3.92 ERA and had allowed a total of 88 hits and walks in 57⅓ innings, was an unlikely save-ior for Boston.

But this, of course, was an unlikely game. And Crawford simply retired the dangerous DeCinces on a fly to shallow right and Grich, the Saturday night hero, on a line drive back to the mound. End of inning, continuation of drama.

In the 10th, the Red Sox had runners on first and third, one out—but Rice grounded into an inning-ending double play. In the Angels' 10th, Rice atoned. With a runner on first and two out, he crashed against the left-field wall to catch a line drive by Pettis.

And then it was the 11th. Moore hit Baylor with a pitch, and for the second time in three innings, that slip-up by an Angels' pitcher was to prove ultra-costly. Evans singled. Gedman's bunt down the third-base line became a single. With the bases loaded and nobody out, Henderson hit the line drive to left-center that was speared by Pettis, but Baylor tagged up and scored easily.

The Red Sox would have had more, but left fielder Downing banged into the wall to grab Ed Romero's line drive, robbing him of a two-run hit. And second baseman Wilfong made a diving spear of Wade Boggs' hard-hopper, ending the inning.

But this time, the one-run lead held. Schiraldi struck out Wilfong, struck out Schofield and got Downing on a foul pop to first baseman Stapleton. The game was over, the series goes on, and the two ships keep circling in the waters.

# JOHN GALLAGHER

*"See you later—I've got to go do my thing."*

This article appeared early in 1986 in *The New York Times Magazine*. Its author also wrote the book *A Thinking Man's Guide to Baseball*—as we well might guess.

# Baseball's Hits and Misses

## LEONARD KOPPETT

BASEBALL FANS have witnessed many developments in their game of choice during the 40 years since the end of World War II, some favorable, some not so. In my opinion, the three worst have been:

1. Artificial turf.

2. Expansion.

3. The evisceration of the minor league system.

The three best developments have been:

1. The television camera.

2. The playoffs.

3. The return of the stolen base.

It is also my opinion that, unfortunately for fans, the worst far outweigh the best.

Before zeroing in on these developments, I should begin by making the following four assumptions:

First, fans dislike change. One of baseball's greatest assets is continuity. If a time machine whisked you back, say, to the 1912 World Series between the New York Giants and the Boston Red Sox, you would have no trouble following the game. All the basic rules and techniques would be the same as they are now. But a 1912 football or basketball or hockey game would mystify anyone who knew only today's rules and styles.

Second, fans like action they can see, which means scoring. A steady diet of 9–7 games with 20 or more hits and the lead changing hands a few times is more enjoyable than a steady diet of 2–1 games, as tense and artistic as these may seem to the professionals involved.

Next, fans like identifiable heroes and exceptional performances. The sports industry pays lip service to "parity" these days, which means spreading victory around to as many markets as possible, but the price of parity is the absence of champions who fire the imagination the way the old New York Yankees, Green Bay Packers, Joe Louis, Muhammad Ali and Arnold Palmer did.

And finally, every fan has a personal Golden Age, coinciding roughly with the first decade of that person's interest in baseball, whether it starts at the age of 6 or 26. That era, for that individual, sets the norm to which everything afterward is related.

For me, that was the decade of the 1930's. But after some 35 years of being paid to watch and report baseball for daily newspapers, mostly in New York, and interacting with those who make their living playing or promoting the game, I've gotten too close to things ordinary fans have no access to. So I no longer qualify as an unadulterated fan and it would be presumptuous to speak as one. On the other hand, all my training, inclination, job requirements and accumulated data have centered on the question, "What does the fan want to know about what happened?" So I don't share the myopia of those who live entirely within the baseball community. I can identify fan concerns with no ax to grind.

All that said, here are my reasons:

ARTIFICIAL TURF: This hard, smooth, homogeneous surface distorts the basic principles of the game: hitting, pitching and fielding. A fundamental esthetic is altered as well: Because of the way artificial turf makes a baseball bounce, the game often looks as if it's being played with a tennis ball.

We think of pitchers as trying to get "outs" and hitters as trying to get "hits." Of course. But outs and hits are consequences of more basic conscious intentions.

A pitcher actually tries to accomplish two things. He wants to upset the batter's timing, so that he can't hit the ball squarely. And, according to the game situation, he wants to induce the batter to hit either a fly ball or a grounder.

A hitter can do nothing more than try to hit the ball hard. He can control its direction to some degree, but he must still hit the ball sharply enough to get it by a fielder.

Traditionally, hitters have wanted line drives and long drives that enable them and base runners to advance more than one base, and pitchers want grounders most of the time. On natural grass, each bounce takes some steam out of a batted ball. Under ordinary conditions, the four infielders and three outfielders can cover the gaps and field balls that aren't hit too sharply, while the offense benefits from balls hit very sharply and very far.

But artificial turf spoils all the formulas and ruins the rhythm of the game, especially in the outfield. A soft fly—in a sense, a victory for the pitcher—that falls in front of an in-rushing outfielder may well bounce over his head. And a modest line drive (or even a grounder) into an outfield gap cannot be cut off before it skids to the fence. To compensate, outfielders must play deeper and come in more cautiously, making the gaps between them even wider. At the same time, though infielders can play deeper—since a bouncing ball reaches them a little sooner, leaving them a bit more time to throw to first—grounders still scoot by them more quickly than they do on natural grass.

The result is more "undeserved" hits, particularly extra-base hits—and a much less attractive game to the spectator's eye. Artificial turf decreases the possibility of the most elegant plays, when fielders move laterally to intercept the ball and throw to a base for a close play.

The surface is enough like a running track to enhance running speed, so fleet outfielders can reach just about any long drive that doesn't hit or clear a fence. But the difficult shoestring catch has become a bad gamble. So we see countless two-base hits on grounders past the second baseman, or pop-fly triples that bounce away, and fewer "authentic" doubles and triples hit over outfielders' heads or out of their reach in the alleys.

If all baseball were played on artificial turf, we would simply adapt to the new parameters. But only 10 of the 26 major league parks have it—enough to make everyone deal with it, not enough to create a new norm. And, of course, in all the habit-forming years from Little League through the minors, players hone their reflexes on natural fields.

EXPANSION: The usual argument against expansion is that it "dilutes" playing talent. This is true but misleading. It is not true that there aren't enough "good" players to go around. Players with enough natural ability to reach the majors improve with the chance to play regularly. The player who would have been on the bench or in the minors behind someone slightly better in the old days now may surpass his original rival after developing on an another team.

What *is* true is that, by definition, the best 400 players, when there were 16 teams, formed a higher density of excellence than the best 650 players on today's 26 teams.

More teams mean basic changes in statistics and schedule. Statistics are a key feature of baseball enjoyment, more so than statistics in other sports, and they became embedded in well-known regularities that existed, roughly, from 1903 to 1960. The 154-game schedule, in each league, had every team playing every other team 22 times. Such milestones as 20 victories for a pitcher or 100 runs batted in for a hitter acquired their significance in that context; but, more important, the frequency and uniformity of matchups among the teams in a league enhanced the "breaks-even-up-over-time" concept that adds to the validity of statistics.

In 1961, the year the American League expanded to 10 teams, the schedule had to be increased to 162 games (with each team meeting each opponent 18 times). And a celebrated flap arose right away, when Roger Maris and Mickey Mantle launched an assault on Babe Ruth's record of 60 homers, set in 1927. Commissioner Ford Frick, once a close friend of Ruth's, declared that a new record "wouldn't count" unless it was accomplished in 154 games—an emotion-driven, illogical, unjustifiable restriction that would poison Maris's achievement of hitting 61, and would make "asterisks" into confusing addenda to all of baseball's record-keeping. The issue had real emotional force, and after leagues were broken into divisions, and more teams produced more players who did not face opponents an equal number of times, many statistics lost their power to excite.

Also weakened has been the fan's capability for attention. In the 16-team days, true fans knew the regular players on all teams, their records and characteristics of their play. Not only were there far fewer players, but each team came to town more often. Now, with 26 teams in action and other sports having gained in both media attention and viewer interest, and with an Oakland coming to New York for only two series three months apart, no fan can keep up with all the players. This increases home-team-only rooting, intensifying partisanship, but attenuating fan involvement in baseball as a whole.

Expansion, of course, benefits fans in cities with new teams. But it does so at the expense of the potential enjoyment of the game by those who had local teams in the old setup, and by the millions who don't live in any major league city but follow the game passionately with free choice of favorites.

In an eight-team league, 10 superstars (in fan perception, aside from statistics) may well be scattered among six teams; in a 14-team league, more than half the teams are likely to be without a superstar.

And too, more sparsely sprinkled talent means that offense suffers. With fewer teams, more good hitters are concentrated in any one batting order, and they "protect" each other. But when a batting order has only one or two outstanding hitters in it, the opposition pitches around them and gives them less opportunity to do damage. It wasn't a coincidence that when Maris hit 61 homers, Mantle (with 54) was hitting behind him, or that Lou Gehrig was on deck when Ruth came to bat.

THE MINORS: It used to take several years of minor league seasoning to produce a major leaguer, and the proportion of top-level minor to major league teams was about 2 to 1. Now the proportion is 1 to 1, and every minor league system is strictly a developmental device for the majors, arousing little local interest.

Why does this concern the major league fan? Because the present system tends to depress offense and retard the development of hitting stars. Pitchers can, by and large, perfect their craft by practicing their deliveries; hitters can become good hitters only by honing their reflexes against good pitchers. A young hitter with natural talent can be ruined if he is overmatched too early, i.e., by bringing him to the majors; but he will stagnate at a certain level if the minor leaguers he faces aren't good enough to keep testing him.

In the old days, the high minors had many experienced pitchers who had been in the majors or would have been there if there had been 26 pitching staffs instead of 16. Young hitters faced them for a couple of years, and either improved or dropped out. Today, minor league rosters consist only of promising youngsters and temporary major league convalescents, with only a few marginals—who are marginal in the context of 26, not 16, teams. Today, potentially talented hitters get minimum minor league experience and rapid promotion to the majors. The best do well enough, but not as many develop to their highest potential as did in the days of the strong minor leagues.

O.K., those are the worst developments. Now what about the best?

THE TELEVISION CAMERA: Thanks to television, fans like my son, who was born in 1967, see more major league baseball and hear more sophisticated discussion of it before the age of 12 than I was exposed to by the time I was 30.

Television's greatest gift to baseball is the camera angle that lets fans see the pitcher-hitter battle as it really takes place.

This, after all, is the whole ball game. It takes exceptionally sharp and well-trained vision to judge the speed and path of a thrown baseball. Managers learn to do it from the dugout, and professional scouts operate behind home plate or in a press box. But how many people sitting in the stands can really pick out the fine, individual qualities of a pitched ball, aside from noting that it is too high, in the dirt, or wild? Fans react to the umpire's signal, the batter's and catcher's movements, and the flight of the batted ball, but they don't really "see" pitching.

On television they do, and with slow-motion replays no less. Fans see it from the catcher-umpire angle sometimes, from the pitcher's angle sometimes, but with center-of-the-screen clarity always.

That alone is blessing enough. But when you add to it close-ups of facial expressions, split screens of base runners taking leads, replays of long hits and funny bounces and spectacular catches—well, television has opened up the richness of baseball details to all fans in a way that only a few professionals actually on the field used to know.

THE PLAYOFFS: Purists scoff at playoffs, but if you think you'd be fascinated watching teams battle for 11th place in late August, or just playing out the string in September, think again. Breaking up leagues into divisions has its drawbacks, as we've seen, but it is the only sensible solution to too many teams. The same forces that created a World Series between two league champions operate to create and hold interest in preliminary rounds. Four "pennant races," whatever their quality, are better than two of the same quality. And the kind of excitement a one-survivor playoff series generates is not obtainable any other way.

THE STOLEN BASE: When Babe Ruth proved what home runs could do, a whole baseball generation converted itself to long-ball thinking. In the process, the attempt to steal a base, a basic scoring weapon before the 1920's, was put aside as a poor risk. The homer or double will score a man from first; a man thrown out stealing won't score when the next man hits a homer, and that out will decrease the number of times the home-run hitters get to bat.

The stand-around-and-wait-for-a-homer style, which prevailed through the 1940's and 1950's, promoted unwanted byproducts: strikeouts and walks. Hitters, swinging from the heels, didn't mind striking out if they connected a few other times. Pitchers, fearing the homer, stayed out of the strike zone.

But fans want to see the batted ball in play. Walks and strikeouts are stop-action plays. By the late 1960's, as factors such as the increasingly effective use of relief pitchers made homers harder to hit, stop-action reached a peak. In 1968, when scoring slumped to a low of 6.8 runs a game (by both teams), about 25 percent of all the players coming to bat walked or struck out—no action one-fourth of the time.

Beginning around 1960, Maury Wills of the Los

Angeles Dodgers and Luis Aparicio of the Chicago White Sox initiated a base-stealing revolution. In the last 25 years, after standing pat for more than four decades, the record for stolen bases in a season has been broken three times, by Wills, by Lou Brock, and finally by Rickey Henderson, who stole 130 for the Oakland A's in 1982. And as a result, many managers have plugged stealing back into their strategies. The threat of a steal worries the pitcher and affects what he throws. It makes infielders move around and affects defensive strategy. Willingness to steal means that the walk ceases to be a stop-action play; it is now perceived as the prelude to a steal attempt.

If you went to 10 games in 1958, you saw, on the average, 86 runs scored, 18 home runs and 6 stolen bases. In 1985, you saw 87 runs scored, 17 home runs and 15 stolen bases. In other words, we haven't lost any of the pleasures of power or production, but we're seeing more action.

Needless to say, there have been other developments that have affected the fan, many of them well-publicized.

There is the recent outrage, for example, over drug use by players, and other factors that have served to alienate the fan from the game: ever-escalating ticket prices; exorbitant player salaries; two player strikes and one umpire strike during the 1980's; the uncertain economics of many franchises; and rowdyism in the stands. But drug abuse, price inflation, labor strife, bad behavior and selfishness are not peculiar to baseball, and as well they're concerns that are tangential to the actual playing of the game, operating outside the baselines.

So what about the ones I've cited? Has the game itself improved for the fan? Is the effect of the bad balanced by the good? I would say no. Artificial turf and expansion have caused far more damage to the game than television and playoff excitement can compensate for. Fortunately, it hasn't been enough to spoil the special pleasures baseball affords, as constantly rising attendance and impassioned literary expressions continue to prove. But is baseball somewhat less fun than it used to be? Alas, yes.

And this raises another question, for each reader to answer alone: what isn't?

These were Charlie Finley's Oakland A's—Sal Bando and Reggie Jackson and Catfish Hunter and Joe Rudi and Vida Blue and Rollie Fingers and Campy Campaneris—who won five straight division titles from 1971 through 1975. But there were other players too: Marquez and Tenace and Mincher and Mangual. They were the ninth-inning heroes in the fourth game of the 1972 World Series, the one that set the A's on course to the first of their three consecutive world championships.

You will note that the title we have assigned to this wacky, wonderful story gives the final score of the game—which is more than the story does. It wouldn't have been as wacky or wonderful a story if it had.

# 1972:
# Oakland A's 3,
# Cincinnati Reds 2

## JOHN KRICH

B Y THE shores of the great bay (one-third filled and seven-eighths surrounded), by the shores of the abundant bay (one-third salmon and seven-eighths oil slick), by the shores of the unnoticed bay (one-third post card and seven-eighths eyewash), we've come for a tribal birth. Fifty-thousand midwives, coaxing, cajoling, armed with scalpels and forceps, ambergris and home-opathy, skulls, and Ju-Ju, we'll whoop and holler while the babe remains silent. Push and pull and boil water and soak towels and look down there between the legs where we're not supposed to look. Find that soft crown and bring forth something pink and cheezy and more alive than we are. Jump-start the battery of our lives, gone dead. Rescue Bump City from the boondocks of history. Get that championship for them A's, them kiss-my-A's, who we'd seen go-in-seven-o and swing-'n'-run in seven-one and sock-it-to for you-know-who in seven-two. Just twenty-seven outs of labor pains, and there would be no turning back.

The amphitheatre will be our operating room. It's waiting for us, all sterilized: such an un-Roman coliseum, grey as the clouds that move in thin steely sheets. Ticket scalpers are doing great business a discreet distance from the surgical gates. The parking lot's full, so I park by the BART stop, where the untouched-by-human-hands system unloads the expectant Moms and Pops. Characteristically, the station's complete, but the pathway from platform to stadium isn't. I follow the most traveled route that crosses two sets of Southern Pacific tracks, an auto demolition works, a trestle bridge over a boggy factory runoff, to a newly-made hole in the Coliseum's fencing. All around are rusting axles and bay estuary sludge and Granny Goose potato chip exhaust.

How far from the places we live are these spectacles we stage: Miami becomes simply the Orange Bowl, Boston is the short porch at Fenway Park, and Oakland is reduced to this bare circle the players have nicknamed "the Mausoleum." But once inside the oval, there's that wonderful first glimpse of green outfield grass, so surprisingly alive and growing. There's the smooth symmetry of the diamond to welcome us, and assure us that all's in order for the birth. There's sausage waftings in the air to alert our canine senses, and a primeval forest's worth of shrill calls from the vendors. There's the pow-wow humming of the stands, like a monotonous chant that alerts us to the coming ritual. Captured by this measured realm, we're willing to suspend all geography. We're ready for Captain Sal and the age of irony.

But where is our cap'n, the brutish Bando, the Catholic rock upon which Finley built his team? Seated high above the right-field line, Section 301, I squint and find Oakland's own L'il Joe Morgan, warming up before the dugout. He's playing catch the way all major leaguers do, with all the seemingly superfluous gestures

**NO PLAY . . .**
Tom Brookens of the Tigers made a crash landing at second base and was safe. What the shortstop, Alfredo Griffin, thought is not recorded. (AP/Wide World Photos)

and ticks that the smallest sandlotters use. It's as though the myth, the uniform, the traditions, are too strong for individual men. This game eats them up. They're still pretending, still dreaming about being ballplayers.

The A's take the field now. They've changed their fuzzy-wuzzy uniforms again. What a headache Finley's clown costumes would be to the chaw-chewing veterans with their superstitions and rabbits' feet hexes! They would have to compute the varying qualities of performance in all six combinations of green, white, and gold. And even as the A's go through their ballet of infield drills and stand with goody-goody white shoes against the clean lye of the foul lines for anthem-time, I'm looking like a good country doctor—we're all looking—for signs of choke. Choke is miscarriage is defects is fear of being born. Choke: the time you didn't and knew you should have. Choke: an uncomfortable escape with everybody watching. Choke isn't even failure, just ambivalence. And every sport fan knows the symptoms—strong conscience, weak constitution. So don't slip, boys. Don't look too closely at what's up ahead. Just slither like spermatozoa. If baseball is a game of inches, then what's conception? Or contraception?

A five-year-old sits down next to me and asks his own question: "Daddy, why is it called the World Series?"

I could tell him. I could recount the bitter corporate rivalry between the greedy American and National Leagues that produced these fall games as a kind of peace treaty. I could name all the winners since '03. Instead of answers, Daddy fills the kid with Fudgsicles and Colossal Dogs and even cheaper "Shaddups!" Behind me, a foghorn voice blasts down at the vacant outfield expanse: "We love you Catfish, oh yes we do. We love you Catfish, and we'll be true . . ." Peeking over my shoulder, I find the song belongs to a Filipino tomgirl in A's cap with black braids tumbling out to her waist, green-and-gold frockery all the way. Her escort is her baby-pink grandpa. Behind them, and filling most of Section 301, is a gaggle of black matrons: all stout, all in knit caps with brims of flattened Coors cans, all clapping and shouting to keep warm. They're placing bets and offering advice and swapping tall tales about past games and future conquests. "Those Reds be bad, but our A's is gonna be monsters!"

The rest of the crowd filtering past me is a unique genetic blend, label it "Mixed Nuts." I look mainly at the feet: white imported shoes skidding past, then tennies, then hiking boots that belong to the backpacking crowd that's just parachuted in. Lower echelon business types drag their wigged wives wearily along, and Hayward pachucos bounce by, grinning to reveal the spaces where they once had front teeth. They're all seated by an usherette with goo-goo eyes and rosy cheeks and a smile that's all gums and hot chocolate.

This must be her thousandth game, but she sways with the organ music and cheers Charlie O., the real-live mule mascot making his customary lap around the warning track's cinder. A proud wagonmaster dug up from the rodeo circuit, reminding us that someplace out there is a land called the West, leads the prized arthritic donkey back to his green-and-gold trailer. The usherette is up on the tip of her Thom McAns, practicing some bouncy routine—poor frustrated cheerleader who never made it past the tryouts. She's leading two sandy-haired executives to the seats on my right. They're arriving just in time, pulling up their tweed suits in the knee as they sit, one of them proclaiming, "How sweet it is!"

I'm glad to have all of them as company. Being alone at the ballpark is like eating alone in a restaurant—I must cheer as I would chomp, hoping no one objects. But first, there's the national anthem to hurdle, and I don't care if it's being played by Harold Farberman and the award-winning Oakland Youth Orchestra. Will I stand for it? The ladies behind me stay seated, and take swigs from their flasks to warm up their hollers. I end up rising but only to catch a glimpse of Charlie O.—the man, not the beast. He's in his imperial box behind the A's dugout, ready to reach for the hot line to his manager, entertaining some politician or beauty queen. Behind him, a field of silver Oakland banners fan.

The Reds are being booed, and a gangling teenager is struggling to place his own banner on the upper deck overhang before me. I recognize him right away as one of those accident-prone drifters, a loser for whom all of life's curveballs have broke wrong. But the A's have made him feel like a winner, and his sign is a thank-you card. It shows a bulbous-nosed Athletic popping a red pill, and reads "DOWN THOSE REDS!" The artist returns to his seat, but the sign is blown loose and flies up to obstruct our section's view of the field. The executives glance at me sadly, and we know what we must do. Tearing wildly, we destroy the banner, letting the pieces bombard the box seats.

Das Spectikal is upon us. As Pete Rose takes his primate stance at the plate, Section 301 and we hold our pencils poised, ready to make the first scratches in our clean scorecards, hoping we'll soon record an A's win, the birth of the manchild. Kenny Holtzman, the Oakland starter, is a stringy Jew who, like his people, always manages to survive. He's also a clubhouse intellect who reads Proust and pitches with a remembrance of games past. Swiveling, barely winding up, he pecks at corners and lives by inches. But the Reds get a rally going at once.

"I'll bet you half our new contract that those runners die right where they are." The young execs starting their own game.

"You're on, pal."

Holtzman ends the threat by getting a loping fly-out to George Hendrick, a.k.a. "Easy Rider," the A's somnambulist centerfielder. His nonchalance makes the nannies cry, "Be careful, Mister Easy Rider, that ball be hard and if you don't watch your bad self, son, why it can kill you!"

Cincinnati's Don Gullett matches Holtzman pitch for pitch and before we know it, the game's bogged down in its silent middle innings. In the bottom of the fifth, Gene Tenace steps up to bat, and the sun breaks through the swift ocean clouds.

"Better soak in those rays while you can, buddy boy," the businessman warns his companion.

"Daddy, what happens if a ball hits a teevee camera?" asks the kid between crunches of Crackerjacks.

"L'il lumber, l'il lumber now!" the beer-bellied mammas plead toward the plate.

And Tenace hears their plea. This fall, he's the meeting point of those concentric circles labeled actuality and hope. Gino hits his third Series home run, and it lands near a sheet hanging from the bleachers with a bull's-eye painted on it and the logo "Tenace's Target." In Section 301, we rise *en masse,* like an opera crowd treated to its favorite aria. But we have no "Bravos!"— just a childish cackle, a growl of delight. The usherette bounces in her crepe soles, and encourages the cheers with a wave of her mittens. The black mammas exult. And Tenace, the coal miner's son, the second-string scrub, does his victory trot. He takes his place in the record books and in R. D. Laing's ledger of pseudo-events. How can we ever experience his experience of our experience of his experience?

It's time for Finley's ball girls to bring coffee (spiked, I presume) to the umps along the first and third base lines. It's really just a chance for these Lolita types to sway their Wedding Gown White tushies, and the crowd claps politely. But there's no room for sex when we hunger for its more potent aftereffects: the child, the child!

The A's don't make a habit of padding their leads, and they do not in the sixth—or the seventh. In the eighth, Holtzman weakens and Concepcion's single sends him from the game. Manager Williams brings on Vida Blue—a lefty to face lefty Joe Morgan, and one of those "percentage" moves that leaves my section to its own mathematics.

"Vida ain't no reliever." The consensus up the aisle.

"I heard that."

"Leave the boy alone, I say. He's angry at The Man. He ain't got room for this shit."

The executives are eager to repeat broadcast clichés.

"He's pitchin' in the kitchen," says one.

"He's so fast he can throw a pork chop past a timberwolf," says the other.

But Blue, who's been punished the whole Series for his early season holdout, is neither angry nor fast. He walks Morgan, and Oakland has advice for its own.

"Don't you be so quick, l'il brother, you hear me?" But Joe has no objective need to heed his off-season neighbors. All butterball-legs pumping, he puts the Reds in front, coming home from first on a crackling, definitive Tolan single.

The mood turns vengeful in Section 301. A loss now would be like a death in the family; the child stillborn. The cheerleading usher has gone glum. Only the execs pretend indifference.

"Back to the drawing board, Charlie O.," one laughs.

"It was a very good year . . ." the other intones in his best Sinatra croon. They pass their money down to me, and I pass them back more "suds."

And the ladies behind me are already passing the word, out the stadium and onto Tobaccy Road: "The brothers are beautiful, but they jus' ain't *ready.*"

The A's have dominated the contest, and the crowd figures they deserve to take it in spite of the tender subtleties involved in either refurbishing or destroying the pitching ego of Vida Blue. There's general relief when he's replaced by Rollie Fingers. That's what a relief pitcher is for.

"Give 'em the finger, Rollie!"

Her grandpa chuckles at the Filipino foghorn's scatology. And Fingers responds by choking off the Reds' rally. The pitcher with the handlebar mustache is taking on Homeric proportions. His consistency of craft placates the crowd. Thanks to Rollie, the A's have one last chance.

"MIKE . . . MIKE . . . MIKE . . ." The scoreboard pacemaker tries to stimulate the comatose crowd.

The Mike being flashed on the big board is Mike Hegan, a pinch-hitter. He grounds out pitifully, and hopes of a miracle finish fade. There are nine Cincinnati gloves poised to make two pitiful outs. But I'm still feeding my fervor with a reminder that the ninth-inning A's are a different franchise, a new team entirely. Like students reluctant to face a written assignment, these A's have always done their best work while facing a deadline. Perhaps the usherette is thinking the same thoughts, since she's clapping her mittened hands together like two stunned fish. A nervy freak, passing in search of his seat, which has disappeared in a Budweiser haze, stops in our aisle.

"Hey," he whispers to the usherette so that only she and I hear, "you're gorgeous! Do you know that? You're really gorgeous!"

The drunk is gone before she can respond, but I watch her permanent stadium rouge deepen. She gets thrilled further when Gonzalo Marquez punches out a single.

He's replaced by Allen Lewis, the Panamanian Express. Once again, whenever it seems to matter most, Gene Tenace is quietly digging his cleats into the batting box's brown dirt.

The Reds send for "The Hawk"—reliever Clay Carroll—to come swooping in for the kill. Tenace chops at the first pitch, and scrambles stubby-legged to first while the ball drops unharmed in that magical dimension between infield and outfield warps.

"Holy Jeez!" The executives are astir.

"Now we gon' get tight!" the sisters cry.

The bleachers rumble in waves of foot-stomping. The fickle-hearted who were headed towards the exits have returned to suffocate the rampways. Contemplations on the miraculous have begun. With one throw, the game could be over, or ready to begin again. How open-ended baseball is! How wisely conceived! How many more possibilities there are on the diamond than in our own lives!

"DON . . . DON . . . DON . . ." This time manager Williams' surprise nominee for sainthood is Don Mincher, and the foghorn chants the catechism. A recycled first baseman, Mincher steps to the plate knowing he's been chosen not for quickness of his wrists, but for the calm of his stomach.

Carroll's next pitch would later be accurately described by Reds' manager Sparky Anderson as "a bum high fastball with nothing on it." Mincher, amazed, responds with marionette reflex. Crack! Bat drawn away to full extension, muscles ripping, the hitter again makes those nine Cincy gloves irrelevant. He sends the pitch to that inner outfield wasteland where no player, living or dead, can get his butt quick enough. The Panamanian Express scores the tying run.

"Holy shit, buddy boy! How sweet it is! You better pinch me, pal, 'cause this I do not believe!"

Even the executives are midwives now, straining to glimpse the emergent skull of our savior.

Mincher leaves the game for a pinch-runner, savoring what was to be his last base-hit before retirement by flinging his cap to the ground with combative bravado. Saint Don has given us the strength to go on, and, under the rules, the chance. The last player on the A's bench is Angel Mangual, and the choir of nannies bless him: "Take it light, Angel darling! What it is and what it's got to be!"

Mangual swings at the first pitch, and we've hardly time to gasp. He appears to have been handcuffed, as the bat-on-ball makes no sound, not a good swing, sending a grounder with delicate tentativeness toward ecstasy.

"Threadin' da needle," it's called. Skipping between first baseman Perez and a desperately lunging Morgan, the ball slows predictably in the dewy outfield grass. Tenace scores the winning run before the ball can be touched.

Clusters of Finley's fireworks look like holy chrysanthemums exploding in the coming night. Below, the Reds depart with the superman speed of all losers, and the A's carry off Mangual like a shimmering gold Madonna. The hero's fist is raised, partisan-style. The ninth-inning A's have pushed the other A's to the point of no return. There is no room now for enough mistakes to deny them the championship.

The Coliseum is one huge orgone box—wired with an affinity that spills down all the ramps, that tramples on the planted slopes around the concrete bowl, that sparkles amidst the parking lot scramble, across the railroads and junkyards, over the little trestle bridge, over fences that are hurdled now with ease, out on the Nimitz, in the clammy bay waters. "By the bay, by the bay, by the beautiful bay . . ." Mister and Missus Baseball Fan U.S.A. are carried along by riotous pleasure. Dazed children wave stiff pennants, looking as though they know that gesture does not do justice to the moment. Their parents are grinning without fear, some whimpering and gasping and hooting, none of them worrying about looking ugly or forming words. Guard railings are casually destroyed on the happy march to the BART station, where the platform overflows with a chanting mob. The traffic cops look scared, but they've no need to be. The chants are not slogans, but odes to the A's. The arriving silver trains look like toys, like kiddie models, in the grip of the crowd's new strength.

Their eyes kicked out by Charlie O. and his mercenary mules, the fans carry visions with them—visions of a new world, visions that rise above the cities like jazz, visions that challenge the stupidity of their sources and actualize so sweet an optimism that even death seems a galaxy away. If only the parking lot had been filled with building blocks instead of chrome-rimmed cars! They would have built a new city for themselves right there, with towers and exalting monuments that would have dwarfed the stadium with their usefulness, declaring: we are more permanent than any of our edifices. A goofy tickle seized the throng, sending it in spasms toward the unseen foe: spontaneity. A spontaneity, like baseball, deserving of a better fate than words. "Why not?" the throng asked itself about almost anything. "Why the fuck not?" Whoever invented this game did it so that ninth innings could be like this.

# 1969:
# New York Mets 5,
# Baltimore Orioles 3

## JACK LANG

THEY SAID man would walk on the moon before the Mets won a championship. Man barely won the race.

Three months after Neil Armstrong took his "one small step for man, one giant leap for mankind," the New York Mets landed on their own moon yesterday and startled the baseball world as well as the Baltimore Orioles by capturing the World Series with a 5–3 victory in the fifth and final game.

Within moments after Jerry Koosman induced Davey Johnson to fly to Cleon Jones in left field for the final out, thousands of fans in the sellout crowd of 57,937 swarmed onto the Shea Stadium diamond to snatch pieces of turf as their personal souvenir of the historic event. In their eyes, they had just witnessed a miracle.

In baseball lore they had. Since 1961, when baseball expanded, there was no worse team in either league than the Mets. In 1962 they established a record by winning only 40 games and losing 120. Then they shocked the baseball establishment this year by first overcoming the veteran Chicago Cubs team to win the Eastern Division title and then by sweeping the Atlanta Braves three straight to win the first ever National League Championship Series.

Entering the World Series with their young club, the Mets were the decided underdogs against the established Baltimore Orioles with their strong pitching staff and renowned sluggers like Boog Powell and Frank Robinson.

And when Orioles leadoff man Don Buford laced Tom Seaver's second pitch in Game No. 1 for a home run, he could not resist a taunt as he rounded second base.

"You ain't seen nothin' yet," Buford chided shortstop Bud Harrelson.

"Neither have you," was Harrelson's bold if unconvincing reply.

Buford's boast would be Baltimore's last. The Orioles, as expected, won the opening game, 4–1, as Mike Cuellar outdueled Seaver. But the rest of the Series belonged to the Mets as they swept the next four games to become the most exuberant, if not the youngest, ever to reign as world champions.

Far into the night, the celebration continued throughout all five boroughs of New York City. Tavern and restaurant owners compared it to the partying of VJ Day or New Year's Eve.

As it did starting in Game No. 2, everything went the Mets' way in the fifth and concluding game. Manager Gil Hodges even managed to convince an American League umpire, Lou DiMuro, that one of his players had been hit with a pitch even though the umpire did not know it at the time.

Jerry Koosman, who got the Mets even with a 2–1 victory in Baltimore in Game No. 2, was victimized for three runs in the third inning. With Dave McNally pitching, that appeared to be a safe lead. But after being held at bay for five innings, the Mets suddenly turned it into a close game with two runs in the sixth.

How the Mets scored those two runs will eventually become as much a part of World Series mystique as the fabulous catches of Tommie Agee and Ron Swoboda in earlier games. If the Orioles could not believe what was happening to them on those spectacular plays, they had to realize they were fighting a higher force after the bizarre "shoe polish" incident.

Cleon Jones, leading off the fifth inning, skipped rope to get out of the way of a low inside pitch by McNally. DiMuro called it a ball and McNally was ready to throw his next pitch when Hodges suddenly appeared from the dugout holding a baseball in his hand. The Mets' manager approached DiMuro and said the ball that Jones had skipped away from actually hit him. Hodges convinced the umpire by showing him a black smudge on the ball: "It can only be shoe polish." DiMuro bought the Hodges version and awarded Jones first base. He had been hit by the pitch, the umpire ruled.

The Orioles, led by Earl Weaver, fussed and fumed to no avail.

No sooner had Jones reached first than Donn Clendenon followed with his third home run of the Series, and the Mets were back in the ball game, trailing by only one run. They got that run one inning later when light-hitting Al Weis took McNally downtown with a shot over the left-field wall. During the regular season, Weis had hit only two home runs and was one of the least likely of all Mets to connect.

Once the score was tied, the Orioles knew their hours were numbered. One inning later, the chaplain arrived to offer last rites.

Jones opened the eighth inning with a double off the left-field wall. Swoboda followed with a sinking liner to left that Buford trapped as Jones raced home with the tie-breaking run.

The great Baltimore defense fell apart to provide the Mets with their fifth and insurance run. First Powell bobbled Jerry Grote's grounder for one error, and then Eddie Watt juggled the ball covering at first and a second error was called. All the while, Swoboda was racing home.

Koosman walked Frank Robinson leading off the ninth but then retired the heart of the Orioles' batting order—Powell, Brooks Robinson and Johnson—to complete the Mets' Miracle.

"The Mets were like an avalanche. There was no way we were going to stop them," said J. Frank Cashen, the Baltimore general manager in the boisterous, victorious Mets' dressing room.

Cashen was right. The Mets were a team of destiny. They had come from a ninth-place finish last year to win 38 of their last 47 games this year and then took 7 out of 8 in postseason play against the Atlanta Braves and Baltimore Orioles.

"If we played until Christmas, no one was going to beat us," Swoboda boasted in the champagne-soaked Mets clubhouse.

Swoboda was right, Santa Claus would have had a tough time against the Mets this year.

Well, maybe they didn't have ground-rule doubles in those days, but that's not going to affect your enjoyment any as you read one of the finest and funniest baseball tales ever. There are players just like Speed Parker in baseball today . . . more than *seventy years* after this story was written!

# Horseshoes

## RING LARDNER

THE SERIES ENDED Tuesday, but I had stayed in Philadelphia an extra day on the chance of there being some follow-up stuff worth sending. Nothing had broken loose; so I filed some stuff about what the Athletics and Giants were going to do with their dough and then caught the eight o'clock train for Chicago.

Having passed up supper in order to get my story away and grab the train, I went to the buffet car right after I'd planted my grips. I sat down at one of the tables and ordered a sandwich. Four salesmen were playing rum at the other table and all the chairs in the car were occupied; so it didn't surprise me when somebody flopped down in the seat opposite me.

I looked up from my paper and with a little thrill recognized my companion. Now I've been experting round the country with ballplayers so much that it doesn't usually excite me to meet one face to face, even if he's a star. I can talk with Tyrus without getting all fussed up. But this particular player had jumped from obscurity to fame so suddenly and had played such an important though brief part in the recent argument between the Macks and McGraws that I couldn't help being a little awed by his proximity.

It was none other than Grimes, the utility outfielder Connie had been forced to use in the last game because of the injury to Joyce—Grimes, whose miraculous catch in the eleventh inning had robbed Parker of a home run and the Giants of victory, and whose own homer—a fluky one—had given the Athletics another World's Championship.

I had met Grimes one day during the spring he was with the Cubs, but I knew he wouldn't remember me. A ballplayer never recalls a reporter's face on less than six introductions or his name on less than twenty. However, I resolved to speak to him and had just mustered

sufficient courage to open a conversation when he saved me the trouble.

"Whose picture have they got there?" he asked, pointing to my paper.

"Speed Parker's," I replied.

"What do they say about him?" asked Grimes.

"I'll read it to you," I said.

" 'Speed Parker, McGraw's great third baseman, is ill in a local hospital with nervous prostration, the result of the strain of the World's Series, in which he played such a stellar role. Parker is in such a dangerous condition that no one is allowed to see him. Members of the New York team and fans from Gotham called at the hospital today, but were unable to gain admittance to his ward. Philadelphians hope he will recover speedily and will suffer no permanent ill effects from his sickness, for he won their admiration by his work in the series, though he was on a rival team. A lucky catch by Grimes, the Athletics' substitute outfielder, was all that prevented Parker from winning the title for New York. According to Manager Mack, of the champions, the series would have been over in four games but for Parker's wonderful exhibition of nerve and——' "

"That'll be a plenty," Grimes interrupted. "And that's just what you might expect from one o' them doughheaded reporters. If all the baseball writers was where they belonged they'd have to build an annex to Matteawan."

I kept my temper with very little effort—it takes more than a peevish ballplayer's remark to insult one of our fraternity; but I didn't exactly understand his peeve.

"Doesn't Parker deserve the bouquet?" I asked.

"Oh, they can boost him all they want to," said Grimes; "but when they call that catch lucky and don't mention the fact that Parker is the luckiest guy in the

world, somethin' must be wrong with 'em. Did you see
the serious?''

"No," I lied glibly, hoping to draw from him the
cause of his grouch.

"Well," he said, "you sure missed somethin'. They
never was a serious like it before and they won't never
be one again. It went the full seven games and every
game was a bear. They was one big innin' every day and
Parker was the big cheese in it. Just as Connie says, the
Ath-a-letics would of cleaned 'em in four games but for
Parker; but it wasn't because he's a great ballplayer—it
was because he was born with a knife, fork and spoon in
his mouth, and a rabbit's foot hung round his neck.

"You may not know it, but I'm Grimes, the guy that
made the lucky catch. I'm the guy that won the serious
with a hit—a home-run hit; and I'm here to tell you that
if I'd had one tenth o' Parker's luck they'd of heard
about me long before yesterday. They say my homer
was lucky. Maybe it was; but, believe me, it was time
things broke for me. They been breakin' for him all his
life.''

"Well," I said, "his luck must have gone back on
him if he's in a hospital with nervous prostration.''

"Nervous prostration nothin','' said Grimes. "He's
in a hospital because his face is all out o' shape and he's
ashamed to appear on the street. I don't usually do so
much talkin' and I'm ravin' a little tonight because I've
had a couple o' drinks; but——''

"Have another," said I, ringing for the waiter, "and
talk some more.''

"I made two hits yesterday," Grimes went on, "but
the crowd only seen one. I busted up the game and the
serious with the one they seen. The one they didn't see
was the one I busted up a guy's map with—and Speed
Parker was the guy. That's why he's in a hospital. He
may be able to play ball next year; but I'll bet my share
o' the dough that McGraw won't reco'nize him when he
shows up at Marlin in the spring.''

"When did this come off?" I asked. "And why?''

"It come off outside the clubhouse after yesterday's
battle," he said; "and I hit him because he called me a
name—a name I won't stand for from him.''

"What did he call you?" I queried, expecting to hear
one of the delicate epithets usually applied by conquered
to conqueror on the diamond.

" 'Horseshoes!' " was Grimes' amazing reply.

"But, good Lord!" I remonstrated, "I've heard of
ballplayers calling each other that, and Lucky Stiff, and
Fourleaf Clover, ever since I was a foot high, and I
never knew them to start fights about it.''

"Well," said Grimes, "I might as well give you all
the dope; and then if you don't think I was justified I'll
pay your fare from here to wherever you're goin'. I
don't want you to think I'm kickin' about trifles—or that

I'm kickin' at all, for that matter. I just want to prove to
you that he didn't have no license to pull that Horseshoes
stuff on me and that I only give him what was comin' to
him.''

"Go ahead and shoot," said I.

"Give us some more o' the same," said Grimes to the
passing waiter. And then he told me about it.

Maybe you've heard that me and Speed Parker was
raised in the same town—Ishpeming, Michigan. We was
kids together, and though he done all the devilment I got
all the lickin's. When we was about twelve years old
Speed throwed a rotten egg at the teacher and I got
expelled. That made me sick o' schools and I wouldn't
never go to one again, though my ol' man beat me up
and the truant officers threatened to have me hung.

Well, while Speed was learnin' what was the principal
products o' New Hampshire and Texas I was workin'
round the freighthouse and drivin' a dray.

We'd both been playin' ball all our lives; and when
the town organized a semipro club we got jobs with it.
We was to draw two bucks apiece for each game and
they played every Sunday. We played four games before
we got our first pay. They was a hole in my pants pocket
as big as the home plate, but I forgot about it and put the
dough in there. It wasn't there when I got home. Speed
didn't have no hole in his pocket—you can bet on that!
Afterward the club hired a good outfielder and I was
canned. They was huntin' for another third baseman too;
but, o' course, they didn't find none and Speed held his
job.

The next year they started the Northern Peninsula
League. We landed with the home team. The league
opened in May and blowed up the third week in June.
They paid off all the outsiders first and then had just
money enough left to settle with one of us two Ishpeming guys. The night they done the payin' I was out to my
uncle's farm, so they settled with Speed and told me I'd
have to wait for mine. I'm still waitin'!

Gene Higgins, who was manager o' the Battle Creek
Club, lived in Houghton, and that winter we goes over
and strikes him for a job. He give it to us and we busted
in together two years ago last spring.

I had a good year down there. I hit over .300 and stole
all the bases in sight. Speed got along good too, and they
was several big-league scouts lookin' us over. The
Chicago Cubs bought Speed outright and four clubs put
in a draft for me. Three of 'em—Cleveland and the New
York Giants and the Boston Nationals—needed outfielders bad, and it would of been a pipe for me to of made
good with any of 'em. But who do you think got me?
The same Chicago Cubs; and the only outfielders they
had at that time was Schulte and Leach and Good and
Williams and Stewart, and one or two others.

Well, I didn't figure I was any worse off than Speed. The Cubs had Zimmerman at third base and it didn't look like they was any danger of a busher beatin' him out; but Zimmerman goes and breaks his leg the second day o' the season—that's a year ago last April—and Speed jumps right in as a regular. Do you think anything like that could happen to Schulte or Leach, or any o' them outfielders? No, sir! I wore out my uniform slidin' up and down the bench and wonderin' whether they'd ship me to Fort Worth or Siberia.

Now I want to tell you about the miserable luck Speed had right off the reel. We was playin' at St. Louis. They had a one-run lead in the eighth, when their pitcher walked Speed with one out. Saier hits a high fly to center and Parker starts with the crack o' the bat. Both coachers was yellin' at him to go back, but he thought they was two out and he was clear round to third base when the ball come down. And Oakes muffs it! O' course he scored and the game was tied up.

Parker come in to the bench like he'd did something wonderful.

"Did you think they was two out?" ast Hank.

"No," says Speed, blushin'.

"Then what did you run for?" says Hank.

"I had a hunch he was goin' to drop the ball," says Speed; and Hank pretty near falls off the bench.

The next day he come up with one out and the sacks full, and the score tied in the sixth. He smashes one on the ground straight at Hauser and it looked like a cinch double play; but just as Hauser was goin' to grab it the ball hit a rough spot and hopped a mile over his head. It got between Oakes and Magee and went clear to the fence. Three guys scored and Speed pulled up at third. The papers come out and said the game was won by a three-bagger from the bat o' Parker, the Cubs' sensational kid third baseman. Gosh!

We go home to Chi and are havin' a hot battle with Pittsburgh. This time Speed's turn come when they was two on and two out, and Pittsburgh a run to the good—I think it was the eighth innin'. Cooper gives him a fast one and he hits it straight up in the air. O' course the runners started goin', but it looked hopeless because they wasn't no wind or high sky to bother anybody. Mowrey and Gibson both goes after the ball; and just as Mowrey was set for the catch Gibson bumps into him and they both fall down. Two runs scored and Speed got to second. Then what does he do but try to steal third—with two out too! And Gibson's peg pretty near hits the left field seats on the fly.

When Speed comes to the bench Hank says:

"If I was you I'd quit playin' ball and go to Monte Carlo."

"What for?" says Speed.

"You're so dam' lucky!" says Hank.

"So is Ty Cobb," says Speed. That's how he hated himself!

First trip to Cincy we run into a couple of old Ishpeming boys. They took us out one night, and about twelve o'clock I said we'd have to go back to the hotel or we'd get fined. Speed said I had cold feet and he stuck with the boys. I went back alone and Hank caught me comin' in and put a fifty-dollar plaster on me. Speed stayed out all night long and Hank never knowed it. I says to myself: "Wait till he gets out there and tries to play ball without no sleep!" But the game that day was called off on account o' rain. Can you beat it?

I remember what he got away with the next afternoon the same as though it happened yesterday. In the second innin' they walked him with nobody down, and he took a big lead off first base like he always does. Benton throwed over there three or four times to scare him back, and the last time he throwed, Hobby hid the ball. The coacher seen it and told Speed to hold the bag; but he didn't pay no attention. He started leadin' right off again and Hobby tried to tag him, but the ball slipped out of his hand and rolled about a yard away. Parker had plenty o' time to get back; but, instead o' that, he starts for second. Hobby picked up the ball and shot it down to Groh—and Groh made a square muff.

Parker slides into the bag safe and then gets up and throws out his chest like he'd made the greatest play ever. When the ball's throwed back to Benton, Speed leads off about thirty foot and stands there in a trance. Clarke signs for a pitch-out and pegs down to second to nip him. He was caught flatfooted—that is, he would of been with a decent throw; but Clarke's peg went pretty near to Latonia. Speed scored and strutted over to receive our hearty congratulations. Some o' the boys was laughin' and he thought they was laughin' with him instead of at him.

It was in the ninth, though, that he got by with one o' the worst I ever seen. The Reds was a run behind and Marsans was on third base with two out. Hobby, I think it was, hit one on the ground right at Speed and he picked it up clean. The crowd all got up and started for the exits. Marsans run toward the plate in the faint hope that the peg to first would be wild. All of a sudden the boys on the Cincy bench begun yellin' at him to slide, and he done so. He was way past the plate when Speed's throw got to Archer. The bonehead had shot the ball home instead o' to first base, thinkin' they was only one down. We was all crazy, believin' his nut play had let 'em tie it up; but he comes tearin' in, tellin' Archer to tag Marsans. So Jim walks over and tags the Cuban, who was brushin' off his uniform.

"You're out!" says Klem. "You never touched the plate."

I guess Marsans knowed the umps was right because

he didn't make much of a holler. But Speed sure got a pannin' in the clubhouse.

"I suppose you knowed he was goin' to miss the plate!" says Hank sarcastic as he could.

Everybody on the club roasted him, but it didn't do no good.

Well, you know what happened to me. I only got into one game with the Cubs—one afternoon when Leach was sick. We was playin' the Boston bunch and Tyler was workin' against us. I always had trouble with lefthanders and this was one of his good days. I couldn't see what he throwed up there. I got one foul durin' the afternoon's entertainment; and the wind was blowin' a hundred-mile gale, so that the best outfielder in the world couldn't judge a fly ball. That Boston bunch must of hit fifty of 'em and they all come to my field.

If I caught any I've forgot about it. Couple o' days after that I got notice o' my release to Indianapolis.

Parker kept right on all season doin' the blamedest things you ever heard of and gettin' by with 'em. One o' the boys told me about it later. If they was playin' a double-header in St. Louis, with the thermometer at 130 degrees, he'd get put out by the umps in the first innin' o' the first game. If he started to steal the catcher'd drop the pitch or somebody'd muff the throw. If he hit a pop fly the sun'd get in somebody's eyes. If he took a swell third strike with the bases full the umps would call it a ball. If he cut first base by twenty feet the umps would be readin' the mornin' paper.

Zimmerman's leg mended, so that he was all right by June; and then Saier got sick and they tried Speed at first base. He'd never saw the bag before; but things kept on breakin' for him and he played it like a house afire. The Cubs copped the pennant and Speed got in on the big dough, besides playin' a whale of a game through the whole serious.

Speed and me both went back to Ishpeming to spend the winter—though the Lord knows it ain't no winter resort. Our homes was there; and besides, in my case, they was a certain girl livin' in the old burg.

Parker, o' course, was the hero and the swell guy when we got home. He'd been in the World's Serious and had plenty o' dough in his kick. I come home with nothin' but my suitcase and a hard-luck story, which I kept to myself. I hadn't even went good enough in Indianapolis to be sure of a job there again.

That fall—last fall—an uncle o' Speed's died over in the Soo and left him ten thousand bucks. I had an uncle down in the Lower Peninsula who was worth fives times that much—but he had good health!

This girl I spoke about was the prettiest thing I ever see. I'd went with her in the old days, and when I blew back I found she was still strong for me. They wasn't a great deal o' variety in Ishpeming for a girl to pick from.

Her and I went to the dance every Saturday night and to church Sunday nights. I called on her Wednesday evenin's, besides takin' her to all the shows that come along—rotten as the most o' them was.

I never knowed Speed was makin' a play for this doll till along last Feb'uary. The minute I seen what was up I got busy. I took her out sleigh-ridin' and kept her out in the cold till she'd promised to marry me. We set the date for this fall—I figured I'd know better where I was at by that time.

Well, we didn't make no secret o' bein' engaged; down in the poolroom one night Speed come up and congratulated me. He says:

"You got a swell girl, Dick! I wouldn't mind bein' in your place. You're mighty lucky to cop her out—you old Horseshoes, you!"

"Horseshoes!" I says. "You got a fine license to call anybody Horseshoes! I suppose you ain't never had no luck?"

"Not like you," he says.

I was feelin' too good about grabbin' the girl to get sore at the time; but when I got to thinkin' about it a few minutes afterward it made me mad clear through. What right did that bird have to talk about me bein' lucky?

Speed was playin' freeze-out at a table near the door, and when I started home some o' the boys with him says:

"Good night, Dick."

I said good night and then Speed looked up.

"Good night, Horseshoes!" he says.

That got my nanny this time.

"Shut up, you lucky stiff!" I says. "If you wasn't so dam' lucky you'd be sweepin' the streets." Then I walks on out.

I was too busy with the girl to see much o' Speed after that. He left home about the middle o' the month to go to Tampa with the Cubs. I got notice from Indianapolis that I was sold to Baltimore. I didn't care much about goin' there and I wasn't anxious to leave home under the circumstances, so I didn't report till late.

When I read in the papers along in April that Speed had been traded to Boston for a couple o' pitchers I thought: "Gee! He must of lost his rabbit's foot!" Because, even if the Cubs didn't cop again, they'd have a city serious with the White Sox and get a bunch o' dough that way. And they wasn't no chance in the world for the Boston club to get nothin' but their salaries.

It wasn't another month, though, till Shafer, o' the Giants, quit baseball and McGraw was up against it for a third baseman. Next thing I knowed Speed was traded to New York and was with another winner—for they never was out o' first place all season.

I was gettin' along all right at Baltimore and Dunnie liked me; so I felt like I had somethin' more than just a one-year job—somethin' I could get married on. It was all framed that the weddin' was comin' off as soon as this season was over; so you can believe I was pullin' for October to hurry up and come.

One day in August, two months ago, Dunnie come in the clubhouse and handed me the news.

"Rube Oldring's busted his leg," he says, "and he's out for the rest o' the season. Connie's got a youngster named Joyce that he can stick in there, but he's got to have an extra outfielder. He's made me a good proposition for you and I'm goin' to let you go. It'll be pretty soft for you, because they got the pennant cinched and they'll cut you in on the big money."

"Yes," I says; "and when they're through with me they'll ship me to Hellangone, and I'll be draggin' down about seventy-five bucks a month next year."

"Nothin' like that," says Dunnie. "If he don't want you next season he's got to ask for waivers; and if you get out o' the big league you come right back here. That's all framed."

So that's how I come to get with the Ath-a-letics. Connie give me a nice, comf'table seat in one corner o' the bench and I had the pleasure o' watchin' a real ball club perform once every afternoon and sometimes twice.

Connie told me that as soon as they had the flag cinched he was goin' to lay off some o' his regulars and I'd get a chance to play.

Well, they cinched it the fourth day o' September and our next engagement was with Washin'ton on Labor Day. We had two games and I was in both of 'em. And I broke in with my usual lovely luck, because the pitchers I was ast to face was Boehling, a nasty left-hander, and this guy Johnson.

The mornin' game was Boehling's and he wasn't no worse than some o' the rest of his kind. I only whiffed once and would of had a triple if Milan hadn't run from here to New Orleans and stole one off me.

I'm not boastin' about my first experience with Johnson though. They can't never tell me he throws them balls with his arm. He's got a gun concealed about his person and he shoots 'em up there. I was leadin' off in Murphy's place and the game was a little delayed in startin', because I'd watched the big guy warm up and wasn't in no hurry to get to that plate. Before I left the bench Connie says:

"Don't try to take no healthy swing. Just meet 'em and you'll get along better."

So I tried to just meet the first one he throwed; but when I stuck out my bat Henry was throwin' the pill back to Johnson. Then I thought: Maybe if I start swingin' now at the second one I'll hit the third one. So I let the second one come over and the umps guessed it was another strike, though I'll bet a thousand bucks he couldn't see it no more'n I could.

While Johnson was still windin' up to pitch again I started to swing—and the big cuss crosses me with a slow one. I lunged at it twice and missed it both times, and the force o' my wallop throwed me clean back to the bench. The Ath-a-letics was all laughin' at me and I laughed too, because I was glad that much of it was over.

McInnes gets a base hit off him in the second innin' and I ast him how he done it.

"He's a friend o' mine," says Jack, "and he lets up when he pitches to me."

I made up my mind right there that if I was goin' to be in the league next year I'd go out and visit Johnson this winter and get acquainted.

I wished before the day was over that I was hittin' in the catcher's place, because the fellers down near the tail-end of the battin' order only had to face him three times. He fanned me on three pitched balls again in the third, and when I come up in the sixth he scared me to death by pretty near beanin' me with the first one.

"Be careful!" says Henry. "He's gettin' pretty wild and he's liable to knock you away from your uniform."

"Don't he never curve one?" I ast.

"Sure!" says Henry. "Do you want to see his curve?"

"Yes," I says, knowin' the hook couldn't be no worse'n the fast one.

So he give me three hooks in succession and I missed 'em all; but I felt more comf'table than when I was duckin' his fast ball. In the ninth he hit my bat with a curve and the ball went on the ground to McBride. He booted it, but throwed me out easy—because I was so surprised at not havin' whiffed that I forgot to run!

Well, I went along like that for the rest o' the season, runnin' up against the best pitchers in the league and not exactly murderin' 'em. Everything I tried went wrong, and I was smart enough to know that if anything had depended on the games I wouldn't of been in there for two minutes. Joyce and Strunk and Murphy wasn't jealous o' me a bit; but they was glad to take turns restin', and I didn't care much how I went so long as I was sure of a job next year.

I'd wrote to the girl a couple o' times askin' her to set the exact date for our weddin'; but she hadn't paid no attention. She said she was glad I was with the Ath-a-letics, but she thought the Giants was goin' to beat us. I might of suspected from that that somethin' was wrong, because not even a girl would pick the Giants to trim that bunch of ourn. Finally, the day before the serious started, I sent her a kind o' sassy letter sayin' I guessed it was up to me to name the day, and askin' whether October twentieth was all right. I told her to wire me yes or no.

I'd been readin' the dope about Speed all season, and I knowed he'd had a whale of a year and that his luck was right with him; but I never dreamed a man could have the Lord on his side as strong as Speed did in that World's Serious! I might as well tell you all the dope, so long as you wasn't there.

The first game was on our grounds and Connie give us a talkin' to in the clubhouse beforehand.

"The shorter this serious is," he says, "the better for us. If it's a long serious we're goin' to have trouble, because McGraw's got five pitchers he can work and we've got about three; so I want you boys to go at 'em from the jump and play 'em off their feet. Don't take things easy, because it ain't goin' to be no snap. Just because we've licked 'em before ain't no sign we'll do it this time."

Then he calls me to one side and ast me what I knowed about Parker.

"You was with the Cubs when he was, wasn't you?" he says.

"Yes," I says; "and he's the luckiest stiff you ever seen! If he got stewed and fell in the gutter he'd catch a fish."

"I don't like to hear a good ballplayer called lucky," says Connie. "He must have a lot of ability or McGraw wouldn't use him regular. And he's been hittin' about .340 and played a bang-up game at third base. That can't be all luck."

"Wait till you see him," I says; "and if you don't say he's the luckiest guy in the world you can sell me to the Boston Bloomer Girls. He's so lucky," I says, "that if they traded him to the St. Louis Browns they'd have the pennant clinched by the Fourth o' July."

And I'll bet Connie was willin' to agree with me before it was over.

Well, the Chief worked against the Big Rube in that game. We beat 'em, but they give us a battle and it was Parker that made it close. We'd gone along nothin' and nothin' till the seventh, and then Rube walks Collins and Baker lifts one over that little old wall. You'd think by this time them New York pitchers would know better than to give that guy anything he can hit.

In their part o' the ninth the Chief still had 'em shut out and two down, and the crowd was goin' home; but Doyle gets hit in the sleeve with a pitched ball and it's Speed's turn. He hits a foul pretty near straight up, but Schang misjudges it. Then he lifts another one and this time McInnes drops it. He'd ought to of been out twice. The Chief tries to make him hit at a bad one then, because he'd got him two strikes and nothin'. He hit at it all right—kissed it for three bases between Strunk and Joyce! And it was a wild pitch that he hit. Doyle scores, o' course, and the bugs suddenly decide not to go home just yet. I fully expected to see him steal home and get away with it, but Murray cut into the first ball and lined out to Barry.

Plank beat Matty two to one the next day in New York, and again Speed and his rabbit's foot give us an awful argument. Matty wasn't so good as usual and we really ought to beat him bad. Two different times Strunk was on second waitin' for any kind o' wallop, and both times Barry cracked 'em down the third-base line like a shot. Speed stopped the first one with his stomach and extricated the pill just in time to nail Barry at first base and retire the side. The next time he throwed his glove in front of his face in self-defense and the ball stuck in it.

In the sixth innin' Schang was on third base and Plank on first, and two down, and Murphy combed an awful one to Speed's left. He didn't have time to stoop over and he just stuck out his foot. The ball hit it and caromed in two hops right into Doyle's hands on second base before Plank got there. Then in the seventh Speed bunts one and Baker trips and falls goin' after it or he'd of threw him out a mile. They was two gone; so Speed steals second, and, o' course, Schang has to make a bad peg right at that time and lets him go to third. Then Collins boots one on Murray and they've got a run. But it didn't do 'em no good, because Collins and Baker and McInnes come up in the ninth and walloped 'em where Parker couldn't reach 'em.

Comin' back to Philly on the train that night, I says to Connie:

"What do you think o' that Parker bird now?"

"He's lucky, all right," says Connie smilin'; "but we won't hold it against him if he don't beat us with it."

"It ain't too late," I says. "He ain't pulled his real stuff yet."

The whole bunch was talkin' about him and his luck, and sayin' it was about time for things to break against him. I warned 'em that they wasn't no chance—that it was permanent with him.

Bush and Tesreau hooked up next day and neither o' them had much stuff. Everybody was hittin' and it looked like anybody's game right up to the ninth. Speed had got on every time he come up—the wind blowin' his fly balls away from the outfielders and the infielders bootin' when he hit 'em on the ground.

When the ninth started the score was seven apiece. Connie and McGraw both had their whole pitchin' staffs warmin' up. The crowd was wild, because they'd been all kinds of action. They wasn't no danger of anybody's leavin' their seats before this game was over.

Well, Bescher is walked to start with and Connie's about ready to give Bush the hook; but Doyle pops out tryin' to bunt. Then Speed gets two strikes and two balls, and it looked to me like the next one was right over the heart; but Connolly calls it a ball and gives him another chance. He whales the groove ball to the fence in left center and gets round to third on it, while Bescher scores. Right then Bush comes out and the Chief goes in. He whiffs Murray and has two strikes on Merkle when Speed makes a break for home—and, o' course, that was the one ball Schang dropped in the whole serious!

They had a two-run lead on us then and it looked like a cinch for them to hold it, because the minute Tesreau showed a sign o' weakenin' McGraw was sure to holler for Matty or the Rube. But you know how quick that bunch of ourn can make a two-run lead look sick. Before McGraw could get Jeff out o' there we had two on the bases.

Then Rube comes in and fills 'em up by walkin' Joyce. It was Eddie's turn to wallop and if he didn't do nothin' we had Baker comin' up next. This time Collins saved Baker the trouble and whanged one clear to the woods. Everybody scored but him—and he could of, too, if it'd been necessary.

In the clubhouse the boys naturally felt pretty good. We'd copped three in a row and it looked like we'd make it four straight, because we had the Chief to send back at 'em the followin' day.

"Your friend Parker is lucky," the boys says to me, "but it don't look like he could stop us now."

I felt the same way and was consultin' the timetables to see whether I could get a train out o' New York for the West next evenin'. But do you think Speed's luck was ready to quit? Not yet! And it's a wonder we didn't all go nuts durin' the next few days. If words could kill, Speed would of died a thousand times. And I wish he had!

They wasn't no record-breakin' crowd out when we got to the Polo Grounds. I guess the New York bugs was pretty well discouraged and the bettin' was eight to five that we'd cop that battle and finish it. The Chief was the only guy that warmed up for us and McGraw didn't have no choice but to use Matty, with the whole thing dependin' on this game.

They went along like the two swell pitchers they was till Speed's innin', which in this battle was the eighth. Nobody scored, and it didn't look like they was ever goin' to till Murphy starts off that round with a perfect bunt and Joyce sacrifices him to second. All Matty had to do then was to get rid o' Collins and Baker—and that's about as easy as sellin' silk socks to an Eskimo.

He didn't give Eddie nothin' he wanted to hit, though; and finally he slaps one on the ground to Doyle. Larry made the play to first base and Murphy moved to third. We all figured Matty'd walk Baker then, and he done it. Connie sends Baker down to second on the first pitch to McInnes, but Meyers don't pay no attention to him— they was playin' for McInnes and wasn't takin' no chances o' throwin' the ball away.

Well, the count goes to three and two on McInnes and

Matty comes with a curve—he's got some curve too; but Jack happened to meet it and—Blooie! Down the left foul line where he always hits! I never seen a ball hit so hard in my life. No infielder in the world could of stopped it. But I'll give you a thousand bucks if that ball didn't go kerplunk right into the third bag and stop as dead as George Washington! It was child's play for Speed to pick it up and heave it over to Merkle before Jack got there. If anybody else had been playin' third base the bag would of ducked out o' the way o' that wallop; but even the bases themselves was helpin' him out.

The two runs we ought to of had on Jack's smash would of been just enough to beat 'em, because they got the only run o' the game in their half—or, I should say, the Lord give it to 'em.

Doyle'd been throwed out and up come Parker, smilin'. The minute I seen him smile I felt like somethin' was comin' off and I made the remark on the bench.

Well, the Chief pitched one right at him and he tried to duck. The ball hit his bat and went on a line between Jack and Eddie. Speed didn't know he'd hit it till the guys on the bench wised him up. Then he just had time to get to first base. They tried the hit-and-run on the second ball and Murray lifts a high fly that Murphy didn't have to move for. Collins pulled the old bluff about the ball bein' on the ground and Barry yells, "Go on! Go on!" like he was the coacher. Speed fell for it and didn't know where the ball was no more'n a rabbit; he just run his fool head off and we was gettin' all ready to laugh when the ball come down and Murphy dropped it!

If Parker had stuck near first base, like he ought to of done, he couldn't of got no farther'n second; but with the start he got he was pretty near third when Murphy made the muff, and it was a cinch for him to score. The next two guys was easy outs; so they wouldn't of had a run except for Speed's boner. We couldn't do nothin' in the ninth and we was licked.

Well, that was a tough one to lose; but we figured that Matty was through and we'd wind it up the next day, as we had Plank ready to send back at 'em. We wasn't afraid o' the Rube, because he hadn't never bothered Collins and Baker much.

The two lefthanders come together just like everybody'd doped it and it was about even up to the eighth. Plank had been goin' great and, though the score was two and two, they'd got their two on boots and we'd hit ourn in. We went after Rube in our part o' the eighth and knocked him out. Demaree stopped us after we'd scored two more.

"It's all over but the shoutin'!" says Davis on the bench.

"Yes," I says, "unless that seventh son of a seventh son gets up there again."

He did, and he come up after they'd filled the bases with a boot, a base hit and a walk with two out. I says to Davis:

"If I was Plank I'd pass him and give 'em one run."

"That wouldn't be no baseball," says Davis—"not with Murray comin' up."

Well, it mayn't of been no baseball, but it couldn't of turned out worse if they'd did it that way. Speed took a healthy at the first ball; but it was a hook and he caught it on the handle, right up near his hands. It started outside the first-base line like a foul and then changed its mind and rolled in. Schang run away from the plate, because it looked like it was up to him to make the play. He picked the ball up and had to make the peg in a hurry.

His throw hit Speed right on top o' the head and bounded off like it had struck a cement sidewalk. It went clear over to the seats and before McInnes could get it three guys had scored and Speed was on third base. He was left there, but that didn't make no difference. We was licked again and for the first time the gang really begun to get scared.

We went over to New York Sunday afternoon and we didn't do no singin' on the way. Some o' the fellers tried to laugh, but it hurt 'em. Connie sent us to bed early, but I don't believe none o' the bunch got much sleep—I know I didn't; I was worryin' too much about the serious and also about the girl, who hadn't sent me no telegram like I'd ast her to. Monday mornin' I wired her askin' what was the matter and tellin' her I was gettin' tired of her foolishness. O' course I didn't make it so strong as that—but the telegram cost me a dollar and forty cents.

Connie had the choice o' two pitchers for the sixth game. He could use Bush, who'd been slammed round pretty hard the last time out, or the Chief, who'd only had two days' rest. The rest of 'em—outside o' Plank— had a epidemic o' sore arms. Connie finally picked Bush, so's he could have the Chief in reserve in case we had to play a seventh game. McGraw started Big Jeff and we went at it.

It wasn't like the last time these two guys had hooked up. This time they both had somethin', and for eight innin's runs was as scarce as Chinese policemen. They'd been chances to score on both sides, but the big guy and Bush was both tight in the pinches. The crowd was plumb nuts and yelled like Indians every time a fly ball was caught or a strike called. They'd of got their money's worth if they hadn't been no ninth; but, believe me, that was some round!

They was one out when Barry hit one through the box for a base. Schang walked, and it was Bush's turn. Connie told him to bunt, but he whiffed in the attempt. Then Murphy comes up and walks—and the bases are

choked. Young Joyce had been pie for Tesreau all day or else McGraw might of changed pitchers right there. Anyway he left Big Jeff in and he beaned Joyce with a fast one. It sounded like a tire blowin' out. Joyce falls over in a heap and we chase out there, thinkin' he's dead; but he ain't, and pretty soon he gets up and walks down to first base. Tesreau had forced in a run and again we begun to count the winner's end. Matty comes in to prevent further damage and Collins flies the side out.

"Hold 'em now! Work hard!" we says to young Bush, and he walks out there just as cool as though he was goin' to hit fungoes.

McGraw sends up a pinch hitter for Matty and Bush whiffed him. Then Bescher flied out. I was prayin' that Doyle would end it, because Speed's turn come after his'n; so I pretty near fell dead when Larry hit safe.

Speed had his old smile and even more chest than usual when he come up there, swingin' five or six bats. He didn't wait for Doyle to try and steal, or nothin'. He lit into the first ball, though Bush was tryin' to waste it. I seen the ball go high in the air toward left field, and then I picked up my glove and got ready to beat it for the gate. But when I looked out to see if Joyce was set, what do you think I seen? He was lyin' flat on the ground! That blow on the head had got him just as Bush was pitchin' to Speed. He'd flopped over and didn't no more know what was goin' on than if he'd croaked.

Well, everybody else seen it at the same time; but it was too late. Strunk made a run for the ball, but they wasn't no chance for him to get near it. It hit the ground about ten feet back o' where Joyce was lyin' and bounded way over to the end o' the foul line. You don't have to be told that Doyle and Parker both scored and the serious was tied up.

We carried Joyce to the clubhouse and after a while he come to. He cried when he found out what had happened. We cheered him up all we could, but he was a pretty sick guy. The trainer said he'd be all right, though, for the final game.

They tossed up a coin to see where they'd play the seventh battle and our club won the toss; so we went back to Philly that night and cussed Parker clear across New Jersey. I was so sore I kicked the stuffin' out o' my seat.

You probably heard about the excitement in the burg yesterday mornin'. The demand for tickets was somethin' fierce and some of 'em sold for as high as twenty-five bucks apiece. Our club hadn't been lookin' for no seventh game and they was some tall hustlin' done round that old ball park.

I started out to the grounds early and bought some New York papers to read on the car. They was a big story that Speed Parker, the Giants' hero, was goin' to be married a week after the end o' the serious. It didn't give the name o' the girl, sayin' Speed had refused to tell it. I figured she must be some dame he'd met round the circuit somewheres.

They was another story by one o' them smart baseball reporters sayin' that Parker, on his way up to the plate, had saw that Joyce was about ready to faint and had hit the fly ball to left field on purpose. Can you beat it?

I was goin' to show that to the boys in the clubhouse, but the minute I blowed in there I got some news that made me forget about everything else. Joyce was very sick and they'd took him to a hospital. It was up to me to play!

Connie come over and ast me whether I'd ever hit against Matty. I told him I hadn't, but I'd saw enough of him to know he wasn't no worse'n Johnson. He told me he was goin' to let me hit second—in Joyce's place—because he didn't want to bust up the rest of his combination. He also told me to take my orders from Strunk about where to play for the batters.

"Where shall I play for Parker?" I says, tryin' to joke and pretend I wasn't scared to death.

"I wisht I could tell you," says Connie. "I guess the only thing to do when he comes up is to get down on your knees and pray."

The rest o' the bunch slapped me on the back and give me all the encouragement they could. The place was jammed when we went out on the field. They may of been bigger crowds before, but they never was packed together so tight. I doubt whether they was even room enough left for Falkenberg to sit down.

The afternoon papers had printed the stuff about Joyce bein' out of it, so the bugs was wise that I was goin' to play. They watched me pretty close in battin' practice and give me a hand whenever I managed to hit one hard. When I was out catchin' fungoes the guys in the bleachers cheered me and told me they was with me; but I don't mind tellin' you that I was as nervous as a bride.

They wasn't no need for the announcers to tip the crowd off to the pitchers. Everybody in the United States and Cuba knowed that the Chief'd work for us and Matty for them. The Chief didn't have no trouble with 'em in the first innin'. Even from where I stood I could see that he had a lot o' stuff. Bescher and Doyle popped out and Speed whiffed.

Well, I started out makin' good, with reverse English, in our part. Fletcher booted Murphy's ground ball and I was sent up to sacrifice. I done a complete job of it—sacrificin' not only myself but Murphy with a pop fly that Matty didn't have to move for. That spoiled whatever chance we had o' gettin' the jump on 'em; but the boys didn't bawl me for it.

"That's all right, old boy. You're all right!" they said on the bench—if they'd had a gun they'd of shot me.

I didn't drop no fly balls in the first six innin's—

because none was hit out my way. The Chief was so good that they wasn't hittin' nothing out o' the infield. And we wasn't doin' nothin' with Matty, either. I led off in the fourth and fouled the first one. I didn't molest the other two. But if Connie and the gang talked about me they done it internally. I come up again—with Murphy on third base and two gone in the sixth, and done my little whiffin' specialty. And still the only people that panned me was the thirty thousand that had paid for the privilege!

My first fieldin' chance come in the seventh. You'd of thought that I'd of had my nerve back by that time; but I was just as scared as though I'd never saw a crowd before. It was just as well that they was two out when Merkle hit one to me. I staggered under it and finally it hit me on the shoulder. Merkle got to second, but the Chief whiffed the next guy. I was gave some cross looks on the bench and I shouldn't of blamed the fellers if they'd cut loose with some language; but they didn't.

They's no use in me tellin' you about none o' the rest of it—except what happened just before the start o' the eleventh and durin' that innin', which was sure the big one o' yesterday's pastime—both for Speed and yours sincerely.

The scoreboard was still a row o' ciphers and Speed'd had only a fair amount o' luck. He'd made a scratch base hit and robbed our bunch of a couple o' real ones with impossible stops.

When Schang flied out and wound up our tenth I was leanin' against the end of our bench. I heard my name spoke, and I turned round and seen a boy at the door.

"Right here!" I says; and he give me a telegram.

"Better not open it till after the game," says Connie.

"Oh, no; it ain't no bad news," I said, for I figured it was an answer from the girl. So I opened it up and read it on the way to my position. It said:

"Forgive me, Dick—and forgive Speed too. Letter follows."

Well, sir, I ain't no baby, but for a minute I just wanted to sit down and bawl. And then, all of a sudden, I got so mad I couldn't see. I run right into Baker as he was pickin' up his glove. Then I give him a shove and called him some name, and him and Barry both looked at me like I was crazy—and I was. When I got out in left field I stepped on my own foot and spiked it. I just had to hurt somebody.

As I remember it the Chief fanned the first two of 'em. Then Doyle catches one just right and lams it up against the fence back o' Murphy. The ball caromed round some and Doyle got all the way to third base. Next thing I seen was Speed struttin' up to the plate. I run clear in from my position.

"Kill him!" I says to the Chief. "Hit him in the head and kill him and I'll go to jail for it!"

"Are you off your nut?" says the Chief. "Go out there and play ball—and quit ravin'."

Barry and Baker led me away and give me a shove out toward left. Then I heard the crack o' the bat and I seen the ball comin' a mile a minute. It was headed between Strunk and I and looked like it would go out o' the park. I don't remember runnin' or nothin' about it till I run into the concrete wall head first. They told me afterward and all the papers said that it was the greatest catch ever seen. And I never knowed I'd caught the ball!

Some o' the managers have said my head was pretty hard, but it wasn't as hard as that concrete. I was pretty near out, but they tell me I walked to the bench like I wasn't hurt at all. They also tell me that the crowd was a bunch o' ravin' maniacs and was throwin' money at me. I guess the ground-keeper'll get it.

The boys on the bench was all talkin' at once and slappin' me on the back, but I didn't know what it was about. Somebody told me pretty soon that it was my turn to hit and I picked up the first bat I come to and starts for the plate. McInnes come runnin' after me and ast me whether I didn't want my own bat. I cussed him and told him to mind his own business.

I didn't know it at the time, but I found out afterward that they was two out. The bases was empty. I'll tell you just what I had in my mind: I wasn't thinkin' about the ball game; I was determined that I was goin' to get to third base and give that guy my spikes. If I didn't hit one worth three bases, or if I didn't hit one at all, I was goin' to run till I got round to where Speed was, and then slide into him and cut him to pieces!

Right now I can't tell you whether I hit a fast ball, or a slow ball, or a hook, or a fader—but I hit somethin'. It went over Bescher's head like a shot and then took a crazy bound. It must of struck a rock or a pop bottle, because it hopped clear over the fence and landed in the bleachers.

Mind you, I learned this afterward. At the time I just knowed I'd hit one somewheres and I starts round the bases. I speeded up when I got near third and took a runnin' jump at a guy I thought was Parker. I missed him

and sprawled all over the bag. Then, all of a sudden, I come to my senses. All the Ath-a-letics was out there to run home with me and it was one o' them I'd tried to cut. Speed had left the field. The boys picked me up and seen to it that I went on and touched the plate. Then I was carried into the clubhouse by the crazy bugs.

Well, they had a celebration in there and it was a long time before I got a chance to change my clothes. The boys made a big fuss over me. They told me they'd intended to give me five hundred bucks for my divvy, but now I was goin' to get a full share.

"Parker ain't the only lucky guy!" says one of 'em. "But even if that ball hadn't of took that crazy hop you'd of had a triple."

A triple! That's just what I'd wanted; and he called me lucky for not gettin' it!

The Giants was dressin' in the other part o' the clubhouse; and when I finally come out there was Speed, standin' waitin' for some o' the others. He seen me comin' and he smiled. "Hello, Horseshoes!" he says.

He won't smile no more for a while—it'll hurt too much. And if any girl wants him when she sees him now—with his nose over shakin' hands with his ear, and his jaw a couple o' feet foul—she's welcome to him. They won't be no contest!

Grimes leaned over to ring for the waiter.

"Well," he said, "what about it?"

"You won't have to pay my fare," I told him.

"I'll buy a drink anyway," said he. "You've been a good listener—and I had to get it off my chest."

"Maybe they'll have to postpone the wedding," I said.

"No," said Grimes. "The weddin' will take place the day after tomorrow—and I'll bat for Mr. Parker. Did you think I was goin' to let him get away with it?"

"What about next year?" I asked.

"I'm goin' back to the Ath-a-letics," he said. "And I'm goin' to hire somebody to call me 'Horseshoes!' before every game—because I can sure play that old baseball when I'm mad."

# Perfection in June

## JOSEPH LAWLER

WHAT IS so rare as a day in June? Why, a perfect game, that's what, the pinnacle of baseball pitching success in which no batter reaches base through all nine innings. It has been accomplished only 13 times in more than a century of major league play, and remarkably, the first two perfect games occurred in New England within five days and 50 miles of each other.

On June 12, 1880, J. Lee Richmond, a Brown University student who pitched for the National League team in Worcester, beat the visiting Cleveland team 1–0. Richmond was a southpaw who made good use that day of a relatively new weapon—the curve ball.

The following week, on June 17, John M. Ward of the Providence Grays beat the Buffalo Bisons 5–0 with nary a Bison reaching base.

The National League did not produce another perfect game for 84 years, until Jim Bunning turned the trick in 1964—in June, naturally!

**OLD-TIMERS . . .**
From the archives at Cooperstown, two nineteenth-century stalwarts—J. Lee Richmond (left) and John M. Ward. And from the Library of Congress, another old-timer—even if he started as a *cat*.

The less-traveled roads of the United States are colored blue on the road map, and that is where William Least Heat Moon got the title *Blue Highways* for his memoir of a journey into Americana on those roads. One of his stopovers was Bagley, North Dakota. And the conversation went as follows.

# From *Blue Highways*

## WILLIAM LEAST HEAT MOON

WITH A bag of blueberry tarts, I went up Main to a tin-sided, false-front tavern called Michel's, just down the street from the Cease Funeral Home. The interior was log siding and yellowed knotty pine. In the backroom the Junior Chamber of Commerce talked about potatoes, pulpwood, dairy products, and somebody's broken fishing rod. I sat at the bar. Behind me a pronghorn antelope head hung on the wall, and beside it a televised baseball game cast a cool light like a phosphorescent fungus. "Hear that?" a dwindled man asked. He was from the time when boys drew "Kilroy-Was-Here" faces on alley fences. "Did you hear the announcer?"

"I wasn't listening."

"He said 'velocity.' "

"Velocity?"

"He's talking about a fastball. A minute ago he said a runner had 'good acceleration.' This is a baseball game, not a NASA shot. And another thing: I haven't heard anybody mention a 'Texas leaguer' in years."

"It's a 'bloop double' now, I think."

"And the 'banjo hitter'—where's he? And what happened to the 'slow ball'?"

"It's a 'change-up.' "

The man got me interested in the game. We watched and drank Grain Belt. He had taught high-school civics in Minneapolis for thirty-two years, but his dream had been to become a sports announcer. "They put a radar gun on the kid's fastball a few minutes ago," he said. "Ninety-three point four miles per hour. That's how they tell you speed now. They don't try to show it to

you: 'smoke,' 'hummer,' 'the high hard one.' I miss the old clichés. They had life. Who wants to hit a fastball with a decimal point when he can tie into somebody's 'heat'? And that's another thing: nobody 'tattoos' or 'blisters' the ball anymore. These TV boys are ruining a good game because they think if you can see it they're free to sit back and psychoanalyze the team. Ask and I'll tell you what I think of it."

"What do you think of it?"

"Beans. And that's another thing too."

"Beans?"

"Names. Used to be players named Butterbean and Big Potato, Little Potato. Big Poison, Little Poison, Dizzy and Daffy. Icehouse, Shoeless Joe, Suitcase, The Lip. Now we've got the likes of Rickie and Richie and Reggie. With names like that, I think I'm watching a third-grade scrub team."

The announcer said the pitcher had "good location."

"Great God in hemock! He means 'nibble the corners.' But which of these throwing clowns nibbles corners? They're obsessed with speed. Satchel Paige— there's a name for you—old Satch could fire the pill a hundred and five miles an hour. He didn't throw it that fast very often because he couldn't make the ball cut up at that speed. And, sure as spitting, his pitching arm lasted just about his whole life."

The man took a long smacking pull on his Grain Belt. "Damn shame," he said. "There's a word for what television's turned this game into."

"What's the word?"

"Beans," he said. "Nothing but beans and hot air."

This story appeared in *Sport* magazine in the early 1950s. It could not have been written today. Somehow, the concepts of the dancing necktie, the jumping plate, and the unnoticeable white powder do not connect with the realities of the present. Well, the unnoticeable white powder, maybe . . . but in this story, all that meant was soap.

# The Other Feller

## HAL LEBOVITZ

A FRIEND was visiting Al Lopez, the Cleveland Indians' manager, in the privacy of his office at Cleveland's lakefront Stadium. Suddenly there was a loud explosion outside Lopez' door. The friend jumped. Lopez said, matter-of-factly, "Feller just came in."

Bob Feller, as everybody knows, is one of the great pitchers of all time, but there is another side to him few people, outside of his family, teammates and close friends, are aware of. It is a side you would be more likely to associate with such eccentrics as Rube Waddell, Dizzy Dean or Lefty Gomez.

Feller is a passionate and dedicated practical joker.

Consider this fireworks incident, if you will, as a typical example of Bob's fun-loving nature. The Indians were traveling by bus to Burbank for an exhibition game with the St. Louis Browns last spring. Seated next to Feller was Bill Grieve, the white-haired veteran American League umpire who had been assigned to the Indians for spring training. Grieve gasped as, without warning, Feller produced a huge, ominous-looking firecracker, lit a match and touched it to the fuse. He casually held the sizzling "cracker" in his hand as Grieve, straining in his seat, howled, "Get rid of it, Bobby! Get rid of it!"

At the last possible moment, Feller casually tossed the explosive out the window onto the sunny street. It immediately burst, the noise reverberating under the wheels of the bus. Grieve dabbed at his perspiring brow and promptly moved to another seat. Twenty minutes later, after the laughter had subsided and the incident remained only a humorous memory, Feller crept behind the dozing umpire's new location, pulled another firecracker from his pocket, lit it and placed the explosive under Grieve's seat.

When the bus eventually reached Burbank, the umpire was in no condition to perform in his usual steady fashion.

Citizens who may have wondered about the unscheduled, mysterious fireworks display in the skies over downtown Cleveland last New Year's Eve will be surprised to learn that the man behind the pyrotechnics was none other than Feller, himself. Bill Veeck, the Indians' former owner, was visiting the city and he invited Bob to his suite high up in the Hotel Carter. What would be more appropriate, thought Firecracker Feller, than noisy, spectacular skyrockets? He smuggled a trunkful up to Veeck's room, and while house detectives went frantic trying to locate the source, he and Veeck had themselves a whiz-bang of a time.

One of Feller's favorite pranks is to plant noisy but harmless bombs in the autos of guests partying at his home. Some explode under the hood when the car starts, others, connected to each tire, erupt periodically after the car is rolling along the highway. "Just want to make sure they don't fall asleep at the wheel," Bob says.

Bob's pretty wife, Virginia, who has had to put up with her husband's shenanigans since he came back from the service in 1945, explains how it all started. "He was sent to Great Lakes to coach the baseball team," she recalls. "Paul Brown was coaching the football team at the time and he and Bob became very close friends. One night at a party, Paul took a scissors out of his pocket, went up to one of the guests, said some magic words and cut off his necktie. It created quite a riot. Just before the party broke up, Paul handed his victim a very expensive necktie as a replacement. After that Bob was 'gone.'

"Now when we go to a party I never know what to expect. Neither does the hostess or the other guests. Once, when we were invited into an especially immaculate home, Bob began to stare at a corner. Then, very deliberately, he walked over to the spot, made a sweep with his hand toward the ceiling and came up with a large, black cobweb. He walked over to a picture, stuck his hand behind it and brought out another cobweb.

"After managing a startled 'Oh!' and 'Oh No!' the hostess became very apologetic. Bob kept a straight face, but finally I burst out laughing. When Bob showed her the cobweb-making stuff he had hidden in his hand she laughed, too. She was an awfully good sport."

At parties, Bob generally pulls appropriate tricks on guests who are in the third-highball stage. He'll drop plastic ice cubes containing fake bugs into their drinks or he'll substitute a leaking glass or a tilted one, giving the illusion it is about to spill. Should they leave the table for a moment, he'll insert a suction device under their drink which prevents the glass from being lifted. He also has a tube which fits under a plate. By pressing a concealed air bulb, he can make the plate jump. He always carries "hot" chewing gum, exploding cigars and cigarettes and matches and a collapsible cushion which emits a Bronx cheer when sat upon.

One of his favorite stunts is his dancing necktie. It takes him about 15 minutes to attach a system of strings and pulleys to his tie. Then by a slight, imperceptible expansion of his stomach muscles the tie rises to a horizontal position. While talking to someone he'll make the tie whisk under the listener's chin, all the while innocently maintaining an "are you crazy?" look at the victim's bewilderment.

Another pet stunt of Bob's is to "doctor" the soap in a friend's home. He sprinkles it with an unnoticeable white powder. When water hits the soap it turns blood red. "It's kind of a delayed-action gag," he explains seriously.

Mrs. Feller, herself, has been an occasional victim. "Once I walked into the shower and there was a snake on the floor," she said. "It was only rubber but it scared the daylights out of me. Another time he put a big fake spider in my bed. When I pulled back the covers, I screamed."

But Virginia doesn't mind Bob's practical jokes. "He likes to make people laugh," she says. "He never tries to hurt anybody. Bob is so serious about his pitching and works so hard on conditioning, that he just needs an outlet. And the way I see it, his gadgets and gimmicks provide it. The war took five years out of his life. It seems to me he has been trying to make up for lost time and lost laughs ever since."

In their ten years of married life, the Fellers have had very few quarrels, "and always about the same two subjects," says Virginia. "We argue about what time

## JOHN GALLAGHER

*"All right, now, who did that?!"*

the children should go to bed and about Bob's airplane. I want the children in bed around seven o'clock, and just about that time, Bob starts to play with them. About the airplane—well, we just don't talk about it any more. We're both too rabid in our views.''

Bob owns a Beechcraft Bonanza. Virginia admits to his excellence as a pilot but wishes he would give up flying. ''I had three bad scares in a row and I shudder when Bob is in the air. But he's promised me he'll never fly in bad weather.

''The Indians' owner once asked me to influence Bob into selling the plane. It was useless, though. My mother was on Bob's side, so I tried to get my Dad's help. He's an inventor, with several successful patents, and Bob idolizes him. He talked to Bob but it worked the wrong way. After their discussion, Dad got the Eaton Manufacturing Company, of which he's a director, to buy its own private plane.''

Bob's in-laws, Mr. and Mrs. Martin Winther, have a 27-acre estate in Gates Mills, Ohio, which is 20 miles from downtown Cleveland. The Fellers live there during the baseball season, and, in fact, most of the year.

Recently Bob had a headline made up in bold railroad type, ''EATON MFG. CO. TO BE INVESTIGATED.'' He casually dropped the phony newspaper on the dinner table. Mr. Winther grabbed for it, exclaiming, ''Hey, let me see that!''

Next day, a board of directors meeting was scheduled at the Eaton Co. Mr. Winther duplicated his son-in-law's performance, tossing the paper on the conference table. ''It would be an understatement to say I obtained the desired effect,'' he grins. ''Wow!''

At the height of the airplane controversy, Bob worked the headline gag again. He had a newspaper faked-up bearing the black lines across the top, ''VIRGINIA FELLER AND SONS FLY LAKE ERIE IN A BONANZA.'' Bob's mother-in-law saw it first and rushed to her daughter with questions. ''We had a good laugh about that one,'' says Virginia. ''It took the edge off our argument.''

Bob keeps his plane at the Lost Nations Airport, near Gates Mills. On game days he drives to the airfield, parks his car, boards his plane and flies it to Cleveland's downtown airport, located about a quarter of a mile from the Stadium. He departs from the plane carrying a small canvas case. He unfolds the case and it becomes a tiny one-cylinder, gasoline-driven kiddie-kar. Bob squats on it bowlegged and chugs in and out of traffic to the ball park, tooting the horn loudly as he enters the clubhouse. He drives right up to his locker, collapses the kiddie-kar and stores it in his locker to be unfolded again when the game is over.

Bob's plane is filled with every safety device known. The cost of the plane was $10,000 but Bob has matched that figure in equipment alone. He carries life preservers, fire extinguishers, parachutes and even radar. He already has the brackets installed for jet propulsion, in anticipation of its release to private planes by the Navy. ''I hope they never release it,'' Mrs. Feller declares fervently.

Bob carries an electric razor in his plane and clips his whiskers as he flies. He also has a shaver in his Cadillac. It's not unusual for him to shave as he waits for a red light to change. He carries cologne and powder to complete the job.

The shaver is only one of the many unusual gadgets attached to his Cadillac. He has two horns, one emitting a blast that sounds like a streamlined train, the other a ''cattle-caller'' for pedestrians which gives out a surprising ''Moo–o–o–o.'' In addition to the regular auto radio, an aircraft radio also has been installed. It reports the weather every half hour. There is also an oil eye. Instead of lifting the hood, a flip of a switch reveals the condition and the exact level of the motor oil.

Bob has two gas pedals. When his right foot becomes tired on long trips, he switches to another near his left foot. In addition to the conventional right-foot brake he has a ''lefty-brake.'' ''Saves wasted motion,'' says the safety-conscious pitcher. ''If my right foot is on the gas, I can use my left foot to stop the car.''

The car has a metallic table that can be swung under the dashboard when not in use. It holds magnetic cups which won't spill the contents no matter how bumpy the road. Perhaps the most unusual contraption is his reading lamp. The car has a 110-volt outlet which enables him to plug in the light. When he and his wife are making a night trip, he hangs the lamp over her seat and she reads to him.

In the Fellers' second car, a station wagon, Bob has installed a foam rubber covering for the floor. ''The kids can play or sleep while we're driving without getting hurt,'' he explains.

Bob finds many of his gadgets in catalogs. ''I'm on every sucker list there is, I guess,'' he often says.

''I feel sorry for our mailman,'' says Mrs. Feller. ''Not only does he bring a pile of fan mail and business letters to our mail box every day, but he's also loaded down with those heavy catalogs.''

Feller's traveling bags are loaded with the gadgets he is constantly purchasing. Most ballplayers are one-suitcase travelers; Feller is a three-bagger. In addition to his suitcases, he carries his clothes on one arm in a cellophane bag and a pile of dated newspapers under the other arm. Bob is so busy he seldom has time to read the papers from day to day, so he saves them up and reads the back copies on train rides.

It's always amusing to Bob's teammates to watch porters dash for Feller's bags. Anticipating a sizeable tip, which they unfailingly receive, the red-caps eagerly grab for Feller's suitcase. Instead of the bag coming up, the porter, after a surprised grunt, sags under the weight. An examination of the contents would be startling to a person unfamiliar with his habits. One bag is jammed with aviation and scientific magazines and catalogs. Another contains a small radio, several cameras, dumbbells for weight-lifting and a hand-squeezer for strengthening the grip. The third holds all sorts of correspondence, including fan mail, which he reads thoroughly, firecrackers and his tricks. Interspersed among this collection is his wearing apparel.

Gadgetman Feller never knows when one of his gimmicks will come in handy but he's always ready to put them to use. One day in Philadelphia a few seasons ago the Indians were taking a rather rough ride from a leather-lunged customer, Pete Adelis, perhaps the most raucous and insulting heckler in the American League. Some of the Tribesmen answered back, making Pete even more vocal. During the fifth inning Feller moved to the top of the dugout steps and hollered, "Pete!" The heckler turned his comments toward Bob. Feller reached into his uniform pocket and pulled out a set of false teeth which he began to jabber up and down. The fans nearby howled and Adelis was silenced for the night.

Once, during the course of a game, manager Lopez noticed Feller, seated at the opposite end of the bench, wearing what appeared to be a hearing aid. "Maybe he's become hard of hearing," thought the manager. But his curiosity was aroused when he noticed the other bench-warmers slide toward Feller and take turns with the ear plug. Upon investigation, Lopez discovered the "hearing-aid" really was a miniature radio. Feller had

been watching the ball game and listening to the play-by-play broadcast at the same time.

Sportswriters aren't spared from Bob's barbs. On a recent train trip, most of the players were relaxing in the dining car after dinner. Ed McAuley, baseball columnist for the Cleveland *News,* pulled out a cigar and began puffing pleasurably on the ten-center. Conspicuously, he was the only cigar smoker in the room. He grew even more conspicuous when the dining car became heavy with cigar ashes—so many, in fact, that they settled on suits like dandruff. McAuley became embarrassed, coughed several times, put out his cigar, murmured an apology, and left the car.

Next day he learned that Feller had been behind him, burning a substance that wafted the ash-like material into the room.

Bob is careful not to pull any of his gags in the locker room after a defeat. But before a game, he believes a laugh helps the club relax. At Briggs Stadium, Detroit, one afternoon in 1948 in the midst of the Indians' hectic drive toward the pennant, Bob placed a bar of white soap between two Nabisco wafers and put the sandwich in the ice cream freezer. Up ambled Satchel Paige, Bob's pitching teammate and barnstorming friend. Satch dug down deep for some cold refreshment and bit in. When Satch reopened his mouth, his bridgework remained behind—stuck in the soap. He walked over to the drinking fountain and washed off his choppers.

"Saves brushing 'em," Satch grinned toothlessly.

That's the other Feller. You'd never suspect it was the same person who is pitching his way into Baseball's Hall of Fame. Maybe the jokes and the laughter have made the way easier.

The book *The 100 Best Companies to Work For in America* was published in 1984. Look who ranks right up there with Time Inc., Delta Air Lines and Goldman, Sachs!

# From *The 100 Best Companies to Work For in America*

## ROBERT LEVERING, MILTON MOSKOWITZ *and* MICHAEL KATZ

LOS ANGELES DODGERS

THE DODGERS OWN one professional major-league baseball team and six minor-league clubs. Employees: 950.

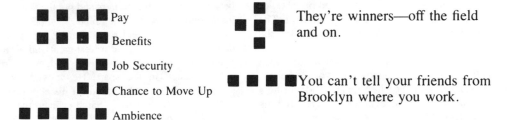

Pay

Benefits

Job Security

Chance to Move Up

Ambience

They're winners—off the field and on.

You can't tell your friends from Brooklyn where you work.

Most people in baseball agree that Dodgertown, in Vero Beach, Florida, is the best spring-training facility in the game. It symbolizes what Dodger employees cite as a principal reason they like the club: "The Dodgers are a first-class organization." Players, front-office people, and even ushers told us that again and again. Dodgertown is also where generation after generation of players acquire the spirit of Dodger Blue.

First opened in 1948, Dodgertown was the first (and is still one of the few) training camps where players from the major and minor leagues practice together. As its name implies, Dodgertown is a little baseball village. Streets such as Duke Snider Road, Jackie Robinson Avenue, Sandy Koufax Lane, and Roy Campanella Drive weave through the 450-acre site. Training coaches include former Dodger greats such as Koufax and Campanella. Off-hours, the players have use of an Olympic-sized pool, two basketball, six tennis, and two shuffleboard courts, and both a 9-hole and an 18-hole golf course (the latter is called Dodger Pines Country Club).

Camaraderie develops among the players at Dodgertown. "When you are together like that, the young players get to see the major leaguers. It means a lot to

those guys," Bill Russell, the team's shortstop, told us. We talked with him during batting practice, shortly before a game between the Dodgers and the Montreal Expos at Dodger Stadium in the summer of 1983. Russell was once in their place, having first gone to Dodgertown in 1967 while a minor leaguer himself. He was promoted to the Dodgers in 1969 and as of 1983 had been with the team longer than any player then on the roster.

Russell says the only significant change in the last 15 years has been the much higher salaries players now receive. "What has not changed is the family feeling of the Dodgers," he said. "They go out of their way to make everybody feel like part of the organization."

The Dodger shortstop believes that the team spirit spills onto the playing field to help the Dodgers win ball games. "Sometimes it makes up for lack of talent," Russell claimed. His explanation may partially account for the Dodgers' success over the years. They've won 13 pennants and 5 World Series championships—more than any other National League club.

The winning attitude is contagious. Steve Sax, 23 and in his second year in the big leagues, told us, "Everyone expects us to win—the fans, the organization, everyone. It just isn't part of the script to lose. Winning is the Dodger tradition.''

Like the majority of Dodgers, Sax and Russell have never played for another professional ball club, something increasingly rare in the major leagues. The Dodgers prefer to find and develop their own talent. Other clubs rely on ''The Bureau,'' a scouting pool that provides tips about promising young players. But the Dodgers employ their own crew of 24 full-time and 22 part-time scouts to comb the United States and Latin America for potential big leaguers. *Forbes* estimated the Dodgers spend about $3 million annually on this operation, which nets only about three new major-league players a year. That's a million dollars per player. But the club believes it is worth the price, since bidding for free agents can cost as much if not more.

Partly because the Dodgers have such a good farm-club system, the club doesn't keep older players around when capable younger ones are in the wings. When

some of these older players have been traded—Steve Garvey, Ron Cey, and Davey Lopes, for instance— they've issued bitter statements to the press. It's hard to accept being kicked out of the family. These trades have had little impact on the morale of the remaining Dodgers.

One testimony to the Dodgers' commitment to their own scouting is a large ledger book hidden in a locked cabinet at Dodger Stadium. The book is the property of Al Campanis, the Dodgers' player-personnel chief. In it, Campanis has written in the team's starting players for the opening game of the season for the next five years. Campanis himself played briefly for the Brooklyn Dodgers in 1943. He became a scout in 1950.

Among those who seem happiest with the Dodgers are players who spent time with other teams. Outfielder Ken Landreaux played with the California Angels and the Minnesota Twins before being traded to the Dodgers in 1981. ''I have been treated better here. The Dodgers treat the players more like human beings,'' he told us. ''I felt the difference as soon as I got here. With the

## GENE MYERS

*''Someone named Keeler is saying, 'Hit 'em where they ain't.' ''*

Twins, you are just like another piece of property that they can use or abuse. With the Angels you're like something they could maneuver with.''

Relief pitcher Pat Zachry, formerly with the Cincinnati Reds and the New York Mets, thinks the Dodgers take care of little things for the players better than he has ever seen before. ''The travel arrangements and the facilities are better than those at other clubs,'' he said. He likes the fact that ''throughout the year they take care of our families. When we are on the road, they have get-togethers where the families can go with the kids. That's important for a ballplayer.'' During spring training, the club hosts other events for the whole family, including a Christmas party with a Santa Claus and imported snow, and barbecues.

The 160 ballplayers make up only part of the Dodger family. There's minimal turnover among the 225 front-office executives and staff, including secretaries. Many, like Bill Schweppe, head of minor-league operations, have been with the club since its days in Brooklyn. (The team's name comes from the nickname of that borough's residents, who were known as ''trolley dodgers.'') ''When we moved from Brooklyn in 1958, more than 50 percent came along, including ticket sellers, ground crew, and secretaries,'' Schweppe said.

Schweppe contrasts the loyalty among Dodger employees with that of other major-league clubs: ''We have a feeling of security here in a business that's very insecure. We have a family-type relaxed atmosphere despite it being such a competitive business.''

Other clubs have absentee owners or new owners every few years. But the Dodgers have been owned by the O'Malley family since 1950; Walter O'Malley brought the club west from Brooklyn. His son Peter, a graduate of the University of Pennsylvania's Wharton business school, started full-time work with the team in 1962 as director of Dodgertown. He began running the club in 1970.

Ken Hasemann, the club's controller and 21-year Dodger veteran, says many of the employees appreciate that ''Mr. O'Malley makes a point to get to know everybody,'' and that his door is always open for employees to talk with him. After the Dodgers won the World Series in 1981, O'Malley took all the department heads and their spouses to Hawaii. Front-office employees also have a profit-sharing plan.

Even the part-time employees—the ushers, ticket sellers, and security guards—speak of being part of the Dodger family. We talked with usher Greg Rigaldo, whose post is outside the Dodgers' locker room. A 30-year veteran of the post office, Rigaldo has been impressed with how the club is so ''well-run'' and how ''the Dodgers take care of their people.'' It's difficult to get a job as an usher at Dodger Stadium. Their base pay is $7.25 an hour, and they are unionized. It helps to be recommended by someone who already works there. Not surprisingly, ''lots of people are related to each other here,'' as Rigaldo told us. ''It's sort of like the movie studios that way.''

Once on board, ushers adhere to a rigid dress code. Men's hair must be cut above their collar, they must be clean-shaven and cannot chew gum on the job. The team provides them with a powder-blue jacket, blue trousers, a Dodgers necktie, and a straw hat. ''I know we're better than ushers at other stadiums,'' Rigaldo asserted. ''I've seen them on TV.''

Nick Cardona, Jr., was working as an usher near the Dodgers' dugout the evening we were there. In his early twenties, Cardona has been ushering for the past five years. He insists that ''this job is not for everybody. You have to like baseball.'' Cardona clearly does. The ushers have their own softball team; they play the security guards at the stadium once a year. The team also throws an annual party for them in the dugout. The main attraction is three six-foot-long submarine sandwiches. ''It's the Dodgers' way of saying thank you,'' Cardona said. The team also gives ushers and other employees the same gifts (Dodger caps, jackets, bats, and so on) that are handed out to the fans during the dozen or so giveaway games each year.

Many players find Dodger Stadium one of the club's principal attractions. The team spent $1 million to landscape the stadium, planting olive and palm trees in the parking lots and a Japanese garden in center field. Fans seem to like it, too. The team leads both leagues in attendance almost every year. With 26,000 season-ticket holders, it's the only team to have had more than three million fans in a year—and it's done it four times, in 1978, 1980, 1982, and 1983. In 1982, only 6 of the 26 major-league teams were estimated to have made any profit at all. None made more than $1.5 million that year. Except for the Dodgers, that is. They are estimated to have cleared a cool $7 million.

Tommy Lasorda has been the Dodgers' manager since 1977. He succeeded Walter Alston, who ran the club from the dugout for 23 years—a major-league record. Lasorda has been with the Dodger organization for 34 years, 11 years as a minor-league pitcher, 5 years as a scout, 7 years as a minor-league manager, and 4 as a Dodger coach. One of baseball's most colorful personalities and prone to hyperbole, Lasorda has often told sports writers of his great love for the Dodger organization. It was no different when we talked with him before the Expos game.

''The Dodgers are the best company to work for in the world, not just in America,'' he asserted. Why? '' 'Cause it's an organization with a heart. The people who run it make those of us who work for them feel very much a part of it. They make us feel appreciated.'' He cited the incident of how the Dodgers gave a job to former Dodger catcher Roy Campanella after he was paralyzed by an auto accident.

Another not-so-well-known example occurred several years ago after ex-Dodger pitcher Don Newcombe had pawned his 1955 World Series ring at a shop in downtown Los Angeles. Newcombe was an alcoholic at the time. When Peter O'Malley heard about the ring, he went to the pawnshop himself and redeemed it. He then went to Newcombe's house and handed the former pitcher the ring, saying it was a present for his son when the boy turned 18. O'Malley later gave Newcombe a job as director of community relations.

Lasorda says his devotion to the Dodgers will extend beyond his retirement. ''I used to tell my wife that when I die, I want it written on my tombstone that Dodger Stadium was his address, but every ball park was his home.''

According to Lasorda, when O'Malley heard of that, he had a plaque printed with Lasorda's preferred epitaph and a heart painted in Dodger blue. ''When I accepted it,

I told Mr. O'Malley, 'I want to go on working for the Dodgers even when I am dead and gone.' Mr. O'Malley said, 'I can understand your feelings, Tommy, but how are you going to work for the Dodgers when you are dead?' I told him, 'Mr. O'Malley, when I die, I want the Dodgers' schedule put on this tombstone. When people are in the cemetery visiting their loved ones, they will say, 'Let's go to Lasorda's grave and find out if the Dodgers are home or away.' ''

**Main employment centers**  Los Angeles and Vero Beach, Florida (Dodgertown). The minor-league clubs are in Albuquerque, New Mexico; San Antonio, Texas; Lodi, California; Vero Beach, Florida; Lethbridge, Alberta, Canada; and Bradenton, Florida.

**Headquarters**   Los Angeles Dodgers
Dodger Stadium
1000 Elysian Park Avenue
Los Angeles, CA 90012
213-224-1500

Born in Philadelphia on March 5, 1888, Fred Lieb began his baseball-writing career in 1911 along with three other newcomers to that craft: Grantland Rice, Heywood Broun and Damon Runyon. Today, all four are in the Baseball Hall of Fame at Cooperstown, New York. They were, Lieb told Jerry Holtzman, "the foremost freshman class that ever broke into the New York press box," and of the four, Lieb lived the longest and became a major historian of the game. He taped these recollections for Holtzman's book *No Cheering in the Press Box* at the age of 85.

# From *No Cheering in the Press Box*

## FRED LIEB

LOU GEHRIG and I always hit it off very well. I suppose it started because of Mom Gehrig. Lou usually would talk German to his mother, and the fact that I could talk German to Mom Gehrig brought a sort of kinship. Lou thought the world of his mother. There was a mother-son complex there that was as bad one way as the other. I remember when we were over in Japan, on one of those postseason exhibition tours, Lou spent something like seven thousand dollars on gifts for his mother—silks and ivory animals, expensive jades and jewels, all kinds of Japanese stuff.

We often went over to her house for dinner. I remember one time she had turkey *and* roast pig. Mom Gehrig was proud of her cooking. It was her way of exhibiting her ego with this thing that she did best, especially when Lou was going with some girl and brought her home for dinner. Mom could be very intimidating.

Mom Gehrig did everything to prevent Lou from getting married. But Mom finally lost. Eleanor won.

On the morning of the wedding—actually it turned out to be just a reception—Lou Gehrig came up to me and said, "Fred, I want you to do me a favor. It's a very important favor, and I don't know anybody but you who could do it. I want you to get Mom to come to the wedding."

"Gosh," I said, "you mean she's not going to the wedding?"

"No, she won't go. But I'm hoping that you and Mary"—that was my wife, Mary—"can talk her into going."

Mom Gehrig was at the ball game that day. She always sat in the same seat, near the Yankee dugout. I went down to see her during the game.

I said, "Mom, Lou just gave me an assignment. It's something he wants me to do."

"What is it?"

"To bring you to the wedding on Long Island tonight."

"I won't go, I won't go!" she said. "I've no intention of going."

I told her, "Now, Mom, that's no way to talk. Nobody knows better than I how close you and Lou have been during the years. If you want that closeness to last, this is a time you have to stand by. Your son is marrying another woman and you now have that choice, whether he's to be married under good circumstances or bad. This could lead to a complete break, which it does sometimes."

Then she said some things about Eleanor, which I won't repeat. And she said, "I'm not going because I'd only raise hell."

I told her, "Mom, I'm going to be by your house at half-past five so we can make the six o'clock ferry. I'm going to honk and I want you to be ready. Mary will be with me."

She said, "It's no use because I won't go."

Anyway, I did go and honked once, and she was there. Everything went off all right. Actually, it was just a reception. Lou was so afraid of Mom's reaction that he and Eleanor had been secretly married the day before by the mayor of New Rochelle.

The only baseball people at the reception were Bill Dickey and his wife, Vi, and myself and my wife and daughter. I had a little more champagne than I usually drink, and on the way home, while we're on the Long Island ferry, I feel someone tugging at my shoulder. I didn't know who it was. I turned around and it was Mom Gehrig and she whispered, "Wasn't I a good girl? I didn't raise any hell."

We retained our friendship with the Gehrigs from the time they were married, and with Mom and Pop, too. There was always friction between them. Mom and Pop had a nine-room house in New Rochelle, that Lou had been buying on time. But after he was married he didn't keep up the payments and they had to let that house go back to the bank. Mom and Pop had to go into a comparatively cheap apartment in Mount Vernon, something like Archie Bunker has in "All in the Family."

One of the reasons for Lou's self-effacement and inner timidity was because of his parents. It wasn't that he was ashamed of them. Really, he was quite proud of them, but he was irritated that Mom and Pop were not more appreciated and that they hadn't made more progress in this country until he, their only surviving child, made it big. Also Lou felt sort of sorry that he was the only one of four Gehrig children who lived past infancy. Once Mom, in explaining her affection for Lou, said, "He's the only big egg I have in my basket. He's the only one of four who lived, so I want him to have the best."

My wife and Eleanor got along pretty good. After we moved to Florida the women kept in touch. Early in the winter of 1939, Eleanor wrote my wife that Lou hadn't been feeling too well. A New Rochelle doctor had diagnosed Lou's trouble as gallbladder and was giving him treatments, or medicine. Lou had been pretty well tied up with some things, and Eleanor thought if he came down here to St. Petersburg about a month early, before the Yankees started spring training, he could put that time into fishing and just lolling around in the sun. She asked if we could get them a house somewhere near us, near the old ball park which is where the Mets practice now, on Thirteenth Avenue and Fourth Street. We got them a place. Shortly, they came around.

The Gehrigs had a ouija board, and one night they brought it over to our house. We were living on Seventh Avenue, that's four blocks north of here. We used to get a contact on this board that called itself "Mark Antony"—without the H. And we really got some amazing stuff which I have in another book, not a baseball book. It's called *Sight Unseen*. Harper put it out in 1939.

We began this session, and almost the first thing was "ELEANOR YOU WILL MEET THE MOST DIFFICULT PROBLEM OF YOUR LIFE."

That may not be the exact words, but that's how I recall it. And "Mark Antony" reiterated that. "Mark Antony" would talk back and forth to us like I'm talking back and forth to you. I can't explain it. It's somehow

the subconscious mind. Whether it was my wife's subconscious mind or not, I don't know. This wasn't an actual voice. The message would be spelled out on the board.

"Mark Antony" spelled this out, repeatedly, and we'd talk back. I would say, "Now, Mark, you're not being fair." Or "That isn't fair. You're telling these people how Eleanor's got this problem, but you don't give us any inkling of what it's about."

"WELL SHE'LL KNOW ABOUT IT SOON ENOUGH."

So then we began asking different questions. I don't recall whether it was Lou or Eleanor who asked if it was about the adopted child.

"Mark Antony" said, "NO."

Lou and Eleanor were married in '33 and this was '39, six years later, and they didn't have any children. She was supposed to be two years younger than Lou. Mom Gehrig always insisted she was two years older. They didn't think they could have any children and had given thought to adopting a child.

As soon as Mom Gehrig heard about that she flew up to the ceiling. If there was going to be a grandchild, and if it wasn't a Gehrig, she wouldn't be interested. They never did adopt a child.

They were both concerned when they left our house, and so were my wife and I. And then the exhibition season opened and Lou got off to quite a bad start. You could tell he was sluggish. He kept saying, "I'm not getting enough work. I'm not in shape."

And I told him, "Hell, Lou, that's stupid. Everybody knows you can hit a ball. Why worry about it if you don't hit down here? It's only spring training."

Lou would come out to the ball park earlier than anybody else and be the last guy to leave. But trying to work out and play ball, with this disease already in his system, only exaggereated the condition. There was one game, a high-scoring game with the Braves. Lou was the clean-up hitter and came up four times and didn't get the ball out of the infield. Finally he came up in the ninth inning with the bases filled and two outs, and the Yankees behind, 7–6, and he popped up to the second baseman.

Lou was very low that night. He kept saying, "What in the hell is the matter with me? What in the hell is the matter with me?"

I said, "You'll snap out of it, Lou. Don't worry."

Eleanor, at that time, had no idea anything was seriously wrong. Later she said she had noticed that when he stepped off a curb, one foot would kind of plop down.

The Yankees left Florida, heading north, and played an exhibition game in Norfolk, and Lou had three home runs. I thought, "Well, he's finally snapped into it." Both my wife and I were overjoyed.

Then the season started and in his first seven games, maybe it was the first nine games, he hit about .145 or something like that. These were the last seven or nine games of that long, Iron Man record.

Later, Lou said the thing that really made him decide to take himself out of the lineup was when he had made a play which any high school first baseman could have made. It was an ordinary ground ball, and he threw the ball underhanded to Johnny Murphy, who was covering first base. Murphy had gone into the game as a relief pitcher. Murphy and Tony Lazzeri put their arms around him and slapped him on the back. "Good play, Lou! Good play, Lou!"

"That hurt me more than anything they could have done," Lou said. "If I'm so bad that when I field an ordinary little grounder I could have eaten up when I went to high school and they say, 'Great play! Great play!' then I know I'm hurting the club."

The Yankees were to open a western trip, and Lou went to Joe McCarthy, the manager, and told McCarthy to play Babe Dahlgren at first base. That's when his streak was broken.

I went up to New York earlier that year than I usually do. We stayed in Mount Vernon because my daughter lived nearby. When we got there I called Eleanor and I said, "We're coming over this afternoon!"

At first she said, "No, Fred, you better not come today." Then she said, "On second thought, I want you to come. I've got a very important phone message coming from Lou, and I'd like to have you with me when I get it."

Lou had called earlier in the day. He was up at the Mayo Clinic, having tests. I was there when he called the second time. Eleanor took the call in another room. And when she came back she said, "I need a drink. I need a drink." She took a stiff hooker of liquor and said, "You know what that Dutchman just told me? 'Don't worry, Eleanor. I have a fifty-fifty chance to live.'"

But soon I found out it wasn't a fifty-fifty chance. It was one out of a hundred. Eleanor found out, too. It was some kind of disease of the spinal column, or the cord. The kind of disease that makes the spinal column turn into chalk. On July 4 of that year, at Yankee Stadium, the people of New York paid Lou Gehrig the finest tribute a ball player has ever received. It was Gehrig Appreciation Day, Lou's farewell. That's when he said that, despite everything, he still felt he was the luckiest man in the world.

The Babe and Lou had been good friends, for about the first eight years that they played together. Quite often the Babe would be a guest at the Gehrig house. He and Mom Gehrig would have a lot of fun. It was there that I first knew that Babe could talk German, really, surpris-ingly well. Eleanor objected to this very much. She always thought they were talking about her.

Gehrig and Ruth were complete opposites. You couldn't find two more different personalities. Lou was a fellow with quite an inferiority complex that followed him into professional baseball. He once told me about the time when his coach at the High School of Commerce asked him to come out to practice for the baseball team. Lou walked around the outside of the field three times, without going in, and then he walked home.

The next day the coach said to him, "Why didn't you show up?"

And Lou said, "I was doing something else."

Lou was sort of ashamed that his father was a janitor in a tenement. He told me one time, when we were on the road, "You know, when some of the writers come up to me and ask me questions, they think that I'm rude because I don't answer right. But I'm so scared I'm almost shitting in my pants."

Lou had a real admiration for the Babe and was content to be in the Babe's shadow. You know, of course, about the Babe's "called shot" homer, the one off Charlie Root in Chicago, in the '32 World Series. There was never any question that Ruth called the shot. I had dinner with Lou the night of that game. Lou hit two home runs himself, but all he could talk about was "What do you think of the nerve of that big monkey calling his shot and taking those two strikes and then hitting the ball exactly where he pointed?" That was how Lou was. He was content to push himself backward and push the Babe forward.

Mom Gehrig thought well of the Babe, too. I don't think she spurred Lou on to exceed the Babe as much as Eleanor did. Once Eleanor told me, "I've got to start a campaign on this Dutchman. He's got this inferiority complex that he's second to Ruth. Now, we know that Ruth is the big man of baseball, but he isn't going to last too much longer and the one who must take his place must, necessarily, be Lou. And I'm trying to build him up to the point where he knows he's good. Babe takes it for granted that he's good. Lou has never had that kind of confidence."

The Gehrigs and the Ruths took part in that Japanese tour of 1934. Something happened on that trip. I think it started with the two ladies, Claire and Eleanor. Whether that had anything to do with the cooling off of their relationship I don't know. But it was about five years before they spoke to each other again, and that was when they met at Lou's farewell at Yankee Stadium.

I still see Eleanor occasionally, usually at the Hall of Fame inductions in Cooperstown. But the old intimacy is gone. We had a falling out after Lou died. I found out that Lou's grave—he's buried in Westchester County—was very much neglected, a lot of weeds, birdshit all over it, and so on. I wrote a letter to a third party about this, to Christy Walsh, the agent. I wrote to him because he was doing some things for Eleanor, following up some deals that Lou had been in, and I said if he didn't do anything about this, about the neglected grave, that I would complain to the commissioner, who was then Chandler.

I thought he would approach Eleanor in a nice way. But he went directly to her with my letter. She called me up, oh, it was about three o'clock in the morning, St. Louis time, and accused me of being a false friend. She said she could sue me, but because of our former relationship she wouldn't. Then she asked to talk to Mary, my wife. Mary objected to Eleanor calling us at that time in the morning. They talked for about a half an hour and finally Mary said, "I don't want to talk anymore."

I've seen the Lou Gehrig movie—*Pride of the Yankees*—several times. They still play it on television. Walter Brennan plays the part of a sportswriter who is Lou's personal friend. I suppose you could say he played my part, though my name isn't mentioned.

I'm mentioned in *The Babe Ruth Story,* which is supposedly based on the book by Bob Considine. The book is under Considine's name, but I gave him most of his information. I dictated that book for about a week prior to the 1947 World Series. I told everything I could recall. Not everything, but everything that could be printed. Considine gave me a copy of the book and inscribed on the title page, "To my good friend Fred Lieb—Without whom this book would not have been possible."

I didn't get in on the royalties, but my name is mentioned in the movie. They said that Fred Lieb measured the six-hundred-foot homer that Ruth hit at Tampa, Florida, during a Red Sox–New York Giant exhibition game in the spring of 1919. Many people believe it was Ruth's longest homer, and he hit it well before he became the nation's home run idol. Actually, the homer was measured by two Boston writers, one of them Mel Webb. I believe I am the only one alive of the New York and Boston writers who covered that game.

I've been somewhat amused this past summer reading about the trouble Hank Aaron was running into when he was chasing Ruth's record. Aaron said—and it came out in the papers—that the fans were writing him abusive letters, calling him "nigger," and he said that Babe Ruth was never confronted with anything like that.

What Aaron doesn't know, and I suppose what most people don't know, is that some of Babe's teammates on the Red Sox were convinced he had Negro blood. There was quite a bit of talk about that. Many of the players, when they wanted to badger him, called him "nigger." Ruth had Negroid features, Negroid nose, mouth, lips.

But when you saw him naked, from the neck down, he was white, a good deal whiter than most men.

Ty Cobb once refused to share a cabin with Ruth. I'm sure of the authenticity of this. They were assigned to the same cabin, but Cobb objected and said, "I've never bedded down with a nigger and I'm not going to start now." This was when they were down at Dover Hall, a hunting lodge near Brunswick, Georgia. A lot of baseball men would go down there in the off-season.

Cobb and Ruth never did get along. Cobb disliked most people, and particularly someone like Ruth who would take any of the glamour off himself. They had a fight once. It was in Detroit. They almost wrecked the place. I've forgotten now why it happened, but they had to call off the game the next day because the fans tore the seats loose and threw them on the field. There must have been five thousand dollars' worth of damage.

The Yankees were at bat and Detroit was in the field. Cobb was the playing manager, and when the fight started he came running in from center field. Ruth got off the bench and ran out to meet him. They met like two football linemen, each trying to put the other out of the play. One shot out in one direction and the other in the other. I have that in my Detroit book. I could look it up if you want me to.

Ruth didn't talk much about Cobb. One time, when I was doing a story on the Babe, I called on him about four in the afternoon and stayed with him until midnight. Despite the fact that Ruth had a sore throat—this was just before he died—we talked for more than eight hours, straight through. He said he thought Cobb was a great ball player but a no-good, mean sonofabitch. Babe wasn't alone on that. Ninety percent of the players felt the same way. Cobb was very much hated. The players hated his guts.

Cobb was a mean, cruel man. I didn't witness this myself, but was told about it by another newspaperman who would have no reason to distort the incident. Cobb was sitting on the porch at Dover Hall with some other baseball men, including some baseball writers. Someone had petted a hunting dog, and the dog came up a few steps on the porch. Cobb got up, almost leaped at this dog, and kicked him about fifteen yards. It wasn't just kicking. He kicked the dog like a football would be kicked, and shouted, very angrily, "That's a hunting dog, not a pet dog. He knows better than this, to come up on the porch." To me, that shows the latent cruelty within Cobb.

Cobb once threatened to punch me in the nose. It was when he was managing Detroit. He was always late sending his lineup to the press box. We had a rather stupid, almost illiterate guy who was the field announcer at Yankee Stadium. He would go on the field before each game and bring the lineups to us. We bawled him out because whenever Detroit was playing he was always late, though I suppose it wasn't all his fault. One time he tried to hurry Cobb into giving him the Detroit lineup. Cobb gave him hell and said, "Why should I worry about those twenty-five and fifty-dollar-a-week sons of bitches?"

I wrote a column the next day blasting Cobb. I headed it with his ridiculing us twenty-five and fifty-dollar-a-week sons of bitches. I said without us there wouldn't be anybody to record his .400 batting average, things like that.

Cobb sent word he wanted to see me. He said, "I didn't like that column you wrote."

I told him, "Well, I only wrote what Jack Lenz told me."

"Who in the hell do you believe? Do you believe that stupid sonofabitch? Or do you believe me?"

I said Lenz had no reason to lie. I believed him.

So Cobb said, "We're going to have this out man-to-man."

I said, "Well, I guess you outweigh me by a few pounds."

Then Cobb relaxed. He smiled and said, "Anyway, you had the guts to come down here. A lot of you sons of bitches wouldn't come down here. I admire you for that."

After that experience Cobb became one of my best friends. It was about this time that we started writing preseason stories on each team, on the prospects of each club and how they figured to do during the season ahead. One spring I couldn't get to see the Tigers. I wrote to Cobb, asking him about his club. And surprisingly enough, he sent me a nine-page handwritten letter telling me who his best new prospects were, things like that. So here the guy is supposed to be so tough, and yet he stayed in his room long enough to write me a long personal letter.

I always thought Cobb was embittered, as a young man, because of the shooting of his father—the way he was killed. His mother shot his father. Supposedly it was an accident, a case of mistaken identity. I know Cobb had a great admiration for his father. He spoke of him often. I never heard him mention his mother.

His father was superintendent of schools for the county they lived in in Georgia. The story was given out that the father was on a trip in one of the more remote parts of the county. He came home unexpectedly and his wife, according to the story, thought he was an intruder and shot and killed him.

This happened right about the time Cobb won his first batting championship. That would be 1907. His father very much opposed his going into baseball. He wanted him to be a doctor and get an education. An older newspaperman told me that Cobb's father told him,

"Well, all right, go ahead and play baseball. But don't come back unless you've made it." Eventually his father was reconciled to his playing baseball.

In his later years, long after he was out of baseball, Cobb tried to change his image. I saw him only a few times in the last years of his life. He was hungry for companionship. He'd want you to have lunch with him, and then he insisted you stay for dinner. It'd be midnight before he let you go. He would talk incessantly. He admitted he didn't have too many friends among the ball players, and he kept repeating he wasn't as mean as people made him out to be. I always had the feeling that if he had had another chance he might have done things differently.

I was in the middle of a famous scoring controversy that involved Cobb. It was in 1922, the last year the Yankees played in the Polo Grounds. The game was being played in the rain, and the other writers, including Jack Kieran, the official scorer, left the press box and scrambled into the top rows of the grandstand for cover.

I stayed in the press stand because I was handling the play-by-play wire for my paper, the New York *Press,* and because I was doing the box score for the Associated Press. Cobb hit a grounder to Everett Scott, the Yankee shortstop. Scott kicked it, fumbled it a bit. The field was wet, and ground balls were difficult to pick up. I figured with Cobb's speed he would have beaten it out for a hit.

If Jack Kieran had been in the press stand, I would have turned to him and asked how he scored it. But he wasn't there. I credited Cobb with a hit in the AP box score and thought no more about it. But Jack, in the official box score which he sent to the league statistician in Chicago, didn't give Cobb a hit. He charged Scott with an error.

This was in August, and nobody noticed until the end of the season when the official averages were tabulated. The AP had been sending out weekly averages which were used by all the newspapers but, of course, were not official. At the end of the season the AP had Cobb hitting .401, but Irwin Howe, in Chicago, the league's official statistician, had Cobb hitting .399.

Howe checked and found this game in August and then made a bad, bad mistake. He decided that since I was the more experienced scorer, my judgment, my decision, should be made official. But there was more to it than that. Howe was working for the president of the league, Ban Johnson, and Johnson wanted the American League to have a .400 hitter, more or less as evidence that the American League was superior to the National League.

I objected to this, but Howe and Johnson insisted they were going to honor my judgment ahead of Kieran's. It so happened that I was the national president of the baseball writers that year, and in the winter I presided at one of the stormiest meetings in our history. We had eleven chapters then—one in each major league city. As I recall, two chapters were not voting, or perhaps they weren't present.

I was really rooting for Cobb's .399. We voted by chapters and the vote was 5–4 in favor of Cobb's .399 and, of course, in favor of Kieran's decision. But Johnson and Howe continued to insist on the .401, and we said if they listed Cobb's .401 in the record books and in the baseball guides, then they should have an asterisk after it, saying, "Not recognized by the Baseball Writers Association." But they never did use an asterisk. That's how Cobb hit .400 for the third time.

I was the official scorer in the first American League game that I attended as a writer because the New York *Press* had befriended the Yankees—they were the Highlanders then—in their early years. So whoever wrote baseball for the *Press* was the official scorer at all Yankee home games.

In the middle of my first year as a scorer, Frank Farrell called me up one day and bawled me out. He owned the Yankees then. He was a politician, a Tammany man. He had been a gambling house owner and collector of a lot of bawdy houses.

Anyway, Farrell called me and said, "You know what I'm paying Jack Knight?"

I didn't know.

"I'm paying him four thousand dollars for playing short, a lot of money for an infielder. He made two errors yesterday, and I pick up my morning paper and I don't see any errors for him."

I explained it was a matter of the judgment of the scorer, that they were difficult chances. But Farrell wasn't interested. The conversation ended with him saying, "Whenever anybody on my club makes an error, I want you to give it to him."

I always had confidence in my ability as an official scorer. I had played a lot of baseball in my early years. That's how I got started in the business. I was a baseball nut, but I was a mediocre player. I played for our church team—the Prince of Peace. We were all Princes of Peace. I had a pretty good left arm, but I was a sucker at the plate and struck out frequently, so the next best thing was to write baseball.

I got started rather early, after high school. I worked in a railroad office in Philadelphia—that's my home town—and I began writing on the side. I contacted *Baseball Magazine,* which was then a new publication. I think it started around 1908 or 1909. In the fall of 1909 they took two of my stories, biographies of Hans Wagner and Ty Cobb, and from there I went to Fred Clarke and Hugh Jennings, the managers of the two World Series clubs of 1909. They liked them and had me do a monthly biography of the great players.

Eddie Collins was the first player I ever talked with. Eddie was pretty nice, but Christy Mathewson was quite reticent, and John McGraw was hard to reach. McGraw would bawl the hell out of you at something that you wrote that displeased him. He would say, "Why don't you come to me when you want some information on this? Why do you just write it?" He bawled me out once for a story about how he let Heinie Wagner go. Heinie was a shortstop for the Red Sox in the 1912 World Series, and McGraw let him get away. It wasn't even an important story, just a fill-in, but McGraw bawled hell out of me anyway.

I also had the good fortune in 1910 to sell two baseball fiction stories to a magazine called *Short Stories.* That was one of the pulps at that time, and later they became an ace in the hole. If I couldn't sell a story to *Top Notch,* or *Popular,* or *Railroad Man's Magazine,* I'd send it to *Short Stories* and invariably they took it.

Then I was briefly with the Philadelphia News Bureau, which was the Philadelphia outlet for the *Wall Street Journal.* My former railroad boss got me acquainted with Clarence Barron, the big boss of Dow-Jones and *Barron's Weekly.* A meeting was arranged for me and Barron, a job interview, at the old Waldorf-Astoria in New York. I met him there, in his room, and the first assignment I had from him was "Draw me a bath."

Barron had one of those big stomachs, and when he lay in the tub this big stomach looked like a big turtle up there. He said, "So you want to write, do you?"

I told him I had visions or ambitions to be a sportswriter, and he says, "Oh, bah, sportswriter! Sportswriters make pennies. Why don't you become a financial writer? That's where all the money is."

Barron was a lineal descendant of Priscilla Alden—you know the Priscilla Alden story—"Speak for yourself, John." I worked for Barron for about four months and then I went to the New York *Press,* which wasn't a great newspaper, but it had two distinctions. At that time it was the only Republican newspaper in New York City, and it gave more space to baseball than any other paper in the country.

That was in 1911. But actually my start as a baseball writer was two years before that, because of those *Baseball Magazine* biographies. That was when Al Spink of *The Sporting News* got out a book on baseball, a *Who's Who, People Worth Knowing in Baseball,* and had me in there as "baseball's foremost biographer." Of course, I was only a kid, twenty-two or twenty-three years old, but it made me think I was a pretty important person.

Armed with these biographies, I got the job at the New York *Press.* I stayed there until 1916, and then I went to the *Morning Sun.* Later I moved to the *Telegram,* then to the *Post.* In 1934 I came down here to St.

Petersburg and began free-lancing full-time, writing books and magazine articles. In the summer I usually went up to *The Sporting News* in St. Louis, as an extra man to help out when others went on vacation. Sometimes I'd spend almost half the year there. Eventually I worked for *The Sporting News* full-time.

This is the sixty-second year that I have a card in the Baseball Writers Association. Only John Wheeler has been a member longer. Wheeler was out of New York City and went into the syndicate business. I believe he's worth several million now. There's nothing else I would have rather done. When I walked into the New York press box for the first time, I couldn't have been happier, not if I'd made the Oval Office in the White House.

# No More Cheers

## BRUCE LOWITT

THERE ARE no more cheers for Steve Howe, only the silence of memories punctuated by the sounds of a distant playoff game he might have been in.

He could have been in the Dodgers' bullpen Wednesday night in Los Angeles, waiting to be summoned to put out a fire on the mound. Instead, he shambles about St. Mary's Rehabilitation Center in Minneapolis, trying to summon up the courage to live the rest of his life free of cocaine.

He had his chances. With the Dodgers. With the Minnesota Twins. He used them up one at a time, like a relief pitcher grooving one fastball after another, watching them explode at the plate until he has nothing left save a trip to the showers, the minors or oblivion.

Once he had it all—all-state in high school, All–Big Ten twice, the winningest pitcher in University of Michigan history, National League Rookie of the Year for the Dodgers in 1980, world champion in 1981.

And in 1985, age 27, when he should be reaching his professional peak, he is looking instead for a way out of the white-powdered valley.

Cocaine, he said on ABC's *Nightline* program last September 12, was not the problem in his life. It was life itself.

"Life in general and people and places and things and success a lot of times are people's problems," he said. "At least it was for me." The day after appearing on the television program, Howe disappeared.

Three days later, he reappeared, met with Twins officials, asked for and was given his release and entered St. Mary's.

"It's bad to have memories dragged up, except by a professional counselor," Jim Hawkins, Howe's lawyer and close friend, said from his office in Westlake Village, California, near Los Angeles. "They recall not only what you saw and heard but what you felt. In his case, they can be extremely negative emotions. Maybe it was bringing up those emotions on the TV program that led to this relapse."

In *Cocaine: Seduction and Solution*, authors Nannette Stone, Marlene Fromme and Daniel Kagan note that people who believe they are unable to love and be loved, and those looking for a way to cope with anxiety, stress and depression, are particularly susceptible to cocaine dependence.

"My sole existence of what I did in life was what I did on the ballfield," Howe said on *Nightline*. "When nothing else matters and you don't feel that you're going to be able to perform up to your capabilities and someone gives you an avenue to deaden that pain . . . you're going to do what you can do so that people are going to like you and accept you."

"I don't know if he did drugs for baseball or baseball made him do drugs," his mother, Barbara, said in an interview. "Whatever it was, he could afford it. The average person can't afford that kind of thing. Maybe the average person becomes an alcoholic because they can afford it. It's cheaper."

Howe and his wife, Cyndy, declined to be interviewed. So did Dr. George Mann, the director of the Twins' employee assistance program and medical director at St. Mary's.

Mann also refused to disclose whether Howe is a patient at St. Mary's. Howard Fox, the Twins' president, and Howe's parents said he is.

His father, Virgil, was once a pretty good sandlot pitcher. Now he and Barbara Howe live in the Detroit suburb of Clarkston and work for General Motors.

"Steven just played ball for so long in his life that—and I'm not saying this is the reason he did what he did with drugs—that there never seemed to be enough time for Steven to do what Steven wanted to do," Virgil said. "He started playing ball when he was 9 years old. That's all he's ever done."

Chris Howe, 24, one of Steve's three younger brothers (he also has a younger sister) and a law student at Michigan's Flint campus, said that as a teenager Steve showed the frustrations of a youngster on a pedestal, believing he had to perform up to someone else's standards.

"I don't think it's accurate to say my father was trying to make Steve into something dad couldn't be, but that's not to say Steve didn't try too hard to please him. He tried to please my father more than anyone else.''

"Oh, it's easy to place blame where there is no blame,'' Barbara, his mother, said. "We have five children and we have one cocaine addict. I would die for my kids. But I will not take the blame for his addiction, any more than his father should. Steven did this all by himself. He chose to do it.''

"I don't feel any sense of failure,'' Virgil, his father, added. "How could we feel we failed with him when we didn't fail with the other four?''

No one is really sure what went wrong with the young left-hander who mastered control of a baseball but not his life.

"When he was a kid, he just said what he was going to do and it came easy,'' Barbara Howe said. "Everything was easy for him and once he got it, it was, 'It's not what I really want.' Personally, if he never plays baseball again, I don't really care, as long as he's OK and can function. But that's up to him. I can't live his life for him. I can't tell him what to do anymore.''

Moby Benedict, the director of intramural athletics at the University of Michigan, was its baseball coach when Howe was one of the Wolverines' star pitchers.

"Steve was a follower more than anything else,'' Benedict said. "Certainly not on the ballfield. Give him the baseball and he became a fierce competitor. . . . Off the field, he was not a leader. The guys would say, 'Let's go,' and he'd go.''

He couldn't say no.

Not to his friends and acquaintances.

Not to the Hollywood crowd which embraced him.

Not to drugs.

"I'd tell him, 'It's against the law and it's harmful to your body,' '' Tom Lasorda, the Dodgers' manager, said. "He'd say to me, 'You're right. You're right.' Then he'd go out and do it.''

Steve Wagner was a teammate at Michigan, another pitcher. He and Howe remained friends beyond college, wound up in California together. When Steve and Cyndy went to spring training at Dodgertown in Vero Beach, Florida, Wagner was their house-sitter.

"I could see a change in him when he got to California,'' said Wagner, now working with his father in the lumber business in Ann Arbor, Michigan. "Steve had been a star in college, but he'd never experienced anything like that—the pressure that someone so young had to face, everybody being on him all the time, everybody wanting a favor. There was always somebody wanting something and Steve could never say he couldn't do it. . . .

"I think he's the kind of guy who can help everybody else deal with their problems and not be able to deal with his own . . . but he was never one to admit it. He would put on a good show about it.''

"Who is the real Steve Howe?'' Barbara, his mother, wonders. "I don't know. I really don't, and I don't think he does. . . . 'Is this the real Steve today? Who are you today? Are you what you want to be or are you what somebody else wants you to be?'

"He's like a chameleon. He'll be whatever you want him to be. He'll see what somebody's looking for and give it to him. He's always been that way. . . . I've told him, 'You've got to live for yourself. You can't please this person, that person and that person.' ''

Barbara Howe sighed. "Maybe when he goes and uses, he says to himself, 'I'm doing this for me.' ''

Mike Hernandez, Sr., owns Camino Real Chevrolet in Monterey Park, five miles east of downtown Los Angeles. He makes a habit of helping young ballplayers with the loan of a car or some money. Maybe a job. In 1980, Howe, married less than a year and with barely half a minor-league season under his belt, made the big leagues.

Hernandez and Manny Mota, the Dodgers' first-base coach, go back a long way. "Manny brought this kid in,'' Hernandez said. " 'He needs a car,' he told me.'' Pretty soon Howe was selling cars for him as well.

"With me and Steve, it quickly became a father-and-son relationship. The second year, I kicked a guy out of here that somehow, in my mind, I felt the guy was a drug pusher. Turned out I was right. I got very upset and scolded Steve and Cyndy. I told him, 'How can you even be walking around with this guy?'

"I don't think Steve was ready to make the kind of money he was making,'' Hernandez said. "I think he got into bad company, not only outside of Dodger Stadium but inside, also.''

A rich young star, even a newly married one, doesn't automatically settle down in the suburbs. Howe didn't. He and Cyndy roared into Marina del Rey, the freeway off-ramp to the California fast lane.

"LA is Media City. TV, movies,'' Hawkins, their lawyer, said. "Steve was invited into those circles, into the Los Angeles celebrity stardom circle. Not just baseball. Actors, directors, producers, fast-movers, the whole crowd. Getting invited into those circles can be a very heady experience for a 22-year-old kid. He was a somebody, very much sought after.''

"Nobody ever told him cocaine was bad,'' his mother said. "Three years ago it was a fun thing. It was Hollywood. It was California. 'Hey, let's do cocaine.' It was party time. It's only been, what, the last year and a half that everybody's realized how evil it is. It was just like marijuana when it started out. 'Let's go smoke pot.' Now we're finding out what it does to your brain cells.''

Dr. Forrest Tennant is executive director of Community Health Project, 25 clinics in southern California. He also is the Dodgers' drug abuse consultant. He was Howe's counselor.

"There are three kinds of cocaine users," Tennant said. "One is the occasional user, the weekend user. He gets his treatment from a minister or a psychologist. Another is the regular user who's not addicted, maybe one, two times a day. He goes into Cocaine Anonymous or a hospital for a 28-day treatment program.

"And there's the chronic, addicted user. He's been to a minister or psychologist. He's been in the hospital or CA. And he's still relapsing because the cocaine has altered his brain chemistry. . . . Simple behavioral treatment isn't enough."

Howe, Tennant said, "is not the same as those players who testified in Pittsburgh," a reference to the seven major leaguers who admitted past cocaine use in the trial of convicted drug dealer Curtis Strong. "Howe is a relapsing user."

"I think I was the first guy to know in '82 that Steve had a problem," Hernandez, the auto dealer, said. "But I'm not his father. I couldn't keep up with the guy."

He called Mota, told him of Howe's problem, asked him to speak quietly to the Dodgers. "He did it and the Dodgers were very concerned, but they didn't do anything until Steve himself—I don't know, maybe he was forced—until he went to the drug center the first time. . . .

"He was taking two [drug] tests a week with the Dodgers," Hernandez said. "I forced him to tell them, 'I want to take it three times.' See, he could con them. The stuff only lasts 72 hours. So he could take a test on Friday, then take dope and not take another test until Monday and it wouldn't show anything. He took three a week for a long time and everything was going fine. Everybody was trying to help him. . . .

"Then all of a sudden he disappeared."

Howe was the Dodgers' No. 1 choice in the June free-agent draft in 1979, spent half a season at San Antonio in the Class AA Texas League, then rode his 94-mile-an-hour fastball to the Dodgers' roster in 1980.

His 17 saves, 2.65 earned-run average and 7–9 record made him the National League Rookie of the Year. In 1981 Howe was 5–3 with a 2.50 ERA and 8 saves, and the next year he led the Dodgers in games (66), saves (13) and ERA (2.08), was 7–5 and a National League All-Star.

By the end of the 1982 season, though, cocaine had become such a part of his life that, after it, he spent five and a half weeks at The Meadows, a clinic in the Arizona desert. "What I did probably saved my career," Howe said on April 27, 1983.

Twenty days later he reentered treatment, this time at the CareUnit Hospital in Orange, California. He returned to the active list on June 29, was fined one month's salary ($53,867), then was suspended by the team on July 16, the day after he arrived half an hour after a game with the Chicago Cubs had begun.

Howe was reinstated the next day after undergoing a drug test, was suspended again on September 23, sat out the rest of the season (he was 4–7 with 18 saves and a 1.44 ERA in 1983) and was suspended for all of 1984 by Bowie Kuhn, then the baseball commissioner.

"I didn't know what Steve's problem was before he admitted it the first time," Lasorda, his manager, said, "but I had suspicions. He'd always have an excuse for being late. I'd tell him, 'You sleep with dogs, you're going to wake up with fleas.' He'd seem all right for a time, then boom, he'd have problems again."

On May 22, 1983, Steve and Cyndy Howe became the parents of Chelsea Leigh Howe, a daughter.

Hawkins met the Howe family for the first time six months later. They'd moved from Marina del Rey to Agoura, a bedroom community 35 miles northwest of Los Angeles. "They were trying very hard to be responsible, parental-type people," the lawyer said.

"They were not the fast-track people anymore. Their emphasis was on church and family. I think that may have added to the frustration. It must have been frustrating to get out of the fast lane and then have everything come down on him when he thought he was in the slow lane."

Howe, anticipating a lengthy suspension, was concerned about paying his bills. Kuhn announced it on December 15. The Howes filed for bankruptcy a week later. They owed about $100,000 more than they had.

On May 15, 1984, Cyndy Howe sued for divorce, citing "irreconcilable differences." The divorce never became final. The Howes are together again.

Steve underwent more drug counseling and rehabilitation during 1984, hoping he could still pitch in the majors.

The Dodgers gave him a one-year contract for 1985.

Al Campanis approached Howe one day at spring training. The Dodgers' vice president of player personnel had read that once someone was addicted to cocaine, it was dangerous to use any other chemical substance, that even smoking could lead to renewed cocaine use.

Howe smoked. Campanis wanted him to stop.

He offered Howe a deal. They would establish a fund for Chelsea. For every one of Howe's smokeless days, Campanis would put in a dollar. For every day he smoked, Howe would kick in two.

It was run on the honor system—but on occasion Campanis would walk up to Howe and say, "Breathe on me."

As Opening Day approached, Howe vowed he had finally beaten cocaine. "Drugs are right where they belong," he said. "In the past."

On June 23, he showed up three hours late for a game against Houston, claiming Cyndy had mistakenly taken the car keys. He was fined $300.

On June 26, in San Diego, he gave up a home run to Steve Garvey in a 10–4 loss. After the game, in Lasorda's office, Howe burst into tears.

"He just came in and said, 'I want to go someplace else. I can't handle this,' " Lasorda said. "He said he had not been involved in cocaine, he was just depressed at the way things were going and he just thought it would be best for him and his family to get somewhere where these things wouldn't happen."

On June 30, he failed to show up for a game against Atlanta.

In 20 games he was 1–1 with 3 saves and a 4.84 ERA.

On July 3, the Dodgers released Steve Howe. He was still smoking cigarettes.

The Twins signed him on August 11.

"Minnesotans are very forgiving people," Fox, the Twins' president, said. "They like to root for underdogs, for people who have made mistakes and are trying to overcome them. That's one reason I gave him an opportunity."

The fans welcomed him warmly. He received a standing ovation the first time he strode to the mound in the Metrodome.

His pitching didn't improve. In 13 games he was 2–3 with no saves and a 6.16 ERA.

Then came the drug trial in Pittsburgh. Steve Howe was mentioned only peripherally. Then came *Nightline*. Then he was gone.

There is fallout from the cocaine cloud under which Steve Howe lives.

"I want to be sympathetic with Steven, but I'm really getting fed up with it all," his mother says. "I don't like picking up the newspaper and reading how my kid's missing from the baseball team again. I'm sick of it, just plain sick of it. I have to get up and go to work every day, his dad has to get up and go to work, he's got brothers in Clarkston who keep hearing, 'I see your druggie brother screwed up again.'

"It hasn't created a problem in the family, although the kids have said things to us, how they feel sorry for us. Not for themselves. Like Michael said, 'Why in the hell doesn't he just get out of baseball and straighten his life out instead of us having to pick up a newspaper all the time and read about him?'

"It's embarrassing, sure. You can say, 'It's no reflection on you.' But it is. That's your kid, and millions of people read about him when he blows his nose or whatever."

Barbara Howe, 43 years old and the mother of a cocaine-addicted former baseball star, sighed once again.

"You know what I think Steven's problem is?" she said. "Everything he ever said he wanted to do, he's done. He's an ordinary kid who got everything he ever wished for. All his dreams came true. And it wasn't enough."

If you have been turning the pages of this book from front to back (not everyone does), then you may already have read Peter Gammons' story on how the Red Sox collapsed in the 1978 pennant race. But at the end they got another chance—the Yankees fell back into a tie and it all came down to a one-game playoff on October 2 for the Eastern Division title of the American League.

Here, then, is that game, reported this time not by Gammons from the press box but by Sparky Lyle from the New York bullpen at Fenway Park.

# From *The Bronx Zoo*

## SPARKY LYLE *and* PETER GOLENBOCK

IT WAS strange, but for a game that was so important to both teams, there was very little tension. Last night a bunch of us went out and had a few drinks, and we were sitting at the hotel bar, and the general consensus was "We're gonna win tomorrow." We just knew we were going to win. And the Red Sox weren't tight because they had just had the Division championship taken away from them, and now they were getting a second chance. So they played as good a game as they could play because they felt they had absolutely nothing to lose.

It was a tremendous day, I'll tell you, it really was. It was like being in the seventh game of the World Series. Gid started and he didn't really have his good stuff 'cause he was going with only three days' rest again, but he was still good enough to hold them to two runs in six and a third, quite an accomplishment for a left-hander in Fenway. In the second Yaz got up, and he knew Gid was going to try to pump a fastball by him, and Gid got the ball up, and Yaz has such power in his hands, he just turned those wrists over and *boom* that ball was gone.

They scored again in the sixth when Rice singled Burleson home. Everything was real quiet in our bullpen, and I said to Tidrow, "We're just teasing them. In the ninth inning, we're gonna win this son of a bitch three to two and go home." Dirt said, "I think we're gonna win eight to two." We were both wrong—the score was actually 5 to 4—but we just knew, we had a feeling out there, that we were going to win. We had all those goose eggs up there on the scoreboard, but the way the game was going, Torrez had been lucky, and there

was no way he was going to shut us out. And there wasn't.

In our half of the seventh Chambliss singled and Roy singled and Bucky Dent got up. Because Willie Randolph's still out, Fred Stanley went in to play second when Lem pinch-hit for Doyle, so they didn't pinch-hit for Bucky like they usually do. Torrez threw Bucky a slider, Bucky swung, and he hit the ball off his ankle. Bucky went down, and when he dragged himself back up, he hobbled over to third-base coach Dick Howser, and he said, "If that son of a bitch comes in there again with that pitch, I'm going to take him into the net." And Torrez threw it in there again, and *bang* there it went. Bucky hit it into the net for a three-run homer.

In the bullpen we were laughing because our shortstops have devastated Torrez. In June, Stanley hit that grand slam off him, and now Bucky hit this three-runner. Seven RBI's in two swings. Torrez just can't get our shortstops out! Then Rivers walked and stole second, and he scored when Thurman doubled off reliever Bob Stanley.

When Reggie got up in the eighth, Mr. October, as he likes to call himself, hit another home run to make it 5 to 2. Despite the fact that Reggie at times can be hard to take, there's no question that in the big games, he can get way up and hit the hell out of the ball. No one's ever denied him that. I can't figure out why he does it, but he does it. I think that in the big games a pitcher has a tendency to be finer around the plate, and that makes the hitter more selective. If Reggie could concentrate all year long like he does in the play-offs and the Series games, his records would be unbelievable. Reggie's so strong, and he has so much power that a pitcher can't fool with him. If he makes a mistake, and Reggie gets his bat on it, Reggie swings such a heavy bat that it's gone.

Goose relieved Gid in the seventh and got the last two outs, but in their half of the eighth, the Red Sox came back with two runs against him. Remy doubled, Yaz singled to drive him in, Fisk singled, and Lynn singled for their fourth run.

They got us out in the top of the ninth, so the score was still 5–4 ours when Boston batted in the bottom of the inning. Goose walked Burleson with one out. Remy then hit a line drive to Piniella in right. Lou lost it in the sun, which was beating right in his eyes, but he pretended he was going to catch it, pounding his glove, so Burleson had to hold up and could only go to second when the ball bounced in front of him. That won the game for us, 'cause Rice flied out, and had Burleson been on third, he would have tagged and scored and tied up the game. With Burleson on second, though, it was just a harmless fly ball.

Now there were two outs in the bottom of the ninth. The Red Sox were down to their last batter: Carl Yastrzemski. I had seen the way the game was going, and I was heating up pretty good in the bullpen 'cause I thought to myself, "Goddamn, the way this is going, I'm going to face Yaz if he comes up in the ninth." Even Tidrow had said, "They're gonna be using you. Stay ready." I guess he figured Yaz is left-handed and they'd bring me in to face the lefty.

If I could have gone in there and gotten him out and saved the game, that one out would have let me be part of something. Just one fucking out, which is all it would have been. I've always been able to get Yaz out, and if ever there was a time to bring me in, this was it.

I stood out in the bullpen waiting for Lemon to come out of the dugout and get Goose. Lemon, however, never left the bench. He left Goose in to pitch to Yaz. I said, "Screw it," and I stopped warming up.

I suppose I should have been annoyed, pissed off, angry, but I wasn't any of those things. You gotta look at it from Lem's way too. When you have a reliever like Goose—just like I was last year—you gotta go with the guy all the way. You can't be making too many moves.

Yaz stepped in, Goose fired the ball in there, and Yaz sent a high pop behind third. When Graig settled under the ball and caught it and the game was over, suddenly I felt a tremendous surge of happiness come over me. Even though I had hardly contributed at all, for the first time since the spring I really felt part of this team. I was proud of what we did, and all the records the team set. I was happy for Guidry, who won his twenty-fifth, and I felt happy for Goose, who got his twenty-seventh save. I was thinking about how we came from 14 games back in July, and how no other team in the entire history of baseball had ever done that. The events were rushing through my mind. There were so many things that happened to this team this year, I'll probably remember this season more than any other season of my baseball career.

We were celebrating in the clubhouse, and I was feeling excited and happy, when I started thinking about what Steinbrenner had said to me during midseason: "I want you to know that just as much as you were responsible for getting us into the play-offs last year, you're just as responsible for our having to struggle so much this year. If you had pitched halfway the way you can, we would have run away with it."

Well, I'll be out of here by Christmas, I guarantee you that, and next year I'll come back and I'll get even with him. I'm going to miss the guys. I have no bitch with them. No team could have as great a bunch of guys as this team. But when I come back to Yankee Stadium, and I'm sitting in the opposite dugout, I'm going to break that man's heart, just like he broke mine. And that's a promise.

Susan McCarthy is the wife of Bill James and one of the contributors to
*The Bill James Historical Baseball Abstract.*

# Uniforms in the 1920s

## ——— SUSAN McCARTHY ———

To LEAD off the twenties, a quote from an ad in the 1923 *Spalding Guide:* "All Spalding base ball uniforms are made by us in our own sanitary factories. They are so built and so maintained. Our employees receive the benefits that an abundance of light and air in the workrooms brings to them. When you put on your Spalding uniform, you have our assurance that it was made under clean and healthful conditions." Just thought you might like to see what kind of stuff was considered important back then.

The ad goes on to describe various styles of uniforms, from the "World Series" down to the "Amateur Special." Two styles of shirts are offered—one with a V-neck collar and the other with a "military" collar (what I've been referring to as a Nehru type). For length of sleeves, there was a choice between full, half, three-quarter, or detachable. The big selection on baseball pants is between elastic or tape bottoms. There was a choice of block or fancy lettering. Colors of suits offered were mostly neutrals (white, pearl gray, brown), but a variety of stripe colors were available for the asking. The cost of the top-of-the-line uniform consisting of cap, shirt, pants, belt, and stockings was $25 to the club, $30 for one suit.

Baseball caps featured in another ad range from the solid-color "Philadelphia Style" to the "Boston Style," which has a solid-color visor but a pinstriped crown. The type of cap now worn by the Pirates was advertised as the "Chicago Style." All styles were fully equipped and ready to wear with "ventilated crowns, no lining . . . stitched visor and perspiration proof sweat-band."

More movement on team name representation. In 1921 the Cleveland Americans chose to identify themselves not by city or symbol but with "World Champions" ablaze across their shirts. The fancy script-style Detroit *D,* still used today, first appeared about 1922. The two Cardinals seesawing on a bat was in place by the same time. (Incidentally, the original nickname for the St. Louis team had nothing to do with birds. It referred to the cardinal red trimming on the uniform first used in the nineteenth century. They were called the "Cardinals" as earlier St. Louis teams had been called "Browns" and "Maroons.") The Boston Nationals had two designs to illustrate their name; one is a circular symbol on the left breast pocket that looks like an emblem of an Indian.

James Michener, Pulitzer-prizewinning author and incurable Phillies fan, was Bangkok-bound in an airliner late one night in October of 1980, when the pilot came on the intercom to announce the Phils had just won their first-ever world championship. Michener's reaction? He seized his pen, and—

# Lines Composed in Exaltation over the North Atlantic

## JAMES MICHENER

Crash the cymbals, blare the trumpets,
Wreathe their noble brows with laurel.
Heap the festive board with crumpets
And with decorations floral.
They deserve the fairest lilies—
Who? The Phillies.

Through the long dark years they stumbled
Scarred with deep humiliations
But our cheering never crumbled
And we kept our expectations.
Yes, we loved them for their sillies—
Who? The Phillies.

Triple plays that did not triple,
Strikeouts with the bases loaded.
Pitchers serving up the cripple,
All our hopes again exploded.
Are they not a bunch of dillies?
Who? The Phillies.

Far behind in early innings,
Doomed to tragedy eternal,
They turn losses into winnings
Through some holy fire internal.
They give enemies the willies—
Who? The Phillies.

Bang the drum and toot the oboes,
Dance until the earth has shaken.
Cheer, for our beloved hoboes
Have at last brought home the bacon.

Garland them with timeless lilies!
Although they are a bunch of dillies
Who give honest men the willies.
We still love them for their sillies—
Hail, The Phillies.

When Jim Murray, the syndicated columnist of *The Los Angeles Times,*
writes about this shortstop, it is a case of the best describing the best.

# Ozzie Smith

## JIM MURRAY

IT'S POSSIBLE no one ever went after a baseball the way
Osborne Earl Smith does, just as it's possible no one
ever went after a high C the way a Caruso did or a Bruch
concerto the way Heifetz did.

With Ozzie Smith, shortstop isn't a position, it's an
art. A yellow-brick road. You watch Ozzie for a while
and you figure he came in with a flying dog. You want
to ask him where the Tin Man went.

God made Ozzie Smith a shortstop the way he made
Tracy an actor or Kelly a dancer. I mean to say, if you
had a license to construct a shortstop, when you got
through putting all the pieces together, it would come
out like Ozzie Smith. The grace, the speed, the leaps,
the rhythmical sweeping motions—Baryshnikov in
cleats. Tchaikovsky would have set music to him. You
get the feeling he's going to turn into a swan any
minute.

He propels his body through the air like a rubber
band. He used to back-flip his way out to his position.
You get the feeling, with Ozzie they shouldn't just let
him field ground balls like every other human being,
they should make him catch them upside-down while
standing on his head and playing Stars and Stripes
Forever on a flute. You feel he could field a ground ball
while juggling three oranges and get the guy out without
dropping a one. Asking Ozzie to make a routine out is
like asking Horowitz to play Chopsticks. Or Hillary to
climb Bunker Hill.

One of the mysteries of baseball is how come he
hasn't won an MVP? On the other hand, it's not such an
enigma. It's been 25 years since a shortstop has won an
MVP in the National League.

There are 153 players in the Hall of Fame. Of those
voted in, only five are shortstops.

Shortstop may be the most overlooked position in the
whole fabric of baseball—with the possible exception of
groundskeeper. Last year, Ozzie Smith led all National
League shortstops in fielding and in chances accepted for

the fifth time in his career and the fourth out of the last
six seasons. And he finished 18th in the MVP balloting
(one guy picked him as the eighth most valuable player
and another, the ninth).

"Baseball is offense-oriented," says Ozzie Smith.
"If you don't do it with the stick, you don't do it."

That may be. But there probably isn't a pitcher in the
game who would vote for Babe Ruth over Ozzie Smith
as MVP. Pitchers, you see, don't like home runs no
matter who hits them. Pitchers like guys who catch or
stop three-base hits, not guys who hit them. "When I
throw a ground ball," the great Warren Spahn used to
say sternly, "I expect it to be an out—maybe two."
Tommy John, who never threw anything but ground
balls, once jumped one club for another because it had a
better third baseman. Geography wasn't as important to
Tommy as geometry.

Still, Ozzie Smith is troubled. Once, years ago, a
scribe complained to the coach, Bob Zuppke, that all the
footballer, Red Grange, could do was run. "Yeah,"
Zuppke is supposed to have retorted, "and all Galli-
Curci could do was sing."

Shortstops are like Grange and Galli-Curci. What they
do is supposed to be enough. For years, the only player
in the Hall of Fame with a batting average under .300
was a shortstop—Rabbit Maranville (.268). The St.
Louis Cardinals cheerfully pay Ozzie Smith millions to
win championships with his glove. Since he joined the
club they have won two pennants and one world championship.

Shortstop is an error position. The record is 95 in a
season. The man held to be the greatest shortstop who
ever played, Honus Wagner, made 676 in his career.
Ozzie Smith made 12 errors in 1984. He made only 14
the next year. And he almost annually leads the league in
chances accepted.

There is a theory that shortstops don't hit because the
position demands full concentration. A right fielder has

nothing else to think about but his next at-bat. With the shortstop the hitting is an afterthought.

Ozzie has decided to rearrange his priorities. He wants to be a .300 hitter and is programming himself to do just that.

There is a risk involved in muscling up to be a better hitter. Do you lift weights to get stronger at the plate but end up clumsier in the field?

Hall of Fame balloters have been hard to please, anyway. Even a player they nicknamed ''Mr. Shortstop'' they failed to vote into the Hall. Couldn't hit, they said of Marty Marion (.263). Then, they got a shortstop who could hit (Arky Vaughan, .385 one season, .318 lifetime) and they wouldn't vote *him* in either. Couldn't field, they said. (Probably not true but the evidence was devastating—.385. How could a guy who could do that have time for fielding?)

Jack Clark of the Cardinals hit the most famous home run of 1985. But it would have been less famous if Ozzie Smith hadn't hit a more astonishing one the game before. Ozzie hit the only home run he has ever hit batting left-handed off Tom Niedenfuer in the ninth inning of Game 5 of the playoffs to give the Cardinals a 3–2 edge in the series and set up Clark's homer.

Ozzie is still 701 homers behind Babe Ruth (and 742 behind Henry Aaron) but he did bat .276 last year, about 40 points above his previous average. And, this year, he is batting right around .300. He has become a super contact hitter—he only struck out 27 times last year.

There is danger in this. The wizard who tied a major league record for most seasons over 500 assists and who got his sixth consecutive gold glove for top-fielding shortstop may find he is turning off the Hall of Fame electorate. If he starts to hit .300, when the time comes to vote on him for the Hall of Fame, they may reject him. ''Couldn't field,'' they may explain. ''How can a guy who hits .300 be a good shortstop? Besides, didn't he win a pennant with a home run once? Call that a shortstop? Rabbit Maranville would be ashamed.''

How about *this* game? The account and box score appear in the Obojoski book *Bush League,* a history of the minors.

# 1923:
# Vernon 35,
# Salt Lake City 11

—— **ROBERT OBOJOSKI** ——

VERNON ROUTED Salt Lake City 35–11 in the latter city on May 11, 1923. In this wild and woolly game, many Pacific Coast League batting and scoring records were set and many may remain on the books for all time. The contest established records for the most runs scored in a game (46) and the most home runs in a game (11). The Vernon team set the following marks for a game: most runs scored (35), most total bases (67), most runs batted in (34), and most home runs (9). Vernon's right-fielder Pete Schneider set six league records in this game and tied another. The marks he established were: most times at bat for a nine-inning game (8), most runs scored (6), most home runs (5), most home runs with the bases filled (2), most total bases (22), most runs batted in (14). (The latter five records are standards for a game of any length.) He tied the record for the most home runs in an inning (2). According to the PCL's historian, William J. Weiss, Schneider in his last time at bat almost clubbed a sixth homer, but the ball missed clearing the fence by a matter of inches and he had to settle for a double.

**BOX SCORE**

| Vernon | AB | H | PO | A | E |
|---|---|---|---|---|---|
| Smith, 3b | 5 | 3 | 3 | 2 | 1 |
| Chadbourne, cf | 4 | 3 | 1 | 0 | 0 |
| O'Brien, cf | 2 | 0 | 0 | 0 | 0 |
| Locker, 1b | 7 | 5 | 10 | 0 | 0 |
| Bodie, lf | 6 | 4 | 1 | 0 | 1 |
| High, lf | 1 | 1 | 2 | 0 | 0 |
| Schneider, rf | 8 | 6 | 4 | 0 | 0 |
| Rader, ss | 5 | 0 | 0 | 5 | 0 |
| Warner, ss | 2 | 1 | 0 | 0 | 0 |
| Sawyer, 2b | 6 | 2 | 3 | 4 | 0 |
| D. Murphy, c | 7 | 4 | 3 | 0 | 1 |
| Dell, p | 7 | 4 | 0 | 0 | 0 |
| Totals | 60 | 33 | 27 | 11 | 3 |

**BOX SCORE**

| Salt Lake City | AB | H | PO | A | E |
|---|---|---|---|---|---|
| Sheean, 2b–p | 6 | 3 | 2 | 2 | 0 |
| Vitt, 3b | 2 | 0 | 0 | 2 | 0 |
| Kerns, 3b | 3 | 0 | 0 | 3 | 0 |
| Frederick, rf | 3 | 2 | 1 | 0 | 0 |
| Strand, cf | 5 | 2 | 6 | 0 | 0 |
| Wilhoit, lf | 4 | 1 | 3 | 0 | 0 |
| Leslie, 1b | 5 | 2 | 11 | 1 | 0 |
| Pearce, ss | 4 | 0 | 1 | 3 | 1 |
| Peters, c | 1 | 1 | 1 | 1 | 0 |
| Anfinson, c–2b | 4 | 3 | 2 | 2 | 0 |
| Coumbe, p | 1 | 0 | 0 | 0 | 0 |
| Kinney, p | 1 | 1 | 0 | 0 | 0 |
| Jenkins, c | 2 | 0 | 0 | 1 | 1 |
| Totals | 41 | 15 | 27 | 15 | 2 |

O'Brien batted for Chadbourne in seventh.
High hit home run for Bodie in seventh.
Warner grounded out for Rader in seventh.

| Vernon | 4 | 3 | 8 | 5 | 0 | 4 | 11 | 0 | 0—35 |
|---|---|---|---|---|---|---|---|---|---|
| Salt Lake City | 0 | 2 | 2 | 0 | 0 | 1 | 0 | 6 | 0—11 |

**PITCHING SUMMARY**

| | IP | AB | R | ER | H | BB | HB | SO | WP |
|---|---|---|---|---|---|---|---|---|---|
| Dell (Winner) | 9 | 41 | 11 | 9 | 15 | 5 | 0 | 2 | 0 |
| Coumbe (Loser) | 2+ | 14 | 12 | 12 | 10 | 1 | 1 | 0 | 0 |
| Kinney | 3⅔ | 23 | 12 | 11 | 11 | 2 | 0 | 1 | 0 |
| Sheehan | 3⅓ | 23 | 11 | 10 | 10 | 3 | 0 | 0 | 0 |

Two-base hits—Dell, Smith, Schneider, Sawyer, Warner, Frederick, Sheehan. Three-base hit—Chadbourne. Home runs—Schneider (5), Murphy, Bodie, Locker, High, Leslie, Strand. Sacrifice hit—Chadbourne. Stolen bases—Leslie (2). Runs batted in—Schneider (14), Locker (6), Bodie (6), Murphy (5), Smith, Chadbourne, High, Sheehan (2), Strand (3), Frederick (2), Wilhoit, Leslie, Peters. Hit by pitcher—Smith by Coumbe. Double play—Vitt to Peters to Leslie. Left on bases—Vernon (8), Salt Lake City (4). Umpires—Ward and Byron. Time—2:11. (Note that the game took only 2 hours and 11 minutes to play despite all the scoring.)

Earlier in these pages we have Joe Durso's account of the home run by Henry Aaron that eclipsed Babe Ruth's lifetime total.

From the fascinating book *A Zen Way of Baseball* comes now the account of the home run that eclipsed Henry Aaron's lifetime total—told by the man who did it.

# 1977: 756

## SADAHARU OH *and* DAVID FALKNER

WHEN NAGASHIMA-SAN took over as manager in 1975, there was big fever over my pursuit of the home-run record. When would I reach 650, 700? When would I finally catch Babe Ruth and overtake Hank Aaron? There was also very big fever over the fate of the Giants. For the first time in ten years we had failed to win the pennant in 1974, finishing a close second to the Chunichi Dragons. Because the Giants had been together successfully for so long, not many people realized that a time of rebuilding was at hand. I think our players may not have realized it either. We did terribly in 1975, worse than anyone expected. We finished last, an almost inconceivable turn of events, given who we were and given the expectations of Nagashima-san's leadership. There was such incredulity over this turn of fortune that even some political and economic writers began wondering aloud whether the fate of the Giants wasn't in some way a foreshadowing of national events. On the final day of the season, Nagashima-san led us from the dugout to stand before our fans and offer them a formal bow of responsibility.

For me, personally, the season was also difficult. I lost a consecutive game streak that year. Over several seasons, well into 1975, I had played in 648 straight games. I had pulled a muscle in my thigh during spring training, and it had never fully healed. Nagashima-san therefore often rested me for parts of games, allowing my streak to continue but conserving my strength at the same time. One day I did not start in a game against the Hanshin Tigers at Osaka. The game progressed and still I did not get in. The game went into extra innings, and at one point Nagashima-san turned to me and said, "Prepare to go in next inning." But there was no next inning. The Tigers won the game then and there with a "sayonara" home run, and my streak was broken. There

was gossip afterward that Nagashima-san did this deliberately, but I never took it that way. A manager's job is always to use his players with regard for the team first and individual records second. It would be perversion for it to be otherwise.

But that might well have been a foreshadowing of the season I was to have. For the first time in fourteen years I failed to win the home-run title. It was a very sad time. A boxer is defeated in a single night, but this was a defeat that lasted many months. It was with me every day when I went to the ball park, and there was nothing I could do about it. Koichi Tabuchi of the Tigers won the crown that year with forty-three homers. I finished tied for third with thirty-three.

I certainly did not believe that I was finished as a player, or even that I was really declining. For the first time since I had begun alternating in third and fourth spots in the batting order, there was no "O-N Cannon." I may have been easier to pitch to than in the past. Also, our team was not nearly as intimidating. Davey Johnson, who joined the Giants that year, perhaps suffered more than anyone, because he was expected to fill the void left by Nagashima-san in the lineup. He did not. Many fans rode him with a chant that was a play on his name. ("J-son! J-son!" they called. *Son* in Japanese means loss.) I was reminded all too well of my own early difficulties, but that changed nothing. The year 1975 was just not a good one for the Giants or for me. When it ended, however, I was thirty-three home runs closer to Babe Ruth. I had also closed the distance between myself and Hank Aaron. I trailed him now by seventy-eight home runs. I had an outside chance of catching Ruth the following season, and sometime after that going beyond Aaron.

I worked as hard that winter as I ever had. I was not

as concerned about Ruth and Aaron as I was about myself. I had one goal for myself from the moment I lost the home-run title—and that was to get it back. I checked what I did against every memorandum I had ever made on batting. I made sure that my condition the following spring would be excellent. When camp came, my motto was that I would be in better shape than even the hungriest rookie. For the Giants and myself, 1976 would be different.

The Giants, to be sure, did not stand still over the winter. In one of the biggest trades in years, we acquired a top hitter from the Pacific League, Isao Harimoto. Mr. Harimoto, like me, was a left-handed batter. He was more of a line-drive hitter than I was, but he could hit home runs, too. The Giants' hope, soon to be borne out, was that the "O-N Cannon" would now be replaced by an "H-O Cannon."

We won the pennant in 1976, edging out the Tigers by just two games. Even though we lost the Japan Series, which followed, we clearly exhibited good fighting spirit. We lost the first three games of the series to a strong Hankyu Braves team. But then we won two games at Nishinomiya and returned to Tokyo. We took a ten-inning victory in the sixth game, tying the series, but then lost the seventh and final game at home, 4–2.

Isao Harimoto finished second in hitting in the Central League. He hit twenty-two home runs, batting ahead of me, driving in ninety-three runs. He was a strong and helpful teammate. He was also a person with more character than people gave him credit for. He came to the Giants with something of a bad-boy reputation. He was not the most admired of players, though clearly the fact that he held the all-time season record for hitting (.383) gained him respect. It turned out, though, that he and I had a good deal in common.

Like myself, Mr. Harimoto, though born in Japan, held a foreign passport. He had never tried to change his Korean identity. He was the same age as I was, entering professional baseball in 1959, the same year I joined the Giants. He lost a sister in childhood, too. He lived in Hiroshima, and his sister was killed in the atom bombing of 1945. He and his mother happened to be walking on a hill just outside the city when the surprise attack occurred, and she shielded him against herself in the shade of a tree. His brother was a survivor, too, and became something of a surrogate parent, working to allow Mr. Harimoto to pursue a career in professional baseball.

But he impressed me most by who he was and not just by what he had been. When he joined the Giants, his position was particularly difficult, because, like Davey Johnson, he had a specific role to fulfill. Unlike Davey Johnson, he was a star within the Japanese baseball system to begin with. Thus he had the dual problem of accepting both more responsibility and somewhat less status. He told me very early on that he had always regarded me as a rival even though we had played in different leagues. As I had set a standard for myself with Nagashima-san, so he had set one with me. But, he said, he had long since given up trying to chase me. Doubling his own effort was the only reasonable way he had of striving as a professional. He wound up asking me to take him to Arakawa-san's to be taught—which I did. It turned out he had a most humble attitude toward this work, the attitude of a beginner though he was a real star. He was a seven-time batting champion, a master at using all ninety degrees of a baseball field (where I could use only forty-five), but he was genuinely humble, and he became my friend. We could equally share the middle of the Giants' batting order and a good round of sake.

The year 1976 marked my return to form, too. I hit forty-nine home runs, drove in 127 runs, and hit .325, and I won two of the three batting titles. But now, no matter what I did, there was this pursuit not only of Japanese records but of world marks as well. With each passing week of the season, particularly as my home-run production ran far ahead of the previous year's pace, the likelihood grew that this would be the year I reached the 700 mark. There was even the chance, growing stronger through the summer, that I would surpass Babe Ruth.

On July 2 I hit my thirtieth home run of the season. The following day, I hit two more, leaving me one shy of 700 career home runs. Till then I had not felt the pressure of having to produce a "special" home run—for myself or for anyone else. All of a sudden, 700 seemed like a real barrier. I found myself trying, and in trying, trying to stop myself from trying. It was an exasperating and peculiar sensation. Of course I knew I would soon get 700, but one week stretched into three before it finally happened. On July 23, in a game against the Taiyo Whales in Kawasaki, in the same park where I took my first swings as a flamingo hitter, I became the only player in Japanese baseball to reach 700 home runs.

By coincidence, Arakawa-san, who had taken a job as a television commentator, was there covering the game that night. I also think Fortune permits you to play-act a little. In line with his official duties, he formally interviewed me after I hit the home run. We met on the field and very seriously shook hands before the cameras.

"Congratulations, Mr. Oh," Arakawa-san said, most soberly standing straight, with one hand behind his back.

"Thank you very much, Arakawa-san."

"Tell me, Mr. Oh, what kind of pitch did you hit?"

"Well, Arakawa-san, I believe it was . . ."

And so on and so on. Afterward, when the crowds were gone, the last interviews and autographs given, we headed off for a little out-of-the-way restaurant where we had *sushi* and sake. I don't know how long we stayed or how much we drank, but our years together made this private celebration the very best imaginable. I did not have a good game the day following.

Because it had taken longer than expected to reach 700, I was not certain that I would surpass Ruth's record that year. I wanted to. I wanted to get past it and reach Aaron's mark as quickly as possible so that I could get back to playing my own game. I believe that records can help a player set standards for his own individual efforts. But they are individual. When they become a planned part of the season, when managers, for example, are pressured to go out of their way to help them along, then the spirit of professional baseball is violated. A record is between a player and himself and cannot be pursued at the expense of his team.

I found myself too caught up in the records ahead. The pressure this brought upon me and my team—not to mention my family—was most unwelcome. And I did not handle it as well as I might have. Yet I could not blame the fans. Their excitement was natural, and their hopes for my success even became a help when I found that my own efforts, so affected by tension, needed something extra.

I did not do especially well after 700. I hit two more home runs in July and then only three in August and none in the first half of September. Fortunately, we were locked in a close pennant race, thus making it easier for me to concentrate. As we fought off the Tigers down the stretch, I began hitting home runs again. From the fourteenth of the month to the end of September, I hit six home runs in twelve games. With season's end sixteen days away, I stood three homers away from passing Babe Ruth.

On October 10, in our 125th game of the year, I hit home runs 713 and 714. I was one away with five games to play. As we were playing at home and as our opponents were the Hanshin Tigers, the expectation became tremendous. We had a full house the following day, and each time I came to the plate I could feel the excitement and the urging of the fans with me. We took an early lead in the game and held it going into the last of the eighth, 4–1. I came up with two men on base, two out, and worked the count full. I connected solidly on the next pitch. The ball rose on a trajectory toward right field. Straight down the line, however. While I knew instantly that I had enough distance on the ball, I didn't know for sure that the ball would stay fair. I watched it for a second or two. It seemed more like a full minute. The ball seemed to be moving in slow motion as it passed just to the inside of the foul pole.

What I did then—what I had never done as a professional before and have never done after—was to joyously leap into the air with both arms extended wide over my head. There was no planning this. It happened almost in spite of myself, as though, perhaps, my "other" had taken over. Oh, yes, how happy I was! I was surely happy for the record. And yet, in thinking about it, I was also happy that the ball was fair and that this home run decisively turned a crucial game in our favor. All of it. But I was surprised at myself nonetheless. Reporters had many times asked me why I didn't show more emotion when I hit home runs, and I always answered as frankly as I could that there was never any point in further punishing an opponent. Photographers, who, after all, had a job to do, always wanted something more than a poker-faced trot about the bases, so I had worked out with them that I would make a happy gesture of some sort, briefly lifting my arms out, for example, so they could get better pictures. This time, my own feelings simply had their way.

The person most affected by this home run—really, I think, by my reaction to it—was my brother. He was, as were other members of my family and the Arakawa-sans, very pleased for me. But, in private, my brother was also very much moved by this reaction of mine. For him it was not a small gesture of triumph but something very different.

"Sada," he told me, "I've been waiting twenty years to say this to you. You remember in high school when I chastised you for being so open about your feelings in the Kanto tournament?"

As if I were likely to forget!

"Well, I've thought about this a great deal, and I must tell you that I was very wrong when I did that."

I, too, was moved when I saw how deeply this affected him and how long he had obviously been living with it.

"I apologize for having done that, Sada! I am deeply sorry. Please, forgive me!"

There was nothing to forgive him for. My brother in recent years had gone from being a kind of elder statesman, with whom only limited confidences could be shared, to being a friend with whom I could share everything. While I surely understood the source of his guilt in this, I wanted to assure him that there really was no need to apologize. If I had had a life not of my own choosing and had so limited my own natural expression, it would have been one thing. But I had spent my life doing what I loved. I certainly envied those who could freely and openly express happy feelings, but I did not really lose because I could not. I gained a peculiar form of self-confidence in the way I limited myself, and I also gained in effectively dealing with opponents. Things are never one-sided, and what is lost in one place is found in another.

Babe Ruth's record, it turned out, was no longer the record by the time I passed it. Ahead was Hank Aaron's.

And the end of the 1976 season marked yet an additional milestone along the way. Hank Aaron retired. For the first time, his home-run record was now fixed at a certain number—755. It was immediately apparent to baseball fans, and many, many others in my country, that sometime in the very near future—the following season or, at the very latest, the season after that—I would pass that mark.

I happened to meet Hank that winter in Hawaii. We talked for a while in a hotel room. I was sorry he had retired, because knowing what he did in America kept me sharper in Japan. We talked a lot about hitting styles. It was odd, though. Hank told me that my swing was artistic and beautiful to watch. I, who certainly had been impressed by his batting form for many years, was struck by the look of gentleness and clarity in his eyes. "I'd like to be there when you break my record," he told me. "I remember Stan Musial greeting me at first base when I got my three hundredth hit."

I finished the 1976 season with 716 career home runs. I needed forty home runs to reach a new record. It was far enough away in needed playing time to afford me an interval of ordinary days before the pressure would again build. But in measuring this, perhaps I was also engaging in some wishful thinking. There was to be no letup now in the fever that swept the country. Every day there were requests for interviews and pictures. What was I doing to prepare for 756? Was I in the best condition? Did I have a target date in my own mind for the world record? Even the press beyond Japan began to take an interest now. With Hank Aaron's retirement and my being in such an obvious position to pass his mark, American journalists reported on my doings. The press in Asia, having regularly reported on Japanese baseball, seemed as eager to pursue the story as media people in Japan.

With the coming of the 1977 season, this "Oh fever" actually became a kind of industry. Everywhere, I am told, baseballs with reproductions of my signature were sold as fast as they could reach the stores; companies began producing medals, towels, T-shirts in advance of the commemorative moment; another company manufactured a plate with my portrait as its principal design; restaurants announced incredible bargains on steak dinners to be offered the day following 756 (the cost of a steak dinner is well beyond the reach of most people in Japan); the media even turned up a story about a Mah-Jongg parlor in Yaesu that happened to have the name Oh and that, as a consequence, announced a 40 percent reduction in prices for the day following the big home run. Whether I wished it to be otherwise or not, there was to be no letup in the pressure surrounding me.

In many ways I was lucky to have had the experience of pursuing an earlier "big" record. It was a kind of rehearsal. I learned from it. I had not handled the pressure as well as I might have. I had also found myself resenting the increased public attention. In a way, that was exactly the problem. All the "atmospherics" surrounding my pursuit of the home-run record had interfered with the way I played the game.

As I had on so many other occasions, I returned to Arakawa-san. In June, while the record was still distant, I worked with him every day for a week. We worked from eleven at night until around two in the morning, just as we had in the past. I approached our training sessions as I always had—bowing to my teacher and formally requesting his instruction. We performed the exercises that by now were familiar but that could not be successfully done unless there was absolute concentration.

I approached the problem of excessive public attention in the only way I knew—by disciplined work as a batsman. The way of the flamingo hitter was something I had grown to love. It had yielded its rewards only with persistent effort. Its promise to me had been a kind of proof that effort does effect change. And the change I was looking for was the one I had always been pursuing—oneness with my skill.

What I found in this "interval" between records was something that I was not quite looking for but that was the very thing I needed most. I came to have a changed attitude toward all the attention I was receiving.

I had become quite conscious that the demands placed upon me by the public—for time, autographs, appearances, interviews, and the like—were interfering not only with my play but my life as well. Because crowds had regularly begun to gather outside my house, for example, it was no longer possible for my daughters to go out and play as ordinary children would. My wife could not go to the market, nor could we, if we wanted, go off to a restaurant or have an evening to ourselves. We had to send out for many of our meals, and our children had to accustom themselves to indoor activities, as though imprisoned in their own house.

During my career I had always made it a point to be accessible to fans. This was never something I did reluctantly. I normally enjoyed the relationship I had with them. I have several fan clubs, for instance, and by participating in their events over the years, I have come to meet many interesting people I might otherwise never have known. Mr. Shimei Cho is the best speaker of Japanese among my many Chinese friends. He organized a club after my fifty-five home-run season consisting of Chinese and Japanese members. They hold various events, as does another club organized in Toyama Prefecture by friends of my mother. I attend the annual parties the clubs hold, and they in turn have been very protective and caring toward me. Members send me gifts and cards, which I always respond to in my own hand,

and they perform helpful services for which I have been deeply grateful. One member of a fan club regularly visits my twin sister's grave and offers prayers and flowers for me during the regular season when I am not able to attend to this myself.

By midsummer in 1977 two things had become clear. One was that the Giants were not nearly as hard pressed in the pennant race as in the season before. We were well on the way to taking the Central League championship, so the pressure to keep pace, though keen, was not really so draining. The other factor was that I had maintained a steady enough home-run pace to bring Aaron's record within reach by the end of the season. I had twenty-six homers by August 1 and needed fourteen for the record.

On August 4 I got my twenty-seventh home run. I homered again on the sixth, twice more on the ninth, then once again on the tenth, eleventh, and twelfth. With rain-outs and breaks in the schedule, we managed to play only three games between the thirteenth and twenty-third. I hit my thirty-fourth home run of the season on the twenty-third, another the following day, two more the day after that. On August 31 I hit career home run number 755. I was one away from the record.

All the while the uproar around my life grew daily. Each day crowds of people gathered at my house, awaiting my comings and goings. The crowds became so regular that police were assigned to the area to keep order. I had no private life of any kind now. From the moment I got up to the moment I went to bed I was accompanied every step of the way by people who awaited this record with me. When I left my house in the morning, I hoped it would give my family some quiet time. It never did. People simply remained or were joined by others awaiting my return. In traffic, cars, camera crews, motorcycles accompanied me, and at stop signals people waved to me and called out greetings. There were times when I could not move from one place to another without benefit of a police escort. Any time I was on a street anywhere, I was sure, in a matter of seconds, to be engulfed by people.

And yet I did not feel as I had earlier. The people who waited for me at my house—children, families—all wished me well and wanted my home run to come soon. When I came down the steps toward my carport, children would hand me bouquets of flowers, some of them quite carefully and beautifully arranged. They had gifts and mementoes, prayers and little capsule messages of good fortune from local shrines. There is a room in my parents' house where all these keepsakes have been preserved. There was a statue of a dragon, my special protection, rising from a baseball; the Overseas Chinese Club presented me with a figure of Hotei, one of the Seven Gods from Chinese mythology, the one who gives

long life and luck; a well-known sculptor did a carving of a fish leaping from the water, this the representation of that in all of us which reaches higher amid the limitations of this world. There were drawings, woodblock prints, dolls, brushwork decorations of every kind. In all of this, instead of resisting a loss of privacy, I took into myself the added strength of these good wishes. I became conscious of how much I was supported in my own efforts.

I had always made it a point to sign autographs. I was never troubled by this, because the time it took cost me so very little. But I had a problem at this time, because the crowds around my house had grown enormously. Over the years I had learned how to sign many autographs in a short while. I could carry on a conversation and sign a baseball or board at the same time. Because it got to the point where I was often faced with many people simultaneously asking for my autograph, I made a study of just how many I could give within a certain period of time. In the past I had not always been able to sign for everyone. It bothered me when this happened, and I did not want it to happen in this special situation at my house.

The best way I could deal with this was to add on an extra fifteen or twenty minutes before I had to leave. I calculated exactly. The greatest number of autographs I could sign in a minute was ten. Before I left the house, I counted the crowd. If there were 150 to 200, I knew that I could sign for everyone within fifteen or twenty minutes. If there were more than 200, then I would sign for no one that day. The point was to sign for all or none. When I got outside, sometimes I would borrow a bullhorn from a policeman and request that people form a line so I could more easily handle their requests for autographs.

There were days when it was impossible to accommodate people. But there were many other days when I could. I was pleased to do this, and in the end I believe it even helped on my way to 756.

On September 1 we finished a series at home against the Taiyo Whales. The next day we began a three-game set against the Yakult Swallows. I was not able to hit the record home run in the final game against the Whales nor in the first game of the following series. If the home run did not come in the next two days, the chances were it would occur on the road, where we would be playing till the middle of the month.

It was strange waiting for this moment. Really, it was as inevitable as something could be, given the finite and unpredictable character of events. Yet it was like living in the midst of a storm. The storm, of course, would pass. But for me the task was to try to find its center so that I could concentrate on what I had to do. One to go. It was almost as though the only place left in the world where I had room to move my arms freely was the playing field during game time. Reporters, photographers, cameramen were with me now even as I took practice, sometimes getting in the way as I tried to run or throw. I realized how fatigued I had become over these many months. Except for sleeping, I could not remember the last time I had really been alone.

The evening of September 3 was filled with the same expectation as the previous evening. Traffic was brought to a halt as I made my way from my home to the ball park. Swarms of people surrounded me right up to game time. I remember sitting on a metal chair in front of my locker after the press had finally cleared the clubhouse. My teammates were milling around, shortly to take the field. I felt drained of all energy, as though I had not slept for days. Suddenly a door opened. I thought for a moment I was imagining things. It was my mother. No one was allowed in the clubhouse at this point, and she was entering an area that was normally closed to the press. I will forever remember the look on her face, sweet and beckoning. She was dressed very plainly, as though the occasion was an ordinary visit with her son. I rose to greet her. Her eyes spoke so much to me— certainty that I would make it that very night and also that it was even more important that I take care of myself.

My mother is a very small woman. As I leaned over to catch her words, I remember wondering, absurdly, when it was that I first became conscious that my mother only reached the middle of my chest.

She reached out and handed me two parcels, one rather large, the other small.

"I brought some apples for you and your teammates," she said. "Please distribute them. The smaller package is for your daughters."

I began to thank her, but she went right on.

"I brought some *suzumushi* for them. Such crickets are hard to find in the cities these days, aren't they? Take good care of them, and take good care of yourself." She then turned and left, heading back for the grandstand.

I brought the packages back to my locker. What a strange gift at such a time! I held the small package to my ear to see if I could hear the crickets inside. Yes! They were quite alive. Their wings whirred and whirred. I became so caught up in listening to them that the noise of the locker room and the heavy sea tide of the crowd in the stadium completely disappeared. There was only the music of these summertime crickets and the immense silence that their voices invoked.

When I left my locker and headed for the field, I had no feeling of tiredness. I could feel in my bones that this indeed was the night. I came upon the lights and noise of Korakuen almost as if they didn't exist. The quietness my mother had brought me surrounded me like a spell.

It was not going to be broken. I hit in the first inning and then in the third. The third inning. One out, no one on base. The pitcher's name, in this twenty-third game of the year against the Swallows, was Kojiro Suzuki. The goal, Arakawa-san had always said, was oneness of mind, body, and skill. You and the opponent together create the moment. The *ma* is the one you create but in which you are not at all separate from your opponent. The pitcher and I, the ball—and the silence my mother gave me—these were all one. In the midst of whatever was going on, there was only this emptiness in which I could do what I wanted to do. The count went full. Mr. Kojiro Suzuki threw a sinker on the outside part of the plate. I followed the ball perfectly. I could almost feel myself waiting for its precise break before I let myself come forward. When I made contact, I felt like I was scooping the ball upward and outward. The ball rose slowly and steadily in the night sky, lit by Korakuen's bright lights. I could follow it all the way, as it lazily reached its height and seemed to linger there in the haze, and then slowly began its descent into the right-field stands.

The crowd erupted, almost as a single voice. A huge banner was suddenly unfurled that read, "Congratulations, World Record!" Everywhere—but on the diamond—people were running and lights were flashing. For me, it was the moment of purest joy I had ever known as a baseball player.

No one can stop a home run. No one can understand what it really is unless you have felt it in your own hands and body. It is different from seeing it or trying to describe it. There is nothing I know quite like meeting a ball in exactly the right spot. As the ball makes its high, long arc beyond the playing field, the diamond and the stands suddenly belong to one man. In that brief, brief time, you are free of all demands and complications. There is no one behind you, no obstruction ahead, as you follow this clear path around all the bases. This is the batsman's center stage, the one time that he may allow himself to freely accept the limelight, to enjoy the sensation of every eye in the stadium fixed on him, waiting for the moment when his foot will touch home plate. In this moment he is free.

Obviously, 756 was special. How could it be otherwise? I know it was not a "world" record (there is no world competition). I don't believe I would have reached 756 if I had played in America. But it was my record and it was baseball's record nevertheless! It was the devotion of a professional's career.

When I reached home plate, all of the noise and excitement I had left behind were there in full force, happy and surging with energy. I don't know where in the midst of all the congratulations that followed it occurred, but someone said to me:

"Your parents, your parents, let your parents come to the field!"

My parents are very shy people, and I was not sure how they would feel in front of so many people. I was uncertain what to do. Also, I did not really want to monopolize things. My home run belonged to many people other than myself. My teammates and my opponents shared in this moment, though no lights found them. I needed no more for myself than my foot touching home plate. But, yes, I did want to share this moment with my parents. If I had planned it exactly, I could not have calculated the depth of thanksgiving and pride I suddenly felt now. By all means, I wanted to stand with them.

Just then a congratulatory message from Hank Aaron flashed on the electronic scoreboard, and, most eerily, his voice boomed out over a loudspeaker as the crowd became hushed. He must have been speaking by telephone hookup.

"Congratulations," his voice resounded. "I had hoped to see you break my record there in Japan, but I haven't been able to make it. . . . Continue slugging for your fans. And again, congratulations."

By now ceremonies were under way. Both teams were lined up in front of their dugouts; a microphone was placed in the center of the diamond. My parents were on the field. They looked so happy and so startled by all the commotion. My mother later told me, contrary to what I saw in her eyes, that she and my father had not really dressed for the occasion because they hadn't expected the home run that night. Just then, my parents impulsively walked over to the players on our team. They bowed to each of them and shook each one's hand, thanking them individually for helping me. It was hard to keep from crying. I was so moved and proud of my parents. I have always believed that success in this life owes to a strong will, and there were no people I knew who were stronger in this way than my mother, who was also tenderhearted, and my father, who had endured so many indignities and who so stubbornly persisted in his dreams anyway. The press made much of how generous I had been to others. In my circumstances, it was easy. My father extended himself when it wasn't so easy. He believed in repaying hatred with virtue not when he was surrounded by an admiring public but when the prejudice of officials and the hands of torturers cut his body and tried his soul. In over seventy years of life he has never once gone back on his deepest belief that the goal of any man's life is to be useful to others.

I was presented with a very large floral award, the official recognition of my achievement. Many cameras were whirring; this was the moment the whole nation had been waiting to celebrate. I could think of nothing more fitting to do then than to bring this award to my parents and offer it to them. I did this. I handed them the award, and I bowed deeply to them—and they to me.

I stood, finally, on the mound with all the lights of the stadium turned off save for a single spot on me. I took my cap off, bowed in four directions, and spoke a few words. I told people that my dream had finally come true, thanks to all those who had given me support. To receive such warm applause and feelings made me a happy man, and I promised to keep playing as long as my body would permit.

Later, I told the press that I was sorry for the pitcher, Suzuki, but that I was relieved to have finally answered the expectations of so many fans. Above all, what I wanted now was to get back to my own style of play. This, however, was still a wish.

There were official parties and functions to attend that night and no end of pursuit by the press. When I got home at two o'clock in the morning, there were over 600 people in front of my house! They greeted me happily and noisily—so much so that my most immediate thought was for the peace and quiet of my neighbors. I had no wish to ruin my fans' happiness either, so rather than have the police ask them to disperse, I signed autographs for them all and to each one said good night.

There was a party in full swing in my house. My parents, my wife, my three daughters, my brother and his family were all there, and so we toasted each other over and over again before we all called it a night.

There was one last matter to attend to. I placed a call to Arakawa-san. He was not with me in the house nor in the entourage that surrounded me before and after the game. I would have liked him to be there, of course, but it was not possible. We might have raised a cup of sake in the midst of all the bedlam, but that would not really have mattered. He knew and I knew—independent of this extraordinary tumult—what we had done together. This night was his, too, and its outcome had been fashioned a long time before.

"Arakawa-san?"

"Yes, it's me."

I said to him what I always said whenever I left one of our training sessions—when I bowed, acknowledging his mastery.

*"Domo arigato Gozaimasu."*

I thanked him with all my heart, because without him there would have been no record.

Daniel Okrent's book *Nine Innings* is about a game played at Milwaukee on June 10, 1982, between the two clubs that went down to the final day of that season to determine the winner of the American League East. The team that won June 10 was the Milwaukee team, which ultimately won the division and went on to win a memorable playoff with the Angels and to lose an equally memorable World Series with the Cardinals. But that is incidental. What you will read here is an account of just the top half of the seventh inning of that game of June 10. That's incidental too. The subtitle of the book called it "The Anatomy of Baseball as Seen Through the Playing of a Single Game." The critics called it "galvanizing" and "fascinating," "amazing" and "unique." One reviewer, in *The St. Louis Post-Dispatch,* called it "The best book about the best game there is."

# 1982:
# Milwaukee Brewers 9,
# Baltimore Orioles 7

## DANIEL OKRENT

TED SIMMONS, who, wrote Roger Angell in *The New Yorker,* "looks very much like an Ivy League football player from the eighteen-nineties," had spent the afternoon in the shade of the bullpen. He was a blocky, solid man with legs one could build a skyscraper on; he became a catcher, he said, "because I looked like one." In uniform, he looked squat and unathletic, especially when compared to his larger or sleeker teammates. In his traditional, Brooks Brothersy street clothes, the illusion no longer held; Simmons then revealed large, strong hands, broad shoulders, and muscular thighs that strained at his tailored chinos. He was clearly too fit to spend his days in a deskbound occupation.

Someday soon enough, Simmons knew, he would leave his bats, his spikes, and his catcher's mitt behind on some ball field and move behind a desk, probably in the financial community. He had served for several years on the board of the Mark Twain Banks of St. Louis, and had just spent an off-season as a bank management trainee. He was an informed and active collector of American furniture, and his interest in the subject, along with his prominence in St. Louis, where he played for the Cardinals for eleven seasons, got him a seat on the board of that city's art museum.

Simmons grew up in the Detroit suburb of Southfield, a community that didn't really exist until the J. L. Hudson Company, Detroit's largest department store firm, opened its Northland Mall in 1954. Northland was the first large-scale suburban shopping center in the nation, and as it prospered, so did Southfield.

By the middle 1960s, Southfield, a largely Jewish community, looked much like hundreds of other instant suburbs that had grown up around the nation's big cities. Large thoroughfares crisscrossed its breadth and length, separating subdivisions thrown up to meet the demands of a suburb-bound population. In the subdivisions, streets curved arbitrarily across a treeless plain, harboring ranch houses, mock colonials, and two-car garages. Near the center of Southfield, the town's high school grew rapidly, almost too fast, becoming an enormous educational factory that accommodated a student population that could easily have filled two or three high schools in a city that had grown more slowly, more organically.

Ted Simmons was perhaps the most prominent person the city and the school produced. He was a running back in football, not terribly fast but extraordinarily strong, and determined and talented enough for the University of Michigan to offer him a football scholarship, which he accepted. In baseball, though, Simmons' star shone even brighter, and the Cardinals drafted him in the first round in 1967. In addition to offering "more money than my family had ever seen," the Cardinals agreed to let him continue (at their expense) his college education while playing in the minors. Simmons signed with St. Louis and gave up his football scholarship. But he enrolled at Michigan that fall and embarked on an academic program. Summers he spent in the St. Louis farm system, and only in the first of three-plus minor league seasons did he hit less than .317.

September to April, Simmons was in Ann Arbor, until he reached the majors. In the late '60s, Ann Arbor was one of the four or five campuses in the country most influenced by the anti–Vietnam War movement and the general rebelliousness of the age. Simmons was no radical, but he was in many ways affected by the campus life that swirled around him; not playing intercollegiate athletics, by dint of his professional baseball contract, he was not isolated by the life of training tables, practice schedules, and athletic dorms that sequestered so many other athletes. He might carry his catcher's mitt around from class to class, but as he got older, as he got a sense of himself, and of the self he wished to create, he was determined not to be perceived as merely a jock.

The Cardinals called Simmons up to the majors to stay in 1970. "I was 20 years old, and they told me I was going to play every day," he remembered. "At the time, I had no basis for understanding how to be a big league catcher." Immediately, though, he made an impact. In 1971, his first full season, he batted .304 while playing in 133 games. He also made an impact with his appearance: this was before he had acquired the Pudge Heffelfinger haircut, parted in the middle, that struck Roger Angell so forcibly, and before he adopted his off-field uniform of pinstriped suits, or blue blazers and cuffed chinos. Simmons wore his hair long, on his shoulders, back when such a coiffure was meant to denote something about its wearer. And his outspokenness confirmed the impression his haircut made: he was against the Vietnam War, determinedly so, and he was in sympathy with his contemporaries on the campuses in more general ways having to do with the direction of American culture, and the generation gap, and that whole bundle of issues and poses that characterized the politics of the day.

At the same time that Ted Simmons emerged from his collegiate life, still brandishing the flag of youthful rebellion, he met a man, fourteen years older, named Robert Gibson. The boy from the suburbs stood in awe of Gibson, as all his St. Louis teammates did—indeed, as the entire National League did. He was a pitcher of uncommon talent, and the talent was made matchless by his preternatural ferocity.

"Gibson as a person was as impressive as Gibson the pitcher," Simmons said in 1981. "He was aggressive, intimidating, awesome. For me, being 20, it was difficult. He wouldn't stand for foolishness. Subtlety wasn't his strong suit. He was the same when he pitched—when he said 'no' to a pitch I called, he'd make it clear why he said 'no.' He taught me how to catch; he taught me how to be a professional baseball player. He also taught me that you can't separate physical talent from emotional talent in baseball."

Bob Gibson had grown up in Omaha, in a four-room wooden shack without heat or electricity. He was one of seven children, their mother a laundress; there was no father in the house. Before his family moved into public housing, Gibson was bitten on the ear by a rat. He struggled throughout his boyhood, in desperate poverty, but finally he, like Simmons, went to college. Indiana University, his first choice, declined to offer Gibson a scholarship; their letter read ". . . an athletic scholarship for Robert Gibson has been denied because we already have filled our quota of Negroes." So Gibson ended up at Omaha's Creighton University, a Jesuit institution, where he played basketball and baseball.

By the time Ted Simmons reached St. Louis and the Cardinals, Gibson's career was at its peak; in 1970, he won 23 games. Catching 133 games for the Cardinals meant Simmons caught for Gibson. "He was the most intimidating player in the league," Simmons recalled. "He'd stare in at the batter, and I could feel his eyes burn. Every pitch was a war for him, every hitter a threat. He never gave in and never gave up. He won by force of his personality, and by his concentration."

Simmons found it hard to explain the actual techniques of calling a game he learned from Gibson; despite his articulateness, and his general willingness to talk, he saw baseball as something that did not reveal itself, except to participants. "It's so subtle," he said, "and so beautiful. You've really got to be out there to understand it, or to appreciate how many different things are going on. Gibson sort of condensed his lifetime into a single pitch; how do you explain that to someone? When you're catching, and you see everything there in front of you, you don't just see batting averages and pitching statistics. You get to the best part of baseball—the mental application of physical skills. You see personalities, and what they think and how they think and how they react in certain situations. Take a guy like Fingers; he's done it all. There's no situation that should be new to him, after all these years, and each time he pitches he's thinking about it like he's never been in this situation before. He just calls on that competitiveness of his, and gets into that game, really into it. It's why he's great."

Off the field, it was hard to see Rollie Fingers as a

great competitor, or a great concentrator, or even a great pitcher. His most distinguishing characteristic was a well-waxed handlebar mustache, an appendage that surely denied Fingers any right to complain about autograph collectors' stopping him on the street or interrupting his dinner in a restaurant; through his long major league career, especially through his five appearances in postseason, prime-time action, millions of Americans had come to recognize Fingers as readily as any other major leaguer simply because of their repeated exposure to his singular upper lip. He was affable and approachable, but it was clear that he retained his affability by failing to make any effort to distinguish among all these new faces—reporters, fans, broadcasters, equipment representatives. He always seemed to be somewhere else, always removed, in some way, from his body, which was going through the motions of social convention and ritual while his mind was off in another place.

Fingers was a smart man, as smart as any on the team, but his was an intelligence called upon only when necessary. Reporters who met him for the first time were astonished by the blandness of his comments, the predictability of virtually everything he said. Fingers actually didn't give a damn, one way or another, about reporters. He was always cordial, always willing to stand still for yet another question, but he answered every question with almost a determined vacuity. He had been asked everything so many times, the answers were all lined up as if he had a Rolodex in his skull, the cards flipping automatically to the right place, providing the predictable response.

What struck one most about Fingers was, first, his apparent placidity—and then, on closer examination, the tension it disguised. He could be loosy-goosy, unconnected, apparently unconcerned. He used to say of Bob Rodgers, "All I want from a manager is that he shouldn't get me up when he isn't going to use me," and then he'd grin and go off to some clubhouse card game or ragging session. In the game of "flip"—a sort of tag with a ball that major leaguers engage in after they are in uniform and before the fans are admitted to the stands—Fingers would stand, open-faced and a little geeky, in the heart of things, amiably taking part. He was rarely serious, never earnest, endlessly jokey, even goofy.

But in other moments, the Fingers who could stand on the mound with the winning runs on base and the count 3 and 0, the icy Fingers who appeared a fearless gunfighter behind his mustache and beneath his narrow, squinted eyes—at other moments, this Fingers became visible. When he arrived in Sun City in '81 for his first Brewer spring training, he brought with him a steel device—it looked like something a dentist might roll out if his mere drill failed him—and daily twisted and pulled

parts of it to strengthen or make more flexible his shoulder, his arm, his wrist. (Fingers called the device "Jaws," and within a day or two of his unveiling of it, the rookies and extra pitchers were fiddling with it, thinking that in this simple isometric device was the clue to Fingers' accomplishment.) He'd stand in front of "Jaws," twisting a handle to relieve the tightness wrought by fifteen years of throwing sliders, and his face would set into hard lines of determination. In a quiet clubhouse, he'd often sit alone in front of his locker, anxiously gulping great quantities of milk, trying to calm a nervous stomach. Doctors who had treated him in San Diego and Oakland said he had a very low pain threshold, and that few pitches—especially the elbow-wrenching slider—were easy for him to throw. He struggled with his cigarette habit, fighting his addiction—and his fear of what the addiction represented, why he *needed* to smoke in the first place. He was a nervous man, and a serious one; he simply seemed not to want his teammates, or his opponents, to know the former, perhaps not wanting himself to know the latter.

To those who traveled with the Brewers, there were in 1982—after Fingers had been named not only the Cy Young Award winner for the American League in 1981 but also the Most Valuable Player (the first time a relief pitcher had ever won that prize in the league)—two incidents that revealed that Fingers' apparent placidity was either crumbling or had been affectation in the first place. The first occurred on May 29, when the Rodgers-led Brewers were struggling along near .500, making little headway. Fingers was brought into a close game against the Angels, and when he gave up a hit that broke Milwaukee's back in the midst of a California rally, he angrily tossed his glove in the air, 20 feet up, in midplay. As Angels raced around the bases, Fingers quickly regained his composure and ran to back up the catcher—bare-handed. No one could believe he had done it, not in the middle of the game; that night, at the bar at the Hyatt in Anaheim where the team was staying, two of the coaches who had been in the dugout when it happened swore that it *didn't* happen—that their drinking companions who had seen it must have been imagining things.

Later on the same road trip, something happened that was even more stunning to those who thought Fingers was the least excitable of ball players, a professional who simply went out and did his job, uncomplaining, never asking to renegotiate, content in his work. When the club reached Seattle, in the process of being consumed by the ill will that occupied the gap between Rodgers and his players, Fingers was warming up during a close game, and Rodgers bypassed him in the ninth inning when Bruce Bochte, a left-handed hitter, came to the plate for the Mariners. Bochte was a good hitter, but

Rodgers was aware that he had been having terrible difficulty with left-handed pitchers this year, and that he had but a .238 lifetime average against Mike Caldwell, who was between starts and thus available to Rodgers. Nevertheless, Bochte reached Caldwell for the hit that tied the game, which the Brewers eventually lost in the eleventh inning.

In a depressed and dispirited clubhouse afterward, Fingers exploded in unwonted rage. "That fucking idiot! This is one more nail in the coffin!" he screamed. "Doesn't he think I can get left-handers out? I get paid a lot of money to do that!" When Rodgers was fired less than forty-eight hours later, Fingers was—along with Simmons, and Caldwell, who had always detested Rodgers—among the most gratified Brewers. But he was also perceived, among the fans, as the villain in a drama that had daily been reported in the Milwaukee papers, a story of the war between a manager and his team. The drone of the call-in shows was punctuated by telephoners who felt that Fingers had cost Rodgers his job, and though Rodgers was no folk hero to the Milwaukee fans, he was perceived as being the victim of a spoiled, underachieving group of overpaid athletes.

On June 10, around 3:45 in the afternoon, Rollie Fingers took the mound for the seventh inning. It was rare for Fingers to be appearing in a game so early, and rarer still to hear a handful of boos. Harry Dalton, the man who had fired Rodgers, was upstairs in his box. Dalton had for a week been telling reporters that Fingers' outburst had had nothing to do with the firing, that he, Dalton, had been on the West Coast trip and had come to realize that the team was simply not in good shape. He had been especially upset by the team's behavior on the flight from Anaheim to Seattle.

Dalton put a high value on dignified comportment in public. The players were required to wear coats and ties while traveling, and Simmons, for one, had once been fined for wearing jeans with his blazer. Howell, Molitor, and Cooper, as well as Simmons and a few others, looked comfortable in their stylish clothing, but to most of the players, coat and tie were alien uniforms. Thomas and Money always wore the same brown leather jackets cut like suit coats, and Caldwell wore various ill-fitting costumes. Vuckovich was a sartorial catastrophe, his sharkskin-type suits, white-on-white shirts, and wraparound sunglasses making him look like a cross between a movie gangster and an overgrown teenager still trying to squeeze into his youthful church-and-wedding suit.

Dalton expected his manager to enforce the dress code, and to control his players' public behavior. The late-May trip to Seattle was made by commercial flight, and members of the team had indeed been behaving badly. Rodgers was either disinclined or unable to do anything about the rowdiness and profanity emanating from the rear cabin. When he rather gently admonished Mike Caldwell for swearing loudly, the pitcher said to his seatmates, "Fuck him. I hope we lose the next ten games so we can get rid of that fucker." Cecil Cooper, sitting nearby, said, "You don't mean that." Caldwell said he didn't, but the intensity of his feeling was clear.

But whether or not Fingers had had anything to do with Rodgers' dismissal, his presence in today's game was indicative of the role he played on Harvey Kuenn's team. Rodgers, too, used him whenever he could, but Kuenn was offering his team on Fingers' altar: if they might need him, they'd use him. Kuenn believed in using Fingers only (and always) when the Brewers were tied or barely ahead—the so-called save situation.

Earlier in the development of the use of relief pitchers, managers used their best bullpen arms to keep their teams in close games in which they were trailing—and a man like Pittsburgh's ElRoy Face, in 1959, could win 18 games in relief. Back then, the standard of measurement of a pitcher, relief or otherwise, was victories; the later recognition of the save as a meaningful statistic actually changed pitching strategies (credit for promulgating the save statistic goes to Chicago writer Jerome Holtzman). In the National League in 1958, there were .32 saves per game played (using the standards of measurement that were established later); twenty years later, there were .43 saves for every game played, an increase of more than 33 percent (in 1938, there were but .18 saves per NL game played, back in the days when managers generally put their least reliable pitchers in the bullpen). With the heralding of the new statistic came an award—the Rolaids Relief Award, licensed by Major League Baseball to an antacid manufacturer—and with the publicity afforded the statistic, and the award, accrued a new regard for the men who came in to shut the other team down. Foremost among these men was Rollie Fingers.

The fact that Fingers hadn't pitched since his one-inning tour against Oakland the previous Sunday was cause for some concern; like most relief pitchers, he thrived on regular work. But he still had a two-run cushion to work with, and today, Milwaukee bats were as alive as Baltimore's. Kuenn had earlier thought the game was Jim Slaton's to win or lose, and Slaton still stood to get credit for the victory if Fingers could pacify Baltimore. The act of bringing him on in the seventh, earlier than he normally would like, and knowing Slaton had the stamina (if not the stuff) to last longer, showed how much Kuenn felt it necessary to win this game and keep the Orioles from capturing four straight victories. "He's always ready for me," Kuenn said later. "You never have to worry about him. In return, I try not to make him get up twice in a game."

Fingers' brief warmup in the sixth had got him ready enough, he felt, and he took his time when he strolled into the infield from the bullpen at the top of the seventh. He handed his warmup jacket to a bat boy, walked casually to the mound, and began to groom the area just in front of the pitcher's rubber, digging a proper toe hole with his spikes, smoothing out the excavations of the other men who had pitched today, tidying up his office. He was in no terrible hurry to take his allotted warmup pitches; his effort in the bullpen was, he felt, sufficient. He had been going through this ritual in the major leagues for fourteen seasons now. Baseball careers stretch long for men of great talent, like Fingers, as well as for men of lesser talent who care for their bodies and work to refine their skills. The California Angels had a pitcher named Steve Renko who was 37 when the 1982 season began—old, but by no means ancient in baseball. Yet by the standards of, say, football, Renko hailed from the prehistoric age: a quarterback at the University of Kansas, he had been a teammate of the great running back Gale Sayers. In the intervening years, Sayers had gone on to an outstanding professional career, retired, been elected to the Football Hall of Fame, and in the minds of football fans was a symbol of a long-ago era. And Steve Renko was still pitching in the major leagues.

Fingers had changed as a thrower but not as a pitcher. The distinction is a cliché, but like most clichés, it is grounded in reality. Like prizefighters who are either boxers or punchers, pitchers live by their skills or simply by their arms. Kuenn thought Fingers was "above average with just his stuff"—which is to say, his arm alone made him a valuable major leaguer. "Add his concentration, though," Kuenn continued, "and he's great. With Rollie Fingers' concentration, anyone would be a better pitcher."

Concentration: it was, in a way, what Ted Simmons thought distinguished Bob Gibson, in his case concentration as it manifested itself in Gibson's ability to focus his energies, his mind, his talents, on a given pitch. It was certainly Cecil Cooper's strength as a hitter, his use of careful analysis and the applied science he brought to every confrontation with a pitcher. Ray Poitevint spoke often about a prospect's "lower half," that part of his makeup that was not visible from skill evaluation lines at the top of scouting forms.

Concentration was a major element of the lower half, and confidence was perhaps the other most important element. Some superb natural athletes may be able to get by on the latter alone—in the sense that, as Yogi Berra reportedly said, "you can't hit and think at the same time." Apart from recognizing that if Yogi Berra actually said everything that has been attributed to him, *Bartlett's* would need a separate edition just to contain his *mots,* there is some wisdom in the comment. There are athletes whose natural skills are so extraordinary that analysis—thinking—can get in the way of innate confidence. The old National League first baseman Buddy Hassett remembered that Hall of Fame hitter Paul Waner "said he just laid his bat on his shoulder, and when he saw a pitch he liked he threw it off." But, on the whole, in the world of major league baseball, which contains only 650 athletes out of a nation (indeed, a hemisphere) of ball-playing boys—in such exclusive territory, few men are so gifted that they can rely solely on skill, and instead need to think, to concentrate, to focus their attention on the athletic problem at hand, season after season, game after game, pitch after pitch. This mental application is, some players maintain, far more grueling than the purely physical aspects of baseball.

Kuenn called Fingers' arm "above average"—meaningful praise but hardly an appraisal that one would expect for one of the two preeminent relief pitchers in all of baseball's history (the other was the old knuckleballer Hoyt Wilhelm, but knuckleballers are a breed apart, freaks in a way, and endlessly downgraded in discussions of greatness conducted by baseball men). But Fingers' knowledge of his own skills, and his limitations, had led him to adjust his game. He had, like most young pitchers, attained prominence on his fastball. He learned to make the fastball more effective by developing a slider. And when he recognized in 1980 that age and innings had taken the sheen off his fastball, and that hitters could afford to concentrate on the slider (especially lefties, who batted .314 against him that year), he developed a forkball—a pitch that ran straight up to the plate and then dropped precipitously. The forkball, popularized in the 1940s by Allie Reynolds and Tiny Bonham, was a good pitch on its own, but not something a pitcher could rely upon exclusively. For Fingers, the threat of the forkball made his fastball more effective with hitters who were ever on the lookout for surprise pitches; and once the fastball was thus reestablished, the slider was renewed.

Over his career, Fingers had pitched 94 innings against the Orioles, with a superb 1.82 earned run average, 7 victories, and 9 saves. But June 10 was the first time he had faced Baltimore in 1982, and in 1981 he had seen the team only twice, for a total of 3⅔ innings. Before 1981, he had for four seasons been in the National League. So his experience against these particular batters was limited, and the first man he would face—the rookie Cal Ripken Jr.—was someone totally new to Fingers.

He relied on his catcher, Moore, and he relied on what he had learned from the other Milwaukee pitchers and from the coaches. Mostly, though, Fingers relied on the generic fact of *pitching*—that there was a certain way one did one's work. He started Ripken with a fastball, but this pitch, the first young Ripken had ever seen from the great Rollie Fingers, was low and inside. Ripken could expect the slider next, probably away—and he proceeded to lunge for a Fingers slider so far away that the end of his bat didn't come within six inches of the ball. He then saw two more Fingers fastballs, the first one up out of the strike zone but the second one a pitch that ran in from the middle of the plate. Ripken sent it on a line into the left field corner, where an alert Oglivie corralled it before it reached the wall and held Ripken to a single.

Dan Ford, he of the extreme, back-to-the-pitcher stance, was next. Fingers, and all the Milwaukee pitchers, knew that the only way to pitch Ford was inside, way inside. So Fingers gave him four straight inside pitches, eventually building the count to 1 and 2. A fifth fastball Ford tipped back toward Moore, who could not hold it. And then Fingers tried a fastball away, and Ford lined it past Money at first. Ripken went to third, where Paul Molitor said to him, "If you're going to keep hitting it down the line, let me know, and I'll play over a bit."

Of course, Molitor wasn't going to move over, not yet, not even if he thought every ball would be hit down the line, as Ripken's had been. Both Ron Hansen, who positioned the infielders for Kuenn, and Kuenn himself had been in baseball too long: you put your first and third basemen on the line when you're one run up and it's the eighth or ninth inning. Until then, it is prudent to give up the potential double inside the bag when one run couldn't hurt you, rather than sacrifice an inning-extending single in the hole between third and short.

By the time Eddie Murray, dangerous and imposing Eddie Murray, came to the plate, Fingers had begun to question whether he had his good fastball today. He had been having difficulty controlling it, and when he came straight with it, neither Ford nor Ripken had had trouble handling it. It was a dilemma, for Murray was one of the best off-speed hitters in the league; he could jump on anything that wasn't a fastball and with his sheer power propel it out of the park in any direction. Fingers determined to pitch Murray low and away, where the hitter would be least dangerous. And he'd leave his fastball out of it; his fastball wasn't doing the job.

His first pitch was a slider, in the dirt, which Moore blocked by moving his body in front of it. It was the sort of work that makes catchers weary, and also the sort of work that saves games; here, it prevented Ripken from scoring on a wild pitch, and kept Ford, the tying run, from moving to second, where Baltimore would have three chances to bring him home. (Ned Yost, the third-string Milwaukee catcher, had actually trained for his vocation by having his high school coach, his teammates, his neighbors—anyone he could corral—

throw balls in the dirt to him for hours on end while he would throw his body at the pitches, keeping them in front of him.)

At 1 and 0, Fingers threw his first forkball of the day. It dropped suddenly, without warning, just as Murray swung, and it went directly under the blur of Murray's bat. Another forkball made it 1 and 2; Fingers was getting into his groove. Each pitch, he'd reach back behind his head with his elastic right arm, then whip through his motion, his arm coming three quarters overhand, then release the pitch—fastball, slider, forkball—at the same point, with the same arm speed, using the same motion he had used since he was a 17-year-old. Expecting a fastball, Murray couldn't adjust for the sharp drop; expecting a forkball, he risked swinging underneath the pitch and popping it up harmlessly. A first fastball—a throwaway pitch, just to show Murray he had one—was out of the strike zone, and Murray fouled it off. The next pitch was another fork, and Murray was too high on it, pounding it into the ground, toward the right-side hole. Money and Gantner raced toward it, Gantner won the race, and Fingers was at first before Murray, to get Gantner's throw for the out. Ripken scored on the play, and Ford moved to second. There was one out, the score now 7–6.

Fingers performed the play perfectly, instinctively calling forth the endless spring training repetition of the pitcher-covers-first exercise. His delivery, which culminated with Fingers storklike and erect on his forward-thrust left leg, employed enough force to carry his weight toward first at its completion anyway. It left him vulnerable to the bunt toward third, or to the smash back at the mound, but these were minor concerns. Nolan Ryan, the outstanding fastball pitcher of the age, had so much force and momentum in his enormous delivery that he'd complete each pitch in an area in front of the mound, way off toward first, his head down, never once seeing a bat hit one of his pitched balls. (He also, not incidentally, fielded his position about as poorly as any pitcher in baseball.)

With their lead down to one run, the Brewers' concern became the man on second. But on Murray's ground ball, Ford came up lame. After calling time, he limped off the base toward the outfield; Cal Ripken Sr., the third base coach, raced over and spoke briefly with Ford. Ripken, now in his twenty-fifth year in baseball—he played in the minors six years, managed there for another twelve, then scouted for one year before joining Weaver's staff in 1976—knelt down next to Ford and grasped the player's left hamstring in his own strong hand, an act he had undoubtedly performed dozens of times before. Earl Weaver came running out, followed by his close friend, the Baltimore trainer, Ralph Salvon, an obese man whose presence on any field but Baltimore's own invariably brought forth hoots and catcalls from the stands. After a few moments of the trainer's ministrations, Ford limped off the field between Ripken and Salvon, Weaver five steps ahead of them, calling for Jim Dwyer in the dugout, beckoning him onto the field to run for Ford. Weaver had asked after Ford's health, and that was that; he had work to do.

Dwyer, the pinch runner, was yet another of the pieces in Weaver's tool kit. He was 32, and had played for St. Louis, Montreal, the New York Mets, the Cardinals again, the Giants, the Red Sox, and now Baltimore. He had never been a regular anywhere. He had a degree in accounting, and he loved to play baseball, even if it was clear he would never amount to more than what he was—a useful and fairly maintenance-free employee who could accept a limited role. He was called "Pigpen," for the usual reasons. He was a left-handed hitter. All of these things made him a perfect Earl Weaver player. That is to say, the sum of his parts was not terribly auspicious, but his parts, considered individually, had real value.

Baltimore continued to chip at Fingers. He tried his fastball again against Al Bumbry, who hit a ground ball that hopped over Fingers' head when he was in his erect-stork position and enabled Dwyer to move to third as Jim Gantner threw the batter out at first. There were two outs when Weaver reached into his tool kit for the last of his outfield parts, John Lowenstein.

If Dwyer was valuable because of his varied attributes, Lowenstein was priceless. If Dwyer was rare—because of his dedication, his itinerant career, his accounting degree, his uncomplaining willingness to adapt—Lowenstein was unique. He was a beak-nosed man of 35 and had played in more than 100 games only twice in his eleven-year major league career. When he was with Cleveland, the Municipal Stadium organist took to playing a different "theme" for each Indian player, and signified Lowenstein with "Hava Nagila"; instructed that Lowenstein wasn't Jewish, the organist switched to "Jesus Christ Superstar." By the time he had his three hundredth major league at-bat, Lowenstein had played every position but pitcher and catcher. He had a B.A. in anthropology from the University of California and was without question the wittiest man in the American League, the ready supplier of cogent and clever quotes for any desperate writer. And he had the engaging quality, desperately rare in baseball, of self-deprecation, ready to turn his wit on himself. In the middle 1970s, he had given an interview to the *Wall Street Journal* in which he made the case for mediocrity in baseball, citing himself as a model example. That was around the same time that Lowenstein, having discouraged some Clevelanders from forming a fan club in his honor, instead gave his blessing to a "John Lowenstein Apathy Club."

But Lowenstein was more than a pleasing ornament to baseball; he had become a fine player, too. He had always had speed, and had employed it well by mastering the walking lead off first base, enabling him to steal bases by surprise and to reach third on routine singles. He knew how to play the outfield, could fill in virtually anywhere else, and had become an able hitter. In 1979, his first Baltimore season, he hit 11 home runs in only 197 at-bats. (By way of comparison, that 1-HR-in-18-at-bats ratio stood up well to, say, Gorman Thomas's 1:17 ratio in 1981, or to the fact that Eddie Murray had only once in his prodigious career exceeded a 1:20 ratio.) In 1980, Weaver used Lowenstein so well that he hit .311 in 104 games. And thus far in 1982, with the season less than one third over, Lowenstein already had 11 home runs while still serving as a platoon player.

In the third inning, when Baltimore had chased Bob McClure and Kuenn countered with Jim Slaton, the lefty-righty switch set in motion Weaver's batting order machinations, with Bumbry hitting for the right-handed Benny Ayala. With that one stroke, he had given the Orioles an offensive edge, and improved the outfield defense as well, placing the experienced and quicker Bumbry in center and moving the able Roenicke to left, where he was a marked improvement over Ayala. Weaver could have had Lowenstein hit for Roenicke then, another righty-lefty switch, a switch to Lowenstein's very hot bat (he was .375 lifetime against Slaton), a switch that would have been at worst a wash defensively. But when one used as many chess pieces as Weaver did, one also learned to save some for the end game.

In the sixth inning, when Singleton's homer halved Milwaukee's lead to 7–5, Lowenstein saw that he would likely have a pinch-hitting opportunity in the game's last innings. Either Slaton was going to settle down, maintaining his lead and getting the lefty-righty edge against both Roenicke and Ford, or, if Slaton crumbled, Kuenn would have to go to Fingers, and the same platoon advantages applied. Lowenstein had spent so much of his career as a part-time player he had learned how to stay in the game mentally, and he had learned as well how to loosen up on short notice. Sometimes Weaver would tell him to get ready; most of the time, he knew when to do so instinctively. He'd go into the clubhouse, or the dugout runway, and swing a bat, do some stretching exercises. By the time the batting order reached Roenicke's spot, Lowenstein was as involved, and as ready, as if he'd been in the starting lineup.

Fingers was less ready. He had allowed the gap to close to one run, and he had put the tying run on third. His fastball was still refusing to come under his control. And in Lowenstein he was facing a batter who, in Fingers' words, was "the toughest out on their team. I don't know why, but nobody for us gets him out. It just doesn't make any difference what you throw him. I don't want to give him anything to pull. I want to spot everything against him, one pitch inside, then outside, I want him to hit my pitch, but he always ends up with his pitch." Fingers might well have listened to Jim Slaton, who said, "I have no idea how to pitch him. I think I should have the catcher *tell* him what's coming—maybe that would make him think too much." And Moore, the catcher, was even more flummoxed: "Forget it—I haven't any idea what to do with him. I've been going against him for nine years. He killed us when he was with Cleveland, he killed us when he was with Texas, and he kills us now. It seems everything we try to do with him is wrong. Every year it's the same—basically, you just throw it up there and hope."

Lowenstein took a spread, knees-bent stance and stared at an outside slider before fouling off Fingers' inside fastball. Fingers then appeared to do what Moore had melancholically suggested—he threw a fastball up there and hoped—and Lowenstein, lifting his front foot with his swing, a curly-haired, mustachioed, modern Mel Ott, slapped a single into right, bringing Dwyer home. Baltimore had come from four runs back and tied the score. At last, Fingers knew for sure not only that his fastball was difficult to spot today but that it was, simply, "horseshit." His shoulders heaved noticeably, and he looked perplexed and somewhat beaten as he rubbed up the ball for the next batter, Ken Singleton.

Singleton was having a bad year, but in this series his bat had enlivened; he was 7 for 17 against Milwaukee pitching. Fingers now had to summon up his concentration, for the game was dangerously close to getting out of control. Wasting a fastball to start, he stuck with his slider, even though he knew Singleton was more vulnerable to fastballs; Moore, in fact, claimed that fastballs inside were the only way to get Singleton consistently. But Fingers was now going with the hoary dictum of "best to best," using his most effective pitch despite the batter's traits. It implied a macho approach, but that wasn't really it. Fingers knew he wasn't going to be able to "think" his way around Singleton. Now it was time for that other element of his "lower half": his confidence, his competitiveness. On the third straight slider, Singleton struck out, and Baltimore's inning was over.

Kuenn later said, "I was concerned. I saw he wasn't pinpoint sharp, and that his fastball wasn't working. But any given pitch can turn Rollie around and make him as sharp as you want him to be." He paused. "I try to keep an even keel, and it's easier to do it when I've got the best relief pitcher in baseball on the mound. I had to have faith in him." It recalled the comment of another manager, Johnny Keane, who said in 1964 about another pitcher, "I had a commitment to his heart." The pitcher was Bob Gibson.

This is hardly the longest historical piece in this book. In its way, though, it might be the most complete.

# From *the wrong season*

## JOEL OPPENHEIMER

john g. ''scissors''
mcilvain, described by
the sporting news as
remarkable, died
in charleroi, pa.,
recently. he was
88. he pitched for
22 minor league teams
in 15 different leagues
and was still in semi-
pro ball in his seventies.
when he won a 4–3 ball
game at seventy-five he
said: i don't see anything
to get excited about. i
think a person should feel
real good when he does
something unexpected.
i expected this. his
big disappointment was
that he never made the
majors, although he won
26 for chillicothe
one season, and 27 the
next. he was, however,
a bird-dog scout for
the indians for several
years. he had been
deaf since 1912.

The piece by Dave Anderson earlier in these pages ends with Reggie Jackson telling Thurman Munson, "You'll be here next year. We'll all be here." That was in 1977, and as baseball prophecy it was true.

In the first week of August, 1979, Munson died when his private plane crashed while he was practicing touch-and-go landings at the Akron-Canton Municipal Airport.

# 1979: Farewell to Thurman

## PHIL PEPE

CANTON, OHIO—It was time to say goodbye, and it was so hard. It was so hard because he was so young, so vibrant, so alive. It was hard because the memories are so vivid, the departure so tragic, the loss so painful.

They came here to say goodbye to Thurman Munson yesterday, his family, his friends, his teammates and their wives, his ex-teammates, his opponents, his neighbors and people who never even knew him.

They came from New York and Cleveland, from Cincinnati and Cooperstown, from Florida and California.

They came to this little town, driving down Market Street past the rows of neat, comfortable tudors and split levels, to the Canton Memorial Civic Center.

They came to pay their respects and to say their goodbyes and to shed their tears for their husband, father, teammate, friend, neighbor, opponent.

The closed casket, an American flag draped upon it, was on the stage that served as an altar and behind the casket, hanging on the wall, was a portrait of him in his Yankee uniform, a beatific smile on his face, so lifelike you expected him to say, "Hiya, buddy."

Alongside the casket, on both sides, were floral pieces, dozens of them, one in the shape of a baseball, one with the NY insignia in it, another with the number 15. They had come from friends and teammates and fans.

The service took an hour and, for most of the 700 in attendance, courage gave way to emotion.

Lou Piniella read from the scriptures and struggled as he delivered a eulogy.

"As a baseball player," Piniella said, "he was one of the best competitors. He played rough, but fair."

He spoke of Thurman Munson the man, "a kind, affectionate, friendly man," and he wondered aloud about the mystery of the death of a friend.

"We don't know why God took Thurman," Piniella said. "But as long as we wear a Yankee uniform, Thurman won't be far from us."

Bobby Murcer spoke eloquently about his longtime friend and teammate, his voice breaking with emotion several times.

Commissioner Bowie Kuhn was there and American League president Lee MacPhail. Gabe Paul and Phil Seghi of the Indians were there and Indian broadcaster Herb Score. Joe Torre of the Mets was there and Al Rosen and Bob Lemon and Dick Howser, who flew up from Florida. Gene Michael and Fritz Peterson were there.

There were ex-teammates in attendance, Sparky Lyle and Doc Medich, Paul Blair and John Ellis, Jay Johnstone and Bobby Bonds, Mickey Rivers and Dell Alston, Scott McGregor and Rick Dempsey, Dave Rajsich and Mike Heath, who played a night game in Seattle Sunday, flew all night, arrived in Cleveland at four in the morning, rented a car and drove to Canton, then returned to Oakland for a game last night, all at his own expense.

There were opposing players, Wayne Garland, Buddy Bell, Toby Harrah and Mike Hargrove, and two American League umpires, Bill Haller and Rich Garcia.

There had been hundreds of telegrams, and four were chosen to be read: from Anita and Lou Piniella, from Eleanor Gehrig, from Reggie Jackson and from Muhammad Ali.

When the services had ended, the friends were asked to leave so that the family and his teammates could have a few moments alone, and then the casket was wheeled outside and placed in the hearse, and outside on the street, Mickey Rivers and Roy White and Dell Alston shed their tears and held on to each other.

Billy Martin had trouble fighting back his tears and he finally gave in to them and Rivers, who had been traded by the Yankees just a week ago, grabbed George Steinbrenner and embraced him and there were tears in the eyes of both men.

And then the hearse rolled away, followed by three busloads of Thurman Munson's friends and teammates and their wives, headed for his final resting place, just a few miles from downtown Canton in the Sunset Hills Burial Park in the beautiful, lush Ohio countryside he loved so much.

As the cortege made its way up the winding road, off to the side of the road, two little boys, who couldn't have been more than six and eight, were standing on the side of a hill and they had removed their baseball caps and they were holding them against their hearts.

At the cemetery, about a mile and a half from the Akron-Canton Airport, site of the fatal crash, there was another brief ceremony. And while the priest prayed in the background, the droning of a light, private airplane could be heard, and Lou Piniella lifted his head and looked at the heavens and followed the flight of the small airplane until it had disappeared from sight.

The breaking of baseball's color line with the signing of Jackie Robinson in 1945 has been a story familiar to fans. Far less familiar are the forces and factors that made integration inevitable.

# From *Only the Ball Was White*

## ROBERT PETERSON

I am an invisible man. No, I am not a spook like those who haunted Edgar Allan Poe; nor am I one of your Hollywood-movie ectoplasms. I am a man of substance, of flesh and bone, fiber and liquids—and I might even be said to possess a mind. I am invisible, understand, simply because people refuse to see me.

—RALPH ELLISON, *Invisible Man*

THE TWO decades between 1900 and 1920—the period when Negro baseball was growing up—were a time when white America's racial attitudes were hardening. The Black Reconstruction had failed and ebbed into history; Jim Crow was firmly embedded, in fact if not in law, both North and South. Racial tensions exploded in 1906 in Atlanta, where ten Negroes and two whites died in a race riot, and in Springfield, Illinois, two years later when two Negroes and four whites were killed. The Great Migration of Negroes from South to North, beginning in 1915, was accompanied by a crescendo of race fury. During World War I race riots in East St. Louis, Missouri, and Houston, Texas, killed at least thirty-nine Negroes and twenty-five whites. After the Houston uprising, thirteen Negroes were hanged and forty-one imprisoned for life. Immediately after the war, in 1919, there were race riots in twenty-six American cities, the worst in Chicago, where twenty-three Negroes and fifteen whites died.

Riding the tide of race hate, segregation calcified during those two decades. But even during this harsh period for the nation's black men, there was still an occasional white voice raised in organized baseball on behalf of the Negro. In 1915, Walter McCredie, manager of Portland in the Pacific Coast League, tried to provide an opening wedge for Negroes by signing an outfielder of Chinese and Hawaiian parentage. His white players immediately rebelled and McCredie was forced to concede defeat. But, he said, "I don't think the color of the skin ought to be a barrier in baseball. . . . If I had my

say the Afro-American would be welcome inside the fold. I would like to have such players as Lloyd and Petway of the Chicago Colored Giants . . ."

Black players also found a champion in *The Sporting News*. In 1923 the baseball weekly (which, when integration finally arrived, was less than enthusiastic) bemoaned the exclusion of Negroes from organized baseball. Calling racial prejudice a "hideous monster," the paper said that it is an "ivory-headed obsession that one man made in God's image is any better than another man made in the same image . . ."

Negro players of that day had little hope that black men would ever play in organized ball. Napoleon Cummings, who began playing with the Bacharach Giants in Atlantic City, N.J., in 1916, remembers, "Yes, we talked about it. We talked about it years back, said there would never be a Negro in the big leagues. But we always used to talk about it among ourselves."

During the late Twenties such talk among players and fans generally receded. Memories that Negroes had once played in organized baseball were dimming, and it seemed more and more the natural order of things that whites played on their teams and Negroes played on theirs. "We never thought much about it," said Bill Yancey, whose career as a professional ballplayer spanned the years from 1923 to 1936. ". . . I remember Rojo [a Cuban-Negro catcher]—he was funny. He didn't speak too much English. He'd see two white kids throwing a baseball and he'd say, 'Byemby, s'ousands of dollars.' "

Rojo's wistfulness mirrored the belief of Negro players of the 1920s that organized baseball, and particularly the big leagues, were forever beyond their aspirations. That belief was reinforced during the carefree years when America was careening on a headlong course toward the Depression of 1929. Rarely was a white man's voice heard to condemn segregation in baseball. In the early Thirties, when the Depression was at its peak and Americans were blinded to social justice by the pervasive, nagging struggle to put food on their tables, Negro players became even more like Ellison's Invisible Man.

In *An American Dilemma*, Gunnar Myrdal put his finger on the attitude of whites toward blacks during this period:

The observer finds that in the North there is actually much unawareness on the part of white people to the extent of social discrimination against Negroes. It has been a common experience of this writer to witness how white Northerners are surprised and shocked when they hear about such things, and how they are moved to feel that something ought to be done to stop it. They often do not understand correctly even the implications of their own behavior and often tell the interviewer that they ''have never thought about it in that light.'' This innocence is, of course, opportunistic in a degree, but it is, nevertheless, real and honest too. It denotes the absence of an explicit theory and an intentional policy. In this situation one of the main difficulties for the Negroes in the North is simply lack of publicity. It is convenient for the Northerners' good conscience to forget about the Negro.

When the question of Negroes playing in the big leagues *was* presented to them, most Northerners did seem to feel that ''something ought to be done.'' In 1928 the New York *Daily News* Inquiring Photographer asked six whites whether they would disapprove of a black player in the big leagues. Four said they would not, and the two who said they would gave as their reason a fear that the fans' race prejudice would inflame the strong feelings aroused by competition on the diamond and possibly lead to riots in the stands. Typical of the favorable replies was this one by a Bronx salesman: ''Certainly not. There shouldn't be any race prejudice. It isn't as bitter now as it used to be, and I think prejudice is gradually dying out. Colored men can enter almost any other field (sic). Why not baseball?''

Why not indeed? Years later, after the color line was finally expunged, Judy Johnson became a scout for the Philadelphia Athletics and a good friend of the A's venerable owner, Connie Mack. Johnson recalls, ''I asked him one day, I said, 'Mr. Mack, why didn't you ever take any of the colored boys in the big leagues?' He said, 'Well, Judy, if you want to know the truth, there

were just too many of you to go in.' As much as to say, it would take too many jobs away from the other boys.''

However, the Negroes who played in the Philadelphia area during this time felt that Mack himself was prepared to accept Negroes if his lodge brothers in the league would not protest too much.

Napoleon Cummings remembers talk around Philadelphia in 1929 that Connie Mack wanted to hire a couple of Negro players:

I remember when they played the '29 World Series, they were short of ballplayers, and there was a rumor around here that they wanted to get somebody from around Philadelphia to help them out because they were short. But they wouldn't let Negroes on that ballclub. I remember that, and I was at the World Series. Connie Mack was trying to get Biz Mackey and Santop and all them. No soap.

If Mack did try to hire Negroes for his Athletics, he did not make sufficient fuss about it for the story to break into print. Why didn't he just go ahead and do it? There was no written rule barring Negroes from organized baseball. What stopped him? Presumably the answer lies in the attitudes of the other major-league operators.

The reasons advanced during this period for baseball's color line (on the rare occasions when it was mentioned) were substantially the same as they were in 1946, when it was finally breached. They can be summarized thus: (1) About a third of all major-league players were Southerners and they would not play with or against Negroes; (2) Negroes could not travel with a big-league club, because hotels would not accommodate them; (3) the clubs trained in the South, where Negroes and whites were forbidden by law to play together; (4) fans might riot in the stands if there was trouble on the field between a white and Negro player; (5) Negroes were not good enough to play in the big leagues anyway.

The first reason given was probably the most serious. It seems likely that some southern players would not have played on the same field with a Negro during the late Twenties and Thirties. But the evidence from the late Forties, when they *were* playing with Negroes, suggests that defections would have been few. Southerners, no less than Northerners, coveted the fame and. fortune offered by major-league baseball.

Reasons 2 and 3 were evasions. Plenty of Negro players would have been perfectly willing to be Jim Crowed in hotels for a chance to play in the majors. As for spring training, Cuba and other areas of Latin America provided acceptable facilities, as the Brooklyn Dodgers would demonstrate when the color bar was crumbling.

Reason 4, the danger of racially motivated skirmishes

in the stands, was a reasonable concern. But in retrospect it seems probable that if the way had been carefully prepared (as it was in Brooklyn), there would have been little trouble among the fans. In addition, some owners feared they would lose their white fans if they played Negroes. After all, organized baseball is a business; it cannot exist without paying customers.

Concerning Reason 5, the quality of Negro players, the testimony is mixed. Many white ballplayers and respected sportswriters believed that at least a few black players were of major-league calibre. Some baseball men were doubtful. In any case, this was not a very good reason, because, if Negroes were truly not ready for the majors, could they not have been initiated into organized baseball in the minors? (In fact, this turned out to be the way the color line was broken.)

Unspoken, but underlying all the stated objections, was the most compelling reason of all: baseball tradition. Organized baseball was steeped—perhaps a better word would be pickled—in tradition. Among the eternal verities were the sun's rising in the east, the sanctity of motherhood, and baseball's status as the National Pastime; and, since there had not been a Negro in the organized leagues in the memory of most baseball men, it must be part of God's plan that there should be none. Tradition is the father of inertia and the balm of the don't-rock-the-boat school.

By the early Thirties, gentle waves were washing against the stately hull of organized baseball. The Negro press had of course been running a low-keyed but persistent campaign to break down the bars for years, but the first powerful voice to raise the issue in the white press was Westbrook Pegler, who denounced baseball for its apartheid in 1931.

Jimmy Powers of the New York *Daily News* soon took up the cudgels and hammered at the ban for several years. In 1933 he conducted his own poll of the dignitaries at the annual Baseball Writers Association dinner on the question of admitting Negroes to the major leagues. Curiously, the only important baseball man who opposed the idea was John J. McGraw, who had tried in vain to sign Charlie Grant for the Baltimore Orioles more than thirty years earlier. Powers did not explain the basis for McGraw's opposition.

One of the problems in breaking down the color bar was the reluctance of baseball's leaders to admit officially that it even existed. John A. Heydler, president of the National League, could say without blushing in 1933, "Beyond the fundamental requirement that a major-league player must have unique ability and good character and habits, I do not recall one instance where baseball has allowed either race, creed or color to enter into its selection of players."

It was becoming increasingly difficult to sustain this sort of nonsense in the face of the performances against big-leaguers in post-season games by men like Satchel Paige, Josh Gibson, Buck Leonard, Slim Jones, and Cool Papa Bell. In 1938, Clark Griffith became the first member of baseball's official family to admit to the possibility that Negroes might one day be in organized baseball. In an interview with Sam Lacy, an enterprising reporter for the Washington *Tribune,* a Negro weekly, Griffith said:

There are few big-league magnates who are not aware of the fact that the time is not far off when colored players will take their places beside those of other races in the major leagues. However, I'm not sure that time has arrived yet . . .

Griffith predicted:

A lone Negro in the game will face caustic comments. He will be made the target of cruel, filthy epithets. Of course, I know the time will come when the ice will have to be broken. Both by the organized game and by the colored player who is willing to volunteer and thus become a sort of martyr to the cause.

There was no shortage of willing volunteers among the black players. No one, not even Griffith, called for them, but the race question appears to have been on his mind as indicated by his talk with Josh Gibson and Buck Leonard in his office after he had watched the two black men belting the ball.

As the third decade of the century neared its close, powerful voices in the press were calling loudly for an end to baseball's discrimination against Negroes. In New York, Heywood Broun and Jimmy Powers were excoriating the major leagues. Shirley Povich of the Washington *Post* wrote after watching Negro clubs train in Florida:

There's a couple of million dollars' worth of baseball talent on the loose, ready for the big leagues, yet unsigned by any major league. There are pitchers who would win 20 games this season for any big-league club that offered them contracts, and there are outfielders who could hit .350, infielders who could win quick recognition as stars, and there is at least one catcher who at this writing is probably superior to Bill Dickey. [The reference is to Josh Gibson.]

Only one thing is keeping them out of the big leagues—the pigmentation of their skin. They happen to be colored. That's their crime in the eyes of the big-league club owners. . . . Their talents are being wasted in the rickety parks in the Negro sections of Pittsburgh, Philadelphia, New York, Chicago and four other cities that comprise the major leagues of

Negro baseball. They haven't a chance to get into the big leagues of the white folks. It's a tight little boycott that the majors have set up against colored players.

A magazine called *Friday* kept the pot simmering in 1940 by soliciting comments from a number of major-league players and managers on the quality of Negro ballplayers. The response of Gabby Hartnett, manager of the Chicago Cubs, is fairly representative: "I am not interested in the color of a player, just his ability," Hartnett said. "If managers were given permission, there'd be a mad rush to sign up Negroes."

Bill McKechnie, Cincinnati Reds manager, and Leo Durocher, then piloting the Brooklyn Dodgers, replied in a similar vein. Stars like Pepper Martin, Luke Hamlin, Bucky Walters, Johnny Vander Meer, and Carl Hubbell praised Negro players. So did William Benswanger, president of the Pittsburgh Pirates, who declared, "If it came to an issue, I'd vote for Negro players. There's no reason why they should be denied the same chance that Negro fighters and musicians are given."

Benswanger had no appetite for the role of pioneer, however, as he proved in 1942, when the *Daily Worker*, a Communist newspaper published in New York, put pressure on the Pirates. In his autobiography, Roy Campanella tells of being approached by a man from the *Worker* (which he did not know was a Communist paper) who said he had arranged a tryout with the Pirates for Campanella, Dave Barnhill, New York Cubans pitcher, and Sammy Hughes, second baseman for the Baltimore Elite Giants. Long afterward, Campanella got a letter from Benswanger saying that the Pirates would be glad to arrange a tryout, "but it contained so many buts that I was discouraged even before I had finished reading the letter." He replied that all he asked for was a chance. The Pirates did not answer his letter.

The *Worker* quoted Leo Durocher, manager of the Brooklyn Dodgers, as blaming the baseball commissioner's office for the color bar. Commissioner Kenesaw Mountain Landis reacted with stern words.

Negroes are not barred from organized baseball by the commissioner and never have been during the twenty-one years I have served. There is no rule in organized baseball prohibiting their participation and never has been to my knowledge. If Durocher, or any other manager, or all of them, want to sign one, or twenty-five, Negro players, it is all right with me. That is the business of the managers and the club owners. The business of the commissioner is to interpret the rules of baseball and to enforce them.

Negro players were not encouraged by the rising level of discussion about the injustice of the color line. Buck Leonard remembers:

We didn't think anything was going to happen. We thought that they were just going to keep talking about it, that's all. They'd talked about it all those years and there'd been nothing done. We just didn't pay it any attention. We'd say, well, if it comes, we hope to have a chance to play, but we just didn't pay it any mind.

Despite the Negro players' fatalism, the quickening tempo of talk about the color bar was significant; it told of subtle changes in America's racial attitudes. Segregation was still the rule, but it was becoming a shaky bulwark against the steady pricking of white America's conscience by the social and economic changes wrought by Roosevelt's New Deal, the Negro's improving educational and living standards, and perhaps most of all, by World War II. With American black men fighting along with whites in the far corners of the globe, it was no longer quite so convenient for whites at home to forget their black compatriots.

Whitey Gruhler, sports columnist of the Atlantic City *Press-Union* and one of the few white writers who had covered Negro baseball regularly, gave voice to the nation's moral crisis in July 1942, when America had been in the war for seven months. Gruhler had been calling in vain for the entry of Negro players into organized baseball for several years; now, with America fighting for its life, he found himself in the mainstream, articulating a thought that had growing echoes:

We are fighting a war—the most terrible war in all history. We are spending billions of dollars. Our youth is shedding barrels and barrels of blood. Every day is one of heartache and tragedy. And what are we fighting for? Freedom and democracy. But some of us seem to have forgotten that freedom and democracy are the human rights for which we fought the Civil War.

But baseball's conservatives were not yet ready for such a drastic step as removal of the color line. *The Sporting News* argued that Negroes were better off in their own leagues and that they were not ready or even willing to mingle with whites. The paper blamed "agitators" who "have sought to force Negro players on the big leagues, not because it would help the game but because it gives them a chance to thrust themselves into the limelight as great crusaders in the guise of democracy." After noting that some Negro baseball men were lukewarm to the idea of integration, *The Sporting News* concluded:

Of course, there are some colored people who take a different view, and they are entitled to their opinions, but in doing so they are not looking at the question from the broader point of view, or for the ultimate good of either the race or the individuals in it. They ought to concede their own people are now protected and that nothing is served by allowing agitators to make an issue of a question on which both sides prefer to be let alone.

Larry MacPhail, president of the Brooklyn Dodgers, echoed this view. When a Brooklyn priest asked Mac-Phail whether the Dodgers would be willing to have Negro players, MacPhail replied that black players had their own leagues which would be wrecked if Negroes were in the majors. "Unfortunately," he added, "the discussion of the problem has been contaminated by charges of racial discrimination—most of it vicious propaganda circulated by professional agitators who do not know what they are talking about."

Other baseball executives, although uncertain that the time was yet ripe for introducing black players into organized baseball, saw that it was coming. Among them was William K. Wrigley, Jr., owner of the Chicago Cubs, who said he foresaw the day—"and soon." But, he declared, "there are men in high places who don't want it."

It was becoming apparent that the color question could not be kept submerged indefinitely, and in 1943 it surfaced in two places 3,000 miles apart. In Los Angeles that spring, Clarence (Pants) Rowland, president of the Pacific Coast League Angels, said trials would be given to three Negro players, Chet Brewer, Howard Easterling, and Nate Moreland. Two weeks later he reneged, apparently under pressure from other league operators, but his retreat brought a flurry of protests. The Los Angeles County Board of Supevisors and the huge local of the United Auto Workers union at North American Aircraft went on record opposing discrimination in the Pacific Coast League. The Angels' park was picketed on opening day.

There was trouble in Oakland, too, where Art Cohn, sports editor of the *Tribune,* scored the Oaks for not trying out Negroes. Oakland owner Vince Devincenzi ordered his manager, Johnny Vergez, to give trials to two Negroes, Chet Brewer and Olin Dial, but Vergez refused, despite the fact that most of the good Oakland players were in service.

Meanwhile, at the other end of the nation, Bill Veeck was trying to dig the grave of the color line. Veeck was a master showman and innovator who had been operating the Milwaukee Brewers of the American Association and who, after the war, would bring pennants to the Cleveland Indians and Chicago White Sox (and, incidentally, introduce the first Negroes into the American

League). He also suffered the ultimate indignity of presiding over the St. Louis Browns.

Veeck's plan was to buy the sinking Philadelphia Phillies franchise and stock the club with Negro stars for the 1944 season. "With Satchel Paige, Roy Campanella, Luke Easter, Monte Irvin, and countless others in action and available, I had not the slightest doubt that in 1944, a war year, the Phils would have leaped from seventh place to the pennant," Veeck says in his book, *Veeck—as in Wreck.*

Jerry Nugent, president of the Phillies, was willing to sell and Veeck had lined up the necessary financing, but, Veeck says, "I made one bad mistake. Out of long respect for Judge Landis, I felt he was entitled to prior notification of what I intended to do. . . . Judge Landis wasn't exactly shocked but he wasn't exactly overjoyed either. His first reaction, in fact, was that I was kidding him."

The plan foundered soon afterward when Veeck learned that Nugent had turned the team back to the National League, and that Ford Frick, the league president, had arranged its sale to William Cox, a lumber dealer, "for about half what I was willing to pay." So that dream died.

The pressures against baseball's segregation were not building up in a vacuum. In 1941, under the threat of a "March on Washington" by thousands of Negroes, President Franklin D. Roosevelt had issued an executive order establishing a Fair Employment Practices Commission. That first FEPC was not a vigorous enforcement agency, but it did turn the spotlight on discriminatory hiring policies in industry, and it paved the way for state laws barring discrimination in employment.

In 1944 the New York State Legislature began considering the Ives-Quinn Bill to forbid discrimination in hiring on the basis of race, creed, color, or national origin. It was not aimed specifically at baseball's color line, but only the most myopic big-league operator could fail to see that it meant eventual legal challenge to the "gentleman's agreement." Given the increasing awareness of white Americans to the insults and outrages suffered daily by black citizens, there was not much question that it would be passed.

So the stage was being set for the climactic scene in the story of Negro baseball. Appropriately it was to be enacted in New York, the big town, which was represented in the six-club Negro National League in 1944 by the weak sisters of the circuit, the New York Black Yankees and the New York Cubans. If Harlem's fans mourned the lowly status of the Black Yankees and Cubans, it was not for long; bigger things were in the air than the final standings of the NNL's pennant race.

I first read Chaim Potok's novel *The Chosen* in 1970—three years after it was published and two years too late to include this chapter in *The Third Fireside Book of Baseball*. That was what started me thinking about a fourth book.

Once it was known that the fourth book was in the works, I've lost track of the number of people who suggested "the softball game in *The Chosen*" for inclusion. I kept saying, "I know, I know."

Here it is.

# From *The Chosen*

## CHAIM POTOK

DANNY AND I probably would never have met—or we would have met under altogether different circumstances—had it not been for America's entry into the Second World War and the desire this bred on the part of some English teachers in the Jewish parochial schools to show the gentile world that yeshiva students were as physically fit, despite their long hours of study, as any other American student. They went about proving this by organizing the Jewish parochial schools in and around our area into competitive leagues, and once every two weeks the schools would compete against one another in a variety of sports. I became a member of my school's varsity softball team.

On a Sunday afternoon in early June, the fifteen members of my team met with our gym instructor in the play yard of our school. It was a warm day, and the sun was bright on the asphalt floor of the yard. The gym instructor was a short, chunky man in his early thirties who taught in the mornings in a nearby public high school and supplemented his income by teaching in our yeshiva during the afternoons. He wore a white polo shirt, white pants, and white sweater, and from the awkward way the little black skullcap sat perched on his round, balding head, it was clearly apparent that he was not accustomed to wearing it with any sort of regularity. When he talked he frequently thumped his right fist into his left palm to emphasize a point. He walked on the balls of his feet, almost in imitation of a boxer's ring stance, and he was fanatically addicted to professional baseball. He had nursed our softball team along for two years, and by a mixture of patience, luck, shrewd manipulations during some tight ball games, and hard,

fist-thumping harangues calculated to shove us into a patriotic awareness of the importance of athletics and physical fitness for the war effort, he was able to mold our original team of fifteen awkward fumblers into the top team of our league. His name was Mr. Galanter, and all of us wondered why he was not off somewhere fighting in the war.

During my two years with the team, I had become quite adept at second base and had also developed a swift underhand pitch that would tempt a batter into a swing but would drop into a curve at the last moment and slide just below the flaying bat for a strike. Mr. Galanter always began a ball game by putting me at second base and would use me as a pitcher only in very tight moments, because, as he put it once, "My baseball philosophy is grounded on the defensive solidarity of the infield."

That afternoon we were scheduled to play the winning team of another neighborhood league, a team with a reputation for wild, offensive slugging and poor fielding. Mr. Galanter said he was counting upon our infield to act as a solid defensive front. Throughout the warm-up period, with only our team in the yard, he kept thumping his right fist into his left palm and shouting at us to be a solid defensive front.

"No holes," he shouted from near home plate. "No holes, you hear? Goldberg, what kind of solid defensive front is that? Close in. A battleship could get between you and Malter. That's it. Schwartz, what are you doing, looking for paratroops? This is a ball game. The enemy's on the ground. That throw was wide, Goldberg. Throw it like a sharpshooter. Give him the ball again.

Throw it. Good. Like a sharpshooter. Very good. Keep the infield solid. No defensive holes in this war.''

We batted and threw the ball around, and it was warm and sunny, and there was the smooth, happy feeling of the summer soon to come, and the tight excitement of the ball game. We wanted very much to win, both for ourselves and, more especially, for Mr. Galanter, for we had all come to like his fist-thumping sincerity. To the rabbis who taught in the Jewish parochial schools, baseball was an evil waste of time, a spawn of the potentially assimilationist English portion of the yeshiva day. But to the students of most of the parochial schools, an inter-league baseball victory had come to take on only a shade less significance than a top grade in Talmud, for it was an unquestioned mark of one's Americanism, and to be counted a loyal American had become increasingly important to us during these last years of the war.

So Mr. Galanter stood near home plate, shouting instructions and words of encouragement, and we batted and tossed the ball around. I walked off the field for a moment to set up my eyeglasses for the game. I wore shell-rimmed glasses, and before every game I would bend the earpieces in so the glasses would stay tight on my head and not slip down the bridge of my nose when I began to sweat. I always waited until just before a game to bend down the earpieces, because, bent, they would cut into the skin over my ears, and I did not want to feel the pain a moment longer than I had to. The tops of my ears would be sore for days after every game, but better that, I thought, than the need to keep pushing my glasses up the bridge of my nose or the possibility of having them fall off suddenly during an important play.

Davey Cantor, one of the boys who acted as a replacement if a first-stringer had to leave the game, was standing near the wire screen behind home plate. He was a short boy, with a round face, dark hair, owlish glasses, and a very Semitic nose. He watched me fix my glasses.

"You're looking good out there, Reuven," he told me.

"Thanks," I said.

"Everyone is looking real good."

"It'll be a good game."

He stared at me through his glasses. "You think so?" he asked.

"Sure, why not?"

"You ever see them play, Reuven?"

"No."

"They're murderers."

"Sure," I said.

"No, really. They're wild."

"You saw them play?"

"Twice. They're murderers."

"Everyone plays to win, Davey."

"They don't only play to win. They play like it's the first of the Ten Commandments."

I laughed. "That yeshiva?" I said. "Oh, come on, Davey."

"It's the truth."

"Sure," I said.

"Reb Saunders ordered them never to lose because it would shame their yeshiva or something. I don't know. You'll see."

"Hey, Malter!" Mr. Galanter shouted. "What are you doing, sitting this one out?"

"You'll see," Davey Cantor said.

"Sure." I grinned at him. "A holy war."

He looked at me.

"Are you playing?" I asked him.

"Mr. Galanter said I might take second base if you have to pitch."

"Well, good luck."

"Hey, Malter!" Mr. Galanter shouted. "There's a war on, remember?"

"Yes, sir!" I said, and ran back out to my position at second base.

We threw the ball around a few more minutes, and then I went up to home plate for some batting practice. I hit a long one out to left field, and then a fast one to the shortstop, who fielded it neatly and whipped it to first. I had the bat ready for another swing when someone said, "Here they are," and I rested the bat on my shoulder and saw the team we were going to play turn up our block and come into the yard. I saw Davey Cantor kick nervously at the wire screen behind home plate, then put his hands into the pockets of his dungarees. His eyes were wide and gloomy behind his owlish glasses.

I watched them come into the yard.

There were fifteen of them, and they were dressed alike in white shirts, dark pants, white sweaters, and small black skullcaps. In the fashion of the very Orthodox, their hair was closely cropped, except for the area near their ears from which mushroomed the untouched hair that tumbled down into the long side curls. Some of them had the beginnings of beards, straggly tufts of hair that stood in isolated clumps on their chins, jawbones, and upper lips. They all wore the traditional undergarment beneath their shirts, and the tzitzit, the long fringes appended to the four corners of the garment, came out above their belts and swung against their pants as they walked. These were the very Orthodox, and they obeyed literally the Biblical commandment *And ye shall look upon it,* which pertains to the fringes.

In contrast, our team had no particular uniform, and each of us wore whatever he wished: dungarees, shorts, pants, polo shirts, sweat shirts, even undershirts. Some of us wore the garment, others did not. None of us wore the fringes outside his trousers. The only element of uniform that we had in common was the small, black skullcap which we, too, wore.

They came up to the first-base side of the wire screen behind home plate and stood there in a silent black-and-white mass, holding bats and balls and gloves in their hands. . . .

A man disentangled himself from the black-and-white mass of players and took a step forward. He looked to be in his late twenties and wore a black suit, black shoes, and a black hat. He had a black beard, and he carried a book under one arm. He was obviously a rabbi, and I marveled that the yeshiva had placed a rabbi instead of an athletic coach over its team.

Mr. Galanter came up to him and offered his hand.

"We are ready to play," the rabbi said in Yiddish, shaking Mr. Galanter's hand with obvious uninterest.

"Fine," Mr. Galanter said in English, smiling.

The rabbi looked out at the field. "You played already?" he asked.

"How's that?" Mr. Galanter said.

"You had practice?"

"Well, sure—"

"We want to practice."

"How's that?" Mr. Galanter said again, looking surprised.

"You practiced, now we practice."

"You didn't practice in your own yard?"

"We practiced."

"Well, then—"

"But we have never played in your yard before. We want a few minutes."

"Well, now," Mr. Galanter said, "there isn't much time. The rules are each team practices in its own yard."

"We want five minutes," the rabbi insisted.

"Well—" Mr. Galanter said. He was no longer smiling. He always liked to go right into a game when we played in our own yard. It kept us from cooling off, he said.

"Five minutes," the rabbi said. "Tell your people to leave the field."

"How's that?" Mr. Galanter said.

"We cannot practice with your people on the field. Tell them to leave the field."

"Well, now," Mr. Galanter said, then stopped. He thought for a long moment. The black-and-white mass of players behind the rabbi stood very still, waiting. I saw Davey Cantor kick at the asphalt of the yard. "Well, all right. Five minutes. Just five minutes, now."

"Tell your people to leave the field," the rabbi said.

Mr. Galanter stared gloomily out at the field, looking a little deflated. "Everybody off!" he shouted, not very loudly. "They want a five-minute warm-up. Hustle, hustle. Keep those arms going. Keep it hot. Toss some balls around behind home. Let's go!"

The players scrambled off the field.

The black-and-white mass near the wire screen remained intact. The young rabbi turned and faced his team.

He talked in Yiddish. "We have the field for five minutes," he said. "Remember why and for whom we play."

Then he stepped aside, and the black-and-white mass dissolved into fifteen individual players who came quickly onto the field. One of them, a tall boy with sand-colored hair and long arms and legs that seemed all bones and angles, stood at home plate and commenced hitting balls out to the players. He hit a few easy grounders and pop-ups, and the fielders shouted encouragement to one another in Yiddish. They handled themselves awkwardly, dropping easy grounders, throwing wild, fumbling fly balls. I looked over at the young rabbi. He had sat down on the bench near the wire screen and was reading his book.

Behind the wire screen was a wide area, and Mr. Galanter kept us busy there throwing balls around.

"Keep those balls going!" he fist-thumped at us. "No one sits out this fire fight! Never underestimate the enemy!"

But there was a broad smile on his face. Now that he was actually seeing the other team, he seemed not at all concerned about the outcome of the game. In the interim between throwing a ball and having it thrown back to me, I told myself that I liked Mr. Galanter, and I wondered about his constant use of war expressions and why he wasn't in the army.

Davey Cantor came past me, chasing a ball that had gone between his legs.

"Some murderers," I grinned at him.

"You'll see," he said as he bent to retrieve the ball.

"Sure," I said.

"Especially the one batting. You'll see."

The ball was coming back to me, and I caught it neatly and flipped it back.

"Who's the one batting?" I asked.

"Danny Saunders."

"Pardon my ignorance, but who is Danny Saunders?"

"Reb Saunders' son," Davey Cantor said, blinking his eyes.

"I'm impressed."

"You'll see," Davey Cantor said, and ran off with his ball.

My father, who had no love at all for Hasidic communities and their rabbinic overlords, had told me about Rabbi Isaac Saunders and the zealousness with which he ruled his people and settled questions of Jewish law.

I saw Mr. Galanter look at his wristwatch, then stare

out at the team on the field. The five minutes were apparently over, but the players were making no move to abandon the field. Danny Saunders was now at first base, and I noticed that his long arms and legs were being used to good advantage, for by stretching and jumping he was able to catch most of the wild throws that came his way.

Mr. Galanter went over to the young rabbi who was still sitting on the bench and reading.

"It's five minutes," he said.

The rabbi looked up from his book. "Ah?" he said.

"The five minutes are up," Mr. Galanter said.

The rabbi stared out at the field. "Enough!" he shouted in Yiddish. "It's time to play!" Then he looked down at the book and resumed his reading.

The players threw the ball around for another minute or two, and then slowly came off the field. Danny Saunders walked past me, still wearing his first baseman's glove. He was a good deal taller than I, and in contrast to my somewhat ordinary but decently proportioned features and dark hair, his face seemed to have been cut from stone. His chin, jaw, and cheekbones were made up of jutting hard lines, his nose was straight and pointed, his lips full, rising to a steep angle from the center point beneath his nose and then slanting off to form a too-wide mouth. His eyes were deep blue, and the sparse tufts of hair on his chin, jawbones, and upper lip, the close-cropped hair on his head, and the flow of side curls along his ears were the color of sand. He moved in a loose-jointed, disheveled sort of way, all arms and legs, talking in Yiddish to one of his teammates and ignoring me completely as he passed by. I told myself that I did not like his Hasidic-bred sense of superiority and that it would be a great pleasure to defeat him and his team in this afternoon's game.

The umpire, a gym instructor from a parochial school two blocks away, called the teams together to determine who would bat first. I saw him throw a bat into the air. It was caught and almost dropped by a member of the other team.

During the brief hand-over-hand choosing, Davey Cantor came over and stood next to me.

"What do you think?" he asked.

"They're a snooty bunch," I told him.

"What do you think about their playing?"

"They're lousy."

"They're murderers."

"Oh, come on, Davey."

"You'll see," Davey Cantor said, looking at me gloomily.

"I just did see."

"You didn't see anything."

"Sure," I said. "Elijah the prophet comes in to pitch for them in tight spots."

"I'm not being funny," he said, looking hurt.

"Some murderers," I told him, and laughed. . . .

The umpire, who had taken up his position behind the pitcher, called for the ball and someone tossed it to him. He handed it to the pitcher and shouted, "Here we go! Play ball!" We settled into our positions.

Mr. Galanter shouted, "Goldberg, move in!" and Sidney Goldberg, our shortstop, took two steps forward and moved a little closer to third base. "Okay fine," Mr. Galanter said. "Keep that infield solid!"

A short, thin boy came up to the plate and stood there with his feet together, holding the bat awkwardly over his head. He wore steel-rimmed glasses that gave his face a pinched, old man's look. He swung wildly at the first pitch, and the force of the swing spun him completely around. His earlocks lifted off the sides of his head and followed him around in an almost horizontal circle. Then he steadied himself and resumed his position near the plate, short, thin, his feet together, holding his bat over his head in an awkward grip.

The umpire called the strike in a loud, clear voice, and I saw Sidney Goldberg look over at me and grin broadly.

"If he studies Talmud like that, he's dead," Sidney Goldberg said.

I grinned back at him.

"Keep that infield solid!" Mr. Galanter shouted from third base. "Malter, a little to your left! Good!"

The next pitch was too high, and the boy chopped at it, lost his bat and fell forward on his hands. Sidney Goldberg and I looked at each other again. Sidney was in my class. We were similar in build, thin and lithe, with somewhat spindly arms and legs. He was not a very good student, but he was an excellent shortstop. We lived on the same block and were good but not close friends. He was dressed in an undershirt and dungarees and was not wearing the four-cornered garment. I had on a light-blue shirt and dark-blue work pants, and I wore the four-cornered garment under the shirt.

The short, thin boy was back at the plate, standing with his feet together and holding the bat in his awkward grip. He let the next pitch go by, and the umpire called it a strike. I saw the young rabbi look up a moment from his book, then resume reading.

"Two more just like that!" I shouted encouragingly to the pitcher. "Two more, Schwartzie!" And I thought to myself, Some murderers.

I saw Danny Saunders go over to the boy who had just struck out and talk to him. The boy looked down and seemed to shrivel with hurt. He hung his head and walked away behind the wire screen. Another short, thin boy took his place at the plate. I looked around for Davey Cantor but could not see him.

The boy at bat swung wildly at the first two pitches and missed them both. He swung again at the third pitch, and I heard the loud *thwack* of the bat as it connected with the ball, and saw the ball move in a swift, straight line toward Sidney Goldberg, who caught it, bobbled it for a moment, and finally got it into his glove. He tossed the ball to me, and we threw it around. I saw him take off his glove and shake his left hand.

"That hurt," he said, grinning at me.

"Good catch," I told him.

"That hurt like hell," he said, and put his glove back on his hand.

The batter who stood now at the plate was broad-shouldered and built like a bear. He swung at the first pitch, missed, then swung again at the second pitch and sent the ball in a straight line over the head of the third baseman into left field. I scrambled to second, stood on the base, and shouted for the ball. I saw the left fielder pick it up on the second bounce and relay it to me. It was coming in a little high, and I had my glove raised for it. I felt more than saw the batter charging toward second, and as I was getting my glove on the ball he smashed into me like a truck. The ball went over my head, and I fell forward heavily onto the asphalt floor of the yard, and he passed me, going toward third, his fringes flying out behind him, holding his skullcap to his head with his right hand so it would not fall off. Abe Goodstein, our first baseman, retrieved the ball and whipped it home, and the batter stood at third, a wide grin on his face.

The yeshiva team exploded into wild cheers and shouted loud words of congratulations in Yiddish to the batter.

Sidney Goldberg helped me get to my feet.

"That momzer!" he said. "You weren't in his way!"

"Wow!" I said, taking a few deep breaths. I had scraped the palm of my right hand.

"What a momzer!" Sidney Goldberg said.

I saw Mr. Galanter come storming onto the field to talk to the umpire. "What kind of play was that?" he asked heatedly. "How are you going to rule that?"

"Safe at third," the umpire said. "Your boy was in the way."

Mr. Galanter's mouth fell open. "How's that again?"

"Safe at third," the umpire repeated.

Mr. Galanter looked ready to argue, thought better of it, then stared over at me. "Are you all right, Malter?"

"I'm okay," I said, taking another deep breath.

Mr. Galanter walked angrily off the field.

"Play ball!" the umpire shouted.

The yeshiva team quieted down. I saw that the young rabbi was now looking up from his book and smiling faintly.

A tall, thin player came up to the plate, set his feet in correct position, swung his bat a few times, then crouched into a waiting stance. I saw it was Danny Saunders. I opened and closed my right hand, which was still sore from the fall.

"Move back! Move back!" Mr. Galanter was shouting from alongside third base, and I took two steps back.

I crouched, waiting.

The first pitch was wild, and the yeshiva team burst into loud laughter. The young rabbi was sitting on the bench, watching Danny Saunders intently.

"Take it easy, Schwartzie!" I shouted encouragingly to the pitcher. "There's only one more to go!"

The next pitch was about a foot over Danny Saunders' head, and the yeshiva team howled with laughter. Sidney Goldberg and I looked at each other. I saw Mr. Galanter standing very still alongside third, staring at the pitcher. The rabbi was still watching Danny Saunders.

The next pitch left Schwartzie's hand in a long, slow line, and before it was halfway to the plate I knew Danny Saunders would try for it. I knew it from the way his left foot came forward and the bat snapped back and his long, thin body began its swift pivot. I tensed, waiting for the sound of the bat against the ball, and when it came it sounded like a gunshot. For a wild fraction of a second I lost sight of the ball. Then I saw Schwartzie dive to the ground, and there was the ball coming through the air where his head had been and I tried for it but it was moving too fast, and I barely had my glove raised before it was in center field. It was caught on a bounce and thrown to Sidney Goldberg, but by that time Danny Saunders was standing solidly on my base and the yeshiva team was screaming with joy.

Mr. Galanter called for time and walked over to talk to Schwartzie. Sidney Goldberg nodded to me, and the two of us went over to them.

"That ball could've killed me!" Schwartzie was saying. He was of medium size, with a long face and a bad case of acne. He wiped sweat from his face. "My God, did you see that ball?"

"I saw it," Mr. Galanter said grimly.

"That was too fast to stop, Mr. Galanter," I said in Schwartzie's defense.

"I heard about that Danny Saunders," Sidney Goldberg said. "He always hits to the pitcher."

"You could've told me," Schwartzie lamented. "I could've been ready."

"I only *heard* about it," Sidney Goldberg said. "You always believe everything you hear?"

"God, that ball could've killed me!" Schwartzie said again.

"You want to go on pitching?" Mr. Galanter said. A thin sheen of sweat covered his forehead, and he looked very grim.

"Sure, Mr. Galanter," Schwartzie said. "I'm okay."

"You're sure?"

"Sure I'm sure."

"No heroes in this war, now," Mr. Galanter said. "I want live soldiers, not dead heroes."

"I'm no hero," Schwartzie muttered lamely. "I can still get it over, Mr. Galanter. God, it's only the first inning."

"Okay, soldier," Mr. Galanter said, not very enthusiastically. "Just keep our side of this war fighting."

"I'm trying my best, Mr. Galanter," Schwartzie said.

Mr. Galanter nodded, still looking grim, and started off the field. I saw him take a handkerchief out of his pocket and wipe his forehead.

"Jesus Christ!" Schwartzie said, now that Mr. Galanter was gone. "That bastard aimed right for my head!"

"Oh, come on, Schwartzie," I said. "What is he, Babe Ruth?"

"You heard what Sidney said."

"Stop giving it to them on a silver platter and they won't hit it like that."

"Who's giving it to them on a silver platter?" Schwartzie lamented. "That was a great pitch."

"Sure," I said.

The umpire came over to us. "You boys planning to chat here all afternoon?" he asked. He was a squat man in his late forties, and he looked impatient.

"No, sir," I said very politely, and Sidney and I ran back to our places.

Danny Saunders was standing on my base. His white shirt was pasted to his arms and back with sweat.

"That was a nice shot," I offered.

He looked at me curiously and said nothing.

"You always hit it like that to the pitcher?" I asked.

He smiled faintly. "You're Reuven Malter," he said in perfect English. He had a low, nasal voice.

"That's right," I said, wondering where he had heard my name.

"Your father is David Malter, the one who writes articles on the Talmud?"

"Yes."

"I told my team we're going to kill you apikorsim this afternoon." He said it flatly, without a trace of expression in his voice.

I stared at him and hoped the sudden tight coldness I felt wasn't showing on my face. "Sure," I said. "Rub your tzitzit for good luck."

I walked away from him and took up my position near the base. I looked toward the wire screen and saw Davey Cantor standing there, staring out at the field, his hands in his pockets. I crouched down quickly, because Schwartzie was going into his pitch.

The batter swung wildly at the first two pitches and missed each time. The next one was low, and he let it go by, then hit a grounder to the first baseman, who dropped it, flailed about for it wildly, and recovered in time to see Danny Saunders cross the plate. The first baseman stood there for a moment, drenched in shame, then tossed the ball to Schwartzie. I saw Mr. Galanter standing near third base, wiping his forehead. The yeshiva team had gone wild again, and they were all trying to get to Danny Saunders and shake his hand. I saw the rabbi smile broadly, then look down at his book and resume reading.

Sidney Goldberg came over to me. "What did Saunders tell you?" he asked.

"He said they were going to kill us apikorsim this afternoon." . . .

The next batter hit a long fly ball to right field. It was caught on the run.

"Hooray for us," Sidney Goldberg said grimly as we headed off the field. "Any longer and they'd be asking us to join them for the Mincha Service."

"Not us," I said. "We're not holy enough."

"Where did they learn to hit like that?"

"Who knows?" I said.

We were standing near the wire screen, forming a tight circle around Mr. Galanter.

"Only two runs," Mr. Galanter said, smashing his right fist into his left hand. "And they hit us with all they had. Now we give them *our* heavy artillery. Now *we* barrage *them!*" His skullcap seemed pasted to his head with sweat. "Okay!" he said. "Fire away!"

The circle broke up, and Sidney Goldberg walked to the plate, carrying a bat. I saw the rabbi was still sitting on the bench, reading. I started to walk around behind him to see what book it was, when Davey Cantor came over, his hands in his pockets, his eyes still gloomy.

"Well?" he asked.

"Well what?" I said.

"I told you they could hit."

"So you told me. So what?" I was in no mood for his feelings of doom, and I let my voice show it.

He sensed my annoyance. "I wasn't bragging or anything," he said, looking hurt. "I just wanted to know what you thought."

"They can hit," I said.

"They're murderers," he said.

I watched Sidney Goldberg let a strike go by and said nothing.

"How's your hand?" Davey Cantor asked.

"I scraped it."

"He ran into you real hard."

"Who is he?"

"Dov Shlomowitz," Davey Cantor said. "Like his name, that's what he is," he added in Hebrew. "Dov" is the Hebrew word for bear.

"Was I blocking him?"

Davey Cantor shrugged. "You were and you weren't. The ump could've called it either way."

"He felt like a truck," I said, watching Sidney Goldberg step back from a close pitch.

"You should see his father. He's one of Reb Saunders' shamashim. Some bodyguard he makes."

"Reb Saunders has bodyguards?"

"Sure he has bodyguards," Davey Cantor said. "They protect him from his own popularity. Where've you been living all these years?"

"I don't have anything to do with them."

"You're not missing a thing, Reuven."

"How do you know so much about Reb Saunders?"

"My father gives him contributions."

"Well, good for your father," I said.

"He doesn't pray there or anything. He just gives him contributions."

"You're on the wrong team."

"No, I'm not, Reuven. Don't be like that." He was looking very hurt. "My father isn't a Hasid or anything. He just gives them some money a couple times a year."

"I was only kidding, Davey." I grinned at him. "Don't be so serious about everything."

I saw his face break into a happy smile, and just then Sidney Goldberg hit a fast, low grounder and raced off to first. The ball went right through the legs of the shortstop and into center field.

"Hold it at first!" Mr. Galanter screamed at him, and Sidney stopped at first and stood on the base.

The ball had been tossed quickly to second base. The second baseman looked over toward first, then threw the ball to the pitcher. The rabbi glanced up from the book for a moment, then went back to his reading.

"Malter, coach him at first!" Mr. Galanter shouted, and I ran up the base line.

"They can hit, but they can't field," Sidney Goldberg said, grinning at me as I came to a stop alongside the base.

"Davey Cantor says they're murderers," I said.

"Old gloom-and-doom Davey," Sidney Goldberg said, grinning.

Danny Saunders was standing away from the base, making a point of ignoring us both.

The next batter hit a high fly to the second baseman, who caught it, dropped it, retrieved it, and made a wild attempt at tagging Sidney Goldberg as he raced past him to second.

"Safe all around!" the umpire called, and our team burst out with shouts of joy. Mr. Galanter was smiling. The rabbi continued reading, and I saw he was now slowly moving the upper part of his body back and forth.

"Keep your eyes open, Sidney!" I shouted from alongside first base. I saw Danny Saunders look at me, then look away. Some murderers, I thought. Shleppers is more like it.

"If it's on the ground run like hell," I said to the

batter who had just come onto first base, and he nodded at me. He was our third baseman, and he was about my size.

"If they keep fielding like that we'll be here till tomorrow," he said, and I grinned at him.

I saw Mr. Galanter talking to the next batter, who was nodding his head vigorously. He stepped to the plate, hit a hard grounder to the pitcher, who fumbled it for a moment then threw it to first. I saw Danny Saunders stretch for it and stop it.

"Out!" the umpire called. "Safe on second and third!"

As I ran up to the plate to bat, I almost laughed aloud at the pitcher's stupidity. He had thrown it to first rather than third, and now we had Sidney Goldberg on third, and a man on second. I hit a grounder to the shortstop and instead of throwing it to second he threw it to first, wildly, and again Danny Saunders stretched and stopped the ball. But I beat the throw and heard the umpire call out, "Safe all around! One in!" And everyone on our team was patting Sidney Goldberg on the back. Mr. Galanter smiled broadly.

"Hello again," I said to Danny Saunders, who was standing near me, guarding his base. "Been rubbing your tzitzit lately?"

He looked at me, then looked slowly away, his face expressionless.

Schwartzie was at the plate, swinging his bat.

"Keep your eyes open!" I shouted to the runner on third. He looked too eager to head for home. "It's only one out!"

He waved a hand at me.

Schwartzie took two balls and a strike, then I saw him begin to pivot on the fourth pitch. The runner on third started for home. He was almost halfway down the base line when the bat sent the ball in a hard line drive straight to the third baseman, the short, thin boy with the spectacles and the old man's face, who had stood hugging the base and who now caught the ball more with his stomach than with his glove, managed somehow to hold on to it, and stood there, looking bewildered and astonished.

I returned to first and saw our player who had been on third and who was now halfway to home plate turn sharply and start a panicky race back.

"Step on the base!" Danny Saunders screamed in Yiddish across the field, and more out of obedience than awareness the third baseman put a foot on the base.

The yeshiva team howled its happiness and raced off the field. Danny Saunders looked at me, started to say something, stopped, then walked quickly away.

I saw Mr. Galanter going back up the third-base line, his face grim. The rabbi was looking up from his book and smiling.

I took up my position near second base, and Sidney Goldberg came over to me.

"Why'd he have to take off like that?" he asked.

I glared over at our third baseman, who was standing near Mr. Galanter and looking very dejected.

"He was in a hurry to win the war," I said bitterly.

"What a jerk," Sidney Goldberg said.

"Goldberg, get over to your place!" Galanter called out. There was an angry edge to his voice. "Let's keep that infield solid!"

Sidney Goldberg went quickly to his position. I stood still and waited.

It was hot, and I was sweating beneath my clothes. I felt the earpieces of my glasses cutting into the skin over my ears, and I took the glasses off for a moment and ran a finger over the pinched ridges of skin, then put them back on quickly because Schwartzie was going into a windup. I crouched down, waiting, remembering Danny Saunders' promise to his team that they would kill us apikorsim. The word had meant, originally, a Jew educated in Judaism who denied basic tenets of his faith, like the existence of God, the revelation, the resurrection of the dead. To people like Reb Saunders, it also meant any educated Jew who might be reading, say, Darwin, and who was not wearing side curls and fringes outside his trousers. I was an apikoros to Danny Saunders, despite my belief in God and Torah, because I did not have side curls and was attending a parochial school where too many English subjects were offered and where Jewish subjects were taught in Hebrew instead of Yiddish, both unheard-of sins, the former because it took time away from the study of Torah, the latter because Hebrew was the Holy Tongue and to use it in ordinary classroom discourse was a desecration of God's Name. I had never really had any personal contact with this kind of Jew before. My father had told me he didn't mind their beliefs. What annoyed him was their fanatic sense of righteousness, their absolute certainty that they and they alone had God's ear, and every other Jew was wrong, totally wrong, a sinner, a hypocrite, an apikoros, and doomed, therefore, to burn in hell. I found myself wondering again how they had learned to hit a ball like that if time for the study of Torah was so precious to them and why they had sent a rabbi along to waste his time sitting on a bench during a ball game.

Standing on the field and watching the boy at the plate swing at a high ball and miss, I felt myself suddenly very angry, and it was at that point that for me the game stopped being merely a game and became a war. The fun and excitement were out of it now. Somehow the yeshiva team had translated this afternoon's baseball game into a conflict between what they regarded as their righteousness and our sinfulness. I found myself growing more and more angry, and I felt the anger begin to focus itself upon Danny Saunders, and suddenly it was not at all difficult for me to hate him.

Schwartzie let five of their men come up to the plate that half inning and let one of those five score. Sometime during that half inning, one of the members of the yeshiva team had shouted at us in Yiddish, "Burn in hell, you apikorsim!" and by the time that half inning was over and we were standing around Mr. Galanter near the wire screen, all of us knew that this was not just another ball game.

Mr. Galanter was sweating heavily, and his face was grim. All he said was, "We fight it careful from now on. No more mistakes." He said it very quietly, and we were all quiet, too, as the batter stepped up to the plate.

We proceeded to play a slow, careful game, bunting whenever we had to, sacrificing to move runners forward, obeying Mr. Galanter's instructions. I noticed that no matter where the runners were on the bases, the yeshiva team always threw to Danny Saunders, and I realized that they did this because he was the only infielder who could be relied upon to stop their wild throws. Sometime during the inning, I walked over behind the rabbi and looked over his shoulder at the book he was reading. I saw the words were Yiddish. I walked back to the wire screen. Davey Cantor came over and stood next to me, but he remained silent.

We scored only one run that inning, and we walked onto the field for the first half of the third inning with a sense of doom.

Dov Shlomowitz came up to the plate. He stood there like a bear, the bat looking like a matchstick in his beefy hands. Schwartzie pitched, and he sliced one neatly over the head of the third baseman for a single. The yeshiva team howled, and again one of them called out to us in Yiddish. "Burn, you apikorsim!" and Sidney Goldberg and I looked at each other without saying a word.

Mr. Galanter was standing alongside third base, wiping his forehead. The rabbi was sitting quietly, reading his book.

I took off my glasses and rubbed the tops of my ears. I felt a sudden momentary sense of unreality, as if the play yard, with its black asphalt floor and its white base lines, were my entire world now, as if all the previous years of my life had led me somehow to this one ball game, and all the future years of my life would depend upon its outcome. I stood there for a moment, holding the glasses in my hand and feeling frightened. Then I took a deep breath, and the feeling passed. It's only a ball game, I told myself. What's a ball game?

Mr. Galanter was shouting at us to move back. I was standing a few feet to the left of second, and I took two steps back. I saw Danny Saunders walk up to the plate, swinging a bat. The yeshiva team was shouting at him in Yiddish to kill us apikorsim.

Schwartzie turned around to check the field. He looked nervous and was taking his time. Sidney Goldberg was standing up straight, waiting. We looked at each other, then looked away. Mr. Galanter stood very still alongside third base, looking at Schwartzie.

The first pitch was low, and Danny Saunders ignored it. The second one started to come in shoulder-high, and before it was two thirds of the way to the plate, I was already standing on second base. My glove was going up as the bat cracked against the ball, and I saw the ball move in a straight line directly over Schwartzie's head, high over his head, moving so fast he hadn't even had time to regain his balance from the pitch before it went past him. I saw Dov Shlomowitz heading toward me and Danny Saunders racing to first and I heard the yeshiva team shouting and Sidney Goldberg screaming and I jumped, pushing myself upward off the ground with all the strength I had in my legs and stretching my glove hand till I thought it would pull out of my shoulder. The ball hit the pocket of my glove with an impact that numbed my hand and went through me like an electric shock, and I felt the force pull me backward and throw me off balance, and I came down hard on my left hip and elbow. I saw Dov Shlomowitz whirl and start back to first, and I pushed myself up into a sitting position and threw the ball awkwardly to Sidney Goldberg, who caught it and whipped it to first. I heard the umpire scream "Out!" and Sidney Goldberg ran over to help me to my feet, a look of disbelief and ecstatic joy on his face. Mr. Galanter shouted "Time!" and came racing onto the field. Schwartzie was standing in his pitcher's position with his mouth open. Danny Saunders stood on the base line a few feet from first, where he had stopped after I had caught the ball, staring out at me, his face frozen to stone. The rabbi was staring at me, too, and the yeshiva team was deathly silent.

"That was a great catch, Reuven!" Sidney Goldberg said, thumping my back. "That was sensational!"

I saw the rest of our team had suddenly come back to life and was throwing the ball around and talking up the game.

Mr. Galanter came over. "You all right, Malter?" he asked. "Let me see that elbow."

I showed him the elbow. I had scraped it, but the skin had not been broken.

"That was a good play," Mr. Galanter said, beaming at me. I saw his face was still covered with sweat, but he was smiling broadly now.

"Thanks, Mr. Galanter."

"How's the hand?"

"It hurts a little."

"Let me see it."

I took off the glove, and Mr. Galanter poked and bent the wrist and fingers of the hand.

"Does that hurt?" he asked.

"No," I lied.

"You want to go on playing?"

"Sure, Mr. Galanter."

"Okay," he said, smiling at me and patting my back. "We'll put you in for a Purple Heart on that one, Malter."

I grinned at him.

"Okay," Mr. Galanter said. "Let's keep this infield solid!"

He walked away, smiling.

"I can't get over that catch," Sidney Goldberg said.

"You threw it real good to first," I told him.

"Yeah," he said. "While you were sitting on your tail."

We grinned at each other, and went to our positions.

Two more of the yeshiva team got to bat that inning. The first one hit a single, and the second one sent a high fly to short, which Sidney Goldberg caught without having to move a step. We scored two runs that inning and one run the next, and by the top half of the fifth inning we were leading five to three. Four of their men had stood up to bat during the top half of the fourth inning, and they had got only a single on an error to first. When we took to the field in the top half of the fifth inning, Mr. Galanter was walking back and forth alongside third on the balls of his feet, sweating, smiling, grinning, wiping his head nervously; the rabbi was no longer reading; the yeshiva team was silent as death. Davey Cantor was playing second, and I stood in the pitcher's position. Schwartzie had pleaded exhaustion, and since this was the final inning—our parochial school schedules only permitted us time for five-inning games—and the yeshiva team's last chance at bat, Mr. Galanter was taking no chances and told me to pitch. Davey Cantor was a poor fielder, but Mr. Galanter was counting on my pitching to finish off the game. My left hand was still sore from the catch, and the wrist hurt whenever I caught a ball, but the right hand was fine, and the pitches went in fast and dropped into the curve just when I wanted them to. Dov Shlomowitz stood at the plate, swung three times at what looked to him to be perfect pitches, and hit nothing but air. He stood there looking bewildered after the third swing, then slowly walked away. We threw the ball around the infield, and Danny Saunders came up to the plate.

The members of the yeshiva team stood near the wire fence, watching Danny Saunders. They were very quiet. The rabbi was sitting on the bench, his book closed. Mr. Galanter was shouting at everyone to move back. Danny Saunders swung his bat a few times, then fixed himself into position and looked out at me.

Here's a present from an apikoros, I thought, and let go the ball. It went in fast and straight, and I saw Danny

Saunders' left foot move out and his bat go up and his body begin to pivot. He swung just as the ball slid into its curve, and the bat cut savagely through empty air, twisting him around and sending him off balance. His black skullcap fell off his head, and he regained his balance and bent quickly to retrieve it. He stood there for a moment, very still, staring out at me. Then he resumed his position at the plate. The ball came back to me from the catcher, and my wrist hurt as I caught it.

The yeshiva team was very quiet, and the rabbi had begun to chew his lip.

I lost control of the next pitch, and it was wide. On the third pitch, I went into a long, elaborate windup and sent him a slow, curving blooper, the kind a batter always wants to hit and always misses. He ignored it completely and the umpire called it a ball.

I felt my left wrist begin to throb as I caught the throw from the catcher. I was hot and sweaty, and the earpieces of my glasses were cutting deeply into the flesh above my ears as a result of the head movements that went with my pitching.

Danny Saunders stood very still at the plate, waiting.

Okay, I thought, hating him bitterly. Here's another present.

The ball went to the plate fast and straight, and dropped just below his swing. He checked himself with difficulty so as not to spin around, but he went off his balance again and took two or three staggering steps forward before he was able to stand up straight.

The catcher threw the ball back, and I winced at the pain in my wrist. I took the ball out of the glove, held it in my right hand, and turned around for a moment to look out at the field and let the pain in my wrist subside. When I turned back I saw that Danny Saunders hadn't moved. He was holding his bat in his left hand, standing very still and staring at me. His eyes were dark, and his lips were parted in a crazy, idiot grin. I heard the umpire yell "Play ball!" but Danny Saunders stood there, staring at me and grinning. I turned and looked out at the field again, and when I turned back he was still standing there, staring at me and grinning. I could see his teeth between his parted lips. I took a deep breath and felt myself wet with sweat. I wiped my right hand on my pants and saw Danny Saunders step slowly to the plate and set his legs in position. He was no longer grinning. He stood looking at me over his left shoulder, waiting.

I wanted to finish it quickly because of the pain in my wrist, and I sent in another fast ball. I watched it head straight for the plate. I saw him go into a sudden crouch, and in the fraction of a second before he hit the ball I realized that he had anticipated the curve and was deliberately swinging low. I was still a little off balance from the pitch, but I managed to bring my glove hand up in front of my face just as he hit the ball. I saw it coming at me, and there was nothing I could do. It hit the finger section of my glove, deflected off, smashed into the upper rim of the left lens of my glasses, glanced off my forehead, and knocked me down. I scrambled around for it wildly, but by the time I got my hand on it Danny Saunders was standing safely on first.

I heard Mr. Galanter call time, and everyone on the field came racing over to me. My glasses lay shattered on the asphalt floor, and I felt a sharp pain in my left eye when I blinked. My wrist throbbed, and I could feel the bump coming up on my forehead. I looked over at first, but without my glasses Danny Saunders was only a blur. I imagined I could still see him grinning.

I saw Mr. Galanter put his face next to mine. It was sweaty and full of concern. I wondered what all the fuss was about. I had only lost a pair of glasses, and we had at least two more good pitchers on the team.

"Are you all right, boy?" Mr. Galanter was saying. He looked at my face and forehead. "Somebody wet a handkerchief with cold water!" he shouted. I wondered why he was shouting. His voice hurt my head and rang in my ears. I saw Davey Cantor run off, looking frightened. I heard Sidney Goldberg say something, but I couldn't make out his words. Mr. Galanter put his arm around my shoulders and walked me off the field. He sat me down on the bench next to the rabbi. Without my glasses everything more than about ten feet away from me was blurred. I blinked and wondered about the pain in my left eye. I heard voices and shouts, and then Mr. Galanter was putting a wet handkerchief on my head.

"You feel dizzy, boy?" he said.

I shook my head.

"You're sure now?"

"I'm all right," I said, and wondered why my voice sounded husky and why talking hurt my head.

"You sit quiet now," Mr. Galanter said. "You begin to feel dizzy, you let me know right away."

"Yes, sir," I said.

He went away. I sat on the bench next to the rabbi, who looked at me once, then looked away. I heard shouts in Yiddish. The pain in my left eye was so intense I could feel it in the base of my spine. I sat on the bench a long time, long enough to see us lose the game by a score of eight to seven, long enough to hear the yeshiva team shout with joy, long enough to begin to cry at the pain in my left eye, long enough for Mr. Galanter to come over to me at the end of the game, take one look at my face, and go running out of the yard to call a cab.

Sergio Ramírez was born in Masatepe, Nicaragua, in 1942. Trained as a lawyer, he served for a time in Costa Rica as the Secretary General of the Council of Central American Universities. From 1973 through 1975 he lived in West Berlin on a writing scholarship and produced the novel *To Bury Our Fathers*, a panoramic story of Nicaraguan history that established him as that country's leading writer of prose.

In 1978 Dr. Ramírez returned home as leader of the ''Group of Twelve,'' a body of influential civilians who gave open support to the Sandinista National Liberation Front against the Somoza dictatorship. After the revolution, he became a civilian member of the governing Sandinista junta, and in 1984 he was elected vice president of Nicaragua.

It is a country with a national passion for baseball, and this is not the only Ramírez story on that subject. But it may be the best. It was written in 1967.

# The Centerfielder

## SERGIO RAMÍREZ *translated by* NICK CAISTOR

THE FLASHLIGHT picked out one prisoner after another until it came to rest on a bed where a man was asleep, his back to the door. His bare torso glistened with sweat.

''That's him, open up,'' said the guard, peering through the bars.

The warder's key hung from a length of electric cable he used as a belt. It grated in the rusty lock. Inside, the guards beat their rifle butts on the bedframe until the man struggled to his feet, shielding his eyes from the glare.

''Get up, you're wanted.''

He was shivering with cold as he groped for his shirt, even though the heat had been unbearable all night, and the prisoners were sleeping in their underpants or stark naked. The only slit in the wall was so high up that the air never circulated much below the ceiling. He found his shirt, and poked his feet into his laceless shoes.

''Get a move on!'' the guard said.

''I'm coming, can't you see?''

''Don't get smart with me, or else . . .''

''Or else what?''

''You know what else!''

The guard stood to one side to let him out of the cell. ''Walk, don't talk,'' he snapped, jabbing him in the ribs with the rifle. The man flinched at the cold metal.

They emerged into the yard. Down by the far wall, the leaves of almond trees glittered in the moonlight. It was midnight, and the slaughtering of animals had begun in the next-door abattoir. The breeze carried a smell of blood and dung.

What a perfect field for baseball! The prisoners must make up teams to play, or take on the off-duty guards. The dugout would be the wall, which left about three hundred and fifty feet from home plate to centerfield. You'd have to field a hit from there running backwards toward the almond trees. When you picked up the ball the diamond would seem far away; the shouts for you to throw would be muffled by the distance; the batter would be rounding second base—and then I'd reach up, catch a branch, and swing myself up. I'd stretch forward, put my hands carefully between the broken bottles on the top of the wall, then edge over with my feet. I'd jump down, ignoring the pain as I crashed into the heap of garbage, bones, bits of horn, broken chairs, tin cans, rags, newspapers, dead vermin. Then I'd run on, tearing myself on thistles, stumbling into a drain of filthy water, but running on and on, as the dry crack of rifles sounded far behind me.

''Halt! Where d'you think you're going?''

''To piss, that's all.''

''Scared are you?''

It is almost identical to the square back home, with the rubber trees growing right by the church steps. I was the only one on our team who had a real leather glove: all the others had to catch barehanded. I'd be out there fielding at six in the evening when it was so dark I could hardly see the ball. I could catch them like doves in my hand, just by the sound.

"Here he is, Captain," the guard called, poking his head around a half-open door. From inside came the steady hum of air conditioning.

"Bring him in, then leave us."

He felt immediately trapped in this bare, whitewashed room. Apart from a chair in the center, and the captain's desk up against the far wall, the only adornments were a gilt-framed portrait and a calendar with red and blue numbers. To judge by the fresh plaster, the air conditioning had only recently been installed.

"What time were you picked up?" the captain asked, without looking up.

He stood there at a loss for a reply, wishing with all his heart that the question had been aimed at somebody else—perhaps at someone hiding under the table.

"Are you deaf—I'm talking to you. What time were you taken prisoner?"

"Sometime after six, I reckon," he mumbled, so softly he was convinced the captain hadn't heard him.

"Why do you think it was after six? Can't you tell me the exact time?"

"I don't have a watch, sir, but I'd already eaten, and I always eat at six."

Come and eat, Ma would shout from the sidewalk outside the house. Just one more inning, I'd say, then I'll be there. But son, it's dark already, how can you see to play? I'm coming, there's only one inning left. The violin and the harmonium would be tuning up for Mass in the church as the ball flew safely into my hands for the last out. We'd won yet again.

"What job do you do?"

"I'm a cobbler."

"Do you work in a shop?"

"No, I do repairs at home."

"You used to be a baseball player, didn't you?"

"Yes, once upon a time."

"And you were known as 'Whiplash' Parrales, weren't you?"

"Yes, they called me that because of the way I threw the ball in."

"And you were in the national team that went to Cuba?"

"That's right, twenty years ago. I went as center-fielder."

"But they kicked you out . . ."

"When we got back."

"You made quite a name for yourself with that arm of yours." The captain's angry stare soon dashed the smile from Parrales' lips.

The best piece of fielding I ever did was at home

when I caught a fly ball on the steps of the church itself. I took it with my back to the bases, but fell sprawling on my face and split my tongue. Still, we won the game and the team carried me home in triumph. My mother left her tortilla dough and came to care for my wound. She was sorry and proud at the same time: "Do you have to knock your brains out to prove you're a real sport?"

"Why did they kick you off the team?"

"On account of my dropping a fly and us losing the game."

"In Cuba?"

"We were playing Aruba. I bungled it, they got two runs, and we'd lost."

"Several of you were booted out, weren't you?"

"The fact is, we all drank a lot, and you can't do that in baseball."

"Aha!"

He wanted to ask if he could sit down because his shins were aching so, but didn't dare move an inch. Instead he stood stock still, as though his shoes were glued to the floor.

The captain laboriously wrote out something. He finally lifted his head, and Parrales could see the red imprint of a cap across his forehead.

"Why did they bring you in?"

He shrugged and stared at him blankly.

"Well, why?"

"No," he answered.

"No, what?"

"No, I don't know."

"Aha, so you don't know."

"No."

"I've got your file here," the captain said, flourishing a folder. "Shall I read you a few bits so you can learn about yourself?" He stood up.

From centerfield you can barely hear the ball smack the catcher's mitt. But when the batter connects, the sound travels clearly and all your senses sharpen to follow the ball. As it flies through the distance to my loving hands, I wait patiently, dancing beneath it until finally I clasp it as though I'm making a nest for it.

"At five p.m. on July 28th a green canvas-topped jeep drew up outside your house. Two men got out: one was dark, wore khaki trousers, and sun glasses. The other was fair-skinned, wore bluejeans and a straw hat. The one with dark glasses was carrying a PamAm dufflebag; the other had an army backpack. They went into your house, and didn't come out again until ten o'clock. They didn't have their bags with them."

"The one with the glasses . . . ," nervous, he choked on endless saliva, "he was my son, the one in glasses."

"I know that."

Again there was silence. Parrales' feet were perspiring

inside his shoes, making them as wet as if he had just crossed a stream.

"The bag contained ammunition for a fixed machine gun, and the rucksack was full of fuses. When had you last seen your son before that?"

"Not for months," he murmured.

"Speak up, I can't hear you."

"Months—I don't remember how many, but several months. He quit his job at the ropeworks one day, and we didn't see him again after that."

"Weren't you worried about him?"

"Of course—he's my son, after all. We asked, made official enquiries, but got nowhere." Parrales pushed his false teeth back into place, worried in case the plate worked loose.

"Did you know he was in the mountains with the rebels?"

"We did hear rumors."

"So when he turned up in the jeep, what did you think?"

"That he was coming home. But all he did was say hello, then leave again a few hours later."

"And ask you to look after his things?"

"Yes, he said he'd send for them."

"Oh, he did, did he?"

The captain pulled more purple-typed sheets out of the folder. He sifted through them, then laid one out on the desk.

"It says here that for three months you were handling ammunition, firearms, fuses and subversive literature, and that you let enemies of the government sleep in your house."

Parrales said nothing. He took out a handkerchief to blow his nose. He looked gaunt and shrunken in the lamplight, as though already reduced to a skeleton.

"And you weren't aware of a thing, were you?"

"You know what sons are."

"Sons of bitches, you mean."

Parrales stared down at the protruding tongues and mud caking his tattered shoes.

"How long is it since you last saw your son?"

He looked the captain full in the face. "You know he's been killed, so why ask me that?"

The last inning of the game against Aruba, zero to zero, two outs, and the white ball was floating gently home to my hands as I waited, arms outstretched; we were about to meet for ever when the ball clipped the back of my hand, I tried to scoop it up, but it bounced to the ground—far off I could see the batter sliding home, and all was lost. Ma, I needed warm water on my wounds, like you always knew, I was always brave out on the field, even ready to die.

"Sometimes I'd like to be kind, but it's impossible," the captain said, advancing around the desk. He tossed the folder back into the drawer, and turned to switch off the air conditioning. Again the room was plunged into silence. He pulled a towel from a hook and draped it about his shoulders.

"Sergeant!" he shouted.

The sergeant stood to attention in the doorway. He led the prisoner out, then reappeared almost immediately.

"What am I to put in the report?"

"He was a baseball player, so make up anything you like. Say he was playing with the other prisoners, that he was centerfielder and chased a hit down to the wall, then climbed up an almond tree and jumped over the wall. Put down that we shot him as he was escaping across the slaughterhouse yard."

This game, the record-breaking fifth no-hitter of Nolan Ryan's career, happened also to be the NBC *Game of the Week* on TV. Nice.

# 1981:
## Houston Astros 5,
## Los Angeles Dodgers 0

### JOSEPH REICHLER

SEPTEMBER 26, 1981, Nolan Ryan had the stamina, the heart, and the marvelous talent to shackle a Dodger offense rated best in the National League. For nine innings, he walked 3, struck out 11, and needed one out-of-the-ordinary defensive play from his Astro teammates to be the first major league pitcher to achieve a fifth no-hitter.

In the Houston Astrodome, 32,115 onlookers were cheering Ryan with each succeeding out, sensing they might be part of baseball history in the making. Only one Astro player was unflappable before and after the last out, securing the record-breaking fifth.

"I don't get emotional about these things anymore," Nolan Ryan explained. "This is something I've wanted for a long time, but I've been too close too many times in the late innings. To tell you the truth, I'd about given up on ever getting another. I've had a few no-hitters going into the seventh and lost them. I was beginning to think I'd lost the stamina for a fifth."

In historical fact, it was in the seventh inning that Terry Puhl made a running catch near the right-center-field wall to gather in Mike Scioscia's long drive and save Nolan's no-hitter. Final score: Houston 5, Los Angeles 0.

Ryan began his string of no-hitters early in the 1970s, notching four in a three-year span. It took another six years to get the one that became the new record, putting him one game ahead of Sandy Koufax, with whom he had shared the record of four. (It might be noted in passing that Ryan also has pitched seven one-hit ball games.)

Pitching this fifth no-hitter offered Ryan other satisfactions. His victims were the Dodgers, who had lost to him only one time in nine previous decisions. In two Astro seasons, he had not had one win over Los

Angeles. This day, the game was being nationally televised and his wife, Ruth, and his mother were in the stands.

Ryan also was able to relish the win as a native of Texas who had come home in the winter of 1979, signing on with the Astros as a free agent. When he signed, it was for the richest sum in baseball history—a four-year pact at $1.125 million per season. Sceptics quickly pointed to his .500 won-and-lost record and wondered whether he was worth the money. True, Ryan owned all kinds of strikeout records, but his career won-and-lost record was 188–174. He also held the unenviable record as baseball's wildest pitcher, with 1,809 bases on balls.

In his first year with the Astros in 1980, Ryan struggled to an 11–10 record and a 3.35 earned run average. In 1981, however, he had one of his best seasons. He recorded 11 wins against 5 losses and a league-leading 1.69 ERA. When he fanned 11 Dodgers on September 26, it was the one-hundred-and-thirty-fifth game in which he had struck out 10 or more.

"I know the National League batters better now," Ryan explained. "I know which pitch to throw to which hitters and where to throw. It means I'm more relaxed out on the mound and more confident."

At 34, Ryan had just about given up hope of ever achieving another no-hitter. "I never envisioned one that day, that's for sure," he recalled. "My back was hurting and I didn't have any rhythm in the early innings."

Nolan issued all three walks in the first three innings, as he struggled with his control. He also uncorked a wild pitch and was continually behind on the count. In the fourth, pitching coach Mel Wright came to the mound to suggest that he might be overstriding. Whatever the reason, Ryan found the groove and not another Dodger reached base. He retired the last 19 batters.

"I let up a little in the late innings," Ryan said. "I didn't get so many strikeouts (ten in the first six innings, only one in the final three) but I had better control."

He certainly didn't let up in the ninth. He threw three straight strikes past leadoff pinch-hitter Reggie Smith. The last was a 97-mile-an-hour fastball. He induced Ken Landreaux to bounce out to the first baseman Denny Walling for the second out. Dusty Baker, a .322 hitter and a clutch performer, represented the last challenge. Ryan's first two pitches were out of the strike zone. The next was a curve. Baker bounced it feebly to Art Howe at third base, whose toss to first for the final out touched off a mob scene on the mound.

## JOHN GALLAGHER

This account was done for inclusion in a splendid collection called *The Ultimate Baseball Book,* which was published in 1979.

# Up from the Minors in Montreal

## MORDECAI RICHLER

PRONOUNCING ON Montreal, my Montreal, Casey Stengel once said, "Well, you see they have these polar bears up there and lots of fellows trip over them trying to run the bases and they're never much good anymore except for hockey or hunting deer."

Alas, we have no polar bears up here, but kids can usually heave snowballs at the outfielders at the opening game of the season, and should the World Series ever dare venture this far north, it is conceivable that a game could be called because of a blizzard. Something else. In April, the loudest cheers in the ball park tend to come when nothing of any consequence seems to have happened on the field, understandably baffling the players on visiting teams. These cheers spring from fans who sit huddled with transistor radios clapped to their ears and signify that something of importance has happened, albeit out of town, where either Guy Lafleur or Pierre Mondou has just scored in a Stanley Cup play-off game.

Baseball remains a popular game here, in spite of the Expos, but hockey is the way of life.

Montreal, it must be understood, is a city unlike any other in Canada. Or, come to think of it, the National League. On the average, eight feet of snow is dumped on us each winter and, whatever the weather, we can usually count on three bank robberies a day here.

This is the city of wonders that gave you Expo in 1967, the baseball Expos a couple of years later and, in 1976, the Olympic Games, its legacy, among other amazing artifacts, a stadium that can seat or intern, as some have it, 60,000 baseball fans. I speak of the monstrous Big O, where our inept Expos disport themselves in summer, their endearing idea of loading the bases being to have two of their runners on second. Hello, hello. Their notion of striking fear into the heart of the opposition being to confront them with muscle, namely one of their pinch-hitting behemoths coming off the bench: group average, .135.

Major league baseball, like the Olympics and the Big

O itself, was brought to this long suffering city through the machinations of our very own Artful Dodger, Mayor Jean Drapeau.

Bringing us the Games, he assured Montrealers that it would be as difficult for the Olympics to cost us money as it would be for a man to have a baby. He estimated the total cost of all facilities at $62.2 million but, what with inflation and unfavorable winds, his calculations fell somewhat short of the mark. Counting stationery and long distance calls, the final cost was $1.2 billion. Never mind. To this day our ebullient mayor doesn't allow that the Games were run at a loss. Rather, as he has put it to the rest of us, there has been a gap between costs and revenue. And, considering the spiffy facilities we have been left with, it would be churlish of us to complain.

Ah, the Big O. The largest, coldest slab of poured concrete in Canada. In a city where we endure seven punishing months of winter and spring comes and goes in an afternoon, it is Drapeau's triumph to have provided us with a partially roofed-over $520 million stadium, where the sun never shines on the fans. Tim Burke, one of the liveliest sportswriters in town, once said to me, "You know, there are lots of summer afternoons when I feel like taking in a ball game, but I think, hell, who wants to sit out there in the dark."

"Shivering in the dark" might be more accurate, watching the boys lose line drives in the seams of the artificial turf.

"The outfield," another wag remarked, "looks just like the kind of thing my aunt used to wear."

Furthermore, come cap day or bat night ours is the only park in the National League that fills a social office, letting the poor know where to get off, which is to say, the scruffy kids in the bleachers are beyond the pale. They don't qualify.

It's a shame, because the Expos, admittedly major league in name only, came to a town rich in baseball history and, to begin with, we were all charged with hope. In their opening game, on April 9, 1969, the Expos took the Mets 11–10 at Shea Stadium, collecting three homers and five doubles. Five days later, the 29,184 fans who turned up for the home opener were electrified by an announcement over the public address system. "When the Expos play a doubleheader," we were informed, "the second game will go the full nine innings, not seven."

Those of us old enough to remember baseball's glory here, the Montreal Royals of the old International League, nodded our heads, impressed. This was the big time. "Montreal," said Warren Giles, president of the National League, "is a growing and vibrant city." Yessirree. And we hollered and stamped our feet as our champions took to the field under the grim gaze of manager Gene Mauch, who had the look of a Marine drill sergeant.

I still have that incomparably bubbly opening day program, *Votre première équipe des ligues majeures*, Vol. 1, No. 1. *Publié par Club de Baseball Montreal Ltée*. "The Expos believe they landed a real prize when they snatched Gary Sutherland from the Philadelphia Phillies. Big things are expected from John Bateman, the former Houston Astros' fine receiver. Bob Bailey impressed everybody with his tremendous hustle. Ty Cline is a two-way player. 'In the field,' said Larry Shepard, manager of the Pittsburgh Pirates, 'Don Bosch can be compared with none other than Willie Mays.' Larry Jaster has youth on his side. This may be the year Don Shaw comes into his own. Angel Hermoso is one of the fine young Expo prospects the scouts have hung a 'can't miss' label on. On a given day, Mike Wegener, only 22, can throw with the best. Don Hahn was a standout performer during spring training. Bob Reynolds' main forte is a blistering fastball. Expansion could be 'just what the doctor ordered' for Coco Laboy."

To be fair, the original Expos included Rusty Staub, sweet Mack Jones and Bill Stoneman, a surprisingly effective player who pitched two no-hitters before his arm gave out. Manny Mota, another original draft choice, was one of the first to be sent packing by a management that was to become celebrated for its lame-headed dealings, its most spectacular blunder being a trade that sent Ken Singleton and Mike Torrez to Baltimore for a sore-armed Dave McNally and a totally ineffective Rich Coggins. It should also be noted that the Expos did take their home opener, defeating the Cardinals 8–7, and that tiny parc Jarry, where they were to play, futile in their fashion, for another eight years, was a charming, intimate stadium with the potential to become another Fenway Park.

Opening day, I recognized many of the plump faces in the box seats on the first-base line. Among them were some of the nervy kids who used to skip school with me

on weekday afternoons to sit in the left-field bleachers of Delormier Downs, cheering on the Royals and earning nickels fetching hot dogs for strangers. Gone were the AZA windbreakers, the bubble gum, the scuffed running shoes, the pale wintry faces. These men came bronzed to the ball park from their Florida condominiums. Now they wore foulards and navy blue blazers with brass buttons; they carried Hudson's Bay blankets in plastic cases for their bejeweled wives; and they sucked on Monte Cristos, mindful not to spill ashes on their Gucci sandals. Above all, they radiated pleasure in their own accomplishments and the occasion. And why not? This was an event and there they were, inside, looking out at last, right on the first-base line. Look at me. "Give it some soul, Mack," one of them shouted.

An article in that memorable opening day program noted that while the province of Quebec had never been known as a hotbed of major league talent, we had nevertheless produced a few ballplayers, among them pitchers Claude Raymond and Ron Piché, and that three more native sons, Roland Gladu, Jean-Pierre Roy and Stan Bréard had once played for another ball club here, the Montreal Royals.

O, I remember the Royals, yes indeed, and if they played in a Montreal that was not yet growing and vibrant, it was certainly a place to be cherished.

Betta Dodd, "The Girl in Cellophane," was stripping at the Gayety, supported by 23 Kuddling Kuties. Cantor Moishe Oysher, The Master Singer of his People, was appearing at His Majesty's. The Johnny Holmes Band, playing at Victoria Hall, featured Oscar Peterson; and a sign in the corner cigar-and-soda warned Ziggy Halprin, Yossel Hoffman and me that

LOOSE TALK COSTS LIVES!
Keep It Under
Your
STETSON

I first became aware of the Royals in 1943. Our country was already 76 years old, I was merely 12, and we were both at war.

MAY U BOAT SINKINGS EXCEED REPLACEMENTS;
KING DECORATES 625 CANADIANS ON BIRTHDAY

Many of our older brothers and cousins were serving overseas. Others on the street were delighted to discover they suffered from flat feet or, failing that, arranged to have an eardrum punctured by a specialist in such matters.

R.A.F. HITS HARD AT COLOGNE AND HAMBURG
2,000 Tons of Bombs
Rain on Rhine City

On the home front, sacrifices were called for. On St. Urbain Street, where we served, collecting salvage, we had to give up American comic books for the duration. Good-bye, Superman, so long, Captain Marvel. Instead, we were obliged to make do with shoddy Canadian imitations printed in black and white. And such was the shortage of ballplayers that the one-armed outfielder, Pete Gray, got to play for the Three Rivers club on his way to the Browns and French Canadians, torn from the local sandlots, actually took to the field for our very own Royals: Bréard, Gladu, Roy.

Even in fabled Westmount, where the very rich were rooted, things weren't the same anymore. H.R., emporium to the privileged, enjoined Westmount to "take another step in further aid of the Government's all out effort to defeat aggression!"

HOLT RENFREW ANNOUNCE THAT BEGINNING JUNE FIRST <u>NO DELIVERIES</u> OF MERCHANDISE WILL BE MADE ON <u>WEDNESDAYS</u>
This forethought will help H.R. to save many gallons of gasoline . . . and many a tire . . . for use by the government. Moreover, will it not thrill you to think that the non-delivery of your dress on Wednesday will aid in the delivery of a 'block-buster' over the Ruhr . . . Naples . . . Berlin . . . and many other places of enemy entrenchment?

Our parents feared Hitler and his Panzers, but Ziggy, Yossel and I were in terror of Branch Rickey and his scouts.

Nineteen thirty-nine was not only the date we had gone to war, it was also the year the management of the Royals signed a contract with Mr. Rickey, making them the number one farm club of the Brooklyn Dodgers. This dealt us young players of tremendous promise, but again and again, come the Dodgers' late-summer pennant drive, the best of the bunch were harvested by the parent team. Before we had even reached the age of puberty, Ziggy, Yossel and I had learned to love with caution. If after the first death there is no other, an arguable notion, I do remember that each time one of our heroes abandoned us for Ebbets Field, it stung us badly. We hated Mr. Rickey for his voracious appetite. "There has been no mention officially that the Dodgers will be taking Flowers," Lloyd MacGowan wrote in the *Star* on a typical day, "but Rickey was in Buffalo to watch the team yesterday. The Dodgers can't take Flowers without sending down a flinger, but chances are the replacement for the burly lefty will hardly be adequate."

The International League, as we knew it in the forties, its halcyon years, was Triple A and comprised of eight teams: Montreal, Toronto, Syracuse, Jersey City, Newark, Rochester, Baltimore and Buffalo. Newark was the number one farm team of the Yankees and Jersey City filled the same office for the Giants. But organized baseball had actually come to Montreal in 1898, the Royals then fielding a team in the old Eastern League, taking the pennant in their inaugural year. In those days the Royals played in Atwater Park, which could seat 12,000, and from all accounts was a fine and intimate stadium, much like parc Jarry. During the 21 years the Royals played there they offered Montreal, as sportswriter Marc Thibault recently wrote, *"du baseball parfois excitant, plus souvent qu'autrement, assez détestable,"* the problem being the troubled management's need to sell off their most accomplished players for ready cash. Be that as it may, in 1914, long before we were to endure major league baseball in name only here, George Herman Ruth came to Atwater Park to pitch for the Baltimore Orioles. Two years later, the team folded, a casualty of World War I, and another 11 years passed before the Royals were resuscitated.

It was 1928 when George Tweedy "Miracle Man" Stallings bought the then-defunct Syracuse franchise and built Delormier Downs, a stadium with a 22,000 capacity, at the corner of Ontario and Delormier streets. An overflow crowd of 22,500, including Judge Kenesaw Mountain Landis, was at the opening game, which the Royals won, defeating the fearsome Reading Keystones, 7–4. Twelve months later Stallings died. In 1929, not a vintage year for the stock market, the Royals finished fourth. Two years later, Delormier Stadium, like just about everybody, was in deep trouble. There were tax arrears and a heavy bank debt to be settled. The original sponsors resigned.

In the autumn of 1931 a new company was formed by a triumvirate which included a man who had made millions in gas stations, the rambunctious, poker-playing J. Charles-Emile Trudeau, father of our present prime minister. Another associate of the newly-formed club, Frank "Shag" Shaughnessy, cunningly introduced the play-off system in 1933, and two years later became the club's general manager. In 1935, fielding a team that included Fresco Thompson, Jimmy Ripple and Del Bissonette, the Royals won their first pennant since 1898. However, they finished poorly in '37 and '38 and, the following year, Mr. Rickey surfaced, sending in Burleigh Grimes to look after his interests.

Redemption was at hand.

Bruno Betzel came in to manage the team in 1944, the year the nefarious Branch Rickey bought the Royals outright, building it into the most profitable club in all of minor league baseball, its fans loyal but understandably resentful of the head office's appetite, praying that this summer the Dodgers wouldn't falter in the stretch, sending down for fresh bats, strong arms, just when we needed them most.

The Royals finished first in 1945, and in '46 and '48 they won both the pennant and the Little World Series. They were to win the pennant again in '51 and '52, under Clay Hopper, and the Little World Series in '53, when they were managed by Walter Alston. The Royals fielded their greatest team in 1948, the summer young Duke Snider played here, appearing in 77 games before he was snatched by Mr. Rickey. Others on that memorable team included Don Newcombe, Al Gionfriddo, Jimmy Bloodworth, Bobby Morgan and Chuck Connors. The legendary Jackie Robinson and Roy Campanella had already come and gone.

Sam Jethroe was here in 1949 and two years later Junior Gilliam was at third and George Shuba hit 20 home runs. In 1952, our star pitcher was southpaw Tommy Lasorda, the self-styled Bob Feller of the International League. Lasorda pitched his last game for the Royals on July 4, 1960, against Rochester, which seemed to be hitting him at will. Reminiscing recently, Lasorda recalled, "I knew I was in trouble when I saw our manager's foot on the top of the dugout step. If the next guy gets on base, I'm going to be out of there. I turned my back to the hitter and looked up toward the sky. Lord, I said, this is my last game. Get me out of this jam. I make the next pitch and the guy at the plate hits the damnedest line drive you ever saw. Our third baseman, George Risley, gets the tips of his fingers on it but can't hang on. The ball bloops over his hand and our shortstop, Jerry Snyder, grabs it. He fires it to Harry Shewman at second base, who relays it to Jimmy Korada at first. Triple play."

A year later the Royals were dissolved and in 1971 the Delormier Stadium was razed to make way for the Pierre Dupuy School.

On weekday afternoons kids were admitted free into the left-field bleachers and by the third inning the more intrepid had worked their way down as far as the first-base line. Ziggy, Yossel and I would sit out there in the sun, cracking peanuts, nudging each other if a ball struck the Miss Sweet Caporal sign, hitting the young lady you-know-where. Another diversion was a porthole in the outfield wall. If a batter hit a ball through it, he was entitled to a two-year supply of Pal Blades. Heaven.

Sunday afternoons the Royals usually played to capacity crowds, but come the Little World Series fans lined up on the roof of the adjoining Grover Knit-To-Fit Building and temporary stands were set up and roped off in center field. Consequently, as my cousin Seymour who used to sit there liked to boast, "If I get hit on the

head, it's a ground rule home run." After the game, we would spill out of the stadium to find streetcars lined up for a half mile, waiting to take us home.

In 1945, the Royals acquired one of ours, their first Jewish player, Kermit Kitman, a William and Mary scholarship boy. Our loyalty to the team was redoubled. Kitman was a centerfielder and an opening day story in *La Presse* declared, "*Trois des meilleurs porte-couleurs du Montréal depuis l'ouverture de la saison ont été ses joueurs de champ: Gladu, Kitman et Yeager. Kitman a exécuté un catch sensationnel encore hier après-midi sur le long coup de Torres à la 8e manche. On les verra tous trois à l'oeuvre cet après-midi contre le Jersey-City lors du programme double de la 'Victoire' au stade de la Rue Delormier.*"

In his very first time at bat in that opening game against the Skeeters, Kitman belted a homer, something he would not manage again until August. Alas, in the later innings he also got doubled off second. After the game, when he ventured into a barbershop at the corner of St. Catherine and St. Urbain, a man in another chair studied him intently. "Aren't you Kermit Kitman?" he asked.

"Yeah," he allowed, grinning, remembering his homer.

"You son-of-a-bitch, you got doubled off second, it cost me five hundred bucks."

Lead-off hitter for the Royals, Kitman was entitled to lower berth one on all their road trips. Only 22 years old, but a college boy, he was paid somewhat better than most: $650 monthly for six months of the year. And if the Royals went all the way, winning the Little World Series, he could earn another $1,800. On the road, his hotel bill was paid and he and the other players were each allowed three bucks a day meal money.

There was yet another sea change in the summer of 1946. After scouting what were then called the Negro Leagues for more than a year, Mr. Rickey brought the first black player into organized baseball. So that spring the Royals could not train in the regular park in Daytona, which was segregated, but had to train in Kelly Field instead.

Actually, Jackie Robinson had been signed on October 23, 1945, in the offices of the Royals at Delormier Stadium, club president Hector Racine saying, "Robinson is a good ball player and comes highly recommended by the Brooklyn Dodgers. We paid him a good bonus to sign with our club."

The bonus was $3,500 and Robinson's salary was $600 monthly.

"One afternoon in Daytona," Kermit Kitman told me, "I was lead-off hitter and quickly singled. Robinson came up next, laying down a sacrifice bunt and running to first. Stanky, covering the sack, tagged him hard and jock-high. Robinson went down, taking a fist in the balls. He was mad as hell, you could see that, but Rickey had warned him, no fights. He got up, dusted himself off and said nothing. After the game, when he was resting, Stanky came over to apologize. He had been testing his temper, under orders from Rickey.''

Kitman, a good glove man, was an inadequate hitter. Brooklyn born, he never got to play there. Following the 1946 season he was offered a place on the roster of another team in the Dodger farm system, but elected to quit the game instead.

The 1946 season opened for the Royals on April 18, with a game in Jersey City. The AP dispatch for that day, printed in the Montreal *Gazette,* ran: ''The first man of his race to play in modern organized baseball smashed a three-run homer that carried 333 feet and added three singles to the Royals' winning 14–1 margin over Jersey City. Just to make it a full day's work, Robinson stole two bases, scored four times and batted in three runs. He was also charged with an error.''

Robinson led the International League in hitting that year with a .349 average. He hit three home runs, batted in 66 runs, stole 40 bases, scored 113 runs and fielded .985 at his second-base position. And, furthermore, Montreal adored him, as no other ballplayer who has been here before or since. No sooner did Robinson reach first base, on a hit or a walk, than the fans roared with joy and hope, our hearts going out to him as he danced up and down the base path, taunting the opposing pitcher with his astonishing speed.

We won the pennant that year and met the Louisville Colonels, another Dodger farm club, in the Little World Series. The series opened in Louisville, where Robinson endured a constant run of racial insults from the Colonels' dugout and was held to a mere single in two games. Montreal evened the series at home and returned to Delormier Downs for the seventh and deciding game. ''When they won it,'' Dick Bacon recently wrote, recalling that game in the 200th anniversary issue of the *Gazette,* ''Jackie was accorded an emotional send-off unseen before or since in this city.

''First they serenaded him in true French Canadien spirit with, *'Il a gagné ses Epaulettes,'* and then clamored for his reappearance on the field.

''When he finally came out for a curtain call, the fans mobbed him. They hugged him, kissed him, cried, cheered and pulled and tore at his uniform while parading him around the infield on their shoulders.

''With tears streaming down his face, Robinson finally begged off in order to shower, dress and catch a plane to the States. But the riot of joy wasn't over yet.

''When he emerged from the clubhouse, he had to bull his way through the waiting crowd outside the stadium. The thousands of fans chased him down Ontario Street for several blocks before he was rescued by a passing motorist and driven to his hotel.

''As one southern reporter from Louisville, Kentucky, was to write afterward:

'' 'It's probably the first time a white mob of rioters ever chased a Negro down the streets in love rather than hate.' ''

That was a long time ago.

I don't know whatever became of Red Durrett. Marvin Rackley, of whom Mr. Rickey once said, ''I can see him in a World Series, running and hitting,'' has also disappeared. Roland Gladu, who got to play 21 games with the old Boston Braves, failed to sign the major league skies with his ability. Robinson died in 1972 and in 1977 a plaque to his memory was installed in the chilly Big O. Jean-Pierre Roy now does the French-language broadcasts for the Expos and a graying but still impressive Duke Snider is also back, doing the color commentary for Expo games on CBC-TV, trying his best to be kind to an uninspired bunch without compromising himself.

The Expos have yet to play .500 ball or, since Mack Jones's brief sojourn here, come up with a player that the fans can warm to. But there is hope. Next year, or maybe five years from now, the Big O will be completed. The retractable roof will be set in place. And, in this city of endless winter and short hot summers, it will be possible to watch baseball played under a roof, on artificial grass, in an air-conditioned, possibly even centrally-heated, concrete tomb.

Progress.

This piece appeared in 1984.

# Monte Irvin

## RAY ROBINSON

On July 6, 1983—the 50th anniversary of baseball's first All-Star Game—Jim Rice of the Boston Red Sox was announced on television as the left fielder for the American League All-Star team. Then the left fielder for the 1933 American League team was announced. His name was Ben Chapman.

What irony, I thought. Chapman, the white Alabaman, who had baited and viciously jockeyed Jackie Robinson when Jackie arrived with the Brooklyn Dodgers in 1947, had now, a half-century later, been introduced along with a black man now playing his position.

My friend, Monte Irvin, who played left field with the New York Giants from 1949 to 1955, helped pave the way for the Jim Rices and so many other black players. Irvin, who retires this week after more than 45 years in the Negro leagues and the major leagues, including 15 years as a special assistant to the baseball commissioner, was not chosen to be the first black in baseball. Many, including Jackie Robinson's mentor, Branch Rickey, thought Monte might have been a better choice. Nor was Irvin a Robinson in temperament, manner or style. He did not "suffer that a hundred Hank Aaronses might bloom," as the author Wilfrid Sheed has written about Robinson.

But Monte, perhaps New York's pre-eminent baseball star following the ascension of Robinson (forgive me, Roy Campanella), brought his own sense of dignity, gentleness, kindness and purpose to what had previously been an all-white world.

Many old-time Giant fans will insist that Irvin only once violated his own sense of privacy to show emotion on a ball field. That was when he fouled out to Gil Hodges, the Dodgers' first baseman, in the ninth inning of the third 1951 National League playoff game, which was won minutes later for the Giants when Bobby Thomson hit his famous home run.

"I didn't throw my bat in anger, because I was never a bat-breaker," recalls Monte. "But I stood there, frustrated, trying to 'root' the ball into the stands and away from Hodges's glove. I kept urging it, with my shoulder and my heart. But it didn't help."

I first met Monte in 1954 at his liquor store in Brooklyn on the same afternoon that I first encountered Howard Cosell. Could anyone imagine two such entirely different men? Cosell was then Monte's lawyer, and he insisted on eavesdropping on the interview that I was doing with Monte, which evolved into an article for a sports magazine. Monte and I have been friends ever since.

Some years after Monte's big league career ended, following a season playing for the Chicago Cubs in 1956, I invited him to visit me with his family at my summer home on Fire Island. The word spread rapidly that the former Giant star was "on the beach." By midafternoon I had persuaded Monte that a bunch of clamorous kids, as well as more than a few worshipful adult fans, wanted to play "catch" with him. So, trailed by a passel of admirers in bathing suits, Monte paraded up to the sand dunes, like a Pied Piper, lugging my ancient black bat in his hands.

With his back to the dunes and facing the sparkling Atlantic (the tide was quite low that day, so a ball could be stroked some 250 feet or so toward the water without its retriever disappearing under the waves), Monte hit his inimitable scorching line drives off a bunch of frustrated batting practice pitchers, including myself. He kept hammering away for hours, as the kids yelled with delight, until, finally, the sun withered away and the blisters sprouted on the palms of his hands.

I cherish hundreds of images and memories connected with baseball. But none of them compare to those moments under a broiling Fire Island sun, with Monte cheerfully complying with the endless shouted requests of his spirited "outfielders."

The next day Monte informed us his watch was missing. We concluded that it had been dropped somewhere on the beach, during the batting session. Within minutes, almost every kid in town was alerted to Monte's misfortune, and a frantic search went on but to no avail.

When Monte returned to my house after the workout, he had removed his watch before showering, placing it on the ledge above the shower. I was surprised when my wife found it later, after Monte had left, for, like all of us in our family, including my two sons and daughter, she is a small woman, who would not think to reach above the shower cage to locate a person's watch. However, it had been an ordinary instinct for a 6-foot-1-inch man, such as Monte, to reach up, like a basketball dunker, and place it there.

In all the years I have known Monte Irvin I have never known him to express bitterness at his fate or for the intemperate actions of others. Yet, he could have been a man devoured by bitterness. After all, he had arrived with the Giants when he was already 30 years old, forfeiting at least a half-dozen productive baseball years. Then, he broke his ankle in a spring training game in 1952 and never again was able to play the way he did in 1951, when he batted .312 and led the National League in runs batted in with 121. Despite his relatively brief major league career, Monte won election to the Hall of Fame in 1973.

With his career over in 1956, he had to wait many disquieting years before baseball summoned him to a spot in the commissioner's office.

\*     \*     \*

Before his career materialized, Monte had been forced to turn down a football scholarship at the University of Michigan because his family couldn't afford the transportation expenses. Then, when playing for the Newark Eagles of the Negro National League, the owner of that club told him he should feel privileged to be able to play for the Eagles, even if only for a few dollars. (Imagine trying that line on any contemporary ballplayer.)

However, Monte is not a stoic, and he has never been insensitive to the indignities that he and others have suffered. He has often spoken privately about his "disappointments" concerning the actions of certain unthinking people.

One distressing story happened just a few years ago, when Monte was attending a Hall of Fame induction ceremony at Cooperstown, N.Y.

"We were posing for a group picture," Monte remembers, "when this great star, a guy I had once idolized, expressed his loud annoyance that there always seemed to be so 'many niggers' voted in every year. I was standing right behind him, but he seemed oblivious to my presence and didn't respect me or my feelings. How much respect could he have had for this wonderful game that made him what he is today?"

Now, at 65, Monte is going to live in Homosassa, Fla. He intends to do some fishing, play a little tennis and get in some shell-hunting.

And maybe he will find some pickup players for some baseball on the beach.

Of baseball and his boyhood, Philip Roth wrote, "I loved the game with all my heart." It was, among other things, the cement that bound a pluralistic society "together in common concerns, loyalties, rituals, enthusiasms, and antagonisms." Is it strange, then, that baseball should find its way so often into Roth's writings, or that he should write an entire book about it and name it *The Great American Novel*?

The answer to that question is no. And neither is it strange that the Ruppert Mundys, losingest team in the Patriot League, here find themselves in the city of Asylum (home of the Keepers, another P. League team), traveling to a real asylum for an exhibition game against the inmates.

# From *The Great American Novel*

## PHILIP ROTH

ONE SUNNY Saturday morning early in August, the Ruppert Mundys boarded a bus belonging to the mental institution and journeyed from their hotel in downtown Asylum out into the green Ohio countryside to the world-famous hospital for the insane, there to play yet another "away" game—a three-inning exhibition match against a team composed entirely of patients. The August visit to the hospital by a P. League team in town for a series against the Keepers was an annual event of great moment at the institution, and one that was believed to be of considerable therapeutic value to the inmates, particularly the sports-minded among them. Not only was it their chance to make contact, if only for an hour or so, with the real world they had left behind, but it was believed that even so brief a visit by famous big league ballplayers went a long way to assuage the awful sense such people have that they are odious and contemptible to the rest of humankind. Of course, the P. League players (who like all ballplayers despised any exhibition games during the course of the regular season) happened to find playing against the Lunatics, as they called them, a most odious business indeed; but as the General simply would not hear of abandoning a practice that brought public attention to the humane and compassionate side of a league that many still associated with violence and scandal, the tradition was maintained year after year, much to the delight of the insane, and the disgust of the ballplayers themselves.

The chief psychiatrist at the hospital was a Dr. Traum, a heavyset gentleman with a dark chin beard, and a pronounced European accent. Until his arrival in America in the thirties, he had never even heard of baseball, but in that Asylum was the site of a major league ball park, as well as a psychiatric hospital, it was not long before the doctor became something of a student of the game. After all, one whose professional life involved ruminating upon the extremes of human behavior, had certainly to sit up and take notice when a local fan decided to make his home atop a flagpole until the Keepers snapped a losing streak, or when an Asylum man beat his wife to death with a hammer for calling the Keepers "bums" just like himself. If the doctor did not, strictly speaking, become an ardent Keeper fan, he did make it his business to read thoroughly in the literature of the national pastime, with the result that over the years more than one P. League manager had to compliment the bearded Berliner on his use of the hit-and-run, and the uncanny ability he displayed at stealing signals during their annual exhibition game.

Despite the managerial skill that Dr. Traum had developed over the years through his studies, his team proved no match for the Mundys that morning. By August of 1943, the Mundys weren't about to sit back and take it on the chin from a German-born baseball manager and a team of madmen; they had been defeated and disgraced and disgraced and defeated up and down the league since the season had begun back in April, and it was as though on the morning they got out to the insane asylum grounds, all the wrath that had been seething in them for months now burst forth, and nothing, but nothing, could have prevented them from grinding the Lunatics into dust once the possibility for victory presented itself. Suddenly, those '43 flops started looking and sounding like the scrappy, hustling, undefeatable Ruppert teams of Luke Gofannon's day—and this despite the fact that it took nearly an hour to complete a single inning, what with numerous delays and interruptions caused by the Lunatics' style of play. Hardly a moment passed that something did not occur to offend the professional dignity of a big leaguer, and yet, through it all, the Mundys on both offense and defense managed to seize hold of every Lunatic mistake and convert it to their advantage. Admittedly, the big right-hander who started for the institution team was fast and savvy enough to hold the Mundy power in check, but playing just the sort of heads-up, razzle-dazzle baseball that used to characterize the Mundy teams of yore, they were able in their first at bat to put together a scratch hit by Astarte, a bunt by Nickname, a base on balls to Big John, and two Lunatic errors, to score three runs—their biggest inning of the year, and the first Mundy runs to cross the plate in sixty consecutive innings, which was not a record only because they had gone sixty-seven innings without scoring earlier in the season.

When Roland Agni, of all people, took a called third strike to end their half of the inning, the Mundys rushed off the bench like a team that smelled World Series loot. "We was due!" yelped Nickname, taking the peg from Hothead and sweeping his glove over the bag—"Nobody gonna stop us now, babe! We was due! We was *over*due!" Then he winged the ball over to where Deacon Demeter stood on the mound, grinning. "Three big ones for you, Deke!" Old Deacon, the fifty-year-old iron-man starter of the Mundy staff, already a twenty-game loser with two months of the season still to go, shot a string of tobacco juice over his left shoulder to ward off evil spirits, stroked the rabbit's foot that hung on a chain around his neck, closed his eyes to mumble something ending with "Amen," and then stepped up on the rubber to face the first patient. Deacon was a preacher back home, as gentle and kindly a man as you would ever want to bring your problems to, but up on the hill he was all competitor, and had been for thirty years now. "When the game begins," he used to say back in his heyday, "charity ends." And so it was that when he saw the first Lunatic batter digging in as though he owned the batter's box, the Deke decided to take Hothead's advice and stick the first pitch in his ear, just to show the little nut who was boss. The Deacon had taken enough insults that year for a fifty-year-old man of the cloth!

Not only did the Deke's pitch cause the batter to go

flying back from the plate to save his skin, but next thing everyone knew the lead-off man was running for the big brick building with the iron bars on its windows. Two of his teammates caught him down the right-field line and with the help of the Lunatic bullpen staff managed to drag him back to home plate. But once there they couldn't get him to take hold of the bat; every time they put it into his hands, he let it fall through to the ground. By the time the game was resumed, with a 1 and 0 count on a new lead-off hitter, one not quite so cocky as the fellow who'd stepped up to bat some ten minutes earlier, there was no doubt in anyone's mind that the Deke was in charge. As it turned out, twice in the inning Mike Rama had to go sailing up into the wall to haul in a long line drive, but as the wall was padded, Mike came away unscathed, and the Deacon was back on the bench with his three-run lead intact.

"We're on our way!" cried Nickname. "We are on our God damn way!"

Hothead too was dancing with excitement; cupping his hands to his mouth, he shouted across to the opposition, "Just watch you bastards go to pieces now!"

And so they did. The Deke's pitching and Mike's fielding seemed to have shaken the confidence of the big Lunatic right-hander whose fastball had reined in the Mundys in the first. To the chagrin of his teammates, he simply would not begin to pitch in the second until the umpire stopped staring at him.

"Oh, come on," said the Lunatic catcher, "he's not staring at *you*. Throw the ball."

"I tell you, he's right behind you and he is too staring. Look you, I see you there behind that mask. What is it you want from me? What is it you think you're looking at, anyway?"

The male nurse, in white half-sleeve shirt and white trousers, who was acting as the plate umpire, called out to the mound, "Play ball now. Enough of that."

"Not until you come out from there."

"Oh, pitch, for Christ sake," said the catcher.

"Not until that person stops staring."

Here Dr. Traum came off the Lunatic bench and started for the field, while down in the Lunatic bullpen a left-hander got up and began to throw. Out on the mound, with his hands clasped behind his back and rocking gently to and fro on his spikes, the doctor conferred with the pitcher. Formal European that he was, he wore, along with his regulation baseball shoes, a dark three-piece business suit, a stiff collar, and a tie.

"What do you think the ol' doc's tellin' that boy?" Bud Parusha asked Jolly Cholly.

"Oh, the usual," the old-timer said. "He's just calmin' him down. He's just askin' if he got any good duck shootin' last season."

It was five full minutes before the conference between the doctor and the pitcher came to an end with the doctor asking the pitcher to hand over the ball. When the pitcher vehemently refused, it was necessary for the doctor to snatch the ball out of his hand; but when he motioned down to the bullpen for the left-hander, the pitcher suddenly reached out and snatched the ball back. Here the doctor turned back to the bullpen and this time motioned for the left-hander *and* a right-hander. Out of the bullpen came two men dressed like the plate umpire in white half-sleeve shirts and white trousers. While they took the long walk to the mound, the doctor made several unsuccessful attempts to talk the pitcher into relinquishing the ball. Finally the two men arrived on the mound and before the pitcher knew what had happened, they had unfurled a straitjacket and wrapped it around him.

"Guess he wanted to stay in," said Jolly Cholly, as the pitcher kicked out at the doctor with his feet.

The hundred Lunatic fans who had gathered to watch the game from the benches back of the foul screen behind home plate, and who looked in their street clothes as sane as any baseball crowd, rose to applaud the pitcher as he left the field, but when he opened his mouth to acknowledge the ovation, the two men assisting him in his departure slipped a gag over his mouth.

Next the shortstop began to act up. In the first inning it was he who had gotten the Lunatics out of trouble with a diving stab of a Bud Parusha liner and a quick underhand toss that had doubled Wayne Heket off third. But now in the top of the second, though he continued to gobble up everything hit to the left of the diamond, as soon as he got his hands on the ball he proceeded to stuff it into his back pocket. Then, assuming a posture of utter nonchalance, he would start whistling between his teeth and scratching himself, as though waiting for the action to *begin*. In that it was already very much underway, the rest of the Lunatic infield would begin screaming at him to take the ball out of his pocket and make the throw to first. "What?" he responded, with an innocent smile. "The ball!" they cried. "Yes, what about it?" "Throw it!" "But I don't have it." "You *do!*" they would scream, converging upon him from all points of the infield, "You do too!" "Hey, leave me alone," the shortstop cried, as they grabbed and pulled at his trousers. "Hey, cut that out—get your hands *out* of there!" And when at last the ball was extracted from where he himself had secreted it, no one could have been more surprised. "Hey, the *ball*. Now who put that there? Well, what's everybody looking at *me* for? Look, this must be some guy's idea of a joke . . . Well, Christ, *I* didn't do it."

Once the Mundys caught on, they were quick to capitalize on this unexpected weakness in the Lunatic defense, pushing two more runs across in the second on two consecutive ground balls to short—both beaten out for hits while the shortstop grappled with the other infielders—a sacrifice by Mike Rama, and a fly to short center that was caught by the fielder who then just stood there holding it in his glove, while Hothead, who was the runner on second, tagged up and hobbled to third, and then, wooden leg and all, broke for home, where he scored with a head-first slide, the only kind he could negotiate. As it turned out, the slide wasn't even necessary, for the center-fielder was standing in the precise spot where he had made the catch—and the ball was still in his glove.

With the bases cleared, Dr. Traum asked for time and walked out to center. He put a hand on the shoulder of the mute and motionless fielder and talked to him in a quiet voice. He talked to him steadily for fifteen minutes, their faces only inches apart. Then he stepped aside, and the center-fielder took the ball from the pocket of his glove and threw a perfect strike to the catcher, on his knees at the plate some two hundred feet away.

"Wow," said Bud Parusha, with ungrudging admiration, "now, that fella has a arm on him."

"Hothead," said Cholly, mildly chiding the catcher, "he woulda had you by a country mile, you know, if only he'd a throwed it."

But Hot, riding high, hollered out, "Woulda don't count, Charles—it's dudda what counts, and I dud it!"

Meanwhile Kid Heket, who before this morning had not been awake for two consecutive innings in over a month, continued to stand with one foot up on the bench, his elbow on his knee and his chin cupped contemplatively in his palm. He had been studying the opposition like this since the game had gotten underway, "You know somethin'," he said, gesturing toward the field, "those fellas ain't thinkin'. No sir, they just ain't usin' their heads."

"We got 'em on the run, Wayne!" cried Nickname. "They don't know *what* hit 'em! Damn, ain't nobody gonna stop us from here on out!"

Deacon was hit hard in the last of the second, but fortunately for the Mundys, in the first two instances the batsman refused to relinquish the bat and move off home plate, and so each was thrown out on what would have been a base hit, right-fielder Parusha to first-baseman Baal; and the last hitter, who drove a tremendous line drive up the alley in left center, ran directly from home to third and was tagged out sitting on the bag with what he took to be a triple, and what would have been one too, had he only run around the bases and gotten to third in the prescribed way.

The quarrel between the Lunatic catcher and the relief pitcher began over what to throw Big John Baal, the lead-off hitter in the top of the third.

"Uh-uh," said the Lunatic pitcher, shaking off the first signal given by his catcher, while in the box, Big John took special pleasure in swishing the bat around menacingly.

"Nope," said the pitcher to the second signal.

His response to the third was an emphatic, "N-O!"

And to the fourth, he said, stamping one foot, "Definitely *not!*"

When he shook off a fifth signal as well, with a caustic, "Are you kidding? Throw him that and it's bye-bye ballgame," the catcher yanked off his mask and cried:

"And I suppose that's what I want, according to you! To lose! To go down in defeat! Oh, sure," the catcher whined, "what I'm doing, you see, is deliberately telling you to throw him the wrong pitch so I can have the wonderful pleasure of being on the losing team again. Oh brother!" His sarcasm spent, he donned his mask, knelt down behind the plate, and tried yet once more.

This time the pitcher had to cross his arms over his chest and look to the heavens for solace. "God give me strength," he sighed.

"In other words," the catcher screamed, "I'm wrong *again*. But then in your eyes I'm *always* wrong. Well, isn't that true? Admit it! Whatever signal I give is *bound* to be wrong. Why? Because *I'm* giving it! I'm daring to give *you* a signal! I'm daring to tell *you* how to pitch! I could kneel here signaling for the rest of my days, and you'd just stand there shaking them off and asking God to give you strength, *because I'm so wrong and so stupid and so hopeless and would rather lose than win!*"

When the relief pitcher, a rather self-possessed fellow from the look of it, though perhaps a touch perverse in his own way, refused to argue, the Lunatic catcher once again assumed his squat behind the plate, and proceeded to offer a seventh signal, an eighth, a ninth, a tenth, each and every one of which the pitcher rejected with a mild, if unmistakably disdainful, remark.

On the sixteenth signal, the pitcher just had to laugh. "Well, that one really takes the cake, doesn't it? That really took brains. Come over here a minute," he said to his infielders. "All right," he called back down to the catcher, "go ahead, show them your new brainstorm." To the four players up on the mound with him, the pitcher whispered, "Catch this," and pointed to the signal that the catcher, in his mortification, was continuing to flash from between his legs.

"Hey," said the Lunatic third-baseman, "that ain't even a finger, is it?"

"No," said the pitcher, "as a matter of fact, it isn't."

"I mean, it ain't got no nail on it, does it?"

"Indeed it has not."

"Why, I'll be darned," said the shortstop, "it's, it's his thingamajig."

"Precisely," said the pitcher.

"But what the hell is that supposed to mean?" asked the first-baseman.

The pitcher had to smile again. "What do you think? Hey, Doc," he called to the Lunatic bench, "I'm afraid my batterymate has misunderstood what's meant by an exhibition game. He's flashing me the signal to meet him later in the shower, if you know what I mean."

The catcher was in tears now. "He made me do it," he said, covering himself with his big glove, and in his shame, dropping all the way to his knees, "everything else I showed him wasn't *good* enough for him—no, he teases me, he taunts me—"

By now the two "coaches" (as they were euphemistically called), who had removed the starting pitcher from the game, descended upon the catcher. With the aid of a fielder's glove, one of them gingerly lifted the catcher's member and placed it back inside his uniform before the opposing players could see what the signal had been, while the other relieved him of his catching equipment. "He provoked me," the catcher said, "he always provokes me—"

The Lunatic fans were on their feet again, applauding, when their catcher was led away from the plate and up to the big brick building, along the path taken earlier by the starting pitcher. "—He won't let me alone, ever. I don't want to do it. I never wanted to do it. I *wouldn't* do it. But then he starts up teasing me and taunting me—"

The Mundys were able to come up with a final run in the top of the third, once they discovered that the second-string Lunatic catcher, for all that he sounded like the real thing—"Chuck to me, babe, no hitter in here, babe—" was a little leery of fielding a bunt dropped out in front of home plate, fearful apparently of what he would find beneath the ball upon picking it up.

When Deacon started out to the mound to pitch the last of the three innings, there wasn't a Mundy who took the field with him, sleepy old Kid Heket included, who didn't realize that the Deke had a shutout working. If he could set the Lunatics down without a run, he could become the first Mundy pitcher to hurl a scoreless game all year, in or out of league competition. Hoping neither to jinx him or unnerve him, the players went through the infield warm-up deliberately keeping the chatter to a minimum, as though in fact it was just another day they were going down to defeat. Nonetheless, the Deke was already streaming perspiration when the first Lunatic stepped into the box. He rubbed the rabbit's foot, said his prayer, took a swallow of air big enough to fill a gallon jug, and on four straight pitches, walked the center-fielder, who earlier in the game hadn't bothered to return the ball to the infield after catching a fly ball, and now, at the plate, hadn't moved the bat off his shoulder. When he was lifted for a pinch-runner (lifted by the "coaches") the appreciative fans gave him a nice round of applause. "That's lookin' 'em over!" they shouted, as he was carried from the field still in the batting posture, "that's waitin' 'em out! Good eye in there, fella!"

As soon as the pinch-runner took over at first, it became apparent that Dr. Traum had decided to do what he could to save face by spoiling the Deacon's shutout. Five runs down in the last inning and still playing to win, you don't start stealing bases—but that was precisely what this pinch-runner had in mind. And with what daring! First, with an astonishing burst of speed he rushed fifteen feet down the basepath—but then, practically on all fours, he was scrambling back. "No! No!" he cried, as he dove for the bag with his outstretched hand, "I won't! Never mind! Forget it!" But no sooner had he gotten back up on his feet and dusted himself off, than he was running again. "Why not!" he cried, "what the hell!" But having broken fifteen, twenty, foot down the basepath, he would come to an abrupt stop, smite himself on his forehead, and charge wildly back to first, crying, "Am I crazy? Am I out of my *mind?*"

In this way did he travel back and forth along the basepath some half-dozen times, before Deacon finally threw the first pitch to the plate. Given all there was to distract him, the pitch was of course a ball, low and in the dirt, but Hothead, having a great day, blocked it beautifully with his wooden leg.

Cholly, managing the club that morning while Mister Fairsmith rested back in Asylum—of the aged Mundy manager's spiritual crisis, more anon—Cholly motioned for Chico to get up and throw a warm-up pitch in the bullpen (one was enough—one was too many, in fact, as far as Chico was concerned) and meanwhile took a stroll out to the hill.

"Startin' to get to you, are they?" asked Cholly.

"It's that goofball on first that's doin' it."

Cholly looked over to where the runner, with time out, was standing up on first engaged in a heated controversy with himself.

"Hell," said Cholly, in his soft and reassuring way, "these boys have been tryin' to rattle us with that there bush league crap all mornin', Deke. I told you fellers comin' out in the bus, you just got to pay no attention to their monkeyshines, because that is their strategy from A to Z. To make you lose your concentration. Otherwise we would be rollin' over them worse than we is. But Deke, you tell me now, if you have had it, if you want for me to bring the Mexican in—"

"With six runs in my hip pocket? And a shutout goin'?"

"Well, I wasn't myself goin' to mention that last that you said."

"Cholly, you and me been in this here game since

back in the days they was rubbin' us down with Vaseline and Tabasco sauce. Ain't that right?"

"I know, I know."

"Well," said the Deke, shooting a stream of tobacco juice over his shoulder, "ain't a bunch of screwballs gonna get my goat. Tell Chico to sit down."

Sure enough, the Deacon, old war-horse that he was, got the next two hitters out on long drives to left. "Oh my God!" cried the base runner, each time the Ghost went climbing up the padded wall to snare the ball. "Imagine if I'd broken for second! Imagine what would have happened then! Oh, that'll teach me to take those crazy leads! But then if you don't get a jump on the pitcher, where are you as a pinch-runner? That's the whole idea of a pinch-runner—to break with the pitch, to break *before* the pitch, to score that shutout-breaking run! That's what I'm in here for, that's my entire purpose. The whole thing is on *my* shoulders—so then what am I doing *not* taking a good long lead? But just then, if I'd broken for second, I'd have been doubled off first! For the last out! But then suppose he hadn't made the catch? Suppose he'd dropped it. Then where would I be? Forced out at second! *Out*—and all because I was too cowardly. But then what's the sense of taking an unnecessary risk? What virtue is there in being foolhardy? None! But then what about playing it too safe?"

On the bench, Jolly Cholly winced when he saw that the batter stepping into the box was the opposing team's shortstop. "Uh-oh," he said, "that's the feller what's cost 'em most of the runs to begin with. I'm afraid he is goin' to be lookin' to right his wrongs—and at the expense of Deacon's shutout. Dang!"

From bearing down so hard, the Deacon's uniform showed vast dark continents of perspiration both front and back. There was no doubt that his strength was all but gone, for he was relying now solely on his "junk," that floating stuff that in times gone by used to cause the hitters nearly to break their backs swinging at the air. Twice now those flutter balls of his had damn near been driven out of the institution and Jolly Cholly had all he could do not to cover his eyes with his hand when he saw the Deke release yet another fat pitch in the direction of home plate.

Apparently it was just to the Lunatic shortstop's liking too. He swung from the heels, and with a whoop of joy, was away from the plate and streaking down the basepath. "Run!" he shouted to the fellow on first.

But the pinch-runner was standing up on the bag, scanning the horizon for the ball.

"Two outs!" cried the Lunatic shortstop. "Run, you idiot!"

"But—where is it!" asked the pinch-runner.

The Mundy infielders were looking skywards themselves, wondering where in hell that ball had been hit to.

"Where *is* it!" screamed the pinch-runner, as the shortstop came charging right up to his face. "I'm not running till I know where the *ball* is!"

"I'm coming into first, you," warned the shortstop.

"But you can't overtake another runner! That's against the law! That's *out!*"

"Then *move!*" screamed the shortstop into the fellow's ear.

"Oh, this *is* crazy. This is exactly what I *didn't* want to do!" But what choice did he have? If he stood his ground, and the shortstop kept coming, that would be the ballgame. It would be all over because he who had been put into the game to run, had simply refused to. Oh, what torment that fellow knew as he rounded the bases with the shortstop right on his tail. "I'm running full speed—and I don't even know where the ball is! I'm running like a chicken with his head cut off! I'm running like a madman, which is just what I don't want to do! Or be! I don't know where I'm going, I don't know what I'm doing, I haven't the foggiest idea of what's happening—and I'm running!"

When, finally, he crossed the plate, he was in such a state, that he fell to his hands and knees, and sobbing with relief, began to kiss the ground. "I'm home! Thank God! I'm safe! I made it! I scored! Oh thank God, thank God!"

And now the shortstop was rounding third—he took a quick glance over his shoulder to see if he could go all the way, and just kept on coming. "Now where's *he* lookin'?" asked Cholly. "What in hell does he see that I can't? Or that Mike don't either?" For out in left, Mike Rama was walking round and round, searching in the grass as though for a dime that might have dropped out of his pocket.

The shortstop was only a few feet from scoring the second run of the inning when Dr. Traum, who all this while had been walking from the Lunatic bench, interposed himself along the foul line between the runner and home plate.

"Doc," screamed the runner, "you're in the way!"

"That's enough now," said Dr. Traum, and he motioned for him to stop in his tracks.

"But I'm only inches from pay dirt! Step aside, Doc—let me score!"

"You just stay vere you are, please."

"*Why?*"

"You know vy. Stay right vere you are now. And giff me the ball."

"What ball?" asked the shortstop.

"You know vat ball."

"Well, I surely don't have any ball. I'm the *hitter.* I'm about *to score.*"

"You are not about to score. You are about to giff me the ball. Come now. Enough foolishness. Giff over the ball."

"But, Doc, I haven't got it. I'm on the offense. It's the *defense* that has the ball—that's the whole idea of the game. No criticism intended, but if you weren't a foreigner, you'd probably understand that better."

"Haf it your vay," said Dr. Traum, and he waved to the bullpen for his two coaches.

"But, Doc," said the shortstop, backpedaling now up the third-base line, "*they're* the ones in the field. *They're* the ones with the gloves—why don't you ask them for the ball? Why me? I'm an innocent base runner, who happens to be rounding third on his way home." But here he saw the coaches coming after him and he turned and broke across the diamond for the big brick building on the hill.

It was only a matter of minutes before one of the coaches returned with the ball and carried it out to where the Mundy infield was now gathered on the mound.

The Deacon turned it over in his hand and said, "Yep, that's it, all right. Ain't it, Hot?"

The Mundy catcher nodded. "How in hell did *he* get it?"

"A hopeless kleptomaniac, that's how," answered the coach. "He'd steal the bases if they weren't tied down. Here," he said, handing the Deacon a white hand towel bearing the Mundy laundrymark, and the pencil that Jolly Cholly wore behind his ear when he was acting as their manager. "Found this on him too. Looks like he got it when he stumbled into your bench for that pop-up in the first."

The victory celebration began the moment they boarded the asylum bus and lasted nearly all the way back to the city, with Nickname hollering out his window to every passerby, "We beat 'em! We shut 'em out!" and Big John swigging bourbon from his liniment bottle, and then passing it to his happy teammates.

"I'll tell you what did it," cried Nickname, by far the most exuberant of the victors, "it was Deacon throwin' at that first guy's head! Yessir! Now that's my kind of baseball!" said the fourteen-year-old, smacking his thigh. "First man up, give it to 'em right in the noggin'."

"Right!" said Hothead. "Show 'em you ain't takin' no more of their shit no more! Never again!"

"Well," said Deacon, "that is a matter of psychology, Hot, that was somethin' I had to think over real good beforehand. I mean, you try that on the wrong feller and next thing they is all of them layin' it down and then spikin' the dickens out of you when you cover the bag."

"That's so," said Jolly Cholly. "When me and the

Deke come up, that was practically a rule in the rule book—feller throws the beanball, the word goes out, 'Drag the ball and spike the pitcher.' Tell you the truth, I was worried we was goin' to see some of that sort of stuff today. They was a desperate bunch. Could tell that right off by their tactics.''

"Well," said the Deke, "that was a chance I had to take. But I'll tell you, I couldn't a done it without you fellers behind me. How about Bud out there, throwin' them two runners out at first base? The right-fielder to the first-baseman, *two times in a row*. Buddy," said the Deacon, "that was an exhibition such as I have not seen in all my years in organized ball."

Big Bud flushed, as was his way, and tried to make it sound easy. "Well, a' course, once I seen those guys wasn't runnin', I figured I didn't have no choice. I *had* to play it to first."

Here Mike Rama said, "Only that wasn't what *they* was figurin', Buddy-boy. You got a one-arm outfielder out there, you figure, what the hell, guess I can get on down the base line any old time I feel like it. Guess I can stop off and get me a beer and a sangwich on the way! But old Bud here, guess he showed 'em!"

"You know," said Cholly, philosophically, "I never seen it to fail, the hitters get cocky like them fellers were, and the next thing you know, they're makin' one dumb mistake after another."

"Yep," said Kid Heket, who was still turning the events of the morning over in his head, "no doubt about it, them fellers just was not usin' their heads."

"Well, maybe they wasn't—but *we* was! What about Hot?" said Nickname. "What about a guy with a wooden leg taggin' up from second and scorin' on a fly to center! How's that for heads-up ball?"

"Well," said Wayne, "I am still puzzlin' that one out myself. What got into that boy in center, that he just sort of stood there after the catch, alookin' the way he did? What in hell did he want to wait fifteen minutes for anyway, before throwin' it? That's a awful long time, don't you think?"

They all looked to Cholly to answer this one. "Well, Wayne," he said, "I believe it is that dang cockiness again. Base runner on second's got a wooden leg, kee-rect? So what does Hot here do—he *goes*. And that swellhead out in center, well, he is so darned stunned by it all, that finally by the time he figures out what hit him, we has got ourselves a gift of a run. Now, if I was managin' that club, I'd bench that there prima donna and slap a fine on him to boot."

"But then how do you figure that shortstop, Cholly?" asked the Kid. "Now if that ain't the strangest ball-playin' you ever seen, what is? Stickin' the ball in his back pocket like that. And then when he is at bat, with a man on and his team down by six, and it is their last

licks 'n all, catchin' a junk pitch like that inside his shirt. Now I cannot figure that out nohow."

"Dang cockiness again!" cried Nickname, looking to Cholly. "He figures, hell, it's only them Mundys out there, I can do any dang thing I please—well, I guess we taught him a thing or two! Right, Cholly?"

"Well, nope, I don't think so, Nickname. I think what we have got there in that shortstop is one of the most tragic cases I have seen in my whole life long of all-field-no-hit."

"Kleptomaniac's what the coach there called him," said the Deacon.

"Same thing," said Cholly. "Why, we had a fella down in Class D when I was just startin' out, fella name a' Mayet. Nothin' got by that boy. Why, Mayet at short wasn't much different than a big pot of glue out there. Fact that's what they called him for short: Glue. Only trouble is, he threw like a girl, and when it come to hittin', well, my pussycat probably do better, if I had one. Well, the same exact thing here, only worse."

"Okay," said Kid Heket, "I see that, sorta. Only how come he run over to field a pop-up and stoled the pencil right off your ear, Cholly? How come he took our towel away, right in the middle of the gosh darn game?"

"Heck, that ain't so hard to figure out. We been havin' such rotten luck this year, you probably forgot just who we all are, anyway. What boy *wouldn't* want a towel from a big league ball club to hang up and frame on the wall? Why, he wanted that thing so bad that when the game was over, I went up to the doc there and I said, 'Doc, no hard feelin's. You did the best you could and six to zip ain't nothin' to be ashamed of against big leaguers.' And then I *give* him the towel to pass on to that there kleptomaniac boy when he seen him again. So as he didn't feel too bad, bein' the last out. And know what else I told him? I give him some advice. I said, 'Doc, if I had a shortstop like that, I'd bat him ninth and play him at first where he don't *have* to make the throw.''

"What'd he say?"

"Oh, he laughed at me. He said, 'Ha ha, Jolly Cholly, you haf a good sense of humor. Who efer heard of a first-baseman batting ninth?' So I said, 'Doc, who ever heard of a fifty-year-old preacher hurlin' a shutout with only three days' rest—but he done it, maybe with the help of interference on the last play, but still he done it.' ''

"Them's the breaks of the game anyway!" cried Nickname. "About time the breaks started goin' our way. Did you tell him that, Cholly?"

"I told him that, Nickname. I told him more. I said, 'Doc, there is two kinds of baseball played in this country, and maybe somebody ought to tell you, bein' a foreigner and all—there is by the book, the way you do it, the way the Tycoons do it—and I grant, those fellers win their share of pennants doin' it that way. But then there is by hook and crook, by raw guts and all the heart you got, and that is just the way the Mundys done here today.' "

Here the team began whooping and shouting and singing with joy, though Jolly Cholly had momentarily to turn away, to struggle against the tears that were forming in his eyes. In a husky voice he went on—"And then I told him the name for that. I told him the name for wanderin' your ass off all season long, and takin' all the jokes and all the misery they can heap on your head day after day, and then comin' on out for a exhibition game like this one, where another team would just go through the motions and not give two hoots in hell how they played—and instead, instead givin' it everything you got. I told the doc the name for that, fellers. It's called courage."

Only Roland Agni, who had gone down twice, looking, against Lunatic pitching, appeared to be unmoved by Cholly's tribute to the team. Nickname, in fact, touched Jolly Cholly's arm at the conclusion of his speech, and whispered, "Somebody better say somethin' to Rollie. He ain't takin' strikin' out too good, it don't look."

So Cholly the peacemaker made his way past the boisterous players and down the aisle to where Roland still sat huddled in a rear corner of the bus by himself.

"What's eatin' ya, boy?"

"Nothin'," mumbled Roland.

"Why don'tcha come up front an'—"

"Leave me alone, Tuminikar!"

"Aw, Rollie, come on now," said the sympathetic coach, "even the best of them get caught lookin' once in a while."

"Caught *lookin'?*" cried Agni.

"Hey, Rollie," Hothead shouted, "it's okay, slugger—we won anyway!" And grinning, he waved Big John's liniment bottle in the air to prove it.

"Sure, Rollie," Nickname yelled. "With the Deke on the mound, we didn't need but one run anyway! So what's the difference? Everybody's gotta whiff sometimes! It's the law a' averages!"

But Agni was now standing in the aisle, screaming, "You think I got caught *lookin'?*"

Wayne Heket, whose day had been a puzzle from beginning to end, who just could not really take any more confusion on top of going sleepless all these hours, asked, "Well, wasn't ya?"

"You bunch of morons! You bunch of idiots! Why,

you are bigger lunatics even than they are! Those fellers are at least locked up!"

Jolly Cholly, signaling his meaning to the other players with a wink, said, "Seems Roland got somethin' in his eye, boys—seems he couldn't see too good today."

"You're the ones that can't see!" Agni screamed. *"They were madmen! They were low as low can be!"*

"Oh, I don't know, Rollie," said Mike Rama, who'd had his share of scurrying around to do that morning, "they wasn't *that* bad."

"They was *worse!* And you all acted like you was takin' on the Cardinals in the seventh game of the Series!"

"How else you supposed to play, youngster?" asked the Deacon, who was beginning to get a little hot under the collar.

"And you! You're the worst of all! Hangin' in there, like a regular hero! Havin' conferences on the mound about how to pitch to a bunch of hopeless maniacs!"

"Look, son," said Jolly Cholly, "just on account you got caught lookin'—"

*"But who got caught lookin'?* How could you get caught lookin' against pitchers *that had absolutely nothin' on the ball!"*

"You mean," said Jolly Cholly, incredulous, "you took a *dive?* You mean you throwed it, Roland? *Why?"*

*"Why?* Oh, please, let me off! Let me off this bus!" he screamed, charging down the aisle toward the door. "I can't take bein' one of you no more!"

As they were all, with the exception of the Deacon, somewhat pie-eyed, it required virtually the entire Mundy team to subdue the boy wonder. Fortunately the driver of the bus, who was an employee of the asylum, carried a straitjacket and a gag under the seat with him at all times, and knew how to use it. "It's from bein' around them nuts all mornin'," he told the Mundys. "Sometimes I ain't always myself either, when I get home at night."

"Oh," said the Mundys, shaking their heads at one another, and though at first it was a relief having a professional explanation for Roland's bizarre behavior, they found that with Roland riding along in the rear seat all bound and gagged, they really could not seem to revive the jubilant mood that had followed upon their first shutout win of the year. In fact, by the time they reached Keeper Park for their regularly scheduled afternoon game, one or two of them were even starting to feel more disheartened about that victory than they had about any of those beatings they had been taking all season long.

Edd Roush owns a highly justified place in baseball's Hall of Fame, with a batting average of .323 for an outfielding career that lasted from 1913 through 1931. "One thing that's always overlooked in the whole mess," he says here, of the fixed 1919 World Series that pitted his Cincinnati Reds against the Chicago "Black Sox," "is that we could have beat them no matter what the circumstances!" (Equally overlooked: Gamblers tried to fix the Reds, too!)

# Rumors Were Flying

## EDD ROUSH

"Who is he, anyhow, an actor?"

"No."

"A dentist?"

". . . No, he's a gambler." Gatsby hesitated, then added coolly: "He's the man who fixed the World's Series back in 1919."

"Fixed the World's Series?" I repeated.

The idea staggered me. I remembered, of course, that the World's Series had been fixed in 1919, but if I had thought of it at all I would have thought of it as a thing that merely *happened,* the end of some inevitable chain. It never occurred to me that one man could start to play with the faith of fifty million people—with the single-mindedness of a burglar blowing a safe.

"How did he happen to do that?" I asked after a minute.

"He just saw the opportunity."

"Why isn't he in jail?"

"They can't get him, old sport. He's a smart man."

—F. Scott Fitzgerald, *The Great Gatsby*

YES, I knew at the time that some finagling was going on. At least that's what I'd heard. Rumors were flying all over the place that gamblers had got to the Chicago White Sox, that they'd agreed to throw the World Series. But nobody knew anything for sure until Eddie Cicotte spilled the beans a year later.

We beat them in the first two games, 9–1 and 4–2, and it was after the second game that I first got wind of it. We played those first two games in Cincinnati, and the next day we were to play in Chicago. So the evening after the second game we were all gathered at the hotel in Cincinnati, standing around waiting for cabs to take us to the train station, when this fellow came over to me. I didn't know who he was, but I'd seen him around before.

"Roush," he says, "I want to tell you something. Did you hear about the squabble the White Sox got into after the game this afternoon?" And he told me some story about Ray Schalk accusing Lefty Williams of throwing the game, and something about some of the White Sox beating up a gambler for not giving them the money he'd promised them.

"They didn't get the payoff," he said, "so from here on they're going to try to win."

I didn't know whether this guy made it all up or not. But it did start me thinking. Later on in the Series the same guy came over to me again.

"Roush," he says, "you remember what I told you about gamblers getting to the White Sox? Well, now they've also got to some of the players on your own ball club."

That's all he said. Wouldn't tell me any more. I didn't

say anything to anybody until we were getting dressed in the clubhouse the next day. Then I got hold of the manager, Pat Moran, just before the pregame meeting.

"Before you start this meeting, Pat," I said, "there's something I want to talk to you about."

"OK," he says, "what is it?"

"I've been told that gamblers have got to some of the players on this club," I said. "Maybe it's true and maybe it isn't. I don't know. But you sure better do some finding out. I'll be damned if I'm going to knock myself out trying to win this Series if somebody else is trying to throw the game."

Pat got all excited and called Jake Daubert over, who was the team captain. It was all news to both of them. So at the meeting, after we'd gone over the White Sox lineup, Moran looked at Hod Eller, who was going to pitch for us that day.

"Hod," he said, "I've been hearing rumors about sellouts. Not about you, not about anybody in particular, just rumors. I want to ask you a straight question and I want a straight answer."

"Shoot," says Hod.

"Has anybody offered you anything to throw this game?"

"Yep," Hod said. Lord, you could have heard a pin drop.

"After breakfast this morning a guy got on the elevator with me, and got off at the same floor I did. He showed me five thousand-dollar bills, and said they were mine if I'd lose the game today."

"What did you say?" Moran asked him.

"I said if he didn't get damn far away from me real quick he wouldn't know what hit him. And the same went if I ever saw him again."

Moran looked at Eller a long time. Finally, he said, "OK, you're pitching. But one wrong move and you're out of the game."

Evidently there weren't any wrong moves. Because ol' Hod went out there and pitched a swell game. He won two of the games in that Series.

I don't know whether the whole truth of what went on there among the White Sox will ever come out. Even today nobody really knows exactly what took place. Whatever it was, though, it was a dirty rotten shame. One thing that's always overlooked in the whole mess is that we could have beat them no matter what the circumstances!

Sure, the 1919 White Sox were good. But the 1919 Cincinnati Reds were *better*. I'll believe that till my dying day. I don't care how good Chicago's Joe Jackson and Buck Weaver and Eddie Cicotte were. *We* had Heinie Groh, Jake Daubert, Greasy Neale, Rube Bressler, Larry Kopf, myself, and the best pitching staff in both leagues. We were a very underrated ball club.

I played center field for that Cincinnati club for 11 straight years, 1916 through 1926. I came to Cincinnati from the Giants in the middle of 1916, along with Christy Mathewson and Bill McKechnie.

Of course I started playing ball long before that, around 1909 or so, right here in Oakland City, Indiana. In those days every little town had an amateur club, and so did Oakland City. Never will forget it. I was only about sixteen at the time. Oakland City had a game scheduled with a neighboring town this day, and one of Oakland City's outfielders hadn't shown up. Everybody was standing around right on the main street of town—only a small town, you know—wondering what to do, when one of the town officials says, "Why not put that Roush kid in?"

I was kind of a shy kid, and I backed away. But the manager says, "Well, that's just what we'll do if he don't show up in five more minutes."

We waited for five minutes and the outfielder never did show, so they gave me a uniform and put me in right field. Turned out I got a couple of hits that day, and I became Oakland City's regular right fielder for the rest of the season.

The next year, of course, I was right in the middle of it. We reorganized the team—the Oakland City Walk-Overs, that's what we called ourselves—and had a pretty good club. In those days, you know, I used to throw with *either* hand. I'm a natural lefty, see, but when I was a kid I never could find a lefty's glove. So I just used a regular glove and learned to throw righty. Batted lefty, but got so I could throw with my right arm almost as well as with my left.

The year after that we got in quite a hassle. That would be 1911. Seems as though some of the Oakland City boys were getting $5 a game, and I wasn't one of them. So I started raising Cain about this under-the-table business and treating some different than others.

Wound up we had such an argument that I quit the home-town club and went over and played with the Princeton team. Princeton is the closest town to Oakland City, about 12 miles due west. And don't think that didn't cause quite a ruckus. Especially when Princeton came over to play Oakland City *at* Oakland City, with me in the Princeton outfield. A fair amount of hard feelings were stirred up, to say the least. I think there are still one or two around here never have forgiven me to this very day.

I played with Princeton about a year and a half, and then a fellow connected with the Evansville club in the Kitty League asked me would I like to play for them in professional baseball. Well, Evansville's only about 30 miles from Oakland City, almost due south, and the idea of getting paid for playing ball sounded real good to me. And Dad thought it was terrific. He'd played semipro ball himself, when he was young. William C. Roush was his name. A darn good ballplayer, too. So I signed with Evansville and finished the 1912 season with them.

I bought a lefty's glove when I started playing with Evansville, figuring I might as well go back to the natural throw. From then on I always threw left-handed, 'cause it didn't carry quite so well when I threw with my right. Wasn't really a natural throw.

After that, things moved quick. Evansville sold me to the Chicago White Sox—of all teams, considering what happened later—in the middle of the following season. I stayed with them a month—Cicotte was there then, and Buck Weaver, and Ray Schalk—and then they optioned me to Lincoln, Nebraska, in the Western League.

The next year the Indianapolis club in the new Federal League got in touch with me and offered me $225 a month, almost twice what I was getting at Lincoln. So I jumped to the Federal League for the next couple of years. That Federal League wasn't a bad league. Too bad it only lasted two years. Ran into a lot of financial troubles and folded in December of 1915. Of course, it was an outlaw league, you know, raiding the other leagues for its players. The established leagues threatened that anybody who jumped to the Feds would never be allowed back in organized ball, but once the Feds broke up they were glad to get us.

We had some good players there the two years the Federal League lived. A lot of old-timers jumped over, like Three-Fingered Brown, Chief Bender, Eddie Plank, Davy Jones, Joe Tinker, Jimmy Delahanty, Al Bridwell, and Charlie Carr, the old Indianapolis first baseman. They didn't care if organized ball never took them back, 'cause they were near the end of the trail anyway.

But there were also a lot of younger players, like Benny Kauff, Bill McKechnie, and myself. All three of us were sold to the New York Giants when the Federal League collapsed, and that's where we reported in the spring of 1916.

Me, I didn't like New York. I'm a small-town boy. I like the Midwest. Well, it wasn't *exactly* that. Not entirely, anyway. It was really McGraw I didn't like. John J. McGraw. I just didn't enjoy playing for him, that's all. If you made a bad play he'd cuss you out, yell at you, call you all sorts of names. That didn't go with me. So I was glad as I could be when he traded me to Cincinnati in the middle of the '16 season. I couldn't have been happier.

McGraw traded Mathewson, McKechnie, and me to Cincinnati for Wade Killefer and Buck Herzog, who had been the Cincinnati manager. Matty was to replace Herzog as the new manager. I still remember the trip the three of us made as we left the Giants and took the train to join the Reds. McKechnie and I were sitting back on the observation car, talking about how happy we were to

be traded. Matty came out and sat down and listened, but he didn't say anything.

Finally I turned to him and said, "Well, Matty, aren't you glad to be getting away from McGraw?"

"I'll tell you something, Roush," he said. "You and Mac have only been on the Giants a couple of months. It's just another ball club to you fellows. But I was with that team for 16 years. That's a mighty long time. To me, the Giants are 'home.' And leaving them like this, I feel the same as when I leave home in the spring of the year.

"Of course, I realize I'm through as a pitcher. But I appreciate McGraw making a place for me in baseball and getting me this managing job. He's doing me a favor, and I thanked him for it. And by the way, the last thing he said to me was that if I put you in center field I'd have a great ballplayer. So starting tomorrow you're my center fielder."

Well, we got to Cincinnati and sure enough, right off Matty puts me in center field. Greasy Neale was the right fielder. It was his first year with the Reds too, but he'd been there since the start of the season and, of course, I was a newcomer. The first game I played there, about three or four fly balls came out that could have been taken by either the center fielder or the right fielder. If I thought I should take it, I'd holler three times: "I got it, I got it, I got it." I'd holler while I was running for it, see.

But Greasy never said a word. Sometimes he'd take it, and sometimes he wouldn't. But in either case he never said a thing. We went along that way for about three weeks. What I finally did was watch *both* him and the ball. If it looked to me like I could catch the ball and get out of his way, I'd holler and take it. But if it looked like it was going to be a tie, I'd just cut behind him and let him take it. He still never hollered, and didn't have too much else to say to me, either. So I didn't have too much to say to him.

You see, I could watch both him and the ball at the same time because I didn't really have to watch the ball. As soon as a ball was hit I could tell where it was going to go, and I'd just take off and not look at it any more till I got there. So I'd take a quick glance at him while I was running.

Finally, one day Greasy came over and sat down beside me on the bench. "I want to end this, Roush," he says to me. "I guess you know I've been trying to run you down ever since you got here. I wanted that center field job for myself, and I didn't like it when Matty put you out there. But you can go get a ball better than I ever could. I want to shake hands and call it off. From now on, I'll holler."

And from then on Greasy and I got along just fine. Grew to be two of the best friends ever. In fact, I made a lot of good friends those years I played in Cincinnati, still my close friends to this day. I think that Cincinnati club from 1916 to 1926 was one of the nicest bunch of fellows ever gathered together.

We even had Jim Thorpe there one year, you know. By thunder, there was a man could outrun a deer. Beat anything I ever saw. I used to be pretty fast myself. Stole close to 300 bases in the Big Leagues. And I had a real long stride, for the simple reason that in the outfield if you don't take a long stride your head bobs up and down too much and makes it hard to follow the flight of the ball. But Jim Thorpe would take only two strides to my three. I'd run just as hard as I could, and he'd keep up with me just trotting along.

One day I asked him, "Jim, anybody in those Olympic games ever make you really run your best?"

"I never yet saw the man I couldn't look back at," he says to me. I believed him.

Well, sir, I really hit my own stride those years in Cincinnati. Led the league in batting twice, hit over .350 three years in a row—'21, '22, and '23—and generally had a ball. The lowest I ever hit while I was there was .321 in 1919, and that was good enough to lead the league that year. We won the pennant and the World Series in 1919, and finished either first, second, or third in seven of the 11 years I was there. Good teams—very much underrated. Like I say, *better* than the 1919 White Sox.

Of course, I hit very different from the way they hit today. I used a 48-ounce bat, heaviest anyone ever used. It was a shorter bat, with a big handle, and I tried to hit to all fields. Didn't swing my head off, just snapped at the ball. Until 1921, you know, they had a dead ball. Well, the only way you could get a home run was if the outfielder tripped and fell down. The ball wasn't wrapped tight and lots of times it'd get mashed on one side. I've caught many a ball in the outfield that was mashed flat on one side. Come bouncing out there like a jumping bean. They wouldn't throw it out of the game, though. Only used about three or four balls in a whole game. Now they use 60 or 70.

Another thing that's different now is the ball parks. Now they have smooth infields and outfields that aren't full of rocks, and they keep them nice. Back in the old days there were parks weren't much better than a cow pasture. Spring training was the worst. Some of those parks they'd want you to play exhibition games in had outfields like sand dunes, and others were hard as a cement sidewalk. The hell with that! I wouldn't go to spring training, that's all.

I used to hold out every year until the week before the season opened. That's the only time they ever had any trouble with me, contract time. Why should I go down there and fuss around in spring training? Twist an ankle,

or break a leg. I did my *own* spring training, hunting quail and rabbits around Oakland City.

After 11 years with the Reds, they traded me to the Giants for George Kelly. That was after the 1926 season. Well, I figured that was it. I was around thirty-four, and I wasn't about to start taking abuse from McGraw that late in life. However, I figured I had one chance: maybe I could get McGraw to trade me.

So in January of '27, when the Giants sent me a contract for $19,000, same as I'd been getting with Cincinnati, I sent it right back and wrote them I wouldn't play in New York. A couple of weeks later another one arrived, calling for $20,000. I figured they hadn't gotten the point. So I wrote a letter telling them I wouldn't play with the Giants for *any* kind of money. And wouldn't you know it, two weeks after that another contract arrived, calling for $21,000. I didn't even bother to send that one back.

Since they didn't seem to get the point the way I was doing it, I finally wrote and said I wanted $30,000. I figured that would sink in and they'd get the idea. Send me to another club.

Well, spring training started—and ended—and the team began to move up north, playing exhibition games along the way. I was still busy hunting quail right here around Oakland City. Then one day I got a call from McGraw. Would I meet him in Chattanooga next week? After thinking it over, I decided I might as well.

I arrived at the hotel in Chattanooga at eight o'clock on a Thursday morning, and when I registered the clerk said to me, "Mr. McGraw left a message for you to come up to his room as soon as you arrive."

Well, it was eight o'clock, and I hadn't had any breakfast. So I went into the dining room and ordered a good meal. About nine o'clock a bellboy comes over and says, "Mr. McGraw would like to see you in room 305."

"All right," I says, "tell him I'll be there."

About that time the ballplayers started to drift in, so I visited with them awhile. One of them gave me a good cigar, so I sat down in a comfortable chair in the lobby and talked to some of the boys while I enjoyed it. About eleven o'clock one of the coaches came over. "McGraw wants to know why you're not up there yet?"

Finally, by about 12:30 or so, after I'd finished visiting with the ballplayers, completed a detailed reading of three newspapers, and had a haircut and a shoeshine, I decided to go upstairs and see Mr. John J. McGraw.

"What the devil's the matter with you, Roush?" he says. "Don't you want to play ball for me?"

"Hell, no," I said. "I don't want to play ball for you. Haven't you figured that out by now?"

"Why not?"

" 'Cause I don't like the way you treat your players, that's why. First time you call me a damn so-and-so, somebody's going to get hurt."

"Listen, we'll get along fine. Don't you worry," he says.

"Yeah. I've heard that one before."

"Sit down," he says, "and listen to me. You know this game as well as I do. You play your own game and I'll never say anything to you."

"That's another one I've heard before."

"Well," he says, "it's the truth."

"The first time something happens out there, and you start on me," I said, "I'm taking off for Oakland City, Indiana. Why don't we stop all this horsing around and you just send me to another ball club?"

"I won't do it," he says. "I've been trying to get you back ever since I traded you away a long time ago. Now you're either going to play for me or you're not going to play ball at all. I'm sure not going to let you go a second time."

"OK," I said, "if that's the way you feel about it. If you give me my salary, I'll try it. But I still say I'll be back in Oakland City, Indiana, in ten days."

"How much do you want?"

"$25,000."

"I can't pay it."

Well, I took my hat and started for the door. "Where do you think you're going?" he says.

"Back to Oakland City, Indiana. Why?"

"Now hold on," he says. "Come back and sit down. I'll tell you what I'll do. I'll give you a three-year contract for $70,000."

"All right," I said, "I'll take it."

I signed the contract, went out to the ball park, got into a uniform, and played six innings that afternoon. Got two hits out of three times up, too.

I played that three-year contract out, and after that I quit, and finally did come back to Oakland City, Indiana. McGraw kept to his word and never bothered me. But it wasn't like playing in Cincinnati. I missed my teammates, and I missed the Cincinnati fans.

I've read where as far as the Cincinnati fans are concerned I'm the most popular player ever wore a Reds' uniform. I don't know about that. It's not for me to say. But—assuming it's true—I'll tell you one thing: the feeling is mutual.

What appears here is, I believe, the only book review in all four volumes of the *Fireside* baseball library, and you may decide it is one of the strangest reviews you ever read. When you consider, however, the Chekhovian cast of the typical Chicago Cubs fan, and that one such fan— the renowned Mike Royko of the *Chicago Tribune*—wrote the review, and that the author of the book in question is Keith Hernandez, who plays for the Mets, then all things fall into place, and there is nothing strange about it at all. It appeared just before the start of the 1987 season.

# A Very Solid Book

## MIKE ROYKO

A NEW YORK publishing house has sent me a copy of a new paperback book it has just brought out.

With it came a note that said: "We take pleasure in presenting you with this review copy and ask that you please send two copies of your notices to our offices."

I seldom review books in my column. The Chicago paper for which I write has a section that takes care of that. But in this case, I'm going to make an exception.

The book is called "If At First . . ." with a subtitle that says "With the exclusive inside story of the 1986 Championship Season."

The author is Keith Hernandez, who is the first baseman on the New York Mets baseball team. Actually, he didn't write it—some professional ghostwriter did. But the words and story originated with Hernandez. I will begin my review by saying that this is a very solid book. The moment I opened the package and saw what it was about, I threw it against my office wall as hard as I could.

Then I slammed it to the floor and jumped up and down on it. I beat on it with a chair for several minutes until I slumped onto my couch, emotionally and physically spent. Although slightly scuffed, the book was still intact.

It is also a book that can cause excitement. I dropped it on the desk of a friend who has had weekend season tickets at Wrigley Field for the past 10 years. It immediately stirred him to emotional heights. He shouted:

"Why are you showing me that piece of (deleted)? I say (deleted) Hernandez and (deleted) the Mets and (deleted) the whole (deleted) city of New York. And (deleted) you, too."

Then he flung it against a wall and gave it a kick. It still remained intact. I told you it was a solid book.

It's a book that can move a sensitive reader to tears, as I discovered when I showed it to a man who has been going to Cub games since 1946, a year that is known as The Beginning of Darkness.

When he looked at the cover, he choked back a sob, a tear trickled down his cheek, and he said: "Why them? Why not us? What was our sin? How can we atone for it? You know, I asked my clergyman that, and he said he wishes he knew, because he lost $50 betting against them."

And it's a powerful book. As reviewers like to say: It can hit you right in the guts. This was proven when I showed it to a confirmed bleacherite who said: "Excuse me. I'm going to throw up."

But enough of generalities. Let us consider the contents of this book.

On the very first page, Hernandez and his ghostwriter say: "ad made the second out on a long the Mets were through for 1986: o out, nobody on, two runs down, ox already leading the World Series en our scoreboard operator at"

And on page 81, Hernandez says: "round during infield practice, I draw a line nan and myself and call our manager over. avy? I ask. He laughs."

Moving to page 125, we find: "Oh, sweet bird of youth. however, were a different story. It's diff- quietly as I work my way out of a bad me to listen to his judgments. I wrong with my swing. I know hot to th hardheaded. Dand and I have had"

I know, it sounds kind of garbled, incomprehensible.

But that's the way a story reads when you rip the pages of a book in half, one by one, as I've been doing.

Don't misunderstand me. I'm not doing that out of spite. I'm a good sport, a cheerful loser. Why, in the last two years, I don't think I've watched my video of the movie "Fail Safe," in which New York City gets nuked, more than 30 or 40 times.

The fact is, I have found this to be a useful book.

I have been tearing out the pages and crumpling them into little wads.

When I have about 30 or 40 of these wads, I put them in my fireplace under the kindling and light them. They're excellent for getting a fire started.

Then I pour myself a drink, lower the lights, sit back and stare at the crackling flames.

And I pretend that I'm looking at Shea Stadium.

## ARNIE LEVIN

*Drawing by Levin; © 1986 The New Yorker Magazine, Inc.*

"This is the way old Casey Stengel ran yesterday afternoon, running his home run home. . . ." So began Damon Runyon's account, included in the first *Fireside Book of Baseball,* of the opening game of the 1923 World Series, and the editor's forenote promised special delight for those readers who thought of Runyon as an author but never as a reporter.

Now, for those who think of Runyon as a reporter but never as an author, another special delight.

# Baseball Hattie

## DAMON RUNYON

IT COMES on springtime, and the little birdies are singing in the trees in Central Park, and the grass is green all around and about, and I am at the Polo Grounds on the opening day of the baseball season, when who do I behold but Baseball Hattie. I am somewhat surprised at this spectacle, as it is years since I see Baseball Hattie, and for all I know she long ago passes to a better and happier world.

But there she is, as large as life, and in fact twenty pounds larger, and when I call the attention of Armand Fibleman, the gambler, to her, he gets up and tears right out of the joint as if he sees a ghost, for if there is one thing Armand Fibleman loathes and despises, it is a ghost.

I can see that Baseball Hattie is greatly changed, and to tell the truth, I can see that she is getting to be nothing but an old bag. Her hair that is once as black as a yard up a stovepipe is gray, and she is wearing gold-rimmed cheaters, although she seems to be pretty well dressed and looks as if she may be in the money a little bit, at that.

But the greatest change in her is the way she sits there very quiet all afternoon, never once opening her yap, even when many of the customers around her are claiming that Umpire William Klem is Public Enemy No. 1 to 16 inclusive, because they think he calls a close one against the Giants. I am wondering if maybe Baseball Hattie is stricken dumb somewhere back down the years, because I can remember when she is usually making speeches in the grandstand in favor of hanging such characters as Umpire William Klem when they call close ones against the Giants. But Hattie just sits there as if she is in a church while the public clamor goes on about her, and she does not as much as cry out robber, or even you big bum at Umpire William Klem.

I see many a baseball bug in my time, male and female, but without doubt the worst bug of them all is Baseball Hattie, and you can say it again. She is most particularly a bug about the Giants, and she never misses a game they play at the Polo Grounds, and in fact she sometimes bobs up watching them play in other cities, which is always very embarrassing to the Giants, as they fear the customers in these cities may get the wrong impression of New York womanhood after listening to Baseball Hattie awhile.

The first time I ever see Baseball Hattie to pay any attention to her is in Philadelphia, a matter of twenty-odd years back, when the Giants are playing a series there, and many citizens of New York, including Armand Fibleman and myself, are present, because the Philadelphia customers are great hands for betting on baseball games in those days, and Armand Fibleman figures he may knock a few of them in the creek.

Armand Fibleman is a character who will bet on baseball games from who-laid-the-chunk, and in fact he will bet on anything whatever, because Armand Fibleman is a gambler by trade and has been such since infancy. Personally, I will not bet you four dollars on a baseball game, because in the first place I am not apt to have four dollars, and in the second place I consider horse races a much sounder investment, but I often go around and about with Armand Fibleman, as he is a friend of mine, and sometimes he gives me a little piece of one of his bets for nothing.

Well, what happens in Philadelphia but the umpire forfeits the game in the seventh inning to the Giants by a score of nine to nothing when the Phillies are really leading by five runs, and the reason the umpire takes this action is because he orders several of the Philadelphia players to leave the field for calling him a scoundrel and a rat and a snake in the grass, and also a baboon, and they refuse to take their departure, as they still have more names to call him.

Right away the Philadelphia customers become infuriated in a manner you will scarcely believe, for ordinarily a Philadelphia baseball customer is as quiet as a lamb, no matter what you do to him, and in fact in those days a Philadelphia baseball customer is only considered as somebody to do something to.

But these Philadelphia customers are so infuriated that they not only chase the umpire under the stand, but they wait in the street outside the baseball orchard until the Giants change into their street clothes and come out of the clubhouse. Then the Philadelphia customers begin pegging rocks, and one thing and another, at the Giants, and it is a most exciting and disgraceful scene that is spoken of for years afterwards.

Well, the Giants march along toward the North Philly station to catch a train for home, dodging the rocks and one thing and another the best they can, and wondering why the Philadelphia gendarmes do not come to the rescue, until somebody notices several gendarmes among the customers doing some of the throwing themselves, so the Giants realize that this is a most inhospitable community, to be sure.

Finally all of them get inside the North Philly station and are safe, except a big, tall, left-handed pitcher by the name of Haystack Duggeler, who just reports to the club the day before and who finds himself surrounded by quite a posse of these infuriated Philadelphia customers, and who is unable to make them understand that he is nothing but a rookie, because he has a Missouri accent, and besides, he is half paralyzed with fear.

One of the infuriated Philadelphia customers is armed with a brickbat and is just moving forward to maim Haystack Duggeler with this instrument, when who steps into the situation but Baseball Hattie, who is also on her way to the station to catch a train, and who is greatly horrified by the assault on the Giants.

She seizes the brickbat from the infuriated Philadelphia customer's grasp, and then tags the customer smack-dab between the eyes with his own weapon, knocking him so unconscious that I afterwards hear he does not recover for two weeks, and that he remains practically an imbecile the rest of his days.

Then Baseball Hattie cuts loose on the other infuriated Philadelphia customers with language that they never before hear in those parts, causing them to disperse without further ado, and after the last customer is beyond the sound of her voice, she takes Haystack

Duggeler by the pitching arm and personally escorts him to the station.

Now out of this incident is born a wonderful romance between Baseball Hattie and Haystack Duggeler, and in fact it is no doubt love at first sight, and about this period Haystack Duggeler begins burning up the league with his pitching, and at the same time giving Manager Mac plenty of headaches, including the romance with Baseball Hattie, because anybody will tell you that a left-hander is tough enough on a manager without a romance, and especially a romance with Baseball Hattie.

It seems that the trouble with Hattie is she is in business up in Harlem, and this business consists of a boarding and rooming house where ladies and gentlemen board and room, and personally I never see anything out of line in the matter, but the rumor somehow gets around, as rumors will do, that in the first place, it is not a boarding and rooming house, and in the second place that the ladies and gentlemen who room and board there are by no means ladies and gentlemen, and especially ladies.

Well, this rumor becomes a terrible knock to Baseball Hattie's social reputation. Furthermore, I hear Manager Mac sends for her and requests her to kindly lay off his ballplayers, and especially off a character who can make a baseball sing high *C* like Haystack Duggeler. In fact, I hear Manager Mac gives her such a lecture on her civic duty to New York and to the Giants that Baseball Hattie sheds tears, and promises she will never give Haystack another tumble the rest of the season.

"You know me, Mac," Baseball Hattie says. "You know I will cut off my nose rather than do anything to hurt your club. I sometimes figure I am in love with this big bloke, but," she says, "maybe it is only gas pushing up around my heart. I will take something for it. To hell with him, Mac!" she says.

So she does not see Haystack Duggeler again, except at a distance, for a long time, and he goes on to win fourteen games in a row, pitching a no-hitter and four two-hitters among them, and hanging up a reputation as a great pitcher, and also as a hundred-precent heel.

Haystack Duggeler is maybe twenty-five at this time, and he comes to the big league with more bad habits than anybody in the history of the world is able to acquire in such a short time. He is especially a great rumpot, and after he gets going good in the league, he is just as apt to appear for a game all mulled up as not.

He is fond of all forms of gambling, such as playing cards and shooting craps, but after they catch him with a deck of readers in a poker game and a pair of tops in a crap game, none of the Giants will play with him any more, except of course when there is nobody else to play with.

He is ignorant about many little things, such as

reading and writing and geography and mathematics, as Haystack Duggeler himself admits he never goes to school any more than he can help, but he is so wise when it comes to larceny that I always figure they must have great tutors back in Haystack's old home town of Booneville, Mo.

And no smarter jobbie ever breathes than Haystack when he is out there pitching. He has so much speed that he just naturally throws the ball past a batter before he can get the old musket off his shoulder, and along with his hard one, Haystack has a curve like the letter $Q$. With two ounces of brains, Haystack Duggeler will be the greatest pitcher that ever lives.

Well, as far as Baseball Hattie is concerned, she keeps her word about not seeing Haystack, although sometimes when he is mulled up he goes around to her boarding and rooming house, and tries to break down the door.

On days when Haystack Duggeler is pitching, she is always in her favorite seat back of third, and while she roots hard for the Giants no matter who is pitching, she puts on extra steam when Haystack is bending them over, and it is quite an experience to hear her crying lay them in there, Haystack, old boy, and strike this big tramp out, Haystack, and other exclamations of a similar nature, which please Haystack quite some, but annoy Baseball Hattie's neighbors back of third base, such as Armand Fibleman, if he happens to be betting on the other club.

A month before the close of his first season in the big league, Haystack Duggeler gets so ornery that Manager Mac suspends him, hoping maybe it will cause Haystack to do a little thinking, but naturally Haystack is unable to do this, because he has nothing to think with. About a week later, Manager Mac gets to noticing how he can use a few ball games, so he starts looking for Haystack Duggeler, and he finds him tending bar on Eighth Avenue with his uniform hung up back of the bar as an advertisement.

The baseball writers speak of Haystack as eccentric, which is a polite way of saying he is a screwball, but they consider him a most unique character and are always writing humorous stories about him, though any one of them will lay you plenty of nine to five that Haystack winds up an umbay. The chances are they will raise their price a little, as the season closes and Haystack is again under suspension with cold weather coming on and not a dime in his pants pockets.

It is sometime along in the winter that Baseball Hattie hauls off and marries Haystack Duggeler, which is a great surprise to one and all, but not nearly as much of a surprise as when Hattie closes her boarding and rooming house and goes to live in a little apartment with Haystack Duggeler up on Washington Heights.

It seems that she finds Haystack one frosty night sleeping in a hallway, after being around slightly mulled up for several weeks, and she takes him to her home and gets him a bath and a shave and a clean shirt and two boiled eggs and some toast and coffee and a shot or two of rye whisky, all of which is greatly appreciated by Haystack, especially the rye whisky.

Then Haystack proposes marriage to her and takes a paralyzed oath that if she becomes his wife he will reform, so what with loving Haystack anyway, and with the fix commencing to request more dough off the boarding-and-rooming-house business than the business will stand, Hattie takes him at his word, and there you are.

The baseball writers are wondering what Manager Mac will say when he hears these tidings, but all Mac says is that Haystack cannot possibly be any worse married than he is single-o, and then Mac has the club office send the happy couple a little paper money to carry them over the winter.

Well, what happens but a great change comes over Haystack Duggeler. He stops bending his elbow and helps Hattie cook and wash the dishes, and holds her hand when they are in the movies, and speaks of his love for her several times a week, and Hattie is as happy as nine dollars' worth of lettuce. Manager Mac is so delighted at the change in Haystack that he has the club office send over more paper money, because Mac knows that with Haystack in shape he is sure of twenty-five games, and maybe the pennant.

In late February, Haystack reports to the training camp down South still as sober as some judges, and the other ballplayers are so impressed by the change in him that they admit him to their poker game again. But of course it is too much to expect a man to alter his entire course of living all at once, and it is not long before Haystack discovers four nines in his hand on his own deal and breaks up the game.

He brings Baseball Hattie with him to the camp, and this is undoubtedly a slight mistake, as it seems the old rumor about her boarding-and-rooming-house business gets around among the ever-loving wives of the other players, and they put on a large chill for her. In fact, you will think Hattie has the smallpox.

Naturally, Baseball Hattie feels the frost, but she never lets on, as it seems she runs into many bigger and better frosts than this in her time. Then Haystack Duggeler notices it, and it seems that it makes him a little peevish toward Baseball Hattie, and in fact it is said that he gives her a slight pasting one night in their room, partly because she has no better social standing and partly because he is commencing to cop a few sneaks on the local corn now and then, and Hattie chides him for same.

Well, about this time it appears that Baseball Hattie

discovers that she is going to have a baby, and as soon as she recovers from her astonishment, she decides that it is to be a boy who will be a great baseball player, maybe a pitcher, although Hattie admits she is willing to compromise on a good second baseman.

She also decides that his name is to be Derrill Duggeler, after his paw, as it seems Derrill is Haystack's real name, and he is only called Haystack because he claims he once makes a living stacking hay, although the general opinion is that all he ever stacks is cards.

It is really quite remarkable what a belt Hattie gets out of the idea of having this baby, though Haystack is not excited about the matter. He is not paying much attention to Baseball Hattie by now, except to give her a slight pasting now and then, but Hattie is so happy about the baby that she does not mind these pastings.

Haystack Duggeler meets up with Armand Fibleman along in midsummer. By this time, Haystack discovers horse racing and is always making bets on the horses, and naturally he is generally broke, and then I commence running into him in different spots with Armand Fibleman, who is now betting higher than a cat's back on baseball games.

It is late August, and the Giants are fighting for the front end of the league, and an important series with Brooklyn is coming up, and everybody knows that Haystack Duggeler will work in anyway two games of the series, as Haystack can generally beat Brooklyn just by throwing his glove on the mound. There is no doubt but what he has the old Indian sign on Brooklyn, and the night before the first game, which he is sure to work, the gamblers along Broadway are making the Giants two-to-one favorites to win the game.

This same night before the game, Baseball Hattie is home in her little apartment on Washington Heights waiting for Haystack to come in and eat a delicious dinner of pigs' knuckles and sauerkraut, which she personally prepares for him. In fact, she hurries home right after the ball game to get this delicacy ready, because Haystack tells her he will surely come home this particular night, although Hattie knows he is never better than even money to keep his word about anything.

But sure enough, in he comes while the pigs' knuckles and sauerkraut are still piping hot, and Baseball Hattie is surprised to see Armand Fibleman with him, as she knows Armand backwards and forwards and does not care much for him, at that. However, she can say the same thing about four million other characters in this town, so she makes Armand welcome, and they sit down and put on the pigs' knuckles and sauerkraut together, and a pleasant time is enjoyed by one and all. In fact, Baseball Hattie puts herself out to entertain Armand Fibleman, because he is the first guest Haystack ever brings home.

Well, Armand Fibleman can be very pleasant when he wishes, and he speaks very nicely to Hattie. Naturally, he sees that Hattie is expecting, and in fact he will have to be blind not to see it, and he seems greatly interested in this matter and asks Hattie many questions, and Hattie is delighted to find somebody to talk to about what is coming off with her, as Haystack will never listen to any of her remarks on the subject.

So Armand Fibleman gets to hear all about Baseball Hattie's son, and how he is to be a great baseball player, and Armand says is that so, and how nice, and all this and that, until Haystack Duggeler speaks up as follows, and to wit:

"Oh, dag-gone her son!" Haystack says. "It is going to be a girl, anyway, so let us dismiss this topic and get down to business. Hat," he says, "you fan yourself into the kitchen and wash the dishes, while Armand and me talk."

So Hattie goes into the kitchen, leaving Haystack and Armand sitting there talking, and what are they talking about but a proposition for Haystack to let the Brooklyn club beat him the next day so Armand Fibleman can take the odds and clean up a nice little gob of money, which he is to split with Haystack.

Hattie can hear every word they say, as the kitchen is next door to the dining room where they are sitting, and at first she thinks they are joking, because at this time nobody ever even as much as thinks of skulduggery in baseball, or anyway, not much.

It seems that at first Haystack is not in favor of the idea, but Armand Fibleman keeps mentioning money that Haystack owes him for bets on the horse races, and he asks Haystack how he expects to continue betting on the races without fresh money, and Armand also speaks of the great injustice that is being done Haystack by the Giants in not paying him twice the salary he is getting, and how the loss of one or two games is by no means such a great calamity.

Well, finally Baseball Hattie hears Haystack say all right, but he wishes a thousand dollars then and there as a guarantee, and Armand Fibleman says this is fine, and they will go downtown and he will get the money at once, and now Hattie realizes that maybe they are in earnest, and she pops out of the kitchen and speaks as follows:

"Gentlemen," Hattie says, "you seem to be sober, but I guess you are drunk. If you are not drunk, you must both be daffy to think of such a thing as phenagling around with a baseball game."

"Hattie," Haystack says, "kindly close your trap and go back in the kitchen, or I will give you a bust in the nose."

And with this he gets up and reaches for his hat, and Armand Fibleman gets up, too, and Hattie says like this:

"Why, Haystack," she says, "you are not really serious in this matter, are you?"

"Of course I am serious," Haystack says. "I am sick and tired of pitching for starvation wages, and besides, I will win a lot of games later on to make up for the one I lose tomorrow. Say," he says, "these Brooklyn bums may get lucky tomorrow and knock me loose from my pants, anyway, no matter what I do, so what difference does it make?"

"Haystack," Baseball Hattie says, "I know you are a liar and a drunkard and a cheat and no account generally, but nobody can tell me you will sink so low as to purposely toss off a ball game. Why, Haystack, baseball is always on the level. It is the most honest game in all this world. I guess you are just ribbing me, because you know how much I love it."

"Dry up!" Haystack says to Hattie. "Furthermore, do not expect me home again tonight. But anyway, dry up."

"Look, Haystack," Hattie says, "I am going to have a son. He is your son and my son, and he is going to be a great ballplayer when he grows up, maybe a greater pitcher than you are, though I hope and trust he is not left-handed. He will have your name. If they find out you toss off a game for money, they will throw you out of baseball and you will be disgraced. My son will be known as the son of a crook, and what chance will he have in baseball? Do you think I am going to allow you to do this to him, and to the game that keeps me from going nutty for marrying you?"

Naturally, Haystack Duggeler is greatly offended by Hattie's crack about her son being maybe a greater pitcher than he is, and he is about to take steps, when Armand Fibleman stops him. Armand Fibleman is commencing to be somewhat alarmed at Baseball Hattie's attitude, and he gets to thinking that he hears that people in her delicate condition are often irresponsible, and he fears that she may blow a whistle on this enterprise without realizing what she is doing. So he undertakes a few soothing remarks to her.

"Why, Hattie," Armand Fibleman says, "nobody can possibly find out about this little matter, and Haystack will have enough money to send your son to college, if his markers at the race track do not take it all. Maybe you better lie down and rest awhile," Armand says.

But Baseball Hattie does not as much as look at Armand, though she goes on talking to Haystack. "They always find out thievery, Haystack," she says, "especially when you are dealing with a fink like Fibleman. If you deal with him once, you will have to deal with him again and again, and he will be the first to holler copper on you, because he is a stool pigeon in his heart."

"Haystack," Armand Fibleman says, "I think we better be going."

"Haystack," Hattie says, "you can go out of here and stick up somebody or commit a robbery or a murder, and I will still welcome you back and stand by you. But if you are going out to steal my son's future, I advise you not to go."

"Dry up!" Haystack says. "I am going."

"All right, Haystack," Hattie says, very calm. "But just step into the kitchen with me and let me say one little word to you by yourself, and then I will say no more."

Well, Haystack Duggeler does not care for even just one little word more, but Armand Fibleman wishes to get this disagreeable scene over with, so he tells Haystack to let her have her word, and Haystack goes into the kitchen with Hattie, and Armand cannot hear what is said, as she speaks very low, but he hears Haystack laugh heartily and then Haystack comes out of the kitchen, still laughing, and tells Armand he is ready to go.

As they start for the door, Baseball Hattie outs with a long-nosed .38-caliber Colt's revolver, and goes root-a-toot-toot with it, and the next thing anybody knows, Haystack is on the floor yelling bloody murder, and Armand Fibleman is leaving the premises without bothering to open the door. In fact, the landlord afterwards talks some of suing Haystack Duggeler because of the damage Armand Fibleman does to the door. Armand himself afterwards admits that when he slows down for a breather a couple of miles down Broadway he finds splinters stuck all over him.

Well, the doctors come, and the gendarmes come, and there is great confusion, especially as Baseball Hattie is sobbing so she can scarcely make a statement, and Haystack Duggeler is so sure he is going to die that he cannot think of anything to say except oh-oh-oh, but finally the landlord remembers seeing Armand leave with his door, and everybody starts questioning Hattie about this until she confesses that Armand is there all right, and that he tries to bribe Haystack to toss off a ball game, and that she then suddenly finds herself with a revolver in her hand, and everything goes black before her eyes, and she can remember no more until somebody is sticking a bottle of smelling salts under her nose.

Naturally, the newspaper reporters put two and two together, and what they make of it is that Hattie tries to plug Armand Fibleman for his rascally offer, and that she misses Armand and gets Haystack, and right away Baseball Hattie is a great heroine, and Haystack is a great hero, though nobody thinks to ask Haystack how he stands on the bribe proposition, and he never brings it up himself.

And nobody will ever offer Haystack any more bribes, for after the doctors get through with him he is shy a left arm from the shoulder down, and he will never pitch a baseball again, unless he learns to pitch right-handed.

The newspapers make quite a lot of Baseball Hattie protecting the fair name of baseball. The National League plays a benefit game for Haystack Duggeler and presents him with a watch and a purse of twenty-five thousand dollars, which Baseball Hattie grabs away from him, saying it is for her son, while Armand Fibleman is in bad with one and all.

Baseball Hattie and Haystack Duggeler move to the Pacific Coast, and this is all there is to the story, except that one day some years ago, and not long before he passes away in Los Angeles, a respectable grocer, I run into Haystack when he is in New York on a business trip, and I say to him like this:

"Haystack," I say, "it is certainly a sin and a shame that Hattie misses Armand Fibleman that night and puts you on the shelf. The chances are that but for this little accident you will hang up one of the greatest pitching records in the history of baseball. Personally," I say, "I never see a better left-handed pitcher."

"Look," Haystack says. "Hattie does not miss Fi-bleman. It is a great newspaper story and saves my name, but the truth is she hits just where she aims. When she calls me into the kitchen before I start out with Fibleman, she shows me a revolver I never before know she has, and says to me, 'Haystack,' she says, 'if you leave with this weasel on the errand you mention, I am going to fix you so you will never make another wrong move with your pitching arm. I am going to shoot it off for you.'

"I laugh heartily," Haystack says. "I think she is kidding me, but I find out different. By the way," Haystack says, "I afterwards learn that long before I meet her, Hattie works for three years in a shooting gallery at Coney Island. She is really a remarkable broad," Haystack says.

I guess I forget to state that the day Baseball Hattie is at the Polo Grounds she is watching the new kid sensation of the big leagues, Derrill Duggeler, shut out Brooklyn with three hits.

He is a wonderful young left-hander.

# Spring Training

## LYNN RIGNEY SCHOTT

The last of the birds has returned—
the bluebird, shy and flashy.
The bees carry fat baskets of pollen
from the alders around the pond.
The wasps in the attic venture downstairs,
where they congregate on warm windowpanes.
Every few days it rains.

This is my thirty-fifth spring;
still I am a novice at my work,
confused and frightened and angry.
Unlike me, the buds do not hesitate,
the hills are confident they will be
perfectly reflected
in the glass of the river.

I oiled my glove yesterday.
Half the season is over.
When will I be ready?

On my desk sits a black-and-white postcard picture
of my father—skinny, determined,
in a New York Giants uniform—
ears protruding, eyes riveted.
Handsome, single-minded, *he* looks ready.

Thirty-five years of warmups.
Like glancing down at the scorecard
in your lap for half a second
and when you look up it's done—
a long fly ball, moonlike,
into the night
over the fence,
way out of reach.

There were the California Angels, one strike away from beating the Red Sox for the 1986 American League pennant, and if you will turn back the pages to Moss Klein's marvelous lead about that game you will be reminded of . . . of *what*? Of what, in an enormous stroke of prescience, Klein described, not just as the curse of the Angels, but the curse of both those teams—*"like two phantom ships, circling in the ocean, trying to elude all the old ghosts that have hounded them for so many years."*

*How did he know?* The Red Sox were in the World Series in 1946, and it went seven games, and they lost it. They were in a one-game pennant playoff with Cleveland in 1948, and they lost it. They closed out their 1949 season with a two-game set against the Yankees, and winning either of those games would have given them the pennant. They lost both. They were in the World Series in 1975, and it went seven games, and they lost it. They were in a one-game division playoff with the Yankees in 1978, and they lost it. Then they beat the Angels in the league playoff in 1986, and now not the Angels but they, the Red Sox, were one strike away, with bases empty and a two-run lead, from winning the World Series from the New York Mets in game six of the World Series.

On three different occasions, with three different hitters at bat in the last half of the tenth inning of that game, they were one strike away from winning it all!

Funny: this was the sixth game, not the seventh. Still time, if the Red Sox lost, to go out and win the seventh game and still emerge as world champs.

Forget the seventh game. Because Glenn Schwartz, who wrote this story on the sixth game for *The San Francisco Examiner,* was just as prescient as Moss Klein in the playoffs. Look at the final sentence of this story.

# 1986:
# New York Mets 6,
# Boston Red Sox 5

## GLENN SCHWARTZ

THE BOSTON Red Sox, one strike away from their first World Series championship in 68 years, lost a game for the ages Saturday night.

The desperate New York Mets pulled off a two-out, three-run rally in the 10th inning to win the sixth game, 6–5, and send the Series to a decisive seventh game Sunday, weather permitting.

"This is not a ballclub that gives up easily," Mets manager Davey Johnson said. "When you're two runs down with two out, and it looks like your season is about to end, that's a huge deficit."

But make no mistake—the Red Sox lost this game more than the Mets won it.

After the Sox scored twice in their half of the 10th, they could've withstood two-out singles by Gary Carter, pinch hitter Kevin Mitchell and Ray Knight off loser Calvin Schiraldi. What the Sox couldn't withstand was Bob Stanley's subsequent 2–2 wild pitch that scored

Mitchell with the tying run nor an error by first baseman Bill Buckner that enabled Knight to carry home the winning run from second.

Mookie Wilson's grounder behind the bag skipped under Buckner's glove and through his legs, turning Shea Stadium into an asylum.

"My only thought was to beat the pitcher to first base," Wilson said. "I thought I had a chance to beat it, and I think Buckner saw that too and tried to rush the play a little bit. It wasn't a very well hit ball, but it had the angle and the spin.

"This whole season has been unbelievable. This should really help us tomorrow," Wilson said. "You don't give up with this club. We could have folded, but everybody battled back. It was up to me to do my part, and I did it."

Now the Red Sox know how the California Angels felt.

"I guess I can associate this to what went on in California when they were down to one out and didn't get it," McNamara said. "Yes, it's disappointing . . . I know nothing about history. Don't tell me anything about choking or any of that crap."

In the American League Championship Series, the Angels were one strike away from winning the pennant when Dave Henderson hit a two-run homer off Donnie Moore. The Red Sox went on to win that game and the next two to qualify for the World Series.

Henderson, the unlikeliest of October heroes, was at it again in Game 6. He led off the 10th inning with a home run off Rick Aguilera. The Sox added a run on Wade Boggs' double and Marty Barrett's single, but as it turned out, they needed more.

Schiraldi, the ex-Met, retired Wally Backman and Keith Hernandez before the Mets' three staying-alive singles, and Boston manager John McNamara summoned Stanley. Schiraldi earlier failed to hold a one-run lead for Roger Clemens in the eighth.

Schiraldi's poor throw to second on a bunt by Lenny Dykstra allowed Lee Mazzilli to reach second after his leadoff single. Following Backman's sacrifice and an intentional walk to Hernandez, Carter tied the game with a sacrifice fly.

What had been arguably the least entertaining Series in years finally served up a game with drama, however flawed by both defenses.

The Red Sox scored two quick runs off Mets starter Bobby Ojeda, Dwight Evans doubling home one in the first and the relentless Barrett singling one in the next inning. But Mets fans were at their loudest from the moment parachutist Michael Sergio landed alongside the mound with the Red Sox batting in the first inning.

The crowd retaliated for the Red Sox fans' taunting of Mets right fielder Darryl Strawberry Thursday night, when the Boston audience sing-songed chants of "Dar-ryl, Dar-ryl, Dar-ryl." The Shea gathering started on Evans with "Doo-ey, Doo-ey, Doo-ey." But the repetitive jeering was directed at Clemens—"Ro-ger, Ro-ger, Ro-ger."

It sounded like an English soccer crowd, at least until the Sox took a 3–2 lead in the seventh against Roger McDowell. Barrett's walk, a throwing error by third baseman Knight and rookie shortstop Kevin Elster's botching of a double play—he missed the bag on his pivot—put the Sox ahead briefly.

The Mets didn't show Clemens the utmost respect before the game.

Strawberry, for one, was more impressed by the pitcher who beat the Mets twice.

"I don't think Clemens is a Bruce Hurst," Strawberry said. "Bruce Hurst is a real pitcher. To me, he's their No. 1 . . . There's a lot of guys on this team who hit fastballs."

It took the Mets a spell to hit anything Clemens threw. He struck out six the first three innings and allowed just one base runner before the fifth.

Strawberry was that one, walking with one out in the second and stealing a base to no avail. But Clemens, blowing on his right hand to warm it in the chill, was throwing a lot of pitches. And the expended energy seemed to weaken him in the fifth.

First, critic Strawberry led off with another walk and steal. Then Knight bounced Clemens' first pitch after the stolen base into center for a single, the Mets' first hit driving in their first run.

Wilson followed with a single to right that surprised right fielder Evans. As he reached down, the ball rabbit-hopped into his chest. The error enabled Knight to take third.

By now, the fan noise was as loud as inside an arena. Some were chanting, some sing-songing, some clapping—all were pleading for more.

They got it, though the way the run scored quieted them. Danny Heep, batting for Rafael Santana, grounded into a double play that moved Knight home.

The "Ro-ger, Ro-ger" taunting of Clemens resumed with one out in the seventh. Backman singled despite a diving stop by shortstop Spike Owen and his strong throw from one knee. Then Hernandez, to that point 4-for-20 in the Series, lined a hit-and-run single that shot Backman to third.

Clemens, however, took a deep breath and went to work on clean-up hitter Carter. Three pitches later, The Kid had struck out with the bat on his shoulder. Clemens subsequently silenced Strawberry on a ground ball.

After the Red Sox regained the lead for him, Clemens pitched a clean seventh and was excused for the night.

The night the Red Sox broke New England's heart—again.

In a sport peopled with flamboyant characters, none was more so than baseball's first high commissioner, Kenesaw Mountain Landis. Yet the fact is that few people really knew much about him—the reality, that is. The remedy is here, in this chapter from the book *Baseball: The Golden Age,* the second volume in Dr. Harold Seymour's magnificent history of the game.

# Residue of Scandal

## HAROLD SEYMOUR

ORGANIZED BASEBALL entered upon the postwar era with a new form of government presided over by Judge Kenesaw Mountain Landis. Few baseball men have been accorded higher place in the industry's pantheon than that scowling, white-haired, hawk-visaged curmudgeon who affected battered hats, used salty language, chewed tobacco, and poked listeners in the ribs with a stiff right index finger. His quarter of a century as Commissioner has been transformed by baseball journalists and "historians" into a legend that still cloaks him. He and Babe Ruth are credited with rescuing professional baseball and restoring it to good repute after the Black Sox scandal: Ruth by extraordinary home-run hitting, Landis by fearless extirpation of wrongdoing. In speaking of his "dedication to justice," one writer said, "He was completely uncompromising in applying the letter of the law to wealthy club owners and second-string players alike." The legends about men live after them; their shortcomings are oft interred with their bones. The legend that covers Landis has proved lasting enough to serve as a gauge against which each of his successors has been measured. It also conceals much of Landis himself.

Landis was thirty-eight years old when President Theodore Roosevelt appointed him judge in the United States District Court for the Northern District of Illinois in 1905. His education and legal training for such a position were skimpy. ·After dropping out of high school at Logansport, Indiana, where he was reared, he taught himself shorthand and secured a job as a court reporter. He finished high school at night and enrolled in a YMCA law school at Cincinnati and then in the Union Law School of Chicago, where he received a law degree and admission to the bar in 1891. He never went to college.

Two years later Judge Walter Q. Gresham, his father's commanding officer in the Civil War, went to Washington as Secretary of State under Grover Cleveland and took Landis with him as his secretary. (Landis was named after Kennesaw Mountain—minus an *n*—where his father had been wounded while serving as a physician.) After Gresham's death two years later, Landis returned to Chicago to practice law and enter Republican politics. Frank Lowden, who was running for governor, put him in charge of his 1904 campaign. After Lowden lost the election he was offered a federal judgeship but declined it and recommended Landis for the post. Roosevelt appointed him.

Landis's meager scholastic background and limited legal training were nothing unusual in a day when academic requirements for the professions were much less stringent. But the combination of this lack and his authoritarian personality restricted his outlook and colored his decisions. Honest and fearless though he was, his spare frame housed a narrow, arbitrary, and vindictive nature. No lacklustre jurist was he. His consummate egotism and flair for showmanship caused a scholar to dub him "the grandstand judge" and Heywood Broun to remark, "His career typifies the heights to which dramatic talent may carry a man in America if only he has the foresight not to go on the stage."

Landis had a deep affection for baseball and looked upon the players more as heroes than as employees. He had a keen aversion to organized labor, liquor, and the New Deal. The rub was that he permitted his personal dislikes to warp his judicial objectivity. Visceral response and caprice often swayed his decisions. Even when lenient he was partial. He made what was probably his most important baseball decision before he became

From Lowell Reidenbaugh's marvelous book, *Take Me Out to the Ball Park:*

It is 1917, and Assistant Secretary of the Navy Franklin D. Roosevelt—not yet a polio victim, let alone President of the United States—leads the opening-day parade at Griffith Stadium in Washington in a salute to the U.S. defense effort.

Now it's 1937, the year of the great flood on the Ohio River. Here is Crosley Field in Cincinnati on opening day that year.

And now it's 1964, and here is Griffith Stadium in Washington once again. The photo tells it all.

All three photos reprinted by permission from *The Sporting News: Take Me Out to the Ball Park,* 1983, St. Louis, The Sporting News Publishing Company.

Commissioner, when he put off a verdict on the Federal League's suit. Afterwards he justified his action on other than legal grounds: "The court's expert knowledge of baseball obtained by more than 30 years of observation of the game as a spectator convinced me that if an order had been entered it would have been, if not destructive, at least vitally injurious to the game of baseball." Landis's career refutes the cliché that in America laws, not men, govern the land.

Rarely was Landis's courtroom dull. His procedure, said the New York *Times* in an understatement, was "unorthodox and shocking to sticklers for legal form." For one thing, Landis ordered people brought before him without subpoenas and held others without warrants. Henry F. Pringle stated that because Landis was a prohibitionist, he gave maximum terms to bootleggers, and in some cases he "blandly ignored the law in the interests of what he conceived to be justice." He indulged in prejudicial outbursts and harangues from the bench and later directed that they be stricken from the record; if an attorney objected, he would be threatened with contempt. Reporters, too, came under the judge's displeasure. Once he referred to the staff of *Sporting*

*News* as "swine"; another time he subjected F. C. Lane of *Baseball Magazine* to such personal abuse in the presence of others that Lane wrote him an open letter protesting his treatment. A New York *Daily Mirror* reporter, Jack Lait, said, "His manner of handling witnesses, lawyers—and reporters—was more arbitrary than the behavior of any jurist I have ever seen."

Landis first achieved national prominence in 1907, two years after Roosevelt appointed him. It was the period of Roosevelt's trust-busting pyrotechnics and the Standard Oil Company's nadir of popularity. Landis, never one to miss a trend, imposed his famous $29,400,000 fine on Standard. The decision was overturned on appeal and the fine was never paid, but Landis won popular acclaim and a place on the front pages for days.

After his setback in the Standard Oil case, higher authority continued to overrule Landis with "startling frequency," notably in cases he adjudicated during and after World War One. When the United States entered the war, Landis not only jumped on the patriotic bandwagon, he helped to drive it along its jingoistic route. An illustration of the hysteria of the times was the declaration made by Elihu Root, Secretary of War under Taft and Roosevelt, at a Union League Club meeting in April 1917: "There are men walking about the streets of this city tonight who ought to be taken out at sunrise tomorrow and shot for treason." As this mood spread, the war to make the world safe for democracy nearly quenched freedom at home. Landis abetted the process. "Few men," wrote Pringle, "have been as zealous in the suppression of minorities, and his charges to juries were dangerously similar to patriotic addresses."

In 1918 more than a hundred members of the radical Industrial Workers of the World, including their leader Big Bill Haywood, were rounded up by agents of Attorney General A. Mitchell Palmer and tried en masse in Landis's court, some of them manacled and all watched over by a hundred guards. The air in the courtroom was reportedly "vibrant with the age-old struggle of the classes." The trial was characterized by H. C. Peterson, an authority on treatment of opponents of the war, as "a weird combination of justice and injustice." The defendants had already been tried in the press as "the Bolsheviki of America"; they were now arraigned on vaguely drawn charges of conspiracy to obstruct the war effort. Old I.W.W. literature, illegally seized, was placed in evidence, but little specific proof of individual unlawful acts was produced. It was soon apparent that what was really on trial was the I.W.W. as an organization.

On the whole, Landis conducted the trial with restraint, despite his reputation as a foe of all radical groups. He also took a personal interest in the prisoners' comfort, even to the extent of ordering sixty "metallic cuspidors" for their quarters. In his charge to the jury he likewise appeared to be unbiased. But when, after an hour's deliberation, the jury rendered a verdict of guilty, Landis reverted to form. He imposed fines totaling $2,300,000 and maximum sentences varying from one to twenty years in Chicago's Bridewell, where, he said, "the work is much harder than in the Federal Prison." He also delivered a tirade from the bench in which he took the view that the Bill of Rights was a luxury that gave only fair-weather protection: "When the country is at peace it is a legal right of free speech to oppose going to war . . . but when once war is declared this right ceases." Big Bill Haywood in his autobiography bitterly commented, "Pontius Pilate or Bloody Jeffreys never enjoyed themselves better than did Judge Landis when he was imposing these terrible sentences upon a group of working men for whom he had no feeling of humanity, no sense of justice." After the war other countries released political prisoners, but in America it was five years before President Coolidge commuted the terms of the convicted I.W.W. members. When he did, in 1923, Landis denounced him.

Landis, like Woodrow Wilson and Theodore Roosevelt, believed that opponents of the war should pay the penalty even after the war was over. The Reverend Mr. David Gerdes, a pacifist, came before Landis after the war accused of having advised against buying Liberty Bonds because to do so was to kill Germans by proxy. "What would you do if a Hun were to attack the honor of your daughter?" Landis asked him and his brother, a member of the congregation. When they answered that they would plead for her in the name of God but would not endanger their souls by killing, Landis shouted, "These men hold their measly little shriveled souls of more importance than the honor of their mother, wife, or daughter," and sentenced Gerdes to ten years in Leavenworth, a sentence later commuted to a year and a day.

The famous postwar trial of Victor Berger and five other socialists surfaced some of Landis's deepest antipathies. Not only were the accused members of a radical party, they were also anti-war, and in addition Berger was a German-Austrian emigré. Berger's attorney requested a change of venue and cited utterances by Landis to show that the judge hated Germans and German-Americans and was personally biased against Berger and the others. For instance, Landis allegedly had said, "One must have a very judicial mind, indeed, not to be prejudiced against the German-Americans in this country. Their hearts are reeking with disloyalty."

Landis denied that he was unqualified and set aside the motion to assign another judge. Berger and the others were given twenty-year sentences for conspiracy. The United States Supreme Court reversed the decision, however, and disqualified Landis on account of his "prejudicial conduct before the trial." The government then abandoned further action. Later Landis himself showed that the Supreme Court was right. In a speech before the American Legion he said, "It was my great disappointment to give Berger only twenty years. . . . I believe the law should have enabled me to have had Berger lined up against a wall and shot." And a month before becoming baseball Commissioner he told a convention of schoolteachers that the opposition of the Socialist Party to the government during the war was "responsible for the fact that the bodies of thousands of American soldiers are now in France."

Landis's decision to retain his judgeship after becoming baseball Commissioner provoked heavy criticism from Congress, the American Bar Association, and the press. If Landis really despised money, as he pretended to do, wrote one critic, he would have turned down the "private sideline," or if his sole desire was to reinstate Organized Baseball to public favor, he could have done the job for nothing. In January 1921 T. J. Sutherland, a Chicago attorney, sent a petition to Congress and a letter to Chicago newspapers protesting Landis's "attempt to mulct the government'' and his ''example of vicious infidelity to public service.'' A month later Congressman B. F. Welty of Ohio introduced a resolution asking for an investigation of the legality of Landis's holding two offices. At the hearing that followed, Welty, calling for Landis's impeachment for ''high crimes and misdemeanors,'' based his demand on five charges.

The most telling charge dealt with conflict of interest. Landis had contracted with Organized Baseball, Welty pointed out, at the very time litigation pertaining to the Black Sox and the Baltimore Federal League club was still pending, and when the latter case was at the stage in which Organized Baseball stood under a $240,000 fine for violation of the anti-trust laws. Welty submitted a letter from an owner, whose name he would not disclose, stating that ''K. M. Landis, lawyer, means nothing to organized baseball, but K. M. Landis, judge of the Federal Court of the United States, was worth any price he might wish to ask.'' Welty considered this letter as evidence that the baseball magnates had in effect bribed Landis to become Commissioner. Welty also brought up the Federal League suit of 1915, which, he said, would have gone through the courts had not Landis arbitrated it. If Landis wished to maintain respect as a judge, declared Welty, he must ''divorce himself from the fleshpots of illegal combinations.'' The congressman further charged Landis with neglect of duty and cited a huge backlog of cases on his docket.

Nothing came of Welty's effort, however. The consensus in the House was that, while Landis had lowered the standards of the bench and of legal ethics, impeachment proceedings would not go far because no law was violated. This prediction proved correct, and the Judiciary Committee buried the matter. Landis himself professed to see nothing unethical in his dual employment. In an address before the Missouri Bar Association he said, ''If there's an impropriety here I haven't seen it.''

In the fall of 1921, the American Bar Association renewed the attack in a resolution expressing ''unqualified condemnation'' of Landis and describing his action as ''derogatory to the dignity of the bench.'' Hampton L. Carson, former attorney general of Pennsylvania, who presented the resolution, stated that Landis was ''soiling the ermine by yielding to the temptation of avarice and private gain.'' Senator N. B. Dial of South Carolina submitted the resolution to the Senate whence, after a hot debate, it was passed on to the Judiciary Committee, but again nothing was done.

Landis finally sent his resignation to President Harding in February 1922, to become effective March 1, after he had held the double job for more than fifteen months. Leslie O'Connor, the able young lawyer whom Landis appointed as his secretary, said much later that Landis would have resigned sooner but delayed until ''one of

those Washington storms blew over'' so it would not appear that he had quit under fire.

As was to be expected in view of Landis's personality and background, he quickly made himself felt as Commissioner of Organized Baseball by proscribing the Black Sox players before their trial and reaffirming his decision after a court of law had acquitted them. But he soon found that the slate of scandal and gambling did not wipe clean so easily. Smudge marks from the past reappeared, and fresh ones were made during the first six years of his administration. Since these form a kind of epilogue to the Black Sox affair, it is convenient to discuss them separately from other aspects of his administration in the 1920's.

In March of 1921, less than two weeks after he banned the Black Sox, Landis added Eugene Paulette to his blacklist. While Paulette was playing for the St. Louis Cardinals in 1919, he had caused ''gossip'' on account of his association with St. Louis gamblers Carl Zork, soon to be a figure in the Black Sox scandal, and Elmer Farrar. The gamblers were said to have urged Paulette to cooperate with them by throwing games, and Paulette had received money from Farrar as a ''loan,'' which he had not repaid. The player had also written Farrar to ask for more money, which he did not obtain, and allegedly offered to throw games. Paulette was traded to the Philadelphia Nationals during 1919. The club owners concerned knew about his associations but accepted his affidavit that he had done nothing crooked and let the matter go at that.

When Landis took office, however, President Baker of the Phillies decided to turn Paulette's incriminating letter over to him. Called before Landis, the player denied having thrown any games and insisted that during the 1920 season he had kept aloof from any ''corrupting influences.'' The Commissioner ordered him to report again at a later date for further questioning, and when he failed to do so, Landis blacklisted him permanently. He asserted that Paulette had ''offered to betray his team and that he put himself in the vicious power of Farrar and Zork.'' Landis was obviously trying to discourage associations between players and gamblers. In doing so, he banned Paulette for life not for throwing games but for allegedly offering to do so and for having, like many players and owners, hobnobbed with gamblers.

In June 1921 Landis banned pitcher Ray Fisher for life. Fisher had nothing to do with crookedness, gambling, or association with gamblers. He merely exercised his right to bargain with others outside Organized Baseball. Fisher had taken a cut of $1000 on his 1920 Cincinnati salary of $5500. Consequently, when he learned just before the season started that a coaching position was open at the University of Michigan, he obtained permission from manager Pat Moran to go to

Ann Arbor for an interview. Having been offered the job, he returned to Cincinnati, met with Moran, Garry Herrmann, and other club officials, and asked to be released from his contract. The club now decided it needed Fisher and offered him a raise to stay. Fisher agreed to do so but, in view of his age (thirty-two), asked for the security of a two-year contract. When this was refused, he decided to accept the Michigan job. Garry Herrmann promised to put him on the voluntarily retired list, and the press so reported. But before long Fisher heard that he was to be placed on the blacklist, and when he chanced upon Landis in a Chicago hotel lobby he introduced himself and explained that he had received permission to go to Michigan. Landis was cordial but noncommital.

Toward the close of the college season the "outlaw" Franklin club of Pennsylvania, believing Fisher would be blacklisted, began dickering with him. After the college season ended, Fisher wired Landis for a decision on his status. Landis put him off and added that he understood Fisher had agreed to sign with the Franklin club. Fisher told him he had not. Nevertheless he soon received a telegram from Landis saying that he was blacklisted. No explanation was given, no charges were made, no hearing was offered; nor did Fisher ever hear from the Cincinnati club or ask for a hearing or apply for reinstatement. He just signed with Franklin.

Thirty years later a document entitled "In Re Reinstatement Application of Player Ray L. Fisher" was found in Landis's files. In it Moran was quoted as saying he "positively refused to grant" Fisher permission to go to Michigan; that the Cincinnati club had offered a "large increase" in salary, but Fisher refused to carry out his contract; that Fisher applied for reinstatement after the college season and, pending consideration thereof, carried on negotiations with the Franklin team, which was composed largely of "contract violators," and had agreed to terms with them in case he was not reinstated. It concluded that "obviously" his application must be denied. Apparently Fisher's crime was his independent attitude in exercising a choice of employment outside Organized Baseball. Whatever the reason, Landis's permanent ban is incomprehensible.

Benny Kauff, outfielder for the New York Giants, was another player who came under the Landis frown of power in 1921. Unlike Paulette, whose alleged transgression at least pertained to baseball, Kauff was put on the "permanently ineligible" list because of an incident that had nothing to do with Organized Baseball.

The Giants had acquired Kauff for a reported $30,000 after the Federal League war, when players were auctioned off. After serving in the military, Kauff returned to the Giants and opened an automobile sales business on the side in partnership with his half brother. In

February 1920 he was arrested and indicted for stealing a car and for receiving stolen cars. Released on bail, he played through the 1920 season, but it was his last. With the case still pending, Landis, declaring that Kauff's indictment showed he was probably guilty, ruled him ineligible just before the start of the 1921 season.

In May Kauff was acquitted in court and applied to the Commissioner for reinstatement, but Landis refused it. In September the player secured a temporary injunction directing the baseball authorities to show cause why they should not be restrained from interfering with Kauff's fulfillment of his contract with the Giants, pending the outcome of his suit for a permanent injunction. Judge Edward O. Whitaker of the New York Supreme Court said he was powerless to grant the injunction because Kauff's contract had expired. In reality, of course, the Giants were ready and willing to use Kauff; however, no New York club official would admit as much in the face of Landis's suspension of the player. Kauff appealed, but his case was dropped when his attorney Emil Fuchs (also attorney for Rothstein and later to become president of the Boston National League club) reached an agreement with Organized Baseball's attorneys John Conway Toole and George Wharton Pepper.

Why was Kauff deprived of his livelihood and the New York club of his services, even though the court had acquitted him? Evidently because the outcome of his trial did not suit Landis. The Commissioner read the trial papers and wrote Kauff that the evidence they disclosed compromised his character and reputation so seriously that his presence in the New York lineup would "burden patrons of the game with grave apprehension as to its integrity." Later Landis took occasion to call Kauff's acquittal "one of the worst miscarriages of justice that ever came under my observation." Judge Whitaker, on the other hand, saw nothing wrong with Kauff's acquittal. On the contrary, even while denying Kauff a permanent injunction, he stated that "an apparent injustice has been done the plaintiff." Apart from the merits of Kauff's acquittal, the fact is that like the Black Sox he was put in double jeopardy. Exonerated under the law of the land, Kauff was still subject to the "law" of that government within a government which is Organized Baseball. Its "law" vested dictatorial power in the Commissioner, making him both judge and jury, and he chose to use that power against Kauff.

In 1922 Landis banished another Giant player, pitcher Phil Douglas, for "treachery." Douglas was a drunkard given to "the disappearing act" and to frequenting "resorts"; he was more a subject for pity than for punishment. He had already knocked about with four major-league clubs before coming to the Giants in a 1919 trade. Manager McGraw, knowing Douglas's frailties, assigned a man to watch him.

Late in August Douglas eluded his latest "keeper," coach Jesse Burkett, an old-time star, and disappeared for several days. Burkett and some detectives finally found him in his room and took him to a sanatarium where he was kept incommunicado for five days while he dried out. After getting out, he was fined $100, suspended five days without pay, and charged with $224.30 for the sanatarium and for taxi fares. He also received one of McGraw's characteristic tongue-lashings.

At this time his club was virtually tied for first place with the St. Louis Cardinals. In a fit of pique Douglas wrote their outfielder, Leslie Mann:

I want to leave here. I don't want to see this guy [McGraw] win the pennant. You know I can pitch, and I am afraid if I stay I will win the pennant for him.

Talk this over with the boys, and if it is all right send the goods to my house at night and I will go to fishing camp. Let me know if you all will do this, and I will go home on the next train.

Whether Douglas was still suffering from the aftereffects of liquor or drugs or was drunk again, he certainly was in a muddled frame of mind. The last person to whom he should have sent such a message was Leslie Mann, a tee-totaling YMCA enthusiast. Mann turned the letter over to Branch Rickey, who forwarded it to the Commissioner. When Douglas admitted writing it, Landis exiled him from Organized Baseball. It was "tragic and deplorable," Landis was quoted as saying, "[but] there is no excuse to be offered for Douglas. He is the victim of his own folly." McGraw denounced Douglas publicly as "the dirtiest ball player I have ever seen." This was quite a superlative, in view of his experience with men like Chase.

After his ouster Douglas engaged an attorney who wrote Landis to ask for a hearing. Landis agreed to give one if the attorney had any new evidence. But shortly Douglas was reported as having "another breakdown," and there was no further mention of a lawsuit. About ten years afterwards a sportswriter led an attempt to get him reinstated, but Landis was adamant, although he did send a check to the player, who was badly off. When Douglas died in 1952 there was a mortgage on his hillside cabin in Tennessee.

Douglas was not a dishonest player; he was an immature and sick man. He threw no games, nor did he offer to throw any, and there is no evidence of any collusion with gamblers. But in a distraught, befuddled, and angry moment he wrote a foolish letter that brought him a harsh punishment.

Landis made a complete turnabout in 1923 by ruling in favor of none other than versatile Rube Benton, whose activities combined pitching, boozing, wenching, and gambling, and who was accused of perjury and possession of "guilty knowledge" of the 1919 World Series plot. Although Benton had admitted knowing of the Black Sox fix beforehand, he had continued to play with the Giants until they shipped him to the minor-league St. Paul team in the middle of 1921. He was more or less persona non grata in the National League, and in the American Ban Johnson made it clear that he was a "tainted" player.

Benton did well with St. Paul, however, so Garry Herrmann decided to bring him back to Cincinnati, where he had begun his big-league career. Heydler opposed the deal and in a guarded public statement said he was confident Cincinnati would not go through with it if the majority of National League clubs did not want Benton back in the league; it was for them to decide, he said. Herrmann's argument was that if Benton was an "undesirable player" for the National League, he should have been equally unfit for the minors. At their February meeting a majority of National League owners backed Heydler—but they also voted to let Landis make the final decision.

Heydler had every reason to believe that the Commissioner would make short work of Benton. But to Heydler's amazement Landis ruled in favor of Benton and excoriated those who wanted to keep him out. Landis's decision was scrupulously fair to the player. The question, he said, was whether Benton was eligible to play anywhere: if he was ineligible to play with Cincinnati, then he was ineligible to play with St. Paul. He pointed out that it had never been contended that Benton was a dishonest player, and the National League had never taken disciplinary action against him. To the contrary, Landis noted—in a pointed thrust at the National League's concealment policy—Benton's "alleged irregularities" had been kept quiet and he was allowed to play with both New York and St. Paul. Certainly the time to bring accusations that could permanently deprive a man of his chief means of livelihood was at the time the alleged irregularities became known, "not at the objectors' discretion upwards of two years later." Landis concluded, "Player Benton is declared eligible."

At this unexpected decision, Heydler at first seemed ready to defy Landis: "It is our judgement that Benton is not the type of character of player we want and therefore I will not sanction his return to our organization." But after conferring privately with Landis, Heydler announced that Benton could play and that the matter was closed.

Landis's complaint against Heydler for waiting two years before trying to ban Benton from baseball might easily have been turned back upon him. As a *Sporting News* editorial pointed out, Landis, "knowing through the records or having read the public prints of the charges made against Rube Benton, himself is to some degree responsible for Benton being permitted to play ball in the seasons of 1921 and 1922, two full years." The editor could have added that Landis also was not bothered by any hobgoblin of consistency. He had banned Buck Weaver and Joe Gedeon for "guilty knowledge" but had kept Benton. He had also banned Paulette on *ex post facto* charges but objected to penalizing Benton for past transgressions. And if Benny Kauff was unfit to be associated with baseball because of his character, Benton was even less so. Landis's decision on Benton, wrote Francis C. Richter, ex-editor of the defunct *Sporting Life,* "did more to affect his dignity and prestige, and to undermine the magnates' faith in his judgment and his fitness for absolute power" than anything since the Black Sox.

These cases involving individual ball players were overshadowed by the O'Connell-Dolan affair, which erupted in 1924. This new scandal, coming as it did while memories of the Black Sox were still fresh, reawakened doubts about the integrity of Organized Baseball and raised questions about what really occurred that have been left unanswered to this day. It also centered upon the New York Giants in a way that curiously paralleled the 1908 episode involving them, the one that resulted in the never fully explained banishment of their team physician, Doc Creamer.

It was near the end of the season, and the Giants held a secure game-and-a-half lead over second-place Brooklyn. They had three games left to play, all with seventh-place Philadelphia, and Brooklyn had only two, with last-place Boston. Two New York victories would clinch the pennant regardless of what Brooklyn did. But, as J. G. Taylor Spink wrote later, there were "persons" who wanted to make the outcome of the pennant race a sure thing.

Before the first game Jimmy O'Connell, a young Giant outfielder, approached the Philadelphia shortstop Heinie Sand and offered him $500 if he would take it easy in the game. The Giants won the game and the pennant too, since Brooklyn lost that day; but meanwhile Sand had reported O'Connell's proposition to his manager, Art Fletcher, who informed John Heydler. Heydler relayed the information to Landis, who came to New York at once. After questioning Sand, Landis called in Charles Stoneham, the Giants' owner, and manager McGraw. McGraw expressed resentment that Heydler had not told him about it before calling Landis.

When Landis summoned O'Connell, the player readily admitted his guilt and said he had followed instructions from Cozy Dolan, a Giant coach variously called McGraw's "Man Friday," "body guard," "gumshoe," and "tale bearer." O'Connell also implicated three Giant stars, Frank Frisch, Ross Youngs, and George Kelly, who he said had inquired afterwards about Sand's response to his proposition. O'Connell gave the impression that others in the Giants' organization knew what was going on too. He later said, "I was working for the Giants and I thought the management wanted me to do it."

Landis next questioned Cozy Dolan, who exasperated him by persistently answering that he did not remember, and also Frisch, Youngs, and Kelly. He then announced that O'Connell and Dolan were permanently blacklisted, Dolan because his "testimony on his own behalf was of such a character as to be unacceptable." The Commissioner completely exonerated the other three players, whose testimony he characterized as "a clear refutation" of O'Connell's charges.

Why had Landis believed O'Connell's accusations against Dolan and not those against Frisch, Youngs, and Kelly? The reason, said a *Sporting News* correspondent, was that Dolan's replies were "evasive" while those of the players were "straight-forward." Within a few months the public discovered just how straightforward the players' replies were. In January 1925 Landis issued the stenographic report of his hearings in order to allay the intimations of sportswriters that he was hiding something. According to the record, part of Youngs's statement was:

> I have heard talking around and such things mentioning it, but I don't remember who by. You hear fellows talking around that boys that are offering money and something like that. I never heard anything like this, offering money here. This is the first I heard of it.

Similarly, Frisch stated: "On a pennant contender, you always hear a lot of stuff like that, a lot of kidding and some other things. That is all I ever hear."

News that Landis had expelled O'Connell and Dolan broke just three days before the World Series. The Commissioner seemed to assume that his action ended the matter, and Heydler declared outright that the case was closed. But many were convinced there was more to it than met the eye. Ban Johnson and Barney Dreyfuss wanted Landis to call off the World Series, but he refused. Johnson, who still nursed his hatred of McGraw and his resentment of Landis, called for a federal investigation. This was tantamount to saying that Landis was unable or unwilling to get to the bottom of the affair. To the further vexation of the Commissioner, Congressman Sol Bloom of New York supported Johnson and called for a federal statute to regulate Organized Baseball as an interstate enterprise.

Johnson then underscored his displeasure with the handling of the case by peevishly absenting himself from the World Series. He also chose this moment, when the information would cause the most embarrassment to McGraw, to produce a hitherto secret affidavit given him in 1923 by Lou Criger, the old-time catcher of the Boston Red Sox, which disclosed an attempted fix of the 1903 World Series. According to Criger's sworn statement, one Anderson, a gambler, approached him at the Monongahela Hotel in Pittsburgh just before the Series and offered him $12,000 to see to it that Pittsburgh won. Criger had spurned the bribe and confided the incident only to his battery mate Cy Young. The story had been kept quiet for twenty years. In revealing the incident, Johnson took pains to point out that the affidavit stated that when Criger was first introduced to the gambler both Wilbert Robinson and John McGraw had been present.

Dreyfuss, whose Pittsburgh Pirates had finished a close third behind New York and Brooklyn, called for a thorough probe. Putting his finger on the crux, he declared it was insulting to the intelligence "to ask people to believe that two rather obscure members [of the Giants] would go and offer to pay somebody $500, solely of their own money, to have something crooked done that would benefit many other persons besides themselves." In addition, Dreyfuss made the cryptic remark: "The New York players change, but the manager remains the same." Dreyfuss followed up by going to Washington, where the Series was about to open, to seek out Landis and give him additional evidence. The Commissioner refused to talk to him and rudely left him and his manager standing in the hotel lobby.

There were reporters, too, who felt the same as Dreyfuss did. *Sporting News* editorialized:

Who is behind this assault and other assaults on the integrity of the sport? . . . Surely no ball player of his own volition will do these things. When is the cleaning out, the general cleaning out, going to begin? That's what the fans want to know. Who inspired Dolan?

Reporter W. O. Phelan was caustic. All those who believed, he wrote, that "a green kid" and "a worn-out coach" devised the plot "without full directions from some crooked brain who neatly used them as a catspaw" should mobilize in the nearest telephone booth, where they would not be crowded. An unidentified New York writer was quoted as saying, "There have been a number of things happen in New York which deserved investigation, but everyone seems to be afraid of Mc-Graw." A story in *Sporting News* claimed that even Landis recognized that the bribe money could not have come from O'Connell personally and therefore must

have been contributed by the team or its management. Frank Richter criticized Landis severely and declared he "exhibited . . . an astonishing incapacity or unwillingness to probe the case to the bottom."

Some new developments helped to keep the murky episode before the public in the months after the World Series. One of them was Cozy Dolan's decision to sue Landis for defamation of character. His attorney was none other than William J. Fallon, counsel for Charles Stoneham and Arnold Rothstein. It was soon learned that McGraw was the one who had sent Dolan to see Fallon and the one who was paying him. Angered by this development, Landis conveyed his sentiments to the New York club's management in pungent language. Abruptly, before Fallon even filed papers, Dolan dropped the suit and left for his home in Oshkosh, Wisconsin.

Another bit of spice went into the stew the following January when it was discovered that George Kelly, one of the three named by O'Connell, and Sammy Bohne, a Cincinnati infielder, had become teammates of O'Connell's on a California basketball team. Heydler, expressing shock and disbelief, warned that Bohne and especially Kelly were jeopardizing their baseball standing, the inference being that association with an outcast contaminates. Garry Herrmann, while not agreeing with Heydler, took no chances on having Bohne blacklisted and ordered him not to play. In a little while, however, the basketball team saved Kelly and Bohne by the simple expedient of firing O'Connell.

Finally, New York District Attorney Joab H. Banton started an investigation and promised to prosecute if he found any violations of the criminal code. Landis sent him what evidence he had but admitted that he had no corroborating evidence against O'Connell. He did not even have O'Connell's original confession because at the time he questioned the player the stenographer was late in arriving, and when he did get there O'Connell was not asked to repeat what he had already told Landis—an oversight that was "puzzling to say the least," said *Sporting News*. After supplying the evidence he had, Landis left for Cuba. The assistant district attorney suggested dryly that the Commissioner might better have devoted less attention to golfing in the tropics and more to the baseball scandal in New York.

The investigation failed to uncover anything. Some ball players testified but not O'Connell, who refused to come east unless given immunity, which the district attorney was unwilling to grant. Neither were officials of the Giants called, nor Dreyfuss, Johnson, or Heydler. In his final report Banton stated that O'Connell "may" have been guilty and that Dolan, in his replies to Landis, "brought suspicion upon himself which has not been removed by my examination of Dolan." The district attorney found no legal evidence against Frisch, Youngs, and Kelly and declared that their "excellent reputations and manner of answering questions . . . points strongly to their innocence." Public opinion became sympathetic toward O'Connell as the unwitting "goat" of the piece, whereas fans booed Sand all over the National League circuit—in keeping with the American habit of venting displeasure more on those who expose wrongdoing than on the wrongdoers themselves.

Time has failed to remove the mystery veiling the O'Connell-Dolan scandal. The stock "explanations" boil down to three: gamblers who could not be reached were behind it; O'Connell, young, naive, or just plain stupid, allowed himself to become the "dupe" of unnamed others; a practical joke perpetrated by teammates hazing O'Connell ended in tragedy for him. But an editorial in *Sporting News* in January 1925 termed the Landis investigation "a screaming farce." And many years later that paper's editor, Taylor Spink, printed the intriguing statement: "Had 'Cozy Dolan,' backed by the Giants, gone through with it [the lawsuit], I believe the Commissioner would have ripped the game wide open."

Landis enjoyed a respite from scandals in 1925, and he almost got through 1926 without any—but not quite. Early in November came the stunning news that Detroit had granted Ty Cobb his unconditional release both as manager and player. Before fans recovered from that jolt they received a second one. A month later they learned that Tris Speaker was resigning as player-manager at Cleveland to enter private business. That these two pillars of the American League should just drop out of baseball was incredible. Although Cobb's managerial ability was debatable, he was still a valuable asset as a player. Speaker's departure was even more inexplicable. He had led the Indians to second place, only three games behind New York, and the club had made money accordingly. Yet all of a sudden, within the space of a month, the two renowned stars had quit. What lay back of it? Rumors spread, and sportswriters pestered baseball officials for more information.

A few days before Christmas it came. Landis made the breathtaking announcement that Cobb and Speaker had been "permitted to resign" in the face of accusations of fixing and betting on a game between Cleveland and Detroit on September 25, 1919. The chief evidence against them consisted of two letters, one written by Cobb and one by "Smokey" Joe Wood, to Hubert "Dutch" Leonard, a retired pitcher. Leonard had recently forwarded the letters to Ban Johnson, who had bought them for the American League. In 1919 Cobb and Leonard had both been on the Detroit team, and Speaker and Wood were with Cleveland. The Indians had already clinched second place, and Detroit had a chance to finish third by winning the game in question. According to Leonard, the four players met under the stands beforehand, and Speaker said something to the effect that Cobb and Leonard should not worry because "your club will win the game." (Detroit did win.) The four decided that since the game was to be a "set-up," they might as well make some money by betting on it.

Leonard's story was only partially substantiated by the letters. The one written by Wood, printed in the *Times,* read:

> Enclosed please find certified check for sixteen hundred and thirty dollars ($1,630.00).
>
> The only bet West* could get down was $600 against $420 (10 to 7). Cobb did not get up a cent. He told us that and I believed him. Could have put up some at 5 to 2 on Detroit, but did not, as that would make us put up $1000 to win $400.
>
> We won the $420. I gave West $30, leaving $390, or $130 for each of us. Would not have cashed your check at all, but West thought he could get it up at 10 to 7, and I was going to put it all up at those odds. We would have won $1,750 for the $2,500 if we could have placed it.
>
> If we ever have another chance like this we will know enough to try to get down early.

The pertinent passages in Cobb's letter were:

> Wood and myself were considerably disappointed in our business proposition, as we had $2,000 to put into it and the other side quoted us $1,400, and when we finally secured that much money it was about 2 o'clock and they refused to deal with us, as they had men in Chicago to take up the matter with and they had no time, so we completely fell down and of course we felt badly over it.
>
> Everything was open to Wood and he can tell you about it when we get together. It was quite a responsibility and I don't care for it again, I can assure you.

Although later in his ghosted book Cobb omitted mention of the incriminating letters and claimed he had never bet on an American League game, at the time of the scandal he admitted he had written the letter and acknowledged that there had been a betting proposition. He said he had always played to win, and that no game he had ever played in was to his knowledge fixed. He attributed Leonard's charges to resentment over his having sent Leonard to the minors and to Speaker's failure to claim him on waivers. Speaker denied all

* Clubhouse man.

knowledge of the affair. He pointed out that there was no letter written by him and that he was not even mentioned in those written by Cobb and Wood.

In releasing the news, Landis dissimulated by telling reporters that it had not been made known earlier because "none of the men involved is now associated with baseball." (Cobb and Speaker had been released, and Wood, who was a coach at Yale, had been out of the major leagues since 1922; little attention was paid to him during the controversy.) In the next breath Landis said he would defer his decision on the accused until later in the winter. "Baseball is again on trial," said the *Times,* "if for no other reason than the peculiar concealment of the Leonard charges."

If Landis was waiting to see which way the winds of public opinion would blow, he soon found out. By this time the public was probably satiated with scandals both in baseball and government. Besides, it was difficult for people to believe that strong competitors like Cobb and Speaker would lose intentionally. Fans and prominent public figures defended the players. If Cobb and Speaker had "been selling out all these years," said Will Rogers, "I would like to have seen them play when they wasn't selling." The Cleveland City Council adopted a resolution expressing confidence in Speaker. Both senators from Georgia, Cobb's home state, vowed to see that he received justice, and some Detroit citizens planned to petition American League owners to prefer charges of incompetence against Landis.

But before the issue was resolved, a new sensation diverted attention from the Cobb-Speaker affair. Swede Risberg, one of the exiled Black Sox, charged that a series of games had been thrown by Detroit in 1917. Manager Clarence "Pants" Rowland, Risberg claimed, had assured him beforehand that "Everything's all fixed," meaning that Detroit was going to "slough off" the two doubleheaders to Chicago on September 2 and 3 in order to put the White Sox at an advantage in their hot battle for first place against the Boston Red Sox. Chicago did win all four games. Later, said Risberg, each man on the Chicago team put up approximately $45 apiece towards a purse of $1100 as a reward for the Detroit pitchers. Players like Eddie Collins, Ray Schalk, and others who had been considered "clean" during the 1919 Series scandal had contributed to the bribe, and Comiskey himself knew about it. Risberg also claimed that two years later, in 1919, "some of our boys" decided to return Detroit's favor of 1917: "We ought to be good to Detroit. . . . So the last two games we had with Detroit we sloughed off." In addition, Risberg maintained that some players on the St. Louis Browns had taken it easy in certain games against Chicago in 1917 in exchange for "gifts." "They pushed Ty Cobb

and Tris Speaker out on a piker bet. I think it's only fair that the 'white lilies' get the same treatment," stated Risberg. Chick Gandil, another of the Black Sox, then came out in support of Risberg's story and claimed he could tell even worse tales.

Landis brought Risberg from Minnesota to Chicago at Organized Baseball's expense and questioned him for two hours on New Year's Day. Landis was acting as though he had never heard of the accusations. Actually, back in 1922 Happy Felsch had made the same charges during his lawsuit against Comiskey, and at that time Landis had shrugged them off as not worth considering. Furthermore, an entry in Harry Grabiner's diary, dated February 16, 1921, shows that Ray Schalk had discussed the matter with Landis then. Another notation in the diary, dated October 10, 1919, stated that Ban Johnson had told District Attorney Hoyne he knew that Chicago players had bribed Detroit to throw games in 1917.

Landis invited some forty players connected with the 1917 White Sox and Tigers to hearings January 5 in Chicago, but before they convened, the defense position had already been staked out by the owners of the clubs involved: they admitted that the pool was collected, but not as a bribe for Detroit to lose to Chicago; they said it was a reward for beating the Boston Red Sox three times straight. Said Comiskey, "This matter was known to everybody. I am not condoning any one or any act." Eddie Collins, former captain of the Clean Sox, explained that the fund was raised more than a month after the series at issue—an implication that time converted a bribe into a gift. "In those days," Collins pointed out, "it was nothing out of the ordinary to give a player on another team some sort of a gift if he went out of the way to turn in a good performance against one of a team's leading rivals in the [pennant] race." Frank admission of this custom was somewhat disillusioning. It ran counter to the article of faith that the heroes were straining their hardest to win at all times.

Barney Dreyfuss then chimed in with a similar story. He charged that in 1921 the New York Giants had offered Brooklyn players money to beat Pittsburgh, the Giants' chief rival for the pennant. McGraw retorted that such a story was "too absurd to discuss," and Brooklyn manager Wilbert Robinson said, "I never heard of it. It is ridiculous." Phil Ball staunchly defended his Browns against having "taken it easy" against Chicago in 1917, although at the time he himself had accused them of not giving their best.

More than thirty players, among them some of the most famous in the American League, and about fifty reporters crowded Landis's office for two days of hearings. In the presence of Risberg and Gandil they generally admitted that a pool had been formed and money had been given to Detroit, but they said that it was a reward for beating Boston, not for losing to Chicago. In a week or so Landis gave the accused blanket exoneration. Terming the pool a "gift fund," he declared the deed "an act of impropriety, reprehensible and censurable, but not an act of criminality."

By this time Landis had had his fill of old scandals. As he remarked off the record, "Won't these God damn things that happened before I came into baseball ever stop coming up?" He therefore decided to establish a five-year statute of limitations on baseball offenses. John Heydler called Landis's acquittal a common-sense view—by which he perhaps meant that the Commissioner could not very well blacklist more than thirty players. He attributed the incident to the "muddled" and "distressing" days when the United States was entering the World War. Ban Johnson was quoted as saying he had known of the fund raised for the Detroit players, but, he explained, "It was simply a reward for a player to use extra effort against a pennant rival. . . . Of course, it was wrong doing . . . yet it was not a criminal act."

In the meantime the fate of Cobb and Speaker remained in abeyance until January 27, when Landis rendered a verdict and a summary of the case. On the basis of this document and other information, it seems that Ban Johnson and the American League believed as far back as early September of 1926 that they possessed sufficient evidence to warrant getting rid of Cobb and Speaker. The two players had requested permission to resign without a hearing, because they believed that unless they could confront their accuser, Dutch Leonard—and he refused to come east from California for a hearing—even a mere announcement of his charges would damage them, experience having shown that "a vindication by baseball authority" based on lack of proof "has been labeled a 'whitewash.' " The American League had honored this request in order to save them and their families embarrassment. Ban Johnson had then turned the letters and other evidence over to Landis, not "to pass the buck," he said later, but as a courtesy. After talking with Cobb and Speaker, Landis acquiesced in their wish to bow out quietly, with the understanding that if the situation changed, a public announcement might be necessary.

As we have seen, the situation did change, to the extent that Landis felt constrained to release the story and the text of the letter just before Christmas. However, by reserving judgment on their guilt or innocence, he left Cobb and Speaker in limbo. Ban Johnson grasped the opportunity to criticize Landis openly and more waspishly than he had in the O'Connell-Dolan case. He was "amazed" that Landis had released the information sent him, which he had no right to do; the reason must have been "a desire for personal publicity." Johnson also proclaimed that Cobb and Speaker would never play in the American League again while he was president. With this attack on Landis, Johnson sounded his own knell in baseball.

When the real reason for their departure from baseball became known, Cobb and Speaker informed Landis of their wish to rescind their withdrawal from baseball and asked that their status be clarified. They also engaged attorneys. It was because of their request, said Landis, not as a result of Johnson's sending him the letters, that he was issuing his summary of the case and his decision. His verdict was practically a foregone conclusion in view of his disposition of the Risberg-Gandil charges and his declared statute of limitations. Landis ruled that the players "have not been, nor are they now, found guilty of fixing a ball game."

The two stars were returned to the reserve lists of Detroit and Cleveland, but since the respective owners, Frank Navin and Jim Dunn, no longer wanted them, they were made free agents. Landis made it plain, however, that they were to play only in the American League, not in the National, some of whose clubs indicated an interest in them. Cobb signed with Connie Mack's Philadelphia Athletics and Speaker with Washington, in spite of Johnson's vow to keep them out.

The entire affair must have been a bit mystifying to the customers, wrote W. O. McGeehan of the New York *Herald Tribune*. "First, they learn that two of the greatest synthetic heroes produced by the national pastime have been ousted for cause. Now they learn that there was no reason at all why they should have left the game excepting their personal differences with their owners." Cobb in his 1961 book attributed the affair to a "plot" hatched against him by Leonard, Navin, Johnson, and Landis: Leonard because of a thirst for "revenge"; Navin because of "acute desire to slide out from under" Cobb's $50,000 contract; Johnson because of "long hatred" of him and Speaker; and Landis because of his "phobia [mania] for projecting himself into the limelight."

In any event, the Commissioner's decision was a popular one and, as McGeehan remarked, "Landis made the best of an unfortunate situation," since the "charges were calculated to do great injury to professional baseball."

No other scandals came to public attention in the few remaining years of the 'twenties or in the 'thirties either. Landis kept some investigations "confidential," but this is not to say that they involved crookedness. New anti-fix rules and penalties recommended by Landis and adopted with slight modifications by the owners at the end of 1927 no doubt helped to keep the slate clean of villainy. Similar rules had existed in the National Agreement since 1903 but had not been enforced. The new rules barred a player for three years for offering or accepting a reward either for extra effort or for "going easy"; made permanently ineligible those players and club officials who bet on a game in which they were involved; suspended for one year those who bet on any other game; and banned for life a player who offered a gift to an umpire or an umpire who accepted one. Under the new National Agreement of 1921 Landis already had the broad power to blacklist a player for "the best interests of the game"; the additional regulations were simply more particularized and provided for the penalty of expulsion.

During his first several years Landis blacklisted some fifteen players permanently, including the eight Black Sox. Others were banned for varying periods for such offenses as participating in games in which ineligible players took part or playing with the outlaws. In 1924 there was a total of fifty-three players on the ineligible list. Landis also had a "secret police system," as the *Times* called it; he employed a detective whom nobody knew, and players discovered to have committed minor infractions were called in and warned.

The Black Sox scandal and those that followed also motivated a number of state legislatures to enact laws providing fines and imprisonment for throwing games and bribing ball players, and in some instances Landis encouraged lobbying for such measures. New York State's statutes, for example, provided for from one to five years in jail and a fine of $10,000 for such offenses and applied to "any professional or amateur game or sport." By 1960 at least thirty-two states had such statutes. They were rarely enforced, however, because of public complacency and the difficulty of discovering dishonesty.

The parent of fixed games, gambling, throve in the 1920's. Betting on the World Series was, as usual, especially heavy, and baseball lotteries and pools continued to flourish. One of the largest and most notorious pools was the Albany (New York) Pool, an outfit that dated back to 1905 and whose continued operation created a scandal because of the complicity of many politicians. In 1927 alone it grossed $4,066,401. Ban Johnson reported to Landis in 1922 that in Chicago pools were operating on a more extensive scale than in any other city, and they mulcted the public of fabulous sums yearly. In Ohio Governor Donahey issued a proclamation calling on mayors and sheriffs to enforce the law against pools and lotteries. "In every important urban center throughout the state," he said, there was gambling on baseball, and through no fault of its own the game had been made a vehicle for corrupting youth by means of punch boards, slot machines, and chances sold on games. "The perils of gambling have not been

removed from baseball," Johnson warned, and "owners must take action if we are to escape another scandal." Landis himself declared that the "loathsome evil" of professional gamblers and pools menaced baseball. "The peril in the situation," he wrote one of the owners, "is that the public may not distinguish this species of gambling from the gambling that corrupts ball games."

To recognize the problem was one thing; to solve it was like trying to tunnel through a mountain with a chisel. Since 1903 the major-minor league agreement had contained a rule against gambling in ball parks which the owners were supposed to enforce. With the Black Sox vividly in mind, the owners now made a renewed bid to stop betting in their parks by employing detectives to evict, arrest, or bar gamblers from their parks altogether. In Brooklyn, for example, Ebbets got city policemen to work without pay on their off-duty days; in exchange, he contributed to the Police Department fund. The National League passed an innocuous resolution calling on state governors to sponsor legislation against gamblers and wagering on baseball. Landis asked newspapermen to stop printing weekly runs-scored tables, and in 1930 he ordered team managers not to announce their starting pitchers until "warmup" time.

Results were negligible. Dreyfuss, for instance, complained that Pittsburgh police did not take the matter seriously and that police magistrates discharged prisoners as fast as they were arrested. When he was told of this, Landis reputedly "roared" in the Schenley lobby, "Politics or no politics, we'll put a stop to gambling." Although betting inside the parks may have been reduced, in 1928 an article in *Outlook* claimed that baseball betting in general exceeded that on horse racing.

In his abhorrence of gambling Landis was driven into conflicts with baseball owners and players over race tracks, where he feared they might be corrupted by gamblers and fixers. His first encounter was with Charles A. Stoneham and John McGraw of the Giants. In 1919 they became owners of the Oriental Park and Jockey Club and the Casino Nacional in Havana. Stoneham was not the first nor would he be the last baseball owner to be involved with horses, but when Landis became Commissioner he informed Stoneham and McGraw that they must choose between racing and baseball, so they divested themselves of their Cuban property, although they continued to frequent the track.

Later that year (1921) Stoneham drew a severe reprimand when Landis learned that Arnold Rothstein had appeared as Stoneham's guest in his private box at the Polo Grounds. Landis extracted a promise from Stoneham not to invite Rothstein to his box again, but he did nothing about Stoneham's business relationship with him.

This relationship was multifaceted. Early on, Rothstein had acted as middleman when Stoneham, McGraw, and another Rothstein friend, Tammany magistrate Francis X. McQuade, bought the Giants. Judge McQuade once dismissed charges against twenty of twenty-one men arraigned after the shooting of three policemen in Rothstein's gambling establishment, the Partridge Club. An investigation of magistrates' courts by Judge Samuel Seabury in the early 1930's caused McQuade's resignation. Stoneham, the chief stockholder of the Giants, was a heavy gambler and, according to Bill Veeck, Jr., a "bookie and a ticket scalper." He was associated with Rothstein in a number of enterprises, including a rum-running deal. Rothstein had also been a partner in the short-lived Stoneham-McGraw race track venture. But it was the operation of Stoneham's brokerage business, in which Rothstein was his closest associate, which was shortly to embarrass the National League.

Stoneham conducted what was known as a bucket shop, an office where orders to buy or sell stock were taken but not executed; instead, the operator pocketed the customer's money and gambled on the possibility of buying the stock later at a lower price or selling it at a higher one. The bucketeer required little margin, operating a kind of cut-rate, bargain-basement securities supermarket, run on the installment plan. At that time there were no federal laws against bucketing, and local restrictions were avoided through political influence and payoffs. Both Stoneham and Rothstein had powerful connections with Tammany Hall, particularly through Boss Tom Foley. Rothstein handled the payoffs, and attorney William J. Fallon was available for legal assistance, including bribery of jurymen and the removal of records.

Stoneham, after making a fortune estimated at ten million dollars, closed his business and referred his customers to a number of other bucketeers, vouching for their moral and financial standing. All went bankrupt, most of them forced shut by the federal government, and their customers lost millions. Subsequent court action involving one of these companies, Fuller & McGee, revealed that Stoneham had continued to supply the firm with funds in the amount of $170,000. Fuller & McGee maintained that Stoneham had invested these funds in the company as a partner and hence was liable for its obligations, whereas Stoneham contended that the money was merely a loan made at the behest of Boss Foley. Stoneham was indicted for perjury and for using the mails to defraud.

The ensuing publicity, particularly the investigations of reporter Nat Ferber of Hearst's New York *American,* put the National League in an awkward position. President Heydler speculated, "Stoneham may feel eventu-ally that for the good of baseball . . . his voluntary sale of the Giants . . . would be a wise move." But there was nothing the league could do, he said, since Stoneham had violated no baseball rule and in his four years in baseball had been an asset to the "sport." Besides, he added, indictment was not conviction.

Far from taking action against Stoneham, the league actually elected him to its board of directors while he was under indictment. Landis also failed to act against Stoneham—an omission that sportswriter Frank Menke pointed out was in sharp contrast with his peremptory dismissal of Benny Kauff. Menke remarked that when Kauff, "merely a ball player, and not possessed of money or power, as is Stoneham, was indicted on the charge of stealing an automobile, Landis became filled with righteous indignation." He "declared that there was no place in the game" for Kauff, and even after the player was acquitted, Landis refused to reinstate him. Stoneham gave no sign of wanting to leave baseball, and although neither the National League nor Landis moved against him, they doubtless were relieved when he was eventually acquitted.

Although Landis succeeded in getting Stoneham and McGraw to give up their race track, he came off second best in other brushes with baseball men over horses. Frank Navin, the Detroit club president, owned a stable and was a big bettor at the track. When Landis asked him to get rid of his racing property, he refused and threatened to take the Commissioner to court.

Rogers Hornsby, the batting star of the National League, was an inveterate bettor who gambled many thousands of dollars on horses. Questioned by Landis, the outspoken Hornsby held his ground. He told the Commissioner that what he did with his money was his own business and that at least he was not gambling other people's money in the stock market. The latter remark was probably a reference to Landis's loss of baseball funds through investments in Sam Insull's rickety utilities empire. However, Landis took a voluntary salary cut to make up for the loss.

When Landis on a visit to New York warned against betting on horses, he very likely had in mind the Yankee players, among whom betting was rampant. Players were checking racing results between innings, Colonel Huston complained. He wanted them to keep their minds on the game, not on a horse three thousand miles away.

Occupied though he was with scandals and related problems in the first years of his administration, Landis was able to take upon himself other issues, some of them of far-reaching importance to the future course of the business. The first noteworthy instance was his blockage of Heinie Groh's transfer from Cincinnati to New York in 1921. Groh, the leading third baseman of the National League, wanted a "little boost" ($2000) in his $10,000 pay of the previous season. Cincinnati refused him an increase, and a stubborn salary fight followed and persisted beyond the deadline for signing—ten days after the start of the season—after which a player automatically landed on Landis's ineligible list.

At length Groh indicated he no longer wanted to play for Cincinnati. He would stay only if he were paid $12,000 but would take $10,000 if he were traded elsewhere. Herrmann explained the situation to the other National League owners and invited bids for Groh, but in order to teach the player an "object lesson," he made the condition that the club that got him would not give him a bonus or restore the back salary he had lost during his holdout.

The Giants made the best offer, $100,000 and three players. In the case of two of them Cincinnati had the choice of taking additional cash in lieu of either or both. Groh signed his contract with Cincinnati in the knowledge that he was going to be traded, and Herrmann then applied to Landis, whom he had kept informed, for the player's reinstatement.

But Landis, after further investigation, cancelled the trade and ordered Groh to play out the season with the Reds, on the ground that permitting him to dictate his terms would set a premium on "rebellious players." Groh objected strenuously, saying the Commissioner had no right to make a man play where he did not want to or to make him accept a salary that did not suit him. However, the owners concerned, Herrmann and Stoneham, resigned themselves to Landis's ruling—in sharp contrast with Ruppert and Huston, who had rebelled against Ban Johnson's interference when Carl Mays was traded under similar circumstances. Groh finished the season with the Reds and, although he did go to the Giants after it was over, the temporary cancellation of the trade served to discourage later dissatisfied players from pressuring a club into trading them. As the New York *Times* put it, the Landis decision was a warning to players that "deserting" a club for real or fancied grievances could not be rewarded by transfer to another club. It added that Landis should have ruled that in future such players would be suspended for a year.

After the 1921 season another big stir occurred over the old problem of post-season barnstorming, but this time it involved the ever famous Babe Ruth, who had already become the most dramatic player in the game. Players tended to consider barnstorming their privilege; however, to avoid the possibility of diminishing the prestige of the World Series, the owners had passed a rule forbidding those who participated in the Series from barnstorming right afterwards. Landis indicated that this rule would be upheld, but Ruth and two other Yankee players, Bob Meusel and Bill Piercy, brazenly defied him. Ruth's position, which had some justification, was

that a player's productive period was short and he should not be deprived of an opportunity to make extra money while he could. Even the Yankee owners recognized that the rule seemed unjust in many respects. Nevertheless, they concurred with Landis that as long as it existed it should be enforced, although they maintained they were powerless to enforce it themselves.

When Ruth and the others went ahead, Landis put his back up, declaring that "this case resolves itself into a question of who is the biggest man in baseball, the Commissioner or the player who makes the most home runs." In any case, the tour was soon abandoned, primarily because of inclement weather, and Ruth switched to vaudeville at $3000 a week for twenty weeks.

December brought a tough announcement from Landis. He declared that Ruth, Meusel, and Piercy had "willfully and defiantly" violated the barnstorming rule in a "mutinous" act and decreed that the three players would not receive their World Series shares. Furthermore, they were suspended until May 20 of the following season, at which time they could apply for reinstatement.

Faced with the loss of Ruth, the biggest attraction in baseball, for such an extended period, Ruppert and Huston sent their attorney to see Landis to plead for an adjustment of the long suspension, since it would hurt them financially even though they were guiltless. Other owners, too, pleaded the losses they would suffer; and Ruth even went to Canossa, but Landis denied him an audience. Despite these and other efforts to have the Commissioner ease up, he held to the suspension, although eventually he did turn over the players' Series money. Ruth's late appearance in the lineup cost him the home-run leadership. His total fell to 35, four fewer than Ken Williams's, and his average dropped to .315.

The rule limiting barnstorming was soon modified. Players wishing to barnstorm could apply for permission from the league president and Landis. They could play through October, although the limit was shortly extended to November 10; any given barnstorming team was limited to three World Series players. But the significant outcome was that Landis had again successfully asserted his authority and made it clear to all that his fiat applied even to the greatest star.

In 1926 Landis interposed his dictum in connection with a player trade that forced Organized Baseball to take a clear-cut position on the problem of conflict of interest. That winter fans and writers were agog over news that the St. Louis Cardinals had swapped Rogers Hornsby to the New York Giants for Frank Frisch and Jimmy Ring. As player-manager, Hornsby had just led the Cardinals to the world championship. The New York *Times* guessed that for such a player as Hornsby the Giants must have thrown in at least $100,000 in cash, but Stoneham insisted that no money had changed hands. The St. Louis press flayed owner Sam Breadon for trading Hornsby away. His loss was "a terrible blow," moaned the St. Louis Chamber of Commerce. St. Louis fans threatened to boycott the team.

Why had Hornsby been traded at such an inopportune time? After all, the Cardinals had turned down a Giant offer of $250,000 for him several years before when they badly needed cash. Breadon's public explanation was that he was afraid Hornsby was on the downgrade as a player, and although he was willing to give Hornsby the $50,000 contract he wanted for one year, he could not risk the club's financial future by acquiescing in the player's demand for a three-year contract at such a figure.

The real reasons lay deeper. They stemmed in large measure from Hornsby's personality. Free-spoken and direct, utterly tactless and aloof—a "loner" among the players—Hornsby in his stiff-necked individualism butted his way through baseball. He quarrelled with a succession of owners and more than once stood up to Landis. Appropriate indeed was the title of his ghosted book: *My Fight with Baseball*.

Such was Hornsby's style on the Cardinals. He did not get along with his predecessor, manager Branch Rickey, and after succeeding Rickey he soon clashed with Sam Breadon. Hornsby had asked Breadon to cancel some late-season exhibition games because the Cardinals, with a genuine chance to win their first pennant, needed the time to rest. After a game Breadon came into the clubhouse, which is traditionally the manager's domain, and told Hornsby that the exhibition games would not be called off. Hornsby, with a volley of choice words, ordered the owner from the clubhouse. Breadon, "blushing and burning," made up his mind that such insults from an employee were intolerable and Hornsby would have to go; hence his transfer to the Giants that winter, despite his success in winning the pennant and the World Series.

But after the trade was completed an obstacle suddenly appeared—interlocking ownership. Hornsby owned 1167 shares of stock in the St. Louis club. How would it look to have the second largest stockholder in the Cardinals playing second base for the Giants? Landis ordered that Hornsby divest himself of his holdings before he could play for New York and more or less left it up to the parties concerned to work out a settlement.

It was not so easily done. Breadon offered to buy the stock from him but only at the price Hornsby had originally paid, about $43 a share. Hornsby had the stock appraised, however, and then demanded $105 a share, which would bring him a profit of something like $72,000. This demand infuriated Breadon, who had helped Hornsby buy the stock in the first place. With the

new season approaching meanwhile, the tension grew. McGraw challenged John Heydler's (not Landis's) right to keep Hornsby from playing with the Giants and threatened legal action. "Heydler can't make new rules," he averred. Heydler repeated Landis's dictum that Hornsby could not play for New York unless he sold the stock: "the National League is against anything that smacks of syndicate baseball and will fight to maintain that stand."

Finally a compromise was reached when Hornsby lowered his price somewhat and the other National League club owners chipped in to help Breadon pay it. Figures vary somewhat, but according to the *Times* Hornsby was paid $100,000 plus $12,000 for legal fees—Breadon putting in $86,000, seven National League clubs $2000 apiece, and New York $12,000. The controversy took on added significance when at the end of the year the major leagues passed a rule that no player could hold stock in one club after his transfer to another in the same league; if he did he would be ineligible to play for or manage his new team. In fact, he would not be permitted to own stock in a club to begin with unless the Advisory Council approved. The majors also put through a rule barring club officials from owning stock in other clubs or lending money to other clubs or players on them.

The year of the difficulty over Hornsby had its brighter side for the National League. In February 1926 it had celebrated its Golden Jubilee with a huge banquet at New York's Hotel Astor. Among the nearly one thousand guests were governors, mayors, authors, publishers, clerics, financiers, officers of the armed forces, and some old-time ball players. A message from President Coolidge read: "Not only because of the nation-wide devotion to this splendid game, but because of my own conviction that it has been a real moral and physical benefit to the nation, I send my congratulations for this occasion."

Landis, too, had his day of personal triumph, although for a time there was some doubt that it would come to pass. At their joint meeting on December 16, 1926, the major-league owners elected him for another seven-year term and raised his salary from $50,000* to $65,000. The minor leagues also endorsed him. Yet the major-league owners had not been altogether enamored of him. After recovering from their panic during the Black Sox scandal, some of them began to grumble about his highhanded way of making decisions without their knowledge or without at least consulting them or working with the Advisory Board.

When Landis heard in 1923 that many of the magnates

---

* His pay had been restored to $50,000 after he resigned his judgeship.

were grousing and wanted to pay him off, he took the offensive and offered to quit if they were dissatisfied, but the owners shied away from such a step. In 1926 the *Times* thought "ominous rumblings" from some quarters presaged a battle over Landis's reappointment. At this juncture John Heydler, long a Landis man, urged his re-election on the ground that his authority was necessary to Organized Baseball. If he "appears" to have "the powers of a Czar or dictator," explained Heydler, "it is because these prerogatives are forced upon him by the unusual nature of all the rivalries that come of keen sports competition."

Immediately after, the National League owners, who had been Landis's most ardent backers from the outset, expressed their continued confidence in him by voting to renew his contract for ten years. The American Leaguers, however, were not quite so eager and it was not until the end of the year that they sent a three-man committee to see Landis. After assuring him of support, the committee discreetly asked for changes in his policy, in particular that he revive the moribund Advisory Board called for in his contract and that he allow Ban Johnson to return to this board, after having been kept off it for two years following his criticism of Landis over the O'Connell-Dolan case. Landis apparently indicated that he was not averse to this provided the owners saw to it that Johnson behaved. At any rate the American League—Comiskey excepted—then voted Johnson back on the board and joined the National League in electing Landis for a second term. Even Johnson gave him a reluctant acceptance: "Landis is all right," he said. "There are lots worse people than the Judge."

But Johnson could no more curb himself than could a hungry wolf in a sheepfold. Never a Landis enthusiast and galled by his appointment, Johnson had grooved his mind against the judge. He had criticized Landis's Standard Oil decision and his handling of the Federal League suit. Then, having failed to keep Landis from being made baseball Commissioner and thus superior in rank to him, Johnson proceeded to hector and embarrass him at every opportunity. Once Johnson even called a meeting of the American League in Chicago on the same date Landis had set for a joint meeting of the majors in New York. Landis, on his part, downgraded Johnson by ignoring the Advisory Board and taking over full control of the World Series. At the end of 1923 Landis presented to the American League owners a bill of particulars against Johnson and gave them to understand that they would have to control him.

The O'Connell-Dolan affair exacerbated the feud between them because of Landis's exclusion of Johnson from the case and Johnson's various expressions of disapproval of Landis's disposition of it. Johnson was even quoted in the press as having called Landis a "wild-eyed crazy nut." Johnson had also tried to usurp Landis's prerogative by taking it upon himself in 1924 to have detectives investigate gamblers who were supposedly tampering with Pacific Coast League players. He presented a report on the subject which aroused the minor leagues to protest and which the majors rejected as unsubstantiated.

The magnates pleaded for an end to the feud. As Ruppert said, two men who themselves had no investment in baseball were, by their inability to get along, threatening the investments of others. But Landis, thoroughly angry, was bent on a showdown. He told a committee that had come to patch up the quarrel that the American League owners must decide between himself and Johnson. The result was that the owners groveled before Landis and beseeched him to overlook Johnson's behavior. Seven of them signed and tendered to Landis an amazing document repudiating Johnson's actions:

> We recognize that conditions have arisen that are gravely harmful to Base Ball and that must be intolerable to you, and that these conditions have been created by the activities of the president of the American League.
>
> While you were dealing promptly and effectively with a most deplorable exception to Base Ball's honorable record [O'Connell-Dolan] our president sought to discredit your action and to cast suspicion upon the 1924 world series.
>
> One year ago you made known to us in his presence various of his activities, and it was our expectation and hope that the unanimous action then taken certainly would operate as a corrective, but in this expectation and hope we have been disappointed.
>
> We don't extenuate these things, nor question their effect on Base Ball. However, he has been president of our league since its inception, and we ask you to again overlook his conduct and accept from us these guarantees:
>
> 1. That his misconduct will cease or his immediate removal from office will follow.
> 2. That legislation will be adopted that will limit his activities to the internal affairs of the American League.
> 3. That any and all measures which you may deem advisable to secure the above will be adopted.

Phil Ball, the lone American Leaguer who did not sign the document so humiliating to Johnson, issued a pointed statement in his defense, calling Johnson "the biggest figure in the national game" and "a victim of the men whose gratitude has bowed to the dollar sign." Recalling the days of the Lasker plan, the editor of *Baseball Magazine,* F. C. Lane, maintained that Johnson had been right in opposing Landis's appointment, because no such power as Landis had should be given any man; it was absurd to hand over "the people's democratic game" to a dictator. Nevertheless, he conceded that Johnson went about things in the wrong way in 1924 by proposing cancellation of the World Series and calling for a federal investigation.

Perhaps to assuage Johnson's feelings, the owners raised his salary from $30,000 to $40,000 at the close of 1925 and extended his contract from 1930 to 1935. At their dinner that winter the Baseball Writers' Association lampooned the Landis-Johnson quarrel with this song:

Ken Landis and Ban Johnson, they had a head-on clash.
Ken Landis got the verdict but Johnson got the cash.
The magnates handed Ken the crown and raised a mighty cheer,
But they raised Ban Johnson's salary ten thousand bucks a year.

Johnson was seemingly pacified, and a semblance of harmony was reached when the American League restored him to the Advisory Board at the end of 1926. But within a week the Cobb-Speaker affair supervened, and Johnson outdid his previous performance in a renewed attack on Landis. Some of his outbursts were so wild and contradictory as to seem almost hysterical, perhaps owing in part to his failing health. This time Landis refused to take any more of Johnson's hectoring and carping. He summoned the American League magnates to a special meeting in Chicago to have it out. Said one reporter, the American League owners "tried a muzzle" on Johnson; this time they "may use a catapult."

He was right. The owners averted a direct confrontation between Landis and Johnson by assembling a day before Landis's meeting and relieving Johnson of his duties for an extended period, no doubt in the hope that the leave would become a permanent one. It was given out that the enforced vacation was for reasons of health, and Johnson's physician certified that he was indeed ill. Navin, vice president of the league, took over the duties of the presidency. The owners also formally repudiated all Johnson's words against Landis. The judge accepted this latest chastisement of Johnson and postponed the meeting he had called.

Although not expected back, Johnson fooled everybody by returning in time for the opening of the next season. He was soon grumbling about Landis again, and in an evident effort to assert his old authority he incensed Connie Mack by imposing unusually stiff penalties on two of his players, Ty Cobb and Al Simmons, after an altercation with an umpire.

The end for Johnson had come. At the request of the owners he called a special meeting for July 8. Johnson, however, shut himself in his hotel room and refused to preside at the meeting, and Frank Navin took charge. A three-man committee consisting of Ball, Griffith, and Ruppert was appointed to negotiate with Johnson—in reality, to persuade him to resign. After the committee's first visit, newsmen were admitted to Johnson's room and found him "wasted away a good deal," his face "drawn and peaked," but vehemently denying that he was going to resign. It took two more visits of the committee before Johnson decided to heed Ruppert's argument: "You can add years to your life by quitting." He wrote a brief statement tendering his resignation as of November 1 or earlier and stipulating that his salary was to stop immediately on his retirement.

It was an ignominious and pathetic end for the man who had for so long been the foremost executive in Organized Baseball. He had stayed too long. Hindsight suggests that he should have left when the American League owners bypassed him and joined with the National League in electing Landis. He could have stepped down then with more grace and dignity.

# Baseball Counts

## MIKE SHANNON

Because it is so much like life,
Because, in fact, it is life
Baseball counts.
Take the matter of justice for example.
What is just in the hitter
Connecting almost perfectly
Smashing the ball so hard down the line
That it curves wickedly
But right into the path of the waiting
Third baseman who makes the catch in
Self-defense?
Hitters say, "It all evens out."
But does it ever?
Do they really believe the old cliche?
As with the rest of life
Believing that it does makes it
Possible to survive the fact that
It doesn't.

Is Dan (*Boston Globe*) Shaughnessy exaggerating when he calls this
"one of the most sensational pitching performances in baseball history"?
No.

# 1986:
# Boston Red Sox 3,
# Seattle Mariners 1

## DAN SHAUGHNESSY

SMOKE GOT IN YOUR EYES. In one of the most
sensational pitching performances in baseball history, Red Sox right-hander Roger Clemens last night
struck out a major league record 20 batters en route to a
three-hit, 3–1 victory over the Seattle Mariners.

Has any pitcher ever been this overpowering? In 111
years of major league baseball, Clemens is the first
pitcher to strike out 20 batters in a nine-inning game. He
walked none.

Watching the Mariners try to hit Clemens was like
watching a stack of waste paper diving into a shredder.
Slumping Seattle is on a record-setting strikeout pace,
and Clemens was at the top of his high-octane game.
You didn't need Dick Albert, Jimmy the Greek Snyder
or Carnac the Magnificent to tell you what was going to
happen. But no one could have envisioned the magnitude
of Clemens' mound mastery.

Sir Roger struck out the side three times. The Mariners
put only ten balls in play. Seattle pulled only two balls
all night. He threw 138 pitches, 97 for strikes.

Clemens tied a league record with 8 straight punch-
outs, broke the single-game Red Sox strikeout record
(17 by Bill Monbouquette in 1961) and shattered the
Fenway Park mark (16 by Jack Harshman of the White
Sox in 1954). They've been playing baseball at Fenway
for 75 years.

He saved the best for last. In the ninth, Clemens
struck out Spike Owen swinging, then fanned Phil
Bradley on three pitches for the magic No. 20. Ken
Phelps grounded to short to end it.

Dwight Evans' three-run, two-out, seventh-inning
homer supplied the punch for the victory, but this was
not a night to talk about hitters.

The major league record for strikeouts in a nine-

inning game had been 19—accomplished by Steve
Carlton, Tom Seaver, Nolan Ryan and Charles Sweeney
(in 1884 while pitching for Providence of the National
League). Clemens broke it in the ninth. The overall
record is 21 by the Washington Senators' Tom Chaney
against the Baltimore Orioles in a 16-inning game
September 12, 1962.

"It's been a long road back," said Clemens. "It feels
good to go out and win like that. . . . I was challenging
guys."

In the middle of the game, Clemens joined Ryan and
Ron Davis as the only American Leaguers to strike out
8 consecutive batters (Seaver holds the major league
record with 10). Boston's 23-year-old phenom made
history in the fourth, fifth and sixth. He fanned 8 straight
Mariners, 4 swinging, 4 called. Owen broke the string
with a two-out fly to center in the sixth.

The fireballing righty was the last thing the Mariners
needed to see. They came into the game with 166
strikeouts, 55 more than the league runners-up (Texas,
111). Seattle is on a pace which would shatter the major
league strikeout record (1,203) by more than 200.

Clemens was perfect in the first three innings. Owen,
Bradley and Ken Phelps all went down swinging in the
first. Gorman Thomas led off the second with a hard
liner to Jim Rice in left, then Jim Presley and Ivan
Calderon (called) struck out. In the third, rookie Danny
Tartabull grounded to second, Dave Henderson was
called out on strikes and Steve Yeager flied to left.
Clemens was in danger of walking five of the first nine
batters, but never threw ball four.

Clemens' no-hitter/perfect game was punctured in the
fourth when Seattle shortstop Owen led off with a single
to right on an 0-2 curve ball. Clemens punished the

Mariners by whiffing the next six batters. He got Bradley and Phelps swinging, then watched Don Baylor (playing first while Bill Buckner DH'd) drop a Thomas pop-up in foul territory. Baylor's blunder served history well. Thomas was called out by Vic Voltaggio on a 3-2 pitch as Clemens closed the door on the fourth.

Clemens brought more high octane to the hill in the fifth. He fanned Presley with a 2-2 heater, then blew Calderon away on three pitches (the third was called). Tartabull worked the count to 2-2 before looking at strike three. Clemens had 12 strikeouts at the end of five.

With an assist from Baylor, Clemens had become the third pitcher in Sox history to fan 6 straight batters. The immortal Buck O'Brien turned the trick against the Senators on April 25, 1913, and Ray Culp punched out 6 straight Angels on May 11, 1970.

O'Brien and Culp fell out of the Sox record book when Henderson fanned on a 2-2 pitch leading off the sixth. Seven straight.

Yeager was next and fell behind 0-2, then looked at a 2-2 curve ball. Eight straight.

Owen broke the string by flying to center to end the sixth. Through six innings, Clemens had fanned 14 and thrown 92 pitches, 60 for strikes. The Mariners had put only four balls into play.

The fires were still burning in the seventh. Bradley and Phelps struck out swinging. With the count 1-2 on Thomas, the crowd was on its feet and roaring. And then it happened. A long fly to deep center landed in the first row of the center-field bleachers. Clemens trailed, 1–0.

Evans got it back, with interest, in the bottom of the seventh. The Sox had already run into three outs and appeared set for one of their most frustrating losses in history. With two outs and no one on, Steve Lyons slapped a single to left off Seattle starter Mike Moore. Glenn Hoffman walked (Ed Romero ran for Hoffman), then Evans drove a 1-0 pitch off the back wall in center for a 3–1 lead.

"That picked me up," said Clemens.

He picked up strikeouts No. 17 and 18 in the eighth. That set up the historic ninth.

What is it the middle-aged father remembers? "The distant, mortal innings of boyhood and youth."

# From *Voices of a Summer Day*

## IRWIN SHAW

THE RED flag was up when he drove up to the house. He went in. The house was silent. "Peggy," he called. "Peggy!" There was no answer. His wife was not there nor either of his children.

He went out and looked at the ocean. The waves were ten feet high and there was about eight hundred yards of foam ripping between the tide line, marked by seaweed, and the whitecaps of the open Atlantic. The beach was deserted except for a tall girl in a black bathing suit, who was walking along the water's edge with two Siamese cats pacing beside her. The girl had long blond hair that hung down her back and blew in the wind. Her legs and arms were pollen-colored against the sea, and the cats made a small pale jungle at her ankles. The girl was not too far away for him to tell whether she was pretty or not and she didn't look in his direction, but he wished he knew her. He wished he knew her well enough to call out and see her smile and wait for him to join her so that they could walk along the beach together, attended by toy tigers, the noise of the surf beating at them as she told him why a girl like that walked alone on an empty beach on a bright summer afternoon.

He watched her grow smaller and smaller in the distance, the cats, the color of the desert, almost disappearing against the sand. She was outlined for a last moment against the dazzle of the waves and then the beach was empty again.

It was no afternoon for swimming, and the girl was gone, and he didn't feel like hanging around the house alone so he went in and changed his clothes and got into the car and drove into town. On the high school field, there was a pickup game of baseball in progress, boys and young men and several elderly athletes who by Sunday morning would regret having slid into second base on Saturday afternoon.

He saw his son playing center field. He stopped the car and got out and lay back in the sun on the hot planks of the benches along the third-base line, a tall, easy-moving man with a powerful, graying head. He was dressed in slacks and a short-sleeved blue cotton shirt, the costume of a man consciously on holiday. On the long irregular face there were not the unexpected signs of drink and overwork. He was no longer young, and, although at a distance his slimness and way of moving gave a deceptive appearance of youth, close-up age was there, experience was there, above all around the eyes, which were deep black, almost without reflections, hooded by heavy lids and a dark line of thick lashes that suggested secret Mediterranean mourning against the olive tint of the skin stretched tight over jutting cheek bones. He greeted several of the players and spectators, and the impression of melancholy was erased momentarily by the good humor and open friendliness of his voice. The combination of voice and features was that of a man who might be resigned and often cynical, but rarely suspicious. He was a man who permitted himself to be cheated in small matters. Taxi drivers, employees, children, and women took advantage of him. He knew this, each time it happened, and promptly forgot it.

On the field, the batter was crouching and trying to work the pitcher for a walk. The batter was fifteen years old and small for his age. The pitcher was six feet three inches tall and had played for Columbia in 1947.

The third baseman, a boy of eighteen named Andy Roberts, called out, "Do you want to take my place, Mr. Federov? I promised I'd be home by four."

"Thanks, no, Andy," Federov said. "I batted .072 last season and I've hung up my spikes."

The boy laughed. "Maybe you'd have a better season this year if you tried."

"I doubt it," Federov said. "It's very rare that your average goes up after fifty."

The batter got his walk, and while he was throwing his bat away and trotting down to first base Federov waved to his son out in center field. His son waved back. "Andy," Federov said, "how's Mike doing?"

"Good field, no hit," Andy said.

"Runs in the family," said Federov. "My father never hit a curve ball in his life either."

The next batter sent a line drive out toward right center, and Michael made a nice running catch over his shoulder and pivoted and threw hard and accurately to first base, making the runner scramble back hurriedly to get there before the throw. Michael was left-handed and moved with that peculiar grace that left-handers always seemed to Federov to have in all sports. There had never been a left-hander before in Federov's family, nor in his wife's family that he knew of, and Federov sometimes wondered at this genetic variance and took it as a mark of distinction, a puzzling designation, though whether for good or ill he could not say. Michael's sister, eleven years old and too smart for her age, as Federov sometimes told her, teased Michael about it. "Sinister, sinister," she chanted when she disagreed with her brother's opinions, "Old Pope Sinister the First."

Old Pope Sinister the First popped up to shortstop his next time at bat and then came over to sit beside his father. "Hi, Dad." He touched his father lightly but affectionately on the shoulder. "How're things in the dirty city?"

"Dirty," Federov said. He and his brother ran a building and contracting business together, and while there was a lot of work unfinished on both their desks, the real reason the brothers had stayed in New York on a hot Saturday morning was to try to arrange a settlement with Louis's third wife, whom he wanted to divorce to marry a fourth wife, and who was all for a vengeful and scandalous action in court. Louis was the architect of the firm, and this connection with the arts, plus his quiet good looks, made him a prey for women and a permanent subsidy for the legal profession.

"Where's your mother?" Federov asked his son.

"The house was empty when I got in."

"Bridge, hairdresser's, I don't know," Michael said carelessly. "You know—dames. She'll turn up for dinner."

"I'm quite sure she will," Federov said.

Michael's side was retired, and he picked up his glove and started toward his position in the field. "Mike," Federov said, "you swung at a high ball, you know."

"I know," Michael said. "I'm a confirmed sinner."

He was thirteen years old but, like his sister, was a ransacker of libraries and often sounded it.

Five minutes later there was a dispute about a close call at first base, and two or three boys shouted, good-naturedly, "Oh, you bum!" and "Kill the umpire!"

"Stop that!" Federov said sharply. Then he was as surprised as the boys themselves by the harshness of his tone. They kept quiet after that, although they eyed him curiously. Ostentatiously, Federov looked away from them. He had heard the cry thousands of times before, just as the boys had, and he didn't want to explain what was behind his sudden explosion of temper. Ever since the President had been shot, Federov, sometimes consciously, sometimes unconsciously, had refrained from using words like "kill" or "murder" or "shoot" or "gun," and had skipped them, when he could, in the things he read, and moved away from conversations in which the words were likely to come up. He had heard about the mocking black-bordered advertisement in the Dallas newspaper that had greeted the President on his arrival in the city, and he had read about the minister who said that schoolchildren in the city had cheered upon being told of the President's death, and he had heard from a lineman friend of his on the New York Giants football team that, after the game they had played in Dallas ten days after the President was killed, an open car full of high school boys and girls had followed the Giants' bus through downtown Dallas, chanting, "Kennedy gawn, Johnson next, Kennedy gawn, Johnson next."

"Kids," the lineman had said wonderingly, "just kids, like anybody else's kids. You couldn't believe it. And nobody tried to stop them."

Kids, just kids. Like the boys on the field in front of him. Like his own son. In the same blue jeans, going to the same kind of schools, listening to the same awful music on radio and television, playing the same traditional games, loved by their parents as he loved his son and daughter. Kids shouting a tribal chant of hatred for a dead man who had been better than any of them could ever hope to be.

The hell with it, he thought. You can't keep thinking about it forever.

With an effort of will he made himself fall back into lazy afternoon thoughtlessness. Soon, lulled by the slow familiar rhythm of the game, he was watching the field through half-dozing, sun-warmed eyes, lying back and not keeping track of what was happening as boys ran from base to base, stopped grounders, changed sides. He saw his son make two good plays and one mediocre one without pride or anxiety. Michael was tall for his age, and broad, and Federov took what he realized was a normal fatherly pleasure in watching his son's movements as, loose-limbed and browned by the sun, he performed in the wide green spaces of the outfield.

Dozing, almost alone on the rows of benches, one game slid into other games, other generations were at play many years before . . . in Harrison, New Jersey, where he had grown up; on college campuses, where he had never been quite good enough to make the varsity, despite his fleetness of foot and surehandedness in the field. The sounds were the same through the years—the American sounds of summer, the tap of bat against ball, the cries of the infielders, the wooden plump of the ball into catchers' mitts, the umpires calling "Strike three and you're out." The generations circled the bases, the dust rose for forty years as runners slid from third, dead boys hit doubles, famous men made errors at shortstop, forgotten friends tapped the clay from their spikes with their bats as they stepped into the batter's box, coaches' voices warned, across the decades, "Tag up, tag up!" on fly balls. The distant, mortal innings of boyhood and youth . . .

## JOHN GALLAGHER

*"That's my bubble gum picture card you're tearing up!"*

Few Pulitzer Prizes have been more deserved than the one that went to Red Smith in 1976 for his syndicated sports columns. Several collections of those columns were published, and this one is from the last of those books, a compendium called *To Absent Friends, from Red Smith*, composed of columns Smith had written about sports figures who had died. He himself died four months before the book was published.

# The Duke of Milwaukee

## RED SMITH

THIS MAY have been Al Simmons's last time at bat in a major league baseball game. At least, it was right around there, for by this time Al was a coach with the Philadelphia Athletics and the only reason for keeping his name on the active list was his hope that he might make the few more hits he needed to achieve a lifetime total of three thousand. He had, like many other ball players, a deep reverence for records. And the three-thousand-hit club is one of baseball's most exclusive fraternities.

Anyhow, he went up as a pinch-hitter this day in Boston, with one out in the ninth inning and the game on the bases. He hit the ball as well as a man could, and it went straight to the shortstop for a double play that ended the game. A rookie who came face to face with him as the play ended was startled beyond the limits of ordinary diplomacy.

"Hey," said the kid, brand new with the club, "what's the matter with you? You're white as a sheet."

"Don't worry about me," Al snapped furiously.

If the rookie was so ignorant he had to be told that Al Simmons didn't choke up in the clutch, then there was no use trying to explain the fact was that to Al baseball was so close to war it affected him as war affects some men; it filled him with a cold, bloodless fury which literally turned him pale.

"When I was hitting," Al said after he was through, "I hated pitchers." This was one of those hit-and-run jumps during spring training like an all-night ride from Los Angeles to Yuma, when the athletes were in bed and their elders sat up over a last beer.

"Pitchers," Al said. "I wanted them dead. Them so-and-so's were trying to take the bread and butter out of my mouth."

He never killed a pitcher, but he made a lot of them wonder why they'd been born.

He never got his three thousand hits, either, but he blamed no pitchers for that, only himself. "If I'd only known as a kid what I know now," he said. This was when he was a coach clinging to the active list and reaching hungrily for a bat whenever Connie Mack nodded his way.

"If I'd ever imagined I could get as close as this, three thousand hits would have been so easy. When I think of the days I goofed off, the times I played sick or something and took myself out of the line-up because the game didn't mean anything, I could cut my throat."

Al was a truly successful man, for he knew he was a great player and a bona fide celebrity and he relished being accepted among them on even terms. The Duke of Milwaukee, they called him, and he had a swagger befitting the rank. He was proud of the title and proud of his hometown, used to boast about other celebrities from Wisconsin like Alfred Lunt and Don Ameche and Pat O'Brien.

Yet he had the gift of self-appraisal. When he started out in baseball he set a financial goal that, having attained it, he raised several times. "When I finally decided I had it made," he said, "I was never again the ball player I was when I was hungry. The only man I ever knew who never lost his fire when he got rich was Ty Cobb."

If Al lost his fire, only he knew it. One summer when a very poor team of Athletics was having an unaccountable hot streak, Connie Mack was asked which player he deemed chiefly responsible. Connie glanced at the only photograph of a ball player that he kept in his office. It was a picture of Simmons at bat, one of those standup jobs mounted on wood and cut out with a scroll saw along the outline of the figure.

"I wish I had nine men like Simm," Connie said, disconcerting his questioner by mentioning a coach instead of a player. "Just coaching there on third base, he does more for the spirit of this club than anybody else on the field."

At a winter meeting in Chicago, Connie told Simm there would always be a place for him in the Philadelphia organization.

"I appreciate that, Mr. Mack," Al said, and he hesitated. "Of course you"—he had started to point out that Connie was getting along in years and wouldn't be around forever. "That is," Al said. "I—well, we don't know how long—"

Connie was chuckling at his embarrassment. "I think my sons know how I feel about it," he said.

"Maybe they do," Al said dubiously, "but would you mind telling them?"

Laughing, Connie said he would. Seems odd, somehow, and sad. Al lived only a few months past Connie's death.

With its quiet, simple title and its quiet, meandering approach, Robert Smith's book *Baseball* is among the most pleasing and satisfying histories of the game. In the chapter reprinted here he goes to one of the most fascinating (and, for today's reader, least familiar) periods—baseball in the years following the Civil War.

# The Age of the Muffin

## ROBERT SMITH

THERE WERE two different kinds of baseball after the Civil War and they were both called "amateur." The great baseball clubs, in this age, while still insisting on the forms and etiquette of amateurism, were professional traveling shows. Clubs which a decade or two earlier had fined members who failed to show up for games now all indulged in open proselytizing and were paying men just to come to practice. Members of the first-string ball team in such clubs as the Olympic of Washington, D.C., or the Atlantic of Brooklyn not only received prizes, expenses, and cuts in the gate receipts (according to merit), but were awarded jobs as "clerks" at three or four times what a clerk was normally paid. One young ballplayer of the 1860's, for instance, found himself "working" (on days when there was no ball game) at a desk next to a youth who was earning ten dollars a week. The ballplayer, ostensibly hired to do the same work, was being paid forty dollars.

But there was plenty of truly amateur baseball. Indeed, popular as the game had become as a spectacle, it was perhaps even more popular as a spare-hour pastime. Every great club had, beside its hired nine, a "muffin" nine, made up of run-of-the-mill members who paid dues for the privilege of playing the game in congenial company. And throughout the land there were surely a thousand organized and uniformed clubs, made up of young men who, bound by the precepts of that age to earn their bread at jobs that would not soil starched collars and cuffs, found in baseball a way to make their blood run hot.

All through the late sixties and the seventies baseball was the young business and professional man's spare-time game, as avidly studied and devoutly pursued as are golf and tennis today. Even spindle-legged clerks and counter jumpers toiled ineptly at the game as a means of affirming the manliness their reluctant beards belied.

Beards and baseball were alike tokens of the American passion for virility which sucked up the country's surplus energy in those years. Out of the few thin dollar bills which a sixty-six-hour work week brought him, a pale, high-collared youngster could always spare a sum to keep him in bottles of Dr. Sevigne's Marvelous Restaurateur Capillaire, or some similar sticky compound, which was reputed to "act upon hair and beard in a miraculous manner" and promised him a beard or mustache within five weeks.

Bearded or not, he could join his "morning-glory" baseball team and meet with his fellows at 4 A.M. to play the noble game before the dew was dry. This meant getting up while it was still dark in his boardinghouse and creeping down the worn staircarpet in the dawn. There would be no noise at that time but the creak of the stairs under his feet, the lilting snore of some fellow boarder asleep behind a blank door, and the tireless exhalation of the small gas flame in the downstairs hall.

Outdoors, daylight would have just begun. The young man, wearing his striped cap, almost like a jockey's except for the tiny bill, his brightly colored dickey-bosom with the insigne of his team, and his ballplayer's brilliant necktie, would not be without embarrassment under the eyes of the few strange folk who might be abroad. The ragged Negro chimneysweeps might snicker and whisper about him when he had passed. A milkman, leading his lumbering cart and announcing his coming by whoops wild enough to stir the dead, might pause to gaze after the young ballplayer down the cobbled street. The scullery maids who crept up out of basement kitchens with their milk pitchers would hide their smiles behind their hands or merely gape in open amazement.

In his pocket, in a hand that was wet with nervous

perspiration, the youth would fondle a small box which held the best baseball spikes a man could buy—detachable ones, sharp as a lumberjack's calks, which he would screw right on to his street shoes when he reached the field, and remove under the admiring eyes of a dozen small boys when the game was over.

The field, reached by horsecar or steam train, might be at Boston Common, or, if the youth was a New Yorker, in Morrisania, where there was deep green grass and fresh country air; or it might be the Red House Grounds in the Bronx, or a field in Brooklyn or Hoboken. If the game was a match game—that is, a contest between two rival clubs—the young man, who had known no more excitement through the week than that offered by gently urging a pen over the silent pages of a ledger, might find his veins very close to bursting when he reached the diamond.

There were always trees around a ball diamond in that age. The game, although deemed a rough and noisy one, still had something of the air of cricket. Spectators gathered in groups where there was shade. The retiring tent for the players seemed to invite repose. The top-hatted umpire, using a bat for a cane and a stool as a rest for one foot, seemed utterly detached. His position was a few strides down the first base line from the batter's box. He was merely a spectator standing rather close to the play. At the other side of home plate, and somewhat behind it, the scorekeeper sat at a big flat table, with pencils, a large book, and often a cold bottle close at hand.

By the time the young clerk reached the field, the Union Club—not the first nine, of course, but the "muffin" team—would be already on the base paths. The warm-up consisted of tossing the ball and calling to each other for a throw. The Union boys handled the ball in a manner so schooled and confident that the young clerk and his companions could only gaze in quiet awe. When their turn came to warm up, they would undoubtedly stumble, encourage each other in doubtful tones, and curse themselves for their awkwardness, convinced that the Unions, gathered there in the tent, were all laughing into their beards.

Despite the earliness of the hour, a good-sized crowd—that is, forty or fifty—had gathered on the surrounding grass by the time play was called. They clapped hands and called greetings to their favorites in a manner almost polite enough for the other favorite sport of that era—croquet. There was a coin toss to decide the order of batting. The umpire solemnly asked the visitors to call while the big fifty-cent piece was spinning in the air. "Tails," said the mustached captain, in a voice which caught in his throat.

The Unions' captain and the captain of the visiting team (named something like the Busy Beavers) bent close to see the coin.

"Tails it is," intoned the umpire. And the Beaver captain, as seemed natural in those days, chose first inning. Well, there was a good omen: winning the first advantage.

Our young clerk was number one at the plate, and his nervousness was so evident as he picked up his long thin bat (not much thicker at the business end than it was at the handle) that a few of the Unions laughed. But there was nothing to laugh about to the clerk, who may have been named Foster Green. Foster's muscles seemed almost paralyzed with weakness and he could not bring himself to offer at a pitch. Ten balls went by. The spectators began to murmur; and the pitcher, with his hands on his hips, looked scornfully down from his "point." Another pitch, waist-high. "Good ball!" said the umpire sharply. Foster swallowed hard. Now he *had* to hit at one of the next two pitches or be "called" out, according to the newest rule. To still his nervousness, Foster kicked the round iron plate that marked home base. He took his stance again, feet in exaggerated "parade-rest" position, left foot pointed toward the pitcher, the bat pointed slightly forward and up, like a gun in the ready position.

The pitcher backed off and prepared to pitch again, holding the ball in his two hands just under his chin, as if he might take a bite of it. Then he bent forward a little, pulled his arm back, took a hop, skip, and jump toward the batter, and let the ball fly with an underhand swing and a twist of his body. It came up straight and fair, about even with Foster's chest. And Foster, his lips pressed tight, swung his long bat. He hit the ball out in front of the plate, with a leathery whack; and the big ball, in the space of a breath, was flying farther than he had ever dreamed, far out over the base lines. It skimmed the turf beyond the base lines and rose in a long silent bound toward the distant trees, with two outfielders converging behind it.

Foster moved like a man possessed, his head back, his arms pumping. His sharp spikes dug into the solid little sandbag that marked first base. He careened in a sudden turn, running far out on the grass, and sped for second with all the strength he owned. He could see the outfielder grab the ball up from the deep grass and turn to throw it in. The ball was in the air, floating in a slow arc toward the second baseman, who stood with one foot firmly planted on the base and both bare hands stiffly extended toward the approaching ball. The ball bounced on the grass some twenty feet away. Foster flung himself headfirst toward the base. He felt the hard gravel dig through his shirt front and scrape his ribs. His straining fingers hit the base. A spiked foot came down on his hand, but he was only faintly aware of the pain.

"Safe!" called the distant umpire. Foster got to his feet and set out to rub the dust from his clothing. He saw the blood streaking the grime on his hand; and he sucked at the small punctures. The ball went back to the pitcher, and Foster took his position just off the base, both feet together, standing erect, ready to fly to third if the ball bounced past the catcher or the batter hit it fair. The style in those days was to use "deception" in stealing—that is, to stand rather indifferently near the base and try to guess when the pitcher was ready to pitch. And even the best of coaches thought that the way to get a flying start was to have both feet together.

But Foster did not need to steal. The catcher had moved "up close" (about six feet behind the batter) so as to be ready to throw in case Foster broke for third base. The batter swung at the first pitch and tipped it; and the ball struck the catcher in the face, necessitating a brief delay while the catcher retrieved the ball and made a futile effort to stem the blood from his split lip.

"Take plenty of ground, Foster!" shouted the coacher near third base. "Take plenty of ground!" Foster moved another step or two away from the base and stared blandly back when the pitcher turned to eye him. The pitcher turned, made his skipping run toward the batter, and let the ball go. It came up in a swift, looping arc, well outside the plate; but the batter swung, caught it on the end of the bat, and sent it high behind first base, about fifteen feet from where the first baseman stood with his foot firmly planted on the sack that was his to guard. The first baseman turned, without removing his foot from the bag, and shouted encouragement to the right fielder, who, starting from about fifty yards beyond the spot where the ball was falling, came running full tilt toward the diamond, with his bare hands vainly out-stretched. The second baseman, who had also planted his foot on his own base, joined in the cry. The right fielder came close. The ball dropped to the turf and bounded high, with the fielder still racing toward it. He stopped and took it in both hands, on the first bounce. The batter was out! But no, the ball seemed to squirm out of the clutching hands of the fielder and squirt away, with the fielder floundering and grabbing at it. Foster, who had foolishly started to run when the ball was in the air (forgetting that he could be "doubled" on a catch), was rounding third base now. "Run!" screamed the coacher. "Leg it, man!" Foster legged it, staring wildly ahead at the looming catcher. Ten feet from the plate he leaped headfirst, tumbling in a heap and whacking the iron plate such a rap with his chin that the metal rang. He rolled over in a half somersault and climbed to his feet in a daze of ecstasy. It was a run! It was an official run! The very first run, *real* run, that is, he had ever scored! That other scoring, in those informal games, didn't count. This was going into the scorebook, for *good,* in the official records, to be preserved forever.

With the dust of the diamond still clinging to him,

Foster, with several of his teammates, crowded at the scorekeeper's shoulder to see the run go down in the big black book. Foster Green: 1. They did not think they could ever get their fill of looking at it.

When the game was over Foster rode home to breakfast in his crumpled uniform, with his cap pushed back and the hair matted on his forehead, the proud sweat still on his face, and not an ounce of embarrass-ment left to unman him in the public eye. He was no longer a gawky clerk who liked to play baseball. He was a *ballplayer;* and he sported his scars as if they were battle wounds.

The rest of the team, too, undoubtedly bore marks from the contest. In those early days many a player caught the ball with fingers stiffly outstretched, not having learned the "Eastern trick" of letting the hands give with the speed of the ball. The catcher, who had to bear in mind the rule that "a tick and a ketch will always fetch," carried the marks of many a foul tick on his fingers and his face. If he escaped a black eye in this game he must at least have had many a sore if not broken finger, possibly a loosened tooth and a swollen lip.

It was a manly game. No matter how many small cuts and bruises a man might have, how badly he limped, or how much his nose bled, there could be no substitution, under the rules of the day, except in the case of obvious serious injury.

No wonder Foster and his office mates were proud to flaunt the trappings of the baseball player. No wonder they conspired to slip a white feather onto the desk of the tall, sharp-featured ledger clerk who had announced that he would be hanged if *he* played any game with that "deuced hard ball."

Although Foster and his mates (whose fellows, like as not, were fighting Indians a-horseback on the plains) were interested in baseball chiefly as a manly exercise, they used to find the game worth watching, too. Hardly a town in the land was too small to earn a visit from a traveling club like the Olympics, the Forest Cities, the Eckfords, the Mutuals, or the Atlantics. And when a famous club came to town, there was a holiday for everyone, not only muffins and sports writers, but for fine ladies and school children—for everyone who could wave a flag or give a welcoming cheer.

These teams used to enter upon their tours like knights-errant. The Olympic team (made up one hundred per cent of young men who had been appointed to government jobs so that they might play ball in Wash-ington) entrained for their first Western tour from a line of carriages all decked out like an inaugural parade. New linen dusters had been bought for the tour. The horses wore plumes or red, white, and blue. Ladies gathered at the railroad station to offer bouquets to each of the players and to pelt them with flowers as they climbed into the cars. There was a brass band to provide the blaring accompaniment when the team and all its followers broke into what was probably the first of many "team songs" of the era:

*We're going Westward Ho! We're going Westward Ho!*
*Here's to all who toss the ball. . . .*

The arrival of the team in a rival town was an occasion of even greater pomp. There were perhaps three different bands at the station to greet them. The rival team turned out, lined up in semimilitary formation, dressed, as many of the well-heeled Western teams were, in Zouave pants and brilliant shirts. The mayor stood on a flag-draped platform to make a speech of welcome. There were welcome signs on fences, bunting tied on every building front, decorated carriages, screaming small boys, and even booming cannon.

Oh, why, some of the essay writers of the day moaned in print, must we Americans go *mad* about everything? Can't we be temperate in *some* things?

We certainly could not be temperate about baseball, even in those distant days. Every good-sized town became a Brooklyn when the Olympics (or whatever the club might be) came to town.

People would crowd into trains with such disregard for fine clothes, comfort, and decency that dainty ladies would take fright. They would hire barouches and buggies, even butcher's wagons and bicycles, cling to horsecars or to the backs of carts, or stream on foot along the clogged and dusty roads that led to the ball park. So many humans would be on the move that it seemed the city had emptied, and still they came, in twos and threes, shouting, sweating, whipping up the horses as game time came close, cutting through fields and woods, leaving their work undone, leading their children, carrying their lunches in baskets, or stopping to buy from peddlers along the way.

At the ball park they might buy strong drink from a man with a hamper full of bottles, then they could wander about to close bets with men they knew, or accept odds from a sweating "pool seller." Or they might simply wager a new hat on the home team. But, as one commentator solemnly pointed out, "hats cost money," so these timid folk were no less abandoned through having retained their technical virtue.

The crowds pouring into the park would spread themselves all over the field. A few would drive their carriages in and remain there, looking out over the heads of the others. Most would pack into the small stand, milling there, shifting seats, craning and shoving until the teams actually appeared.

The speculating element would collect in front of the clubhouse veranda, there to shout odds, drip sweat, rush to close wagers, and yell entreaties to the players. These made a solemn crowd, despite the noise they raised; and there would be expressions here as strained as you might find on the floor of the stock exchange. There would be liquor peddlers among them and professional bookmakers, their faces reddened by shouting, with bandanna handkerchiefs shoved inside their melting collars and their hats jammed down tight.

On the clubhouse veranda the really select folk would lounge, conversing ostentatiously with the players, sipping mixed drinks, tending to the needs and curiosity of voluminously dressed ladies in pert hats. And all through the outfield the more rabid fans would range, along with self-important correspondents from the sporting and local press, who moved about as if they were covering a battle and needed to watch each phase of the attack from every point.

In the matter of controlling these swarming crowds, baseball then was much like professional football in the days before it became organized. There was no more than a formal effort to keep the spectators from getting so close to the play as to interfere with it. "Cranks" (the old-time name for fans) with a few uneasy dollars riding on the game could curse into the very face of a player who missed a chance to make victory sure. And more than a few times a frenzied partisan entered the field of play to give his favorites what aid he could manage.

In the "national-championship" game between the invincible Cincinnati Reds and the unbeaten Atlantics of Brooklyn, played in Brooklyn on June 14, 1870, a spectator whose devotion to the Atlantics (or to the dollars he had placed on them) got the better of him really turned the tide. The Reds had been all over the nation, trimming amateur teams by scores that, nowadays, would sound fantastic even for football (86–8; 103–8; etc.). Now they were leading the Atlantics by two runs, with Smith of the Atlantics on third, when Joe Start, the Atlantics' "Old Reliable" first baseman (he caught all the throws) stepped to bat. Start drove a long fly out toward Calvin McVey in right field. The crowd gave way to permit McVey to field the ball, which fell, almost dead, on a slope. But as Cal stooped to retrieve it, he was suddenly sent sprawling to his hands and knees. A spectator had jumped on his back. By the time McVey had freed himself, flung the fan aside, and recovered the ball, Smith had scored and Start had gone all the way to third, with the tying run. Bob Ferguson, who later became famed as an umpire of unimpeachable honesty, batted left-handed, so as not to risk hitting the ball to George Wright, then playing shortstop for the Reds. Bob brought in the tying run with a daisy-cutter between first and second bases, then scored the winning run himself, when nervous fielding allowed him to circle the bases. It was the first defeat in two years for the Cincinnati Reds.

The Reds, incidentally, were the first openly professional club. They were an outgrowth of the Cincinnati Cricket Club; and when they turned to baseball, with Harry Wright, the elder of the Wright brothers, as manager, they named themselves the Red Stockings and announced publicly that they were going to pay each player a regular stipend each season. The salaries were not high—they ranged from $800 to $1400—but the shamelessness of the matter brought indignant comment in the polite press. And when a group of men in Chicago formed a stock company to sponsor the White Stockings Baseball Club, and even undertook a pay dividends out of the gate receipts, there were open expressions of horror. In commenting on that disgraceful event, a writer in the *Lakeside Monthly* found occasion to extenuate the shame of the Reds, inasmuch as the profits for the first season ($7000) had been used for "decorating the clubhouse, etc." Nor were the Reds, like the White Stockings, just a crowd of shiftless young men who took money for having fun. One was a "respectable broker" in private life.

The Reds, even though they admitted their professionalism, still paid homage to the amateur tradition. Their arrivals and departures were as festive as those of the Olympics; and they, too, had their traveling song, with a verse for every player:

> *Hurrah! Hurrah! For the noble game, hurrah!*
> *Red Stockings all, we'll toss the ball*
> *And shout our loud hurrah!*

The Red Stockings found some intimations of what the world, or at least the game of baseball, was coming to when they journeyed to Philadelphia to play the old Athletics (which had no connection whatever with the modern club). Riding out to the park in their four-horse, flag-decorated omnibus, they were escorted by many boys of assorted sizes, barefoot, ragged, some wearing grown men's clothes rolled up and tucked in at needful places.

"You're a-goin' to get beat!" sang the boys.

When the Reds rode back to the station, triumphant, the same boys darted out from the gutters to shake their dirty little fists. "Go to hell!" they screamed. "Go to hell!"

On the ball field, too, the tradition of chivalry began to tarnish badly, even though the great figures of the game were at some pains to maintain its glow. The traveling clubs usually brought their own umpire with them; and he was never in the least doubtful as to which side of his bread held the margarine. And the managers of the clubs were not above using the mask of chivalry as a means of helping them achieve the prime purpose: winning the game. For instance, when the Forest City

club of Rockford, Illinois, appeared in Marshalltown, Iowa, in 1867, and beat the locals by only 18–3 (a tight score in those times), Manager Spalding had to polish up his famous strategy in order to save his team's reputation. His request for a second game happily granted, the eloquent gentleman explained that he knew to what expense the home team had already gone in the matter of equipment and entertainment and he offered to supply the baseball for the second game. The Marshalltown boys gratefully accepted. It was not until they had watched the ball flying over their heads for several innings that the home team began to wonder, somewhat timorously, if the ball was indeed the "Ryan Dead" that the rules called for. They looked the ball over, and it did indeed bear the Ryan name. But when the game was over, the Spalding team having won 35–5, the Marshalltown players learned that inside the Ryan cover was not the legitimate ball at all but a "Bounding Rock," one of the liveliest balls ever made. They realized then why the Forest City outfielders had played so much deeper in the second game and why the Marshalltown outfielders had seen so many hits take wings and light far out of reach.

Incidents of this sort helped to kindle the fierce local pride and yearning for vindication which have been meat and drink to the national game ever since. Of course, in the beginning most town teams were honestly teams of the town, with not a foreign face in the line-up; and even the professional teams, which began to spring up haphazardly throughout the land in the seventies, made such a serious effort to nourish this spirit that many a "crank" thought that the Red Stockings, for instance, had been on hand as long as there was a Cincinnati. One sage, before the Red Stockings established themselves as the greatest ball team in the land, allowed that it would kill the game deader than a frozen fish if players were brought in from other cities. When, within a few months, an entire team of professionals had been gathered from Eastern cities, one local writer took public pride in the fact that the team had at least been "secured by a Cincinnatian."

It was not long before intertown competition, particularly in the Midwest, waxed so hot that a peg like this was all the home-town folk needed to hang their pride on. Many a ballplayer who later, when the leagues were formed, earned for himself a name that still lives in the records made his first good-sized stake by serving as a ringer in some small-town series, particularly in the Midwest, where betting on ball games was enriching a few farmers and small-town sports faster than the railroad was bringing cattle money into Dodge City and Abilene.

Ted Sullivan, that thrifty manager from Dubuque, whose name still lives on the tongues of professional ballplayers who ride the Sullivan Sleepers (day coaches) to the training camp, tells a story of the rivalry between two Iowa teams, Cresco and Decorah. Decorah first beat Cresco by using a collection of professionals from the Chicago City League, who had been qualified for the intertown game by being given jobs without work in and around Decorah for a week or two. The farmers and merchants of Cresco, after observing that they had been bilked, determined to win back their hats, horses, currency, and a little to boot. They sent to Dubuque, whose "Rabbits" were the champions of the Northwest League (the first minor league), to hire the famous battery: Radbourne (soon to become the National League's "Old Hoss") and Billy Taylor, who later served as both pitcher and catcher for Pittsburgh. Taylor and Radbourne were "hired" to work on a near-by farm, where they loafed through a few chores or just killed time in the barnyard, waiting for the day of the game. Meanwhile, the crafty Decorah boys, suspecting that Cresco might have learned some tricks in their recent defeat, had spies watching the workouts of the Cresco nine, on the lookout for ringers. Right up to the eve of the game, no new faces appeared, so Decorah sports began to dig deep into their socks for cash to lure in some of the Cresco sucker money. Betting on this game almost put a stop to commerce.

The day for the game was a warm one. The railroads had scheduled excursion trains to bring in farmers from the whole county; and wagons creaked into town from early morning on. Milk soured, cattle went untended, and pigs grunted hungrily in their sties. There was no admission charge to the ball field, for it was marked off only by stakes and a rope. Farm wagons and carriages provided an informal grandstand. Small boys scampered barefoot across the stubble. Men hawked liquor from bottles, and ladies unhappily tried to keep their Sunday finery straight in the crush. The sun settled into midafternoon, and the crowd, who had been howling and applauding as the two nines worked out on the baking diamond, began to murmur for action. The Decorah captain was ready. How about getting started? "No," said the Cresco captain, "my battery isn't here yet. They're a little slow in coming from the farm."

Meanwhile, a farmer drove into the field with a tremendous load of hay and ten overalled farm hands riding the load. He took his wagon right to the ropes. Hold up there! the players told him. Get her out of there, Si. You'll have to pull over there beyond the first-base line. The farmer whopped his horses, yelled, heaved the reins, frightened a few ladies, and took his lumbering load off out of the way. The sun grew older and the sweating crowd began to complain more steadily: Come on! Play ball!

The newly arrived farmer climbed off his wagon and asked what was holding up the game. Thought she'd be nearly half done by now. No, the players told him, no pitcher and catcher yet.

"Well, Jinkers," said the farmer, "take a couple of my hands here. You're welcome to them."

"No," said the Cresco captain, "we've got our regular pitcher and catcher coming. This game is too important to take any chances on."

The afternoon burned on for several more long minutes.

"Oh, come on," said the Decorah man, "we came here to play ball. Use a couple of those hayshakers until your boys get here. We ain't got nobody that'll hit them far," he said, winking at a couple of the grinning Chicago pros.

The Cresco captain grimaced, eyed the impatient crowd, who were beginning to straggle beyond the ropes, and finally gave in. Two of the strongest-looking farm hands climbed off the load, set their straw hats down, and walked out on the diamond. "Hey, Rube!" one of the spry young Chicago pros cried; and his mates and followers punched each other in glee.

But the "farmers" were Radbourne and Taylor; and before the first inning was out the big city boys realized they were up against something faster than they had ever heard tell of back in the Chicago league. Decorah and her ringers never had a chance that day. Some of her partisans even left their teams and wagons behind, in payment of their wagers, when they set out for home that evening, returning with nothing but the clothes on their backs and a wry amazement at the speed and spin which that big farmer could give to a baseball.

Radbourne, of course, was no farmer. He was a railroad brakeman from Bloomington, Illinois, and first played ball in Peoria. People can still be found who will insist, from the records and from what a few men can remember, that Charles G. "Old Hoss" Radbourne was the greatest pitcher who ever lived. He did have the quality that all great athletes have had in common, a burning desire to win. He also, despite his supposedly "weak" character (he was given to drink and to associating with ladies of easy virtue), possessed an almost idealistic loyalty toward his team, which prompted him to drive himself through the most intense physical agony.

In 1884, to wander just a few years ahead, Radbourne was one of the two regular pitchers carried by Providence of the National League. The other was Charles Sweeney, a young speed-ball specialist from California. The right fielder, Miller, was the "change" pitcher—that is, the man who would come in and toss the ball up if the regular pitcher wobbled or tired. As has already been noted, the rules did not permit the sending in of a substitute: the game had to be played out with the men who were on the field at the start, unless one were incapacitated by injury right on the field.

In a tight game with Philadelphia, when Providence and Philadelphia were fighting out the championship of the league, Sweeney faltered and the manager ordered him to right field to change places with Miller. ''Nothing doing,'' said Sweeney, who walked right off the field, out of the park, and signed with the St. Louis team of the new Union Association. The Providence team had to complete the game with only eight men on the field; and they could not begin to hold the fast Philadelphia club even.

That night the club directors met to discuss calling the whole season off; but Radbourne, who was under suspension at the time because of ''misconduct,'' allowed that he could carry the entire load—thirty-odd more games—and win the pennant into the bargain. He was a short, solidly built man, with one of the droopiest mustaches ever described; and he spoke quietly, without a hint of bragging. He was immediately reinstated and pitched twenty-seven games. He won twenty-six of them, but at the price of excruciating muscular pain. Most of the time he could not use his right arm at all, except when he was pitching, and only then after hours of careful limbering up or massage. He would grimace in pain for an hour after he had started his tedious warm-up. And after the game he could not lift his hand high enough to brush his hair. Yet he pitched with tremendous speed and great craft. He could curve the ball both ways and had a dazzling change of pace. It was said of him that he never threw a wild pitch. Like so many ''Iron Man'' pitchers, he always threw underhand, even when the rules were changed to permit overhand throwing.

After he won the pennant for Providence, he became the most famous player in the country. Illinois Wesleyan College used him as a pitcher in Bloomington against the local semi-pros, in order to fatten the gate, thus giving rise to a persistent fable that Radbourne attended that college. Inasmuch as he had no contract with Providence for the following season, he received offers from baseball clubs the country over, at salaries higher than he had ever thought of earning. But he signed with Providence. And in spite of the fact that Manager Allen of Providence offered to let him fill in his own salary on the contract, he gave himself only a modest advance in wages.

He pitched successfully for several more years, including a season with the Boston club of the Players' League; but he never earned the sort of money a great pitcher can hope for now. His career was shortened by a siege of jaundice, a sore arm (blamed on the lively ball of the Players' League), and finally paresis, which manifested itself just before his death. In 1891, he retired from baseball and bought himself a poolroom. He lost an eye by the accidental discharge of a gun—he had been a great hunter and outdoorsman—and from that time on he sat in a dark corner of his pool hall while the disease ate into his brain. The Old Hoss, who had numbered his good friends in hundreds, became more morose and antisocial each day. He gave up all activity and practically all his friends and died in obscurity in 1897, at the age of forty-three.

**EVOLUTION OF A BALL PARK . . .**
New York's Polo Grounds:
first, in 1890; then, just after
the turn of the century; then,
in the 1920s. (Photos by
Brown Brothers)

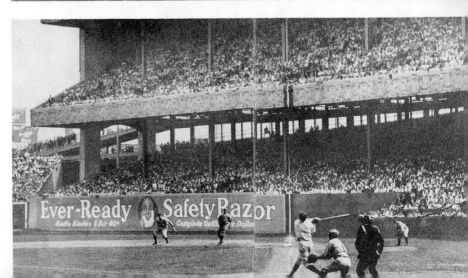

This listing was published in the May, 1986, issue of *Inside Sports* magazine.

# Rating the Baseball Movies

## BERT RANDOLPH SUGAR

THROUGHOUT THE ages, or at least since the subject of baseball was first introduced to the screen in the 1899 one-reeler "Casey at the Bat," baseball has served as both the subject and backdrop for many a motion picture. Two of the films that have used baseball merely as a point of departure include "Strategic Air Command"—in which the world's oldest third baseman, Jimmy Stewart, is prevailed upon to desert the diamond and join SAC in order to "keep America strong"—and "The Odd Couple"—in which Oscar Madison covers a game that, not incidentally, features a triple play hit into by Bill Mazeroski (a proud Roberto Clemente having refused the honor of participating).

But in researching my upcoming book, "The Baseball Trivia Book To End All Baseball Trivia Books," I was more concerned with the 36 pictures that have used baseball as their subject (see below). And in compiling my list, I came to the realization that, like Orwell's pigs, not all of them were created equal. In fact, some of them are far more equal than others. And this gave rise to two other lists: The 10 Best and the 10 Worst Baseball Movies of All Time. With apologies to Rex Reed, I herewith present those lists for your consideration and consternation.

### THE 10 BEST MOVIES

1. "The Pride of the Yankees" (RKO, 1942—Gary Cooper, Teresa Wright). A three-handkerchiefer, which could almost be retitled, "Mr. Deeds goes to Yankee Stadium."

2. "Bang the Drum Slowly" (Paramount, 1973—Robert De Niro, Michael Moriarty). Another tear-jerker. It is a movie with a message: "Don't rag on nobody," and also possesses much of the two-fer spirit made popular by "The Sting."

3. "Damn Yankees" (Warner Bros., 1958—Tab Hunter, Gwen Verdon). Damn good musical and

excellent treatment of the stage play, which was developed from Douglas Wallop's "The Year the Yankees Lost the Pennant."

4. "Fear Strikes Out" (Paramount, 1957—Anthony Perkins, Karl Malden). One of the father-son conflict films done in the late '50s. It hits a home run—even if all Jimmy Piersall remembered about its star was that "shaking Anthony Perkins' hand was like holding a dead fish."

5. "Casey at the Bat" (Paramount, 1927—Wallace Beery, ZaSu Pitts). Magnificent tour de force for Beery and fun for all as he leaves the audience in stitches and Blake still "ahugging third."

6. "The Bingo Long Traveling All-Stars and Motor Kings" (UA, 1976—Billy Dee Williams, Richard Pryor, James Earl Jones). A tour, a romp, and a trip well worth taking in this throwback to days of yore when, as Billy Dee Williams said, "Niggers ain't allowed."

7. "Elmer the Great" (Warner Bros., 1933—Joe E. Brown). Brown came up to the Pirates in 1920, but Pittsburgh opted to keep their other third baseman, Pie Traynor. He's as much fun to watch on the screen as Ring Lardner's original.

8. "The Stratton Story" (MGM, 1949—Jimmy Stewart, June Allyson). This is baseball's answer to "Song of Bernadette," an uplifting any-man-can saga.

9. "Angels in the Outfield" (MGM, 1951—Paul Douglas, Jean Peters). A turn on the old Stephen Vincent Benet theme. The Pittsburgh Pirates needed all the help they could get, and being on the side of the Angels didn't hurt.

10. "The Bad News Bears" (Paramount, 1976—Walter Matthau, Tatum O'Neal). "Our Gang" updated with a fresh look.

THE 10 WORST MOVIES

1. "Safe at Home" (Columbia, 1962—Mickey Mantle, Roger Maris, Bill Frawley). Mantle and Maris should of stood at home instead of trying to be safe at home. The audiences did!

2. "The Babe Ruth Story" (Allied Artists, 1948—William Bendix, Claire Trevor, Charles Bickford). There was no way Ruth's life could be captured on film. Especially when the title role was played by William Bendix. In short, it was ruthless as well as Ruthless.

3. "Take Me Out to the Ballgame" (MGM, 1949—Gene Kelly, Frank Sinatra, Esther Williams). This movie was as padded as Esther Williams' bra and was the greatest dive since the 1919 Black Sox scandal in Chicago.

4. "The Bad News Bears Go to Japan" (Paramount, 1978—Tony Curtis). Baseball's version of "Rocky II," this should have been subtitled "The Bad News Bears Go Ca-Ca."

5. "The Natural" (Tri-Star, 1984—Robert Redford, Robert Duvall, Glenn Close). A rape of Bernard Malamud's book. As writer Peter Golenbock, in his review, said, "They should have shot the director instead of Roy Hobbs."

6. "Rhubarb" (Paramount, 1955—Ray Milland, Jan Sterling). This remake of a delightful H. Allen Smith novella about a cat that owns a ballclub somehow gets lost somewhere between the screen and a litterbox.

7. "The Winning Team" (Warner Bros., 1952—Ronald Reagan, Doris Day). Grover Cleveland Alexander an epileptic? Come on, now. He was one of the great all-time drunks, one who could, in the words of his St. Louis manager, Rogers Hornsby, "pitch better, drunk or sober, than anyone else in baseball." A shame the picture was so sterile. But then again, what else can we expect from George Gipp in a baseball uniform?

8. "The Great American Pastime" (MGM, 1956—Tom Ewell). This film proves that the real "Great American Pastime" at the time was watching Marilyn Monroe, which Ewell had done in his previous movie, "The Seven-Year Itch."

9. "The Pride of St. Louis" (20th Century Fox, 1952—Dan Dailey, Joanne Dru). Dan Dailey playing Dizzy Dean? This whole movie, as the Diz would have said, "slud." And even worse.

10. "Here Come the Tigers" (American International, 1978). The "Bad News Bears" growing up and changing their name to Tigers.

EVERY BASEBALL MOVIE EVER MADE

"Alibi Ike" (Warner Bros., 1935—Joe E. Brown and Olivia de Havilland)

"Angels in the Outfield" (MGM, 1951—Paul Douglas, Jean Peters, Ed Begley)

"The Babe Ruth Story" (AA, 1948—William Bendix, Claire Trevor, Charles Bickford)

"Bang the Drum Slowly" (Paramount, 1973—Robert De Niro, Michael Moriarty)

"The Bad News Bears" (Paramount, 1976—Walter Matthau, Tatum O'Neal)

"The Bad News Bears Go to Japan" (Paramount, 1978—Tony Curtis)

"The Bad News Bears in Breaking Training" (Paramount, 1977)

"The Big Leaguer" (MGM, 1953—Edward G. Robinson, Vera Ellen)

"The Bingo Long Traveling All-Stars and Motor Kings" (UA, 1976—Billy Dee Williams, Richard Pryor, James Earl Jones)

"The Bush Leaguer" (Warner Bros., 1927—Monte Blue)

"Casey at the Bat" (Paramount, 1927—Wallace Beery, ZaSu Pitts, Ford Stirling)

"College" (UA, 1927—Buster Keaton)

"Damn Yankees" (Warner Bros., 1958—Tab Hunter, Gwen Verdon)

"Death on the Diamond" (MGM, 1934—Robert Young)

"Elmer the Great" (Warner Bros., 1933—Joe E. Brown)

"Fast Company" (Paramount, 1929—Jack Oakie)

"Fear Strikes Out" (Paramount, 1957—Anthony Perkins, Karl Malden)

"Fireman Save My Child" (Warner Bros., 1932—Joe E. Brown)

"The Great American Pastime" (MGM, 1956—Tom Ewell, Anne Francis, Ann Miller)

"Here Come the Tigers" (American International, 1978)

"It Happened in Brooklyn" (20th Century Fox, 1942—Lloyd Nolan)

"It Happens Every Spring" (Walt Disney, 1949—Ray Milland)

"The Jackie Robinson Story" (Eagle Lion, 1950—Jackie Robinson, Ruby Dee)

"The Kid from Cleveland" (Republic, 1949—Russ Tamblyn, George Brent, "And 30 Godfathers, the Cleveland Indians")

"The Kid from Left Field" (20th Century Fox, 1953—Dan Dailey)

"Kill the Umpire" (Columbia, 1950—William Bendix, Una Merkel)

"Ladies Day" (RKO, 1943—Eddie Albert)

"The Natural" (Tri-Star, 1984—Robert Redford, Robert Duvall, Glenn Close)

"The Pride of St. Louis" (20th Century Fox, 1952—Dan Dailey)

"The Pride of the Yankees" (RKO, 1942—Gary Cooper, Teresa Wright)

"Rhubarb" (Paramount, 1955—Ray Milland, Jan Sterling)

"Safe at Home" (Columbia, 1962—Mickey Mantle, Roger Maris, Bill Frawley)

"The Stratton Story" (MGM, 1949—Jimmy Stewart, Frank Morgan, June Allyson)

"Take Me Out to the Ballgame" (MGM, 1949—Gene Kelly, Frank Sinatra, Esther Williams)

"Whistling in Brooklyn" (MGM, 1943—Red Skelton, Ann Rutherford, and the entire Brooklyn Dodgers team)

"The Winning Team" (Warner Bros., 1952—Ronald Reagan, Doris Day)

# The Spring We Ran Out of Bats

## ED SUNDT

WE HAD always played ball, even with coats and gloves on, in New England springs when the base valleys were filled with water, patches of snow decorated the soggy outfield, and a scrap of paper became first or second. But 1948 was different: we began to run out of bats.

Bats cost a lot, and when Jordan's Hardware Store raised the price another quarter, nobody would let anybody else use his bat. Nothing brought about more bad feelings at school that spring. Once we chased one of the twins for ten minutes, even cutting illegally through the playground hedges and risking a hair pulling by the principal, just because Twinny had supposedly stepped on Ronnie's bat and "spiked" it (put little dents into it from his spiked shoes). Only he didn't have spikes on and he weighed only 40 pounds, so his black sneakers wouldn't have dented an ant hill. We were just frustrated.

We did have one bat, a skinny-handled one that everybody used. But when it cracked, its handle was so thin that we couldn't nail it or screw it back together. The heavy wrapping of friction tape changed its feel, and you could feel it give when you swung.

The season began to look endless and boring. We'd get together and use the old taped bat to hit out some flies, but with so many guys jumping up and shoving each other as the ball came down, it was clear somebody was going to get beaned, and it would all be for nothing.

My grandfather must have noticed that something was wrong. Grandpa had his own lumber business, with lots of machinery and sawdust piles and mountains of slabs all over his yard. He had been old ever since I knew him, with a gray bristly mustache and a hawk nose under spectacles, a dark, wear-softened hat with sawdust on it, bib overalls, steel-toed shoes, and a thumb missing. He was also an inventor. He designed and manufactured sawmills and parts, and cant hooks to help men roll huge logs onto the sawmills' carriages.

One May afternoon Grandma came to where I was out back, digging out sawdust, and said, "Grandpa wants to see you in his office."

This was a scary thing to hear. Sometimes we played checkers or pinochle in the evening, if he wasn't listening to Fulton Lewis Junior, and then went to bed. But he had never called me into his office.

The room was yellowy-dim and all in reddish wood. It had a big roll-top desk, a black mechanical adding machine on one stand, and a huge old spidery typewriter on another. He sat in a creaky swivel chair by the desk, a green ledger book in front of him.

His chair barked a loud noise when he swung around suddenly. "You've been around the house a lot lately," he said sternly.

"Look in that closet door." It was the one where he kept his guns, one that I was forbidden to go near.

There was a tense silence. The clock ticked.

"Go ahead," he said.

I opened the tall, thin, oil-smelling door. There were the dark shotguns and rifles leaning. But then I noticed the bats. Two white baseball bats.

"Go ahead," he said.

I took one out and gripped it, swinging it in a short arc so as not to hit the desk. I rubbed my hand along the smooth barrel and it bumped over the rough trademark my grandfather had burned in: "Willington Slugger" it said. And in an oval it read, "C.S. Amidon & Sons, Sawmills and Supplies, East Willington, Conn."

"I guess a lathe that can make a cant hook can make a baseball bat," he said, accenting the "ball."

The two Willington Sluggers went to school with me the next day. I had the rarest gifts, the greatest power: not one new bat, but two. Fashioned from ash, honed and polished, without knots and of smooth grain that curved beautifully over the top of the barrel, the bats began their magic that morning at recess and we had to be ordered to come back in at 10:15 to study arithmetic.

But it was only like a rain delay; it was the beginning of a most wonderful season.

It is only recently that it's occurred to me: how did he know how long to make them? How did he know what bats should weigh? How did he know how to make a knob that felt just right? He died when I was in high school, that gruff, taciturn old man who probably never saw a baseball game and who even pronounced the word oddly, but who made Willington Sluggers for me and my friends.

This is a quiet piece about a private man. But when Marilyn Monroe said, "You never heard such cheering," he could answer, "Yes I have." The article appeared in *Esquire* in 1966.

# The Silent Season of a Hero

## GAY TALESE

"I would like to take the great DiMaggio fishing," the old man said. "They say his father was a fisherman. Maybe he was as poor as we are and would understand."

—ERNEST HEMINGWAY, *The Old Man and the Sea*

IT WAS not quite spring, the silent season before the search for salmon, and the old fishermen of San Francisco were either painting their boats or repairing their nets along the pier or sitting in the sun talking quietly among themselves, watching the tourists come and go, and smiling, now, as a pretty girl paused to take their picture. She was about twenty-five, healthy and blue-eyed and wearing a red turtleneck sweater, and she had long, flowing blond hair that she brushed back a few times before clicking her camera. The fishermen, looking at her, made admiring comments but she did not understand because they spoke a Sicilian dialect; nor did she notice the tall gray-haired man in a dark suit who stood watching her from behind a big bay window on the second floor of DiMaggio's Restaurant that overlooks the pier.

He watched until she left, lost in the crowd of newly arrived tourists that had just come down the hill by cable car. Then he sat down again at the table in the restaurant, finishing his tea and lighting another cigarette, his fifth in the last half hour. It was eleven-thirty in the morning. None of the other tables was occupied, and the only sounds came from the bar, where a liquor salesman was laughing at something the headwaiter had said. But then the salesman, his briefcase under his arm, headed for the door, stopping briefly to peek into the dining room and call out, "See you later, Joe." Joe DiMaggio turned and waved at the salesman. Then the room was quiet again.

At fifty-one, DiMaggio was a most distinguished-looking man, aging as gracefully as he had played on the ballfield, impeccable in his tailoring, his nails manicured, his 6-foot 2-inch body seeming as lean and capable as when he posed for the portrait that hangs in the restaurant and shows him in Yankee Stadium swinging from the heels at a pitch thrown twenty years ago. His gray hair was thinning at the crown, but just barely, and his face was lined in the right places, and his expression, once as sad and haunted as a matador's, was more in repose these days, though, as now, tension had returned and he chainsmoked and occasionally paced the floor and looked out the window at the people below. In the crowd was a man he did not wish to see.

The man had met DiMaggio in New York. This week he had come to San Francisco and had telephoned several times but none of the calls had been returned because DiMaggio suspected that the man, who had said he was doing research on some vague sociological project, really wanted to delve into DiMaggio's private life and that of DiMaggio's former wife, Marilyn Monroe. DiMaggio would never tolerate this. The memory of her death is still very painful to him, and yet, because he keeps it to himself, some people are not sensitive to it. One night in a supper club a woman who had been drinking approached his table, and when he did not ask her to join him, she snapped:

"All right, I guess I'm *not* Marilyn Monroe."

He ignored her remark, but when she repeated it, he replied, barely controlling his anger, "No—I wish you were, but you're not."

The tone of his voice softened her, and she asked, "Am I saying something wrong?"

"You already have," he said. "Now will you please leave me alone?"

His friends on the wharf, understanding him as they

do, are very careful when discussing him with strangers, knowing that should they inadvertently betray a confidence he will not denounce them but rather will never speak to them again; this comes from a sense of propriety not inconsistent in the man who also, after Marilyn Monroe's death, directed that fresh flowers be placed on her grave "forever."

Some of the old fishermen who have known DiMaggio all his life remember him as a small boy who helped clean his father's boat, and as a young man who sneaked away and used a broken oar as a bat on the sandlots nearby. His father, a small mustachioed man known as Zio Pepe, would become infuriated and call him *lagnuso* (lazy) *meschino* (good-for-nothing) but in 1936 Zio Pepe was among those who cheered when Joe DiMaggio returned to San Francisco after his first season with the New York Yankees and was carried along the wharf on the shoulders of the fishermen.

The fishermen also remember how, after his retirement in 1951, DiMaggio brought his second wife, Marilyn, to live near the wharf, and sometimes they would be seen early in the morning fishing off DiMaggio's boat, the *Yankee Clipper*, now docked quietly in the marina, and in the evening they would be sitting and talking on the pier. They had arguments, too, the fishermen knew, and one night Marilyn was seen running hysterically, crying as she ran, along the road away from the pier, with Joe following. But the fishermen pretended they did not see this; it was none of their affair. They knew that Joe wanted her to stay in San Francisco and avoid the sharks in Hollywood, but she was confused and torn then—"She was a child," they said—and even today DiMaggio loathes Los Angeles and many of the people in it. He no longer speaks to his onetime friend, Frank Sinatra, who had befriended Marilyn in her final years, and he also is cool to Dean Martin and Peter Lawford and Lawford's former wife, Pat, who once gave a party at which she introduced Marilyn Monroe to Robert Kennedy, and the two of them danced often that night, Joe heard, and he did not take it well. He was very possessive of her that year, his close friends say, because Marilyn and he had planned to remarry; but before they could she was dead, and DiMaggio banned the Lawfords and Sinatra and many Hollywood people from her funeral. When Marilyn Monroe's attorney complained that DiMaggio was keeping her friends away, DiMaggio answered coldly, "If it weren't for those friends persuading her to stay in Hollywood she would still be alive."

Joe DiMaggio now spends most of the year in San Francisco, and each day tourists, noticing the name on the restaurant, ask the men on the wharf if they ever see him. Oh yes, the men say, they see him nearly every day; they have not seen him yet this morning, they add,

but he should be arriving shortly. So the tourists continue to walk along the piers past the crab vendors, under the circling sea gulls, past the fish 'n' chip stands, sometimes stopping to watch a large vessel steaming toward the Golden Gate Bridge which, to their dismay, is painted red. Then they visit the Wax Museum, where there is a life-size figure of DiMaggio in uniform, and walk across the street and spend a quarter to peer through the silver telescopes focused on the island of Alcatraz, which is no longer a Federal prison. Then they return to ask the men if DiMaggio has been seen. Not yet, the men say, although they notice his blue Impala parked in the lot next to the restaurant. Sometimes tourists will walk into the restaurant and have lunch and will see him sitting calmly in a corner signing autographs and being extremely gracious with everyone. At other times, as on this particular morning when the man from New York chose to visit, DiMaggio was tense and suspicious.

When the man entered the restaurant from the side steps leading to the dining room, he saw DiMaggio standing near the window, talking with an elderly maître d' named Charles Friscia. Not wanting to walk in and risk intrusion, the man asked one of DiMaggio's nephews to inform Joe of his presence. When DiMaggio got the message he quickly turned and left Friscia and disappeared through an exit leading down to the kitchen.

Astonished and confused, the visitor stood in the hall. A moment later Friscia appeared and the man asked, "Did Joe leave?"

"Joe who?" Friscia replied.

"Joe DiMaggio!"

"Haven't seen him," Friscia said.

"You haven't *seen* him! He was standing right next to you a second ago!"

"It wasn't me," Friscia said.

"You were standing next to him. I saw you. In the dining room."

"You must be mistaken," Friscia said, softly, seriously. "It wasn't me."

"You *must* be kidding," the man said, angrily, turning and leaving the restaurant. Before he could get to his car, however, DiMaggio's nephew came running after him and said, "Joe wants to see you."

He returned expecting to see DiMaggio waiting for him. Instead he was handed a telephone. The voice was powerful and deep and so tense that the quick sentences ran together.

*"You are invading my rights, I did not ask you to come, I assume you have a lawyer, you must have a lawyer, get your lawyer!"*

"I came as a friend," the man interrupted.

"That's beside the point," DiMaggio said. "I have my privacy, I do not want it violated, you'd better get a lawyer. . . ." Then, pausing, DiMaggio asked, "Is my nephew there?"

He was not.

"Then wait where you are."

A moment later DiMaggio appeared, tall and red-faced, erect and beautifully dressed in his dark suit and white shirt with the gray silk tie and the gleaming silver cuff links. He moved with big steps toward the man and handed him an airmail envelope, unopened, that the man had written from New York.

"Here," DiMaggio said. "This is yours."

Then DiMaggio sat down at a small table. He said nothing, just lit a cigarette and waited, legs crossed, his head held high and back so as to reveal the intricate construction of his nose, a fine sharp tip above the big nostrils and tiny bones built out from the bridge, a great nose.

"Look," DiMaggio said, more calmly. "I do not interfere with other people's lives. And I do not expect them to interfere with mine. There are things about my life, personal things, that I refuse to talk about. And even if you asked my brothers they would be unable to tell you about them because they do not know. There are things about me, so many things, that they simply do not know. . . ."

"I don't want to cause trouble," the man said. "I think you're a great man, and. . . ."

"I'm not great," DiMaggio cut in. "I'm not great," he repeated, softly. "I'm just a man trying to get along."

Then DiMaggio, as if realizing that he was intruding upon his own privacy, abruptly stood up. He looked at his watch.

"I'm late," he said, very formal again. "I'm ten minutes late. *You're* making me late."

The man left the restaurant. He crossed the street and wandered over to the pier, briefly watching the fishermen hauling their nets and talking in the sun, seeming very calm and contented. Then, after he had turned and was headed back toward the parking lot, a blue Impala stopped in front of him and Joe DiMaggio leaned out the window and asked, "Do you have a car?" His voice was very gentle.

"Yes," the man said.

"Oh," DiMaggio said. "I would have given you a ride."

Joe DiMaggio was not born in San Francisco but in Martinez, a small fishing village twenty-five miles northeast of the Golden Gate. Zio Pepe had settled there after leaving Isola delle Femmine, an islet off Palermo where the DiMaggios had been fishermen for generations. But in 1915, hearing of the luckier waters off San Francisco's wharf, Zio Pepe left Martinez, packing his boat with furniture and family, including Joe who was one year old.

San Francisco was placid and picturesque when the DiMaggios arrived, but there was a competitive undercurrent and struggle for power along the pier. At dawn the boats would sail out to where the bay meets the ocean and the sea is rough, and later the men would race back with their hauls, hoping to beat their fellow fishermen to shore and sell it while they could. Twenty or thirty boats would sometimes be trying to gain the channel shoreward at the same time, and a fisherman had to know every rock in the water, and later know every bargaining trick along the shore, because the dealers and restaurateurs would play one fisherman off against the other, keeping the prices down. Later the fishermen became wiser and organized, predetermining the maximum amount each fisherman would catch, but there were always some men who, like the fish, never learned, and so heads would sometimes be broken, nets slashed, gasoline poured onto their fish, flowers of warning placed outside their doors.

But these days were ending when Zio Pepe arrived, and he expected his five sons to succeed him as fishermen, and the first two, Tom and Michael, did; but a third, Vincent, wanted to sing. He sang with such magnificent power as a young man that he came to the attention of the great banker, A. P. Giannini, and there were plans to send him to Italy for tutoring and the opera. But there was hesitation around the DiMaggio household and Vince never went; instead he played ball with the San Francisco Seals and sportswriters misspelled his name.

It was DeMaggio until Joe, at Vince's recommendation, joined the team and became a sensation, being followed later by the youngest brother, Dominic, who was also outstanding. All three later played in the big leagues and some writers like to say that Joe was the best hitter, Dom the best fielder, Vince the best singer, and Casey Stengel once said: "Vince is the only player I ever saw who could strike out three times in one game and not be embarrassed. He'd walk into the clubhouse whistling. Everybody would be feeling sorry for him, but Vince always thought he was doing good."

After he retired from baseball Vince became a bartender, then a milkman, now a carpenter. He lives forty miles north of San Francisco in a house he partly built, has been happily married for thirty-four years, has four grandchildren, has in the closet one of Joe's tailor-made suits that he has never had altered to fit, and when people ask if he envies Joe he always says, "No, maybe Joe would like to have what I have. He won't admit it, but he just might like to have what I have." The brother Vince most admired was Michael, "a big earthy man, a dreamer, a fisherman who wanted things but didn't want to take from Joe, or to work in the restaurant. He wanted a bigger boat, but wanted to earn it on his own. He never got it." In 1953, at the age of forty-four, Michael fell from his boat and drowned.

Since Zio Pepe's death at seventy-seven in 1949, Tom, at sixty-two the oldest brother—two of his four sisters are older—has become nominal head of the family and manages the restaurant that was opened in 1937 as Joe DiMaggio's Grotto. Later, Joe sold out his share, and now Tom is the co-owner of it with Dominic. Of all the brothers, Dominic, who was known as the "Little Professor" when he played with the Boston Red Sox, is the most successful in business. He lives in a fashionable Boston suburb with his wife and three children and is president of a firm that manufactures fiber-cushion materials and grossed more than $3,500,000 last year.

Joe DiMaggio lives with his widowed sister, Marie, in a tan stone house on a quiet residential street not far from Fisherman's Wharf. He bought the house almost thirty years ago for his parents, and after their death he lived there with Marilyn Monroe; now it is cared for by Marie, a slim and handsome dark-eyed woman who has an apartment on the second floor, Joe on the third. There are some baseball trophies and plaques in the small room off DiMaggio's bedroom, and on his dresser are photographs of Marilyn Monroe, and in the living room downstairs is a small painting of her that DiMaggio likes very much: it reveals only her face and shoulders and she is wearing a very wide-brimmed sun hat, and there is a soft sweet smile on her lips, an innocent curiosity about her that is the way he saw her and the way he wanted her to be seen by others—a simple girl, "a warm big-hearted girl," he once described her, "that everybody took advantage of."

The publicity photographs emphasizing her sex appeal often offended him, and a memorable moment for Billy Wilder, who directed her in *The Seven Year Itch*, occurred when he spotted DiMaggio in a large crowd of people gathered on Lexington Avenue in New York to watch a scene in which Marilyn, standing over a subway grating to cool herself, had her skirts blown high by a sudden wind below. "What the hell is going on here?" DiMaggio was overheard to have said in the crowd, and Wilder recalled, "I shall never forget the look of death on Joe's face."

He was then thirty-nine, she was twenty-seven. They had been married in January of that year, 1954, despite disharmony in temperament and time: he was tired of publicity, she was thriving on it; he was intolerant of tardiness, she was always late. During their honeymoon in Tokyo, an American general had introduced himself and asked if, as a patriotic gesture, she would visit the troops in Korea. She looked at Joe. "It's your honey-

moon," he said, shrugging, "go ahead if you want to."

She appeared on ten occasions before 100,000 servicemen, and when she returned she said, "It was so wonderful, Joe. You never heard such cheering."

"Yes I have," he said.

Across from her portrait in the living room, on a coffee table in front of a sofa, is a sterling-silver humidor that was presented to him by his Yankee teammates at a time when he was the most talked-about man in America, and when Les Brown's band had recorded a hit that was heard day and night on the radio:

> . . . From Coast to Coast, that's all you hear
> Of Joe the One-Man Show
> He's glorified the horsehide sphere,
> Jolting Joe DiMaggio . . .
> Joe . . . Joe . . . DiMaggio . . . we want you on our
> side. . . .

The year was 1941, and it began for DiMaggio in the middle of May after the Yankees had lost four games in a row, seven of their last nine, and were in fourth place, five-and-a-half games behind the leading Cleveland Indians. On May 15th, DiMaggio hit only a first-inning single in a game that New York lost to Chicago, 13–1; he was barely hitting .300, and had greatly disappointed the crowds that had seen him finish with a .352 average the year before and .381 in 1939.

He got a hit in the next game, and the next, and the next. On May 24th, with the Yankees losing 6–5 to Boston, DiMaggio came up with runners on second and third and singled them home, winning the game, extending his streak to ten games. But it went largely unnoticed. Even DiMaggio was not conscious of it until it had reached twenty-nine games in mid-June. Then the newspapers began to dramatize it, the public became aroused, they sent him good-luck charms of every description, and DiMaggio kept hitting, and radio announcers would interrupt programs to announce the news, and then the song again: "Joe . . . Joe . . . DiMaggio . . . we want you on our side. . . ."

Sometimes DiMaggio would be hitless his first three times up, the tension would build, it would appear that the game would end without his getting another chance—but he always would, and then he would hit the ball against the left-field wall, or through the pitcher's legs, or between two leaping infielders. In the forty-first game, the first of a doubleheader in Washington, DiMaggio tied an American League record that George Sisler had set in 1922. But before the second game began a spectator sneaked onto the field and into the Yankees' dugout and stole DiMaggio's favorite bat. In the second game, using another of his bats, DiMaggio lined out twice and flied out. But in the seventh inning, borrowing one of his old bats that a teammate was using, he singled and broke Sisler's record, and he was only three games away from surpassing the major-league record of forty-four set in 1897 by Willie Keeler while playing for Baltimore when it was a National League franchise.

An appeal for the missing bat was made through the newspapers. A man from Newark admitted the crime and returned it with regrets. And on July 2, at Yankee Stadium, DiMaggio hit a home run into the left-field stands. The record was broken.

He also got hits in the next eleven games, but on July 17th in Cleveland, at a night game attended by 67,468, he failed against two pitchers, Al Smith and Jim Bagby, Jr., although Cleveland's hero was really its third baseman, Ken Keltner, who in the first inning lunged to his right to make a spectacular backhanded stop of a drive and, from the foul line behind third base, he threw DiMaggio out. DiMaggio received a walk in the fourth inning. But in the seventh he again hit a hard shot at Keltner, who again stopped it and threw him out. DiMaggio hit sharply toward the shortstop in the eighth inning, the ball taking a bad hop, but Lou Boudreau speared it off his shoulder and threw to the second baseman to start a double play and DiMaggio's streak was stopped at fifty-six games. But the New York Yankees were on their way to winning the pennant by seventeen games, and the World Series too, and so in August, in a hotel suite in Washington, the players threw a surprise party for DiMaggio and toasted him with champagne and presented him with this Tiffany silver humidor that is now in San Francisco in his living room. . . .

Marie was in the kitchen making toast and tea when DiMaggio came down for breakfast; his gray hair was uncombed but, since he wears it short, it was not untidy. He said good-morning to Marie, sat down and yawned. He lit a cigarette. He wore a blue wool bathrobe over his pajamas. It was eight A.M. He had many things to do today and he seemed cheerful. He had a conference with the president of Continental Television, Inc., a large retail chain in California of which he is a partner and vice-president; later he had a golf date, and then a big banquet to attend, and, if that did not go on too long and he were not too tired afterward, he might have a date.

Picking up the morning paper, not rushing to the sports page, DiMaggio read the front-page news, the people-problems of '66: Kwame Nkrumah was overthrown in Ghana, students were burning their draft cards (DiMaggio shook his head), the flu epidemic was spreading through the whole state of California. Then he flipped inside through the gossip columns, thankful they did not have him in there today—they had printed an item about his dating "an electrifying airline hostess" not long ago, and they also spotted him at dinner with Dori Lane, "the frantic frugger" in Whiskey à Go Go's glass cage—and then he turned to the sports page and read a story about how the injured Mickey Mantle may never regain his form.

It had all happened so quickly, the passing of Mantle, or so it seemed; he had succeeded DiMaggio as DiMaggio had succeeded Ruth, but now there was no great young power hitter coming up and the Yankee management, almost desperate, had talked Mantle out of retirement; and on September 18, 1965, they gave him a "day" in New York during which he received several thousand dollars' worth of gifts—an automobile, two quarter horses, free vacation trips to Rome, Nassau, Puerto Rico—and DiMaggio had flown to New York to make the introduction before 50,000: it had been a dramatic day, an almost holy day for the believers who had jammed the grandstands early to witness the canonization of a new stadium saint. Cardinal Spellman was on the committee, President Johnson sent a telegram, the day was officially proclaimed by the Mayor of New York, an orchestra assembled in center field in front of the trinity of monuments to Ruth, Gehrig, Huggins; and high in the grandstands, billowing in the breeze of early autumn, were white banners that read: "Don't Quit Mick," "We Love the Mick."

The banners had been held by hundreds of young boys whose dreams had been fulfilled so often by Mantle, but also seated in the grandstands were older men, paunchy and balding, in whose middle-aged minds DiMaggio was still vivid and invincible, and some of them remembered how one month before, during a pre-game exhibition at Old-timers' Day in Yankee Stadium, DiMaggio had hit a pitch into the left-field seats, and suddenly thousands of people had jumped wildly to their feet, joyously screaming—the great DiMaggio had returned, they were young again, it was yesterday.

But on this sunny September day at the Stadium, the feast day of Mickey Mantle, DiMaggio was not wearing No. 5 on his back nor a black cap to cover his graying hair; he was wearing a black suit and white shirt and blue tie, and he stood in one corner of the Yankees' dugout waiting to be introduced by Red Barber, who was standing near home plate behind a silver microphone. In the outfield Guy Lombardo's Royal Canadians were playing soothing soft music; and moving slowly back and forth over the sprawling green grass between the left-field bullpen and the infield were two carts driven by grounds keepers and containing dozens and dozens of large gifts for Mantle—a 6-foot, 100-pound Hebrew National salami, a Winchester rifle, a mink coat for Mrs. Mantle, a set of Wilson golf clubs, a Mercury 95-horse power outboard motor, a Necchi portable, a year's supply of Chunky Candy. DiMaggio smoked a cigarette, but cupped it in his hands as if not wanting to be caught in the act by teen-aged boys near enough to peek down into the dugout. Then, edging forward a step, DiMaggio poked his head out and looked up. He could see nothing above except the packed towering green grandstands that seemed a mile high and moving, and he could see no clouds or blue sky, only a sky of faces. Then the announcer called out his name—*"Joe DiMaggio!"*—and suddenly there was a blast of cheering that grew louder and louder, echoing and reechoing within the big steel canyon, and DiMaggio stomped out his cigarette and climbed up the dugout steps and onto the soft green grass, the noise resounding in his ears, he could almost feel the breeze, the breath of 50,000 lungs upon him, 100,000 eyes watching his every move and for the briefest instant as he walked he closed his eyes.

Then in his path he saw Mickey Mantle's mother, a smiling elderly woman wearing an orchid, and he gently reached out for her elbow, holding it as he led her toward the microphone next to the other dignitaries lined up on the infield. Then he stood, very erect and without expression, as the cheers softened and the Stadium settled down.

Mantle was still in the dugout, in uniform, standing with one leg on the top step, and lined on both sides of him were the other Yankees who, when the ceremony was over, would play the Detroit Tigers. Then into the dugout, smiling, came Senator Robert Kennedy, accompanied by two tall curly-haired young assistants with blue eyes, Fordham freckles. Jim Farley was the first on the field to notice the Senator, and Farley muttered, loud enough for others to hear, "Who the hell invited *him?*"

Toots Shor and some of the other committeemen standing near Farley looked into the dugout, and so did DiMaggio, his glance seeming cold, but he remaining silent. Kennedy walked up and down within the dugout shaking hands with the Yankees, but he did not walk onto the field.

"Senator," said the Yankees' manager, Johnny Keane, "why don't you sit down?" Kennedy quickly shook his head, smiled. He remained standing, and then one Yankee came over and asked about getting relatives out of Cuba, and Kennedy called over one of his aides to take down the details in a notebook.

On the infield the ceremony went on, Mantle's gifts continued to pile up—a Mobilette motor bike, a Sooner Schooner wagon barbecue, a year's supply of Chock Full O'Nuts coffee, a year's supply of Topps Chewing Gum—and the Yankee players watched, and Maris seemed glum.

"Hey, Rog," yelled a man with a tape recorder, Murray Olderman, "I want to do a thirty-second tape with you."

Maris swore angrily, shook his head.

"It'll only take a second," Olderman said.

"Why don't you ask Richardson? He's a better talker than me."

"Yes, but the fact that it comes from you . . ."

Maris swore again. But finally he went over and said in an interview that Mantle was the finest player of his era, a great competitor, a great hitter.

Fifteen minutes later, standing behind the microphone at home plate, DiMaggio was telling the crowd, "I'm proud to introduce the man who succeeded me in center field in 1951," and from every corner of the Stadium the cheering, whistling, clapping came down. Mantle stepped forward. He stood with his wife and children, posed for the photographers kneeling in front. Then he thanked the crowd in a short speech, and turning, shook hands with the dignitaries standing nearby. Among them now was Senator Kennedy, who had been spotted in the dugout five minutes before by Red Barber, and been called out and introduced. Kennedy posed with Mantle for a photographer, then shook hands with the Mantle children, and with Toots Shor and James Farley and others. DiMaggio saw him coming down the line and at the last second he backed away, casually, hardly anybody noticing it, and Kennedy seemed not to notice it either, just swept past shaking more hands. . . .

Finishing his tea, putting aside the newspaper, DiMaggio went upstairs to dress, and soon he was waving good-bye to Marie and driving toward his business appointment in downtown San Francisco with his partners in the retail television business. DiMaggio, while not a millionaire, has invested wisely and has always had, since his retirement from baseball, executive positions with big companies that have paid him well. He also was among the organizers of the Fisherman's National Bank of San Francisco last year, and, though it never came about, he demonstrated an acuteness that impressed those businessmen who had thought of him only in terms of baseball. He has had offers to manage big-league baseball teams but always has rejected them, saying, "I have enough trouble taking care of my own problems without taking on the responsibilities of twenty-five ballplayers."

So his only contact with baseball these days, excluding public appearances, is his unsalaried job as a batting coach each spring in Florida with the New York Yankees, a trip he would make once again on the following Sunday, three days away, if he could accomplish what for him is always the dreaded responsibility of packing, a task made no easier by the fact that he lately has fallen into the habit of keeping his clothes in two places—some hang in his closet at home, some hang in the back room of a saloon called Reno's.

Reno's is a dimly lit bar in the center of San Francisco. A portrait of DiMaggio swinging a bat hangs on the wall, in addition to portraits of other star athletes, and the clientele consists mainly of the sporting crowd and newspapermen, people who know DiMaggio quite well and around whom he speaks freely on a number of subjects and relaxes as he can in few other places. The owner of the bar is Reno Barsocchini, a broad-shouldered and handsome man of fifty-one with graying wavy hair who began as a fiddler in Dago Mary's tavern thirty-five years ago. He later became a bartender there and elsewhere, including DiMaggio's Restaurant, and now he is probably DiMaggio's closest friend. He was the best man at the DiMaggio-Monroe wedding in 1954, and when they separated nine months later in Los Angeles, Reno rushed down to help DiMaggio with the packing and drive him back to San Francisco. Reno will never forget the day.

Hundreds of people were gathered around the Beverly Hills home that DiMaggio and Marilyn had rented, and photographers were perched in the trees watching the windows, and others stood on the lawn and behind the rose bushes waiting to snap pictures of anybody who walked out of the house. The newspapers that day played all the puns—"Joe Fanned on Jealousy"; "Marilyn and Joe—Out at Home"—and the Hollywood columnists, to whom DiMaggio was never an idol, never a gracious host, recounted instances of incompatibility, and Oscar Levant said it all proved that no man could be a success in two national pastimes. When Reno Barsocchini arrived he had to push his way through the mob, then bang on the door for several minutes before being admitted. Marilyn Monroe was upstairs in bed, Joe DiMaggio was downstairs with his suitcases, tense and pale, his eyes bloodshot.

Reno took the suitcases and golf clubs out to DiMaggio's car, and then DiMaggio came out of the house, the reporters moving toward him, the lights flashing.

"Where are you going?" they yelled. "I'm driving to San Francisco," he said, walking quickly.

"Is that going to be your home?"

"That *is* my home and always has been."

"Are you coming back?"

DiMaggio turned for a moment, looking up at the house.

"No," he said, "I'll never be back."

Reno Barsocchini, except for a brief falling out over something he will not discuss, has been DiMaggio's trusted companion ever since, joining him whenever he can on the golf course or on the town, otherwise waiting for him in the bar with other middle-aged men. They may wait for hours sometimes, waiting and knowing that when he arrives he may wish to be alone; but it does not seem to matter, they are endlessly awed by him, moved by the mystique, he is a kind of male Garbo. They know that he can be warm and loyal if they are sensitive to his wishes, but they must never be late for an appointment to meet him. One man, unable to find a parking place, arrived a half-hour late once and DiMaggio did not talk to him again for three months. They know, too, when dining at night with DiMaggio, that he generally prefers male companions and occasionally one or two young women, but never wives; wives gossip, wives complain, wives are trouble, and men wishing to remain close to DiMaggio must keep their wives at home.

When DiMaggio strolls into Reno's bar the men wave and call out his name, and Reno Barsocchini smiles and announces, "Here's the Clipper!", the "Yankee Clipper" being a nickname from his baseball days.

"Hey, Clipper, Clipper," Reno had said two nights before, "where you been, Clipper? . . . Clipper, how 'bout a belt?"

DiMaggio refused the offer of a drink, ordering instead a pot of tea, which he prefers to all other beverages except before a date, when he will switch to vodka.

"Hey, Joe," a sportswriter asked, a man researching a magazine piece on golf, "why is it that a golfer, when he starts getting older, loses his putting touch first? Like Snead and Hogan, they can still hit a ball well off the tee, but on the greens they lose the strokes. . . ."

"It's the pressure of age," DiMaggio said, turning around on his bar stool. "With age you get jittery. It's true of golfers, it's true of any man when he gets into his fifties. He doesn't take chances like he used to. The younger golfer, on the greens, he'll stroke his putts better. The old man, he becomes hesitant. A little uncertain. Shaky. When it comes to taking chances the younger man, even when driving a car, will take chances that the older man won't."

"Speaking of chances," another man said, one of the group that had gathered around DiMaggio, "did you see that guy on crutches in here last night?"

"Yeah, had his leg in a cast," a third said. "Skiing."

"I would never ski," DiMaggio said. "Men who ski must be doing it to impress a broad. You see these men, some of them forty, fifty, getting onto skis. And later you see them all bandaged up, broken legs. . . ."

"But skiing's a very sexy sport, Joe. All the clothes, the tight pants, the fireplace in the ski lodge, the bear rug—Christ, nobody goes to ski. They just go out there to get it cold so they can warm it up. . . ."

"Maybe you're right," DiMaggio said. "I might be persuaded."

"Want a belt, Clipper?" Reno asked.

DiMaggio thought for a second, then said, "All right—first belt tonight."

\*     \*     \*

Now it was noon, a warm sunny day. DiMaggio's business meeting with the television retailers had gone well; he had made a strong appeal to George Shahood, president of Continental Television, Inc., which has eight retail outlets in Northern California, to cut prices on color television sets and increase the sales volume, and Shahood had conceded it was worth a try. Then DiMaggio called Reno's bar to see if there were any messages, and now he was in Lefty O'Doul's car being driven along Fisherman's Wharf toward the Golden Gate Bridge en route to a golf course thirty miles upstate. Lefty O'Doul was one of the great hitters in the National League in the early thirties, and later he managed the San Francisco Seals when DiMaggio was the shining star. Though O'Doul is now sixty-nine, eighteen years older than DiMaggio, he nevertheless possesses great energy and spirit, is a hard-drinking, boisterous man with a big belly and roving eye; and when DiMaggio, as they drove along the highway toward the golf club, noticed a lovely blond at the wheel of a car nearby and exclaimed, "Look at *that* tomato!" O'Doul's head suddenly spun around, he took his eyes off the road, and yelled, "Where, *where?*" O'Doul's golf game is less than what it was—he used to have a two-handicap—but he still shoots in the 80s, as does DiMaggio.

DiMaggio's drives range between 250 and 280 yards when he doesn't sky them, and his putting is good, but he is distracted by a bad back that both pains him and hinders the fullness of his swing. On the first hole, waiting to tee off, DiMaggio sat back watching a foursome of college boys ahead swinging with such freedom. "Oh," he said with a sigh, "to have *their* backs."

DiMaggio and O'Doul were accompanied around the golf course by Ernie Nevers, the former football star, and two brothers who are in the hotel and movie-distribution business. They moved quickly up and down the green hills in electric golf carts, and DiMaggio's game was exceptionally good for the first nine holes. But then he seemed distracted, perhaps tired, perhaps even reacting to a conversation of a few minutes before. One of the movie men was praising the film *Boeing, Boeing,* starring Tony Curtis and Jerry Lewis, and the man asked DiMaggio if he had seen it.

"No," DiMaggio said. Then he added, swiftly, "I haven't seen a film in eight years."

DiMaggio hooked a few shots, was in the woods. He took a No. 9 iron and tried to chip out. But O'Doul interrupted DiMaggio's concentration to remind him to keep the face of the club closed. DiMaggio hit the ball. It caromed off the side of his club, went skipping like a rabbit through the high grass down toward a pond. DiMaggio rarely displays any emotion on a golf course,

but now, without saying a word, he took his No. 9 iron and flung it into the air. The club landed in a tree and stayed up there.

"Well," O'Doul said, casually, "there goes *that* set of clubs."

DiMaggio walked to the tree. Fortunately the club had slipped to the lower branch and DiMaggio could stretch up on the cart and get it back.

"Every time I get advice," DiMaggio muttered to himself, shaking his head slowly and walking toward the pond, "I shank it."

Later, showered and dressed, DiMaggio and the others drove to a banquet about ten miles from the golf course. Somebody had said it was going to be an elegant dinner, but when they arrived they could see it was more like a county fair; farmers were gathered outside a big barnlike building, a candidate for sheriff was distributing leaflets at the front door, and a chorus of homely ladies were inside singing *You Are My Sunshine*.

"How did we get sucked into this?" DiMaggio asked, talking out of the side of his mouth, as they approached the building.

"O'Doul," one of the men said. "It's his fault. Damned O'Doul can't turn *anything* down."

"Go to hell," O'Doul said.

Soon DiMaggio and O'Doul and Ernie Nevers were surrounded by the crowd, and the woman who had been leading the chorus came rushing over and said, "Oh, Mr. DiMaggio, it certainly is a pleasure having you."

"It's a pleasure being here, ma'am," he said, forcing a smile.

"It's too bad you didn't arrive a moment sooner, you'd have heard our singing."

"Oh, I heard it," he said, "and I enjoyed it very much."

"Good, good," she said. "And how are your brothers Dom and Vic?"

"Fine. Dom lives near Boston. Vince is in Pittsburgh."

"Why, *hello* there, Joe," interrupted a man with wine on his breath, patting DiMaggio on the back, feeling his arm. "Who's gonna take it this year, Joe?"

"Well, I have no idea," DiMaggio said.

"What about the Giants?"

"Your guess is as good as mine."

"Well, you can't count the Dodgers out," the man said.

"You sure can't," DiMaggio said.

"Not with all that pitching."

"Pitching is certainly important," DiMaggio said.

Everywhere he goes the questions seem the same, as if he has some special vision into the future of new heroes, and everywhere he goes, too, older men grab his hand and feel his arm and predict that he could still go out there and hit one, and the smile on DiMaggio's face is genuine. He tries hard to remain as he was—he diets, he takes steam baths, he is careful; and flabby men in the locker rooms of golf clubs sometimes steal peeks at him when he steps out of the shower, observing the tight muscles across his chest, the flat stomach, the long sinewy legs. He has a young man's body, very pale and little hair; his face is dark and lined, however, parched by the sun of several seasons. Still he is always an impressive figure at banquets such as this—an *immortal,* sportswriters called him, and that is how they have written about him and others like him, rarely suggesting that such heroes might ever be prone to the ills of mortal men, carousing, drinking, scheming; to suggest this would destroy the myth, would disillusion small boys, would infuriate rich men who own ballclubs and to whom baseball is a business dedicated to profit and in pursuit of which they trade mediocre players' flesh as casually as boys trade players' pictures on bubble-gum cards. And so the baseball hero must always act the part, must preserve the myth, and none does it better than DiMaggio, none is more patient when drunken old men grab an arm and ask, "Who's gonna take it this year, Joe?"

Two hours later, dinner and the speeches over, DiMaggio is slumped in O'Doul's car headed back to San Francisco. He edged himself up, however, when O'Doul pulled into a gas station in which a pretty red-haired girl sat on a stool, legs crossed, filing her fingernails. She was about twenty-two, wore a tight black skirt and tighter white blouse.

"Look at *that,*" DiMaggio said.

"Yeah," O'Doul said.

O'Doul turned away when a young man approached, opened the gas tank, began wiping the windshield. The young man wore a greasy white uniform on the front of which was printed the name "Burt." DiMaggio kept looking at the girl, but she was not distracted from her fingernails. Then he looked at Burt, who did not recognize him. When the tank was full, O'Doul paid and drove off. Burt returned to his girl; DiMaggio slumped down in the front seat and did not open his eyes again until they'd arrived in San Francisco.

"Let's go see Reno," DiMaggio said.

"No, I gotta go see my old lady," O'Doul said. So he dropped DiMaggio off in front of the bar, and a moment later Reno's voice was announcing in the smoky room, "Hey, here's the Clipper!" The men waved and offered to buy him a drink. DiMaggio ordered a vodka and sat for an hour at the bar talking to a half dozen men around him. Then a blond girl who had been with friends at the other end of the bar came over, and somebody introduced her to DiMaggio. He bought her a drink, offered

her a cigarette. Then he struck a match and held it. His hand was unsteady.

"Is that me that's shaking?" he asked.

"It must be," said the blond. "I'm calm."

Two nights later, having collected his clothes out of Reno's back room, DiMaggio boarded a jet; he slept crossways on three seats, then came down the steps as the sun began to rise in Miami. He claimed his luggage and golf clubs, put them into the trunk of a waiting automobile, and less than an hour later he was being driven into Fort Lauderdale, past palm-lined streets, toward the Yankee Clipper Hotel.

"All my life it seems I've been on the road traveling," he said, squinting through the windshield into the sun. "I never get a sense of being in any one place."

Arriving at the Yankee Clipper Hotel, DiMaggio checked into the largest suite. People rushed through the lobby to shake hands with him, to ask for his autograph, to say, "Joe, you look great." And early the next morning, and for the next thirty mornings, DiMaggio arrived punctually at the baseball park and wore his uniform with the famous No. 5, and the tourists seated in the sunny grandstands clapped when he first appeared on the field each time, and then they watched with nostalgia as he picked up a bat and played "pepper" with the younger Yankees, some of whom were not even born when, twenty-five years ago this summer, he hit in fifty-six straight games and became the most celebrated man in America.

But the younger spectators in the Fort Lauderdale park, and the sportswriters, too, were more interested in Mantle and Maris, and nearly every day there were news dispatches reporting how Mantle and Maris felt, what they did, what they said, even though they said and did very little except walk around the field frowning when photographers asked for another picture and when sportswriters asked how they felt.

After seven days of this, the big day arrived—Mantle and Maris would swing a bat—and a dozen sportswriters were gathered around the big batting cage that was situated beyond the left-field fence; it was completely enclosed in wire, meaning that no baseball could travel more than thirty or forty feet before being trapped in rope; still Mantle and Maris would be swinging, and this, in spring, makes news.

Mantle stepped in first. He wore black gloves to help prevent blisters. He hit right-handed against the pitching of a coach named Vern Benson, and soon Mantle was swinging hard, smashing line drives against the nets, going *ahhh ahhh* as he followed through with his mouth open.

Then Mantle, not wanting to overdo it on his first day, dropped his bat in the dirt and walked out of the batting cage. Roger Maris stepped in. He picked up Mantle's bat.

"This damn thing must be thirty-eight ounces," Maris said. He threw the bat down into the dirt, left the cage and walked toward the dugout on the other side of the field to get a lighter bat.

DiMaggio stood among the sportswriters behind the cage, then turned when Vern Benson, inside the cage, yelled, "Joe, wanna hit some?"

"No chance," DiMaggio said.

"Com'on, Joe," Benson said.

The reporters waited silently. Then DiMaggio walked slowly into the cage and picked up Mantle's bat. He took his position at the plate but obviously it was not the classic DiMaggio stance; he was holding the bat about two inches from the knob, his feet were not so far apart, and, when DiMaggio took a cut at Benson's first pitch, fouling it, there was none of that ferocious follow through, the blurred bat did not come whipping all the way around, the No. 5 was not stretched full across his broad back.

DiMaggio fouled Benson's second pitch, then he connected solidly with the third, the fourth, the fifth. He was just meeting the ball easily, however, not smashing it, and Benson called out, "I didn't know you were a choke hitter, Joe."

"I am now," DiMaggio said, getting ready for another pitch.

He hit three more squarely enough, and then he swung again and there was a hollow sound.

"Ohhh," DiMaggio yelled, dropping his bat, his fingers stung, "I was waiting for that one." He left the batting cage rubbing his hands together. The reporters watched him. Nobody said anything. Then DiMaggio said to one of them, not in anger nor in sadness, but merely as a simply stated fact, "There was a time when you couldn't get me out of there."

If you tell me the White Sox beat the Indians 9 to 4 in 14 innings, I can tell you where the game was played. For a few other facts about what happens to visiting and home teams and players, meet John Thorn, editor of *The National Pastime,* a journal of baseball history, and Pete Palmer, statistician for the American League. Both are members of the Society for American Baseball Research—SABR, by the acronym—an offshoot of the computer age. And they joined forces to produce a delightful book from which one chapter, "There's No Place Like Home," has been taken for use here.

(Note—that 9–4 game had to be at Cleveland. After 8½ innings, no home team can win by more than four runs. Think about it.)

# From *The Hidden Game of Baseball*

## JOHN THORN *and* PETE PALMER

FAMILIARITY BREEDS success. Every team is expected to win more games at home than it does on the road, to the extent that if it only breaks even on the road it is deemed to have a shot at the pennant. In 1983, for example, only three National League clubs had plus .500 records on the road (and none won more than 43 games); in 1981 Montreal finished 8 games *under* .500 away from home yet topped the National League East.

Hitters' park or pitchers' park, the home team should take advantage of its pecularities better than the visiting team. The Houston Astros may score fewer runs at home than they do on the road, but their *differential* between runs scored and runs allowed will be greater than their run differential on the road. The Boston Red Sox may allow more runs at home than they do on the road, yet the result should be the same: Their run differential, and thus their won-lost record, should be better at Fenway than in the hinterlands. If it's not—and it was not in 1983—shake up that front office.

Why would a team, strong or weak, perform better in their own park than on the road? The players benefit from home stands of reasonable duration—say, eight to thirteen games—when they live in their own residences, sleep at more nearly regular times, play before appreciative fans, and benefit from the physical park conditions which to some degree may have made their organizations acquire them in the first place. It is difficult for fans to grasp the difficulty of playing on a travel day or of adjusting to jet lag and hotel "comforts."

In 1983, when, as noted above, only three NL clubs had winning records on the road, only one (the Reds) was a loser at home. Almost anybody, it seems—which is to say, the Mets and Cubs of '83—can play .500 ball at home. This is somewhat deceptive, for while the team that goes 81–81 on the season is by definition an average team, to be an average performer at home requires a team to win 54 percent of its games. Substantiation for this assertion rests in the table below, which gives the home won-lost percentages of the American and National (and Federal) Leagues for every decade since 1900. Totaling all the games played at home by all the teams, we come up with a record of 62,205 wins and 52,426 losses, a winning percentage of .543. The inverse, .457, is the average road record.

TABLE V, 1. HOME-PARK WON-LOST RECORDS

|  | National League | | | American League | | |
|---|---|---|---|---|---|---|
| 1900–10 (1901 AL) | 3489 | 2995 | .538 | 3345 | 2530 | .569 |
| 1911–20 | 3189 | 2755 | .537 | 3201 | 2754 | .537 |
| 1921–30 | 3360 | 2770 | .548 | 3344 | 2787 | .545 |
| 1931–40 | 3353 | 2760 | .549 | 3349 | 2753 | .549 |
| 1941–50 | 3319 | 2823 | .540 | 3383 | 2754 | .551 |
| 1951–60 ('61 NL) | 3681 | 3098 | .543 | 3291 | 2863 | .535 |
| 1961–68 ('62 NL) | 3075 | 2591 | .543 | 3462 | 3003 | .535 |
| 1969–76 | 4088 | 3638 | .529 | 4142 | 3568 | .537 |
| 1977–82 | 3023 | 2473 | .550 | 3451 | 2951 | .539 |
|  | 30,577 − 25,903 = .541 | | | 30,968 − 25,963 = .544 | | |

|  | Federal League | | |
|---|---|---|---|
| 1914–15 | 660 − 560 = .541 | | |
| TOTAL | 62,205 − 52,426 = .543 | | |

If the average home winning percentage is .543, then an average team (defined as 81–81) should be expected to go 45–36 at home and 36–45 on the road. What this means is that breaking even on the road (impossible in ordinary practice, but say 41–40 or 40–41) represents a performance that is distinctly *above* average. Only six teams in this century have won pennants with below-average road records. The worst on a percentage basis was the Expo team of 1981; the others were the 1902 Athletics, the 1944 Browns, the 1974 Pirates, and the Phillies and Royals of 1978. Not a single one won a World Series, and in the four cases in which the teams were divisional champions, not one made it to the World Series. There is no statistical reason for this; we offer simply a cautionary tale.

Just as in the previous chapter we indicated how runs scored and runs allowed might predict won-lost records, now we move backward from won-lost records—the actual home-park norm of 45–36, which is about 10 percent better than the theoretical norm of 41–40—to examine runs scored and runs allowed. It develops that individuals bat and pitch at a rate 10 percent higher at home, on average. That is, On Base Average and slugging percentage each tend to be 5 percent higher (when combined to create OPS, they are 10 percent higher); batting average will be 5 percent higher too. Linear Weights, because it is denominated in runs, will be 10 percent higher at home, while earned run average, for the same reason, will be 10 percent lower. These statements are true on average, but in some cases home-park variations may run considerably higher or lower: The ERAs of Red Sox pitchers may soar 20 or 30 percent, and the OPS of Astro batters may plummet by as much.

Keeping in mind that the home record of the average hitter, as reflected in his OPS, should be 1.10 times his OPS on the road, let's look at the lifetime ratio of Normalized OPS at home to NOPS on the road for some leading American League batters.

TABLE V, 2. LIFETIME RATIOS OF NORMALIZED OPS AT HOME TO NOPS ON THE ROAD

| | |
|---|---|
| Ty Cobb, 1.03 | Mickey Mantle, 1.07 |
| Joe DiMaggio, 0.88 | Babe Ruth, 1.04 |
| Jimmie Foxx, 1.24 | Tris Speaker, 1.22 |
| Lou Gehrig, 0.94 | Ted Williams, 1.09 |

Speaker and Foxx derived more than average benefit from their home parks to a staggering degree while the others, notably DiMaggio and Gehrig, had their batting performance suffer for playing where they did (Williams took nearly average—1.10—benefit of Fenway). Thus the batting statistics of all eight men—like those of every man who ever played the game—reflect not only how

they played, but *where* they played, with the latter proposition having enormous effect on those batters blessed to have played half their games in Shibe Park, Fenway, or Wrigley Field and on those cursed to have been denizens of Yankee Stadium, San Diego Stadium, or the Astrodome. For pitchers, naturally, the stigmata are reversed.

For hard luck in home parks, it is tough to top the record of Dave Winfield, who has had the misfortune to call both San Diego and Yankee Stadiums home. Through 1982, his lifetime OPS, normalized to league average but not adjusted for park effects, was 102nd best on the all-time list of those playing in 1000 games. Had he played his home games instead in Fenway Park, his NOPS would have projected to the 25th best of all time. (The statistical method by which such projections are made is explained below.)

If we desire to remove the silver spoon or the millstone that a home park can be, and measure individual ability alone, we must create a statistical balancer which diminishes the individual batting marks created in parks like Fenway and augments those created in San Diego. Pete has developed an adjustment which enables us, for the first time, to measure a player's accomplishments apart from the influence of his home park.

Parks differ in so many ways that it may be hard to imagine how their differences can be quantified. The most obvious way in which they differ is in their dimensions, from home plate to the outfield walls, and from the base lines to the stands. The older arenas—Fenway Park, Wrigley Field, Tiger Stadium—tend to favor hitters in both regards, with reasonable fences and little room to pursue a foul pop. The exception among the older parks is Chicago's Comiskey which, in keeping with the theories of Charles Comiskey back in 1910 and the team's perceived strength, was built as a pitchers' park. Yet two parks can have nearly equal dimensions, like Pittsburgh's Three Rivers Stadium and Atlanta's Fulton County Stadium, yet have highly dissimilar impacts upon hitters because of climate (balls travel farther in hot weather), elevation (travel farther above sea level), and playing surface (travel faster and truer on artificial turf). Yet another factor is how well batters think they see the ball; Shea Stadium is notorious as a cause of complaints.

And perhaps more important than any of the objective park characteristics, suggested Robert Kingsley in a 1980 study of why so many homers were hit in Atlanta, is the attitude of the players, the way that the park changes their view of how the game must be played in order to win. Every team that comes into Atlanta in August knows that the ball is going to fly and, whether it is a team designed for power or not, it plays ball there as if it were the 1927 Yankees. In their own home park the Astros may peck and scratch for runs, but in Atlanta they will put the steal and hit-and-run in mothballs. Conversely, a team which comes into the Astrodome and plays for the big inning will generally get what it deserves—a loss. The successful team is one that can play its game at home—the game for which the team was constructed—yet is flexible enough to adapt when on the road. How to quantify attitude?

Rather than try to assign a numerical value to each of the six or more variables that might go into establishing an estimator of home-park impact, Pete looked to the single measure in which all these variables are reflected—runs. After all, why would we assign one value to dimensions, another to climate, and so on, except to identify their impact on scoring? If a stadium is a "hitters' park," it stands to reason that more runs would be scored there than in a park perceived as neutral, just as a "pitcher's park" could be expected to depress scoring.

To measure park impact, Pete looks not at the runs scored by the home team, which may have been put together specifically to take advantage of a park's peculiar features, but rather those scored by the visiting teams. By totaling the runs allowed at home for all teams in a league year and dividing that figure by the runs allowed by all teams in their road games, we take the first step in determining the Park Factor, which may be applied to a team's batters and pitchers (it might also be applied to base stealers, inasmuch as Craig Wright's studies have shown that it is 12 percent easier to steal on artificial surfaces, and fielders, who also benefit from the carpet, as shown by Paul Schwarzenbart's study in *The Baseball Analyst;* however, this task awaits another day).

The succeeding steps, alas, become increasingly complicated, and for this reason the full explanation for the computation of the Park Factor is left to the footnote, where hardy readers might consider taking a peek right now.[1] For most of us, though, it will be enough to understand that the Park Factor consists mainly of the team's home-road ratio of runs allowed, computed as it was above for the league, compared to the league's home-road ratio. The batter adjustment factor, or Batter Park Factor (BPF), consists of (1) the Park Factor and (2) an adjustment for the fact that the batter does not have to face his own pitchers. The pitcher adjustment factor, or Pitcher Park Factor (PPF), likewise consists of the Park Factor and an adjustment for the fact that the pitcher does not have to face his own team's batters.

The BPF and PPF are expressed in relation to the average home-park factor, which is defined mathematically as 1.00. A park which featured 5 percent more scoring than the average park would have a BPF of 1.05, while the same park's PPF might be 1.04 or 1.06, for instance, because it is adjusted differently (correcting for

the absence of home team batters rather than that of home team pitchers). In practice, a BPF might be used in this way: To express the individual batting performance of, say, Joe Morgan in 1976, take his Normalized On Base Plus Slugging (NOPS) of 1.91 and simply divide that by his Batter Park Factor that year, which was 1.08: the result is 1.77, which is the NOPS that Morgan would have totaled had he played in a average home park, not deriving the 8 percent additional benefit of Riverfront Stadium. (Batter and Pitcher Park Factors for each year since 1901 are listed in the team stats section of the year-by-year record at the back of the book.) Analogously, the normalized earned run average of Cincinnati pitcher Pat Zachry in that year (league ERA of 3.51 over Zachry's ERA of 2.74, or 1.28) is bettered by *multiplying* the NERA by the Pitcher Park Factor of 1.06 (result: an NERA of 1.36, or an ERA of 2.58).

To apply Batter Park Factor to any other average—On Base, slugging, Isolated Power, batting average—use the square root of the BPF. This is done so that run scoring for teams, which is best mirrored by On Base Average *times* slugging percentage, can be represented clearly:

$$\frac{OBA}{\sqrt{BPF}} \times \frac{SLG}{\sqrt{BPF}} = \frac{O \times S}{BPF}$$

The application of the Batter Park Factor to Linear Weights, which is not an average, is more complicated—the explanation will be found in the footnotes—but Park Adjusted figures are offered in the tables for the top three in LWTS for batters and starting pitchers for all years since 1900 and for relievers since 1946.[2]

The previous chapter presented the top ten Linear Weights performances since 1961 in batting and pitching without adjustment for home park. Here are those same lists with Park Factors incorporated (the superscript numbers indicate ranking in unadjusted LWTS).

### TABLE V, 3. BATTERS' LINEAR WEIGHTS

| | LWTS | BPF | LWTS (Adjusted for park) |
|---|---|---|---|
| 1. 1961 Norm Cash, DET[1] | 86.1 | 1.003 | 85.8 |
| 2. 1961 Mickey Mantle, NY[3] | 76.3 | .908 | 83.4 |
| 3. 1969 Willie McCovey, SF[4] | 76.1 | 1.004 | 75.8 |
| 4. 1962 Frank Robinson, CIN[8] | 66.6 | .921 | 73.2 |
| 5. 1966 Frank Robinson, BAL[5] | 73.6 | 1.023 | 72.0 |
| 6. 1977 Rod Carew, MIN | 67.0 | .980 | 68.7 |
| 7. 1972 Dick Allen, CHI (A)[9] | 66.1 | .978 | 67.3 |
| 8. 1970 Carl Yastrzemski, BOS[6] | 71.7 | 1.067 | 66.6 |
| 9. 1970 Willie McCovey, SF | 62.0 | .940 | 66.5 |
| 10. 1969 Harmon Killebrew, MIN[10] | 65.6 | .996 | 65.9 |

Note that the second place finisher in the earlier ranking drops off the list entirely (Carl Yastrzemski, 1967) thanks to a BPF of 1.174 in that year, which meant that playing half his games in Fenway boosted the totals of all visiting players by some 17 percent (who said it was a righthanded hitters' park?). However, that extreme BPF does not mean that Yaz in particular benefited by 17 percent; in fact, an analysis of his record reveals that he hit only 10 percent better than average at home. To perform this kind of home-road breakdown for every player in every season is beyond human capacity, so a Batter Park Factor remains the best method for adjusting the records of all hitters. An aside: Much of the reason for the dominance of such early 1960s types as Cash, Mantle, and Robinson lies in the higher run-scoring pattern of the period. If we divide the Park Adjusted LWTS by the number of runs required to produce an additional win, Dick Allen rises to fifth and Frank Robinson in 1962 falls to sixth; also, Reggie Jackson's 1969 season finds its way onto the list, along with Yaz's 1967.

### TABLE V, 4. PITCHERS' LINEAR WEIGHTS WITH PARK FACTORS

| | LWTS | PPF | LWTS (Adjusted) |
|---|---|---|---|
| 1. 1973 Bert Blyleven, MIN | 47.0 | 1.131 | 65.1 |
| 2. 1971 Vida Blue, OAK[7] | 57.2 | 1.059 | 64.3 |
| 3. 1978 Ron Guidry, NY[3] | 62.0 | 1.016 | 63.9 |
| 4. 1971 Wilbur Wood, CHI(A)[6] | 57.7 | 1.040 | 62.8 |
| 5. 1965 Juan Marichal, SF | 46.0 | 1.120 | 59.9 |
| 6. 1966 Sandy Koufax, LA[1] | 67.4 | .940 | 59.7 |
| 7. 1968 Bob Gibson, STL[2] | 63.2 | .948 | 57.9 |
| 8. 1972 Steve Carlton, PHI[8] | 56.9 | .990 | 55.6 |
| 9. 1969 Bob Gibson, STL | 49.5 | 1.041 | 54.7 |
| 10. 1972 Gaylord Perry, CLE | 44.0 | 1.079 | 53.3 |

This list underwent drastic revision once home-park influences were discounted. Bert Blyleven, whose unadjusted LWTS of 47.0 did not make the top ten, zooms to first on the list when the hardships of trying to hold down the score in the old Minnesota stadium are considered. On the other side of the coin, Dean Chance's LWTS of 61, which was the fourth best of the expansion era, dropped off the list entirely because of the Chavez Ravine Pitcher Park Factor of .887, by far the lowest for any pitcher in the list of top 100 season performances.

This is not to say Chance had anything but a marvelous year: 20 wins, a 1.65 ERA, and 11 shutouts are hard to argue with; yet he was aided considerably by park conditions which were not available to, say, Blyleven in 1973. In 81 home games in 1964, the Angels allowed 226 runs; in 81 games on the road, they allowed 325— 44 percent more, where a 10 to 11 percent increase would have been normal. If you are to compare Chance and Blyleven fairly, you must deny one of the benefit of his home park and remove from the other the onus of his. This is what Park Factor does.

For decades, the all-time scoring squelcher was Chicago's South Side Park, which saw service at the dawn of the American League. From 1901 through 1909, its last full year of service to the White Sox, this cavernous stadium produced home run totals like the 2 in 1904, 3 in 1906, and 4 in 1909; in two years the Sox failed to hit *any* homers at home, thus earning the nickname "Hitless Wonders." In 1906, Chicago pitchers held opponents to 180 runs at South Side Park, an average of 2.28 runs per game, earned *and* unearned, in a decade when 4 of every 10 runs were unearned. This mark held until 1981, when the Astrodome intimidated opposing hitters to such a point that in the 51 home dates of that strike-shortened season, Astro hurlers were touched for only 106 runs— 2.08 per game. The Pitcher Park Factor of .871 for the Astrodome was the lowest ever. Those who suspected that men like Joe Niekro, Don Sutton, Vern Ruhle, et al., were perhaps not worldbeaters after all were right: Look at the ERAs the Astro starters registered that year, and what these ERAs might have been in an average park like Shea that year (BPF: 1.00) or a moderately difficult pitchers' park like San Francisco (BPF: 1.06).

### TABLE V, 5. HOUSTON PITCHERS, 1982

| | ERA | BPF:1.00 | BPF:1.06 |
|---|---|---|---|
| Nolan Ryan | 1.69 | 2.07 | 2.19 |
| Joe Niekro | 2.82 | 3.43 | 3.64 |
| Vern Ruhle | 2.91 | 3.56 | 3.77 |
| Bob Knepper | 2.18 | 2.66 | 2.82 |
| Don Sutton | 2.60 | 3.17 | 3.36 |
| HOUSTON (all) | 2.66 | 3.24 | 3.44 |
| SAN FRANCISCO (all) | 3.28 | 3.09 | 3.28 |

Some observations prompted by this table: San Francisco with its team ERA of 3.28 had a better pitching staff than Houston with its 2.66; and Houston batters, regarded as a Punch-and-Judy crew by all observers, must have been a lot more effective than heretofore suspected. In fact, when Houston batters' totals (eighth in runs scored, eighth in LWTS) are adjusted for park, the Astros emerge on ability as the *best* hitting team in the National League of 1981! Even without the application of Park Factor, one might have come to a similar conclusion by examining the runs scored totals for all NL clubs on the road in 1981. Houston's total was exceeded only by those of the Dodgers and Reds.

Proceeding from a similar hunch, we may look at the batting record of the "Hitless Wonders" of 1906, who won the pennant (and the World Series, in four straight over a Cubs team which went 116–36 during the season). Baseball lore has it that a magnificent pitching staff (Ed Walsh, Doc White, Nick Altrock, and others) overcame a puny batting attack (BA of .230, 6 homers, slugging percentage of .286). In fact, the Sox scored more runs on the road than all but one AL team, and their Batting Linear Weights, when adjusted for park, was third in the league—the same rank achieved by their pitching. (How they won the pennant remains a mystery, for both Cleveland and New York had vastly superior teams on paper.)

There have been nine other notable "pitchers' parks" since 1900, those that held scoring down at a rate 15 percent or more below normal.

### TABLE V, 6. WORST HITTERS' PARKS SINCE 1900

| | | |
|---|---|---|
| 1981 | Houston | .817 |
| 1906 | Chicago (A) | .820 |
| 1981 | Texas | .821 |
| 1918 | Boston (A) | .822 |
| 1958 | Milwaukee | .825 |
| 1926 | Boston (N) | .832 |
| 1976 | Houston | .838 |
| 1950 | Boston (N) | .843 |
| 1953 | Cleveland | .844 |
| 1975 | Oakland | .844 |

The great hitters' parks—those providing 15 percent greater run scoring than normal—have been more numerous, but these are the top ten, in order.

### TABLE V, 7. BEST HITTERS' PARKS SINCE 1900

| | | |
|---|---|---|
| 1955 | Boston | 1.22 |
| 1970 | Chicago (N) | 1.19 |
| 1972 | Detroit | 1.19 |
| 1957 | Brooklyn | 1.18 |
| 1968 | Cincinnati | 1.17 |
| 1967 | Boston | 1.17 |
| 1977 | Boston | 1.17 |
| 1981 | Toronto | 1.17 |
| 1917 | Cleveland | 1.17 |
| 1911 | New York (A) | 1.16 |

Looking at the most recent of these, Exhibition Stadium in Toronto, one wonders how the Blue Jays' young staff managed to avoid a mass nervous breakdown in 1981, let alone post an ERA of 3.82 which, when adjusted for park, proved second best in the AL.

Illuminating as the application of Park Factor can be to team results, it is positively mind-bending when applied to individuals. Here is a sampling of the revelations which emerge from a casual perusal of the data on the subject.

- In 1981, Houston's Art Howe was the third best hitter in the National League.
- The superstar numbers posted by Jim Rice would be hardly as impressive if the Fenway Park Factor were taken into account (through 1982, slugging percentage home/away for Rice, .584/.476; LWTS home/away, 211.2/85.2).
- Of the 815 men who have played in 1000 or more games since 1900, no batter has suffered more for

his "choice" of home park than Houston's José Cruz (Winfield's home-park advantage is nearly as poor).

- Of the top 100 lifetime marks in park-adjusted Batters' LWTS, only three have been achieved despite Park Factors 5 percent below average, those of Lou Gehrig, Gene Tenace, and Dave Winfield. And Cesar Cedeno, whose career is universally regarded as one of failed expectations, occupies the 117th spot on the list, his accomplishments adjusted for a low Park Factor of .95.
- When measuring batting by OPS adjusted for park, the list of top 100 seasons includes such unexpected delights as: Harry Lumley, the Dodger first sacker whose 1906 season (PF: .91) ranks 76th; or Frank Howard, whose 1968 season (PF: .89) ranks 81st; or Bobby Murcer in 1974 (PF: .94), who takes the 88th spot. These men were stars of the first magnitude, but did not receive their due until now. Howard's lifetime NOPS, in fact, is the 35th best of all time. In the 1983 Hall of Fame election, he received no votes (Ray Sadecki got two).
- Among the top fifty seasons posted by pitchers, as measured by LWTS, the 4th best of all time was the 1944 campaign of Dizzy Trout, who had to contend with a Park Factor of 1.15. Other perhaps unexpected occupants on the list: Bert Blyleven in 1973 (11th best), Steve Rogers in 1982 (42nd best), and Frank Sullivan in 1955 (43rd).
- Of the top fifty lifetime LWTS by pitchers, the greatest park handicap had to be overcome by Phil Niekro (10th best); others who have spent their careers in home parks 5 percent more conducive to hitting were Fergy Jenkins, Dizzy Trout, Hal Newhouser, and Virgil Trucks.
- Nolan Ryan's lifetime ERA, an impressive 3.11, has been hugely helped by the fact that he has pitched all his home games in pitchers' parks, first Shea, then Anaheim, now the Astrodome. His lifetime PF of .942 is lower than that of all the top 100 pitchers except Warren Spahn, Lefty Gomez, and Don Sutton. Ryan's ERA at home through 1982, in fact, was 2.41, while on the road it was 3.75—not even a league average performance.

Of the top thirty hitters of all times, as measured by their NOPS, it is strange that the two who played in the worst hitters' parks were men whose rankings did not need the boost of their Park Factors: Babe Ruth and Lou Gehrig. Their totals are so awesome that no matter what measure of offense you use, no matter what adjustments you make, Ruth is going to rank first and Gehrig third, with Ted Williams second. However, the gap between Williams and Gehrig narrows considerably once each record is adjusted for park. What would Gehrig have done in almost any other park in the American League at that time? In 1930 he drove in 177 runs *on the road*, with 27 homers and a .405 BA. Lifetime, his road BA was .351; at home—where his batting average should have been, with a normal home-park advantage, .372—it was "only" .329.[3]

Oddly, just as Babe Ruth's star was dimming in the late '30s. Gehrig seems to have concentrated more on pulling the ball for homers, with the result that in 1934, '36, and '37, he hit 30, 27, and 24 homers at home, a level previously unreached. Indeed, in 1934 he had one of the great *home* records of all time, with a BA of .414, 98 RBIs, and a NOPS of 2.48. In recent years, one of the best home batting marks has been that of Fred Lynn in 1979, when he batted .386 with 28 homers, 83 RBIs, and a NOPS of 2.50; since moving to Anaheim in 1981, he has not accomplished in a full season what he did in that half season.

A few other notable home hitting records:

- In 1912 Joe Jackson hit .483 at home. which was Cleveland's League Park.
- In 1920 Babe Ruth slugged .985 and had a NOPS of 3.10—more than three times the league average!—at the Polo Grounds (Yankee Stadium was not built until 1923).
- Also in 1920, George Sisler hit .473 at Sportsman's Park in St. Louis. Two years later, when he hit .453 there, teammate Ken Williams chipped in with 32 homers and 103 RBIs at home, and the Browns made their first serious run at pennant.
- In 1936 Cleveland's Hal Trosky hit 30 homers and drove in 99 runs at home.
- In 1938 Hank Greenberg hit an all-time-high 39 fourbaggers at Briggs Stadium and Jimmie Foxx hit 35 homers at Fenway to go with his all-time high 104 RBIs.
- In 1941 Ted Williams had an On Base Average of .541 in Boston.

Pitchers, too, have compiled unbelievable home records. In the early part of the century:

- In 1908 Ed Walsh went 23–5 in 241 innings pitched at Chicago's South Side Park with an ERA of 1.04. That's a full season's work and then some.
- Joe Wood was 18–2 at home for the 1912 Red Sox (of course, he was impartial, going 16–3 away).
- Chief Bender won 11 and lost only 1 for the 1914 A's.

In 1916, pitching in tiny Baker Bowl, Pete Alexander hurled 9 shutouts. But the most astounding record may be that of Lefty Grove, who showed his partiality to home cooking throughout his career, in two cities. Here is his record with the A's between 1929 and 1933:

TABLE V, 8. LEFTY GROVE, HOME/AWAY, 1929–1933

|      | HOME | AWAY | TOTAL |
|------|------|------|-------|
| 1929 | 9–2  | 11–4 | 20–6  |
| 1930 | 17–2 | 11–3 | 28–5  |
| 1931 | 17–1 | 14–3 | 31–4  |
| 1932 | 16–4 | 9–6  | 25–10 |
| 1933 | 16–2 | 8–6  | 24–8  |

Obviously, the man's road record of 53–22 over the five years wasn't too shabby, but it pales before the otherworldly home mark of 75–11, a winning percentage of .872. How to explain it? Shibe Park did not favor pitchers except in 1933; if anything, it is conventionally regarded as having been a very friendly place for righthanded hitters like Jimmie Foxx or Al Simmons. Even in Grove's later years, when he lost his fastball and was traded to the Red Sox—to pitch in Fenway, another park congenial to righthanded batters—he maintained his mastery at home, going 18–0 there over a three-year period.

TABLE V, 9. TEAM HOME/AWAY RECORDS, TOP FIVE SINCE 1900*

*Best Winning Percentage (Home)*

| 1932 | Yankees | .805 |
|------|---------|------|
| 1961 | Yankees | .802 |
| 1931 | Athletics | .800 |
| 1949 | Red Sox | .792 |
| 1946 | Red Sox | .792 |

*Best Winning Percentage (Away)*

| 1939 | Yankees | .730 |
|------|---------|------|
| 1933 | Senators | .697 |
| 1928 | Cardinals | .688 |
| 1971 | Athletics | .688 |
| 1923 | Yankees | .684 |

*Most Runs Scored Per Game (Home)*

| 1950 | Red Sox | 8.12 |
|------|---------|------|
| 1932 | Athletics | 7.43 |
| 1931 | Yankees | 7.08 |
| 1930 | Athletics | 7.05 |
| 1930 | Cardinals | 7.03 |

*Most Runs Scored Per Game (Away)*

| 1939 | Yankees | 7.80 |
|------|---------|------|
| 1930 | Yankees | 7.57 |
| 1936 | Yankees | 7.35 |
| 1931 | Yankees | 6.69 |
| 1932 | Yankees | 6.58 |

*Fewest Runs Allowed Per Game (Home)**

| 1981 | Astros | 2.08 |
|------|---------|------|
| 1964 | White Sox | 2.63 |
| 1968 | Dodgers | 2.65 |
| 1966 | White Sox | 2.68 |
| 1958 | Braves | 2.69 |

*Fewest Runs Allowed Per Game (Away)**

| 1968 | Yankees | 2.83 |
|------|---------|------|
| 1972 | Orioles | 2.84 |
| 1968 | Tigers | 2.87 |
| 1972 | Tigers | 2.90 |
| 1954 | White Sox | 2.95 |

*Worst Winning Percentage (Home)*

| 1939 | Browns | .234 |
|------|---------|------|
| 1911 | Braves | .260 |
| 1923 | Phillies | .267 |
| 1915 | Athletics | .267 |
| 1962 | Mets | .275 |

*Worst Winning Percentage (Away)*

| 1935 | Braves | .167 |
|------|---------|------|
| 1916 | Athletics | .169 |
| 1945 | Athletics | .171 |
| 1909 | Senators | .195 |
| 1904 | Senators | .197 |

*Fewest Runs Scored Per Game (Home)**

| 1942 | Phillies | 2.46 |
|------|---------|------|
| 1968 | Dodgers | 2.62 |
| 1972 | Padres | 2.71 |
| 1968 | Mets | 2.73 |
| 1972 | Angels | 2.76 |

*Fewest Runs Scored Per Game (Away)**

| 1972 | Indians | 2.65 |
|------|---------|------|
| 1981 | Cubs | 2.73 |
| 1942 | Phillies | 2.75 |
| 1963 | Mets | 2.78 |
| 1963 | Colt .45s | 2.82 |

*Most Runs Allowed Per Game (Home)*

| 1930 | Phillies | 8.36 |
|------|---------|------|
| 1923 | Phillies | 7.96 |
| 1929 | Phillies | 7.63 |
| 1939 | Browns | 7.19 |
| 1936 | Browns | 7.17 |

*Most Runs Allowed Per Game (Away)*

| 1930 | Phillies | 7.03 |
|------|---------|------|
| 1932 | White Sox | 6.76 |
| 1936 | Athletics | 6.68 |
| 1901 | Brewers | 6.59 |
| 1950 | Athletics | 6.58 |

*Most Homers Hit Per Game (Home)*

| 1947 | Giants | 1.72 |
|------|---------|------|
| 1956 | Reds | 1.66 |
| 1970 | Indians | 1.64 |
| 1954 | Giants | 1.58 |
| 1977 | Red Sox | 1.55 |

*Most Homers Hit Per Game (Away)*

| 1957 | Braves | 1.61 |
|------|---------|------|
| 1982 | Brewers | 1.57 |
| 1961 | Yankees | 1.56 |
| 1980 | Brewers | 1.41 |
| 1963 | Twins | 1.41 |

| *Fewest Homers Hit Per Game (Home)** | | |
|---|---|---|
| 1924 | Senators | .013 |
| 1945 | Senators | .013 |
| 1927 | Reds | .038 |
| 1928 | Reds | .038 |
| 1921 | Red Sox | .039 |
| 1924 | Reds | .039 |
| 1920 | Red Sox | .039 |

| *Fewest Homers Hit Per Game (Away)** | | |
|---|---|---|
| 1920 | Athletics | .114 |
| 1920 | Pirates | .130 |
| 1920 | Dodgers | .143 |
| 1944 | White Sox | .156 |
| 1928 | Browns | .156 |

| *Best Batting Teams (Batter Run Rating)†* | | |
|---|---|---|
| 1913 | Athletics | 1.43 |
| 1947 | Yankees | 1.40 |
| 1933 | Yankees | 1.40 |
| 1931 | Yankees | 1.38 |
| 1930 | Yankees | 1.37 |

| *Worst Batting Teams (Batter Run Rating)* | | |
|---|---|---|
| 1981 | Blue Jays | .664 |
| 1942 | Phillies | .672 |
| 1910 | Braves | .682 |
| 1903 | Senators | .719 |
| 1932 | Red Sox | .720 |

| *Best Pitching Teams (Pitcher Run Rating)*** | | |
|---|---|---|
| 1906 | Cubs | .644 |
| 1909 | Cubs | .686 |
| 1907 | Cubs | .694 |
| 1926 | Athletics | .700 |
| 1905 | Cubs | .722 |

| *Worst Pitching Teams (Pitcher Run Rating)* | | |
|---|---|---|
| 1915 | Athletics | 1.42 |
| 1911 | Braves | 1.38 |
| 1953 | Tigers | 1.36 |
| 1904 | Senators | 1.35 |
| 1968 | Senators | 1.33 |

* In some cases—particularly, fewest runs scored and allowed per game and fewest homers hit—the tables present post-1920 data to avoid total dominance in these categories by dead-ball era teams.
† The Batter Run Rating is the team's runs scored per inning, normalized to league average and adjusted for home park.
** The Pitcher Run Rating is the team's runs allowed per inning, normalized to league and adjusted for park.

In recent years, the best home pitching record has been that of Ron Guidry in 1978, when he was 13–1, however, he was scarcely less effective on the road at 12–2. In between Grove and Guidry, a supposedly washed-up Billy Pierce pitched the Giants to the 1962 flag by starting 12 games at home and winning all of them, the most wins without a loss either at home or on the road. And Mel Parnell, a lefthander, was 16–3 at Fenway in 1949.

The best and worst records by teams in this century, home and away, are perhaps best presented in tabular form (see Table V, 9). With so many factors going into a team's winning percentage, its runs scored and allowed, its home runs, etc., it may be useful to think of the *road* record as the best index of ability pure and portable. The New York Giants may have hit 131 homers at home in 1947, but we ought to be more impressed by the 124 hit away from home by the Milwaukee Braves ten years later—or by the Milwaukee Brewers in 1982, with 127 on the road. The Phillies of 1930 may have scored 7.05 runs a game at home, but we rub our eyes in disbelief at the road record of the 1939 Yankees: 7.8 runs scored per game, only 3.9 allowed (and that was the year in which Gehrig was replaced in May by a .235-hitting Babe Dahlgren).

The Houston Astros have always done well at home, even before they were a .500 team overall and before there was an Astrodome. Visiting teams hated to play in the heat before 1965 and have hated to play in the air conditioning since. In 1969 the eventual champion Mets lost all their games in Texas; that year produced an Astro record of 52–29 at home, best in the league, and a symmetrical 29–52 on the road.

Occasionally an organization runs out of kilter and gathers, somehow, an overabundance of players ill-equipped to take advantage of its home park. Imagine Richie Zisk and Pat Putnam in Houston, or Terry Puhl and José Cruz in Boston; or reflect back to when San Diego paid big money to acquire first Gene Tenace, then Oscar Gamble. The customary way out of such a fix is to swing a deal, or to go out in the free-agent mart and buy what you need to redress the team's balance. Occasionally a franchise has opted to keep the personnel and change the park, as the Cleveland Indians did in 1970 when they moved the fences in to such an extent that the number of homers hit in Municipal Stadium jumped from 116 to 236 (the Indians themselves jumped only one place, from last to next-to-last). An equally bizarre leap of the imagination was George Steinbrenner's decision in the winter of 1981 that speed was the wave of the future; overnight, he transformed the Yankees' traditional posture from power and pitching, which had been good enough since their park was built in 1923, to a team of jackrabbits and slap hitters. In came Dave Collins and Ken Griffey, out went Reggie Jackson and Bob Watson, among others. These moves made a fifth-place finisher of a pennant-winning club, and the Yankees' speed era came to a speedy conclusion, as the next winter's shopping expedition brought Don Baylor and Steve Kemp.

A home park with extreme charcteristics—heavily favoring pitchers or batters, lefty or righty—can be a problem. In Fenway visiting teams almost never start a lefthander because the Red Sox have historically stacked their lineup with righthanded hitters who can pull 350-foot fly balls over The Wall. (Hall of Famer Whitey Ford had an ERA of 6.16 in Fenway Park—things got so bad that the Yanks eventually decided to skip his turn in the rotation if they happened to be in Boston.)

This dearth of lefthanded opposition negates much of the presumed advantage that the Sox front office has labored to construct. Likewise, the Sox have rarely had a first-rate lefthanded pitcher on their own staff for the same reason: dread of The Wall. However, this has left Boston hurlers very vulnerable to lefthanded-hitting lineups in their road games. In this regard, it will be interesting to see Boston's road record in 1984, considering the club's 1983 acquisition of yet another righthanded slugger in Tony Armas when they knew Yaz was on the way out, taking with him the only lefthanded power they had. Entering 1984 without acquiring at least one more lefthanded hitter will be perilous indeed. Overreliance upon a strength can become, in the end, a weakness.

Home park characteristics certainly are on the minds of management as they contemplate trades. They may even have been on the minds of Messrs. Ruppert and Huston back in 1920 when they brought Babe Ruth to New York by giving to cash-strapped Red Sox owner Harry Frazee $100,000 and a $350,000 mortgage on Fenway Park. Ruth had been a sensation in 1919, hitting 29 homers to set a new baseball record. What has not been examined until now, but may have been known to the Yankees, was that of Ruth's 29 homers, only 9 were hit in his 63 games in Fenway Park, while 4 were hit in the Polo Grounds in the 11 games he played against the Yankees. A simple projection from these figures would indicate a plausible home-run mark for Ruth in 1920, playing 77 games in the Polo Grounds, of 28 homers in N.Y. plus 20 more on the road, with Fenway replacing the Polo Grounds as a road park. In fact, Ruth hit 54, which has been universally attributed to the introduction of the lively ball that year. Had he played with the same ball used in 1919, however, he figured to hit about that many anyway.

The classic "What if?" proposition regarding home parks also involved New York and Boston, the fancied trade of Ted Williams, a lefthanded pull hitter in a park that was thought to benefit only righthanded hitters (in fact it benefits all hitters) for Joe DiMaggio, a righthanded power hitter playing in a stadium that was cavernous in left and cozy in right. The thinking behind the proposed deal was that Williams, playing in Yankee Stadium, would have a shot at Ruth's home run marks and would hit for an even higher average, while DiMaggio would benefit in like fashion from Fenway. This hypothetical exchange of titans was very nearly consummated in 1949, long after the point at which it might have been a trade of equals, for DiMaggio's career would end in 1951 while Williams's would continue through 1960.

What if the deal had been completed a decade earlier? Park Factor, useful tool though it may be, should not be employed as if it were a magical button on your Betamax; it does not permit a "true" replay of seasons long past with the characters transported to different locales or new characters introduced. Park Factor offers a *suggestive* truth, one that is essentially and logically plausible, but not "verifiable" statistically (statistics never *prove,* anyway—they are estimations of truth). So, we really shouldn't be doing this, but what the hell. Here are the lifetime batting average and home run totals of Joe DiMaggio and Ted Williams as they might have looked if each had played his entire career in the other's uniform.

TABLE V, 10. DiMaggio with Boston, Williams
with New York

Joe DiMaggio, NY BA: .325; HR: 361
Joe DiMaggio, BOS BA: .340; HR: 417
Ted Williams, BOS BA: .344 HR: 521
Ted Williams, NY BA: .328* HR: 497*

The basis of these calculations is not simply Park Factor, but the precise batting data for each player at Boston, at New York, and elsewhere. Williams hit much better at Fenway over his career than he did in Yankee Stadium (BA, .361 to .309; SLG, .652 to .543) but his homers at Boston came at about the same rate as they did in New York. DiMaggio hit no better at Fenway than he did in

* Williams's figures in Yankee pinstripes would be higher still—a .340 BA and 513 homers—if we adjust for the fact that he would have been batting against Red Sox pitching rather than against Yankee pitching. Yankee pitchers were 7 percent better than the league average during 1939–60, William's span, while the Red Sox hurlers performed at the league average for DiMaggio's span, the period 1936–51.

**CAREW AND CLEMENTE . . .**
Two of the all-time greats. First, Rod Carew in the simple performance of his great specialty—hitting a baseball.
Next, Roberto Clemente doing everything—hitting, fielding, scoring. The final picture shows Clemente's
teammate Willie Stargell and his wife, and other Pittsburgh teammates, leaving the funeral services for Clemente,
who was killed on New Year's Eve in the crash of the plane he chartered to help victims of the Nicaraguan
earthquake of Dec. 23, 1972. (All photos AP/Wide World Photos)

the average of all the other road parks, but he *did* hit much better there than at Yankee Stadium (BA: .334 to .315; SLG, .605 to .546).

Bottom line? The trade was better off not being made as far as the Red Sox were concerned. DiMaggio would have built up more impressive career totals had he come up with the Red Sox in 1936, but by 1949 it was too late.

[1] PARK ADJUSTMENT: (Step 1) Add up runs allowed at home for all teams in the league (ROH—Runs, Opposition, Home) and runs allowed away for all teams in the league (ROA—Runs, Opposition, Away). Form a league average home/road ratio of HRL = ROH/ROA, where HRL is the home/road ratio of the league. (Step 2) Find games, losses, and runs allowed for each team at home and on the road. Take runs per game allowed at home over runs per game allowed on road, all over HRL. (Step 3) Make corrections for innings pitched at home and on the road. This is a bit complicated. First find the league average road winning percentage (wins on road over games on road). For each team compare its road winning percentage to the league average. If it is higher, this means the innings pitched on the road are higher because the other team is batting more often in the last of the ninth. This rating is divided by the Innings Pitched Corrector (IPC):

IPC = 1 + (Road Win Percentage, League − Road Win Percentage, Team) × .113

(Step 4) Make corrections for the fact that the other road parks' total difference from the league average is offset by the park rating of the club which is being rated. Multiply rating by this Other Parks Corrector (OPC):

$$\text{OPC} = \text{No. of teams} - \frac{\text{Run Factor, team}}{\text{No. of teams} - 1}$$

*Example:* In 1982, the runs allowed at home by all teams in the National League was 3993; on the road it was 3954. Thus the home/road ratio (HRL) is 1.010. Atlanta allowed 387 runs at home in 81 games, 315 runs allowed on the road in 81 games. The initial factor is (387/81) / (315/81) / 1.010 = 1.216. The league road winning percentage was .487 (473 wins in 972 games). The Braves' road record was 47–34, or .580. Thus the IPC = 1 + (.487 − .580) × .113 = .989. The team rating is now 1.216/.989 = 1.230. The OPC = (12 − 1.230) / (12 −1) = .979. The final rating is 1.230 × .979, or 1.204.

We warned you it wouldn't be easy.

The batter adjustment factor is composed of two parts, one the park factor and the other the fact that a batter does not have to face his own pitchers. The initial correction takes care of only the second factor. For the first start with the following:

SF = Scoring Factor, previously determined (for Atlanta, 1.204)

SF1 = Scoring Factor of the other clubs (NT = number of teams);

$$1 - \frac{\text{SF} - 1}{\text{NT} - 1}$$

Next is an iterative process in which the initial team pitching rating is assumed to be one, and the following factors are employed:

RHT, RAT = Runs per game scored at home (H), away (A) by team

OHT, OAT = Runs per game allowed at home, away, by team

RAL = Runs per game by both teams

Now, with the Team Pitching Rating (TPR) = 1, we proceed to calculate Team Bat Rating (TBR):

$$\text{TBR} = \left(\frac{\text{RAT}}{\text{SF1}} + \frac{\text{RHT}}{\text{SF}}\right)\left(1 + \frac{\text{TPR} - 1}{\text{NT} - 1}\right)\Big/\text{RAL}$$

$$\text{TPR} = \left(\frac{\text{OAT}}{\text{SF1}} + \frac{\text{OHT}}{\text{SF}}\right)\left(1 + \frac{\text{TBR} - 1}{\text{NT} - 1}\right)\Big/\text{RAL}$$

The last two steps are repeated three more times. The final batting corrector (BF) is:

$$\text{BF} = \frac{(\text{SF} + \text{SF1})}{\left(2 \times \left[1 + \dfrac{\text{TBR} - 1}{\text{NT} - 1}\right]\right)}$$

Similarly, the final pitching corrector (PF) is:

$$\text{PF} = \frac{(\text{SF} + \text{SF1})}{\left(2 \times \left[1 + \dfrac{\text{TBR} - 1}{\text{NT} - 1}\right]\right)}$$

Now an example, using the 1982 Atlanta Braves once more.

$$\text{RHT} = \frac{388}{81} = 4.79 \qquad \text{RAT} = \frac{351}{81} - 4.33$$

$$\text{OHT} = \frac{387}{81} = 4.78 \qquad \text{OAT} = \frac{315}{81} = 3.89$$

$$\text{RAL} = \frac{7947}{972} = 8.18 \qquad \text{NT} = 12$$

$$\text{SF} = 1.204 \qquad \text{SF1} = 1 - \left(\frac{1.204 - 1}{11}\right) = .981$$

$$\text{TBR} = \left(\frac{4.33}{.981} + \frac{4.79}{1.20}\right)\left(1 + \frac{1 - 1}{11}\right)\Big/8.18 = 1.027$$

$$\text{TPR} = \left(\frac{3.89}{.981} + \frac{4.78}{1.20}\right)\left(1 + \frac{1.027 - 1}{11}\right)\Big/8.18 = .974$$

Repeating these steps give a TBR of 1.02 and a TPR of .97. The batting corrector is:

$$\text{BF} = \frac{(1.204 + .981)}{\left(2 \times \left[1 + \dfrac{.97 - 1}{11}\right]\right)} = 1.09$$

This is not a great deal removed from taking the original ratio,

$$\frac{1.216 + 1}{2},$$ which is 1.11.

The pitching corrector may be calculated in analogous fashion.

[2] To apply the Batter Park Factor to Linear Weights, one must use this formula:

$$\begin{array}{ccc} \text{LWT} & = & \text{LWT} & + & \dfrac{\text{Runs (league)}}{(\text{AB} + \text{BB} + \text{HBP})} \\ \text{corrected} & & \text{uncorrected} & & \text{league} \end{array}$$

$$\times \ (\text{BF} - 1) \times (\text{AB} + \text{BB} + \text{HBP})$$
$$\text{player or team}$$

For example, if a player produces 20 runs above average in 700 plate appearances with a Batter Park Factor of 1.10, and the league average of runs produced per plate appearance was .11, this means that his uncorrected LWT was 20 over the zero point of 700 × .11 (77 runs). In other words, 77 runs is the average run contribution expected of this batter had he played in an average home park. But because his Batter Park Factor was 1.10, which means his home park was 10 percent kinder to hitters, you would really expect an average run production of 1.1 × 77, or 85 runs. Thus the player whose uncorrected LWT was 97 with a BF of 1.1 was only + 12 runs rather than + 20, and 12 is his Park Adjusted Linear Weights Runs.

$$12 = 20 + .11 \times (1.10 - 1) \times 700$$

[3] Some other great road batting marks: Harry Heilmann had a BA of .456 in his away games of 1925; Gehrig slugged .805 away in 1927; and Ted Williams had an OBA of .528 on the road in 1957, with a NOPS of 2.68. The last men to post batting averages over .400 on the road were Lou Boudreau and Stan Musial, both in 1948.

# AMADEE

The first *Fireside Book of Baseball,* published in 1956, carried drawings of six major-league ballparks by Gene Mack of *The Boston Globe.* Three of the six—Fenway Park in Boston, Tiger Stadium in Detroit, and Wrigley Field in Chicago—are still with us. But when Lowell Reidenbaugh of *The Sporting News* wanted to update the other three for his book *Take Me Out to the Ball Park,* he chose Amadee Wohlschlaeger, for many years the sports cartoonist for the *St. Louis Post-Dispatch,* to update them. Amadee's drawings of the newer parks in the majors also appear in Reidenbaugh's book, and we have chosen four of them to reproduce here. (Reprinted by permission from *The Sporting News: Take Me Out to the Ball Park,* 1983, St. Louis, The Sporting News Publishing Company)

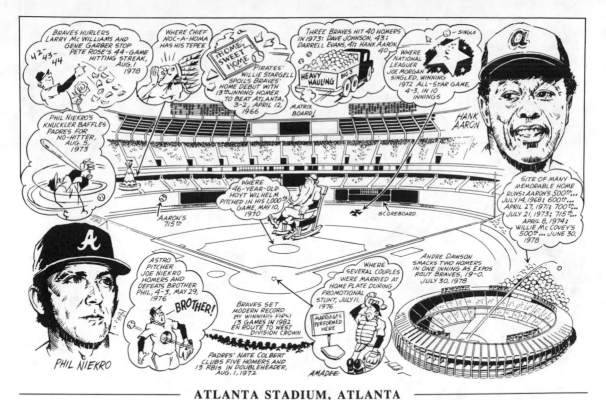

## ATLANTA STADIUM, ATLANTA
### Seating Capacity 52,785—First Game April 12, 1966

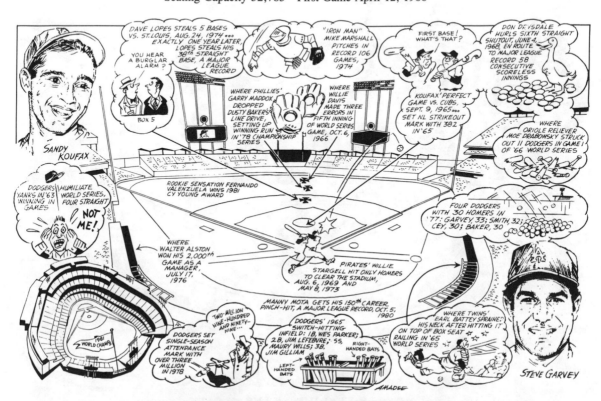

## DODGER STADIUM, LOS ANGELES
### Seating Capacity 56,000—First Game April 10, 1962

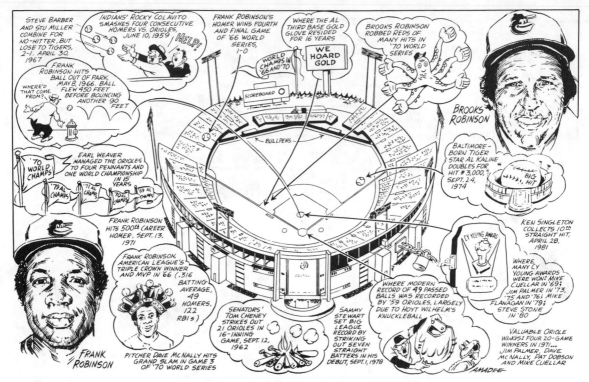

## MEMORIAL STADIUM, BALTIMORE

Seating Capacity 53,208—First Game April 15, 1954

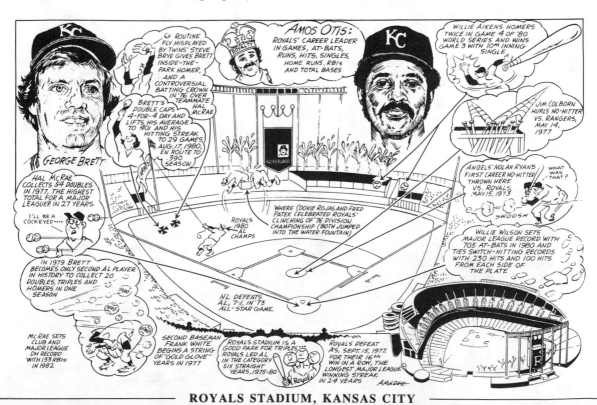

## ROYALS STADIUM, KANSAS CITY

Seating Capacity 40,635—First Game April 10, 1973

Novelist, critic, short story writer, John Updike is essayist and poet as well, and in those two forms his love of baseball has had extraordinary results. One was his 1960 article in *The New Yorker* about Ted Williams' last game (it was reprinted in *The Third Fireside Book of Baseball* and many other places). Another is this poem, written more than thirty years ago.

# Tao in the Yankee Stadium Bleachers

## JOHN UPDIKE

Distance brings proportion. From here
the populated tiers
as much as players seem part of the show:
a constructed stage beast, three folds of Dante's rose,
or a Chinese military hat
cunningly chased with bodies.
"Falling from his chariot, a drunk man is unhurt
because his soul is intact. Not knowing his fall,
he is unastonished, he is invulnerable."
So, too, the "pure man"—"pure"
in the sense of undisturbed water.

"It is not necessary to seek out
a wasteland, swamp, or thicket."
The old men who saw Hans Wagner
scoop them up in lobster hands,
the opposing pitcher's pertinent hesitations,
the sky, this meadow, Mantle's thick baked neck,
the old men who in the changing rosters see
a personal mutability,
green slats, wet stone are all to me
as when an emperor commands
a performance with a gesture of his eyes.

"No king on his throne has the joy of the dead,"
the skull told Chuang-tzu.
The thought of death is peppermint to you
when games begin with patriotic song
and a democratic sun beats broadly down.
The Inner Journey seems unjudgeably long
when small boys purchase cups of ice
and, distant as a paradise,
experts, passionate and deft,
wait while Berra flies to left.

Did Jane Austen invent baseball in 1792?

# Baseball in Wales

## GEORGE VECSEY

ON OUR first morning in Wales, our host Alastair made a pot of tea and announced, "So, we're off to a baseball game on Saturday." We indulgently ascribed his talk to Celtic mysticism, vision of long lost cities in the driving surf, ancient Druid deities in the mist. If Alastair thought he could find a baseball game in Wales, more power to him.

Alastair's stone cottage looks out on a rolling valley with a rushing river, a scenic canal, two brands of sheep grazing on separate farms and a mountain range in the distance. Only two miles from his home is a thriving market town where one can find just enough Caerphilly cheese and Jan Morris books to revive the dream of Getting Away From It All.

The exact name and location of Alastair's town will remain a secret, lest this damp little version of paradise become Hamptonized. There are enough public footpaths and castles and Roman gold mines and rocky promontories overlooking the sea to make a New Yorker get over the fact that Len Dykstra and Kevin Mitchell are nearly 3,000 miles away.

On Friday night, we sat in yet another picturesque pub, drinking cider and eating grilled trout, when Alastair said, "Well folks, tomorrow is the baseball game in Cardiff."

The day of the alleged big game dawned bright and clear, and we drove through twisting mountain roads to the defunct coal mines of the Rhondda Valley until we reached Cardiff, capital of a nation with no government, whose last prince, Llewelyn, was murdered seven centuries ago.

We found Roath Park, a long green strip with stone row houses on one side and a grove of trees on the other—as urban oasis something like Memorial Stadium in Baltimore, without the stadium.

Shortly after two o'clock, there was a bustle of robust men in bright uniforms of cleated shoes, short-sleeved shirts and bright shorts, like soccer players. They carried a few bats, rounded on one side, flat on the other; a few baseballs slightly smaller and slightly softer than the American brand, and they began warming up in what any American baseball buff would immediately recognize as a game of pepper.

Then an umpire arrived, and they began playing a game that seemed halfway between North American baseball and the cricket played in the rest of the English-speaking world. Ten fielders aligned themselves in a 360-degree circle around a batter, while the pitcher, or "hurler," fired his missile from an underhand position, much like Dan Quisenberry of the Kansas City Royals.

The basic idea is that the batter tries to catch a piece of the ball and slice it or hook it "where they ain't" as Wee Willie Keeler was supposed to have said. What would be a foul ball in the United States can become a four-base wallop, with a fielder chasing the ball into the street behind home plate while the batter rounds the bases, tapping four poles inserted in the ground.

The catcher wears two gloves that fit snugly over both hands, but nobody else wears gloves. The players position themselves depending on the hitting skills of the batter and, occasionally, make nifty diving catches of slashing fly balls. The teams keep batting until every man has been retired once: Two full innings constitutes a game.

Midway through the game, it became apparent that the hurler for the Llanrumney team, a burly right-hander with straight sandy hair, a droopy sandy mustache and a solid athlete's paunch, was one tough Welshman. His best pitch was a spinning, rising fastball straight at the chin—the top of the strike zone. He reminded one touring Yank of Billy Smith, the gruff hockey goalkeeper of the New York Islanders, and, it turned out, he was himself a Smith, named John.

"He is the most capped Welsh player in history," explained William Barrett, a headmaster by profession who helps run the Welsh league. "John Smith has played 13 straight years against the English in our annual international match.''

As Llanrumney, champions for 12 years, scampered from post to post on this brisk afternoon, William Barrett told how Jane Austen had differentiated between cricket and baseball in ''Northanger Abbey,'' written in 1792, or 47 years before Abner Doubleday was supposed to have created baseball in Cooperstown, N.Y.

The game took hold in Newport and Cardiff in south Wales in the late 19th century and also surfaced in Merseyside, England. William Barrett filled us in on the exploits of the great Fred Fish, who once hit 11 homers in 12 times up; the immortal Tommy Denning who was capped 12 times against England; the Irish immigrant, Paddy Hennessey, who allowed the tiny sum of six runs in one inning to England in 1964, and how American sailors from the Manley had played both versions of the game with Welshmen in World War II.

Only a few relatives and a few fans were watching this game, a far cry from the crowds of 4,000 to 5,000 that used to come out. ''Too much else to do now,'' Barrett noted, proudly adding that thousands of Welsh boys and girls play baseball as their main summer sport.

After slashing hits to the four points of the compass, burly John Smith was finally retired, and wandered over to talk a little baseball. He is a docker in the fading port of Cardiff, who pays one British pound (currently nearly $1.50) to play on weekends and 50 pence on week nights.

''I don't make anything from baseball,'' he said, ''but it's a nice feeling when the youngsters come up to you and say, 'Don't you play for Wales?' ''

Standing on the grass in Cardiff, this most amateur of athletes sounded as professional as any hurler in one of the enclosed baseball parks in the New World. He readily agreed: ''Yes, I do aim at their chins. It puts pressure on them. That's what this game is all about, pressure.

''One day I'll pressure them and the next day they'll pressure me. There are lots of batters who can hit me. They learn to use the pace on my ball to their advantage.

''I'm 34 now, getting on in years, and I don't throw as hard as I used to. But the beauty of this game is that you learn to get them out other ways. I'm trying to place my fielders more now. Let them get the batters out for me.

John Smith looked blank when the visiting Yank compared him to another aging hurler named Tom Seaver, who had learned, years ago, to compensate for loss of velocity.

Smith seemed to know little about American baseball except that those players make money at the game, but the discrepancy did not seem to trouble him as he swaggered back to the field to aim a few more fastballs at a few more chins.

At about the same time this poem was appearing in *The Atlantic Monthly*, another magazine, *Yankee*, was explaining the obvious baseball connection: "Wiffleball. . . . the ball that could curve all by itself was invented by David Mullany, a salesman for an auto polish manufacturer. After watching his son 'tearing his arm out trying to make a ball curve,' he got a dozen plastic globes from a nearby perfume factory where they were used to hold perfume. Then he went to work at his kitchen table cutting slits in them with a razor blade."

# Wiffle Ball

## RONALD WALLACE

Doing my best to hit
the bat, I serve the pitch up
on a platter.
Limp-wristed and slithery
she spins full around
and falls to the ground
dizzy, a fizzle.
Despair floats out
to the makeshift mound
and I catch it.
So I explain
stance, the snap
of the wrist, the quick
eye and level swing, the love
of the game—
all curve balls
to her blunt stare.
And what do I care
anyway? She's nine, and I
can't make her do
anything she doesn't
want to, so there!
She stumps off adjusting
her mask and pads,
shaking off all my signs.

# Anthem

## WILLIAM (SUGAR) WALLACE

Catfish, Mudcat, Ducky, Coot.
The Babe, The Barber, The Blade, The Brat.
Windy, Dummy, Gabby, Hoot.
Big Train, Big Six, Big Ed, Fat.

Greasy, Sandy, Muddy, Rocky.
Bunions, Twinkletoes, Footsie. The Hat.
Fuzzy, Dizzy, Buddy, Cocky.
The Bull, The Stork, The Weasel, The Cat.
    Schoolboy, Sheriff,
    Rajah, Duke,
    General, Major,
    Spaceman, Spook.

The Georgia Peach, The Fordham Flash,
The Flying Dutchman. Cot.
The People's Cherce, The Blazer. Crash.
The Staten Island Scot.
    Skeeter, Scooter,
    Pepper, Duster,
    Ebba, Bama, Boomer, Buster.

The Little Professor, The Iron Horse. Cap.
Iron Man, Iron Mike, Iron Hands. Hutch.
Jap, The Mad Russian, Irish, Swede. Nap.
Germany, Frenchy, Big Serb, Dutch,
    Turk. Tuck, Tug, Twig.
    Spider, Birdie, Rabbit, Pig.

Fat Jack, Black Jack, Zeke, Zack. Bloop.
Peanuts, Candy, Chewing Gum, Pop.
Chicken, Cracker, Hot Potato, Soup.
    Ding, Bingo.
    Hippity-Hopp.

Three-Finger, No-Neck, The Knuck, The Lip.
Casey, Gavvy, Pumpsie, Zim.
Flit, Bad Henry. Fat Freddie, Flip.
Jolly Cholly, Sunny Jim.
    Shag, Schnozz,
    King Kong, Klu.
    Boog, Buzz,
    Boots, Bump, Boo.

King Carl, The Count. The Rope, The Whip.
Wee Willie, Wild Bill, Gloomy Gus. Cy.
Bobo, Bombo, Bozo. Skip.
Coco, Kiki, Yo-yo. Pie.
 Dinty, Dooley,
 Stuffy, Snuffy,
 Stubby, Dazzy,
 Daffy, Duffy.

Baby Doll, Angel Sleeves, Pep, Sliding Billy,
Buttercup, Bollicky, Boileryard, Juice.
Colby Jack, Dauntless Dave, Cheese,
 Gentle Willie,
Trolley Line, Wagon Tongue, Rough,
 What's the Use.

 Ee-yah,
 Poosh 'Em Up,
 Skoonj, Slats, Ski.
 Ding Dong,
 Ding-a-Ling,
 Dim Dom, Dee.

Famous Amos. Rosy, Rusty.
Handsome Ransom. Home Run, Huck.
Rapid Robert. Cactus, Dusty.
Rowdy Richard. Hot Rod, Truck.
 Jo-Jo, Jumping Joe,
 Little Looie,
 Muggsy, Moe.

Old Folks, Old Pard, Oom Paul. Yaz.
Cowboy, Indian Bob, Chief, Ozark Ike.
Rawhide, Reindeer Bill. Motormouth. Maz.
Pistol Pete, Jungle Jim, Wahoo Sam. Spike.
 The Mad Hungarian.
 Mickey, Minnie.
 Kitten, Bunny.
 Big Dan, Moose.
 Jumbo, Pee Wee; Chubby, Skinny.
 Little Poison.
  Crow, Hawk, Goose.

Marvelous Marv.
 Oisk, Oats, Tookie.
Vinegar Bend.
 Suds, Hooks, Hug.
Hammerin' Hank.
 Cooch, Cod, Cookie.
Harry the Horse.
 Speed, Stretch, Slug.

The Splendid Splinter. Pruschka. Sparky.
Chico, Choo Choo, Cha-Cha, Chub.
Dr. Strangeglove. Deacon. Arky.

Abba Dabba. Supersub.
Bubbles, Dimples, Cuddles, Pinky.
Poison Ivy, Vulture, Stinky.
  Jigger, Jabbo
  Jolting Joe
  Blue Moon
  Boom Boom
  Bubba
  Bo

Outfielders Paul and Lloyd Waner were known as "Big Poison" and "Little Poison," and Lee Allen recorded that this was not because of what they meant to enemy pitchers but a corruption of "person." It came into being, Allen wrote, "when a baseball writer overheard an Ebbets Field fan continually say, in Brooklynese, as the Waners came to bat, 'Here comes that big poison' or 'Here comes that little poison.' "

Lawrence Ritter has noted that Paul Waner stood only five feet eight inches tall, and weighed less than 150 pounds, and brother Lloyd was even smaller. *The Baseball Encyclopedia* says Paul was three pounds heavier but half an inch shorter than Lloyd. According to that, we have two little poisons. According to pitchers, they were both big poisons: Paul had 3,152 hits lifetime and Lloyd 2,459—a combined total exceeding, as Ritter points out, the total hits of all three DiMaggio brothers by more than 500 and all *five* Delahanty brothers by more than 1,000!

(In this piece, from Ritter's *The Glory of Their Times,* Big Poison does indeed refer to Little Poison as his "little brother.")

# "I *Liked* to Be Booed"

## PAUL WANER

I COME from a little town right outside of Oklahoma City, a town by the name of Harrah. You can spell that backwards or forwards. From there I went to State Teachers' College at Ada. And you can spell that backwards or forwards, too. Which just naturally explains why I've always been a fuddle-dee-dud!

I went to State Teachers' College at Ada for three years, although I didn't really intend to be a teacher. Maybe for a little while, but not forever. What I wanted to be was a lawyer, and I figured sooner or later I'd go to law school. Eventually I was going to go to Harvard Law School, I reckon. That was my ambition, anyway.

But all at once baseball came up, and that changed everything all around. Of course, I was playing ball on amateur and semipro teams all the while I was in high school and college. In those days, you know, every town that had a thousand people in it had a baseball team. That's not true any more. But in those days there were so many teams along there in the Middle States, and so few scouts, that the chances of a good player being "discovered" and getting a chance to go into organized ball were one in a million. Good young players were a dime a dozen all over the country then.

How did they find me? Well, they found me because

a scout went on a drunk. Yes, that's right, because a scout went on a bender. He was a scout for the San Francisco Seals of the Pacific Coast League, and he was in Muskogee looking over a player by the name of Flaskamper that Frisco wanted to buy. He looked him over, and sent in a recommendation—that was late in the summer of 1922—and then he went out on a drunk for about ten days. They never heard a thing from him all this while, didn't know anything about him or where the heck he was.

He finally got in shape to go back to the Coast, but on the way back a train conductor by the name of Burns— you know how they used to stop and talk with you and pass the time of day—found out that this fellow was a baseball scout. Well, it so happened that I went with this conductor's daughter—Lady Burns—at school. So naturally—me going with his daughter and all—what the heck—he couldn't wait to tell this scout how great I was. How I could pitch and hit and run and do just about everything. He was such a convincing talker, and this scout needed an excuse so bad for where he'd been those ten days, that the scout—Dick Williams was his name— decided, "Doggone it, I've got something here."

When he got back to San Francisco, of course they

wanted to know where the heck he'd been and what had happened. "Well," he said, "I've been looking over a ballplayer at Ada, Oklahoma. His name is Paul Waner and he's only nineteen years old, and I think he's really going to make it big. I've watched him for ten days and I don't see how he can miss."

Then Dick quickly wrote me a letter. He said, "I've just talked to the Frisco ball club about you. I heard about you through this conductor, Burns. I told them that I saw you and all that, and I want you to write me a letter and send it to my home. Don't send it to the ball club, send it to my home. Tell me all about yourself: your height, your weight, whether you're left-handed or right-handed, how fast you can run the hundred, and all that. So I'll know, see, really know."

So I wrote him the letter he wanted, and sent it to his home, not really thinking too much about it at the time. But the next spring, darned if they didn't send me a contract. However, I sent it right back, 'cause my Dad always wanted me to go to school. He didn't want me to quit college. My father was a farmer and he wanted his sons to get a good education.

But they sent the contract right back to me, and even upped the ante some. So I said, "Dad, I'll ask them for $500 a month, and if they give it to me will you let me go?"

He thought about it awhile, and finally said, "Well, if they'll give you $500 a month starting off, and if you'll promise me that if you don't make good you'll come right back and finish college, then it's OK with me."

"Why surely, I'll do that," I said.

So I told the Frisco club about those conditions. But it didn't make any difference to them. Because they could offer you any salary at all and look you over, and if you weren't really good they could just let you go and they'd only be out expenses. They had nothing to lose.

So out I went to San Francisco for spring training. That was in 1923. I was only nineteen years old, almost twenty, just an ol' country boy. I didn't even know, when I got there, that they had a boat going across to San Francisco. My ticket didn't call for any boat trip. But after the train got into Oakland you got on a ferry and went across San Francisco Bay. Boy, as far as I was concerned that was a huge ocean liner!

I had hardly arrived out there before I met Willie Kamm, Lew Fonseca, and Jimmy O'Connell. Those three used to pal around together a lot, because they all came from the Bay Area. I was anxious to be friendly and all, so I said to them, real solicitous-like, "Well, do you fellows think you'll make good up here?" (All the while thinking to myself, you know, "Gee, you sure don't look like it to me.")

## JOHN GALLAGHER

*"You wanna talk? I'm his agent."*

How was I to know that all three of them *already* were established Big Leaguers? It turned out that they were just working out with the Frisco club until their own training camps opened. But I didn't know that. That was a big joke they never let me forget—a kid like me asking them did they think they'd make good!

Anyway, there I was, a rookie who'd never played a game in organized ball, at spring training with the San Francisco club in the Coast League, which was the highest minor league classification there was. I was a pitcher then, a left-handed pitcher. At Ada I'd played first base and the outfield when I wasn't pitching, but the Frisco club signed me as a pitcher.

The first or second day of spring training we had a little game, the Regulars against the Yannigans—that's what they called the rookies—and I was pitching for the Yannigans. The umpire was a coach by the name of Spider Baum. Along about the sixth inning my arm started to tighten up, so I shouted in, "Spider, my arm is tying up and getting sore on me."

"Make it or break it!" he says.

They don't say those things to youngsters nowadays. No, sir! And maybe it's just as well they don't, because what happened was that, sure enough, I *broke* it! And the next day, gee, I could hardly lift it.

I figured that was the end of my career, and in a few weeks I'd be back in Ada. I was supposed to be a pitcher, and I couldn't throw the ball ten feet. But just to keep busy, and look like I was doing something, I fooled around in the outfield and shagged balls for the rest of them. I'd toss the ball back underhanded, because I couldn't throw any other way. I did that day after day, but my arm didn't get any better.

After the regular day's practice was over, the three Big Leaguers—Willie Kamm, Lew Fonseca, and Jimmy O'Connell—would stay out an extra hour or so and practice hitting, and I shagged balls for them, too. I figured I'd better make myself useful in any way I could, or I'd be on my way back to Oklahoma.

I don't know which one of them mentioned it to the others, but after about a week or so of this they decided that maybe I'd like a turn at hitting. Especily since if I quit shagging for them, they'd have to go chase all those balls themselves. And they didn't relish the idea of doing that.

So they yelled, "Hey, kid! You want to hit some?"

"Sure I do," I said.

So they threw, and I hit. They just let me hit and hit and hit, and I really belted that ball. There was a carpenter building a house out just beyond the right-field fence, about 360 or 370 feet from home plate. He was pounding shingles on the roof, and he had his back to us. Well, I hit one, and it landed on the roof, pretty close to him. He looked around, wondering what the devil was

going on. The first thing you know, I slammed another one out there and it darned near hit him. So he just put his hammer down, and sat there and watched. And I kept right on crashing line drives out there all around where he was sitting. Of course, they were lobbing the ball in just right, and heck—I just swished and away it went.

When we were finished, we went into the clubhouse and nobody said a word to me. Not a word. And there was only dead silence all the while we showered, and got dressed, and walked back to the hotel. We sat down to dinner, and still not a single one of them had said "You looked good," or "You did well," or anything like that.

But when we were almost through eating dinner the manager, Dots Miller, came over to my table. He said, "Okie, tomorrow you fool around in the outfield. Don't throw hard, just toss 'em in underhanded. And you *hit* with the regulars."

Well, boy, that was something! I gulped, and felt like the cat that just ate the canary. And from then on I was with the regulars, and I started playing.

Luckily, my arm came back a month or two later, a few weeks after the season started. We went into Salt Lake City, and was it ever hot. Suddenly, during fielding practice, my arm felt like it stretched out at least a foot longer, and it felt real supple and good. It caught me by surprise, and I was afraid to really throw hard. But I did, a little more each time, and it felt fine!

Duffy Lewis was managing Salt Lake City and he knew about my bad arm, so he'd told his players, "Run on Waner. Anytime the ball goes to him, just duck your head and start running, because he can't throw."

There was a pretty short right-field wall at Salt Lake City, and in the first or second inning one of their players hit one off the wall. I took it on the rebound and threw him out at second by 15 feet. Someone tried to score from second on a single to right, and I threw him out at home. Gee whiz, I could throw all the way from the outfield to home plate! I threw about four men out in nothing flat, and after that they stopped running on me. I never had any trouble with my arm after that. It never bothered me again.

I had a good year in the Coast League that first season; hit about .370. Then the next season I did the same thing, got over 200 hits, and batted in about 100 runs. I was figuring by then that maybe I should be moving up to the Big Leagues. Joe Devine, a Pittsburgh scout, was trying to get the Pirates to buy me, but the San Francisco club wanted $100,000 for me, and the Pittsburgh higher-ups thought that that was a little too much for a small fellow like me. I only weighed 135 pounds then. I never weighed over 148 pounds ever, in all the years I played.

So Joe said to me, "Paul, it looks like you'll have to hit .400 to get up to the majors."

"Well, then," I said, "that's just exactly what I'll do."

I was kidding, you know. But darned if I didn't hit .401 in 1925. I got 280 hits that season, and at the end of the year the Pirates paid the $100,000 for me. San Francisco sold Willie Kamm to the Big Leagues for $100,000 in 1922, and then did the same thing with me three years later.

After I got to Pittsburgh early in 1926, I told Mr. Dreyfuss, the president of the club, that I had a younger brother who was a better ballplayer than I was. So the Pirates signed Lloyd and sent him to Columbia in the Sally League to see how he'd do. Well, Lloyd hit about .350 and was chosen the league's Most Valuable Player.

The Pirates took Lloyd along to spring training in 1927, mostly just to look at him a little closer. They never thought he could possibly make the team, 'cause Lloyd only weighed about 130 pounds then. He was only twenty years old, and was even smaller than me.

Our outfield that season was supposed to be Kiki Cuyler, Clyde Barnhart, and myself. But Barnhart reported that spring weighing about 260 or 270 pounds. He was just a butterball. They took him and did everything they could think of to get his weight down. They gave him steam baths, and exercised him, and ran him, and ran him, and ran him. Well, they got the weight off, all right, but as a result the poor fellow was so weak he could hardly lift a bat.

So on the trip back to Pittsburgh from spring training, Donie Bush came to me and said, "Paul, I'm putting your little brother out there in left field, and he's going to open the season for us."

"Well, you won't regret it," I said. "Lloyd will do the job in first-rate style."

And he did, too, as you know. We won the pennant that year, with Lloyd hitting .355. I hit .380 myself, and between the two of us we got 460 base hits that season: 223 hits for Lloyd and 237 for me. It's an interesting thing that of those 460 hits only 11 were home runs. They were mostly line drives: singles, doubles, and a lot of triples, because both of us were very fast.

Don't get the idea that we won the pennant for Pittsburgh all by ourselves that year, though, because that sure wasn't so. We had Pie Traynor at third base, you know, and Pie hit about .340 that season. Pie was a great ballplayer, I think the greatest third baseman who ever lived. A terrific hitter and a great fielder. Gosh, how he could dive for those line drives down the third base line and knock the ball down and throw the man out at first! It was remarkable. Those two Boyer brothers who are playing now are both great fielding third basemen, but Pie could do all they can and more. In addition to his hitting and fielding, Pie

was a good base runner, too. Most people don't remember that.

It's a funny thing, but Pie always said that I was the best first baseman he ever threw to. I played first once in a while, not too much, but every so often. I didn't know very much about how to play first base at the beginning, but one of the greatest fielding first basemen of all time practiced and practiced with me, until I knew my way around the bag well enough to make do. That was Stuffy McInnis, the great first baseman of the Philadelphia Athletics' "$100,000 infield" back in 1911 and 1912 and around there.

When I joined the Pirates in 1926, Stuffy was there as a substitute first baseman. He must have been close to forty at the time, and I think that was his last year in baseball. He'd been in the Big Leagues since 1910 or so. But he could still field that position like nobody's business, and he tried to teach me all he knew. I was his roommate in 1926, before Lloyd came up the next year, and Stuffy would spend hours with me in the room showing me how to play first base, using a pillow as a base. Gee, even at that age he was just a flow of motion out there on the field, just everywhere at once and making everything look so easy.

Actually, I was a little too small to make a good first baseman. On the other hand, I was almost as tall as Stuffy McInnes and George Sisler. Neither of them were six-footers. They were a lot bigger than I was, of course. They must have weighed at least 170 or 180. But neither of them was real tall, like most first basemen are.

They say Hal Chase was the greatest fielding first baseman of all time. I never saw him, so I don't know about that. But I did see Stuffy McInnes and George Sisler, and I don't see how he could have been better than them. They were the best I ever saw. I guess every generation has its own, and it's hard to compare between generations.

Although I did see Honus Wagner play, I really did. Honus came back as a coach with the Pirates during the 'thirties. He must have been sixty years old easy, but goldarned if that old boy didn't get out there at shortstop every once in a while during fielding practice and play that position. When he did that, a hush would come over the whole ball park, and every player on both teams would just stand there, like a bunch of little kids, and watch every move he made. I'll never forget it.

Honus was a wonderful fellow, so good-natured and friendly to everyone. Gee, we loved that guy. And the fans were crazy about him. Yeah, everybody loved that old Dutchman! If anyone told a good joke or a funny story, Honus would slap his knee and let out a loud roar and say, "What about *that!*"

So whenever I'd see him, the first thing I'd say would be, "What about *that,* Honus," and both of us would laugh. I guess there's no doubt at all that Honus was the most popular player who ever put on a Pittsburgh uniform. Those Pittsburgh fans were always fine fans, did you know that? They sure were. And I presume they still are, for that matter.

I remember soon after I came up, Pie Traynor said to me, "Paul, you're going to be a very popular ballplayer. The people like to pull for a little fellow."

And that's the way it turned out. In all the 15 years I played with Pittsburgh, I was never booed at home. Not even once. The same with Lloyd. No matter how bad we were, no booing. We never knew what it was like to be booed at home. I don't imagine it would help a fellow any.

Now on the road, I *liked* to be booed. I really did. Because if they boo you on the road, it's either 'cause you're a sorehead or 'cause you're hurting them. Either one or the other. In my first year in the Big Leagues, the players all told me to watch out for the right-field fans in St. Louis. "That right-field stand is tough," they said. "They ride everybody." And, of course, the fellows didn't know whether I could take a riding in the majors or not.

So the first time we went into St. Louis, I figured if they jumped on me I'd have a little fun. And sure enough, as soon as I showed up in right field they started in and gave me a terrible roasting. I turned around and yelled, "They told me for years about all you fans in St. Louis, that all the drunken bums in the city come here. And now that I'm here, I see it's true." I said it real serious and madlike, you know, never cracked a smile.

Oh, did they scream! Well, such as that went on back and forth between us for two or three months. Then one day in the middle of the summer we were giving them an awful licking. I bounced a triple out to right center and drove in two or three runs, and after the inning was over and I came running out to my position they stood up and gave me the very devil. And then, for the first time, I laughed and waved to them.

It so happened that on the very last out of that game a fly ball was hit out to me. I caught it, and then ran over to the stands and handed it to some old fellow that I'd noticed out there every time we played in St. Louis. Well, by golly, they started to clap, and soon all of them were cheering, and do you know that from then on all of them were for me. And that old fellow, any time I got the last ball after that I'd run over and give it to him.

Anyway, like I was saying, we won the pennant in 1927, the first year Lloyd and I played together in the Pittsburgh outfield. That was a great thrill for us, naturally. We even brought Mother and Dad and our sister to the World Series. But then the Yankess beat us four straight, so we weren't very happy about Mother and Dad seeing *that*.

The one thing I remember best about that Series is that I didn't seem to actually realize I was really playing in a World Series until it was all over. The first time we came to bat in the first game, Lloyd singled and I doubled, and from then on the two of us just kept on hitting like it was an ordinary series during the regular season. Neither of us was a bit nervous.

Finally, we came into the bottom of the ninth of the fourth game, with the score tied, 3–3. We were playing at Yankee Stadium, and the Yankees had already beaten us three times in a row. Before I knew what had happened, the Yankees had loaded the bases: Babe Ruth was on first base, Mark Koenig on second, and Earle Combs on third. And there were none out. But then Johnny Miljus, who was pitching for us, struck out Lou Gehrig and Bob Meusel, and it looked like we'd get out of it. While he was working on Tony Lazzeri, though, Johnny suddenly let loose a wild pitch that sailed over catcher Johnny Gooch's shoulder, and in came Combs with the run that won the game, and the Series, for the Yankees.

Out in right field, I was stunned. And that instant, as the run that beat us crossed the plate, it suddenly struck me that I'd actually played in a World Series. It's an odd thing, isn't it? I didn't think, "It's all over and we lost."

What I thought was, "Gee, I've just played in a World Series!"

And you know, I think that's the first time I really realized it. It's funny how much your frame of mind has to do with your ability to play ball. I guess I forced myself not to think about playing in a World Series, so I wouldn't get nervous.

It's the same way with superstitions. Most ballplayers know that such things are silly. But if it gives you a feeling of confidence in yourself, then it'll work. You figure, "If it helps, why not? What have I got to lose?"

Like the time I got six straight hits in a game. That was in 1926, my first year up. I used six different bats, and swung six different times, and came up with six different hits. You just know there has to be a lot of luck in a thing like that. It so happened that Bill McKechnie, who was our manager that year, changed our batting order a little that day, and I was put hitting second instead of third, where I usually hit. So I was in the corner of the dugout, smoking a cigarette, not figuring it was my turn yet, when somebody yelled, "Hey, Paul, hurry up, you're holding up the parade. Get up to bat."

I hustled out to the plate and just grabbed a bat on the way, any bat, I didn't even look. And I got a hit. So I thought, well, maybe that's not such a bad way to do. The next time up I did the same thing, just grabbed a bat blind, not looking, and off came another hit. So I did that all day. Six bats and six hits. (However, that system stopped working the next day, unfortunately.)

After that disastrous World Series, Mom and Dad and Lloyd and I went back home to Oklahoma, and darned if they didn't have a parade and all for us in our home town. Everybody was so happy that I was hard put to figure it out. After all, we hadn't won the Series, we'd lost it, and in four straight games to boot.

Well, it turned out that there had been a lot of money bet there, but it hadn't been bet on the Pirates against the Yankees. It had been bet on the Waner brothers against Ruth and Gehrig. And our combined batting average for the Series had been .367, against .357 for Ruth and Gehrig. So that's why everybody was so happy.

Well, after that 1927 pennant we never won another one, not one single one, all the years Lloyd and I played in Pittsburgh. Gee, that was tough to take. We ended second about four times, but never could get back on top again. We had good teams, too. You know, Pie, Arky Vaughan, Gus Suhr, Bill Swift, Mace Brown, Ray Kremer, all good boys. But we never quite made it.

It'd just tear you apart. We'd make a good start, but before the season was over they'd always catch up with us. And when you're not in the race any more, it gets to be a long season, really long.

The closest we came was in 1938. God, that was awful! That's the year Gabby Hartnett hit that home run. We thought we had that pennant sewed up. A good lead in the middle of September, it looked like it was ours for sure. Then the Cubs crept up and finally went ahead of us on that home run, and that was it.

It was on September 28, 1938. I remember it like it just happened. We were playing in Chicago, at Wrigley Field, and the score was tied, 5–5, in the bottom of the ninth inning. There were two out, and it was getting dark. If Mace Brown had been able to get Hartnett out, the umpires would have had to call the game on account of darkness, it would have ended in a tie, and we would have kept our one-half-game lead in first place. In fact, Brown had two strikes on Hartnett. All he needed was one more strike.

But he didn't get it. Hartnett swung, and the damn ball landed in the left-field seats. I could hardly believe my eyes. The game was over, and I should have run into the clubhouse. But I didn't. I just stood out there in right field and watched Hartnett circle the bases, and take the lousy pennant with him. I just watched and wondered, sort of objectively, you know, how the devil he could ever get all the way around to touch home plate.

You see, the crowd was in an uproar, absolutely gone wild. They ran onto the field like a bunch of maniacs, and his teammates and the crowd and all were mobbing Hartnett, and piling on top of him, and throwing him up in the air, and everything you could think of. I've never seen anything like it before or since. So I just stood there

in the outfield and stared, like I was sort of somebody else, and wondered what the chances were that he could actually make it all the way around the bases.

When I finally did turn and go into the clubhouse, it was just like a funeral. It was terrible. Mace Brown was sitting in front of his locker, crying like a baby. I stayed with him all that night, I was so afraid he was going to commit suicide. I guess technically we still could have won the pennant. There were still a couple of days left to the season. But that home run took all the fight out of us. It broke our hearts.

I still see Mace every once in a while, when he comes down this way on a scouting trip. He's a scout for the Boston Red Sox. Heck of a nice guy, too. He can laugh about it now, practically 30 years later. Well, he can almost laugh about it, anyway. When he stops laughing, he kind of shudders a bit, you know, like it's a bad dream that he can't quite get out of his mind.

Well, there's a lot of happiness and a lot of sadness in playing baseball. The last full season that Lloyd and I played together on the Pirates was 1940. That was my fifteenth year with Pittsburgh, and Lloyd's fourteenth. Heck, I was thirty-seven by then, and Lloyd was thirty-four. Of course, we hung on in the Big Leagues with various teams for about five more years, but that was only on account of the war. With the war and all, they couldn't get young players, so I played until I was forty-two, and then my legs just wouldn't carry me any more.

I remember one day when I was with the Boston Braves in 1942. Casey Stengel was the manager. I was supposed to be just a pinch hitter, but in the middle of the summer, with a whole string of doubleheaders coming up, all the extra outfielders got hurt and I had to go in and play center field every day. Oh, was that ever rough! One doubleheader after the other.

Well, that day—I think we were in Pittsburgh, of all places—in about the middle of the second game, one of the Pittsburgh players hit a long triple to right center. I chased it down, and came back with my tongue hanging out. I hardly got settled before the next guy hit a long triple to left center, and off I went after *it*. Boy, after that I could hardly stand up.

And then the next guy popped a little blooper over second into real short center field. In I went, as fast as my legs would carry me. Which wasn't very fast, I'll tell you. At the last minute I dove for the ball, but I didn't quite make it, and the ball landed about two feet in front of me and just *stuck* in the ground there. And do you know, I just lay there. I *couldn't* get up to reach that ball to save my live! Finally, one of the other outfielders came over and threw it in.

That's like in 1944, when I was playing with the Yankees. I finished up my career with them. Some fan in the bleachers yelled at me, "Hey Paul, how come you're in the outfield for the Yankees?"

"Because," I said, "Joe DiMaggio's in the army."

Of course, in a sense, I've never really left baseball, because I've been a batting coach most of the years since I quit playing. I coached two years with the Phillies, two with the Cardinals, six with Milwaukee, and some with the Red Sox. I took the whole organization, not just the Big League club. When the parent team was at home, I'd usually be there. Then, when they went on the road, I'd start flying to all their minor-league clubs.

Even as a batting coach, you know, my small size has helped me. Because the youngsters figure that, me being small and all, I must know *something* about how to hit.

It's obvious I can't strong-back the ball, and yet they know I got over 3,000 hits, over 600 doubles, and all that. So they say to themselves, "Gee, he must know the secret." And they listen.

So that's the way it was. Those 24 years that I played baseball—from 1923 to 1946—somehow, it doesn't seem like I played even a month. It went *so fast*. The first four or five years, I felt like I'd been in baseball a long time. Then, suddenly, I'd been in the Big Leagues for ten years. And then, all at once, it was twenty.

You know . . . sitting here like this . . . it's hard to believe it's more than a quarter of a century since Lloyd and I played together. Somehow . . . I don't know . . . it seems like it all happened only yesterday.

If you were tuned to any TV news show the night of Thursday, September 25, 1986, but the sound was off and what you saw was the Houston first baseman fielding a grounder, beating the batter to the base, and then joining in the avalanche of teammates mobbing the pitcher, your first thought could have been to wonder what happened: were the Astros celebrating a division title or a no-hitter?

For the first time in baseball history, the answer was: both.

# 1986:
# Houston Astros 2,
# San Francisco Giants 0

## TOM WEIR

THIS HARDLY began as though it would be Mike Scott's day. His first pitch hit San Francisco Giants batter Dan Gladden.

It was not the start Scott had dreamed of when he came to the Astrodome Thursday with a chance to clinch the National League West title for Houston.

"I was so pumped up I was trying to throw it through everybody. I almost threw it through Gladden," Scott said. "I thought I better get my act together."

That act came together as never before in a championship-clinching game. When Houston's 2–0 victory was complete, San Francisco had no base hits to go with its one hit batter.

As Houston reliever Charlie Kerfeld said in between showering everyone in sight with champagne: "Shakespeare couldn't have written it any better."

Nor could Olivier have acted it out in finer fashion.

Scott's first professional no-hitter climaxed what will have to stand as three of the best consecutive pitching performances ever by a team.

Jim Deshaies opened with a record-setting eight strikeouts while two-hitting Los Angeles Tuesday. Next, Nolan Ryan worked six hitless innings against the Giants Wednesday before finishing with a combined two-hitter.

Then came Scott's grand finale that left Houston with only four hits allowed and 35 strikeouts in 27 innings.

"It's the best three pitching performances I've ever seen back-to-back-to-back," Houston manager Hal Lanier said.

No one was more nervous than Ryan, who has an easier time throwing no-hitters than watching them.

"Yeah, I get real nervous because I know what they mean," said Ryan, the all-time no-hit leader with five. "And I know how little a thing can make them go wrong."

A little thing had undone Ryan's bid the night before: Mike Aldrete's soft single.

Thursday, Aldrete again produced the Giants' best offensive effort, an eighth-inning fly ball to the edge of the warning track. Billy Hatcher made the catch on the run and held on tight as his momentum carried him into the wall. The wall shook, but Scott didn't.

Scott had been in this situation only once before while throwing a collegiate no-hitter at Pepperdine.

"I think it was against Cal Lutheran," he said. "Some power like that."

Aldrete's fly was only the second ball San Francisco managed to get beyond the infield. In the Giants dugout, manager Roger Craig had to be feeling both pride and anguish as Scott struck out 13.

Craig, while still the Detroit Tigers pitching coach, taught Scott the split-fingered fastball that has made him a Cy Young Award candidate.

Even with a no-hitter and a title on the line, Scott's thoughts drifted over to Craig a couple of times.

"If it wasn't for him, I probably wouldn't be out there doing what I'm doing," Scott said.

And if not for Craig's help, it might be the Giants, instead of the Astros, who are headed for the playoffs.

Initially, Scott wasn't the best of pupils.

"The first three times I worked with him he didn't pick it up," Craig said. "Then he got it. I knew he was going to have a good one, but I didn't think it was going to be this good.

"Scott, at this point, has the best one of anyone I ever taught. Him and (Detroit right-hander) Jack Morris. You saw the ultimate today."

When the ultimate moment of his ultimate game came—the game-ending grounder by Will Clark to Glenn Davis at first base—Scott backed off.

"I told him to take it himself," Scott said. "I didn't want to go over and bobble it."

Craig has no regrets about turning around Scott's career.

"When I did it I did it in good faith," he said. "I was in the other league."

Opposing pitchers still ask for lessons, but Craig, understandably, said those days are over. The would-be students have Scott to thank for that.

# G. B. TRUDEAU

© 1986 Universal Press Syndicate

This piece was written in 1978, and one senses that its famous author was as embittered as his famous subject at the absence of an Enos Slaughter plaque in baseball's Hall of Fame. "He can only hope that the Veterans' Committee might choose him," Tom Wicker wrote here. Six years later, the Veterans' Committee did choose him.

# Enos Slaughter, on His Toes

## TOM WICKER

WHEN BILLY Southworth came to Martinsville, Va., in 1935 to look over St. Louis Cardinals farmhands playing in the Class D Bi-State League, he spotted a stocky young outfielder with one glaring weakness and one promising statistic. The kid was hitting a mediocre .275—but more than a third of his hits were going for extra bases. So he hit with power; but to Southworth's experienced eye, he looked too slow of foot for the major leagues. Southworth took the rookie aside and told him he'd have to learn to run. Get out there in the outfield, he said, demonstrating a proper running stride, and start running on your toes. Get off that flat-footed gait or you're going home to plant some more tobacco.

To Enos Bradsher Slaughter, aged 19 and a short jump away from semi-pro ball and the Cavel Manufacturing Company team in his native Roxboro, N.C., that was a life or death choice. Not that $75 a month was much of a fortune even in Depression days, although room and board in Martinsville came to only five dollars a week. It wasn't even that the big leagues, if he could make it that high, offered something nearer wealth, although it was certainly a better deal than the hardscrabble life on a Person County tobacco farm, like the one on which Slaughter had grown up.

It was rather that baseball *was* life to Enos Slaughter—a fact not particularly unusual in his generation of ballplayers, most of them farm boys or slum kids, at a time when the game was truly the national pastime. It was a leisurely era before technology and affluence pushed American life so near hysteria, in the last years before the old game became modern big business.

To be cut in 1935 would have been worse than merely the end of a professional career, even as bad as that would have been: condemnation to semi-pro, with its cheap uniforms, skinned infields, smelly locker rooms (if any). It would have been worse than that, because making it in baseball in 1935 was not just fun and money in the pocket but living up to a myth.

So young Slaughter took Billy Southworth at his word, went to the outfield and started running on his toes; he ran and then he ran some more. Just four days after Southworth's ultimatum, Enos Slaughter went down the first-base line in *four steps fewer* than he had ever before. If a man worked at it, he observed, he could make himself do more than he had thought he could do; that was baseball, and that was America.

In 1936, the Cards sent the Tar Heel rookie with the newly developed speed to the Columbus, Ga., Redbirds of the Class B Sally League—not a bad jump in one season. At Columbus, the home dugout was set back a long way from the base line. In an early game, Slaughter came running in from the outfield to the line; then he walked to the dugout.

Manager Eddie Dyer met him at the steps. "Son, if you're tired," Dyer said, "we'll try to get you some help."

Enos Slaughter never walked to the bench again—or to his position, or to first base if a pitcher gave him a base on balls, or anywhere else on a baseball field. Dyer later taught him the strike zone and how to throw home on one bounce, but running became Slaughter's obsession, partly to keep his legs in shape, mostly because he believed it was part of the game that was his life. A ballplayer ran, because if he didn't he was out—out at first, out at home, out of the game, out of place in baseball.

So on October 14, 1946, when Enos Slaughter took a steal signal from Eddie Dyer, it was nothing unusual for Slaughter to be off and running; that was his style. But this time he wasn't running in the outfield at Martinsville or across the old ballfield at Columbus; this was Sportsman's Park in St. Louis, the big time—in fact, the eighth inning of the seventh game of the World Series. Enos Slaugher, on first base with a single to center, represented the go-ahead run and perhaps the championship of the world.

The score was tied—the Cards 3, the Boston Red Sox 3—when Slaughter led off the home eighth with his hit. He had watched impatiently from first as Bob Klinger retired Whitey Kurowski and catcher Del Rice, playing for the injured Joe Garagiola. Then, with Harry Walker at the plate and Klinger concentrating on the third out, Dyer, in the Series in his first year as a big league manager, flashed the steal sign.

Slaughter got his usual jump and was tearing for second at high speed, running on his toes, when the left-handed Walker popped a weak fly into center field. Rounding second, cutting his turn short and charging for third, Slaughter saw from the corner of his eye that Leon Culberson was moving to field the ball and that shortstop Johnny Pesky was already running out for a possible relay. To Slaughter, the ball Walker had hit looked like a "dying seagull"; he saw it was going to fall in front of Culberson and the thought flashed through his mind, *I can score on this guy.*

The inning before, the Red Sox had tied the game when Dominic DiMaggio, with runners on second and third, doubled into right field off relief pitcher Harry Brecheen. But DiMaggio had pulled up lame at second with a torn muscle in his leg; Culberson, his replacement, was no DiMaggio in center field and Slaughter knew Culberson's arm was weak. And now, putting his head down, charging around second and digging hard, Slaughter knew what no one else in Sportsman's Park knew—that he was going all the way home.

Third base coach coach Mike Gonzalez gave no signal at all ("I think he was flabbergasted," Slaughter says) as the runner began to make the turn toward home with no sign of slowing. Behind him, Culberson fielded Walker's hit and threw to Johnny Pesky, still coming out with his back to the infield. Pesky's play was orthodox; Walker had singled with a man on first, and even with Slaughter's jump on the play, the sensible expectation was that he would pull up at third.

So when Pesky took Culberson's throw, he turned *toward second,* cocking his arm to throw, against the remote possibility that Walker would try to pick up an extra base. By then, the wide sleeves of his old-style baseball shirt flapping like wings, Slaughter was around third—hitting the bag at full speed with his left foot, as he had learned to do long before in the minors—and striding on his toes for home, with 36,143 fans standing and screaming him on.

Just as Pesky set himself for a possible throw to second, he caught sight of Slaughter tearing toward home. He reacted quickly enough, but from a disadvantage. He was set for a throw to second and had to shift quickly to his right to make the throw home, a move that would put any right-hand thrower somewhat off balance. Probably as a result, Pesky's peg was short, and it was late.

Red Sox catcher Roy Partee had to come out into the infield in front of the plate to field the ball. Slaughter, racing down the base line at top speed, could have scored standing up, but he didn't. He slid across the plate, climaxing one of the great individual plays in World Series history not with an unnecessary bit of showboating but with an Enos Slaughter trademark. He *always* slid into every base but first, no matter how badly he had a throw beaten, because Enos Slaughter knew he would never be a better ballplayer than the legs that carried him around the bases and over the outfield, and he had seen too many other players go lame—little Dom DiMaggio just the inning before—by having to pull up sharply, from top speed, in order not to overrun a base. He believed it was safer to slide.

So Slaughter turning third, Pesky's fatal "hesitation" (although Slaughter has always defended the shortstop's turn toward second as the proper play in most circumstances), the hurtling slide home all passed into the bottomless repository of baseball lore. There was more drama to come, as there often is in a World Series game; in the Red Sox ninth, Brecheen gave up singles to Rudy York and Bobby Doerr, then forced three straight batters to hit the ball on the ground for infield outs, no one scoring. The Cat became the ninth pitcher in Series history to win three games (he had won two complete games previously, one of them the day before) and the first since Stan Coveleski of the Indians in 1920.

But with that heat-down, game-winning, 270-foot dash from first to home on a weak single (Walker did go to second and got a softhearted scorer's "official" double for his dying seagull), Slaughter became *the* Series star and one of baseball's most memorable heroes—if not quite one of its certified immortals. When all else about the 1946 Series, a cliffhanging upset for the Cards, has been reduced to bloodless statistics, Enos Slaughter's break for home will be remembered, retold, elevated into the kind of myth baseball and America love the most—a story of individual effort, "hustle," playing hard, putting out the extra effort that wins the day.

And if the making of that play actually began far away and 11 years earlier in Martinsville with a desperate rookie trying to teach himself to run on his toes, the play itself was not an isolated moment. However orthodox Pesky's handling of the situation, he should have known by then—as Slaughter had known about Culberson's weak arm—that with Enos Slaughter on base and the game and Series possibly at stake, *something* out of the ordinary was likely to happen.

That could have been learned in the fourth game of that same Series, played in Fenway Park. In the sixth inning of the fourth game, the Cards leading 7 to 1, the Red Sox had loaded the bases with one out and had Cardinal pitcher George Munger (who had got out of the service only in August) on the ropes after a walk and singles by Doerr and Pinky Higgins. Hal Wagner ripped into a Munger pitch and, as Arthur Daley wrote in *The New York Times,* ". . . Rudy York was on third when Hal Wagner's towering smash backed Slaughter to the bullpen. York tagged up and raced home, knowing he couldn't be headed off. A throw was so impossibly far that it wouldn't even be attempted. But Slaughter, who never gave up on anything, threw out York at the plate.

" 'What kind of ball do those fellows play?' asked the flabbergasted Rudy. 'No one else would even have attempted that throw'."

Now that quote from York probably should be taken with a grain of salt, since it doesn't sound like any ballplayer of the day, or any day, let alone Rudy York, and since Arthur Daley just naturally loved Enos Slaughter. Another time, Daley wrote: "On the ballfield he [Slaughter] is perpetual motion itself . . . he would run through a brick wall, if necessary, to make a catch, or slide into a pit of ground glass to score a run." But Slaughter's remarkable throw to take the Red Sox out of a possible big inning can't be questioned; there it is in the box score, under "double plays"—"Slaughter and Garagiola."

Arthur Daley also frequently told a story about the fifth game of that Cards-Sox series. A pitch from Joe Dobson caught Slaughter in the elbow, causing agonizing pain. Slaughter "stoically pattered down to first," Daley recalled in a column nearly 20 years later. Then he attributed to Slaughter a quote that may be as fanciful as the supposed words of Rudy York the day before: " 'I wouldn't give nobody the satisfaction of knowin' I was hurt,' said this Spartan."

Quote or no quote, Enos Slaughter promptly stole second base with his arm still wracked with pain. But the Cards lost that day, to return to St. Louis down three games to two. That night on the train, the Cards' team doctor packed the injured arm in ice and told Slaughter he was through for the Series.

"The fellers need me," Slaughter said, or so Daley reported. "No matter what you say, I'm playin'."

So in the sixth game he singled home a run in the winning rally, and in the seventh he dashed to glory. In neither game did the Red Sox try to run on him—the throw to double York at the plate had convinced them he

had a gun for an arm, and he never let on that Dobson's pitch had incapacitated it for the rest of the Series. That year, Enos Slaughter was 30 years old, having lost what probably were his three best years physically to the Army Air Corps; the Cards were paying him less than $25,000.

Enos Slaughter's baseball career was destined to last through 1959, a startling 24 years from its beginning in Martinsville. From 1938 on, he was a big leaguer, playing 19 seasons—he was in the Air Corps in 1943, 1944 and 1945—with the Cards, the Yankees in two different tours, the Kansas City Athletics and the Milwaukee Braves. Slaughter was 43 years old when he ended his last season—typically playing hurt, after hitting a foul ball off his own foot, as Milwaukee finally lost the 1950 National League pennant to Los Angeles in a play-off.

He might have hung on another season or two—into his fourth decade of major league ball—as a pinch hitter, but in 1960 Slaughter took a fling at managing (with Houston, then in the American Association).

He retired with a lifetime batting average of exactly .300 for those 19 big league seasons, and given his total of 2,383 major league hits, it's not inconceivable that if he hadn't lost those three vital years to the Air Corps (when he was 27, 28, 29 years old), he'd have reached the rarefied level of 3,000 hits.

A power hitter, but not a home run-or-strikeout muscle man, Slaughter blasted 148 triples and 413 doubles, as well as 169 home runs, thus maintaining for his career the old Martinsville pace that had first caught Billy Southworth's eye—more than a third of his hits were for extra bases. And in almost 8,000 at bats, he struck out only 538 times.

On the pennant-winning Cardinals of 1942 ("by far the best team I ever played on," he says today. "We had everything, we just felt we could beat anybody . . ."), Slaughter led the league in hits with 188, led the club and was second in the league with a .318 average and starred in the World Series the Cards won from the Yankees, hitting a home run in the fifth game.

In the Cards' pennant-winning year 1946, coming out of his three years in service, Slaughter hit .300 and led both leagues in runs batted in with 130. In 10 consecutive All-Star games, Slaughter hit .381 for the National League, and when St. Louis traded him to the Yankees in 1954, of all players then active in both leagues, only Stan Musial had more hits, 2,223 to 2,064, and only Ted Williams of the Red Sox had batted in more runs, 1,298 to 1,148.

When the Yankees traded Slaughter to Kansas City in 1955, he was 39 years old; he hit .315 for the Athletics, playing most of the time, and was voted the team's "most popular" player in a year when he took the field—still running—for his 2,000th game.

The next year, at 40, Slaughter was hitting .279 and had played in 90 games—today's brittle stars, take note—when the Yankees sent cash and Bob Cerv to the Athletics (for delivery in 1957) to get him back a week before the September 1 World Series eligibility deadline. The Yanks released Phil Rizzuto to make room on the roster, whereupon Slaughter played six Series games, hit a game-winning three-run homer in the third game and wound up the Series batting .350, including two of the Yankees' five hits off that other indestructible, Sal Maglie, during Don Larsen's perfect fifth game.

But Slaughter, for all his success on the field, never had any financial luck. That year, for example, the Yankees (who won the Series in seven games) voted Rizzuto a full share of the winners' swag, or $8,714. Slaughter was supposedly due only a half-share, but second baseman Jerry Coleman went to Commissioner Ford Frick and asked on behalf of the other players that Slaughter's cut be raised to a three-quarter share. Frick agreed and Slaughter took down $6,536. Yankee clubhouse steward Pete Sheehy got a three-quarter share, too.

At 41 and 42, Slaughter then put in a couple of solid years with the Yankees—.254 in 96 games in 1957, plus .250 in five World Series games against the Braves; then .304, mostly as a pinch hitter with 138 at bats in 77 games in 1958, with another Yankees-Braves Series following.

Late in 1959, still making a contribution to the Yankees, nearly bald by then but still running on and off the field and weighing only three pounds more than the 188 he had hustled along the Martinsville basepaths 24 years earlier, the 43-year-old Slaughter fouled a pitch off his own foot and was out for a week. Then Casey Stengel asked him how he'd like a shot at his sixth World Series; the Yankees were out of the running in the American League, but over in the National Milwaukee, in a stretch race with the Dodgers, needed a left-handed pinch hitter.

The Yankees hadn't bothered to X-ray Slaughter's injured foot; he recalls that he "hobbled" into general manager George Weiss's office and protested, not the proposed deal, but that his foot might prevent him from helping the Braves. Weiss telephoned John McHale of the Braves with the injury news; but McHale told Slaughter, "If you can swing the bat, we can get a runner for you."

So at an age at which almost all his contemporaries were retired, unable to run in his trademark style, but dead game and still eager to play ball, Enos Slaughter went back to the National League, to his fourth club, to another pennant race, and in his first game delivered a pinch-hit single against Bob Purkey of Cincinnati.

The Braves made it through a last road trip to a dead heat with the Dodgers, but lost the play-offs in two games, and Slaughter finished his playing career on a downbeat. Milwaukee took an 8–4 lead into the home ninth of the second game in the Dodgers' temporary home, the infamous Coliseum, a converted football stadium with a short left-field wall that made Fenway Park look like a pitcher's haven. The Dodgers scored five runs in that ninth inning and it was all over. If some heroics of his could have saved it for Milwaukee, as so often they had for St. Louis, that would have made a better ending; but Enos Slaughter's long day was done at last.

Maybe they still play his kind of tough, shrewd baseball in 1978—Thurman Munson of the Yankees comes to mind, and so does Lou Piniella's smart handling of a crucial hit to right field in that year's Yankee-Red Sox play-off game. Piniella couldn't see the ball in the sun but pretended he was making the catch; that held up baserunner Rick Burleson between second and first long enough so that when the ball dropped, Piniella could grab it and fire to third in time to halt Burleson at second. That could be a story about Slaughter, but few play that hard or smart today, and certainly not for the kind of small change Enos Slaughter was paid throughout his career.

From the start, he had given baseball all he had, but baseball gave him little in return except the fun of the game—admittedly no small reward. Even in the fall of 1934, when on the recommendation of Fred Haney, a baseball writer for the Durham, N.C., *Herald*, the Cardinals invited him to a tryout camp in Greensboro, general manager Branch Rickey made it clear that young Slaughter would have to pay his own expenses if the club didn't sign him.

After his 1937 season in Columbus, Ohio, of the American Association—the highest minor league classification—Slaughter thought his league-leading .382, 27 home runs and 122 runs batted in were worth something more than the $150 a month he'd been paid. Hadn't those statistics made him the MVP? Eddie Dyer was later to recall the heyday of the minor leagues and the farm system as a time when "if you needed help you could reach down to Columbus, Ohio, for a broad-tailed kid named Slaughter who was hitting .382."

So Slaughter went to the top. "Mister Rickey," he asked when the season was over, "how about a bonus?" Forty years later he remembered with a chuckle how Rickey "jumped down my throat and said the older fellows had been talkin' to me, puttin' ideas in my head."

No bonus, naturally. And when Slaughter went up to the Cards in 1938, it was for the munificent sum of $400 a month—not for 12 months, of course, but for the five and a half months of the major league season. The old Gas House Gang was breaking up (Dizzy Dean had just been traded to the Cubs), but some of Slaughter's teammates were legitimate stars—Johnny Mize, Joe Medwick, Pepper Martin, Terry Moore ("the greatest defensive centerfielder I ever played with. . . . I've never been back to the wall at no time that he wasn't there to tell you how much room there was and what base to throw to. . . ."). Catcher Bill DeLancey was a particular hero to Slaughter; after a bad case of tuberculosis, DeLancey played in 1940 with only one lung.

Even now, Slaughter professes not to know what any of these fabled ballplayers were being paid—although on the Cardinals of those years it couldn't have been much ("we didn't make no money with the Cards, they all said we was hungry ballplayers"). Back then, he insists, money wasn't much talked about and "nobody ever talked salary in the clubhouse"—maybe because no one had anything much to brag about. Today, with free agents and million-dollar contracts, the publicized jealousies of such as Billy Martin for the monstrous salaries of such as Reggie Jackson not only dominate the headlines but some clubhouses, too.

Slaughter hit .350 for the first three months of his first big league year, then tailed off to .276, an average that would earn a rookie a fat contract in 1978—and which brought him up to $600 a month for the 1939 season, when Ray Blades's Cards finished second; that year, the young outfielder hit .320 and led the league in doubles. That was worth $750 a month to the Cardinals for 1940, and Slaughter responded with an early-season batting tear.

Then came an Eastern road trip that he recalls as if it were yesterday, but not with pleasure. "I left St. Louis hittin' .371 and came back hittin' .216. I went three for 82, the worst slump I ever had" (perhaps not least because of a personal nemesis, one Jumbo Brown, a 295-pound relief pitcher for the Giants, who knew how to get Slaughter out).

That season the Cards were in the race all the way and once Slaughter shook his slump, he was a leading factor in another second place finish, finally batting .306 for the year. He hit a solid .311 in 1941, and on the great 1942 team could pocket $9,000 for the season, plus a Series winner's share.

Slaughter played that Series as an enlisted man in the Air Corps, having signed up in August, and spent the next three years on what sound like some pretty good service ball clubs at Lackland Air Base, Hickam Field in Hawaii and in the southwest Pacific—where the players often had to build the field before they could play their morale-building exhibitions for the GIs. Birdie Tebbetts, Joe Gordon, Howard Pollet, Taft Wright, Ferris Fain,

Tex Hughson—Slaughter remembers playing with or against them all, once on Iwo Jima just after its capture.

He came out of the service to give several great years to the Cardinals and in 1949 he hit .336 and led the league in triples, which earned him a $25,000 contract for 1950—the best he ever had. That season, he batted .290 ("a guy'd own a franchise, he hit that much today") and the niggardly Cardinals proceeded to hand him a 10 percent pay cut.

But baseball was beginning to change and TV was waiting in the wings to wipe out the minors and the farm systems and change the atmosphere and traditions of the game. Night World Series competition in the chill of October, for example, would have been unthinkable before TV; so would players who'd had their basic experience not at Martinsville or Columbus but at Arizona State and Southern Cal. Not far ahead were designated hitters, interchangeable parts for pitching staffs, uniforms gaudy as those of a marching band, rugs for playing surfaces and a time when a hangnail or a wounded ego could become a major factor in a pennant race.

Above all, television put money—big money—in the pockets of owners and players alike, and its largesse ultimately permitted free agentry to make capitalists out of second-string outfielders. But Enos Slaughter, who played his 19 major league seasons without an agent or a holdout, just missed the fat years; as they came in, he was past his prime.

Still, when the Cards traded him to the Yankees in 1954, he wept: *The New York Times* ran a picture of one of baseball's celebrated hard guys with his face in his hands. Even though St. Louis president August Busch blustered that he hated to trade "one of the greatest baseball players in the history" of the Cards, but had to in order to build a younger team, and manager Eddie Stanky mealymouthed that "a champion baseball player is going to a champion baseball club," the truth was apparent. Slaughter spoke it through his tears.

"I've given my life to this organization, and they let you go when you're getting old."

That is also the story of baseball, the dark side of the myth, and in Slaughter's case, even the Russians recognized it. In *Soviet Sport,* the Soviet Union's leading sports magazine, the Slaughter trade was singled out as an example of "flesh-peddling in disregard of the player's wishes and rights . . . a typical example of beer and beizbol. The beizbol bosses care nothing about sport or their athletes but only about profits."

Right on, in 1954, and another of the reasons for free agentry today, as well as the fact that the Slaughter deal could not now be made without his consent. But he might not have vetoed it even if he could have, and not just because it got him away from the one pitcher who seemed to have his number, Carl Erskine of the Dodgers; but because for all his fire and dash on the field, in the clubhouse Enos Slaughter was a company man. He never caused trouble for the club, never groused about his paycheck, never gave anything but his best for whatever he was being paid. And it never occurred to him to do anything else.

So he went to Casey Stengel when he reported to the Yankees during a series in Washington, and told the manager he was ready to give him 100 percent; no doubt Stengel already knew that, but when the 38-year-old Slaughter added that he wanted to play regularly (at a time when the Yankee outfield consisted of Mickey Mantle, Hank Bauer and Irv Noren, with Gene Woodling and Bob Derv in reserve), Stengel told him: "My boy, you play when I tell you to play, and you'll stay up here a long time."

Slaughter did; and Stengel, he says, played him against the "tough clubs" and especially against "the tough lefthanders," because for some reason the left-hand hitting Slaughter feasted on left-hand pitching; over his career, he hit better off lefties than off right-handers. One of his special pleasures is that, at 40, he hit the marvelous Billy Pierce "pretty good," and Herb Score, too. He was playing the outfield for the Yankees the day Gil McDougald's line drive hit Score in the eye and doomed his career—a memory that puts Slaughter in mind of a young pitcher he recalls only as "Slayball" who in the early fifties was hit in the eye by a line drive and injured so badly his eyeball was "hangin' out on his cheek." But "he pitched the next year in Double-A," which to Enos Slaughter was the natural order of things. ("Slayball" was actually Bobby Slaybaugh, who indeed lost his eye in the accident—and who nonetheless attempted a comeback the following year.)

After his seasons with Kansas City, Slaughter didn't want to come back to the Yankees, where he feared he'd play less, and he was saddened to be the cause of Rizzuto's release; but baseball was still his life and he flew dutifully to Detroit, where at the age of 40 he went five for nine playing both ends of a Sunday doubleheader on his first day back under Stengel's command. In those last seasons, the Yankees paid him $18,000 a year, more or less.

After his last stand with the Braves, he went off to manage at Houston in 1960. His team finished third and Slaughter was released; after he paid his own way to the minor league meetings in 1961, he was signed to manage Raleigh (not far from Roxboro) in the Class B Carolina League. That was a farm club of the embryonic Mets and at the Mobile, Ala., training base, Slaughter looked over his "talent" and bluntly notified the higher-ups: "They ain't even Class D players."

He was told rather indignantly that he had at least 15 major league prospects on the Raleigh roster; as it turned out, he took just one of the 15 back to Raleigh, and that year 52 different Met farmhands, he says, paraded through the Raleigh clubhouse, all going nowhere, like the club itself. At the end of the season, Slaughter was released again.

That was the last of organized ball for one of its most dedicated performers; the myth was finished with him. He was never again offered a job, despite innumerable applications over the next few years. Maybe he was too demanding for today's ballplayers; he wouldn't have understood a player begging off the All-Star game with a sore toe. Or maybe he was too hardbitten for jetset owners and youngsters who hadn't been happy to get $75 a month playing baseball in order to get out of the tobacco fields. Maybe his talent evaluations were too merciless for his bosses.

To an interviewer's suggestion that maybe baseball also feared that a rural Southerner of his generation couldn't deal with blacks, he snorted: "Long as they produce for me I don't care if they're red." He'd had blacks at both Houston and Raleigh, he said, and had no trouble, and he'd managed to bridge baseball's lily-white years and the coming of the blacks in the fifties.

In 1970, Duke University's athletic director, Eddie Cameron, hired Slaughter to coach baseball at a school where it was a secondary sport. He had no scholarships to offer, and often lost his best players to a rule that football scholarship men could play baseball only in conference games. Still, he was 16–15 his first year, and usually won a dozen to 15 games in each of the next six seasons, before he was retired.

Meanwhile, in 1966, when he turned 50 years old, Enos Slaughter applied for the pension organized baseball promises its players and which TV supposedly had inflated. He drew his first monthly check—for $400, the same as his first major league salary—in July, 1966; it was not until six months later, just too late, that he learned that the complicated pensions rules would have entitled him to $800 a month if he'd waited until 1967 to start taking payments. Years of complaints, to various Commissioners of Baseball and to the Players Association have failed to redress this grievance; in fact, Slaughter says his baseball pension, for some quirky reason, has declined to $379 a month. He had paid into the plan for 20 years.

But there was a final way Slaughter might have been rewarded beyond the fun of he game for his 22 professional seasons of dedicated play, hard running and hard hitting. He had earned little money, been shipped like a chattel among unfeeling teams, found no further place in the game that had been his life, and been shortchanged—at least by his reckoning—on his pension. But the baseball writers, if not baseball's officials, could do something. They had the power to vote him into the Hall of Fame.

That alone, to a man who believed he had given the best of his life to baseball, would have been compensation enough, better than any conceivable perquisite or financial reward, final security within the myth. But the writers have not recognized Enos Slaughter either. In 1978, they chose Eddie Mathews, a home run hitter, with Slaughter coming in second. His last chance was 1979, when the 15 years of his eligibility to be voted in came to an end; after that, he can only hope that the Veterans' Committee might choose him—which is less desirable than selection by the writers.

Why the Hall of Fame has eluded a player of Slaughter's caliber and longevity is a mystery. It's true that writers for the West Coast and Canadian teams, Texas, Houston, Atlanta, never saw him play; it's true also that (to Slaughter's undisguised disgust) home run hitting is the name of the game in Cooperstown—"You hit a few home runs, don't matter you got a lifetime average .270, .280, you go in. . . . I got the pinky on that thing."

One outfielder he played against—a home-hitter of brief fame—had an arm so weak, he recalls, "he caught a fly 30 feet behind third base. I'd go home on him." But he's in and Slaughter's not.

Whatever the reason, Slaughter tried to console himself that Red Ruffing and Joe Medwick, "who should have been there earlier," didn't make it until their fifteenth years of eligibility; but an interviewer could sense that he didn't really expect any longer to make it. And he is too honest to act as if he doesn't care.

Exclusion from the Hall of Fame seems to have embittered him far more than the shabby treatment he's had from baseball, which he follows fairly closely. He thinks he could have made more hits in modern ballparks with their symmetrical distances and artificial surfaces, and he thinks that although there are "some great ballplayers today," no team has 25 "top-notch major league players. You hit .275, you're a superstar." He doesn't exactly begrudge today's big salaries but—still the company man who respects the boss—he suggests "they've got out of hand a little bit"; and he sees little of his own hustle and desire in today's players, although he likes to point out that "there's been many a game

won by runnin' out a pop fly, 'cause if it falls you're on second base." In 1938, he remembers, he hit a grounder back to Bill Lee, pitching for the Cubs, "and he looked at it a couple of times and when he looked up I was almost on first. He was so surprised he threw it away and I wound up on third. A fly ball got me home and we won the game."

But that's all in the past, however alive that past still seems (Slaughter exemplies William Faulkner's belief that the past not only isn't dead, "it isn't even past"). Now Enos Slaughter farms six acres of tobacco in Person County, N.C., which, after all, he escaped only temporarily back in 1935. He manages about 2,100 pounds to the acre and brief leaf goes these days for at least $1.50 a pound. There's plenty of time left over for fishing at Kerr Lake, where over the 1978 Fourth of July weekend he and Max Crowder, the Duke trainer, pulled in 53 stripers in four days; and there's good hunting every day in the autumn deer season.

The night Junior Gilliam died ("hell of a ballplayer, I saw him break in with the Dodgers"), just before the 1978 World Series opened, with Helen Slaughter pottering in the kitchen and their daughter Rhonda watching television, Slaughter—aged 62, up to 208 pounds and more than ever fitting the nickname "Country" that Burt Shotton hung on him 40 years ago—summed up his life in baseball:

"I really enjoyed baseball. It was my livelihood. If they wanted me at the ballpark at eight in the morning, I'd be there. I asked no odds and I give none. A guy got in my way, I run over him. If they knocked me down at the plate, I said nothin'. You can't steal first base but if they hit me, I'm on first. And if you don't get on first, you can't score a run."

In the fading light of the myth Enos Slaughter lived—not just the myth of baseball, but the American myth itself—doesn't that get close to a truth? *If you don't get on first, you can't score a run.* So do anything, accept anything, knock down and be knocked down, to get on first, score a run, win the game.

And then what? Don't they let you go when you're gettin' old? And not even the Hall of Fame will bring back a broad-tailed kid who hit .382 at Columbus and ran on his toes everywhere he went.

# Louisville Slugger

## GEORGE F. WILL

LOUISVILLE, KY.—I don't want to wax mystical and metaphysical about this, but . . .

Stop. I want to wax. If an American boy can't get all worked up about a genuine "powerized" Louisville Slugger baseball bat, what use is the First Amendment's guarantee of the free exercise of religion?

When Thomas Aquinas was ginning up proofs of God's existence, he neglected to mention the ash tree. It is the source of the Louisville Slugger; and hence is conclusive evidence that a kindly mind superintends the universe.

The Big Bang got the universe rolling and produced among the celestial clutter one planet, Earth, enveloped in an atmosphere that causes rain to patter on Pennsylvania ridgetops where ash trees grow. They grow surrounded by other trees that protect the ash trees from wind-twisting and force them to grow straight toward sunlight. The result is wood with the perfect strength required for the musical "crack" that is the sound the cosmos makes each spring when it clears its throat and says, "We made it."

It is spring and a young man's fancy lightly turns to thoughts of . . . well, to that, too, but also to baseball and its instruments. Baseballs are made in Haiti and many gloves are made in the Orient, but the bats that put people on the path to Cooperstown are made, one at a time, where you would expect, in mid-America.

Wood lathes at Hillerich & Bradsby's "Slugger Park" plant take just eight seconds to make a bat for the masses. But craftsmen—the junior member of the work force has 17 years seniority—take longer to make bats for hitting artists. The makers of bats must take care. Ted Williams once returned a batch of bats because the grips did not feel right. They were found to be 5/1000 of an inch wrong.

Hillerich & Bradsby charges $12 for each major leaguer's bat, and loses about $13 on the deal. They do it for the prestige. They must have been relieved when Orlando Cepeda retired. He used to discard a bat after getting a hit. His reasoning, in which I find no flaw, was that there are only so many hits in a bat, that you can't tell how many there are in bat and that he did not want to risk using a bat from which all the hits had been taken.

The production of real bats has declined because of a monstrous development—the popularity of aluminum bats. Hillerich & Bradsby makes such ersatz Sluggers, but commits that unnatural act in Southern California, a region of novelties and regrets.

Colleges, those incubators of heresies, use aluminum bats for a grotesque reason: They last longer. But immortality is not a virtue in things that should not exist at all. Because metal bats are livelier than wooden bats, they distort the game. Scoring soars, 200-minute games become common and some teams—yes, teams—have batting averages over .350. Aluminum bats in the big leagues would produce every fan's ultimate nightmare: a blizzard of asterisks in the record book, denoting records set after baseball became subservient to the science of metallurgy.

People who will not recognize tradition as a sufficient argument should bow to aesthetic as well as scientific considerations. Aluminum hitting horsehide makes a sound as grating as fingernails scraping a blackboard. If the sound of the aluminum bat were a food, it would be lima beans. Imagine a balmy summer evening, the portable radio on the front porch emitting the soft sizzle of crowd noise. The announcer says: "Here's the pitch—and the runner is off at the ping of the bat!" "Ping"? The prosecution rests.

A. Ray Smith never rests. Louisville, like Renaissance Florence, is not especially large but is immoderately drenched with the finest art of its century, which in the case of Louisville is baseball. Smith has not gotten the word from French philosophers that angst is the right response to the 20th century. But it is hard to get the hang of existential despair when your Triple-A Louisville Redbirds recently drew 1,062,000 fans, more than five major-league teams.

A few of those fans probably were H&B craftsmen who went to the ballpark to see their handiwork put to work. Imagine, working amidst ash chips, which smell better than bacon in the morning. It is enough to make a boy wax poetical: I think that I shall never see a tree as lovely as what folks here make from some of them.

Meet the official scorer. At long last!

# They Call It a Hit in Detroit

## DICK YOUNG

THE TRIM-BEARDED ballplayer threw a soiled towel angrily to the ground, mumbled something that sounded vaguely like "key-ryst!" then stormed up to the older man in the tall hat, the man standing near first base, and shouted: "How could you call that an error?"

It happened on June 19, 1846. It was on that day, at the Elysian Fields in Hoboken, New Jersey, that the first baseball game was played, and how could the first baseball game have been played without somebody, some ballplayer, second-guessing the official scorer?

Being human, the official scorer will, upon occasion, make a mistake, which in turn explains why he will be second-guessed. It is not necessary to be mistaken, however, in order to be second-guessed. Inasmuch as the function of an official scorer involves judgment (is it a hit or is it an error?), there is always the implicit invitation for the ballplayer to disagree.

There are written guidelines for scoring, but how do you put down in writing that which man must adjudge? Good shall prevail, says The Big Book, but as long as *you* think vanilla is good and *I* think vanilla is vomitous, it cannot be incontrovertibly written.

Scoring a ball game, therefore, is in the eyes of the beholder. Nobody can, with absolute precision describe for you what is a hit and what is an error. I can tell you only how I do it. I cannot tell you it is the best way; I can tell you that I have found it best for me.

I employ a negative technique, a circuitous approach. I say to myself, "If the fielder had made the play, would it have been an unusually fine play?" If the answer comes back yes, then I do not charge the man with an error. He is not required to make an unusually fine play. The words "with ordinary effort" recur in the official scorer's manual. That much is written.

My negative technique therefore combines judgment and the written word to produce—what? Infallibility? To produce that which one man believes to be proper and fair, based on his experience, his judgment, his bold integrity. Two men still may see the same play differ-

ently. The same man, on two successive days, may see virtually the same play differently. This is the human factor—to be lived with.

What makes me an official scorer? Somewhere in the convenient past it was decided by the leagues that qualified newspapermen should be the official scorers of baseball games. They had the first requisite: they were there. They were deemed qualified on the basis of extreme exposure to the sport. And they would work reasonably cheap.

The Baseball Writers Association of America (which calls itself the BBWAA under the mistaken idea that baseball is two words) has set up qualifications for scorers as follows: A reporter must have covered a minimum of one hundred games a year for three years to be eligible.

That is it. It might also help to insist that a scorer be color-blind, so as not to be able to distinguish between the colors of the home-team uniform and those of the visitor, but this is not required. Nor is the scorer asked to take an oath that he will not be a homer, a homer being one who favors, in his decision-making, members of the home club. It is simply presumed that he, like the umpire, is impartial.

However, a New York baseball writer scores only for games played in New York, a Chicago writer in Chicago, and so on. No city has a monopoly on objectivity, although the ballplayer in any city is convinced that the scoring for the home team is more lenient (considerate?) in another town. A classic ballplayer-scorer exchange goes like this:

"They call that a hit in Detroit."

"I don't give a damn what they do in Detroit. It's an error."

"If a man doesn't get those kinds of hits at home, where can he get them?"

"A hit is a hit, no matter where, and an error is an error. Just because somebody else is a homer, don't ask me to be one."

Around and around we go. The player is convinced the scorer is out to get him; the scorer is convinced the player wants something for nothing, a bloody beggar.

Official scorers should not be influenced by the post-game persuasion of a hit-hungry ballplayer, nor coerced by his anger. Neither should a scorer be so intractable as to be deaf to reasonable appeal. I do not mean appeal to his judgment, but occasionally a ball does take a bad hop that is not clearly visible at press-box level, or a throw does nick a man caught in a rundown just before the ball is dropped, and the true blame escapes the scorer.

There is one key word: blame. It is the essence of scoring. All too often, the official scorer becomes too technical, officious, a slave to the written rule. He will go thumbing through the pages of the manual looking for hidden meanings, seeking complications—and then one day, when the obscure play occurs, he will announce his gem triumphantly in the press box—instant expert.

Common sense is a better servant. Common sense serves the true duty of the official scorer, for what is his purpose? To reward the deserving; to blame those responsible. Thus two key words: reward, blame. Keeping those in mind, the scorer doesn't find himself trapped by technical verbiage.

Some years ago when a team called the New York Giants played in a place called the Polo Grounds, somebody hit a high fly to left field, slightly toward center. It was a geographic peculiarity of the Polo Grounds that if the outfielders weren't careful they would step on one another. Thus, quite often, a man camped under a high fly would feel the warm breath of a colleague on his earlobe while hearing the encouragement, ''You got it, old buddy.''

In this particular case, the old buddy had it, then didn't have it. The ball hit into his glove and somehow curled out of it, fortunately on the side of the rooting teammate, who simply raised his glove and caught the evasive thing. The official scorer gave the ultimate fielder the put-out, which was fine, then added an assist for the juggler, which raised something of a stink in the press box and beyond.

''How in the world can you reward a man who has muffed a ball?'' demanded the commonsense advocates.

''He touched the ball, didn't he?'' said the official scorer, ''therefore, he gets an assist,'' and no amount of dissuasion could convince him otherwise. Thus the undeserving left fielder was awarded an assist, just as surely as if he had thrown out a runner at the plate. (A footnote was later added to the scorers' manual, stating that ''mere ineffective contact with the ball shall not be considered an assist.'')

Periodically, displeasure over some outlandish scoring decision leads some fan to write a letter to the editor, or if the feelings are strong, to the league president, wondering why the duties of official scorer are not given to the umpire or perhaps to some overage ballplayer.

If the scorer were to be an umpire, he would have to be an added umpire, a fifth man who would sit at the press-box level, for a man on the field does not have the perspective to view all plays clearly. This would seem to be a good idea, with the fifth man rotating every day with the other four. However, such a man would be salaried at, say, $15,000, and his travel expenses would be roughly another $15,000. A twelve-team major league would require six such fifth men at an overall cost of $180,000. Put this alongside the $34,000 that the league now pays for scoring fees. And add the fact that there would be no guarantee of improved service to any degree, for the same human factors, the same variance of judgments and the same prejudices pertain to umpires as to reporter-scorers.

Official scorers are paid on a per-game basis. Since 1970, the major-league fee has been $35. This was part of the American inflationary spiral. The year before it was $30, and a few years prior to that, $25. As a rule, the eighty-one home games are divided among the newsmen regularly assigned to the ball club. Thus, in a two-newspaper city like Pittsburgh, each man will score forty or forty-one games, whereas in New York, four men do sixteen, one seventeen.

This is no grand lagniappe. In addition to making the calls, after each game the official scorer must fill out a statistical form and mail it to the league's sports bureau. The way modern managers throw the troops into battle, the official box score often takes longer to fill out than tax form 1040.

For the most part, newspapermen do not score only for the money. They do it for the participation, perhaps for the prestige. Baseball receives, as a bonus, the gratis service of leading newspapermen on special committees. The constant review of scoring rules and statistical records, with an eye toward revision and modernization, is the function of such groups. At every meeting of the BBWAA such matters are debated openly—and beneficial change evolves.

The abolition of the free sacrifice bunt was the result of one of these get-togethers. Until a few years ago, any batter who advanced a runner with a bunt, regardless of the score or inning, was credited with a sacrifice and not charged with a time-at-bat if retired. This led to some very unsacrificial sacrifices. It was decided to give the official scorer latitude. If common sense dictates that the batter obviously is bunting to get on base rather than to advance a runner (his team trailing 6–0 in the ninth inning), he shall be charged with a time-at-bat, regardless of the fact that a runner advances, and not credited with a sacrifice.

A giant stride forward in the scoring of games may be in the offing: the establishment of a team-error category. For years, scorers have been handicapped by the insistence that a specific fielder be charged with the error on a misplay that permits a man to reach base or to advance an additional base. There are several instances when this is patently unfair, when a play should have been made, but no one individual can be singled out as the culprit (fly ball lost in the sun; Alphonse-Gaston act by two fielders under pop fly; perfectly thrown ball that strikes sliding base runner, permitting further advance and so forth).

It is felt that the charging of an error to the offending team as a whole would serve the cause of justice by not rewarding pitchers with hits (and earned runs) they do not deserve and by not blaming fielders who might be blameless. There are, of course, opponents to the team-error concept, pure-thinking men who believe too much is being left to the scorer's judgment.

But is not all scoring judgment? Is that not the essence of an official scorer's prime duty—the exercise of judgment? There are some who contend that the latitude does not go far enough, that the taboo on misjudged balls and mental errors should be lifted, enabling the official scorer to say, and make it stick, "That ball should have been caught" or "That man would have been out had the pitcher covered first base."

Perhaps in time. For the present, judgment is restricted to some extent by the written word ("mental mistakes or misjudgments are not to be scored as errors . . ."), but there is steady progress.

Not that a degree of perfection will be reached that abolishes all controversy. Who could stand it? It would mean the end of baseball, death by sheer boredom. Argument is beautiful when concretely founded.

It should be emphasized that no official scorer can influence the outcome of a game. The scoring of a hit or an error in no way impedes or aids the advancement of a base runner. Such decisions belong only to umpires, and they can have it. The scorer can, however, influence the course of baseball history upon occasion, and has.

In 1923, a fine pitcher named Howard Ehmke, having been traded by Detroit to the Boston Red Sox, worked something of a miracle by winning 20 games for his new tail-end club. In the process, he pitched a no-hit game against the Philadelphia Athletics on September 7 and started next against the Yankees in New York.

The first batter to face him, Whitney Witt, sent a small bouncer toward third. The ball escaped the protruding hands of Howard Shanks, bounced abruptly upward and struck him in the chest while Witt raced safely to first.

Fred Lieb, the official scorer and a journalistic giant in his time, decreed it a hit for Witt. Not only was that the

only hit by the Yankees that day, but Witt was the only baserunner. As the game progressed and it became increasingly apparent that Ehmke was to be deprived of a second consecutive no-hitter because of the first-inning decision, extreme press box pressure was exerted on Lieb to alter his call.

The scorer held fast and when, sure enough, the game ended with only the questionable hit, friends of Ehmke petitioned the league president, Ban Johnson, to reverse the official scorer. Among the evidence present in support of Ehmke was an opinion by umpire Tommy Connolly that the ball should have been scored an error. Ban Johnson, to his credit, backed the official scorer. Thus it remained for Johnny Vander Meer, in 1938, to become the first pitcher (and the only one) to achieve successive no-hitters.

Fred Lieb was involved in one of the most hectic batting-average disputes—on an occasion when, oddly enough, he was not the official scorer. At least he was not the *official* official scorer.

The year was 1922. Ty Cobb, the Detroit superstar, was in fierce battle with that inanimate rival, the .400 batting average. If he made it, it would be the third time for the fearsome Tyrus, a feat accomplished by only one man before him. Cobb finished with .401, but a tremendous outcry was raised against the figure's authenticity.

Crux of the dispute was a base hit credited to Cobb during a rainy midsummer game in New York. The official scorer was John Kieran, then a baseball writer for the *New York Tribune,* subsequently a celebrity involved with such exercises as "Information Please," the original radio quiz show.

Cobb hit a ground ball in the vicinity of Everett Scott, Yankee shortstop. Kieran scored it an error. At that instant, the rain was driving into the exposed press section to the extent that Fred Lieb, covering for the *New York Press,* sought refuge in the covered grandstand to the rear. Over his shoulder as he fled, he glimpsed the play and hastily marked a base hit for Cobb in his scorebook.

You may ask why the opinion of Fred Lieb, the non-scorer, should overrule the judgment of John Kieran, the official scorer. Good question. In addition to working for the *New York Press,* Lieb kept daily box scores for the Associated Press. Irwin Howe, head man of the American League's statistical bureau, located in Chicago, frankly admitted that, in tabulating Cobb's day-to-day batting average, he had used the AP box score for that day rather than the official score sheet eventually mailed to his office by John Kieran.

The one hit was important. Had Howe accepted Kieran's official version, Cobb would have finished with .399, not .401.

Irwin Howe said he deferred to Lieb on the basis of

superior scoring experience, and Ban Johnson upheld that version. In New York, where Cobb was not exactly the most popular ballplayer alive, a furor erupted over The Case of the Two-Point Base Hit. The New York chapter of the Baseball Writers Association brought it to the floor of the national BBWAA for a vote—the irony being that Lieb then was president of the BBWAA.

The Association voted against Lieb's version by a narrow margin, insisting that Cobb's average be recognized at .399. But the Reach and Spalding Baseball Guides for the following year carried it at .401. And so it stands today in all official records—an unofficial base hit.

It could not happen today. While it is possible for a league president to overrule a scorer on the matter of rule interpretation, it is unlikely he would second-guess the judgment of an official scorer. He certainly would not give precedence to an AP boxscore.

So while an official scorer cannot influence a game's outcome, he can influence something near and dear to the ballplayer—his personal record. Thus the occasional friction between player and scorer.

It must be remembered, however, that the ballplayer is not the most objective person involved in such matters, nor is the manager. This is why it is best for an official scorer to disregard the suggestion of a complaining ballplayer to "go ask Joe about it"—Joe being (a) a teammate, (b) the player on the other team who did not handle the ball or (c) the manager.

The apparent weakness in seeking such advice is that (a) the teammate is for his buddy, (b) the opposing player often will make a beau geste and (c) the manager invariably will take the side of his player, hopeful of ingratiating himself with all the players. There are many instances of managers waving a towel from the dugout toward the press box, or exhibiting some other form of histrionic criticism of a scoring decision, and there are cases on record of the league president warning, even fining, such a manager for his unprofessional actions.

In a grand spirit of camaraderie, major-league ballplayers have been known to become similarly demonstrative, even physical. There was a case, not too many years ago, when a violent argument erupted around the Cincinnati batting cage over a scoring decision of the previous day. Oddly, the two men doing the most vociferous arguing had not been directly involved: the player was defending a viewpoint and a teammate, while the baseball writer supported the rule-interpretation of the scorer.

Things heated up to the point where the angered player took a halfhearted swing with the bat he was holding, meaning to frighten the newsman, not hit him. But the bat struck a glancing blow on the shoulder. Bystanders were aghast, save one.

"Huh," snarled the struck newsman at the ballplayer who had been benched for poor hitting, "you even fouled me off."

Dist. News America Syndicate, 1986

As NEWSMAN, novelist, columnist, screenwriter and prizewinning author Charles Einstein has published 36 books and more than 400 magazine articles and stories, and has television credits ranging from "Playhouse 90" to "Lou Grant." But for all seasons, there is no question which is his favorite. A lifetime member of the Baseball Writers' Association of America, he covered his first World Series in 1945 and since then has written millions of words about the game. Regarded as one of the sport's foremost historians, he has, in addition to his wire service, newspaper, magazine and TV output, more than a dozen books to his credit, including his editorship of the four-volume *Fireside* library, a 31-year labor of love that has been called "baseball literature's greatest monument."

Other books have included collaborations with Orlando Cepeda, Juan Marichal and Willie Mays, as well as *Willie's Time,* the widely acclaimed Mays biography. The father of four grown children, including three sons, Mr. Einstein put in more than one man's share of time as a Little League manager, coach and official. One result was his authoritative manual *How to Coach, Manage & Play Little League Baseball*, a perennial best-seller ever since its initial publication in 1968.